Lecture Notes in Computer Science

3053

Commenced Publication in 1973
Founding and Former Series Editors:
Gerhard Goos, Juris Hartmanis, and Jan van Leeuwen

Editorial Board:

Springer
Berlin
Heidelberg
New York
Hong Kong
London
Milan
Paris
Tokyo

Christoph Bussler   John Davies
Dieter Fensel   Rudi Studer (Eds.)

The Semantic Web: Research and Applications

First European Semantic Web Symposium, ESWS 2004
Heraklion, Crete, Greece, May 10-12, 2004
Proceedings

Springer

Volume Editors

Christoph Bussler
Digital Enterprise Research Institute (DERI)
National University of Ireland
Galway, Ireland
E-mail: Chris.Bussler@DERI.ie

John Davies
British Telecommunications plc
Orion 5/12, Adastral Park
Ipswich IP5 3RE, UK
E-mail: john.nj.davies@bt.com

Dieter Fensel
Digital Enterprise Research Institute (DERI)
National University of Ireland
Galway, Ireland
University of Innsbruck, Austria
E-mail: dieter.fensel@deri.org

Rudi Studer
University of Karlsruhe
76128 Karlsruhe, Germany
E-mail: studer@aifb.uni-karlsruhe.de

Library of Congress Control Number: Applied for

CR Subject Classification (1998): H.4, H.3, C.2, H.5, I.2, K.4, D.2

ISSN 0302-9743
ISBN 3-540-21999-4 Springer-Verlag Berlin Heidelberg New York

Springer-Verlag is a part of Springer Science+Business Media

springeronline.com

© Springer-Verlag Berlin Heidelberg 2004
Printed in Germany

Typesetting: Camera-ready by author, data conversion by Boller Mediendesign
Printed on acid-free paper   SPIN: 11007722   06/3142   5 4 3 2 1 0

Preface

These proceedings contain the papers accepted for presentation at the First European Semantic Web Symposium (ESWS 2004) held on Crete, Greece, May 10–12, 2004.

Given its status as an inaugural event, the organizers were delighted to receive 79 high-quality submissions. Most papers were reviewed by at least three referees, with the review results coordinated by the academic and industrial track chairs. In total, 27 papers were accepted for the academic track and 6 papers were accepted for the industrial track. The papers span a wide range of topics from the Semantic Web area, from infrastructure and ontology engineering to applications.

The high quality of this symposium is due to the efforts of many people. Jos de Bruijn in particular worked hard in a number of areas, including submissions management, publicity and the poster program. We would also like to thank Martin Doerr for local arrangements, Johannes Breitfuss for the WWW site, the Program Committee and additional reviewers for their invaluable support and the sponsors for their financial support.

March 2004

Christoph Bussler
John Davies
Dieter Fensel
Rudi Studer

Organization

Organizing Committee

Academic Track: Dieter Fensel (DERI, Austria)
                                         Rudi Studer (University of Karlsruhe, Germany)
Tutorial Program and Proceedings: John Davies (BT, UK)
Industrial Track and Demo Chair: Christoph Bussler (DERI, Ireland)
Local Arrangements and Posters: Jos de Bruijn (DERI, Austria)
                                         Martin Doerr (ICS-FORTH, Greece)

Scientific Program Committee

Andreas Eberhart	University of Karlsruhe, Germany
Asun Gomez-Perez	Universidad Politécnica de Madrid, Spain
Carole Goble	University of Manchester, UK
Christine Golbreich	University of Rennes, France
Daniel Schwabe	PUC-Rio, Brazil
Deborah McGuinness	Stanford University, USA
Dunja Mladenic	J. Stefan Institute, Slovenia
Enrico Franconi	Free Univ. Bozen, Italy
Enrico Motta	The Open University, UK
Frank van Harmelen	Vrije Universiteit Amsterdam, The Netherlands
Guus Schreiber	Vrije Universiteit Amsterdam, The Netherlands
Hamish Cunningham	University of Sheffield, UK
Heiner Stuckenschmidt	Vrije Universiteit Amsterdam, The Netherlands
Ian Horrocks	University of Manchester, UK
Jerome Euzenat	INRIA, Rhône-Alpes, France
John Davies	BT, UK
Mark Musen	Stanford University, USA
Martin Doerr	ICS-FORTH, Greece
Michael Kifer	University at Stony Brook, USA
Nigel Shadbolt	University of Southampton, UK
Norman Sadeh	Carnegie Mellon University, USA
Raphael Volz	University of Karlsruhe, Germany
Richard Benjamins	iSOCO, Spain
Riichiro Mizoguchi	Osaka University, Japan
Robert Meersman	Vrije Universiteit Brussels, Belgium
Stefan Decker	DERI, Ireland
Stefanos Kollias	National Technical University of Athens, Greece
Steffen Staab	University of Karlsruhe, Germany
Wolfgang Nejdl	University of Hannover, Germany
Ying Ding	DERI, Austria
Yolanda Gil	ISI USC, USA
York Sure	University of Karlsruhe, Germany

Industrial Program Committee

Alain Leger	France Telecom, France
Alistair Duke	BT, UK
Arian Zwegers	European Commission, Brussels
David Trastour	HP, UK
Dean Allemang	Boston University, USA
Frank Leymann	IBM, Germany
Jürgen Angele	Ontoprise, Germany
Kim Elms	SAP, Australia
Leo Obrst	MITRE, USA
Mari Georges	ILOG, France
Mike Dean	BBN, USA
Naso Kiryakov	Sirma AI, Bulgaria
Peter Smolle	NetDynamics, Austria
Ralph Traphoener	Empolis, Germany
Satish Thatte	Microsoft, USA
Stuart Williams	HP, UK
Vipul Kashyap	National Library of Medicine, USA

Additional Reviewers

Arthur Stutt	The Open University, UK
Atanas Kiryakov	Sirma AI, Bulgaria
Bo Hu	University of Southampton, UK
Daniel Oberle	University of Karlsruhe, Germany
Daniele Turi	University of Manchester, UK
Dmitry Tsarkov	University of Manchester, UK
Donovan Artz	ISI – USC, USA
Dumitru Roman	DERI, Ireland
Erik van Mulligen	Vrije Universiteit Amsterdam, The Netherlands
Farshad Hakimpor	The Open University, UK
Francis Kwong	University of Manchester, UK
Gary Wills	University of Southampton, UK
Holger Wache	Vrije Universiteit Amsterdam , The Netherlands
Hongsuda Tangmunarunkit	University of Manchester, UK
Janez Brank	J. Stefan Institute, Slovenia
Jeen Broekstra	Vrije Universiteit Amsterdam, The Netherlands
Jeff Z Pan	University of Manchester, UK
Jesús Barrasa Rodríguez	Universidad Politécnica de Madrid, Spain
Jos de Bruijn	DERI, Austria
Lei Li	University of Manchester, UK
Marc Spraragen	ISI – USC, USA
Maria Vargas-Vera	The Open University, UK
Mariano Fernandez Lopez	Universidad Politécnica de Madrid, Spain
Martin Dzbor	The Open University, UK
Matthew Horridge	University of Manchester, UK

Table of Contents

Knowledge Representation

Applications

Content Management

Information Management and Integration

Towards On-the-Fly Ontology Construction - Focusing on Ontology Quality Improvement

Naoki Sugiura[1], Yoshihiro Shigeta[1], Naoki Fukuta[1], Noriaki Izumi[2], and Takahira Yamaguchi[1]

[1] Shizuoka University, 3-5-1 Johoku, Hamamatsu, Shizuoka 432-8011, Japan,
`sugiura@ks.cs.inf.shizuoka.ac.jp`,
http://mmm.semanticweb.org
[2] National Institute of AIST, 2-41-6, Aomi, Koto-ku, Tokyo, Japan

Abstract. In order to realize the on-the-fly ontology construction for the Semantic Web, this paper proposes DODDLE-R, a support environment for user-centered ontology development. It consists of two main parts: pre-processing part and quality improvement part. Pre-processing part generates a prototype ontology semi-automatically, and quality improvement part supports the refinement of it interactively. As we believe that careful construction of ontologies from preliminary phase is more efficient than attempting generate ontologies full-automatically (it may cause too many modification by hand), quality improvement part plays significant role in DODDLE-R. Through interactive support for improving the quality of prototype ontology, OWL-Lite level ontology, which consists of taxonomic relationships (class - sub class relationship) and non-taxonomic relationships (defined as property), is constructed efficiently.

1 Introduction

As the scale of the Web becomes huge, it is becoming more difficult to find appropriate information on it. When a user uses a search engine, there are many Web pages or Web services which are syntactically matched with user's input words but semantically incorrect and not suitable for user's intention. In order to defeat this situation, Semantic Web[1] is now gathering attentions from researchers in wide area. Adding semantics (meta-data) to the Web contents, software agents are able to understand and even infer Web resources. To realize such paradigm, the role of ontologies[2][3] is important in terms of sharing common understanding among both people and software agents[4]. On the one hand, in knowledge engineering field ontologies have been developed for particular knowledge system mainly to reuse domain knowledge. On the other hand, for the Semantic Web, ontologies are constructed in distributed places or domain, and then mapped each other. For this purpose, it is an urgent task to realize a software environment for rapid construction of ontologies for each domain. Towards the on-the-fly ontology construction, many researches are focusing on

J. Davies et al. (Eds.): ESWS 2004, LNCS 3053, pp. 1–15, 2004.

automatic ontology construction from existing Web resources, such as dictionaries, by machine processing with concept extraction algorithms. However, even if the machine produces ontologies automatically, users still need to check the output ontology. It may be a great burden for users to check all the correctness of the ontology and modify it, especially if the scale of automatically produced ontology is large. Considering such situation, we believe that the most important aspect of the on-the-fly ontology construction is that how efficiently the user, such as domain experts, are able to check the output ontology in order to make Semantic Web contents available to the public. For this reason, ontologies should be constructed not fully automatically, but through interactive support by software environment from the early stage of ontology construction. Although it may seem to be contradiction in terms of efficiency, the total cost of ontology construction would become less than automatic construction because if the ontology is constructed with careful interaction between the system and the user, less miss-construction will be happened. It also means that high-quality ontology would be constructed. In this paper, we propose a software environment for user-centered on-the-fly ontology construction named DODDLE-R (Domain Ontology rapiD DeveLopment Environment - RDF[5] extension). The architecture of DODDLE-R is re-designed based on DODDLE-II [6], the former version of DODDLE-R. Although DODDLE-II has already provided interactive support for ontology construction, the system architecture is not well-considered and sophisticated. The DODDLE-R system is modularized into machine-processing module and user-interaction module in order to separate pre-processing part and user-centered quality management part specifically. Especially, to realize the user-centered environment, DODDLE-R dedicates to the quality improvement part. It enables us to develop ontologies with interactive indication of which part of ontology should be modified. The system supports the construction of both taxonomic relationships and non-taxonomic relationships in ontologies. Additionally, because DODDLE-II has been built for ontology construction not for the Semantic Web but for typical knowledge systems, it needs some extensions for the Semantic Web such as OWL (Web Ontology Language) [7] import and export facility. DODDLE-R supports OWL-Lite level ontology construction because if we think of user-centered ontology construction, OWL-DL or OWL-Full sounds too complicated for human to understand thoroughly. DODDLE-R contributes the evolution of ontology construction and the Semantic Web.

2   System Design of DODDLE-R

Fig. 1 shows the overview of DODDLE-R. The main feature of DODDLE-R is the modularized two parts - pre-processing part and quality improvement part. In pre-processing part, the system generates the basis of the ontology, a taxonomy and extracted concept pairs, by referring to WordNet[8] as an MRD (Machine Readable Dictionary) and domain specific text corpus. A taxonomy is a hierarchy of IS-A relationship. Concept pairs are extracted based on co-occurrence by using statistic methods. These pairs are the candidates which has

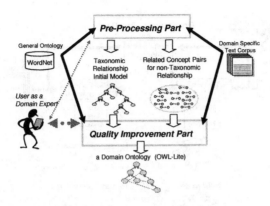

Fig. 1. DODDLE-R overview

significant relationships. A user identifies some relationship between concepts in the pairs. In quality improvement part, the prototype ontology produced by pre-processing part is modified by a user through interactive support by the system.

2.1 Pre-processing Part

In pre-processing part, the system generates the basis of output ontology for further modification by a user. Fig. 2 describes the procedure of pre-processing part. This part consists of three sub-parts: input concept selection, taxonomy building, and related concept pair acquisition. First, as input of the system, several domain specific terms are selected by a user. The system shows a list of noun concepts in the domain specific text corpus as candidates of input concept. At this phase, a user also identifies the sense of terms to map those terms to concepts in WordNet.

For building taxonomic relationship (class - sub class relationship) of an ontology, the system attempts to extract "best-matched concepts". That is, "concept matching" between input concepts and WordNet concepts is done, and matched nodes are extracted, and then merged at each root nodes. To extract related concept pairs from domain specific text corpus as a basis of identifying non-taxonomic relationships (such as "part-of" relationship), statistic methods are applied. In particular, WordSpace[9] and an association rule algorithm[10] are used in this part and these methods attempt to identify significantly related concept pairs.

Construction of WordSpace WordSpace is constructed as shown in Fig.3.
1. Extraction of high-frequency 4-grams Since letter-by-letter co-occurrence information becomes too much and so often irrelevant, we take term-by-term co-occurrence information in four words (4-gram) as the primitive to make up co-

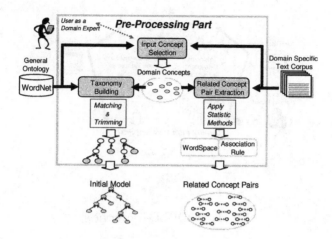

Fig. 2. Pre-processing Part

occurrence matrix useful to represent context of a text based on experimented results. We take high frequency 4-grams in order to make up WordSpace.

2. Construction of collocation matrix A *collocation matrix* is constructed in order to compare the context of two 4-grams. Element $a_{i,j}$ in this matrix is the number of 4-gram f_i which comes up just before 4-gram f_j (called *collocation area*). The collocation matrix counts how many other 4-grams come up before the target 4-gram. Each column of this matrix is the *4-gram vector* of the 4-gram f.

3. Construction of context vectors A *context vector* represents context of a word or phrase in a text. A sum of 4-gram vectors around appearance place of a word or phrase (called *context area*) is a context vector of a word or phrase in the place.

4. Construction of word vectors A word vector is a sum of context vectors at all appearance places of a word or phrase within texts, and can be expressed with Eq.1. Here, $\tau(w)$ is a vector representation of a word or phrase w, $C(w)$ is appearance places of a word or phrase w in a text, and $\varphi(f)$ is a 4-gram vector of a 4-gram f. A set of vector $\tau(w)$ is WordSpace.

$$\tau(w) = \sum_{i \in C(w)} (\sum_{f \text{ close to } i} \varphi(f))$$ (1)

5. Construction of vector representations of all concepts The best matched "synset" of each input terms in WordNet is already specified, and a sum of the word vector contained in these synsets is set to the vector representation of a concept corresponding to a input term. The concept label is the input term.

6. Construction of a set of similar concept pairs Vector representations of all concepts are obtained by constructing WordSpace. Similarity between concepts is obtained from inner products in all the combination of these vectors. Then we

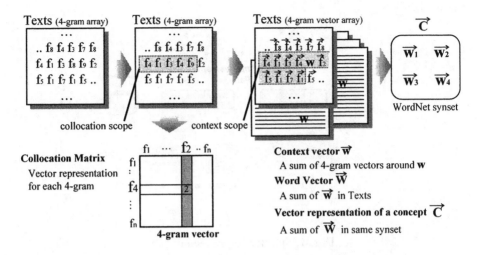

Fig. 3. Construction flow of WordSpace

define certain threshold for this similarity. A concept pair with similarity beyond the threshold is extracted as a similar concept pair.

Finding Association Rules between Input Terms The basic association rule algorithm is provided with a set of transactions, $T := \{t_i \mid i = 1..n\}$, where each transaction t_i consists of a set of items, $t_i = \{a_{i,j} \mid j = 1..m_i, a_{i,j} \in C\}$ and each item $a_{i,j}$ is form a set of concepts C. The algorithm finds association rules $X_k \Rightarrow Y_k : (X_k, Y_k \subset C, X_k \cap Y_k = \{\})$ such that measures for support and confidence exceed user-defined thresholds. Thereby, support of a rule $X_k \Rightarrow Y_k$ is the percentage of transactions that contain $X_k \cup Y_k$ as a subset (Eq.2) and confidence for the rule is defined as the percentage of transactions that Y_k is seen when X_k appears in a transaction (Eq.3).

$$support(X_k \Rightarrow Y_k) = \frac{\mid \{t_i \mid X_k \cup Y_k \subseteq t_i\} \mid}{n} \qquad (2)$$

$$confidence(X_k \Rightarrow Y_k) = \frac{\mid \{t_i \mid X_k \cup Y_k \subseteq t_i\} \mid}{\mid \{t_i \mid X_k \subseteq t_i\} \mid} \qquad (3)$$

As we regard input terms as items and sentences in text corpus as transactions, DODDLE-R finds associations between terms in text corpus. Based on experimented results, we define the threshold of support as 0.4% and the threshold of confidence as 80%. When an association rule between terms exceeds both thresholds, the pair of terms are extracted as candidates for non-taxonomic relationships.

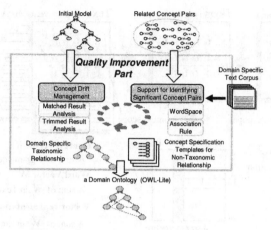

Fig. 4. Quality improvement part

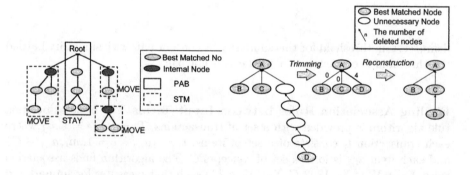

Fig. 5. Matched Result Analysis   **Fig. 6.** Trimmed Result Analysis

2.2   Quality Improvement Part

In order to improve the quality of the pre-processed ontology, the quality improvement part works interactively with a user. Fig. 4 shows the procedure of this part. Because the pre-processed taxonomy is constructed from a general ontology, we need to adjust the taxonomy to the specific domain considering an issue called Concept Drift. It means that the position of particular concepts changes depending on the domain. For concept drift management, DODDLE-R applies two strategies: Matched Result Analysis (Fig. 5) and Trimmed Result Analysis (Fig. 6).

In Matched Result Analysis, the system divides the taxonomy into PABs (PAths including only Best matched concepts) and STMs (SubTrees that includes best-matched concepts and other concepts and so can be Moved) and indicates on the screen. PABs are paths that include only best-matched concepts that have senses suitable for the given domain. STMs are subtrees of which root is an internal concept of WordNet and its subordinates are all best-matched concepts. Because the sense of an internal concept has not been identified by a user yet, STMs may be moved to other places for the concept adjustment to the domain. In addition, for Trimmed Result Analysis, the system counts the number of internal concepts when the part was trimmed. By considering this number as the original distance between those two concepts, the system indicates to move the lower concept to other places.

As a facility for related concept pair discovery, there are functions that allow users to attempt some ways to improve the quality of extracted concept pairs through trial and error by changing parameters of statistic methods. Users can re-adjust the parameters of WordSpace and association rule algorithm and check the result. After that, the system generates "Concept Specification Templates" from by using the results. It consists of some concept pairs which have considerable relationship considering the result value of statistic methods.

By referring to the constructed domain specific taxonomic relationship and the "Concept Specification Templates", a user develops a domain ontology.

3 Implementation

In this section, we describe the system architecture from the aspect of system implementation. DODDLE-R support environment for ontology construction is realized in conjunction with MR^3 (Meta-Model Management based on RDF(S)[11] Revision Reflection) [12]. MR^3 is an RDF(S) graphical editor with meta-model management facility such as consistency checking of classes and a model in which these classes are used as the type of instances. Fig. 7 shows the relationship between DODDLE-R and MR^3 in terms of system implementation. Both MR^3 and DODDLE-R are implemented in Java language (works on Java 2 or higher). MR^3 is implemented using JGraph[13] for RDF(S) graph visualization, and Jena 2 Semantic Web Framework[14] for enabling the use of

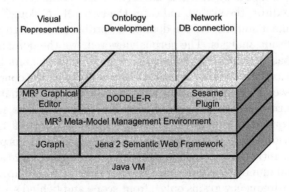

Fig. 7. DODDLE-R architecture

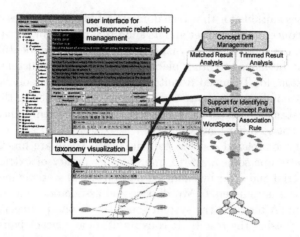

Fig. 8. Quality improvement process with DODDLE-R graphical user interface

Semantic Web standards such as RDF, RDFS, N-triple and OWL. By using these libraries, MR^3 is implemented as an environment for graphical representation of the Semantic Web contents. Additionally, because MR^3 also has plug-in facility to extend its functionality, it can provide some other functions such as the connectivity to Sesame RDF(S) server [15].

On top of MR^3 base environment, DODDLE-R is implemented as a support environment for ontology construction. Fig. 8 depicts the procedure of quality improvement with graphical user interface of the system. DODDLE-R's graphical user interface consists of an ontology information viewer, a corpus viewer and a non-taxonomic relationship acquisition window as in Fig. 9. The ontology information viewer shows the information about particular concepts such as the dictionary definition of the concept, the distance from default root node of ontology. In addition, generated hierarchies are visualized by MR^3 graph editor. On the editor, the system indicates the parts of ontologies which may be modified to make it suitable for the domain according to matched result analysis and trimmed result analysis. The corpus viewer shows the domain specific text corpus which has been referred to acquire related concept pairs by WordSpace and an association rule. When the user clicks a concept on the concept hierarchy, the corpus viewer highlights related terms in the corpus so that the user can see how the term or concept is used in the actual text. The non-taxonomic relationship acquisition window is used for setting parameters for WordSpace and an association rule to apply for the domain specific text corpus in order to generate significantly related concept pairs. For WordSpace, there are parameters such as the gram number (default gram number is four), minimum N-gram count (to extract high-frequency grams only), front scope and behind scope in the text. For an association rule, minimum confidence and minimum support are able to be set by the user.

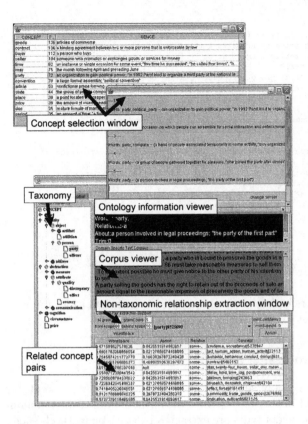

Fig. 9. A graphical user interface for non-taxonomic relationship management

4 An Example of Ontology Construction with DODDLE-R

In this section, we show a brief example of an ontology construction with DODDLE-R. As a domain specific text corpus for the reference of this ontology construction, we selected the text in CISG (Contracts for the International Sale of Goods)[16] for the particular field of law to compare with the case study which has been done by using DODDLE-II. This corpus is composed of approximately 10,000 words.

4.1 Input Concept Selection

Before starting pre-processing part, a user needs to select some terms as the input. As input of DODDLE-R, the user needs to associate those terms with concepts in WordNet. For example, the user decide which "concept" (or synset) in WordNet is suitable for the term "party" (the noun "party" has 5 senses as in

```
Sense 1
party, political party -- (an organization to gain political power;
 "in 1992 Perot tried to organize a third party at the national level")
        => organization, organisation -- (a group of people who work
           together)
           => social group -- (people sharing some social relation)
              => group, grouping -- (any number of entities (members)
                 considered as a unit)
Sense 2
party -- (an occasion on which people can assemble for social
 interaction and entertainment; "he planned a party to celebrate
 Bastille Day")
        => affair, occasion, social occasion -- (a vaguely specified
           social event; "the party was quite an affair")
           => social event -- (an event characteristic of persons
              forming groups)
              => event -- (something that happens at a given place
                 and time)

...
```

Fig. 10. WordNet concepts for the word "party"

Fig. 10). By referring to the synset and term's definition, the user selects Sence 3 as a concept for the word "party".

4.2   Pre-processing Part

After the user apply selected concepts for the system, a prototype ontology is produced. (A) in Fig. 11 describes the initial model of the taxonomic relationsip. Also related concept pairs are extracted by statistic methods such as WordSpace and assocciation rule by default parameter.

4.3   Quality Improvement Part

After the pre-processing part, there are prototype taxonomy and candidates of concept pairs for concept specification. However, they are just processed automatically and we need to adjust them to actual domain.

(B) in Fig. 11 shows the display of concept drift management. The system indicates some groups of concepts in the taxonomy so that the user can decide which part should be modified.

Also the related concept pairs may be re-extracted by setting the parameters of statistic methods and attempting to get suitable number of concept pairs.

As a result, the user got a domain ontology as in Fig. 12

5   Related Work

Navigli et,al. proposed OntoLearn [17][18], that supports domain ontology construction by using existing ontologies and natural language processing techniques. In their approach, existing concepts from WordNet are enriched and

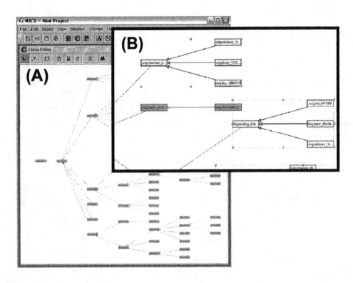

Fig. 11. The initial model of the domain taxonomy (A) and the concept drift management (B)

pruned to fit the domain concepts by using NLP (Natural Language Processing) techniques. They argue that the automatically constructed ontologies are practically usable in the case study of a terminology translation application. However, they did not show any evaluations of the generated ontologies themselves that might be done by domain experts. Although a lot of useful information is in the machine readable dictionaries and documents in the application domain, some essential concepts and knowledge are still in the minds of domain experts. We did not generate the ontologies themselves automatically, but suggests relevant alternatives to the human experts interactively while the experts' construction of domain ontologies. In another case study [19], we had an experience that even if the concepts are in the MRD (Machine Readable Dictionary), they are not sufficient to use. In the case study, some parts of hierarchical relations are counterchanged between the generic ontology (WordNet) and the domain ontology, which are called "Concept Drift". In that case, presenting automatically generated ontology that contains concept drifts may cause confusion of domain experts. We argue that the initiative should be kept not on the machine, but on the hand of the domain experts at the domain ontology construction phase. This is the difference between our approach and Navigli's. Our human-centered approach enabled us to cooperate with human experts tightly.

From the technological viewpoint, there are two different related research areas. In the research using verb-oriented method, the relation of a verb and nouns modified with it is described, and the concept definition is constructed from this information (e.g. [20]). In [21], taxonomic relationships and Subcategorization Frame of verbs (SF) are extracted from technical texts using a machine learning

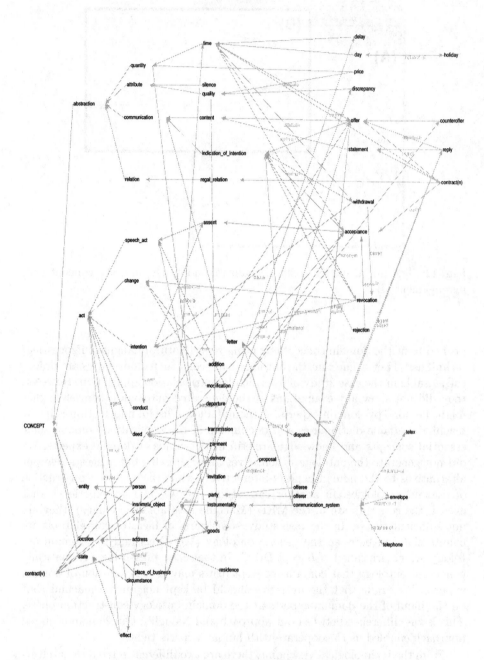

Fig. 12. Constructed CISG ontology

method. The nouns in two or more kinds of different SF with the same frame-name and slot-name are gathered as one concept, base class. And ontology with only taxonomic relationships is built by carrying out clustering of the base class further. Moreover, in parallel, Restriction of Selection (RS) which is slot-value in SF is also replaced with the concept with which it is satisfied instantiated SF. However, proper evaluation is not yet done. Since SF represents the syntactic relationships between verb and noun, the step for the conversion to non-taxonomic relationships is necessary.

On the other hand, in ontology learning using data-mining method, discovering non-taxonomic relationships using an association rule algorithm is proposed by [22]. They extract concept pairs based on the modification information between terms selected with parsing, and made the concept pairs a transaction.

By using heuristics with shallow text processing, the generation of a transaction more reflects the syntax of texts. Moreover, RLA, which is their original learning accuracy of non-taxonomic relationships using the existing taxonomic relations, is proposed. The concept pair extraction method in our paper does not need parsing, and it can also run off context similarity between the terms appeared apart each other in texts or not mediated by the same verb.

6   Conclusion and Future Work

In this paper, we presented a support environment for ontology construction named DODDLE-R, which is aiming at becoming a total support environment for user-centered on-the-fly ontology construction. Its main principle is that high-level support for users through interaction and low dependence on automatic machine processing. First, a user identifies the input concepts by associating WordNet concepts with terms extracted from a text corpus. Then, pre-processing part generates the basis of ontology in the forms of taxonomy and related concept pairs, by referring to WordNet as an MRD and a domain specific text corpus. The quality improvement part provides management facilities for concept drift in the taxonomy and identifying significant concept pairs in extracted related concept pairs. In these management, MR^3 provides significant visualization support for the user in graph representation of ontologies. As a case study, we have constructed an ontology in law domain by exploiting articles in CISG as a domain specific text corpus. Comparing with former ontology construction study with DODDLE-II, even though the first step, input concept selection phase, takes time, other phases are processed fairly well because of the re-organized system architecture and the improved user interface in conjunction with MR^3. Finally, the user constructed a law domain ontology by interactive support of DODDLE-R and produced an OWL-Lite file, which is able to put on public as a Semantic Web ontology.

We plan further improvement of DODDLE-R to be more flexible ontology development environment. At this point, the user interface of DODDLE-R is not completely supports users' trial and error (in other words, go forward and come back to particular phases of ontology construction seamlessly) in ontology construction. Since we believe that the user interface is one of the most important facilities of support tool for ontology construction, it should be improved to the point of supporting the user seamlessly. In addition, although DODDLE-R extracts domain concepts from text corpus, the extracted terms might be suitable not for concepts (classes) but for relationships (properties) or instances (individuals). For example, the term "time" may be concept or property (or other kind of attributes). Because the collaboration with MR^3 realized total management of OWL classes, properties and instances (by its editors for each in sub windows and its meta-model management facility), DODDLE-R may be able to support the construction of not only ontologies, but also models, which consist of individuals and their relationships (properties). Furthermore, we plan to implement import facility of other statistic methods. Although DODDLE-R does not emphasize the function in pre-processing part, it would be better to prepare the import facility of other methods. For instance, there is a machine learning software Weka [23], and it contains several machine learning algorithms, which may be suitable for extracting related concept pairs from text corpus. If we look at quality improvement part of DODDLE-R, there may be many additional functions. For instance, for related concept pair extraction by statistic methods, a line graph window is suitable for showing the result of applying statistic methods, also to check the current status of recall and precision. Additionally, in terms of adaptation to the Semantic Web standards, the import and export support of other ontology languages, such as DAML+OIL, must be helpful for interoperability across other ontology tools.

Acknowledgements

This work is supported by Takeshi Morita, a creator of MR^3 and a student in Shizuoka University, Japan.

References

[1] Berners-Lee, T., Hendler, J., Lassila, O.: The Semantic Web. Scientific American (2001)
[2] Gruber, T.: Ontolingua: A Mechanism to Support Portable Ontologies. Version 3.0 TR, KSL (1992)
[3] Heijst, G.V.: The Role of Ontologies in Knowledge Engineering. Dr.thesis, University of Amsterdam (1995)
[4] Ding, Y., Foo, S.: Ontology Research and Development, Part 1 – a Review of Onlotogy. Journal of Information Science (2002) pp.123–136
[5] Lassila, O., Swick, R.R.: Resource Description Framework(RDF) Model and Syntax Specification (1999) http://www.w3.org/RDF/.
[6] Sugiura, N., et al.: A Domain Ontology Engineering Tool with General Ontologies and Text Corpus. Proceedings of the 2nd Workshop on Evaluation of Ontology based Tools (2003) pp.71–82
[7] Michael K. Smith, C.W., McGuinness, D.L.: OWL Web Ontology Language Guide (2004) http://www.w3.org/TR/owl-guide/.

[8]   G.A.Miller: WordNet: A Lexical Database for English. ACM (1995) pp.39–41
[9]   Marti A. Hearst, H.S.: Customizing a Lexicon to Better Suit a Computational
      Task. Corpus Processing for Lexical Acquisition (1996) pp.77–96
[10] Agrawal, R., Srikant, R.: Fast algorithms for mining association rules. Proceedings
      of VLDB Conference (1994) pp.487–499
[11] Brickley, D., Guha, R.: RDF Vocabulary Description Language 1.0: Rdf Schema.
      W3C Proposed Recommendation (2003) http://www.w3.org/TR/2004/REC-rdf-
      schema-20040210/.
[12] Noriaki Izumi, Takeshi Morita, N.F., Yamaguchi, T.: RDF-based Meta-Model
      Management Environment. Proceedings of The 6th SANKEN (ISIR) International
      Symposium (2003)
[13] Alder, G.: Jgraph. (2003) http://www.jgraph.com.
[14] HP Labs: Jena Semantic Web Framework. (2003)
      http://jena.sourceforge.net/downloads.html.
[15] Jeen Broekstra, A.K., Harmelen, F.V.: Sesame: A Generic Architecture for Storing
      and Querying RDF and RDF Schema. Towards the Semantic Web (2002) pp.71–
      88 http://sesame.aidministrator.nl.
[16] Sono, K., Yamate, M.: United Nations Convention on Contracts for the Interna-
      tional Sale of Goods. Seirin Shoin (1993)
[17] Navigli, R., Paola Velardi: Automatic Adaptation of WordNet to Domains. Pro-
      ceedings of International Workshop on Ontologies and Lexical Knowledge Bases
      (2002)
[18] P. Velardi, M.M., Fabriani, P.: Using Text Processing Techniques to Automati-
      cally enrich a Domain Ontology. Proceedings of ACM Conf. On Formal ontologies
      and Information Systems (ACM FOIS) (2001) pp.270–284
[19] Yamaguchi, T.: Constructing domain ontologies based on concept drift analy-
      sis. Proceedings of the IJCAI99 Workshop on Ontologies and Problem Solving
      methods(KRR5) (1999)
[20] Hahn, U., Schnattingerg, K.: Toward text knowledge engineering. AAAI-98 pro-
      ceedings (1998) pp.524–531
[21] Faure, D., Nédellec, C.: Knowledge Acquisition of Predicate Argument Structures
      from Technical Texts. Proceedings of International Conference on Knowledge
      Engineering and Knowledge Management (1999)
[22] Maedche, A., Staab, S.: Discovering Conceptual Relations from Text. Proceedings
      of 14th European Conference on Artificial Intelligence (2000) pp.321–325
[23] Weka: Machine Learning Software in Java (2004)
      http://www.cs.waikato.ac.nz/~ml/weka/index.html.

OntoEdit Empowering SWAP: a Case Study in Supporting DIstributed, Loosely-Controlled and evolvInG Engineering of oNTologies (DILIGENT)

Sofia Pinto[1,2], Steffen Staab[2], York Sure[2], and Christoph Tempich[2]

[1] Dep. de Engenharia Informática, Instituto Superior Técnico, Lisboa, Portugal
http://www.dei.ist.utl.pt/
sofia.pinto@dei.ist.utl.pt
[2] Institute AIFB, University of Karlsruhe, 76128 Karlsruhe, Germany
http://www.aifb.uni-karlsruhe.de/WBS/
{staab,sure,tempich}@aifb.uni-karlsruhe.de

Abstract. Knowledge management solutions relying on central repositories sometimes have not met expectations, since users often create knowledge ad-hoc using their individual vocabulary and using their own decentral IT infrastructure (e.g., their laptop). To improve knowledge management for such decentralized and individualized knowledge work, it is necessary to, first, provide a corresponding IT infrastructure and to, second, deal with the harmonization of different vocabularies/ontologies. In this paper, we briefly sketch the technical peer-to-peer platform that we have built, but then we focus on the harmonization of the participating ontologies.

Thereby, the objective of this harmonization is to avoid the worst incongruencies by having users share a core ontology that they can expand for local use at their will and individual needs. The task that then needs to be solved is one of distributed, loosely-controlled and evolving engineering of ontologies. We have performed along these lines. To support the ontology engineering process in the case study we have furthermore extended the existing ontology engineering environment, OntoEdit. The case study process and the extended tool are presented in this paper.

1 Introduction

The knowledge structures underlying today's knowledge management systems constitute a kind of ontology that may be built according to established methodologies *e.g.* the one by [1]. These methodologies have a centralized approach towards engineering knowledge structures requiring *knowledge engineers*, *domain experts* and others to perform various tasks such as *requirement analysis* and *interviews*. While the user group of such an ontology may be huge, the development itself is performed by a — comparatively — small group of domain experts who *represent* the user community and ontology engineers who *help structuring*.

In Virtual Organizations [2], organizational structures change very often, since organizations frequently leave or join a network. Therefore, working based on traditional, centralized knowledge management systems becomes infeasible. While there are some

J. Davies et al. (Eds.): ESWS 2004, LNCS 3053, pp. 16–30, 2004.

technical solutions toward Peer-to-Peer knowledge management systems (e.g., [3]) — and we have developed a technically sophisticated solution of our own as part of our project, SWAP — Semantic Web and Peer-to-Peer [4], traditional methodologies for creating and maintaining knowledge structures appear to become unusable like the systems they had been developed for in the first place.

Therefore, we postulate that ontology engineering must take place in a Distributed, evolvInG and Loosely-controlled setting. With DILIGENT we here provide a process template suitable for distributed engineering of knowledge structures that we plan to extend towards a fully worked out and multiply tested methodology in the long run. We here show a case study we have performed in the project SWAP using DILIGENT with a virtual organization. DILIGENT comprises five main activities of ontology engineering: **build, local adaptation, analysis, revision**, and **local update** (cf. Section 3).

The case study (cf. Section 4) suggests that the resulting ontology is indeed shared among users, that it adapts fast to new needs and is quickly engineered. With some loose control we could ensure that the core ontology remained consistent, though we do not claim that it gives a complete view on all the different organizations.

In the following, we briefly introduce the organizational and technical setting of our case study (Section 2). Then we sketch the DILIGENT process template (Section 3), before we describe the case study (Section 4).

2   Problem Setting

2.1   Organizational Setting at IBIT Case Study

In the SWAP project, one of the case studies is in the tourism domain of the Balearic Islands. The needs of the tourism industry there, which is for 80% of the islands' economy, are best described by the term 'coopetition'. On the one hand the different organizations *compete* for customers against each other. On the other hand, they must *cooperate* in order to provide high quality for regional issues like infrastructure, facilities, clean environment, or safety — that are critical for them to be able to compete against other tourism destinations.

To collaborate on regional issues a number of organizations now collect and share information about *indicators* reflecting the impact of growing population and tourist fluxes in the islands, their environment and their infrastructures. Moreover, these indicators can be used to make predictions and help planning. For instance, organizations that require *Quality & Hospitality management* use the information to better plan, *e.g.*, their marketing campaigns. As another example, the governmental agency IBIT[3], the Balearic Government's co-ordination center of telematics, provides the local industry with information about *new technologies* that can help the tourism industry to better perform their tasks.

Due to the different working areas and objectives of the collaborating organizations, it proved impossible to set up a centralized knowledge management system or even a centralized ontology. They asked explicitly for a system without a central server, where

---

[3] http://www.ibit.org

knowledge sharing is integrated into the normal work, but where very different kinds of information could be shared with others.

To this end the SWAP consortium — including us at Univ. of Karlsruhe, IBIT, Free Univ. Amsterdam, Meta4, and empolis — have been developing the SWAP generic platform and we have built a concrete application on top that allows for satisficing the information sharing needs just elaborated.

2.2   Technical Setting at SWAP

The SWAP platform (Semantic Web And Peer-to-peer; short Swapster) [4] is a generic infrastructure, which was designed to enable knowledge sharing in a distributed network. Nodes wrap knowledge from their local sources (files, e-mails, etc.). Nodes ask for and retrieve knowledge from their peers. For communicating knowledge, Swapster transmits RDF structures [5], which are used to convey conceptual structures (e.g., the definition of what a conference is) as well as corresponding data (e.g., data about ESWS-2004). For structured queries as well as for keyword queries, Swapster uses SeRQL, an SQL-like query language that allows for queries combining the conceptual and the data level and for returning newly constructed RDF-structures.

In the following we describe only the SWAPSTER components that we refer to later in this document (for more see [4]).

Knowledge Sources: Peers may have local sources of information such as the local file system, e-mail directories, local databases or bookmark lists. These local information sources represent the peer's body of knowledge as well as its basic vocabulary. These sources of information are the place where a peer can physically store information (documents, web pages) to be shared on the network.

Knowledge Source Integrator: The Knowledge Source Integrator is responsible for the extraction and integration of internal and external knowledge sources into the Local Node Repository. This task comprises (1) means to access local knowledge sources and extract an RDF(S) representation of the stored knowledge, (2) the selection of the RDF statements to be integrated into the Local Node Repository and (3) the annotation of the statements with metadata. These processes utilize the SWAP metadata model presented later in this section.

Local Node Repository: The local node repository stores all information and its meta information a peer wants to share with remote peers. It allows for query processing and view building. The repository is implemented on top of Sesame [6].

User Interface: The User Interface of the peer provides individual views on the information available in local sources as well as on information on the network. The views can be implemented using different visualization techniques (topic hierarchies, thematic maps, etc). The *Edit* component described here is realized as a plug-in of the OntoEdit ontology engineering environment.

Communication Adapter: This component is responsible for the network communication between peers. Our current implementation of the Communication Adapter is build on the JXTA framework [7].

Information and Meta-information. Information is represented as RDF(S) statements in the repository. The SWAP meta model[4] (*cf.* [4]) provides meta-information about the statements in the local node repository in order to memorize where the statements came from and other meta-information. The SWAP meta model consists of two RDFS classes, namely Swabbi and Peer. Every resource is related to an instance of Swabbi in order to describe from which instances of Peer it came from, etc.

Besides the SWAP meta data model the SWAP environment builds on the SWAP common ontology.[5] The SWAP common model defines concepts for *e.g.* File and Folder. Purpose of these classes is to provide a common model for information usually found on a peer participating in a knowledge management network.

Querying for Data. SeRQL[8] is an SQL like RDF query language comparable to *e.g.* RQL [9]. The main feature of SeRQL that goes beyond the abilities of existing languages is the ability to define structured output in terms of an RDF graph that does not necessarily coincide with the model that has been queried. This feature is essential for defining personalized views in the repository of a SWAP peer.

OntoEdit. [10] is an ontology engineering environment which allows for inspecting, browsing, codifying and modifying ontologies. Modelling ontologies using OntoEdit means modelling at a conceptual level, *viz.* (i) as much as possible independent of a concrete representation language, (ii) using graphical user interfaces (GUI) to represent views on conceptual structures, *i.e.* concepts ordered in a concept hierarchy, relations with domain and range, instances and axioms, rather than codifying conceptual structures in ASCII.

3 DILIGENT Process

3.1 Process Overview

As we have described before, decentralized cases of knowledge sharing, like our example of a virtual organization, require an ontology engineering process that reflects this particular organizational setting [11].[6] Therefore, we have drafted the template of such a process — we cannot claim that it is a full-fledged methodology yet. The result, which we call DILIGENT, is described in the following. In particular, we elaborate on the high-level process, the dominating roles and the functions of DILIGENT, before we go through the detailed steps in Sections 3.2. Subsequently, we give the concrete case in Section 4 as an indicator for the validity of our ontology engineering process design.

Key roles: In DILIGENT there are several experts, with different and complementary skills, involved in collaboratively building the same ontology. In a virtual organization they often belong to competing organizations and are geographically dispersed. Ontology builders may or may not use the ontology. Vice versa, most ontology users will typically not build or modify the given ontology.

Overall process: An initial ontology is made available and users are free to use it and modify it locally for their own purposes. There is a central board that maintains and

---

[4] http://swap.semanticweb.org/2003/01/swap-peer#

[5] http://swap.semanticweb.org/2003/01/swap-common#

[6] In fact, we conjecture that the majority of knowledge sharing cases falls into this category.

---

assures the quality of the shared core ontology. This central board is also responsible for deciding to do updates to the core ontology. However, updates are mostly based on changes re-occurring at and requests by *decentral*ly working users. Therefore the board only *loosely controls* the process. Due to the changes introduced by the users over time and the on-going integration of changes by the board, the ontology *evolves*. Let us now survey the DILIGENT process at the next finer level of granularity. DILIGENT comprises five main steps: (1) **build**, (2) **local adaptation**, (3) **analysis**, (4) **revision**, (5) **local update** (*cf.* Figure 1).

Build. The process starts by having *domain experts, users, knowledge engineers* and *ontology engineers* **build** an initial ontology. In contrast to existing ontology engineering methodologies (cf. [12–16]), we do not require completeness of the initial shared ontology with respect to the domain. The team involved in building the initial ontology should be relatively small, in order to more easily find a small and consensual first version of the shared ontology.

Local adaptation. Once the core ontology is available, users work with it and, in particular, adapt it to their local needs. Typically, they will have their own business requirements and correspondingly evolve their local ontologies (including the common core) [17, 18]. In their local environment, they are also free to change the reused core ontology. However, they are not allowed to directly change the core ontology from which other users copy to their local repository. Logging local adaptations (either permanently or at control points), the control board collects change requests to the shared ontology.

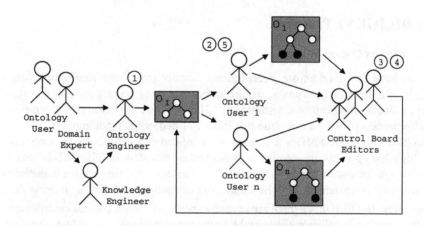

Fig. 1. Roles and functions in distributed ontology engineering

Analysis. The board **analyzes** the local ontologies and the requests and tries to identify similarities in users' ontologies. Since not all of the changes introduced or requested by the users will be introduced to the shared core ontology,[7] a crucial activity of the board is deciding which changes are going to be introduced in the next version of the shared ontology. The input from users provides the necessary arguments to underline change

---

[7] The idea in this kind of development is not to merge all user ontologies.

requests. A balanced decision that takes into account the different needs of the users and meets user's evolving requirements[8] has to be found.

Revise. The board should regularly **revise** the shared ontology, so that local ontologies do not diverge too far from the shared ontology. Therefore, the board should have a well-balanced and representative participation of the different kinds of participants involved in the process: knowledge providers, domain experts, ontology engineers and users. In this case, users are involved in ontology development, at least through their requests and re-occurring improvements and by evaluating it, mostly from an usability point of view. Knowledge providers in the board are responsible for evaluating the ontology, mostly from a technical and domain point of view. Ontology engineers are one of the major players in the analysis of arguments and in balancing them from a technical point of view. Another possible task for the controlling board, that may not always be a requirement, is to assure some compatibility with previous versions. Revision can be regarded as a kind of ontology development guided by a carefully balanced subset of evolving user driven requirements. Ontology engineers are responsible for updating the ontology, based on the decisions of the board. Revision of the shared ontology entails its evolution.

Local update. Once a new version of the shared ontology is released, users can **update** their own **local** ontologies to better use the knowledge represented in the new version. Even if the differences are small, users may rather reuse *e.g.* the new concepts instead of using their previously locally defined concepts that correspond to the new concepts represented in the new version.

3.2   Tool Support for DILIGENT Steps

We support the participants in the DILIGENT process with a tool (*cf.* Figure 2). It is an implementation of the *Edit* component of the SWAP environment, thus it works on the information stored in the local node repository, and is realized as an OntoEdit plug-in. We will now describe in detail how the tool supports the actions **building**, **locally adapting**, **analyzing**, **revising** and **locally updating**.

Build

The first step of the ontology engineering task is covered by established methodologies and by common OntoEdit functions. Some major tool functionality includes support for knowledge elicitation from domain experts by means of competency questions and mind maps and further support for the refinement process.

In contrast to a common full ontology engineering cycle the objective of this Build task is not to generate a complete and evaluated ontology but rather to *quickly* identify and formalize the main concepts and main relations.

---

[8] This is actually one of the trends in modern software engineering methodologies (see Rational Unified Process).

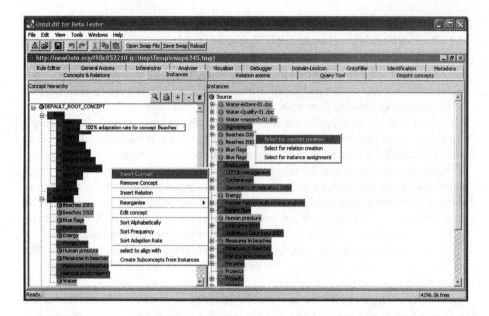

Fig. 2. OntoEdit plug-in to support DILIGENT

Local Adaptation

We distinguish two main types of users. The less frequent type is the user with ontology engineering competence who analyzes his personal needs, conceptualizes and
formalizes them. He uses established ontological guidelines [19] in order to maintain
soundness and validity. Besides, he annotates his knowledge according to his locally
extended ontology.

The more common type of user reuses the categorizations he had defined in his daily
work before (*e.g.* his folder structures) and just aligns them with the shared ontology. To
illustrate this use case we must point forward to some issues we found in the case study.
In the case study, users expect from a peer-to-peer system primarily the possibility to
share their documents with others. Users already organize their files in folder structures
according to their individual views. Hence, they will extend the core ontology with
concepts and relations corresponding to folder structures found in their file or email
system.

Concept creation. Our tool supports the creation of concepts and thus the extension of
the shared ontology in two ways. The reader may note that both methods have been
heavily influenced by our targeted system, SWAPSTER, and may be supplemented or
overridden by other methods for other target systems:

1. OntoScrape — part of the SWAPSTER knowledge source integrator — can extract
   information from the user's local file and email system. OntoScrape extracts *e.g.* the
   folder hierarchy and builds up an RDFS representation in which the folder names
   are used to create instances of class **Folder**. This information is stored in the local

node repository. Then, the user can pick a set of instances of Folder and create concepts or relations using the folder names. In case of "concept creation" he would select a certain concept and the system would subclass that concept using the names of the previously selected folders.

The user may also reuse the folder hierarchy given by the inFolder relation to construct a subClassOf hierarchy.

2. Furthermore, a user can query other participants for their local subconcepts of the core ontology. He can use the gathered information to directly extend his own structures by integrating retrieved information. Alternatively, he may use the query result only for inspiration and create own extensions and modifications.

SWAPSTER integrates a component for semi-automatic alignment. Alignment detection is based on similarities between concepts and relations(cf., *e.g.*, [20]). The user may either select a set of classes and ask for proposed alignment for these classes, or he can look for alignments for the entire class hierarchy. The reader may note that even the best available alignment methods are not very accurate and hence some user involvement is required for aligning ontologies.

We are well aware of the drawbacks of this approach since the created structures will not be "clean" ontologies. However, as our case study indicates the created structures are good enough to be a fair input for the revision phase.

Instance assignment. Besides instances of the created concepts the user has mainly instances of concept Source *e.g.* Folder and File and wants to relate them to his concepts. In particular, documents play a predominant role in our case study. Since the global ontology certainly differs from existing local structures, we face the typical bootstrapping problem that the documents need to be aligned with the defined concepts. Our tool offers two possibilities to facilitate the assignment of documents to classes.

Manual Assignment Instances of concept Source can manually be selected and assigned to any concept in the ontology.

Automatic Assignment Automatic text classification is nowadays very effective. Hence we provide an interface for classifiers to suggest document classifications. Classifier training can take place remotely for the core ontology or according to established procedures [21]. The classifier has to produce a set of RDFS statements, stating which files should be classified where in the concept hierarchy. This has not been implemented yet.

Analyzing

As described in the methodology, the board will come together in fixed time lines or when a certain threshold of change requests has been reached. They will subsequently analyze the activities which have taken place. They will gather the ontologies from all participating peers on one central peer. The main task of the board is to incorporate the change requests into the core ontology and to identify common usage patterns. Our tool supports the board members in different ways to fulfill their task.

View selection. The number of newly created concepts within the peer network can be large. The board members can use queries to select only parts of the ontology to be visualized. Instead of loading the entire local node repository, a SeRQL query can be used to generate a view on the repository. Queries can be defined manually, or predefined ones — visualizing certain branches of the ontology — can be selected.

Colors. The board needs to separate extensions made by different users and is interested in their relative activity. Since each peer uses its own name space to create URIs, extensions to the core made by different peers can be distinguished. The tool highlights the concepts, relations and instances of different peers by changing their background color. The saturation and brightness of the color indicates the number of concepts coming from a particular peer.[9] White is preserved for name spaces which the users can chose not to highlight (*e.g.* the local, swap-peer and swap-common name space are excluded from highlighting by default).

Adaptation rate. The averaged adaptation rate[10] of concepts from the core ontology and also of concepts from different users is an indicator of how well a concept fits the user needs. If a concept of the core ontology was not accepted by the users it probably has to be changed. Alternatively, a concept introduced by a user which has been reused by many other users can easily be integrated into the core ontology. The adaptation rate is visualized as a tool tip. In our case study *e.g.* the concept **beaches** was adapted by all users. It is calculated from the information stored in the SWAP data model.

Visualizing alignments. Instead of reusing concepts from other users, they can align them. The semantics of both actions is very similar. However, alignment implies, in most cases, a different label for the concept, which is determined by the board.

Sorting. To facilitate the analysis process, concepts, relations and instances may be sorted alphabetically, according to their adaptation rate or the peer activity. Concepts with the same label, but from different peers can be identified. Equally the concepts reused by most peers may be recognized.

Revision

The analysis is followed by the revision of the core ontology. The change requests as well as the recognized common usage patterns are integrated. In a traditional scenario the knowledge engineer introduces the new concepts and relations or changes the existing ones while the system meets the requirements described in [18]. The ontology changes must be resolved taking into account that the consistency of the underlying ontology and all dependent artifacts are preserved and may be supervised.

Additionally we require, that the reasons for any change do not require too much effort from the individual user. In particular, changes to the core ontology made because of overarching commonalities should be easy to integrate for users who created the concepts in the first place.

Local Update

The changes to the core ontology must be propagated to all peers afterwards. The list of changes is transmitted to the different peers by the *Advertisement* component. Maedche

---

[9] Brighter and less saturated means less concepts than darker and more saturated.

[10] The adaptation rate of a concept indicates how many users have included the concept into their

local ontology: adaptation rate $:= \dfrac{\text{No of participant who have locally included the concept}}{\text{No of participants}}$

et al. describes in [22] the necessary infrastructure to enable consistent change propagation in a distributed environment. We do not require that all users adapt their ontology to the changes introduces by the board members. Furthermore, we allow that they use different evolution strategies when they accept changes (see [18] for an overview of different strategies).

After the *local update* took place the iteration continues with *local adaptation*. During the next *analysis* step the board will review which changes were actually accepted by the users.

4 Case Study

We are now going to describe how DILIGENT ontology engineering is taking place in the IBIT case study and how OntoEdit is supporting it.

In the case study one organization with seven peers took part. The case study lasted for two weeks. The case study will be extended in the future to four organizations corresponding to 21 peers and it is expected that the total number of organizations will grow to 7 corresponding to 28 peers.

Building. In the IBIT case study two knowledge engineers were involved in building the first version of the shared ontology with the help of two ontology engineers. In this case, the knowledge engineers were at the same time also knowledge providers. In addition they received additional training such that later, when the P2P network is going to be up and running on a bigger scale, they will be able to act as ontology engineers on the board. This they did already during this study — together with two two experts from the domain area.

The ontology engineering process started by identifying the main concepts of the ontology through the analysis of competency questions and their answers. The most frequent queries and answers exchanged by peers were analyzed. The identified concepts were divided into three main modules: "Sustainable Development Indicators", "New Technologies" and "Quality&Hospitality Management". From the competency questions we quickly derived a first ontology with 22 concepts and 7 relations for the "Sustainable Development Indicator" ontology. This was the domain of the then participating organizations. The other modules will be further elaborated in future efforts.

Based on previous experience of IBIT with the participants we could expect that users would mainly specialize the modules of the shared ontology corresponding to their domain of expertise and work. Thus, it was decided by the ontology engineers and knowledge providers involved in building the initial version that the shared ontology should only evolve by addition of new concepts, and not from other more sophisticated operations, such as restructuring or deletion of concepts.

Local Adaptation. The developed core ontology for "Sustainable Development Indicator" was distributed among the users and they were asked to extend it with their local structures. With assistance of the developers they extracted on average 14 folders. The users mainly created sub concepts of concepts in the core ontology from the folder names. In other cases they created their own concept hierarchy from their folder structure and aligned it with the core ontology. They did not create new relations. Instance assignment took place, but was not significant. We omitted the use of the automatic functions to get a better grasp of the actions the users did manually.

Analyzing. The members of the board gathered the evolving structures and analyzed them with help of the OntoEdit plug-in. The following observations were made:

Concepts matched A third of the extracted folder names was directly aligned with the core ontology. A further tenth of them was used to extend existing concepts.

Folder names indicate relations In the core ontology a relation inYear between the concept Indicator and Temporal was defined. This kind of relation is often encoded in one folder name. *e.g.* the folder name "SustInd2002" matches the concepts Sustainable Indicator and Year[11]. It also points to a modelling problem, since Sustainable Indicator is a concept while "2002" is an instance of concept Year.

Missing top level concepts The concept project was introduced by more than half of the participants, but was not part of the initial shared ontology.

Refinement of concepts The top level concept Indicator was extended by more than half of the participants, while other concepts were not extended.

Concepts were not used Some of the originally defined concepts were never used. We identified concepts as used, when the users created instances, or aligned documents with them. A further indicator of usage was the creation of sub concepts.

Folder names represent instances The users who defined the concept project used some of their folder names to create instances of that concept *e.g.* "Sustainable indicators project".

Different labels The originally introduced concept Natural spaces was often aligned with a newly created concept Natural environments and never used itself.

Ontology did not fit One user did create his own hierarchy and could use only one of the predefined concepts. Indeed his working area was forgotten in the first ontology building workshop.

From the discussions with the domain experts we have the impression that the local extensions are a good indicator for the evolution direction of the core ontology. However, since the users made use of the possibility to extend the core ontology with their folder names, as we expected, the resulting local ontologies represent the subjects of the organized documents. Therefore, a knowledge engineer is still needed to extend the core ontology, but the basis of his work is being improved significantly. From our point of view there is only a limited potential to automate this process.

Revision. The board extended the core ontology where it was necessary and performed some renaming. More specifically the board introduced (1) one top level concept (Project) and (2) four sub concepts of the top level concept Indicator and one for the concept Document. The users were further pointed to the possibility to create instances of the introduced concepts. *E.g.* some folder names specified project names, thus could be enriched by such an annotation.

Local update. The extensions to the core ontology were distributed to the users. The general feedback of the users was generally positive. However, due to the early development stage of the SWAP environment a prolonged evaluation of the user behavior and second cycle in the ontology engineering process has not yet been performed.

---

[11] Year is sub class of class Temporal

5   Lessons Learned

The case study helped us to generally better comprehend the use of ontologies in a peer-to-peer environment. First of all our users did understand the ontology mainly as a classification hierarchy for their documents. Hence, they did not create instances of the defined concepts. However, our expectation that folder structures can serve as a good input for an ontology engineer to build an ontology was met.

Currently we doubt that our manual approach to analyzing local structures will scale to cases with many more users. Therefore, we look into technical support to recognize similarities in user behavior. Furthermore, the local update will be a problem when changes happen more often. Last, but not least, we have so far only addressed the ontology creation task itself – we have not yet measured if users get better and faster responses with the help of DILIGENT-engineered ontologies. All this remains work to be done in future.

In spite of the technical challenges, user feedback was very positive since (i) the tool was integrated into their daily work environment and could be easily used and (ii) the tool provided very beneficial support to perform their tasks.

6   Related Work

An extensive state-of-the-art overview of methodologies for ontology engineering can be found in (cf. [14]). We here briefly present some of the most well-known ontology engineering methodologies.

CommonKADS [1] is not per se a methodology for ontology development. It covers aspects from corporate knowledge management, through knowledge analysis and engineering, to the design and implementation of knowledge-intensive information systems. CommonKADS has a focus on the initial phases for developing knowledge management applications, one can therefore make use of CommonKADS e.g. for early feasibility stages.

Methontology [14] is a methodology for building ontologies either from scratch, reusing other ontologies as they are, or by a process of re-engineering them. The framework consists of: identification of the ontology development process where the main activities are identified (evaluation, configuration, management, conceptualization, integration implementation, etc.); a lifecycle based on evolving prototypes; and the methodology itself, which specifies the steps to be taken to perform each activity, the techniques used, the products to be output and how they are to be evaluated.

Even though Methontology already mentions evolving prototypes, none of these (and similar others) methodologies responds to the requirements for distributed, loosely controlled and dynamic ontology engineering.

There exists a plethora of 'ontology editors'. We briefly compare two of the most well-known ones to OntoEdit viz. Protégé and WebODE. The design of Protégé [23] is very similar to OntoEdit since it actually was the first editor with an extensible plug-in structure and it also relies on the frame paradigm for modelling. Numerous plug-ins from external developers exist. WebODE [24] is an ontology engineering workbench that provides various services for ontology engineering. Similar to OntoEdit it is accompanied by a sophisticated methodology of ontology engineering, see above Methontology. However, no support of these tools is so far known for distributed, loosely controlled and evolving ontology engineering such as we have presented for OntoEdit.

There are a number of technical solutions to tackle problems of remote collaboration, *e.g.* ontology editing with mutual exclusion [25, 26], inconsistency detection with a voting mechanism [27] or evolution of ontologies by different means [17, 18, 22]. APECKS [28] allows users to discuss different modelling decisions online. All these solutions address the issue of keeping an ontology consistent. Obviously, none supports (and do not intend to) the work process of the ontology engineers by way of a methodology.

The development of the National Cancer Institute Thésaurus [29] could be an interesting application scenario for DILIGENT, because their processes seem to follow our process templates. However, they focus on the creation of the thésaurus itself rather than on a generalizable methodology.

7   Conclusion

It is now widely agreed that ontologies are a core enabler for the Semantic Web vision. The development of ontologies in centralized settings is well studied and established methodologies exist. However, current experiences from projects suggest, that ontology engineering should be subject to continuous improvement rather than a one time action and that ontologies promise the most benefits in decentralized rather than centralized systems. Hence, a methodology for distributed, loosely-controlled and dynamic ontology engineering settings is needed. The current version of DILIGENT is a step towards such a methodology.

DILIGENT comprises the steps **Build**, **Local Adaptation**, **Analysis**, **Revision** and **Local Update** and introduces a board to supervise changes to a shared core ontology. The DILIGENT methodology is supported by an OntoEdit plug-in, which is an implementation of the *Edit* component in the SWAP system. The plug-in supports the board mainly in recognizing changes to the core ontology by different users during the analysis and revision steps and highlights commonalities. It thus supports the user in extending and changing the core.

We have applied the methodology with good results in a case study at IBIT, one of the partners of the SWAP project. We found that the local extensions are very document centered. Though we are aware that this may often lead to unclean ontologies, we believe it to be one (of many) important step(s) towards creating a practical semantic web in the near future.

Acknowledgements. Research reported in this paper has been partially financed by EU in the IST project SWAP (IST-2001-34103), the IST thematic network OntoWeb (IST-2000-29243), the IST project SEKT (IST-2003-506826) and Fundação Calouste Gulbenkian (21-63057-B). In particular we want to thank Immaculada Salamanca and Esteve Lladó Martí from IBIT for the fruitful discussions and the other people in the SWAP team for their collaboration towards SWAPSTER.

References

1. Schreiber, G., et al.: Knowledge Engineering and Management — The CommonKADS Methodology. The MIT Press, Cambridge, Massachusetts; London, England (1999)
2. Camarinha-Matos, L.M., Afsarmanesh, H., eds.: Processes and Foundations for Virtual Organizations. Volume 262 of IFIP INTERNATIONAL FEDERATION FOR INFORMATION PROCESSIN. Kluwer Academic Publishers (2003)
3. Bonifacio, M., Bouquet, P., Mameli, G., Nori, M.: Peer-mediated distributed knowldege management. [30] To appear 2003.
4. Ehrig, M., Haase, P., van Harmelen, F., Siebes, R., Staab, S., Stuckenschmidt, H., Studer, R., Tempich, C.: The swap data and metadata model for semantics-based peer-to-peer systems. In: Proceedings of MATES-2003. First German Conference on Multiagent Technologies. LNAI, Erfurt, Germany, Springer (2003)
5. Klyne, G., Carroll, J.J.: Resource Description Framework (RDF): Concepts and abstract syntax. http://www.w3.org/TR/rdf-concepts/ (2003)
6. Broekstra, J., Kampman, A., van Harmelen, F.: Sesame: A generic architecture for storing and querying RDF and RDFSchema. [31] 54–68
7. Gong, L.: Project JXTA: A technology overview. Technical report, Sun Micros. Inc. (2001)
8. Broekstra, J.: SeRQL: Sesame RDF query language. In Ehrig, M., et al., eds.: SWAP Deliverable 3.2 Method Design. (2003) 55–68
9. Karvounarakis, G., et al.: Querying RDF descriptions for community web portals. In: Proceedings of The French National Conference on Databases 2001 (BDA'01), Agadir, Maroc (2001) 133–144
10. Sure, Y., Angele, J., Staab, S.: OntoEdit: Multifaceted inferencing for ontology engineering. Journal on Data Semantics, LNCS **2800** (2003) 128–152
11. Pinto, H.S., Martins, J.: Evolving Ontologies in Distributed and Dynamic Settings. In Fensel, D., Giunchiglia, F., McGuinness, D., Williams, M., eds.: Proc. of the 8th Int. Conf. on Principles of Knowledge Representation and Reasoning (KR2002), San Francisco, Morgan Kaufmann (2002) 365–374
12. Staab, S., Schnurr, H.P., Studer, R., Sure, Y.: Knowledge processes and ontologies. IEEE Intelligent Systems **16** (2001) Special Issue on Knowledge Management.
13. Gangemi, A., Pisanelli, D., Steve, G.: Ontology integration: Experiences with medical terminologies. In Guarino, N., ed.: Formal Ontology in Information Systems, Amsterdam, IOS Press (1998) 163–178
14. Gómez-Pérez, A., Fernández-López, M., Corcho, O.: Ontological Engineering. Advanced Information and Knowlege Processing. Springer (2003)
15. Pinto, H.S., Martins, J.: A Methodology for Ontology Integration. In: Proc. of the First Int. Conf. on Knowledge Capture (K-CAP2001), New York, ACM Press (2001) 131–138
16. Uschold, M., King, M.: Towards a methodology for building ontologies. In: Proc. of IJ-CAI95's WS on Basic Ontological Issues in Knowledge Sharing, Montreal, Canada (1995)
17. Noy, N., Klein, M.: Ontology evolution: Not the same as schema evolution. Knowledge and Information Systems (2003)
18. Stojanovic, L., et al.: User-driven ontology evolution management. In: Proc. of the 13th Europ. Conf. on Knowledge Eng. and Knowledge Man. EKAW, Madrid, Spain (2002)
19. Guarino, N., Welty, C.: Evaluating ontological decisions with OntoClean. Communications of the ACM **45** (2002) 61–65
20. Noy, N., Musen, M.: The PROMPT suite: Interactive tools for ontology merging and mapping. Technical report, SMI, Stanford University, CA, USA (2002)
21. Sebastiani, F.: Machine learning in automated text categorization. ACM Computing Surveys **34** (2002) 1–47

22. Maedche, A., Motik, B., Stojanovic, L.: Managing multiple and distributed ontologies on the semantic web. The VLDB Journal **12** (2003) 286–302
23. Noy, N., Fergerson, R., Musen, M.: The knowledge model of Protégé-2000: Combining interoperability and flexibility. In Dieng, R., Corby, O., eds.: Proc. of the 12th Int. Conf. on Knowledge Eng. and Knowledge Man.: Methods, Models, and Tools (EKAW 2000). Volume 1937 of LNAI., Juan-les-Pins, France, Springer (2000) 17–32
24. Arpírez, J.C., et al.: WebODE: a scalable workbench for ontological engineering. In: Proceedings of the First Int. Conf. on Knowledge Capture (K-CAP) Oct. 21-23, 2001, Victoria, B.C., Canada. (2001)
25. Farquhar, A., et al.: The ontolingua server: A tool for collaborative ontology construction. Technical report KSL 96-26, Stanford (1996)
26. Sure, Y., Erdmann, M., Angele, J., Staab, S., Studer, R., Wenke, D.: OntoEdit: Collaborative ontology development for the semantic web. [31] 221–235
27. Pease, A., Li, J.: Agent-mediated knowledge engineering collaboration. [30] 405–415
28. Tennison, J., Shadbolt, N.R.: APECKS: a Tool to Support Living Ontologies. In Gaines, B., Musen, M., eds.: 11th Knowledge Acquisition for Knowledge-Bases Systems Workshop (KAW98). (1998) 1–20
29. Golbeck, J., Fragoso, G., Hartel, F., Hendler, J., Parsia, B., Oberthaler, J.: The national cancer institute's thesaurus and ontology. Journal of Web Semantics **1** (2003)
30. van Elst, L., et al., eds. LNAI. Springer, Berlin (2003)
31. Horrocks, I., Hendler, J., eds. In Horrocks, I., Hendler, J., eds.: Proc. of the 1st Int. Semantic Web Conf. (ISWC 2002). Volume 2342 of LNCS., Sardinia, IT, Springer (2002)

A Protégé Plug-In for Ontology Extraction from Text Based on Linguistic Analysis

Paul Buitelaar[1], Daniel Olejnik[1], Michael Sintek[2]

[1] DFKI GmbH, Language Technology, Stuhlsatzenhausweg 3,
66123 Saarbruecken, Germany
{paulb, olejnik}@dfki.de

[2] DFKI GmbH, Knowledge Management, Erwin-Schrödinger-Straße,
67608 Kaiserslautern, Germany
sintek@dfki.de

Abstract. In this paper we describe a plug-in (OntoLT) for the widely used Protégé ontology development tool that supports the interactive extraction and/or extension of ontologies from text. The OntoLT approach provides an environment for the integration of linguistic analysis in ontology engineering through the definition of mapping rules that map linguistic entities in annotated text collections to concept and attribute candidates (i.e. Protégé classes and slots). The paper explains this approach in more detail and discusses some initial experiments on deriving a shallow ontology for the neurology domain from a corresponding collection of neurological scientific abstracts.

1   Introduction

With a recent increase in developments towards knowledge-based applications such as Intelligent Question-Answering, Semantic Web Services and Semantic-Level Multimedia Search, the interest in large-scale ontologies has increased. Additionally, as ontologies are domain descriptions that tend to evolve rapidly over time and between different applications (see e.g. Noy and Klein, 2002) there has been an increasing development in recent years towards learning or adapting ontologies dynamically, e.g. by analysis of a corresponding knowledge base (Deitel et al., 2001, Suryanto and Compton, 2001) or document collection.

Most of the work in ontology learning has been directed towards learning ontologies from text[1]. As human language is a primary mode of knowledge transfer, ontology learning from relevant text collections seems indeed a viable option as illustrated by a number of systems that are based on this principle, e.g. ASIUM (Faure et al., 1998), TextToOnto (Maedche and Staab, 2000; Maedche) and Ontolearn (Navigli et al., 2003). All of these combine a certain level of linguistic analysis with machine

---

[1] See for instance the overview of ontology learning systems and approaches in OntoWeb deliverable 1.5 (Gomez-Perez et al., 2003).

J. Davies et al. (Eds.): ESWS 2004, LNCS 3053, pp. 31-44, 2004.

learning algorithms to find potentially interesting concepts and relations between them (see also Maedche, 2003).

A typical approach in ontology learning from text first involves term extraction from a domain-specific corpus through a statistical process that determines their relevance for the domain corpus at hand. These are then clustered into groups with the purpose of identifying a taxonomy of potential classes. Subsequently also relations can be identified by computing a statistical measure of 'connectedness' between identified clusters.

The OntoLT approach follows a similar procedure, but we aim also at more directly connecting ontology engineering with linguistic analysis. Through the use of mapping rules between linguistic structure and ontological knowledge, linguistic knowledge (context words, morphological and syntactic structure, etc.) remains associated with the constructed ontology and may be used subsequently in its application and maintenance, e.g. in knowledge markup, ontology mapping and ontology evolution.

2   OntoLT

The OntoLT approach (introduced in Buitelaar et al., 2003) is available as a plug-in for the widely used Protégé ontology development tool[2], which enables the definition of mapping rules with which concepts (Protégé classes) and attributes (Protégé slots) can be extracted automatically from linguistically annotated text collections. A number of mapping rules are included with the plug-in, but alternatively the user can define additional rules.

The ontology extraction process is implemented as follows. OntoLT provides a precondition language, with which the user can define mapping rules. Preconditions are implemented as XPATH expressions over the XML-based linguistic annotation. If all constraints are satisfied, the mapping rule activates one or more operators that describe in which way the ontology should be extended if a candidate is found.

Predefined preconditions select for instance the predicate of a sentence, its linguistic subject or direct object. Preconditions can also be used to check certain conditions on these linguistic entities, for instance if the subject in a sentence corresponds to a particular lemma (the morphological stem of a word). The precondition language consists of Terms and Functions, to be discussed in more detail in section 4.2.

Selected linguistic entities may be used in constructing or extending an ontology. For this purpose, OntoLT provides operators to create classes, slots and instances. According to which preconditions are satisfied, corresponding operators will be activated to create a set of candidate classes and slots that are to be validated by the user. Validated candidates are then integrated into a new or existing ontology.

---

[2] http://protégé.stanford.edu

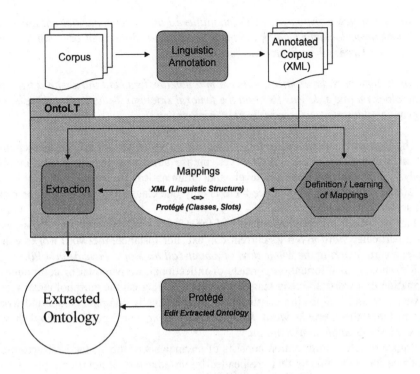

Figure 1: Overview of the OntoLT Approach

3   Linguistic Annotation

Linguistic annotation is not integrated with OntoLT, but is accessed via an XML-based exchange format, which integrates multiple levels of linguistic and semantic analysis in a multi-layered DTD with each analysis level (e.g. morphological, syntactic and dependency structure) organized as a separate track with options of reference between them via indices[3].

Linguistic annotation is currently provided by SCHUG, a rule-based system for German and English analysis (Declerck, 2002) that implements a cascade of increasingly complex linguistic fragment recognition processes. SCHUG provides annotation of part-of-speech (through integration of TnT: Brants, 2000), morphological inflection and decomposition (based on Mmorph: Petitpierre and Russell, 1995), phrase and dependency structure (head-complement, head-modifier and grammatical functions).

In Figure 2, we present a section of the linguistic annotation for the following sentence (German with corresponding sentence from the English abstract):

---

[3] The format presented here is based on proposals and implementations described in (Buitelaar et al., 2003) and (Buitelaar and Declerck, 2003).

An 40 Kniegelenkpräparaten wurden mittlere Patellarsehnendrittel mit einer neuen Knochenverblockungstechnik in einem zweistufigen Bohrkanal bzw. mit konventioneller Interferenzschraubentechnik femoral fixiert.

(In 40 human cadaver knees, either a mid patellar ligament third with a trapezoid bone block on one side was fixed on the femoral side in a 2-diameter drill hole, or a conventional interference screw fixation was applied.)

The linguistic annotation for this sentence consists of part-of-speech and lemmatization information in the <text> level, phrase structure (including head-modifier analysis) in the <phrases> level and grammatical function analysis in the <clauses> level (in this sentence there is only one clause, but more than one clause per sentence is possible).

Part-of-speech information consists of the correct syntactic class (e.g. noun, verb) for a particular word given its current context. For instance, the word *works* will be either a verb *(working the whole day)* or a noun *(all his works have been sold).*

Morphological information consists of inflectional, derivational or compound information of a word. In many languages other than English the morphological system is very rich and enables the construction of semantically complex compound words. For instance the German word *Kreuzbandverletzung* corresponds in English with three words: *cruciate ligament injury.*

Phrase structure information consists of an analysis of the syntactic structure of a sentence into constituents that are headed by an adjective, a noun or a preposition. Additionally, the internal structure of the phrase will be analyzed and represented, which includes information on modifiers that further specify the head. For instance, in the nominal phrase *neue Technik (new technology)* the modifier *neu* further specifies the head *Technik.*

Clause structure information consists of an analysis of the core semantic units (clauses) in a sentence with each clause consisting of a predicate (mostly a verb) with its arguments and adjuncts. Arguments are expressed by grammatical functions such as the subject or direct object of a verb. Adjuncts are mostly prepositional phrases, which further specify the clause. For instance, in *John played football in the garden* the prepositional phrase *in the garden* further specifies the clause *"play (John, football)".*

All such information is provided by the annotation format that is illustrated in Figure 2 below. For instance, the direct object (**DOBJ**) in the sentence above (or rather in clause **cl1**) covers the nominal phrase **p2**, which in turn corresponds to tokens **t5** to **t10** (*mittlere Patellarsehnendrittel mit einer neuen Knochenverblockungstechnik*). As token **t6** is a German compound word, a morphological analysis is included that corresponds to lemmas **t6.l1, t6.l2, t6.l3.**

```
<sentence id="s3" stype="decl" corresp=" ">

 <clauses>
  <clause id="cl1" from="p1" to="p5" pred="p5" type="pass">
    <arg id="a1" type="SUBJ" phrase="none" />
    <arg id="a2" type="IOBJ" phrase="p1"/>
    <arg id="a3" type="DOBJ" phrase="p2" />
    <arg id="a4" type="PP_ADJ" phrase="p3"/>
  </clause>
 </clauses>

 <phrases>
   ...
  <phrase id="p2" from="t5" to="t10" type="NP">
    <mod from="t5" to="t5" />
    <head from="t6" to="t6" />
    <mod_post from="t7" to="t10" />
  </phrase>
   ...
 </phrases>

 <text>
  <token id="t1" pos="APPR" str="An">
   <lemma id="t1.l1">an</lemma>
  </token>
  <token id="t2" pos="CARD" str="40" />
  <token id="t3" pos="NN" str="Kniegelenkpraeparaten">
   <lemma id="t3.l1">Kniegelenk</lemma>
   <lemma id="t3.l2">Praeparat</lemma>
  </token>
  <token id="t4" pos="VAFIN" str="wurden">
   <lemma id="t4.l1">werden</lemma>
  </token>
  <token id="t5" pos="ADJA" str="mittlere">
   <lemma id="t5.l1">mittler</lemma>
  </token>
  <token id="t6" pos="NN" str="Patellarsehnendrittel">
   <lemma id="t6.l1">patellar</lemma>
   <lemma id="t6.l2">Sehne</lemma>
   <lemma id="t6.l3">Drittel</lemma>
  </token>
   ...
  <token id="t19" pos="ADJD" str="femoral" />
  <token id="t20" pos="VVPP" str="fixiert">
   <lemma id="t6.l1">fixieren</lemma>
  </token>
  <token id="t21" pos="PUNCT" str="." />
 </text>
</sentence>
```

Figure 2: Linguistic Annotation Example

4   Ontology Extraction from Text with OntoLT

The ontology extraction process is implemented as follows. OntoLT provides a pre-condition language with which the user can define mapping rules. Preconditions are implemented as XPATH expressions over the linguistic annotation. If the precondition is satisfied, the mapping rule activates one or more operators that describe in which way the ontology should be extended if a candidate is found.

4.1   Mapping Rules

A number of mapping rules are predefined and included with the OntoLT plug-in, but alternatively the user may define additional mapping rules, either manually or by the integration of a machine learning process. In Figure 3, two rules are defined for mapping information from the linguistic annotation to potential Protégé classes and slots:

- **HeadNounToClass_ModToSubClass** maps a head-noun to a class and in combination with its modifier(s) to one or more sub-class(es)

- **SubjToClass_PredToSlot_DObjToRange** maps a linguistic subject to a class, its predicate to a corresponding slot for this class and the direct object to the "range" of this slot.

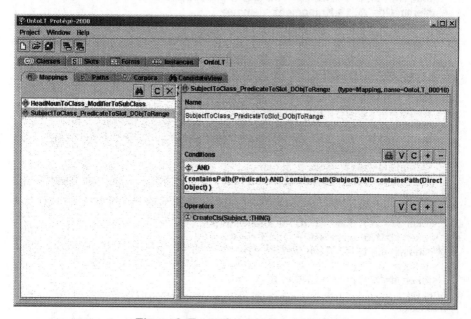

Figure 3: Example Mappings in OntoLT

4.2   Precondition Language

OntoLT provides a precondition language for defining mapping rules, which allows for the selection of particular linguistic entities in the annotated documents. Predefined predicates[4] of the precondition language select, e.g., the pred (linguistic predicate) of a sentence, its subject or object. Preconditions can also be used to check certain conditions on these linguistic entities, for instance if the subject corresponds to a certain semantic class[5]. Correspondingly, the precondition language consists of terms (constants and functions) and predicates.

Predicates can be one of[6]:

containsPath	:	returns true/false if a certain path is contained in the source or not
HasValue	:	returns true/false if a certain path has a specified value or not
HasConcept	:	returns true/false if a certain path corresponds to a specified concept code (e.g. a EuroWordNet sense)
AND	:	Boolean 'and'
OR	:	Boolean 'or'
NOT	:	Boolean 'not'
EQUAL	:	tests if two terms are equal

Currently, the only supported function is:

ID	:	returns the ID of a node of the XML-source

Selection of the pred, object and subject of a sentence can then be implemented by the definition of the precondition that was shown in Figure 3., which checks if there are any valid XPATH expressions for subject, object and pred.

```
(containsPath(Pred) AND
containsPath(Subject) AND
containsPath(Object))
```

---

[4] Unfortunately, we need to use the word "predicate" in two different meanings, either as: 1. a predicate of the precondition language; 2. a predicate in the linguistic analysis. To distinguish the two meanings, we will write pred for the linguistic use of "predicate".

[5] Semantic class information may be provided by a lexical semantic resource, such as WordNet (Miller, 1995) for English or EuroWordNet (Vossen, 1997) for various other languages, or by a domain-specific thesaurus or ontology, such as MeSH (Medical Subject Headings) for the biomedical domain: http://www.nlm.nih.gov/mesh/meshhome.html

[6] In the current implementation, with more predicates (and functions) to be added upon need.

4.3   Operators

Selected linguistic entities may be used in constructing or extending an ontology. For this purpose, OntoLT provides operators to create classes, slots and instances:

CreateCls   : create a new class
AddSlot   : add a slot to a class or create it if non-existing
CreateInstance   : introduce a new instance for an existing or new class
FillSlot   : set the value of a slot of an instance

OntoLT executes all mapping rules collectively. Therefore, according to which preconditions are satisfied, all corresponding operators will be activated to create a set of candidate classes and slots that are to be validated by the user. According to this interactive process, classes and slots will be automatically generated into a new ontology or integrated into an existing ontology.

4.4   Statistical Preprocessing

In order to use only extracted linguistic information that is relevant for the domain, the approach includes a statistical preprocessing step. Here we base our approach on the use of the "chi-square" function in (Agirre et al., 2001) for determining domain relevance[7]. This function computes a relevance score by comparison of frequencies in a domain corpus under consideration with that of frequencies in a reference corpus. In this way, word use in a particular domain is contrasted with that of more general word use.

4.5   Semi-automatic Generation of Mapping Rules

The statistical preprocessing step also allows for a semi-automatic generation of mapping rules. For this purpose, we can simply generate mapping rules for all possible XML-elements in the linguistic annotation (e.g. pred, mod, head) constrained to only those words that were selected by the chi-square measure. User interaction will however still be needed to specify the operators associated with these generated conditions for the mapping rules to be defined. For instance, it would need to be decided if the lemma of a pred should be generated as a class, or rather as a slot for a class that should be generated for the lemma of a particular head, or if a class should be generated for the lemma of the modifier (mod), etc. In future work, also this aspect could be further supported by inclusion of a machine-learning component based on active learning (see e.g. Finn and Kushmerick, 2003) that would enable the automatic generation of operators given a training process on previous specifications by the user.

---

[7] The chi-square function gives a good indication of relevance, but experiments showed that also absolute frequency is an important indication of relevance. We therefore additionally multiply the chi-square score by absolute frequency to obtain a combined measure of frequency and relevance.

5   Experiment: Extracting an Ontology for Neurology

In order to test our approach in a realistic setting, we defined the following experiment. Given a corpus of medical texts in the neurology domain, we applied OntoLT in combination with linguistic annotation as described above to extract a shallow ontology for this domain.

The neurology corpus that we used in the experiment is a section of the bilingual (English-German) medical corpus that was constructed within the MuchMore project on cross-lingual information retrieval in the medical domain. The MuchMore corpus includes around 9000 scientific abstracts in various medical sub-domains[8] with around 1 million tokens for each language (see Buitelaar et al., 2004). The neurology section of the MuchMore corpus consists of 493 abstracts.

As a first step, the neurology corpus is linguistically analyzed and annotated with SCHUG, according to the XML-format presented in section 3 above. In all further steps, this linguistically annotated version of the corpus is used rather than the original text version.

5.1   Statistical Preprocessing of the Neurology Corpus

To extract only relevant linguistic entities from the neurology corpus, we applied the chi-square measure as discussed above. The rest of the MuchMore corpus was used in this process as a contrasting reference corpus (representing the medical domain in general) that allowed for the identification of those linguistic entities that are specific to neurology.

In the following tables, a selection of extracted 10 topmost relevant linguistic entities (head, mod, pred) are given for the neurology corpus (German with English translations):

	Dysgenesie (dysgenesia)
	Denkstörung (thought disorder)
	Epilepsie (epilepsia)
	Psychiater (psychiatrist)
head	*Aura (aura)*
	Tremor (tremor)
	Asystolie (asystole)
	Dopaminfreisetzung (dopamine release)
	Obdachlose (homeless)
	Aphasie (aphasia)

Table 1: 10 topmost relevant Heads in the Neurology corpus

---

[8] The MuchMore corpus and related evaluation resources and interactive demos are publicly available from the project website: http://muchmore.dfki.de

	schizophren (schizophrenic)
	epileptisch (epileptic)
	transkraniel
	paranoid (paranoid)
mod	*neuroleptisch (neuroleptic)*
	neuropsychriatisch (neuro psychiatric)
	serotonerg
	impulsiv (impulsive)
	intraventrikulär (intra ventricular)
	neuropsychologisch (neuro psychological)

Table 2: 10 topmost relevant Modifiers in the Neurology corpus

	zuerkennen (to adjudicate, award)
	staerken (to boost, encourage, strengthen)
	sparen (to conserve, save)
	betreten (to enter)
pred	*hervorbringen (to create, produce)*
	befuerworten (to support, advocate)
	gebrauchen (to employ, use)
	begreifen (to apprehend, understand)
	ueben (to exercise, practice)
	imitieren (to copy, imitate, mimic)

Table 3: 10 topmost relevant Predicates in the Neurology corpus

5.2   Definition of Mapping Rules for Neurology

The results of the statistical processing are now used to generate one or more mappings between selected elements in the linguistic annotation (e.g. head, mod, pred) and Protégé classes and or slots. Here we present two examples.

HeadNounToClass_ModToSubClass

This mapping generates classes for all head-nouns (head) that were determined to be statistically relevant for the domain. For instance, classes are generated for the head-nouns *Dysgenesie (dysgenesia)* and *Epilepsie (epilepsia)*. Further, for each of these, sub-classes are generated for corresponding modifiers (mod). For the two classes just mentioned, the following sub-classes are generated:

Dysgenesie	:	Dysgenesie_kortikal *(cortical)*
Epilepsie	:	Epilepsie_myoklonisch *(myoclonic)*
		Epilepsie_idiopathisch *(idiopathic)*
		Epilepsie_fokal *(focal)*

SubjToClass_PredToSlot_DObjToRange

This mapping generates for all statistically relevant predicates (pred) a class for the head of the subject, a slot for the pred and a corresponding slot-range for the head of the object. For instance, consider the sentence:

Transitorische ischaemische Attacken imitieren in seltenen Fällen einfache fokale motorische Anfälle.

("Transient ischemic attacks mimicking in some cases simple partial motor seizures.")

In this case, a class is generated for the head of the subject *Attacke (attack)* and for the head of the object *Anfall (seizure)*. Further, a slot imitieren *(to mimic)* is generated for the new class attacke with the new class anfall as its range (i.e. the class of possible fillers for this slot).

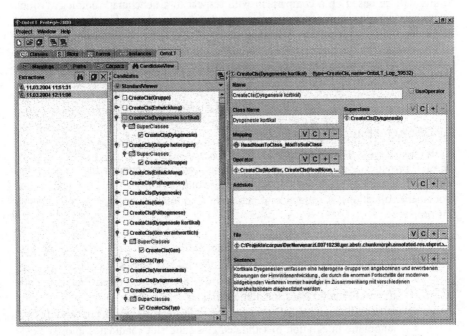

Figure 4: Class Candidates Generated by HeadNounToClass_ModToSubClass

6   Future Work

OntoLT allows for the semi-automatic extraction of shallow ontologies from German and English text collections. Future work will be concerned with providing further automatic support in the definition of mapping rules by refining and extending the statistical preprocessing step and by including an active learning approach (see also section 4.5).

Other aspects that will be worked on include: integration of linguistic annotation over a web service; integration of an information extraction approach for ontology population (identifying class instances); definition and implementation of an evaluation platform to evaluate extracted ontologies in a quantitative (technical performance) and qualitative (user satisfaction) way.

As discussed before, a number of different methods for text-based ontology extraction and learning have developed over recent years. However, in order to compare the performance of OntoLT with these and other methods, a proper evaluation framework needs to be set up. Currently it is very hard to compare methods and approaches, due to the lack of a shared understanding of the task at hand. Future work will therefore be concerned also with a contribution towards the development of such a shared understanding and an appropriate evaluation framework accordingly.

We expect that the general problem of ontology extraction and learning can be decomposed into a set of simpler tasks, which can be addressed with well-established evaluation methodologies (i.e. *precision* and *recall*). The assessment of the system results will be based on a comparison with respect to a benchmark ontology, which has to be manually produced by domain experts taking into consideration the content that is implicitly available in a corresponding text collection. Evaluation measures will be defined on the basis of the benchmark, according to the experience of related evaluation efforts in information retrieval (TREC[9], CLEF[10]) and natural language processing (SENSEVAL[11]).

7   Conclusions

OntoLT provides a middleware solution in ontology development that enables the ontology engineer to bootstrap a domain-specific ontology from a relevant text corpus (document collection). A sequence of automatic and interactive steps are involved in this process:

- automatic linguistic analysis and annotation
- automatic statistical preprocessing of extracted linguistic entities
- interactive definition of mapping rules between extracted linguistic entities and Protégé class and slot candidates
- interactive user validation of generated Protégé class and slot candidates
- automatic integration of validated class and slot candidates into an existing or new ontology

---

[9] http://trec.nist.gov/
[10] http://clef.iei.pi.cnr.it:2002/
[11] http://www.senseval.org/

Acknowledgements

This research has in part been supported by EC grants IST-2000-29243 for the OntoWeb project, IST-2000-25045 for the MEMPHIS project and IST-2001-34373 for the ESPERONTO project.

Special thanks also to our colleagues at Saarland University (Thierry Declerck, Mihaela Hutanu, Alexander Schutz) for making available the SCHUG linguistic analysis tool and for their cooperation in the neurology experiment.

References

Agirre E., Ansa O., Martinez D., Hovy E. Enriching WordNet concepts with topic signatures. In: Proceedings NAACL WordNet Workshop, 2001.

Brants, T. TnT - A Statistical Part-of-Speech Tagger. In: Proceedings of 6th ANLP Conference, Seattle, 2000.

Buitelaar P., Declerck Th., Sacaleanu B., Vintar Š., Raileanu D., Crispi C. A Multi-Layered, XML-Based Approach to the Integration of Linguistic and Semantic Annotations. In: Proceedings of EACL 2003 Workshop on Language Technology and the Semantic Web (NLPXML'03), Budapest, Hungary, April 2003.

Buitelaar P. and Declerck Th. Linguistic Annotation for the Semantic Web. In: Handschuh S., Staab S. (eds.) Annotation for the Semantic Web, IOS Press, 2003.

Buitelaar P., Olejnik D. and Sintek M. OntoLT: A Protégé Plug-In for Ontology Extraction from Text In: Proceedings of the Demo Session of the International Semantic Web Conference ISWC-2003, Sanibel Island, Florida, October 2003.

Buitelaar P., Steffen D., Volk M., Widdows D., Sacaleanu B., Vintar Š., Peters S. and Uszkoreit H. Evaluation Resources for Concept-based Cross-Lingual Information Retrieval in the Medical Domain. In: Proceedings of LREC2004.

Declerck Th. A set of tools for integrating linguistic and non-linguistic information. Proceedings of the SAAKM workshop at ECAI, Lyon, 2002.

Deitel A., Faron C. and Dieng R. Learning Ontologies from RDF Annotations In: Proceedings of the IJCAI Workshop on Ontology Learning, Seattle, Washington, 2001.

Faure D., Nédellec C. and Rouveirol C. Acquisition of Semantic Knowledge using Machine learning methods: The System ASIUM. Technical report number ICS-TR-88-16, 1998.

Finn A. and Kushmerick N. Active Learning Strategies for Information Extraction In: Proceedings of the ECML/PKDD Workshop on Adaptive Text Extraction and Mining (ATEM), Cavtat-Dubrovnik, Croatia, September 22nd, 2003.

Gomez-Perez A. and Manzano-Macho D. A Survey of Ontology Learning Methods and Techniques. Deliverable 1.5, OntoWeb Project, 2003.

Gruber T. Towards principles for the design of ontologies used for knowledge sharing. Int. Journal of Human and Computer Studies 43(5/6), 1994, 907-928.

Maedche A. Ontology Learning for the Semantic Web. The Kluwer International Series in Engineering and Computer Science, Volume 665, 2003.

Maedche, A., Staab, S. Semi-automatic Engineering of Ontologies from Text. In: Proceedings of the 12th International Conference on Software Engineering and Knowledge Engineering, 2000.

Miller, G.A. WordNet: A Lexical Database for English. Communications of the ACM 11. 1995.

Navigli R., Velardi P., Gangemi A. Ontology Learning and its application to automated terminology translation. IEEE Intelligent Systems, vol. 18:1, January/February 2003.

Noy N. F. and Klein M. Ontology Evolution: Not the Same as Schema Evolution In: Knowledge and Information Systems, in press. Available as technical report SMI-2002-0926, 2002.

Petitpierre, D. and Russell, G. MMORPH - The Multext Morphology Program. Multext deliverable report for the task 2.3.1, ISSCO, University of Geneva. 1995.

Skut W. and Brants T. A Maximum Entropy partial parser for unrestricted text. In: Proceedings of the 6th ACL Workshop on Very Large Corpora (WVLC), Montreal. 1998.

Suryanto H. and Compton P. Discovery of Ontologies from Knowledge Bases In: Proceedings of the First International Conference on Knowledge Capture, Victoria, BC, Canada, October 2001.

Vossen P. EuroWordNet: a multilingual database for information retrieval. In: Proc. of the DELOS workshop on Cross-language Information Retrieval, March 5-7, Zürich, Switzerland, 1997.

Formal Support for Representing and Automating Semantic Interoperability

Yannis Kalfoglou[1] and Marco Schorlemmer[2]

[1] School of Electronics and Computer Science, University of Southampton, UK
y.kalfoglou@ecs.soton.ac.uk
[2] E. U. de Tecn. d'Informació i Comunicació,
Universitat Internacional de Catalunya, Spain
marco@cir.unica.edu

Abstract. We discuss approaches to semantic heterogeneity and propose a formalisation of semantic interoperability based on the Barwise-Seligman theory of information flow. We argue for a theoretical framework that favours the analysis and implementation of semantic interoperability scenarios relative to particular understandings of semantics. We present an example case of such a scenario where our framework has been applied as well as variations of it in the domain of ontology mapping.

1 Introduction

The problem of resolving semantic heterogeneity has been identified in the past in the field of federated databases as one of the core challenges for achieving semantic interoperability [22]. Despite collective efforts from researchers and industrialists it remains largely unsolved. Recently, the same challenge surfaced again in a different context, that of the Semantic Web. It has different characteristics though, which make it even harder to tackle, because we are dealing with a distributed and deregulated environment where the assurances of a strictly monitored database management system no longer hold.

One of the core premises of the Semantic Web vision is that systems should be able to exchange information and services with one another in semantically rich and sound manners [5]. The semantics of one system should therefore be exposed to the environment in such a way that other systems can interpret it correctly and use it to achieve interoperability, which is vital for distributed reasoning in order to support applications and services alike. However, there are numerous ways of expressing, exposing and understanding semantics, which leads to heterogeneity, more specifically, semantic heterogeneity. Lessons learned from previous attempts to resolve semantic heterogeneity—and also from peripheral areas where inconsistency has shown that semantic heterogeneity is an endemic characteristic of distributed systems and we should learn to live with it [10]—has prompted us to look at this challenge from another angle: to achieve the necessary and sufficient semantic interoperability even if it means that we will not resolve semantic heterogeneity completely.

J. Davies et al. (Eds.): ESWS 2004, LNCS 3053, pp. 45–60, 2004.

To understand the necessary and sufficient conditions for achieving semantic interoperability we need to look what the minimal requirements for interoperability are. For two systems to interoperate there must be an established form of communication and the right means to achieve this efficiently and effectively. An established form of communication clearly resembles the idea of agreed standards, and there has been considerable effort in the knowledge engineering community to come up with the right technologies for enforcing them. Ontologies are among the most popular ones, which act at the protocol to which systems have to adhere in order to establish interoperability. Although ontologies provide the means to establish communication efficiently there are not always effective. The crux of the problem is the increasing proliferation of domain and application ontologies on the Semantic Web, and, since they were built independently by distinct groups, they are semantically heterogeneous, hence outweighing the benefits of having an ontology in the first place. Enforcing a single standard ontology (or a set of standard ontologies) could alleviate the problem, but history of computing has taught us that this is a long process with arguable results. If we accept that ontologies are necessary for expressing and exposing semantics of systems and domains to the Semantic Web, then we have to anticipate different versions of them which are semantically heterogeneous and have to be shared in order to achieve interoperability.

2 Semantic Interoperability and Integration

Semantic interoperability and semantic integration are much contested and fuzzy concepts, which have been used over the past decade in a variety of contexts and works. As reported in [21], in addition, both terms are often used indistinctly, and some view these as the same thing.

The ISO/IEC 2382 Information Technology Vocabulary defines interoperability as "the capability to communicate, execute programs, or transfer data among various functional units in a manner that requires the user to have little or no knowledge of the unique characteristics of those units." In a debate on the mailing list of the IEEE Standard Upper Ontology working group, a more formal approach to semantic interoperability was advocated: to use logic in order to guarantee that, after data were transmitted from a sender system to a receiver, all implications made by one system had to hold and be provable by the other, and that there should be a logical equivalence between those implications.[3]

With respect to integration, Uschold and Grüninger argue that "two agents are semantically integrated if they can successfully communicate with each other" and that "successful exchange of information means that the agents understand each other and there is guaranteed accuracy" [26]. According to Sowa, to integrate two ontologies means to derive a new ontology that facilitates interoperability between systems based on the original ontologies, and he distinguishes three levels of integration [23]: *Alignment*—a mapping of concepts and relations to

---

[3] Message thread on the SUO mailing list initiated at http://suo.ieee.org/email/msg07542.html.

indicate equivalence—, *partial compatibility*—an alignment that supports equivalent inferences and computations on equivalent concepts and relations—, and *unification*—a one-to-one alignment of all concepts and relations that allows any inference or computation expressed in one ontology to be mapped to an equivalent inference or computation in the other ontology.

The above definitions reveal a common denominator, that of *communication*. As we said in the introduction, since ontologies have been established as the preferable means for supporting communication, the research issue is the following: *Having established a protocol to which communication will be based, i.e., ontologies, what is the best way to effectively make those semantically interoperable?*

A practical angle of viewing this problem is to focus on the notion of equivalence. That is, we would like to establish some sort of correspondence between the systems and, subsequently, their ontologies, to make them interoperable; this could be done by reasoning about equivalent constructs of the two ontologies. However, equivalence is not a formally and consensually agreed term, neither do we have mechanisms for doing that. Hence, if we are to provide a formal, language-independent mechanism of semantic interoperability and integration, we need to use some formal notion of equivalence. And for a precise approximation to equivalence the obvious place to look at is Logic.

In this sense first-order logic seems the natural choice: among all logics it has a special status due to its expressive power, its natural deductive systems, and its intuitive model theory based on sets. In first-order logic, equivalence is approximated via the precise model-theoretic concept of *first-order equivalence*. This is the usual approach to formal semantic interoperability and integration; see e.g., [4,6,20,26] and also those based on Description Logics [1]. In Ciocoiu and Nau's treatment of the translation problem between knowledge sources that have been written in different knowledge representation languages, semantics is specified by means of a common ontology that is expressive enough to interpret the concepts in all agents' ontologies [6]. In that scenario, two concepts are equivalent if, and only if, they share exactly the same subclass of first-order models of the common ontology.

But this approach also has its drawbacks. First, such formal notion of equivalence requires the entire machinery of first-order model theory, which includes set theory, first-order structures, interpretation, and satisfaction. This appears to be heavyweight for certain interoperability scenarios. Madhavan et al. define the semantics in terms of instances in the domain [16]. This is also the case, for example, in Stumme and Maedche's ontology merging method, FCA-Merge [24], where the semantics of a concept symbol is captured through the instances classified to that symbol. These instances are documents, and a document is classified to a concept symbol if it contains a reference that is relevant to the concept. For FCA-Merge, two concepts are considered equivalent if, and only if, they classify exactly the same set of documents. Menzel makes similar objections to the use of first-order equivalence and proposes an axiomatic approach instead, inspired on property theory [25], where entailment and equivalence are not model-theoretically defined, but axiomatised in a logical language for ontology theory [19].

Second, since model-theory does not provide proof mechanisms for checking model equivalence, this has to be done indirectly via those theories that specify the models. This assumes that the logical theories captured in the ontologies are complete descriptions of the intended models (Uschold and Grüninger call these *verified ontologies* [26]), which will seldom be the case in practice. Furthermore, Corrêa da Silva et al. have shown situations in which even a common verified ontology is not enough, for example when a knowledge base whose inference engine is based on linear logic poses a query to a knowledge base with the same ontology, but whose inference engine is based on relevance logic [7]. The former should not accept answers as valid if the inference carried out in order to answer the query was using the contraction inference rule, which is not allowed in linear logic. Here, two concepts will be equivalent if, and only if, we can infer exactly the same set of consequences on their distinct inference engines.

A careful look at the several formal approaches to semantic integration mentioned above reveals many different understandings of semantics depending on the interoperability scenario under consideration. Hence, what we need in order to successfully tackle the problem of semantic interoperability is not so much a framework that establishes a particular semantic perspective (model-theoretic, property-theoretic, instance-based, etc.), but instead we need a framework that successfully captures semantic interoperability despite the different treatments of semantics.

3   An Approach Based on Information-Flow Theory

We observe that, in order for two systems to be semantically interoperable (or semantically integrated) we need to align and map their respective ontologies such that *the information can flow*. Consequently, we believe that a satisfactory formalisation of semantic interoperability can be built upon a mathematical theory capable of describing under which circumstances information flow occurs.

Although there is no such theory yet, there have been many notable efforts [9,8,3]. A good place to start establishing a foundation for formalising semantic interoperability is Barwise and Seligman's channel theory, a mathematical model that aims at establishing the laws that govern the flow of information. It is a general model that attempts to describe the information flow in any kind of distributed system, ranging form actual physical systems like a flashlight connecting a bulb to a switch and a battery, to abstract systems such as a mathematical proof connecting premises and hypothesis with inference steps and conclusions.

A significant effort to develop a framework around the issues of organising and relating ontologies based on channel theory is Kent's Information Flow Framework (IFF) [14], which is currently developed by the IEEE Standard Upper Ontology working group as a meta-level foundation for the development of upper ontologies[13].

3.1   IF Classification, Infomorphism, and Channel

In channel theory, each component of a distributed system is represented by an *IF classification* $\mathbf{A} = \langle tok(\mathbf{A}), typ(\mathbf{A}), \models_{\mathbf{A}} \rangle$, consisting of a set of *tokens*, $tok(\mathbf{A})$, a set of *types*, $typ(\mathbf{A})$, and a *classification relation*, $\models_{\mathbf{A}} \subseteq tok(\mathbf{A}) \times typ(\mathbf{A})$, that classifies tokens to types.[4] It is a very simple mathematical structure that effectively captures the local syntax and semantics of a community for the purpose of semantic interoperability.

For the problem that concerns us here the components of the distributed systems are the ontologies of the communities that desire to communicate. We model them as IF classifications, such that the syntactic expressions that a community uses to communicate constitute the types of the IF classification, and the meaning that these expressions take within the context of the community are represented by the way tokens are classified to types. Hence, *the semantics is characterised by what we choose to be the tokens of the IF classification*, and depending on the particular semantic interoperability scenario we want to model, types, tokens, and its classification relation will vary. For example, in FCA-Merge [24], types are concept symbols and tokens particular documents, while in Ciocoiu and Nau's scenario [6] types are expressions of knowledge representation languages and tokens are first-order structures. The crucial point is that *the semantics of the interoperability scenario crucially depends on our choice of types, tokens and their classification relation for each community*.

The flow of information between components in a distributed system is modelled in channel theory by the way the various IF classifications that represent the vocabulary and context of each component are connected with each other through *infomorphisms*. An infomorphism $f = \langle f^{\wedge}, f^{\vee} \rangle : \mathbf{A} \rightleftarrows \mathbf{B}$ from IF classifications $\mathbf{A}$ to $\mathbf{B}$ is a contravariant pair of functions $f^{\wedge} : typ(\mathbf{A}) \rightarrow typ(\mathbf{B})$ and $f^{\vee} : tok(\mathbf{B}) \rightarrow tok(\mathbf{A})$ satisfying, for each type $\alpha \in typ(\mathbf{A})$ and token $b \in tok(\mathbf{B})$, the fundamental property that $f^{\vee}(b) \models_{\mathbf{A}} \alpha$ iff $b \models_{\mathbf{B}} f^{\wedge}(\alpha)$:[5]

$$
\begin{array}{ccc}
\alpha & \xrightarrow{\;\;f^{\wedge}\;\;} & f^{\wedge}(\alpha) \\
{\scriptstyle \models_{\mathbf{A}}} \Big| & & \Big| {\scriptstyle \models_{\mathbf{B}}} \\
f^{\vee}(b) & \xleftarrow[\;\;f^{\vee}\;\;]{} & b
\end{array}
$$

A *distributed IF system* $\mathcal{A}$ consists then of an indexed family $cla(\mathcal{A}) = \{\mathbf{A}_i\}_{i \in I}$ of IF classifications together with a set $inf(\mathcal{A})$ of infomorphisms all having both domain and codomain in $cla(\mathcal{A})$.

A basic construct of channel theory is that of an *IF channel*—two IF classifications $\mathbf{A}_1$ and $\mathbf{A}_2$ connected through a core IF classification $\mathbf{C}$ via two infomorphisms f_1 and f_2:

---

[4] We are using the prefix 'IF' (information flow) in front of some channel-theoretic constructions to distinguish them from their usual meaning.

[5] Such contravariance is a recurrent theme in logic and mathematics and has been thoroughly studied within the context of Chu spaces [2,12]; it also underlies the mathematical theory of concept formation [11].

$$
\begin{array}{ccc}
 & \xrightarrow{\ f^\wedge_1\ } typ(\mathbf{C}) \xleftarrow{\ f^\wedge_2\ } & \\
typ(\mathbf{A}_1) & \quad\vert \vDash_{\mathbf C} & typ(\mathbf{A}_2) \\
\vert \vDash_{\mathbf A_1}\ \vert & \quad tok(\mathbf{C}) & \vert \vDash_{\mathbf A_2} \\
tok(\mathbf{A}_1) & \xleftarrow{f^\vee_1}\qquad\xrightarrow{f^\vee_2} & tok(\mathbf{A}_2)
\end{array}
$$

This basic construct captures the information flow between components $\mathbf{A}_1$ and $\mathbf{A}_2$. Note that, in Barwise and Seligman's model it is the particular tokens that carry information and that information flow crucially involves both types and tokens.

In fact, our approach uses this model to approximate the intuitive notion of equivalence necessary for achieving semantic interoperability with the precise notion of a type equivalence that is supported by the connection of tokens from $\mathbf{A}_1$ with tokens from $\mathbf{A}_2$ through the tokens of the core IF classification $\mathbf{C}$. This provides us with the general framework of semantic interoperability we are after, one that accommodates different understandings of semantics—depending on the particularities of the interoperability scenario—whilst retaining the core aspect that will allow communication among communities: a connection through their semantic tokens.

The key channel-theoretic construct we are going to exploit in order to outline our formal framework for semantic interoperability is that of a *distributed IF logic*. This is the logic that represents the information flow occurring in a distributed system. In particular we will be interested in a restriction of this logic to the language of those communities we are attempting to integrate. As we proceed, we will hint at the intuitions lying behind the channel-theoretical notions we are going to use; for a more in-depth understanding of channel theory we point the interested reader to [3].

3.2   IF Theory and Logic

Suppose two communities $\mathbf{A}_1$ and $\mathbf{A}_2$ need to interoperate, but are using different ontologies. To have them semantically interoperating will mean to know the semantic relationship in which they stand to each other. In terms of the channel-theoretic context, this means to know an *IF theory* that describes how the different types from $\mathbf{A}_1$ and $\mathbf{A}_2$ are logically related to each other.

Channel theory has been developed based on the understanding that information flow results from regularities in a distributed system: information of some components of a system carries information of other components because of the regularities among the connections. These regularities are implicit in the representation of the systems' components and its connections as IF classifications and infomorphisms, but in order to derive a notion of equivalence on the type-level of the system we need to capture this regularity in a logical fashion. This is achieved with IF theories and IF logics in channel theory.

An *IF theory* $T = \langle typ(T), \vdash \rangle$ consists of a set $typ(T)$ of types, and a binary relation $\vdash$ between subsets of $typ(T)$. Pairs $\langle \Gamma, \Delta \rangle$ of subsets of $typ(T)$ are called *sequents.* If $\Gamma \vdash \Delta$, for $\Gamma, \Delta \subseteq typ(T)$, then the sequent $\Gamma \vdash \Delta$ is called a *constraint.* T is *regular* if for all $\alpha \in typ(T)$ and all sets $\Gamma, \Gamma', \Delta, \Delta', \Sigma', \Sigma_0, \Sigma_1$ of types:

1. *Identity:* $\alpha \vdash \alpha$
2. *Weakening:* If $\Gamma \vdash \Delta$, then $\Gamma, \Gamma' \vdash \Delta, \Delta'$
3. *Global Cut:* If $\Gamma, \Sigma_0 \vdash \Delta, \Sigma_1$ for each partition $\langle \Sigma_0, \Sigma_1 \rangle$ of Σ', then $\Gamma \vdash \Delta$.[6]

Regularity arises from the observation that, given any classification of tokens to types, the set of all sequents that are satisfied by all tokens always fulfill these three properties. In addition, given a regular IF theory T we can generate a classification $Cla(T)$ that captures the regularity specified in its constraints. Its tokens are partitions $\langle \Gamma, \Delta \rangle$ of $typ(T)$ that are *not* constraints of T, and types are the types of T, such that $\langle \Gamma, \Delta \rangle \models_{Cla(T)} \alpha$ iff $\alpha \in \Gamma$.[7]

The IF theory we are after in order to capture the semantic interoperability between communities $\mathbf{A}_1$ and $\mathbf{A}_2$ is an IF theory on the union of types $typ(\mathbf{A}_1) \cup typ(\mathbf{A}_2)$ that respects the local IF classification systems of each community—the meaning each community attaches to its expressions—but also interrelates types whenever there is a similar semantic pattern, i.e., a similar way communities classify related tokens. This is the type language we speak in a semantic interoperability scenario, because we want to know when type α of one component corresponds to a type β of another component. In such an IF theory a sequent like $\alpha \vdash \beta$, with $\alpha \in typ(\mathbf{A}_1)$ and $\beta \in typ(\mathbf{A}_2)$, would represent an implication of types among communities that is in accordance to how the tokens of different communities are connected between each other. Hence, a constraint $\alpha \vdash \beta$ will represent that every α is a β, together with a constraint $\beta \vdash \alpha$ we obtain type equivalence.

Putting the idea of an IF classification with that of an IF theory together we get an *IF logic* $\mathfrak{L} = \langle tok(\mathfrak{L}), typ(\mathfrak{L}), \models_{\mathfrak{L}}, \vdash_{\mathfrak{L}} \rangle$. It consists of an IF classification $cla(\mathfrak{L}) = \langle tok(\mathfrak{L}), typ(\mathfrak{L}), \models_{\mathfrak{L}} \rangle$ and a regular IF theory $th(\mathfrak{L}) = \langle typ(\mathfrak{L}), \vdash_{\mathfrak{L}} \rangle$, such that all tokens $tok(\mathfrak{L})$ satisfy all constraints of $th(\mathfrak{L})$;[8] a token $a \in tok(\mathfrak{L})$ satisfies a constraint $\Gamma \vdash \Delta$ of $th(\mathfrak{L})$ if, when a is of all types in Γ, a is of some type in Δ.

3.3   Distributed IF Logic

The sought after IF theory is the IF theory of the distributed IF logic of an IF channel

---

[6] A partition of Σ' is a pair $\langle \Sigma_0, \Sigma_1 \rangle$ of subsets of Σ', such that $\Sigma_0 \cup \Sigma_1 = \Sigma'$ and $\Sigma_0 \cap \Sigma_1 = \emptyset$; Σ_0 and Σ_1 may themselves be empty (hence it is actually a quasi-partition).

[7] These tokens may not seem obvious, but these sequents code the content of the classification table: The left-hand sides of the these sequents indicate to which types they are classified, while the right-hand sides indicate to which they are not.

[8] Properly speaking this is the definition of a *sound* IF logic. Channel theory has room for unsound IF logics, but they are not needed for the purpose of this paper.

that represents the information flow between A_1 and A_2. This channel can either be stated directly, or indirectly by some sort of partial alignment of A_1 and A_2 (as we show, e.g., in Section 4.2).

The logic we are after is the one we get from *moving* a logic on the core C of the channel to the sum of components $A_1 + A_2$: The IF theory will be induced at the core of the channel; this is crucial. The distributed IF logic is the *inverse image* of the IF logic at the core.

Given an infomorphism $f : A \rightleftarrows B$ and an IF logic $\mathcal{L}$ on B, the *inverse image* $f^{-1}[\mathcal{L}]$ of $\mathcal{L}$ under f is the IF logic on A, whose theory is such that $\Gamma \vdash \Delta$ is a constraint of $th(f^{-1}[\mathcal{L}])$ iff $f^\wedge[\Gamma] \vdash f^\wedge[\Delta]$ is a constraint of $th(\mathcal{L})$.

The type and tokens system at the core and the IF classification of tokens to types will determine the IF logic at this core. We usually take the *natural IF logic* as the IF logic of the core, which is the IF logic $Log(C)$ generated from an IF classification C: its classification is C and its regular theory is the theory whose constraints are the sequents satisfied by all tokens. This seems natural, and is also what happens in the various interoperability scenarios we have been investigating.

Given an IF channel $\mathcal{C} = \{f_{1,2} : A_{1,2} \rightleftarrows C\}$ and an IF logic $\mathcal{L}$ on its core C, the *distributed IF logic*, $DLog_C(\mathcal{L})$, is the inverse image of $\mathcal{L}$ under the sum infomorphisms $f_1 + f_2 : A_1 + A_2 \rightleftarrows C$. This sum is defined as follows: $A_1 + A_2$ has as set of tokens the Cartesian product of $tok(A_1)$ and $tok(A_2)$ and as set of types the disjoint union of $typ(A_1)$ and $typ(A_2)$, such that for $\alpha \in typ(A_1)$ and $\beta \in typ(A_2)$, $\langle a, b \rangle \models_{A_1+A_2} \alpha$ iff $a \models_{A_1} \alpha$, and $\langle a, b \rangle \models_{A_1+A_2} \beta$ iff $b \models_{A_2} \beta$. Given two infomorphisms $f_{1,2} : A_{1,2} \rightleftarrows C$, the sum $f_1 + f_2 : A_1 + A_2 \rightleftarrows C$ is defined by $(f_1 + f_2)^\wedge(\alpha) = f_i(\alpha)$ if $\alpha \in A_i$ and $(f_1 + f_2)^\vee(c) = \langle f^\vee_1(c), f^\vee_2(c) \rangle$, for $c \in tok(C)$.

4   Representing Semantic Interoperability

In this section we illustrate, by means of an example, our approach to semantic interoperability via IF channels. Suppose that we are dealing with a situation where an agent or a group of agents (human or artificial) are faced with the task of aligning organisational structures and responsibilities of ministries across different governments. This is a realistic scenario set out in the domain of e-governments. Our agents have to align UK and US governments, by focusing on governmental organisations, like ministries. The focal point of this alignment is not only the structural and taxonomic differences of these ministries but the way in which responsibilities are allocated in different departments and offices within these ministries. This constitutes the semantics of our interoperability scenario, and consequently this will determine our choice of types, tokens and their classification relation for each community, as already pointed out in Section 3.1.

For the sake of brevity and space reasons, we only describe here four ministries: The UK Foreign and Commonwealth Office, the UK Home Office, the US Department of State, the US Department of Justice (hereafter, FCO, HO,

DoS and DoJ, respectively). We gathered information related to these ministries from their web sites[9] where we focused on their organisational structures, assuming that the meaning of these structures is in accordance to the separation of responsibilities. These structures were trivial to extract, either from the hierarchical lists of departments, agencies, bureau, directorates, divisions, offices (which we shall commonly refer to as *units*) within these ministries, or organisational charts and organograms publicly available on the Web. The extraction of responsibilities and their units though, requires an intensive manual knowledge acquisition exercise. At the time of our experiments, the ministries' taxonomies ranged from 38 units comprising the US DoJ to 109 units for the UK HO.

In order to capture semantic interoperability via IF channels we devised the following four steps:

1. Define the various contexts of each community by means of a distributed IF system of IF classifications;
2. Define an IF channel—its core and infomorphisms—connecting the IF classifications of the various communities;
3. Define an IF logic on the core IF classification of the IF channel that represents the information flow between communities;
4. Distribute the IF logic to the sum of community IF classifications to obtain the IF theory that describes the desired semantic interoperability.

These steps illustrate a theoretical framework and need not to correspond to actual engineering steps; but we claim that a sensible implementation of semantic interoperability can be achieved following this framework, as it constitutes the theoretical foundation of a semantic interoperability scenario. In fact, we have proposed an IF-based method to assist in ontology mapping [15], and in Section 5 we briefly discuss how it relates to this framework.

4.1 Community IF Classifications

UK and US governments use different ontologies to represent their respective ministries; therefore, we shall be dealing with two separate sets of types, $typ(\mathbf{UK}) = \{\text{FCO,HO}\}$ and $typ(\mathbf{US}) = \{\text{DoS,DoJ}\}$. We model the interoperability scenario using a separate IF classification for each government, **UK** and **US**, whose types are ministries.

To have UK and US ministries semantically interoperable will mean to know the semantic relationship in which they stand to each other, which we take, in this particular scenario, to be their set of responsibilities. It is sensible to assume that there will be no obvious one-to-one correspondence between ministries of two governments because responsibilities of a ministry in one government may be spread across many ministries of the other, and vice versa. But we can attempt to derive an IF theory that describes how the different ministry types are logically related to each other—an IF theory on the union of ministry types $typ(\mathbf{UK}) \cup typ(\mathbf{US})$ in which a constraint like FCO ⊢ DoS would represent the

---

[9] Accessible from www.homeoffice.gov.uk, www.fco.gov.uk, www.state.gov and www.usdoj.gov.

fact that a responsibility of the UK Foreign and Commonwealth Office is also a responsibility of the US Department of State.

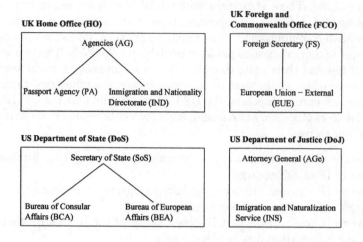

Fig. 1. Hierarchical structures of government ministries

We shall construct the IF channel that will allow us to derive the desired IF theory using the hierarchical structure of units shown in Figure 1. Within the context of one government, different ministries represent already the top-level separation of responsibilities. From the hierarchical structures we extract an IF theory on unit types for each government. Following are the two IF theories of UK and US units, respectively:

$$\vdash AG, FS \qquad IND \vdash AG \qquad\qquad \vdash SoS, AGe \qquad BEA \vdash SoS$$
$$AG, FS \vdash \qquad PA, IND \vdash \qquad\qquad SoS, AGe \vdash \qquad BCA, BEA \vdash$$
$$PA \vdash AG \qquad EUE \vdash FS \qquad\qquad BCA \vdash SoS \qquad INS \vdash AGe$$

By extracting responsibilities from the units' web sites we are able to define an IF classification for each government whose tokens are responsibilities and types are ministry units, and then classify responsibilities to their respective units. In the table below, we list the extracted responsibilities for both UK and US ministries along with their IDs, which we will use in sequel for the sake of brevity.

ID	UK responsibilities	ID	US responsibilities
r_1	issues UK passports	s_1	US passport services and information
r_2	regulate entry and settlement in the UK	s_2	promotes US interests in the region
r_3	executive services of the HO	s_3	heading the DoS
r_4	promote productive relations	s_4	facilitate entry to the US
r_5	responsible for the work of FCO	s_5	supervise and direct the DoJ

The IF classifications will have to be in accordance to the hierarchy as represented in the IF theories. That is, if a responsibility is classified to a unit, it shall also be classified to all its supra-units. This can be done automatically. The

IF classifications $\mathbf{A}_{UK}$ and $\mathbf{A}_{US}$ for UK and US units, respectively, along with their abbreviated responsibilities is as follows:

	AG	PA	IND	FS	EUE
r_1	1	1	0	0	0
r_2	1	0	1	0	0
r_3	1	0	0	0	0
r_4	0	0	0	1	1
r_5	0	0	0	1	0

	SoS	BCA	BEA	AGe	INS
s_1	1	1	0	0	0
s_2	1	0	1	0	0
s_3	1	0	0	0	0
s_4	0	0	0	1	1
s_5	0	0	0	1	0

To represent how ministry types (like FCO,HO, etc.) from the IF classification **UK** relate to the IF classification $\mathbf{A}_{UK}$ of ministerial units, we will use the *flip* $\mathbf{A}_{UK}^{\perp}$[10] of the IF classification table and its *disjunctive power* $\vee \mathbf{A}_{UK}^{\perp}$[11]. The flip classifies ministerial units to responsibilities, and for the UK case is shown in Figure 2 (a). The disjunctive power of this flip classifies ministerial units to sets of responsibilities, whenever at least one of its responsibilities are among those in the set. A fragment of this IF classification is shown in Figure 2 (b).

	r_1	r_2	r_3	r_4	r_5
AG	1	1	1	0	0
PA	1	0	0	0	0
IND	0	1	0	0	0
FS	0	0	0	1	1
EUE	0	0	0	1	0

	$\{r_1,r_2,r_3,r_4,r_5\}$	$\cdots$	$\{r_1,r_2,r_3\}$	$\cdots$	$\{r_4,r_5\}$
AG	1		1		0
PA	1		1		0
IND	1		1		0
FS	1		0		1
EUE	1		0		1

(a)   (b)

Fig. 2. Flip and disjunctive power of a classification

The way ministries relate to these sets of responsibilities can then be represented with an infomorphism $h_{UK} : \mathbf{UK} \rightleftarrows \vee \mathbf{A}_{UK}^{\perp}$; and each context for a government, with its ministries, their respective units, and hierarchy captured by an IF theory, is then represented as a distributed IF system of IF classifications. For the UK government this distributed system is $\mathbf{UK} \xrightarrow{h_{UK}} \vee \mathbf{A}_{UK}^{\perp} \xleftarrow{\eta_{\mathbf{A}_{UK}^{\perp}}} \mathbf{A}_{UK}^{\perp}$, with $h_{UK}(\text{HO}) = \{r_1, r_2, r_3\}$ and $h_{UK}(\text{FCO}) = \{r_4, r_5\}$.

4.2   The IF Channel

We construct an IF channel from a partial alignment of some of the responsibilities extracted from the ministerial units' web sites. This is the crucial aspect of

---

[10] The flip $\mathbf{A}^{\perp}$ of an IF classification $\mathbf{A}$ is the classification whose tokens are $typ(\mathbf{A})$ and types are $tok(\mathbf{A})$, such that $\alpha \models_{\mathbf{A}^{\perp}} a$ iff $a \models_{\mathbf{A}} \alpha$

[11] The disjunctive power $\vee \mathbf{A}$ of an IF classification $\mathbf{A}$ is the classification whose tokens are the same as $\mathbf{A}$, types are subsets of $typ(\mathbf{A})$, and given $a \in tok(\mathbf{A})$ and $\Phi \subseteq typ(\mathbf{A})$, $a \models_{\vee \mathbf{A}} \Phi$ iff $a \models_{\mathbf{A}} \sigma$ for some $\sigma \in \Phi$. There exists a natural embedding $\eta_{\mathbf{A}} : \mathbf{A} \rightleftarrows \vee \mathbf{A}$ defined by $\eta_{\mathbf{A}}(\alpha) = \{\alpha\}$ and $\eta^{\check{}}_{\mathbf{A}}(a) = a$, for each $\alpha \in typ(\mathbf{A})$ and $a \in tok(\vee \mathbf{A})$

the semantic interoperability, since it is the point where relations in meaning are established. We assume a partial alignment, that is, one where not all responsibilities r_1 to r_5 are related to responsibilities s_1 to s_5. In particular we shall assume the alignment of UK responsibilities r_1, r_2 and r_4 with US responsibilities s_1, s_4 and s_2. An agreed description of these responsibilities is the following:

- (a) passport services: $r_1 \longleftrightarrow s_1$
- (b) immigration control: $r_2 \longleftrightarrow s_4$
- (c) promote productive relations: $r_4 \longleftrightarrow s_2$

The focus of this paper is not how this partial alignment is established; various heuristic mechanisms have been proposed in the literature (see e.g., [20]), as well as mapping methods based on information-flow theory (see [15] and Section 5). We assume that we have already applied one of those heuristics or methods and come up with the agreed descriptions given above.

The above partial alignment is a binary relation between $typ(\mathbf{A}_{UK}^\perp)$ and $typ(\mathbf{A}_{US}^\perp)$. In order to represent this alignment as a distributed IF system in channel theory, we decompose the binary relation into a couple of total functions $g\hat{}_{UK}, g\hat{}_{US}$ from a common domain $typ(\mathbf{A}) = \{a, b, c\}$. (For example $g\hat{}_{UK}(b) = r_2$ and $g\hat{}_{US}(b) = s_4$.) This will constitute the type-level of a couple of infomorphisms. We complete the alignment to a system of IF classifications $\mathbf{A}_{UK}^\perp \xleftarrow{g_{UK}} \mathbf{A} \xrightarrow{g_{US}} \mathbf{A}_{US}^\perp$ by generating the IF classification on $typ(\mathbf{A})$ with all possible tokens, which we generate formally, and their classification. To satisfy the fundamental property of infomorphisms, the token-level of g_{UK}, g_{US} must be as follows:

	a b c
n_0	0 0 0
n_1	0 0 1
n_2	0 1 0
n_3	0 1 1
n_4	1 0 0
n_5	1 0 1
n_6	1 1 0
n_7	1 1 1

$g\check{}_{UK}(\mathsf{AG}) = n_6$ $g\check{}_{US}(\mathsf{SoS}) = n_5$
$g\check{}_{UK}(\mathsf{PA}) = n_4$ $g\check{}_{US}(\mathsf{BCA}) = n_4$
$g\check{}_{UK}(\mathsf{IND}) = n_2$ $g\check{}_{US}(\mathsf{BEA}) = n_1$
$g\check{}_{UK}(\mathsf{FS}) = n_1$ $g\check{}_{US}(\mathsf{AGe}) = n_2$
$g\check{}_{UK}(\mathsf{EUE}) = n_1$ $g\check{}_{US}(\mathsf{INS}) = n_2$

Obviously, not all tokens of $\mathbf{A}$ will be in the images of $g\check{}_{UK}$ and $g\check{}_{US}$.

This alignment allows us to generate the desired channel between **UK** and **US** that captures the information flow according to the aligned responsibilities. This is done by constructing a classification $\mathbf{C}$ and a couple of infomorphisms $f_{UK} : \vee\mathbf{A}_{UK}^\perp \rightleftarrows \mathbf{C}$ and $f_{US} : \vee\mathbf{A}_{US}^\perp \rightleftarrows \mathbf{C}$ that correspond to a category-theoretic colimit [18] of the following distributed IF system, which includes the alignment and the contexts of each government:

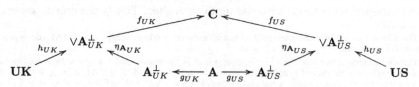

4.3   The IF Logic on the Core

This is how colimit **C** is constructed: its set of types $typ(\mathbf{C})$ is the disjoint union of types of $\vee\mathbf{A}_{UK}^{\perp}$ and $\vee\mathbf{A}_{US}^{\perp}$; its tokens are connections—pairs of tokens—that connect a token a of $\vee\mathbf{A}_{UK}^{\perp}$ with a token b of $\vee\mathbf{A}_{US}^{\perp}$ only when a and b are send by the alignment infomorphisms g_{UK} and g_{US} to tokens of the alignment IF classification **A** that are classified as of the same type. For example, the core **C** will have a token $\langle$AG,SoS$\rangle$ connecting $\vee\mathbf{A}_{UK}^{\perp}$-token AG with $\vee\mathbf{A}_{US}^{\perp}$-token SoS, because $g\breve{\ }_{UK}(\mathrm{AG}) = n_6$ and $g\breve{\ }_{US}(\mathrm{SoS}) = n_5$, and both n_5 and n_6 are of type a in **A**.

The following is a fragment of the IF classification on the core (not all types are listed, but all tokens are):

	$\{r_1,r_2,r_3\}$	$\{r_4,r_5\}$	$\{s_1,s_2,s_3\}$	$\{s_4,s_5\}$
$\langle$FS,BEA$\rangle$	0	1	1	0
$\langle$EUE,BEA$\rangle$	0	1	1	0
$\langle$FS,SoS$\rangle$	0	1	1	0
$\langle$EUE,SoS$\rangle$	0	1	1	0
$\langle$IND,AGe$\rangle$	1	0	0	1
$\langle$IND,INS$\rangle$	1	0	0	1
$\langle$AG,AGe$\rangle$	1	0	0	1
$\langle$PA,BCA$\rangle$	1	0	1	0
$\langle$PA,SoS$\rangle$	1	0	1	0
$\langle$AG,BCA$\rangle$	1	0	1	0
$\langle$AG,SoS$\rangle$	1	0	1	0

It shows the IF classification of all connections to those types of the core that are in the image of $f_{UK} \circ h_{UK}$ and $f_{US} \circ h_{US}$, which are the infomorphisms we will use in the next step to distribute the IF logic on the core to the IF classifications **UK** and **US**.

As the IF logic on the core we will take the natural IF logic of the IF classification **C**, whose constraints are:

$$\{r_4,r_5\} \vdash \{s_1,s_2,s_3\} \qquad\qquad \{s_4,s_5\} \vdash \{r_1,r_2,r_3\}$$
$$\{r_1,r_2,r_3\},\{r_4,r_5\} \vdash \qquad\qquad \vdash \{r_1,r_2,r_3\},\{r_4,r_5\}$$
$$\{s_1,s_2,s_3\},\{s_4,s_5\} \vdash \qquad\qquad \vdash \{s_1,s_2,s_3\},\{s_4,s_5\}$$

The natural IF logic is the one that captures in its constraints a complete knowledge of the IF classification. Since we have constructed the IF classification from those in the distributed system—which captured the contexts of governments together with the alignment of certain responsibilities—the natural IF logic will have as its IF theory all those sequents that conform to the government's contexts as well as to the alignment, which is what we desire for semantic interoperability.

4.4   The Distributed IF Logic

The natural IF logic has an IF theory whose types are sets of responsibilities taken from UK or US web sites, but we want to know how this theory translates to government ministries, by virtue of what responsibilities each ministry has. Hence we take the IF theory of the distributed IF logic of the IF channel $\mathbf{UK} \xrightarrow{f_{UK} \circ h_{UK}} \mathbf{C} \xleftarrow{f_{US} \circ h_{US}} \mathbf{US}$:

$$\mathrm{FCO} \vdash \mathrm{DoS} \qquad \mathrm{DoJ} \vdash \mathrm{HO}$$
$$\mathrm{HO,FCO} \vdash \qquad\qquad \vdash \mathrm{HO,FCO}$$
$$\mathrm{DoS,DoJ} \vdash \qquad\qquad \vdash \mathrm{DoS,DoJ}$$

which is the inverse image along $(f_{UK} \circ h_{UK}) + (f_{US} \circ h_{US})$ of the natural IF logic $Log(\mathbf{C})$ generated from the core IF classification. Its theory has the constraints shown above and captures the semantic interoperability between all ministries in our scenario.

5   Toward Automating Semantic Interoperability

The case described above showed the four steps of the proposed framework for representing semantic interoperability through an example scenario. As these steps exemplify the application of a theoretical framework to a test case, they do not correspond to actual engineering processes. Furthermore, when it comes to implementation we do not impose any specific requirements as to what formalisms or inference engine will be used, or how it will be deployed on the Web. It depends on the interoperability scenario at question. For example, in our previous work we focused on ontology mapping and devised the IF-Map method, which comprises four phases: *acquisition, translation, infomorphism generation*, and *map projection*. The IF-Map method is described in detail in [15], but here we recapitulate on some key parts and draw an analogy with the generic framework proposed above.

The *acquisition* and *translation* phases of IF-Map fall into the first step of our framework. In particular, they support the definition of the contexts of each community by representing source ontologies as IF classifications. The *acquisition* phase actually supports the harvesting of ontologies from various sources when these are not immediately available. IF-Map's next phase, *infomorphism generation*, supports the generation of the IF channel, which constitutes the second step in our framework. In the example of Section 4 we used an alignment structure to generate the desired channel between IF classifications **UK** and **US**. The IF-Map method is able to support and automate the generation of the necessary infomorphisms of this alignment structure, and also of the infomorphisms of the IF channel. The third and fourth steps of our framework—the generation of the IF logic at the core and its distribution to the sum of communities in order to obtain the distributed IF logic—do not have a direct counterpart in the IF-Map method as it would have been if we were interested in representing the integration of the two ontologies. Finally, the last phase of IF-Map, *map projection*, projects and stores the generated infomorphisms into RDF stores, which lies outside the scope of the theoretical framework presented here. We currently represent infomorphisms as custom-made RDF statements but we could have also used the OWL construct `owl:sameAs`. As it is reported in [17], `owl:sameAs` constructs could be used to represent links from one individual to another individual, and in more expressive versions of the language, like OWL Full, `owl:sameAs` could be used to define class equality, thus indicating that two concepts have the same intentional meaning. As the semantics of `owl:sameAs` do not impose a particular form of equality—only indicating individuals which share the same identity or sets of individuals (classes) that are interpreted intentionally as equal—we could see them as candidates for representing equivalence between types (a.k.a. classes).

6 Conclusions

We elaborated on the efforts been made to formalise and to provide automated support to semantic interoperability. We argued for the need to represent semantic interoperability in such a way that different understandings of semantics can be accommodated and potentially automated. We presented a theoretical framework for achieving this based on Information-Flow theory and illustrated an example scenario. Variations of this framework have been used in our recent work on mapping for Semantic Web ontologies. In the future, we plan to apply this framework to different semantic interoperability scenarios and to focus on semantic integration of distinct ontologies on the Semantic Web.

Acknowledgments. Yannis Kalfoglou is supported by the Advanced Knowledge Technologies (AKT) IRC, which is sponsored by UK EPSRC grant GR/N15764/01 and comprises the Universities of Aberdeen, Edinburgh, Sheffield, Southampton and the Open University. Marco Schorlemmer is supported by a 'Ramón y Cajal' Fellowship from the Spanish Ministry of Science and Technology.

References

1. F. Baader, D. Calvanese, D. McGuinness, D. Nardi, and P. Pater-Schneider. *The Description Logic Handbook.* Cambridge University Press, 2003.
2. M. Barr. The Chu construction. *Theory and Applications of Categories,* 2(2):17–35, 1996.
3. J. Barwise and J. Seligman. *Information Flow.* Cambridge University Press, 1997.
4. T. Bench-Capon and G. Malcolm. Formalising ontologies and their relations. *Database and Expert Systems Applications, Proc. 10th Int. Conf.,* LNCS 1677, pp. 250–259, Springer, 1999.
5. T. Berners-Lee, J. Hendler, and O. Lassila. The Semantic Web. *Scientific American,* May 2001.
6. M. Ciocoiu and D. Nau. Ontology-based semantics. *Proc. 7th International Conference on the Principles of Knowledge Representation and Reasoning,* pp. 539–548, 2000.
7. F. Corrêa da Silva, W. Vasconcelos, D. Robertson, V. Brilhante, A. de Melo, M. Finger, and J. Agustí. On the insufficiency of ontologies: Problems in knowledge sharing and alternative solutions. *Knowledge Based Systems,* 15(3):147–167, 2002.
8. K. Devlin. *Logic and Information.* Cambridge University Press, 1991.
9. F. Dretske. *Knowledge and the Flow of Information.* MIT Press, 1981.
10. A. Finkelstein, D. Gabbay, A. Hunter, J. Kramer, and B. Nuseibeh. Inconsistency handling in multi-perspective specifications. *IEEE Trans. on Software Engineering,* 20(8):569–578, 1994.
11. B. Ganter and R. Wile. *Formal Concept Analysis.* Springer, 1999.
12. V. Gupta. *Chu Spaces: A Model of Concurrency.* PhD thesis, Stanford University, 1994.
13. R. Kent. A KIF formalization of the IFF category theory ontology. *Proc. IJCAI'01 Workshop on the IEEE Standard Upper Ontology,* 2001.

14. R. Kent. The IFF foundation for ontological knowledge organization. *Knowledge Organization and Classification in International Information Retrieval*, Cataloging and Classification Quarterly, The Haworth Press Inc., 2003.

15. Y. Kalfoglou and M. Schorlemmer. IF-Map: an ontology-mapping method based on information-flow theory. *Journal on Data Semantics I*, LNCS 2800, pp. 98–127, Springer, 2003

16. J. Madhavan, P. Bernstein, P. Domingos, and A. Halevy. Representing and reasoning about mappings between domain models. *Proc. 18th Nat. Conf. on AI*, 2002.

17. D. McGuinness and F. van Harmelen, eds. OWL Web Ontology Language. W3C Recommendation, 10 February 2004. http://www.w3.org/TR/2004/REC-owl-reatures-20040210/

18. S. McLane. *Categories for the Working Mathematician*. Springer, 2nd edition, 1998.

19. C. Menzel. Ontology theory. *Ontologies and Semantic Interoperability, Proc. ECAI-02 Workshop*, CEUR-WS 64, 2002.

20. P. Mitra and G. Wiederhold. Resolving terminological heterogeneity in ontologies. *Ontologies and Semantic Interoperability, Proc. ECAI-02 Workshop*, CEUR-WS 64, 2002.

21. J. Pollock. The Web Services Scandal: How data semantics have been overlooked in integration solutions. *eAI Journal*, pp. 20–23, August 2002.

22. A. Sheth and J. Larson. Federated database systems for managing distributed, heterogeneous, and autonomous databases. *ACM Computing Surveys*, 22(3):183–230, 1990.

23. J. Sowa. *Knowledge Representation*. Brooks/Cole, 2000.

24. G. Stumme and A. Maedche. FCA-Merge: Bottom-up merging of ontologies. *Proc. 17th International Joint Conference on Artificial Intelligence*, pp. 225–230, 2001.

25. R. Turner. *Properties, propositions and semantic theory*. Computational linguistics and formal semantics, chapter 5. Cambridge University Press, 1992.

26. M. Uschold. Creating semantically integrated communities on the World Wide Web. *WWW'02 Semantic Web Workshop*, 2002.

S-Match: an Algorithm and an Implementation of Semantic Matching

Fausto Giunchiglia, Pavel Shvaiko, Mikalai Yatskevich

Dept. of Information and Communication Technology
University of Trento,
38050 Povo, Trento, Italy
{fausto, pavel, yatskevi}@dit.unitn.it

Abstract. We think of *Match* as an operator which takes two graph-like structures (e.g., conceptual hierarchies or ontologies) and produces a mapping between those nodes of the two graphs that correspond semantically to each other. Semantic matching is a novel approach where semantic correspondences are discovered by computing, and returning as a result, the semantic information implicitly or explicitly codified in the labels of nodes and arcs. In this paper we present an algorithm implementing semantic matching, and we discuss its implementation within the *S-Match* system. We also test *S-Match* against three state of the art matching systems. The results, though preliminary, look promising, in particular for what concerns precision and recall.

1 Introduction

We think of *Match* as an operator that takes two graph-like structures (e.g., conceptual hierarchies, database schemas or ontologies) and produces mappings among the nodes of the two graphs that correspond semantically to each other. *Match* is a critical operator in many well-known application domains, such as schema/ontology integration, data warehouses, and XML message mapping. More recently, new application domains have emerged, such as catalog matching, where the match operator is used to map entries of catalogs among business partners; or web service coordination, where *Match* is used to identify dependencies among data sources.

We concentrate on *semantic matching*, as introduced in [4], based on the ideas and system described in [17]. The key intuition behind semantic matching is that we should calculate mappings by computing the semantic relations holding between the concepts (and not labels!) assigned to nodes. Thus, for instance, two concepts can be equivalent, one can be more general than the other, and so on. We classify all previous approaches under the heading of *syntactic matching*. These approaches, though implicitly or explicitly exploiting the semantic information codified in graphs, differ substantially from our approach in that, instead of computing semantic relations between nodes, they compute syntactic "similarity" coefficients between labels, in the [0,1] range. Some examples of previous solutions are [11], [1], [14], [18], [3], [9]; see [4] for an in depth discussion about syntactic and semantic matching.

J. Davies et al. (Eds.): ESWS 2004, LNCS 3053, pp. 61-75, 2004.
© Springer-Verlag Berlin Heidelberg 2004

In this paper we propose and analyze in detail an algorithm and a system implementing semantic matching. Our approach is based on two key notions, the notion of *concept of/at a label*, and the notion of *concept of/at a node*. These two notions formalize the set of documents which one would classify under a label and under a node, respectively. We restrict ourselves to trees, and to the use of hierarchies (e.g., ontologies, conceptual hierarchies) for classification purposes. While the classification of documents is undoubtably the most important application of classification hierarchies, a new set of interesting applications have lately been found out. For instance in [7], classification hierarchies are used to classify nodes, databases and database contents (but in this latter set of applications we need to deal with attributes, a topic not discussed in this paper) in the Semantic Web.

The system we have developed, called *S-Match*, takes two trees, and for any pair of nodes from the two trees, it computes the *strongest semantic relation* (see Section 2 for a formal definition) holding between the concepts of the two nodes. The current version of *S-Match* is a rationalized re-implementation of the CTXmatch system [17] with a few added functionalities. *S-Match* is schema based, and, as such, it does not exploit the information encoded in documents. We have compared *S-Match* with three state of the art, schema based, matching systems, namely Cupid [11], COMA [1], and Similarity Flooding (SF) [14] as implemented within the Rondo system [13]. The results, though preliminary, look very promising, in particular for what concerns precision and recall.

The rest of the paper is organized as follows. Section 2 provides, via an example, the basic intuitions behind our algorithm and introduces the notions of concept of/at a label and of concept of/at a node. The algorithm is then articulated in its four macro steps in Section 3, which also provides the pseudo-code for its most relevant parts. Then, Section 4 describes *S-Match*, a platform implementing semantic matching, while Section 5 presents some preliminary experimental results. Finally, Section 6 provides some conclusions.

2 Semantic Matching

We introduce semantic matching by analyzing how it works on the two concept hierarchies of Figure 1 (a very simplified version of a catalog matching problem).

Preliminary to the definition of semantic matching is the definition of *concept of/at a node*, which, in turn, is based on the notion of *concept of/at a label*. Let us analyze these two notions in turn, starting from the second.

The trivial but key observation is that labels in classification hierarchies are used to define the set of documents one would like to classify under the node holding the label. Thus, when we write *Images* (see the root node A1 in Figure 1), we do not really mean "images", but rather "the documents which are (about) images". Analogously, when we write *Europe* (see the root node of A2 in Figure 1), we mean "the documents which are about Europe". In other words, a label has an intended meaning, which is what this label means in the world. However, when using labels for classification purposes, we use them to denote the set of documents which talk about their intended meaning. This consideration allows us to generalize the example definitions of

Images and *Europe* and to define the *"concept of/at a label"* as *"the set of documents that are about what the label means in the world"*.

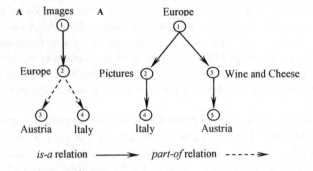

Fig.1. Two simple concept hierarchies

Two observations. First, while the semantics of a label are the real world semantics, the semantics of the concept of a label are in the space of documents; the relation being that the documents in the extension of the concept of a label are about what the label means in the real world. Second, concepts of labels depend only on the labels themselves and are independent of where in a tree they are positioned.

Trees add structure which allows us to perform the classification of documents more effectively. Let us consider, for instance, the node with label *Europe* in A1. This node stands below the node with label *Images* and, therefore, following what is standard practice in classification, one would classify under this node the set of documents which are images and which are about Europe. Thus, generalizing to trees and nodes the idea that the extensions of concepts range in the space of documents, we have that *"the concept of/at a node"* is *"the set of documents that we would classify under this node"*, given it has a certain label and it is positioned in a certain place in the tree. More precisely, as the above example has suggested, a document, to be classified in a node, must be in the extension of the concepts of the labels of all the nodes above it, and of the node itself. Notice that this captures exactly our intuitions about how to classify documents within classification hierarchies.

Two observations. First, concepts of nodes always coincide with concepts of labels in the case of root nodes, but this is usually not the case. Second, when computing concepts of nodes, the fact that a link is *is-a* or *part-of* or *instance-of* is irrelevant as in all cases, when we go down a classification, we only consider concepts of labels.

We can now proceed to the definition of semantic matching. Let a *mapping element* be a 4-tuple $< ID_{ij}, n1_i, n2_j, R >$, $i=1,...,N1$; $j=1,...,N2$; where ID_{ij} is a unique identifier of the given mapping element; $n1_i$ is the *i-th* node of the first graph, $N1$ is the number of nodes in the first graph; $n2_j$ is the *j-th* node of the second graph, $N2$ is the number of nodes in the second graph; and R specifies a *semantic relation* which holds between the concepts of nodes $n2_j$ and $n1_i$. Possible semantic relations are: *equivalence* ($=$), *more general* ($\sqsupseteq$), *less general* ($\sqsubseteq$), *mismatch* ($\perp$), *overlapping* ($\sqcap$). Thus, for instance, the concepts of two nodes are equivalent if they have the same extension, they mismatch if their extensions are disjoint, and so on for the other relations. We order these relations as they have been listed, according to their binding strength, from the strongest to the weakest, with *less general* and *more general* having the same binding power. Thus, *equivalence* is the strongest binding relation since the mapping tells us that the concept of the second node has exactly the same extension ad the first, *more general* and *less general* give us a containment information with respect to the extension of the concept of the first node, *mismatch* provides a containment information with respect to the extension of the complement of the concept of the first node, while, finally, *overlapping* does not provide any useful information, since we have containment with respect to the extension of both the concept of the first node and its negation.

Semantic matching can then be defined as the following problem: given two graphs $G1$, $G2$ compute the $N1 \times N2$ mapping elements $<ID_{ij}, n1_i, n2_j, R'>$, with $n1_i \in G1$, $i=1,...,N1$, $n2_j \in G2$, $j=1,...,N2$ and R' the strongest semantic relation holding between the concepts of nodes $n1_i, n2_j$. Notice that the strongest semantic relation always exists since, when holding together, more general and less general are equivalent to equivalence. We define a *mapping* as a set of mapping elements.

Thus, considering the mapping between the concepts of the two root nodes of A1 and A2 we have (the two *1*'s are the identifiers of the two nodes in the two trees):

$$< ID_{11}, 1, 1, \sqcap >$$

This is an obvious consequence of the fact that the set of images has a non empty intersection with the set of documents which are about Europe and no stronger relation exists. Building a similar argument for node *2* in A1 and node *2* in A2, and supposing that the concepts of the labels *Images* and *Pictures* are synonyms, we compute instead

$$<ID_{22}, 2, 2, = >$$

Finally, considering also the mapping between node *2* in A1 and the nodes with labels *Europe* and *Italy* in A2, we have the following mapping elements:

$$<ID_{21}, 2, 1, \sqsubseteq >$$
$$<ID_{24}, 2, 4, \sqsupseteq >$$

3   The Algorithm

Let us introduce some notation (see also Figure 1). Nodes are associated a number and a label. Numbers are the unique identifiers of nodes, while labels are used to identify concepts useful for classification purposes. Finally, we use "C" for concepts of nodes and labels. Thus, C_{Europe} and "C_2 in A1" are, respectively, the concept of label *Europe* and the concept of node 2 in A1.

The algorithm is organized in the following four macro steps:

Step 1: for all labels L in the two trees, compute C_L
Step 2: for all nodes N in the two trees, compute C_N
Step 3: for all pairs of labels in the two trees, compute relations among C_L
Step 4: for all pairs of nodes in the two trees, compute relations among C_N

Thus, as from the example in Section 2, when comparing C_2 in A1 and C_2 in A2 (the nodes with labels *Europe* and *Pictures*) we first compute C_{Images}, C_{Europe}, $C_{Pictures}$ (step 1); then we compute C_2 in A1 and C_2 in A2 (step 2); then we realize that C_{Images}= $C_{Pictures}$ (step 3) and, finally (step 4), we compare C_2 in A1 with C_2 in A2 and, in this case, we realize that they have the same extension. The detail of how these steps are implemented is provided below. Here it is important to notice that steps 1 and 2 can be done once for all, for all trees, independently of the specific matching problem. They constitute a phase of *preprocessing*. Steps 3 and 4 can only be done at run time, once the two graphs which must be matched have been chosen. Step 3 produces a matrix, called C_L *matrix*, of the relations holding between concepts of labels, while step 4 produces a matrix, called C_N *matrix*, of the strongest relations holding between concepts of nodes. These two matrixes constitute the main output of our matching algorithm.

Let us consider these four steps in detail, analyzing in turn the preprocessing phase, the computation of the C_L matrix and, finally, the computation of the C_N matrix.

3.1 The Preprocessing Phase

As from above, the first step is the computation of the concept of a label. The most natural choice is to take the label itself as a placeholder for its concept. After all, for instance, the label *Europe* is the best string which can be used with the purpose of characterizing "all documents which are about Europe". This is also what we have done in the examples in Section 2: we have taken labels to stand for their concepts and, when computing the concepts of nodes, we have reasoned about their extensions.

Collapsing the notions of label and of concept of label is in fact a reasonable assumption, which has been implicitly made in all the previous work on syntactic matching (see, e.g., [11], [1]). However, it does have a major drawback in that labels are most often written in some (not well defined) subset of natural language and, as we all know, natural language presents lots of ambiguities and complications. Thus, for instance, there are many possible different ways to state the same concept (as we have with *Images* and *Pictures*); dually, the same sentence may mean many different things (e.g., think of the label *tree*); *Image* and *Images*, though being different words, for our purposes have the same classification role; labels may be composed of multiple words as, for instance, *wine and cheese* in Figure 1; and so on.

The key idea underlying semantic matching is that labels, which are written in some *external language*, should be translated into an *internal language*, the language used to express concepts. The internal language should have precisely defined syntax and semantics, thus avoiding all the problems which relate to the problem of understanding natural language. We have chosen, as internal language, a logical propositional language where atomic formulas are atomic concepts, written as single words, and complex formulas are obtained by combining atomic concepts using the connectives of set theory. These connectives are the semantic relations introduced in Section 2, plus *union* (⊔). The semantics of this language are the obvious set-theoretic semantics.

Various work on translating natural language into more or less precisely defined internal forms has been done. We have implemented the ideas first introduced in [17],

[12] which specifically focus on the interpretation of labels, as used within classification hierarchies. We provide here only the main ideas, as they are needed in order to understand the overall matching algorithm, and refer to [17], [12] for the details. The core idea is to compute atomic concepts, as they are denoted by atomic labels (namely, labels of single words), as the *senses* provided by WordNet [15]. In the simplest case, an atomic label generates an atomic concept. However, atomic labels with multiple senses or labels with multiple words generate complex concepts. Following [17] and [12], we have implemented the translation process from labels to concepts where the main steps are as follows:

1. *Tokenization.* Labels at nodes are parsed into tokens by a tokenizer which recognises punctuation, cases, digits, etc. Thus, for instance, *Wine and Cheese* becomes *<Wine, and, Cheese>*.
2. *Lemmatization.* Tokens at labels are lemmatized, namely they are morphologically analyzed in order to find all their possible basic forms. Thus, for instance, *Images* is associated with its singular form, *Image*.
3. *Building atomic concepts.* WordNet is queried to extract the senses of lemmas at tokens identified during step 2. For example, the label *Images* has the only one token *Images*, and one lemma *Image*, and from WordNet we find out that *Image* has eight senses, seven as a noun and one as a verb.
4. *Building complex concepts.* When existing, all tokens that are prepositions, punctuation marks, conjunctions (or strings with similar roles) are translated into logical connectives and used to build complex concepts out of the atomic concepts built in step 3 above. Thus, for instance, commas and conjunctions are translated into disjunctions, prepositions like *of, in* are translated into conjunctions, and so on. For instance, the concept of label *Wine and Cheese*, $C_{Wine\ and\ Cheese}$ is computed as $C_{Wine\ and\ Cheese}$ = $<wine, \{senses_{WN}\#4\}>\sqcup<cheese, \{senses_{WN}\#4\}>$ where $<cheese, \{senses_{WN}\#4\}>$ is taken to be union of the four senses that WordNet attaches to *cheese*, and similarly for *wine*.

After the first phase, all labels have been translated into sentences of the internal concept language. From now on, to simplify the presentation, we assume that the concept denoted by a label is the label itself. The goal of the second step is to compute concepts at nodes. These are written in the same internal language as concepts of labels and are built suitably composing them. In particular, as discussed in Section 2, the key observation is that a document, to be classified in a certain node, must be in the extension of the concepts of the labels of all the nodes above the node, and also in the extension of the concept of the label of the node itself. In other words, the concept C_n of node n, is computed as the intersection of the concepts at labels of all the nodes from the root to the node itself. Thus, for example, C_4 in A1 in Figure 1 (the node with label *Italy*) is computed by taking the intersection of the concepts of labels *Images*, *Europe* and *Italy*, namely

$$C_4 = Images \sqcap Europe \sqcap Italy$$

The pseudo-code of a basic solution for the off-line part is provided in Figure 2.

```
1.   concept: wff;
2.   node: struct of {
3.               nid: int;
4.               lab: string;
5.              clab: concept;
6.              cnod: concept;
7.                    };
8.   T: tree of(node);

9. function TreePrep(T){
10.   foreach node∈T do{
11.        node.clab:= BuildClab(node.lab);
12.        node.cnod:= BuildCnod(node,T);
13.                    }}

14. function BuildCnod(node, T){
15.   return Filter(mkwff(⊓, GetCnod(GetParent(node, T)),
16.                          node.clab));}
```

Fig.2. The tree preprocessing algorithm

Let us analyze it in detail. Lines 1-8 define variables and data types. clab and cnod are used to memorize concepts of labels and concepts of nodes, respectively. They are both of type Concept, which, in turn, is of type wff (remember that concepts are codified as propositional formulas). A node is a 4-tuple <nid, lab, clab, cnod> representing the node unique identifier, the node label, the concept of the label C_L, and the concept of the node C_N.

T is our tree. Initially, the nodes in T contain only their unique identifiers and labels. Lines 9-13 describe the function TreePrep which gradually enriches the tree nodes with semantic information, by doing all the needed preprocessing. TreePrep starts from the root node and progresses top-down, left-to-right, and for each node it computes first the concept of the label and then the concept of the node. To guarantee this we assume that, as in the example of Figure 1, nodes are lexicographically ordered, starting from the root node. The function BuildClab, which is called at line 11, builds a concept for any label it takes in input. BuildClab implements the four steps briefly described above in this section. The only further observation to be made is that, in case Wordnet returns no senses, BuildClab returns the label itself, suitably manipulated to be compatible with the senses returned by Wordnet.

Lines 14-16 illustrate how BuildCnod constructs the concept of a node. In doing so, BuildCnod uses the concept of the parent node (thus avoiding the recursive climbing up to the root) and the concept of the label of that node. The concept at a node is built as the intersection of the concepts of labels of all the node above the node being analyzed. Mkwff takes a binary connective and two formulas and builds a formula out of them in the obvious way. The Filter function implements some heuristics whose aim is to discard the senses which are inconsistent with the other senses; see [17], [12] for the details.

3.2 The Computation of the C_L Matrix

At run time the first step (step 3 above) is to compute the C_L matrix containing the relations existing between any two concepts of labels in the two trees. This step requires a lot of a priori knowledge ([17] distinguishes it in lexical and domain knowledge). We use two sources of information:

1. We use a library of what we have called in [4] *"weak semantics element level machers"*. These matchers basically do string manipulation (e.g., prefix, postfix analysis, n-grams analysis, edit distance, soundex, data types, and so on) and try to guess the semantic relation implicitly encoded in similar words. Typical examples are discovering that *P.O.* and *Post Office* are synonyms and the same for *phone* and *telephone*. Element level weak semantics matchers have been vastly used in previous syntactic matchers, for instance in [11] and [1]. However there are two main differences. The first is that our matchers apply to concepts of labels and not to labels. Thus, on one side, their implementation is simplified by the fact that their input has been somehow normalized by the previous translation step. However, on the other side, they must be modified to take into account the specific WordNet internal form. The second and most important difference is that our matchers return a semantic relation, rather an affinity level in the range [0,1].

2. We use a library of what we have called in [4] *"strong semantics element level machers"*. These matchers extract semantic relations existing between concepts of labels using oracles which memorize the necessary lexical and domain knowledgdge (possible oracles are, for instance, WordNet, a domain ontology, a thesaurus). Again, following the work described in [17], our current implementation computes semantic relations in terms of relations between WordNet senses. We have the following cases: *equivalence:* one concept is equivalent to another if there is at least one sense of the first concept, which is a synonym of the second; *more general:* one concept is more general than the other if there exists at least one sense of the first concept that has a sense of the other as a hyponym or as a meronym; *less general:* one concept is less general than the other iff there exists at least one sense of the first concept that has a sense of the other concept as a hypernym or as a holonym; *mismatch:* two concepts are mismatched if they have two senses (one from each) which are different hyponyms of the same synset or if they are antonyms. For example, according to WordNet, the concept denoted by label *Europe* has the first sense which is a holonym to the first sense of the concept denoted by label *Italy*, therefore *Italy* is less general than *Europe*. Notice that, with WordNet, we cannot compute *overlapping,* and that the fact that WordNet does not provide us with any information is taken to be that two concepts have no relation.

A vanilla pseudo-code implementing this step is reported in Figure 3.

T1 and T2 are trees preprocessed by the code in Figure 2. n1 and n2 are nodes of T1 and T2 respectively, while N1 and N2 are the number of concepts of labels occurring in T1 and T2, respectively. ClabMatrix is the bidimensional array memorizing the C_L matrix. GetRelation tries WordNet first and then, in case WordNet returns no relation (it returns a blank), it tries the library of weak semantics element level matchers. In case also this attempt fails, no relation (a blank character) is returned.

```
1.  i, j: int;
2.  N1, N2:int;
3.  n1, n2: node;
4.  T1, T2: tree of (node);
5.  relation = {=,⊑,⊒,⊥,⊓};
6.  clabreltemp, ClabMatrix(N1,N2): relation ;

7.     function mkClabMatrix(T1,T2){
8.        for (i = 0; i < N1; i++ ) do
9.          for (j = 0; j < N2; j++ ) do
10.           ClabMatrix(i,j):= GetRelation(T1(i).clab,T2(j).clab)}

11.    function GetRelation(clab1, clab2){
12.       clabreltemp:= GetRelFromWordNet(clab1, clab2);
13.       if (clabreltemp == `` '')
14.        return GetRelFromMatcherLibrary(clab1, clab2);
15.       else
16.        return clabreltemp;}
```

Fig. 3. Computing the C_L matrix

If we apply the code in Figure 3 to the example in Figure 1, we obtain the results in Table 1. In this case, given the input, only WordNet returns useful results.

Table 1: The computed C_L matrix of the example in Figure 1

A1＼A2	C_{Europe}	$C_{Pictures}$	C_{Wine}	C_{Cheese}	C_{Italy}	$C_{Austria}$
C_{Images}		=				
C_{Europe}	=				⊒	⊒
$C_{Austria}$	⊑				⊥	=
C_{Italy}	⊑				=	⊥

Notice that we have one row for each label in A2 and one column for each label in A1. Each intersection between a row and a column contains a semantic relation. An empty square means that no relations have been found.

3.3 The Computation of the C_N Matrix

The second step at run time (step 4 above) computes the relations between concepts at nodes. This problem cannot be solved simply by asking an oracle containing static knowledge. The situation is far more complex, being as follows:

1. We have a lot of background knowledge computed in the C_L matrix, codified as a set of semantic relations between concepts of labels occurring in the two

graphs. This knowledge is the background theory/axioms which provide the context (as defined in [4]) within which we reason.

2. Concepts of labels and concepts of nodes are codified as complex propositional formulas. In particular concepts of nodes are intersections of concepts of labels.

3. We need to find a semantic relation (e.g., equivalence, more general, mismatch) between the concepts of any two nodes in the two graphs.

As discussed in [4], the key idea behind our approach is to translate all the semantic relations into propositional connectives in the obvious way (namely: equivalence into equivalence, more general and less general into implication, mismatch into negation of the conjunction) and then to prove that the following formula:

$$Context \rightarrow rel(C_i, C_j)$$

is valid; where C_i is the concept of node i in graph 1, C_j is the concept of node j in graph 2, *rel* is the semantic relation (suitably translated into a propositional connective) that we want to prove holding between C_i and, C_j, and *Context* is the conjunction of all the relations (suitably translated) between concepts of labels mentioned in C_i and, C_j. The key idea is therefore that the problem of matching has been translated into a validity problem where the holding of a semantic relation between the concepts of two nodes is tested assuming, as background theory (context), all we have been able to infer about the relations holding among the concepts of the labels of the two graphs. Figure 4 reports the pseudo code describing step 4.

```
1.  i, j, N1, N2: int;
3.  context, goal: wff;
4.  n1, n2: node;
5.  T1, T2: tree of (node);
6.  relation = {=,⊑,⊒,⊥,⊓};
8.  ClabMatrix(N1,N2),CnodMatrix(N1,N2),relation:relation

9.    function mkCnodMatrix(T1,T2,ClabMatrix){
10.     for (i = 0; i < N1; i++) do
11.       for (j = 0; j < N2; j++) do
12.         CnodMatrix(i,j):=NodeMatch(T1(i),T2(j),ClabMatrix)}

13. function NodeMatch(n1,n2,ClabMatrix){
14.     context:=mkcontext(n1,n2, ClabMatrix, context);
15.     foreach (relation in < =,⊑,⊒,⊥ >) do{
16.       goal:= w2r(mkwff(relation, GetCnod(n1), GetCnod(n2)));
17.       if VALID(mkwff(→, context, goal))
18.         return relation;}
19.     return ⊓ ;}
```

Fig.4. Computing the C_N matrix

CnodMatrix is the bidimensional array memorizing the C_N *matrix*. mkcontext at line 14 builds the context against which the relation is tested. **foreach** at line 15 tests semantic relations with decreasing binding power. w2r at line 16 translates a relation between two formulas containing only set theoretic connectives into a propositional formula. VALID at line 17 is tested by taking the negation of the formula and by testing unsatisfiability by running a SAT decider, namely a decider for propositional satisfiability (a formula is valid if and only if its negation is unsatisfiable). In case **foreach** fails on all the semantic relations in his argument, NodeMatch returns intersection. That this must be the case can be easily proved by reasoning by cases. In fact, given two sets one of the following relations =,⊑,⊒,⊥,⊓, must be the case.

The semantic relations computed between all the pairs of C_Ns for the hierarchies shown in Figure 1 are summarized in Table 2.

Table 2: The computed C_N matrix of the example in Figure 1

A1＼A2	C_1	C_2	C_3	C_4	C_5
C_1	⊓	⊒	⊓	⊒	⊓
C_2	⊑	=	⊓	⊒	⊓
C_3	⊑	⊑	⊓	⊥	⊓
C_4	⊑	⊑	⊓	=	⊥

Each intersection between a row and a column reports the strongest semantic relation that the code of Figure 4 has been able to infer. For example, the concept at node *Images* (C_1) in A1, is more general then the concept at node *Pictures* (C_2) in A2. Notice that this table, contrarily to Table 1, is complete in the sense that we have a semantic relation between any pair of concepts of nodes. However, the situation is not as nice as it looks as, in most matching applications, intersection gives us no useful information (it is not easy to know which documents should be discarded or kept). [4] suggests that, when we have intersection, we iterate and refine the matching results; however, so far, we have not been able to pursue this line of research.

4   A Platform Implementing Semantic Matching

Matching is a very hard task. Semantic matching does not have some of the problems that syntactic matchers have. Its major advantage is that the algorithm we have proposed is correct and complete in the sense that it always computes the strongest semantic relation between concepts of nodes (contrarily to what happens with syntactic matchers, see also the discussion of the testing results in the next section). This is, in fact, an obvious consequence of the fact that we have translated the problem of computing concepts of nodes (step 4) into a validity problem for the propositional calculus. However still a lot of problems exist which make it unlikely that we will ever be able to build the "ultimate good-for-all" semantic matcher. Thus, in practice, in semantic matching we have not eliminated the problem of incorrectness and incompleteness. We have only limited it to the translation of labels into concepts of labels (step 1) and to the computation of the semantic relations existing between pairs of concepts of labels (step 3). Steps 2 and 4, instead guarantee correctness and completeness. However, while, if step 2 is uncontroversial, step 4 still presents problems.

These problems are due to the fact that, we have codified the semantic matching problem into a CO-NP problem (as it is the validity problem for the propositional calculus). Solving this class of problems requires, in the worst case, exponential time. Furthermore there is no SAT solver which always performs better than the others and at the moment we have no characterization of our matching problems which allows us to choose the "best" solver and heuristics (even if we have some preliminary evidence that most of our examples are in the "easy" part of the "easy-hard-easy" SAT phase transition).

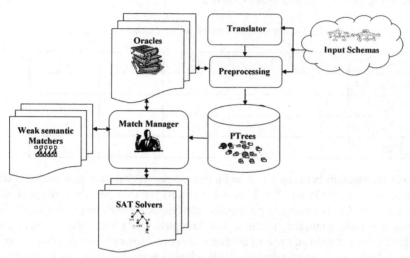

Fig. 5. Architecture of the S-match platform

Our approach is therefore that of developing a *platform* for semantic matching, namely a highly modular system where single components can be plugged, unplugged or suitably customized. The logical architecture of the system we have developed, called *S-Match,* is depicted in Figure 5. Let us discuss it from a data flow perspective. The module taking input schemas does the *preprocessing.* It takes in input trees codified into a standard internal XML format. This internal format can be loaded from a file manually edited or can be produced from a input format dependent *translator.* This module implements the preprocessing phase and produces, as output, enriched trees which contain concepts of labels and concepts of nodes. These enriched trees are stored in an internal database (the database labeled *PTrees* in figure 5) where they can be browsed, edited and manipulated. The preprocessing module has access to the set of *oracles* which provide the necessary *a priori* lexical and domain knowledge. In the current version WordNet is the only oracle we have. The *Matching Manager* coordinates the execution of steps 3 and 4 using the *oracles* library (used here as element level *strong semantics matchers*), the library of element level *weak semantic matchers*, and the library of *SAT solvers* (among the others, the SAT decider that we are currently testing is JSAT [10]).

S-Match is implemented in Java 1.4 and the total amount of code (without optimizations!) is around 60K.

5   A Comparative Evaluation

We have done some preliminary comparison between *S-Match* and three state of the art matching systems, namely Cupid [11], COMA [1], and SF [14] as implemented within the Rondo system [13]. All the systems under consideration are fairly comparable because they are all only schema-based, and they all utilize linguistic and graph matching techniques. They differ in the specific matching techniques they use and in how they combine them.

In our evaluation we have used three examples: the simple catalog matching problem, presented in the paper and two small examples from the academy and business domains. The business example describes two company profiles: a standard one (mini) and Yahoo Finance (mini). The academy example describes courses taught at Cornell University (mini) and at the University of Washington (mini).[1] Table 3 provides some indicators of the complexity of the test schemas.

Table 3: Some indicators of the complexity of the test schemas

	Images/Europe	Yahoo(mini)/Standard (mini)	Cornell(mini)/ Washington (mini)
#nodes	4/5	10/16	34/39
max depth	2/2	2/2	3/3
#leaf nodes	2/2	7/13	28/31

As match quality measures we have used the following indicators: *precision, recall, overall, F-measure, overall* (from [8]) and *time* (from [19]). *precision* varies in the [0,1] range; the higher the value, the smaller is the set of wrong mappings (false psotives) which have been computed. *precision* is a correctness measure. *recall* varies in the [0,1] range; the higher the value, the smaller is the set of correct mappings (true positives) which have not found. *recall* is a completeness measure. *F-measure* varies in the [0,1] range. The version computed here is the harmonic mean of precision and recall. It is global measure of the matching quality, growing with it. *overall* is an estimate of the post match efforts needed for adding false negatives and removing false positives. *overall* varies in the [-1, 1] range; the higher it is, the less post-match efforts are needed. *Time* estimates how fast matchers are in when working fully automatically. *Time* is very important for us, since it shows the ability of matching systems to scale up to the dimensions of the Semantic Web, providing meaningful answers in real time.

For what concerns the testing methodology, to provide a ground for evaluating the quality of match results, all the pairs of schemas have been manually matched to produce *expert mappings*. The results produced by matchers have been compared with expert mappings. In our experiments each test has two degrees of freedom: *directionality* and *use of oracles*. By directionality we mean here the direction in which mappings have been computed: from the first graph to the second one (forward direction), or vice versa (backward direction). For lack of space we report results obtained only with direction forward, and use of oracles allowed.

---

[1] Source files and description of the schemas tested can be found at our project web-site, experiments section: http://www.dit.unitn.it/~p2p/

All the tests have been performed on a P4-1700, with 256 MB of RAM, with the Windows XP operating system, and with no applications running but a single matcher. The evaluation results are shown in Figure 6. From the point of view of the quality of the matching results *S-Match* clearly outperforms the other systems. As a consequence of the fact that the computation of concept of nodes is correct and complete, given the same amount of information at the element level, *S-Match* will always perform the best and the other matchers can only approximate its results.

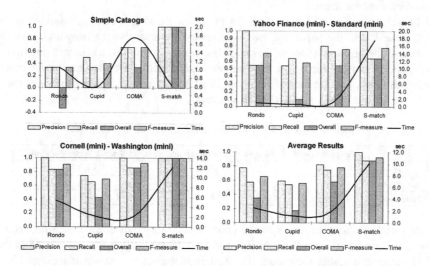

Fig.6. Experimental results

As a matter of fact, the only case where *S-Match* does not compute precision and recall at their maximum value is due to a mistake in computing the relation between two pairs of concepts of labels. From the point of view of time, *S-Match* is the lowest, this due to the fact that that the computation of mappings in *S-Match* is translated into a validity problem. However these results do not look so bad as the ratio is always relatively small and, as stated above, the e current version of our system has no optimizations.

6   Conclusion

We have presented an algorithm implementing semantic matching and its preliminary implementation within a semantic matching platform, *S-Match*. We have tested our current implementation against three state of the art systems and the results look very promising, with a point of attention on computation times.

This is only a first step and many issues still need to be dealt with. Some examples are: extend the current algorithm to dealing with attributes (this is of fundamental importance in order to move to the database domain), optimize the algorithm and its implementation, implement iterative semantic matching (as first defined in [4]), do a thorough testing of the system, which in turn will require the definition of a testing methodology, and so on.

Acknowledgments

Thanks to Luciano Serafini, Paolo Bouquet, Bernardo Magnini and Stefano Zanobini for many discussions on CTXmatch. We also thank to Phil Bernstein, Hong Hai Do and Erhard Rahm, Sergey Melnik for providing us with the Cupid, COMA and Rondo prototypes.

References

1. Bergamaschi S., Castano S., Vincini M.: Semantic Integration of Semistructured and Structured Data Sources. SIGMOD Record, 28(1) (1999) 54-59.
2. Do H.H., Rahm E.: COMA – A System for Flexible Combination of Schema Matching Approach. Proceedings of VLDB'02, (2002) 610-621.
3. Doan A., Madhavan J., Domingos P., Halvey A.: Learning to map between ontologies on the semantic web. Proceedings of WWW'02, (2002) 662-673.
4. Giunchiglia F.: Contextual reasoning. *Epistemologia, special issue on "I Linguaggi e le Macchine"*, vol. XVI, (1993) 345-364.
5. Giunchiglia F., Shvaiko P.: Semantic Matching. To appear in "The Knowledge Engineering Review" journal 18(3). Short versions: Proceedings of Ontologies and distributed systems workshop at IJCAI'03 and Semantic Integration workshop at ISWC'03, (2003).
6. Giunchiglia F., Zaihrayeu I.: Making peer databases interact - a vision for an architecture supporting data coordination. Proceedings of CIA'02, (2002) 18-35.
7. Giunchiglia F., Zaihrayeu I.: Implementing database coordination in P2P networks. Submitted to ESWS' 04 (2004).
8. Do H.H., Melnik S., Rahm E.: Comparison of schema matching evaluations. Proceedings of workshop on Web and Databases, (2002).
9. Kang J., Naughton J.F.: On schema matching with opaque column names and data values. Proceedings of SIGMOD'03, (2003) 205-216.
10. Le Berre D. JSAT: The java satisfiability library. http://cafe.newcastle.edu.au/daniel/JSAT/. (2001).
11. Madhavan J., Bernstein P., Rahm E.: Generic schema matching with Cupid. Proceedings of VLDB'01, (2001) 49-58.
12. Magnini B., Serafini L., Speranza M.: Making Explicit the Semantics Hidden in Schema Models. Proceedings of workshop on Human Language Technology for the Semantic Web and Web Services at ISWC'03 (2003).
13. Melnik S., Rahm E., Bernstein P.: Rondo: A programming platform for generic model management. Proceedings of SIGMOD'03, (2003) 193-204.
14. Melnik, S.,Garcia-Molina H., Rahm E.: Similarity Flooding: A Versatile Graph Matching Algorithm. Proceedings of ICDE, (2002) 117-128.
15. Miller, A.G.: Wordnet: A lexical database for English. Communications of the ACM, 38(11) (1995) 39-41.
16. Rahm E., Bernstein P.: A survey of approaches to automatic schema matching. VLDB Journal, 10(4) (2001) 334-350.
17. Serafini L., Bouquet P., Magnini B., Zanobini S.: Semantic Coordination: A new approach and an application. Proceedings of ISWC'03, (2003) 130-145.
18. Xu L., Embley D.W.: Using domain ontologies to discover direct and indirect matches for schema elements. Proceedings of Semantic Integration workshop at ISWC'03, (2003).
19. Yatskevich M.: Preliminary Evaluation of Schema Matching Systems. DIT Technical Report, DIT-03-028, (2003).

Ontology Mapping - An Integrated Approach

Marc Ehrig and York Sure

Institute AIFB, University of Karlsruhe
{ehrig,sure}@aifb.uni-karlsruhe.de

Abstract. Ontology mapping is important when working with more than one ontology. Typically similarity considerations are the basis for this. In this paper an approach to integrate various similarity methods is presented. In brief, we determine similarity through rules which have been encoded by ontology experts. These rules are then combined for one overall result. Several boosting small actions are added. All this is thoroughly evaluated with very promising results.

1 Introduction

The Semantic Web community has achieved a good standing within the last years. As more and more people get involved, many individual ontologies are created. Interoperability among different ontologies becomes essential to gain from the power of the Semantic Web. Thus, mapping and merging of ontologies becomes a core question. As one can easily imagine, this can not be done manually beyond a certain complexity, size, or number of ontologies any longer. Automatic or at least semi-automatic techniques have to be developed to reduce the burden of manual creation and maintenance of mappings.

One specific application at Karlsruhe, which requires mapping and merging is derived from the SWAP project (Semantic Web and Peer-to-Peer). The SWAP project[1] wants to enable individuals to keep their own work views and at the same time share knowledge across a peer-to-peer network. For this reason tools are provided for each peer to easily create an own ontology. This ontology represents the view on the local file system, emails, or bookmarks. Through the peer-to-peer network communication between the individual peers becomes possible without relying on a central instance. Formal queries are sent around in this network, and peers which know an answer reply to these queries. (Natural language) Examples for such queries could be: "What is the the email address of York?" or "Which documents on Marc's computer are about similarity?". This knowledge can then be integrated into the knowledge repository of the original asking peer. Additionally every peer advertises the topics he has most information on; this expertise is saved by the other peers.
In our scenario mapping becomes necessary for different tasks. Mapping is required every single time a decision is taken on which peer has knowledge about a certain topic, and thus will be addressed with the query. Naturally, a foreign peer can only answer incoming queries, if it can interpret the entities with respect to its own knowledge base.

---

[1] http://swap.semanticweb.org

J. Davies et al. (Eds.): ESWS 2004, LNCS 3053, pp. 76–91, 2004.

Query rewriting is required [5]. Finally, the originally asking peer receives answers. When including this information into the own local knowledge base, the new knowledge has to be linked to already existing knowledge. Equal entities have to be identified.

In this paper we present an approach to combine different similarity measures to find mapping candidates between two or more ontologies. **As our hypothesis H we expect better mapping results from intelligent approaches in combining different similarity identifying measures than today's approaches can provide.**

The next section defines and explains general concepts this work is based on: ontology, similarity, and mapping. In section 3 the similarity methods based on rules derived by human experts are introduced. The section 4 presents our approach for combining and integrating these various methods. In section 5 a thorough evaluation is performed showing the strengths of our approach. Finally related work, the next steps, and a conclusion are given.

2 Definitions

In this section our understanding of ontologies is presented. For clarification we also discuss the general meaning of similarity. Additionally follow ideas on how to bring the two worlds together. Our notion of mapping will be presented at the end.

2.1 Ontologies

In philosophy an ontology is *a particular theory about the nature of being or the kinds of existents*. The following short definition describes ontologies as used in our scenario. In the understanding of this paper they consist of both schema and instance data.

$$O := (C, H_C, R_C, H_R, I, R_I, A)$$

An ontology O consists of the following. The concepts C of the schema are arranged in a subsumption hierarchy H_C. Relations R_C exist between single concepts. Relations (properties)[2] can also be arranged in a hierarchy H_R. Instances I of a specific concept are interconnected by property instances R_I. Additionally one can define axioms A which can be used to infer knowledge from already existing one. An extended definition can be found in [21]. Common languages to represent ontologies are RDF(S)[3] or OWL[4], though one should note that each language offers different modelling primitives and, thus, a different level of complexity.

2.2 Similarity

We start with a short definition of similarity from Merriam Webster's Dictionary: *having characteristics in common: strictly comparable*. From our point of view we want to

---

[2] In this paper we treat the words *relation* and *property* as synonyms.
[3] http://www.w3.org/RDFS/
[4] http://www.w3.org/OWL/

strictly compare two entities to find identity among them. The definition already gives us a hint on how to check for similarity: two entities need common characteristics to be similar. We also give a short formal definition of similarity here derived from [3]:

- $sim(x,y) \in [0..1]$
- $sim(x,y) = 1 \rightarrow x = y$: two objects are identical.
- $sim(x,y) = 0$: two objects are different and have no common characteristics.
- $sim(x,y) = sim(y,x)$: similarity is symmetric.

2.3 Similarity for Ontologies

What is the meaning of similarity in the context of ontologies? The basic assumption is that knowledge is captured in an arbitrary ontology encoding. Based on the consistent semantics the coherences modelled within the ontology become understandable and interpretable. From this it is possible to derive additional knowledge such as, in our case, similarity of entities in different ontologies. An example shall clarify how to get from encoded semantics to similarity: by understanding that labels describe entities in natural language one can derive that entities having the same labels are similar. A formal definition of similarity for ontologies follow:

- O_i: ontology, with ontology index $i \in \mathbb{N}$
- $sim(x,y)$: similarity function
- e_{ij}: entities of O_i, with $e_{ij} \in \{C_i, R_i, I_i\}$, entity index $j \in \mathbb{N}$
- $sim(e_{i_1 j_1}, e_{i_2 j_2})$: similarity function between two entities $e_{i_1 j_1}$ and $e_{i_2 j_2} (i_1 \neq i_2)$; as shown later this function makes use of the ontologies of the entities compared

The paper focuses on the similarity of pairs of single entities from different ontologies. At the current stage we do not compare whole ontologies or parts larger than one entity.

2.4 Mapping

Due to the wide range of expressions used in this area (merging, alignment, integration etc.), we want to describe our understanding of the term "mapping". We define mapping as cf. [22]: "Given two ontologies A and B, mapping one ontology with another means that for each concept (node) in ontology A, we try to find a corresponding concept (node), which has the same or similar semantics, in ontology B and vice verse." We want to stick to this definition, more specific we will demand the *same* semantic meaning of two *entities*.

Formally an ontology mapping function can be defined the following way:

- $map : O_{i_1} \rightarrow O_{i_2}$
- $map(e_{i_1 j_1}) = e_{i_2 j_2}$, if $sim(e_{i_1 j_1}, e_{i_2 j_2}) > t$ with t being the threshold
  entity $e_{i_1 j_1}$ is mapped onto $e_{i_2 j_2}$; they are semantically identical, each entity $e_{i_1 j_1}$ is mapped to at most one entity $e_{i_2 j_2}$

The central contribution of this paper is to present an approach for defining this mapping function. We only consider one-to-one mappings between single entities. Neither do we cover mappings of whole ontologies or sub-trees, nor complex mappings as concatenation of literals (e.g. name corresponds to first name plus last name) or functional transformation of attributes (e.g. currency conversions).

3 Similarity Measures

Our mapping approach is based on different similarity measures. In this section we want to describe how the various similarity methods have been created.

3.1 Manual Rules

Our implemented approach is based on manually encoded mapping rules. Please note that the mappings itself are not yet encoded through rules (as in [15]). We are using rules to identify possible mappings. This manual effort is necessary because coherences in ontologies are too complex to be directly learned by machines. An expert understanding the encoded knowledge in ontologies formulates machine-interpretable rules out of the information. Each rule shall give a hint on whether two entities are identical, but no rule for itself provides enough support to unambiguously identify a mapping. Naturally, evaluation of these manually created rules has to be a core element of the overall process.

3.2 Similarity Stack

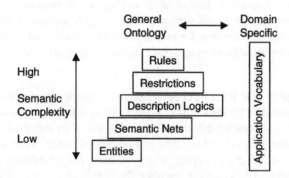

Fig. 1. Similarity stack

The presented general idea will now be explicitly used to determine similarity between ontologies. To get a better understanding, the rules are categorized in a similarity stack as shown in graph 1. Ontologies are based on certain vocabularies which are well-defined, well-understood, and with a generally accepted meaning. The left part shows these aspects arranged along their complexity, which is derived from the "layer cake" of [2]. Special shared ontology domains e.g. SWAP-common in the mentioned SWAP project, have their own additional vocabulary. The right part therefore covers domain-specific aspects. As this domain-specific knowledge can be situated at any level of ontological complexity, it is presented as a box across all of them. In the next paragraphs the general semantic meaning of features is described followed by the concrete derived rules, being tagged with a number ($\mathbf{R}n$) with $n \in (1, ..17)$. As many of the rules are derived from existing literature, we give references where applicable.

Entities The first level describes entities as is. No ontological considerations are needed for these features. Labels are human identifiers (names) for entities, normally shared by a community of humans speaking a common language. We can therefore infer that *if labels are the same, the entities are probably also the same* (**R1**, see example 1). Several ideas have already been created to compare labels, e.g. the edit distance[11]. Dictionaries (e.g. WordNet) can further be used for comparisons even across languages, although some restrictions apply. Another feature of objects can be an identifier such as URIs, which are unique for every entity. Therefore we know that *if two entities have the same identifier they are identical* (**R2**).

```
<owl:Class rdf:ID=''id1''>
    <rdfs:label>telephone number</label>
</owl:Class>
<owl:Class rdf:ID=''id2''>
    <rdfs:label>phone number</label>
</owl:Class>
```
Example 1. Two entities id1 and id2 with similar labels.

Semantic Nets The second level is the level of Semantic Nets as e.g. introduced by [17]. A concept is a general class of objects. They are in relation to others through attributes or properties. *If the properties of two concepts are equal, the concepts are also equal* (**R3**). The same is true for properties. *If the domain and range (the original and the result concept) of two properties are equal, the properties are also* (**R4**).

Description Logics The third level described here covers ontologies which have the complexity as provided by Description Logics [1]. A taxonomy can be created over concepts, in which a concept inherits all the relations of its super-concepts. Another rule is that if concepts are the same, they will probably have the same super-concepts. We turn the rule around: *if super-concepts are the same, the actual concepts are similar to each other* (**R5**). In practice we calculate the degree of overlap of the two super-concept sets, which provides a number between 0% and 100% [6]. And finally the sub-concepts of two equal classes will also be the same. *If sub-concepts are the same, the compared concepts are similar* (**R6**) [12]. Also, *if concepts have similar siblings (i.e. children of parents), they are also similar* (**R7**). It is also possible to group properties into a taxonomy, with the corresponding rules resulting: *super-properties* (**R8**) and *sub-properties* (**R9**). The next piece of information which can be added are instances. An instance is a specific entity of a general class from which it inherits all the relations. A concept on the other hand can also be defined as a representative for a set of instances. We can therefore infer that *concepts that have the same instances are the same* (**R10**) [9]. Vice versa, *instances that have the same mother concept are similar* (**R11**). It is also interesting to have a look at the possible distribution of instances on concepts. *If concepts have a similar low/high fraction of the instances, the concepts are similar* (**R12**). Like concepts are interconnected via properties, instances are also regarded to be interconnected via properties instances. This means that *if two instances are linked to another instance via the same property, the two original instances are similar* (**R13**).

To a certain degree we can also turn this around: *if two properties connect the same two instances, the properties can be similar* (**R14**).

Restrictions We continue with ontologies using restrictions. This is covered by e.g. the ontology language OWL. In OWL there are properties such as "sameIndividualAs" or "sameClassAs". *They explicitly state that two entities are the same* (**R15**). A number of further features from OWL could be used, but are discarded at this time, as they do not have any wide distribution yet: property characteristics as symmetry, restrictions of values, equivalence, set operators, enumeration, and disjointness. From all of them new rules to determine similarity can be derived.

Rules Higher levels of the ontology "layer cake" [2] can also become interesting for similarity considerations. Especially if similar rules between entities exist, these entities will be regarded as similar. For this one would have to process higher-order relationships. Unfortunately there has not been sufficient research and practical support for the rule layer in the Semantic Web in general, not at all for similarity considerations.

Application-Specific Vocabulary One can also exploit clearly defined application-specific vocabulary for similarity considerations. As an example we take the ontology used within the SWAP project, in which every file has a unique hash-code assigned. *If the hash-codes of two files are the same, one can infer that they are the same* (**R16**). Additionally, *files with the same MIME-type are similar*, at least in their format (**R17**).

Similarity Paths In a bigger environment one can expect to have to do more complex mapping e.g. of elements of multiple ontologies. In this case we can use the notion of similarity itself to receive information on other mappings. Similarity as defined here has transitive characteristics if A is similar to B, and B is similar to C, A is similar to C. Some relaxation has to be added when the paths become too long.

4 Integrated Approach

4.1 Combination

According to our hypothesis, a combination of the so far presented rules leads to better mapping results compared to using only one at a time. Clearly not all introduced similarity methods have to be used for each aggregation, especially as some methods have a high correlation. We present both manual and automatic approaches to learn how to combine the methods. Even though quite some methods exist, no research paper focused on the combination and integration of these methods yet.

Summarizing A general formula for this integration task can be given by summarizing over the n weighted similarity methods.

$$sim(e_{i_1j_1}, e_{i_2j_2}) = \sum_{k=1}^{n} w_k sim_k(e_{i_1j_1}, e_{i_2j_2})$$

with w_k being the weight for a specific method sim_k and $n \in \mathbb{N}$

Please note our assumption that similarities can be aggregated and are increasing strictly. The weights could be assigned manually or learned e.g. through maximization of the f-measure (see section 5) of a training set. In our approach we are basically looking for similarity values supporting the thesis that two entities are equal. If a measure doesn't support the thesis, it still doesn't mean that it's opposing it. These considerations are directly derived from the open world assumption which we respect in this paper.

Sigmoid Function A more sophisticated approach doesn't only weight the similarity methods but performs a functional computation on each of them. In the given case the most promising function would be the sigmoid function, which has to be shifted to fit our input range of $[0 \ldots 1]$ (see figure 2).

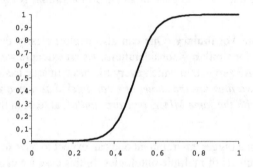

Fig. 2. Sigmoid function

$$sim(e_{i_1j_1}, e_{i_2j_2}) = \sum_{k=1}^{n} w_k \times sig_k(sim_k(e_{i_1j_1}, e_{i_2j_2}) - 0.5)$$

with $sig(x) = \frac{1}{1+e^{-ax}}$ and a being a parameter for the slope

The idea behind using a sigmoid function is quite simple: a high similarity value should be weighted over-proportionally whereas a low value practically can be abandoned. An example shall make this clear. When comparing two labels the chance of having the same entity if only one or two letters are different is very high. On the other hand if only three or four letters match there is no information in this similarity at all. The parameters of the sigmoid function can be regarded as an extension of the similarity methods, as they have to be adjusted according to the method they are applied to.

Machine Learning with Neural Networks A very convenient way of determining how to combine the methods is to use a machine learning approach. As we have continuous inputs, only some machine learning approaches make sense. In our work we focus on neural networks [10], as they represent an appropriate way to learn non-linear functions. Specifically we choose a three layer fully connected neural network consisting of a linear input layer, a hidden layer with a tanh-function, and a sigmoid output function. A lot of literature discusses how to choose the number of layers, nodes, and edges. We will stick to a simple approach, as we focus on similarity considerations rather than efficient machine learning. Support vector machines are another alternative. Unfortunately one needs a large number of examples for training, which is currently difficult to obtain.

4.2 Cut-Off

After the just described steps we have a list which consists of the most similar entities of two ontologies plus the corresponding similarity value. Now remains the question which level of similarity is appropriate to indicate equality for the mapping and which strongly indicates inequality? It is important to make the decision where to put the cut-off[8]. Every similarity value above the cut-off indicates a match; everything below the cut-off is dismissed.

Constant Similarity Value For this method a fixed constant c is taken as cut-off.

$$b = c, \text{ with } b \text{ being the cut-off}$$

The difficulty is to determine this value. Possible approaches are to take an average which maximizes the f-measure in several test runs. Alternatively it might make sense to let experts determine the value, which only works if the similarity value can be interpreted completely (e.g. with the sigmoid summarization).

Delta Method For this method the cut-off value for similarity is defined by taking the highest similarity value of all and subtracting a fixed value c from it.

$$b = max(sim(e_{i_1 j_1}, e_{i_2 j_2}) | \forall e_{i_1 j_1} \in O_{i_1}, e_{i_2 j_2} \in O_{i_2}) - c$$

N Percent This method is closely related to the former one. Here we take the highest similarity value and subtract a fixed percentage p from it.

$$b = max(sim(e_{i_1 j_1}, e_{i_2 j_2}) | \forall e_{i_1 j_1} \in O_{i_1}, e_{i_2 j_2} \in O_{i_2})(1 - p)$$

The latter two approaches are motivated from the idea that similarity is also dependent on the domain. The calculated maximum similarity can be an indicator for this and is fed back into the algorithm.

Our approach focuses on classifying the found mappings into two groups: equal or not equal. As a potential extension in future we foresee a *three layer semi-automatic* approach having: correct mappings, mappings to be confirmed manually, and dismissed mappings.

4.3 Additional Actions

Using small additional actions can lead to significantly better results.

Multiple Rounds For calculating the similarity of one entity pair many of the described methods rely on the similarity input of other entity pairs. The first round always has to be a general method like the comparison based on labels, which does not rely on any other pairs. By doing the calculation in several rounds one can then access the already calculated pairs and receive a better similarity. Several possibilities when to stop the calculations have been described in the literature: a fixed number of rounds, no changes in the mappings, changes below a certain threshold, or dynamically depending on how much time and calculation power can be provided.

Best Mappings Only When having more than one round of calculation the question arises if the results of each round should be converted/adjusted before they are fed back for the next round. One approach is to reuse only the similarity of the best mappings found. A possible way could be to give the best match a weight of 1, the second best of $\frac{1}{2}$, and the third of $\frac{1}{3}$. Potentially correct mappings are kept with a high probability but leave a path for second best mappings to replace them. The danger of having the system being diverted by low similarity values is minimized.

Deletion of Doubles The goal of the current approach is to gain a single mapping between two entities from the best similarity values. As there can be only one *best* match, every other match is a potential mistake, which should be dropped. Practically we do cleansing in the mapping table by removing entries with already mapped entities.

4.4 Process

All the ideas presented so far describe how two entities can be compared to one another and determine a mapping measure between them. We use the following methodology (see figure 3):

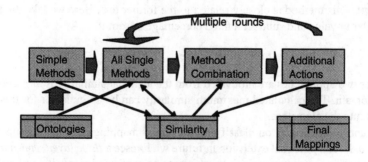

Fig. 3. Mapping Process

1. Starting point are two ontologies which have to be mapped. We will therefore calculate the similarities between any valid pair of entities.

2. In a first round basic similarities are set via measures which are independent of other similarities. In our case we rely on the label similarity, equal URIs, or the sameAs relation (**R1, R2,** and **R15**). The complete similarity matrix is calculated from this.

3. In a second step the overall similarities between the entities are calculated based on all the introduced similarity measures (**R1** through **R17**), always using the now existing previous similarities of other entities if required.

4. Following the presented additional actions steps two and three are repeated for multiple rounds (either a fixed number of times, or until the number of changes per round drops below a threshold value). In a last step doubles are deleted and similarities which are too little (i.e. below the cut-off value and therefore not worth to mention) are removed and only the best similarities are displayed.

5. These will then be used as the final mapping table. They will be evaluated as explained in the next section.

5 Evaluation

The problem of mapping between ontologies already produced some interesting approaches. A thorough evaluation of our new approach is presented here.

5.1 Evaluation Scenario

Our evaluation is based on the introductory example given in section 1. We have presented an application scenario for mappings at the beginning of this paper.

We basically take two ontologies and create mappings between the entities based on a given strategy. These mappings are validated against the correct mappings which had been created in beforehand. Our goal was to reach the best number of mappings, which is quantified in the f-measure (see next section). As the absolute quality of mappings is highly dependent of the complexity of the ontologies themselves, we focus on the relative performance of different mapping strategies.

The implementation itself was done in Java using the KAON-framework[5] for ontology access and maintenance. All the tests were run on a standard notebook.

5.2 Metrics

To allow for comparability not only between our own test series, but also with existent literature we will focus on using standard information retrieval metrics. The definitions of precision and recall is adapted by us to fit the given evaluation scenario.

Recall $r = \frac{\#correct\_found\_mappings}{\#possible\_existing\_mappings}$

Precision $p = \frac{\#correct\_found\_mappings}{\#all\_found\_mappings}$

F-Measure combines the two mentioned measures [23].

$f = \frac{(b^2+1)pr}{b^2p+r}$ with $b = 1$ being a factor to weight precision and recall.

---

[5] http://kaon.semanticweb.org/

11-Point Measure is the 11-point interpolated average precision at the TREC[6]. We adjusted it to the similarity scenario: eleven points are equally distributed between the best match and the least match. This way we can gain an average precision, recall, or f-measure.

Measures at Cut-Off takes into account how well the algorithm can determine which mappings are still valid and which should be dismissed.

5.3 Data Sets

Four data sets each consisting of at least two ontologies were used for evaluation purposes. From the differences of them we expect a representative evaluation.

Russia 1 In this first set we have two ontologies describing Russia. The ontologies were created by students with the task to represent the content of two independent travel websites about Russia. These ontologies have approximately 400 entities, including concepts, relations, and instances. The total number of theoretical mappings is at 280, which have been assigned manually. This scenario is an easy scenario, with which many individual methods can be tested.

Russia 2 The second set again covers Russia. This time the two ontologies have been additionally altered by deleting entities and changing the structure as well as the labels at random. Each ontology has about 300 entities with 215 possible mappings, which were captured during the generation. Many of these mappings can not even be identified by humans any longer.

Tourism Two ontologies which were created separately by different groups of people describe the tourism domain. Both ontologies consist each of about 500 concepts and relations, but no instances though. 300 manual mappings were created.

SWRC The SWRC (Semantic Web Research Community) ontology describes the domain of universities and research. Its size is about 300 entities, with very little instances. For this setting three more very small ontologies (about 20 entities each) were created. In total we have 20 possible mappings (manually determined) against the SWRC ontology. This scenario was derived from the SWAP case where small queries (plus additional context) are sent to an existing ontology for validation.

5.4 Strategies

For the tests we chose to use five similarity strategies:

Label (S1) For this strategy only the labels of entities were regarded (**R1**). This strategy can be regarded as the baseline against which we need to evaluate the other strategies with more advanced measures.

All (S2) As a next step all described similarity methods (**R1** through **R15**) are integrated through simple addition.

Weighted (S3) All similarity methods are integrated including different weights for each method. The weights were calculated by maximizing the overall f-measure in the four test data sets. Additionally five rounds of similarity calculation are done and doubles are removed.

---

[6] http://trec.nist.gov/

Sigmoid (S4) Again all methods (**R1** to **R15**) are taken, but they are weighted with the sigmoid function. The parameters of the sigmoid functions were assigned manually with respect to the underlying similarity method. In the five rounds only the best results were fed back into the next round. Finally doubles were removed. A constant was used to determine the cut-off.

Neural Nets (S5) The results of the methods are fed into a neural network. A fraction (20%) of the evaluation examples was taken for training purposes. The rest was then used for evaluation. A constant value for cut-off was determined from the same training set manually.

5.5 Results

For space purposes we will only present an excerpt of the concrete results as to be published in an upcoming technical report[7]. We will focus on the averaged table for the discussion, which already covers the complete results.

In figure 4 we present the results of the first data set with the two strategies S1 Labels and S4 Sigmoid. All mappings are arranged by their similarity value - with the left side of the graph showing the highest value and the right side showing the lowest value. With each new mapping we recalculate the other measures. The graphs show the respective precision, recall, and f-measure values. The marked points show the cut-off border. This is the point we have to measure if we are looking for exactly one value. Alternatively we also measured the 11-point average to gain a view of the whole curve.

We will now compare the two strategies with respect to the defined evaluation measures. The highest mappings are all correct, what one can see from the precision value of 1 for both strategies. But what one can also see is that S4 Sigmoid keeps the precision value high for many more mappings than S1 Label (97% vs. 80% at cut-off). Recall only reaches a medium level for S1 Label; the final level is much higher for S4 Sigmoid: 0.75 vs. 0.5. A consequence of these two measures is that the f-measure is also higher for the advanced approach in comparison to the naive approach.

A word about the other strategies: all lie in between the two presented approaches. However, determining the cut-off point was much more difficult in those strategies. They often missed the highest f-measure value considerably. A general comparison graph is plotted in figure 4. This comparison graph shows the average results over all four data sets, each with the different strategies. Precision, recall, and f-measure reach their highest values with S4 Sigmoid. In general one can say that there is an increase with the rise of strategy complexity. For S1 to S3 we plotted the two results from different cut-offs. We will now discuss these results in more detail.

5.6 Discussion

Our original hypothesis H is widely fulfilled:

Semantics can help to determine better mappings (S1 vs. S4).

---

[7] We refer to http://www.aifb.uni-karlsruhe.de/WBS/meh/publications/ESWS for the complete graphs as well as the used ontologies.

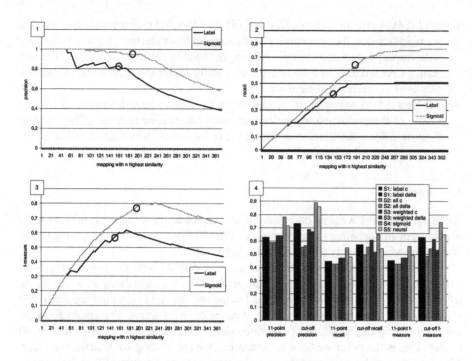

Fig. 4. Results of strategies on dataset Russia1 (1. precision, 2. recall, 3. f-measure); Average results of all strategies over all test scenarios (4.)

Precision is considerably higher for the more advanced combination methods. Especially interesting is the fact that precision generally is higher for these methods, no matter where the cut-off is placed in the mapping table. This is important when thinking of full-automatic solutions, where we want to keep the wrong mappings as low as possible.

Recall also rises along the richness of methods.

F-measure as our core evaluation measure reaches the highest value for the S4 Sigmoid strategy for every data set.

Average Increase of 20% in precision, recall and f-measure.

Naive Combinations of mapping methods often do not make the results better, but worse (S2 All, and even S3 Weighted) . The effort for advanced carefully determined methods is therefore very important.

Machine Learning might help (S5). The problems we encountered are general problems of machine learning such as over-fitting. We also faced the problem that the additional actions could not be completely integrated into the machine learning approach, which lead to lower results.

6   Outlook

6.1   Related Work

Most of the ideas for measuring similarity are derived from common sense and can be easily understood. To our knowledge existing approaches focus on specific methods to determine similarity rather than using an overall integrating approach.

Some authors have tried to find a general description of similarity with several of them being based on knowledge networks. [19] give a general overview of similarity. As the basic ontology mapping problem has been around for some years first tools have already been developed to address this. The tools PROMPT and AnchorPROMPT [16] use labels and to a certain extent the structure of ontologies. Their focus lies on ontology merging i.e. how to create one ontology out of two. [9] already used a general approach of relaxation labelling in their tool GLUE. Most of their work is based on the similarity of instances only. [14] created a tool for mapping called Chimaera. Potential matches are presented to the user in all mentioned tools for confirmation. In their tool ONION [15] the authors take up the idea of using rules and inferencing for mapping, but the inferencing is based on manually assigned mappings or simple heuristics (as e.g. label comparisons). Besides equality first steps are taken in the direction of complex matches. These could also include concatenation of two fields such as "first name" and "last name" to "name" [4]. Despite the large number of related work, there are very little approaches on how to combine the many methods as we do. The other mentioned tools do not raise the issue, they presumably use only naive summarization approaches.

[18] express their insights from a database view. Many ideas from the database community, especially concerning efficiency [13], should also be regarded. Another community involved in similarity and mapping are object-oriented representations in which little work seems to has been done, [20] for UML being an exception. Agent communication greatly benefits from mapping as shown in [24].

6.2   Problems and Future Steps

Even though the shown approach retrieves good results, the results do not reach 100% correctness. Unfortunately, if full-automatic mapping is done, and inferencing builds on top of it, wrong results can bring down the value of the whole mapping process. Implications of fuzzy inferencing[7] will have to be understood well when using it. Semi-automatic processing is a common approach to circumvent this problem. Another problem is a general problem when doing comparisons. Especially with big ontologies complexity of similarity calculations can grow dramatically. In our approach one can expect a complexity of $O(log^2(n) \times n^2)$. It is derived from: $O(log(n))$ for entity access, $O(log(n))$ for the method complexity, and $O(n^2)$ for the full comparison of all possible pairs. Approaches to reduce complexity from other domains (e.g. databases) might be a good start. As data in ontologies expresses certain semantics the calculations might be channelled using these semantics e.g. starting with comparisons of top-level elements in the hierarchy. Both problem areas have potential for future work.

6.3 Conclusion

The mapping problem arises in many scenarios. We have shown a methodology for identifying mappings between two ontologies based on the intelligent combination of manually encoded rules. Evaluation proved our initial hypothesis, i.e. the combination of our presented similarity measures leaded to considerably better results than the usage of one at a time. One can summarize that precision, recall, and f-measure increase by 20% compared to label-based approaches. Semantics helps bridging the mapping gap.

Acknowledgements. Research reported in this paper has been partially financed by EU in the IST projects SWAP (IST-2001-34103) and SEKT (IST-2003-506826). Many thanks to our colleagues for the fruitful discussions.

References

[1] F. Baader, D. L. McGuinness, D. Nardi, and P. F. Patel-Schneider. *The Description Logic Handbook*. 2003.
[2] T. Berners-Lee, J. Hendler, and O. Lassila. The Semantic Web. *Scientific American*, 284(5):34–43, 2001.
[3] G. Bisson. Why and how to define a similarity measure for object based representation systems. *Towards Very Large Knowledge Bases*, pages 236–246, 1995.
[4] P. Bouquet, B. Magnini, L. Serafini, and S. Zanobini. A SAT-based algorithm for context matching. Technical report, University of Trento, Trento, Italy, 2003.
[5] D. Calvanese, G. D. Giacomo, D. Lembo, M. Lenzerini, and R. Rosati. What to ask to a peer: Ontology-based query reformulation. In *Proc. of the 9th Int. Conf. on the Principles of Knowledge Representation and Reasoning (KR 2004)*, 2004.
[6] S. V. Castano, M. G. D. Antonellis, B. Fugini, and C. Pernici. Schema analysis: Techniques and applications. *ACM Trans. Systems*, 23(3):286–333, 1998.
[7] Z. Ding and Y. Peng. A probabilistic extension to ontology language owl. In *Proceedings of the 37th Hawaii International Conference On System Sciences (HICSS-37)*, Big Island, Hawaii, January 2004.
[8] H. Do and E. Rahm. Coma - a system for flexible combination of schema matching approaches. In *Proc. of the 28th VLDB Conference*, Hong Kong, China, 2002.
[9] A. Doan, J. Madhavan, P. Domingos, and A. Halevy. Learning to map between ontologies on the semantic web. In *Proc. to the WWW-11*, Honolulu, USA, 2002.
[10] J. Heaton. *Programming Neural Networks in Java*. 2002.
[11] I. V. Levenshtein. Binary codes capable of correcting deletions, insertions, and reversals. *Cybernetics and Control Theory*, 1966.
[12] A. Maedche, B. Motik, N. Silva, and R. Volz. Mafra - a mapping framework for distributed ontologies. In *Proc. of the EKAW 2002*, 2002.
[13] A. McCallum, K. Nigam, and L. H. Ungar. Efficient clustering of high-dimensional data sets with application to reference matching. In *Knowledge Discovery & Data Mining*, 2000.
[14] D. L. McGuinness. Conceptual modeling for distributed ontology environments. In *International Conference on Conceptual Structures*, pages 100–112, 2000.
[15] P. Mitra, G. Wiederhold, and M. Kersten. A graph-oriented model for articulation of ontology interdependencies. *Lecture Notes in Computer Science*, 1777:86+, 2000.
[16] N. F. Noy and M. A. Musen. Anchor-PROMPT: Using Non-Local Context for Semantic Matching. In *WS Ontologies & Information Sharing at IJCAI-2001*, Seattle, USA, 2001.

[17] M. R. Quillan. Word concepts: A theory and simulation of some basic capabilities. *Behavioral Science*, 12:410–430, 1967.

[18] J. Roddick, K. Hornsby, and D. de Vries. A unifying semantic distance model for determining the similarity of attribute values. In *Proc. of ACSC2003*, Adelaide, Australia, 2003.

[19] M. Rodríguez and M. Egenhofer. Determining semantic similarity among entity classes from different ontologies. *IEEE Trans. on Knowledge and Data Eng.*, 15(2):442–456, 2003.

[20] R. Rufai. Similarity metric for UML models. Master's thesis, King Fahd University of Petroleum and Minerals, 2003.

[21] G. Stumme et al. The Karlsruhe View on Ontologies. Technical report, University of Karlsruhe, Institute AIFB, 2003.

[22] X. Su. A text categorization perspective for ontology mapping. Technical report, Norwegian University of Science and Technology, Norway, 2002.

[23] C. J. Van Rijsbergen. *Information Retrieval, 2nd edition*. Dept. of Computer Science, University of Glasgow, 1979.

[24] P. C. Weinstein and W. P. Birmingham. Agent communication with differentiated ontologies. Technical Report CSE-TR-383-99, 7, 1999.

Application of Ontology Techniques to View-Based Semantic Search and Browsing

Eero Hyvönen, Samppa Saarela, and Kim Viljanen

Helsinki Institute for Information Technology (HIIT) / University of Helsinki
P.O. Box 26, 00014 UNIV. OF HELSINKI, FINLAND
{Eero.Hyvonen, Samppa.Saarela, Kim.Viljanen}@cs.Helsinki.FI
http://www.cs.helsinki.fi/group/seco/

Abstract. We show how the benefits of the view-based search method, developed within the information retrieval community, can be extended with ontology-based search, developed within the Semantic Web community, and with semantic recommendations. As a proof of the concept, we have implemented an ontology- and view-based search engine and recommendation system Ontogator for RDF(S) repositories. Ontogator is innovative in two ways. Firstly, the RDFS-based ontologies used for annotating metadata are used in the user interface to facilitate view-based information retrieval. The views provide the user with an overview of the repository contents and a vocabulary for expressing search queries. Secondly, a semantic browsing function is provided by a recommender system. This system enriches instance level metadata by ontologies and provides the user with links to semantically related relevant resources. The semantic linkage is specified in terms of logical rules. To illustrate and discuss the ideas, a deployed application of Ontogator to a photo repository of the Helsinki University Museum is presented.

1 Introduction

This paper addresses two problems encountered when using keyword search. Firstly, the precision and recall of keyword-based search methods is lowered since they are based on words instead of the underlying concepts [4]. For example, a keyword in a document does not necessarily mean that the document is relevant, relevant documents may not contain the explicit keyword, synonyms lower recall rate, homonyms lower precision rate, and semantic relations such as hyponymy, meronymy, and antonymy [6] are not taken into account. A prominent solution approach to these problems is to use *ontology-based information retrieval* [21, 22]. Secondly, keyword search methods are not easy to use in situations where the user does not know the terminology used in annotating the contents or does not have an explicit target to be retrieved in mind but rather wants to learn what the database in general contains. A prominent solution approach to information retrieval in this kind of situations is the *multi-faceted* or *view-based search* method[1] [19, 9]. Here the idea is to organize the terminological keywords of the underlying database into orthogonal hierarchies and use them extensively in the

---

[1] See http://www.view-based-systems.com/history.asp for a historical review of the idea.

J. Davies et al. (Eds.): ESWS 2004, LNCS 3053, pp. 92–106, 2004.

user interface in helping the user to formulate the queries, in navigating the database, and in grouping the results semantically.

We describe a system called Ontogator, a semantic search engine and browser for RDF(S)[2] repositories. Its main novelty lays in the idea of combining the benefits of ontology-based and view-based search methods with semantic recommendations. To test and validate the ideas presented, Ontogator has been applied to a real-life system Promoottori that is in daily use at the Helsinki University Museum[3].

In the following, keyword, view-based and ontology-based approaches to information retrieval are first discussed. After this Ontogator and its application to Promoottori are discussed. In conclusion, contributions of this paper are summarized, related work discussed, the lessons learned listed, and a further application of Ontogator to a deployed semantic web portal is pointed out.

2 View-Based Search

The content of data records in a database is often described by associating each record with a set of keywords. Keywords can be selected from controlled vocabularies or thesauri [7] in order to create coherent annotations and to ease image retrieval. In view-based information retrieval, the keywords—to be called *categories*—are organized systematically into a set of hierarchical, orthogonal taxonomies, such as "Artifacts", "Places", "Materials" etc. The taxonomies are called subject *facets* or *views*.

A search query in view-based search is formulated by selecting categories of interest from the different facets. For example, by selecting the category "Floora's day" from a time facet, and "Building" from a location facet, the user can express the query for retrieving all images that are taken during Floora's day *and* at *any* building that is defined as a subcategory of "Building" (at any depth), such as "Old Student Union house". Intuitively, the query is a conjunctive constraint over the facets with disjunctive constraints over the sub-categories in each facet.

More formally, if the categories selected are $C_1, ..., C_n$ and the subcategories of $C_i, i = 1...n$, including C_i itself are $S_{i,1}, S_{i,2}..., S_{i,k}$, respectively, then this selection corresponds to the following boolean AND-OR-constraint:

$$(S_{1,1} \lor ... \lor S_{1,k}) \land (S_{2,1} \lor ... \lor S_{2,l}) \land ... \land (S_{n,1} \lor ... \lor S_{n,m}) \tag{1}$$

Facets can be used for helping the user in information retrieval in many ways. Firstly, the facet hierarchies give the user an overview of what kind of information there is in the repository. Secondly, the hierarchies can guide the user in formulating the query in terms of appropriate keywords. Thirdly, the hierarchies can be used to disambiguate homonymous query terms. Fourthly, the facets can be used as a navigational aid when browsing the database content [9]. Fifthly, the number of hits in every category that can be selected next can be computed *beforehand* and be shown to the user [19]. In this way, the user can be hindered from making a selection leading to an empty result set—a recurring problem in IR systems—and is guided toward selections that are likely to constrain (or relax) the search appropriately.

---

[2] http://www.w3.org/RDF
[3] http://www.helsinki.fi/museo/

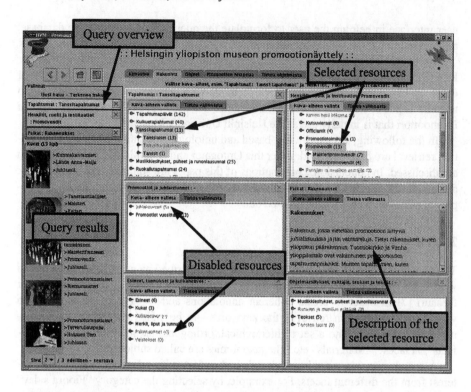

Fig. 1. Ontogator user interface for view-based multi-facet search in Promoottori.

Figure 1 shows the search interface of Ontogator in the Promoottori application. It is used by museum clients for finding photographs related to the historical promotion ceremonies of the University of Helsinki. The contents of the photos are semantically complicated and the vocabulary used in describing the ceremonies largely unknown to the users. The goal of Promoottori is to provide the museum guest with an easy to use image information retrieval system for investigating the contents of the promotion photo database, and in this way to illustrate the inner life and traditions of the university.

On the right, six facet hierarchies are shown (in Finnish): "Events", "Promotions", "Performances", "Persons and roles", "Physical objects", and "Places". For example, the Events facet (Tapahtumat) classifies the various traditional events that take place during the ceremonies. It gives the user an overview of the whole ceremony process and the vocabulary for formulating queries. The facet hierarchies are visualized like hierarchical folders in Windows Explorer. By clicking on the symbol in front of the category name, the category is expanded into sub-categories.

A query is formulated by selecting (sub-)categories in hierarchies, at most one selection from each facet. A category is selected into the query by clicking on its name. When the user selects a new category c, the system constrains the search further by leaving in the current result set only such images that are annotated with some sub-category of c. After each selection the result set is recomputed for each category in the opened hierarchies, and a number n is shown to the user. It tells that if the category is selected next, then there will be n images in the result set. A selection leading to empty result set ($n = 0$) is disabled and shown in gray color. The query can be relaxed by making a new selection on a higher level of the facets or by dismissing the facet totally from the query.

The idea of view-based search idea has been used, e.g., in the HiBrowse system [19] in the 90's. A later application of the approach is the Flamenco system [9] and the first web-based prototype of Ontogator [11]. Extensive user studies [16, 5] have recently been carried out to show that a direct Google-like keyword search interface is preferred over view-based search if the users know precisely what they want. However, if this is not the case, then the view-based search method with its "browsing the shelves" sensation is clearly preferred over keyword search or using only a single facet. The latter approach is commonly used for finding resources on the web, e.g., in the Open Directory Project[4] and in Yahoo.

3   Extending Views with Ontologies

View-based search is based on hierarchically organized category labels. They are related with each other by the hierarchical inclusion relation within a single classification. By using semantically richer ontologies the following benefits can be obtained. Firstly, ontologies can be used to describe the domain knowledge and the terminology of the application in more detail. For example, relations between categories in different views can be defined. Secondly, ontologies can be used for creating semantically more accurate annotations [21, 22] in terms of the domain knowledge. Thirdly, with the help of ontologies, the user can express the queries more precisely and unambiguously, which leads to better precision and recall rates. Fourthly, through ontological class definitions and inference mechanisms, such as property inheritance, instance-level metadata can be enriched semantically.

Ontogator combines the benefits of view-based and ontology-based search methods. It provides the user with a view-based interface by which he can easily get an overview of the database contents, learn the terminology in use, and formulate the queries (cf. figure 1). However, the categories in the views are not keyword hierarchies but projected resources from the underlying ontologies by which the contents have been annotated. The domain knowledge, annotations and information retrieval is based on semantically rich ontological structures instead of simple keyword classifications. As a result, more developed inference mechanisms can be employed for performing the search and for creating additional services. In Ontogator, for example, a semantic recommendation system has been implemented for browsing the data resources.

Figure 2 depicts the overall architecture of Ontogator. The system is used by the Content Browser and is based on two information sources: Domain Knowledge and Annotation Data. Domain Knowledge consists of ontologies that define the domain concepts and the individuals. Annotation Data describes the metadata of the data resources represented in terms of the annotation and domain ontologies. The subject of a

---

[4] http://dmoz.org

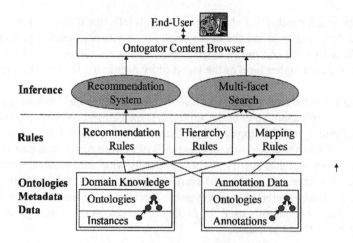

Fig. 2. Architecture of Ontogator.

data resource (image in Promoottori) is described by associating it with a set of RDF(S) resources of the domain knowledge that describe its content (in Promoottori, these resources occur in the image). The difference with keyword annotations is that the associated resources are not words but URIs of the domain ontology knowledge base, which disambiguates the meaning of annotations (synonym/homonym problem) and provides additional implicit semantic metadata through the RDF graph. The domain and annotation ontologies used in the Promoottori application are described in more detail in [13].

Based on the domain knowledge and the annotation data, Ontogator provides the user with two services:

Multi-facet search The underlying domain ontologies are projected into facets that facilitate multi-facet search.

Recommendation system After finding an image of interest by multi-facet search, Domain Knowledge and Annotation Data are used to recommend the user to view other related data resources shown as hypertext links. The labels of the links are used to explain the semantic relation to the user. For example, in Promoottori links to photos of the relatives of a person in a photo are recommended.

These two services are connected with the information sources by three sets of rules: Hierarchy Rules, Mapping Rules, and Recommendation Rules (cf. figure 2).

3.1 Hierarchy Rules

The hierarchy rules tell how to construct the facet hierarchies from the domain ontologies. Hierarchy rules are needed in order to make the classifications shown to the user independent from the design choices of the underlying Domain Ontologies. The view-based search system itself does not differentiate between differently projected hierarchies.

The specification of a facet hierarchy consists of the following parts: 1) Selection of the top resource (root) for the facet in a domain ontology. 2) Specification of the relation through which the (sub)categories are found from the root in the domain ontology. In Ontogator and Promoottori, as described in this paper, hierarchy projections are created using Java but in the recent server version on Ontogator, hierarchy projections are specified in logic and Prolog is used as in [15].

An obvious way to extract a facet hierarchy from the RDF(S)-based domain knowledge is to use the subclass-of hyponymy relation. Then the inner nodes of the hierarchy consist of the classes of the domain ontology, and the leaves are the direct instances of these classes. Using only hyponymy for facet projections would, however, be a limitation in the general case. For example, places may constitute a part-of hierarchy, and this would be a natural choice for a facet in the user interface.

Hierarchy rules tell how the views are projected logically. A separate question is how these hierarchies should be shown to the user. Firstly, the ordering of the sub-resources may be relevant. In Promoottori, for example, the sub-happenings of an event should be presented in the order in which they take place and persons be listed in alphabetical order. In Ontogator, ordering of the sub-nodes can be specified by a configurable property; the sub-categories are sorted based on the values of this property. Second, one may need a way to filter unnecessary resources away from the user interface. For example, in Promoottori the ontology was created partly before the actual annotation work and had more classes and details than were actually needed. In Ontogator, empty categories can be pruned out. A hierarchy may also have intermediate classes that are useful for knowledge representation purposes but are not very natural categories to the user. Such categories should be present internally in the search hierarchies but should not be shown to the user. Third, the names for categories need to be specified. For example, in Promoottori the label for a person category should be constructed from the last and first names represented by distinct property values.

3.2   Mapping Rules

In Promoottori, an image is annotated by associating it with a set of domain knowledge resources describing its content. This set is, however, not enough because there may be also *indirect* relations between images and the annotations. Mapping rules can be used to specify what indirect resources describe the images in addition to the direct ones. Through such rules it is possible to achieve a search system that is independent of both the annotation scheme and the domain ontology design. The search system does not make any distinction between the ways in which data resources may be related with their annotations.

For example, in Promoottori there are the classes Role and Person in the domain ontology. The subclasses of Role, such as Master and Doctor Honoris Causa, are used to annotate the role in which a person appears in a picture. If the role r of a person p is known, then the picture is annotated by an instance of the Role. As a result, the picture is found using r in the multi-facet search through the "Roles" facet, but not with p through the "Persons" facet, which would be unsatisfactory. The problem can be solved by using a mapping rule telling that the images, that are about an instance of Role are also images about the person (in that role).

Mapping rules are given as RDF traversal paths using the N3 notation[5]. For example, the description below tells that any instance p of the class Person (or its subclasses) is mapped to an image, if there is a related_instances arc from the image to resource r and then a persons_in_role arc from there to p (notation ^ denotes traversal through an RDF arc in the opposite direction). The tag labelRegex illustrates how category labels are constructed in Ontogator from different resources using templates. The label for the person categories is concatenated from the property values of lastName and firstName, separated by a comma and space (e.g., "Smith, John").

```
<?xml version='1.0' encoding='ISO-8859-1'?>
<!DOCTYPE rdf:RDF [
    <!ENTITY rdf 'http://www.w3.org/1999/02/22-rdf-syntax-ns#'>
    <!ENTITY Promotion
            'http://www.cs.helsinki.fi/Promotion#'>
    <!ENTITY yom 'http://www.cs.helsinki.fi/yomuseo/yom#'>
    <!ENTITY rdfs 'http://www.w3.org/TR/1999/PR-rdf-schema-19990303#'>
]>
<rdf:RDF xmlns:yom="&yom;" xmlns:rdf="&rdf;"
        xmlns:Promotion="&Promotion;" xmlns:rdfs="&rdfs;">
...
<rdf:Description rdf:about="&Promotion;Person">
  <yom:relatedDocumentMapping>
    ^Promotion:persons_in_role
    ^Promotion:related_instances
  </yom:relatedDocumentMapping>
  <yom:labelRegex>${Promotion:lastName}, ${Promotion:firstName}
  </yom:labelRegex>
</rdf:Description>
...
</rdf:RDF>
```

All mappings between facet resources and the data resources are determined when constructing the system's internal representation of the facet hierarchies. Computing mappings during the startup makes the search system faster but at the price of the memory needed for the search data structures.

4   Recommendation System

Ontogator's Recommendation System (figure 2) is a mechanism for defining and finding semantic relations in the underlying RDF(S) knowledge base, i.e. Domain Knowledge and Annotation Data. The relations of interest to the user in an application are described by a set of logical Recommendation Rules. The recommendations are shown as labeled navigational links relating data resources with each other. Figure 3 illustrates their usage in Promoottori. The user has selected a photo from the Query results provided by the multi-facet search engine on the left. Ontogator shows the image with its metadata in the middle. On the right, the Recommendations for the selected image are seen in groups. Each group is based on a recommendation rule. A group may contain several images that can be viewed one after another in the group pane. The title of the group pane gives a general, rule level explanation for the semantic recommendation, such as

---

[5] http://www.w3.org/DesignIssues/Notation3.html

"next event" (seuraava tapahtuma). In addition, every recommended photo is described and (if possible) given a natural language explanation of how the current image is related to the recommended one. For example, if the current image presents Ms. Laura Hautamäki, then the system recommends images containing images about her father with an explanation "The father of Laura Hautamäki" under the group title "Related persons".

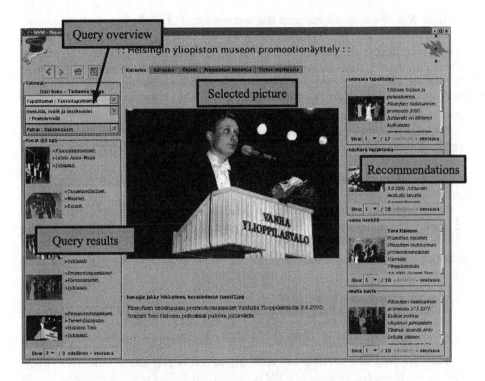

Fig. 3. Screenshot of the recommendation system in Promoottori.

Promoottori currently contains rules for determining photos of the preceding event and the next event based on the promotion procedure, rules for determining photos depicting related persons (family relations), rules for showing other images of the persons in the selected image, rules for showing photos taken in the same place, rules for showing images from the same promotion, and rules for showing photos from the same era.

4.1 Recommendation Rules

The recommendation rules are defined in terms of logical Horn clauses and are implemented using SWI-Prolog[6] and its RDF parser. For example, the "Related persons"

---

[6] SWI-Prolog version 5.1.5, http://www.swi-prolog.org/

-rule links a person with other persons through family relations described in the underlying RDF graph. If the user selects an image exposing a person p, then images exposing persons in different family relations with p are recommended to the user. The following predicate is used for defining the recommendation rule:

$$\text{rec\_related\_persons}(X,Y,RecType,Relation,Desc,RevDesc,Priority) \qquad (2)$$

Here X is the selected resource that we are searching links for, Y is the recommended resource, RecType is the topic title for this recommendation rule to be shown in the group pane in the user interface, Relation is the property (URI) which connects X and Y (if exists), Desc is a natural language description for the relation $X \to Y$ (e.g., "X is the father of Y"), RevDesc a reverse description for the relation $Y \to X$ (e.g., "Y is a child of X"), and Relevance is an integer that is used to sort the recommendations in a relevance order in the user interface. In essence, the rule defines 1) a set of RDF triples (recommendation links) between the resources and 2) attaches with each triple additional information to be used in showing the recommendation to the end-user. The same predicate structure is used for all recommendation rules. The definition of the predicates can be programmed freely in Prolog and depends on the ontologies and metadata of the application.

The Promotion ontology contains a class Persons that has the properties father-of, mother-of, and spouse. The related persons may be found by simply following the RDF triplet connecting two person instance resources. The central part in defining the predicate rec_related_persons is to specify when two persons are related with each other by some of these properties. In this case, the simple definition below can be used:

```
related_persons(X, Y, Relation) :-
    rdf(X, rdf:type, 'http://www.cs.helsinki.fi/Promotion#Persons'),
    rdf(X, Relation, Y),
    rdf(Y, rdf:type, 'http://www.cs.helsinki.fi/Promotion#Persons').
```

Here the predicate rdf matches RDF triples and is provided by the SWI-Prolog RDF parser. If needed, other rules could be defined for finding more complicated family relations, such as grand children or cousins.

The rec_related_persons predicate also has to create for each recommendation triple the explanatory strings RecType, Expl, and RevExpl to be used in the user interface visualization, and a value for the relevance. These values can either be given explicitly or computed, e.g., by concatenating the labels of the RDF graph.

For reasons of efficiency, the recommendations are generated into an XML-file in a batch process before using the application. This recommendation file is loaded into the Ontogator browser at the application startup. A limitation of this static approach is that it is not possible to create on-line dynamic recommendations based on the user's profile and usage of the system. (An online-version of the relation generation engine has been implemented in [10].)

Two recommendations for a photo resource are shown in XML below. The first recommendation (rec tag) is based on the logical relation "same century". The URI of the related resource (relatedInstance) is given (here "..." for short) with the label "Promotions in the 19th century". The tag and attribute names used correspond to the

variable names in predicate (2). For example, the priority attribute of the recommendation tells the relevance order in which the recommendations are shown to the user.

```xml
<?xml version="1.0" encoding="ISO-8859-1"?>
<recommendations>
...
<recs about=
  "http://www.cs.helsinki.fi/Promotion#Promotion_02311">
  <rec priority="3">
    <relatedInstance uri="...">Promotions in the 19th century
    </relatedInstance>
      <relation name="same century"/>
      <rectype>same century</rectype>
      <description>Promotions in the 19th century</description>
  </rec>
  <rec priority="8">
      <relatedInstance uri="...">Theological Faculty</relatedInstance>
      <relation name="same promotion"/>
      <rectype>same promotion</rectype>
      <description>Theological Faculty, June 15, 1818</description>
  </rec>
  ...
</recs>
...
</recommendations>
```

The recommendation system is divided into three modules: domain specific recommendation rules, RDF Schema specific rules (such as rules implementing the transitive
subclass-of closure), and system specific rules (the "main" program creating the recommendations). The domain specific rules are application dependent and are created by a
domain specialist. RDF Schema specific and system specific rules are independent of
the application.

When processing the data, the program iterates through all images and their metadata. The recommendation rules are applied to every different resource r describing the
content of some image. If recommendations are found, they are stored as recommendations for r. In order to minimize the number of recommendation links represented in
the XML-file the recommendations are created only for each metadata resource r and
not for each image. The Ontogator browser then shows, as the recommendations of an
image, the recommendations related to each resource r used in the image's metadata.

The recommendation system creates recommendation descriptions to the user in
natural language using templates such as "*Person X is a child of Person Y*". The definition of the reverse description (RevDesc in predicate (2)) facilitates symmetric usage of
the recommendation associations. The texts are based on the labels of the resources defined in the RDF descriptions and some simple Prolog rules describing typical Finnish
conjugation rules. For example, the genetive form for the last name "Virtanen" is "Vir-
tasen" but "Mannerheim" is in genetive form "Mannerheimin".

4.2 Strategies for Creating Recommendations

Recommendations can be created in various ways [20]. In our work, we have been
considering the following alternatives:

User *profile-based recommendations* are based on information collected by observing the user, or in some cases by asking the user to explicitly define the interest profile. Based on the user's profile, recommendations are then made to the user either by comparing the user's profile to other users' profiles (collaborative filtering/recommending) or by comparing the user's profile to the underlying document collection (content-based recommending). The strength of user profile-based recommendations is that they are personalized and hence serving better the user's individual goals. In our case application, personalization is however difficult, because the users cannot be identified. It is not even known when the user's session begins and when it ends because the users are using the same physical kiosk interface located in the museum. The profiling must be easy for the user because most of the users use the system perhaps only once in their lifetime. Finally, it is difficult to identify whether the user liked or disliked the current image without asking the user to rate every image explicitly. A weakness of collaborative filtering is that explaining the recommendations to the user can be difficult, because they are mostly based on heuristic measures of the similarity between user profiles and database contents, and on the user's actions.

With *similarity-based recommendations* we refer to the possibility to compare the semantical distance between the metadata of resources. The nearest resources are likely to be of more interest and could be recommended to the user. A difficulty of this recommendation method is how to measure the semantical distance between metadata. For example, in Promoottori the most similar image may not the most interesting one but rather just another picture of the same event. One method is to use the count of common or intersecting annotation resources as a distance measure [23].

The idea of *rule-based recommendations* used in Ontogator is that the domain specialist explicitly describes the notion of "interesting related image" with generic logic rules. The system then applies the rules to the underlying knowledge base in order to find interesting images related to the selected one. This method has several strengths. Firstly, the rule can be associated with a label, such as "Images of the previous event", that can be used as the explanation for the recommendations found. It is also possible to deduce the explanation label as a side effect of applying the rule. Recommendation rules are described by the domain specialist. The rules and explanations are explicitly defined, not based on heuristic measures, which could be difficult to understand and motivate. Secondly, the specialist knows the domain and may promote the most important relations between the images. However, this could also be a weakness if the user's goals and the specialists thoughts about what is important do not match, and the user is not interested in the recommendations. Thirdly, the rule-based recommendations do not exclude the possibility of using other recommendation methods but provides an infrastructure for running any rules. For example, the recommendation rules could perhaps be learned by observing the users actions and then used in recommending images for the current or future users.

In the initial version of Promoottori [14], we implemented a profile-based and similarity-based recommendation system that recommended semantically similar images. The recommendations were not static but were modified dynamically by maintaining a user profile and a history log of image selections. Then a rule-based recommendation system was implemented due to the benefits discussed above and is in use in the Promoottori application.

5   Conclusions

5.1   Contributions

We developed methods for combining the benefits of RDF(S)-based knowledge representation, the multi-facet search method, and knowledge-based recommendations. The ideas have been implemented as the Ontogator tool. In Ontogator, facet hierarchies projected from ontologies are used to help the user in formulating the information need and the corresponding query. After finding a relevant document with view-based search, the recommender system provides the user with a semantic browsing facility linking semantically related images. The mapping between the user interface functionalities (searching and browsing) and the underlying knowledge base is specified by hierarchy, mapping, and recommendation rules. By changing the rules, Ontogator can be applied to different domains and annotation schemas. As an example, application of Ontogator to a deployed image retrieval system, Promoottori, was discussed.

5.2   Related Work

The idea of viewing an RDF(S) knowledge base along different hierarchical projections has been applied, e.g., in the ontology editor Protégé-2000[7] where it is possible to choose the property by which the hierarchy of classes is projected to the user. However, in our case a much more complex specification of the projection than a single property is needed. For example, the hyponymy projection already employs two properties (rdfs:subClassOf and rdf:type). Furthermore, in Ontogator the idea of mapping rules was developed for associating indirectly related resources with views.

The idea of semantic browsing was inspired by the idea of Topic Maps [18, 17]. However, while the links in a Topic Map are given by a map, the links in Ontogator are inferred based on logic rules and the underlying knowledge base. The idea of semantic browsing is also related to research on recommender systems [20]. In Ontogator, the recommendation system is used for searching labeled relations between data resources. This approach is different from knowledge-based recommender systems [1], such as the FindMe systems [2], where browsing is based on altering the characteristics of a found prototype. Logic and dynamic link creation on the semantic web have been discussed, e.g., in [8, 3].

The search interface of Ontogator is based on the HiBrowse model [19]. However, in our case the whole hierarchy, not only the next level of subcategories, can be opened for selections. Moving between hierarchy levels is more flexible because at any point any new selection in the opened hierarchy is possible. In addition, the "browsing the shelves" sensation is provided by a separate recommendation system based in the underlying ontological domain knowledge. This provides a semantically richer basis for

---

[7] http://protege.stanford.edu

browsing than the keyword hierarchies used in traditional view-based search engines, such as Flamenco [9].

The idea of ontology-based image retrieval has been discussed, e.g., in [21, 22]. By annotating data with concepts instead of words more precise information retrieval is possible. The price to be paid is that more work is needed when constructing the ontologies and during the content annotation phase.

5.3 Lessons Learned

The main difficulty in integrating the view-based and ontology-based search paradigms is how to model and deal with the indirect relations between the images and domain ontology resources, and how to project the facet hierarchies from the RDF(S) knowledge base. If not properly modeled, the precision and recall rates of the system are lowered.

A reason for choosing RDF(S) for the knowledge representation language was its domain independent nature and openness. This makes it possible to apply the content and Ontogator more easily to different applications. During our work, we actually reused the promotion ontology and instance data easily in another application for generating automatically semantically linked web pages from RDF(S) data [15].

In our work, logic programming turned to be a very flexible and effective way to handle RDF(S) data by querying and inferring when compared with RDF query languages, such as RDQL and RQL. The definition of the recommendation rules requires programming skills and may be difficult to a domain specialists who is not familiar with logic languages. A problem encountered there is how to test and verify that the recommendations for all images are feasible without having to browse through the whole database. Computational efficiency and central memory requirements can be a problem if the RDF knowledge base is very large and if the rules are complex.

During our work, Protégé-2000 was used as the ontology editor. Jena's[8] basic main memory -based model (ModelMem) was employed to load the RDF(S)-models into Ontogator's internal representation form. Protégé turned out to be a versatile tool with an intuitive user interface that even for a non-programmer could use for constructing ontologies. A good thing about Protégé is that it is not limited to RDF(S) semantics only, but enables and enforces the use of additional features.

Ontology evolution poses a problem with Protégé-2000 even in the simple case that a name (label) of some class changes. Protégé derives URI's of the classes from their names, and if a name changes then the classes URI (ID) changes also. This leads to configurational problems. Rules and mappings for one version of the ontology do not apply to the new version, even though the actual classes have not changed, only their labels. Multi-instantiations would have been desirable in some situations but this is not possible with Protégé.

The major difficulty in the ontology-based approach is the extra work needed in creating the ontology and the detailed annotations. We believe, however, that in many applications such as Promoottori this price is justified due to the better accuracy obtained in information retrieval and to the new semantic browsing facilities offered to the end-

---

[8] http://www.hpl.hp.com/semweb/jena.htm

user. The trade-off between annotation work and quality of information retrieval can be balanced by using less detailed ontologies and annotations, if needed.

Evaluating the quality and relevance of recommendations can only be based on the user's opinions. In our case, only a small informal user study of has been conducted using the personnel of the museum. The general conclusion was that the idea seems useful in practice.

5.4   A Further Application on the Web

A server-based version of Ontogator, Ontogator 2, has been developed and is used as the search engine of the "MuseumFinland — Finnish Museums of the Semantic Web" portal [10] that is available on the web[9]. The first version of this application contains 4,000 images of museum collection objects from three different museums. The metadata is given in terms of seven RDF(S) ontologies that consist of some 10,000 concepts and individuals. First experiments with the implementation indicate that the technology scales up to at least tens of thousands of images and ontological resources. In Ontogator 2, the recommendation system has been separated into a SWI-Prolog HTTP-server of its own called Ontodella. Ontodella is used dynamically for creating the view hierarchies (by a combination of hierarchy and mapping rules in Prolog) and for generating the recommendations for a given resource.

Acknowledgments

Kati Heinämies and Jaana Tegelberg of the Helsinki University Museum provided the content material for Promoottori. Avril Styrman created most of the promotion ontologies and annotated the images. Our work was mainly funded by the National Technology Agency Tekes, Nokia, TietoEnator, the Espoo City Museum, the Foundation of the Helsinki University Museum, the National Board of Antiquities, and the Antikvariagroup.

References

[1] R. Burke. Knowledge-based recommender systems. In A. Kent, editor, *Encyclopaedia of Library and Information Sciences*. Marcel Dekker, 2000.

[2] R. Burke, K. Hammond, and B. Young. The FindMe approach to assisted browsing. *IEEE Expert*, 12(4), 1997.

[3] P. Dolong, N. Henze, and W. Neijdl. Logic-based open hypermedia for the semantic web. In *Proceedings of the Int. Workshop on Hypermedia and the Semantic Web, Hypertext 2003 Conference, Nottinghan, UK*, 2003.

[4] D. Fensel (ed.). The semantic web and its languages. *IEEE Intelligence Systems*, Nov/Dec 2000.

[5] J. English, M. Hearst, R. Sinha, K. Swearingen, and K.-P. Lee. Flexible search and navigation using faceted metadata. Technical report, University of Berkeley, School of Information Management and Systems, 2003. Submitted for publication.

---

[9] http://museosuomi.cs.helsinki.fi

[6] C. Fellbaum, editor. *WordNet. An electronic lexical database.* The MIT Press, Cambridge, Massachusetts, 2001.

[7] D. J. Foskett. Thesaurus. In *Encyclopaedia of Library and Information Science, Volume 30*, pages 416–462. Marcel Dekker, New York, 1980.

[8] C. Goble, S. Bechhofer, L. Carr, D. De Roure, and W. Hall. Conceptual open hypermedia = the semantic web? In *Proceedings of the WWW2001, Semantic Web Workshop, Hongkong*, 2001.

[9] M. Hearst, A. Elliott, J. English, R. Sinha, K. Swearingen, and K.-P. Lee. Finding the flow in web site search. *CACM*, 45(9):42–49, 2002.

[10] E. Hyvönen, M. Junnila, S. Kettula, , E. Mäkelä, S. Saarela, M. Salminen, A. Syreeni, A. Valo, and K. Viljanen. MuseumFinland—Finnish Museums on the Semantic Web. User's perspective. In *Proceedings of Museums and the Web 2004 (MW2004), Arlington, Virginia, USA*, 2004. http://www.cs.helsinki.fi/u/eahyvone/publications/ MuseumFinland.pdf.

[11] E. Hyvönen, S. Kettula, V. Raatikka, S. Saarela, and Kim Viljanen. Semantic interoperability on the web. Case Finnish Museums Online. In Hyvönen and Klemettinen [12], pages 41–53. http://www.hiit.fi/publications/.

[12] E. Hyvönen and M. Klemettinen, editors. *Towards the semantic web and web services. Proceedings of the XML Finland 2002 conference. Helsinki, Finland*, number 2002-03 in HIIT Publications. Helsinki Institute for Information Technology (HIIT), Helsinki, Finland, 2002. http://www.hiit.fi/publications/.

[13] E. Hyvönen, A. Styrman, and S. Saarela. Ontology-based image retrieval. In Hyvönen and Klemettinen [12], pages 15–27. http://www.hiit.fi/publications/.

[14] E. Hyvönen, A. Styrman, and S. Saarela. Ontology-based image retrieval. In Hyvönen and Klemettinen [12], pages 15–27. http://www.hiit.fi/publications/.

[15] E. Hyvönen, A. Valo, K. Viljanen, and M. Holi. Publishing semantic web content as semantically linked HTML pages. In *Proceedings of XML Finland 2003, Kuopio, Finland*, 2003. http://www.cs.helsinki.fi/u/eahyvone/publications/ xmlfinland2003/swehg_article_xmlfi2003.pdf.

[16] K.-P. Lee, K. Swearingen, K. Li, and M. Hearst. Faceted metadata for image search and browsing. In *Proceedings of CHI 2003, April 5-10, Fort Lauderdale, USA*. Association for Computing Machinery (ACM), USA, 2003.

[17] Jack Park and Sam Hunting, editors. *XML Topic Maps. Creating and using Topic Maps for the Web.* Addison-Wesley, New York, 2003.

[18] Steve Pepper. The TAO of Topic Maps. In *Proceedings of XML Europe 2000, Paris, France*, 2000. http://www.ontopia.net/topicmaps/materials/rdf.html.

[19] A. S. Pollitt. The key role of classification and indexing in view-based searching. Technical report, University of Huddersfield, UK, 1998. http://www.ifla.org/IV/ifla63/63polst.pdf.

[20] J. Ben Schafer, Joseph A. Konstan, and John Riedl. E-commerce recommendation applications. *Data Mining and Knowledge Discovery*, 5(1/2):115–153, 2001.

[21] A. T. Schreiber, B. Dubbeldam, J. Wielemaker, and B. J. Wielinga. Ontology-based photo annotation. *IEEE Intelligent Systems*, 16:66–74, May/June 2001.

[22] G. Schreiber, I. Blok, D. Carlier, W. van Gent, J. Hokstam, and U. Roos. A mini-experiment in semantic annotation. In I. Horrocks and J. Hendler, editors, *The Semantic Web – ISWC 2002. First international semantic web conference*, number 2342 in LNCS, pages 404–408. Springer–Verlag, Berlin, 2002.

[23] Nenad Stojanovic, Rudi Studer, and Ljiljana Stojanovic. An approach for the ranking of query results in the semantic web. In Dieter Fensel, Katia Sycara, and John Mylopoulos, editors, *The Semantic Web – ISWC 2003. Second international semantic web conference*, number 2870 in LNCS, pages 500–516. Springer–Verlag, Berlin, 2003.

Active Ontologies for Data Source Queries*

Jos de Bruijn and Holger Lausen

Digital Enterprise Research Institute (DERI), location
Institute for Computer Science, University of Innsbruck
Innsbruck, Austria
{jos.de-bruijn, holger.lausen}@deri.ie
http://deri.semanticweb.org/

Abstract. In this paper we describe the work that was done in the Corporate Ontology Grid (COG) project on the querying of existing legacy data sources from the automotive industry using ontology technology and a conceptual ontology query language. We describe the conceptual ontology query language developed by Unicorn, the querying support provided by the Unicorn Workbench, and describe the use of these queries in the run-time architecture built in the COG project.

1 Introduction

In this paper we describe the work that was done in the Corporate Ontology Grid (COG) project on the querying of existing legacy data sources using ontology technology and a conceptual ontology query language. Our aim in the COG project was to create an application using the Semantic Information Management [4] methodology in which several real-life heterogeneous data sources are integrated using ontology technology (for more information on the COG project see [1, 2]). The Unicorn Workbench[1] tool was used to integrate legacy data sources in CFR (Centro Richerche Fiat) through the mapping to a central Information model, or ontology.

The central ontology together with the mappings to the local data sources enable the user to discover data residing at different location in the organization, to automatically transform instance data from one representation to another, and to query instance data residing in the disparate data sources. This paper focuses on the latter. We discuss the querying problem, the querying support in the Unicorn Workbench tool and the application of this querying support in the COG Architecture.

In the COG project, several existing heterogeneous data sources from the automotive industry, which used different underlying platforms and (syntactically and semantically) different data schemas, were integrated by creating a central

---

* The research presented in this paper was funded by the European Commission in the context of the COG project (http://www.cogproject.org/), under contract number IST-2001-38491. Some materials presented in this paper are the copyright of Unicorn Solutions, Inc. and are used with permission.
[1] A component, part of the Unicorn System http://www.unicorn.com/

J. Davies et al. (Eds.): ESWS 2004, LNCS 3053, pp. 107–120, 2004.
© Springer-Verlag Berlin Heidelberg 2004

ontology and mapping the data sources to the central ontology. By creating these mappings between the source schemas and the ontology, an integrated unified global virtual view [3] was created of the information present in the disparate data sources throughout the enterprise, enabling the querying of the disparate data sources through the central ontology. Figure 1 depicts the integration paradigm used in the COG project. The "spokes" are related to each other via the "hub", which is the central ontology, or information model.

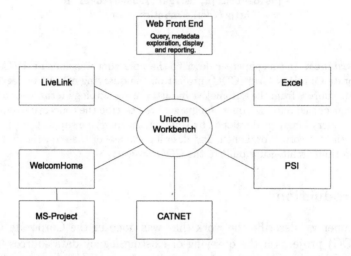

Fig. 1. The hub-and-spoke model for information integration used in the COG project.

This paper is organized as follows: we will first introduce the querying support of the Unicorn Workbench tool [5], which has been used for the implementation of the COG project, in section 2. Then, we will show how this querying support was leveraged in the architecture of the COG project and the extensions of this querying capability required for the COG project, in section 3. Finally, we provide conclusions in section 4.

2   Querying Disparate Data Sources Using the Unicorn Workbench

In this section, we present the support in the Unicorn Workbench tool for the conceptual querying of an ontology (the Information Model) and the subsequent translation to asset queries. With asset queries we mean queries that can actually be executed on the native platforms of the external assets that have been mapped to the central ontology in the Unicorn Workbench.

The Unicorn Workbench has a facility to create SQL-like queries on the ontology. In the query, a number of properties are selected from a certain class using a boolean condition (specified in the 'where' clause). The condition can be created using the Unicorn conversion langauge [5], which is also used for the specification of business rules[2] in the Unicorn Workbench (cf. [2]). The Unicorn conversion language is based on the Python language and enables transformation of data values and basic boolean operations (e.g. equality, greater-then, etc.).

These queries are issued against a single data source and are translated automatically by Unicorn into a correct query in the native language of the data source platform. This translated query can be automatically retrieved (via the operational API) by the (custom) run-time architecture or can be manually executed in the data source platform. The COG architecture, presented in section 3.1, contains such a run-time engine, which retrieves parameterized queries from the Unicorn Workbench.

We distinguish two main Use Cases for creating queries in the Workbench:

- During *design-time* the ontology can be manually evaluated by creating queries on the ontology, translating them to SQL queries for the data source and execute them to verify that the expected results are returned.
- During *run-time*, when an information architecture is set up, using the Information Model in the Unicorn Workbench, queries can be created on the Information Model, where the Unicorn Workbench would translate them into the native format used in the data sources. The middle-ware would then take care of executing the query in the data source platform and retrieving the results for the front-end application.

In this section, we first introduce the querying capabilities presented by the Unicorn Workbench, after which we show the translation of conceptual queries into actual SQL queries, which can be executed on the native data source platform. We finish with discussing some limitations of the querying functionality in the Workbench.

2.1   Queries in the Unicorn Workbench

Unicorn has developed a conceptual query language for querying ontologies in the Unicorn Workbench. With this query language, the user can specify conceptual queries on classes in the ontology (Information Model). These conceptual queries are, with the use of mappings to data schemas, automatically translated into instance queries that can be executed on the platform of the data source. Queries created in the Unicorn Workbench are instance queries; only queries on instances can be created. It is as yet not possible to query the ontology itself.

The query itself consists of the following five parts:

- A *name*, identifying the query.
- A *select* clause, which specifies which (indirect) properties to retrieve. These properties can only be of fundamental data types and can be converted using the Python-based Unicorn Conversion Language [5].

---

[2] Business rules restrict the values of properties by specifying a relation between properties or by restricting the value of the property to a limited set of possible value.

- A *from* clause, which specifies which class in the ontology is queried.
- A *where* clause, which specifies which additional conditions the instances need to satisfy to be selected. Here also the Unicorn Conversion Language can be used for transforming values.
- An *on database* clause, which specifies which data source to query.

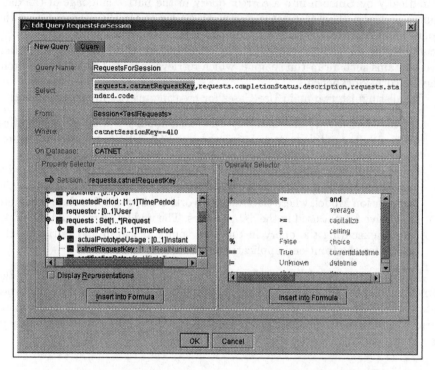

Fig. 2. Example query in the Unicorn Workbench

An example query is shown in Figure 2. At the top of the figure we see the query name, which is `RequestsForSession`. Below that we see the properties to be selected, under the heading 'Select'. One of the selected properties is highlighted, namely the property `requests.catnetRequestKey`. Note that this same property is selected in the property selector at the bottom left of the figure. We must also note here that only properties that refer to classes in the "fundamental" package[3] (see [2]) can be selected here. This is because the query is translated to the native query language of a data(base) platform, where only built-in data types can be selected. Note that because of the mechanism of indirect properties (cf. [2]), it is possible to select properties that belong to properties of the class on which the query is performed, as indeed is done here

---

[3] The fundamental package is shipped with the Unicorn Workbench and contains fundamental data types such as integer, string, date, etc...

with the catnetRequestKey property of the Request class, which is the type of the requests property in the Session class, on which we perform the query.

The next caption, 'From', is fixed to Session (the 'Session' concept will be explained in more detail in section 3) in the example, because in the Workbench a query is performed on one class. In our example, the 'Where' clause specifies the condition that the value of the catnetSessionKey property is '420'. The last part, 'On Database', contains the data source on which we want to perform the query. A query can only be translated to the native query language of one platform so the data source on which the query is to be executed, must be selected. In our case we chose to query the database CATNET.

The panel at the bottom left of the query editing window is the Property Selector, which can be used to conveniently select properties from the class (and related classes) to be used in the query, thereby saving lookup time and preventing typing mistakes. The panel at the bottom right is the Operator Selector, where boolean, string, and integer operators can be selected, which can be used in the 'Select' and the 'Where' clauses. In fact, in Figure 2 we already see the boolean equality operator put to use in the 'Where' clause to check the equality of the catnetSessionKey property and the number 420.

The problem with the example outlined above is that it is not possible to reuse this query for different session keys. In order to overcome this problem, it is possible to *parameterize* the query. An arbitrary number of parameters can be used in a query; these parameters are replaced with actual values when the queries are extracted during run-time. For example, we can replace the value '420' in Figure 2 with a generic parameter, allowing us to reuse the query for different sessions (a session is uniquely identified by the catnetSessionKey). In section 3.1 we show how this parameterization works in practice.

2.2 Transforming Conceptual Queries into Physical Queries

There is no query execution engine in Unicorn; instead, the query is translated into the native language of the data source platform, which can be manually executed in an external data source. The fact that the query can currently only be translated to a SQL database query is a limitation. The wrappers currently used for the Asset API do not support the translation of queries to the native platform. This translation is currently done by a separate component, which limits generality of the query.

There are, however, efforts under way to generate Query Planners, in the same way Transformation Planners[4] work for transformations.

Queries that are created are stored in the Unicorn project along with the SQL translation and possibly some descriptor information provided by the user. The queries can be updated when the ontology or the mappings to the data assets are updated. Unicorn will warn the user when a query has possibly become invalid.

---

[4] A Transformation Planner is an XML document describing which the composites and atoms from the source schema are to be mapped to which composites and atoms from the target schema. This XML document can be used to develop the actual transformation.

```
SELECT
      CATNETREQUESTKEY AS BR      /* BR is business rule
                                     requests.catnetRequestKey */,
      DESCRIPTION AS BR1     /* BR1 is business rule
                                requests.completionStatus.description */,
      CODE AS BR2     /* BR2 is business rule requests.standard.code */
FROM
      (
      SELECT
            A.AK_7RCH AS CATNETREQUESTKEY     /* CATNETREQUESTKEY is property
                                                 requests.catnetRequestKey */,
            B.DESCRIZIONE AS DESCRIPTION     /* DESCRIPTION is property
                                                requests.completionStatus.description */,
            A.COD_NORMA AS CODE     /* CODE is property requests.standard.code */,
            C.AK_7SEL AS CATNETSESSIONKEY     /* CATNETSESSIONKEY is property
                                                 catnetSessionKey */
      FROM
            COG.TAJO7RCH A,
            COG.TAJO2STA B,
            COG.TAJO7SEL C
      WHERE
            C.AK_7RCH = A.AK_7RCH AND
            A.COD_STATO_RICHIESTA = B.COD_STATO_RICHIESTA AND
            B.COD_STATO_RICHIESTA = A.COD_STATO_RICHIESTA
      ) SESSION     /* SESSION is class Session in package TestRequests */
WHERE
      CATNETSESSIONKEY=410
```

Fig. 3. Example SQL translation of an ontology query

In figure 3 we see the SQL translation of the ontology query shown in figure 2. We see here that the SQL query has been annotated with comments that specify the parts in the query that correspond to the properties that were specified in the ontology query.

We can reconstruct the SQL presented in Figure 3 as follows. We see a nested **SELECT** statement, where the inner statement is used to reconstruct, using a join operation[5], the ontology class **Session**, including the required indirect properties, from the tables in the data source that have been mapped to the class.

In the outer **SELECT** statement the requested properties are selected from the inner statement using the 'Where' condition specified in the ontology query and translated to the language of the specific data platform. Note that only the atoms necessary in the outer **SELECT** statement are selected.

2.3   Limitations of the Current Approach

With the current version (2.6.1) of the Unicorn Workbench it is not possible to use a single query for multiple data source. In fact, only relational databases can be queried with the Unicorn tool at the moment. To query multiple databases,

---

[5] Notice that the last two clauses in the 'WHERE' clause of the inner SELECT statement are actually equivalent and thus redundant. This is apparently a bug in the current version of the software; this bug will not cause many problems because any optimizer will filter out such redundancies before query execution.

it is necessary to create the same conceptual query several times, where each query differs only in the data source to which it refers. This creates maintenance problems.

A disadvantage of the query support in the Unicorn Workbench is that only fundamental data types (i.e. integer, string, etc. . .) can eventually be queried. This means that the user usually has to drill down the indirect properties in order to find the required data type to be retrieved from the data source. When that specific data value happens to be residing in a different data source, it is not possible to retrieve it in the same query. The user needs to create a new query in order to retrieve the value from the other data source.

Another drawback of the current version of the Unicorn tool is that it is not possible to automatically retrieve the results of a query from a data source. In this scenario it also doesn't make any sense to query multiple data source at the same time. This only makes sense if multiple sources are automatically queried and if the results are integrated into a unified view for the user. In the querying scenario as envisioned by Unicorn, the run-time architecture will take care of the querying of the data sources and the integration of the results into a unified view for the user. In this case, the run-time architecture can use the Unicorn Query API to specialize the queries for the different data sources from which the query results need to be integrated.

3   Querying Disparate Data Source in the COG Project

One of the goals of the COG project was to create a platform-independent semantic querying tool to query the disparate data sources through the central ontology. The ontology has been implemented using the Unicorn Workbench, a tool supporting the Semantic Information Management ([4]). Unicorn provides basic ontology querying support, which was described in detail in the previous section. The querying support is further expanded in the COG run-time architecture.

In this section we first describe the overall COG run-time architecture with respect to the querying support. Then, we provide an example of the application of querying in the COG showcase, after which we briefly explain how the COG architecture overcomes some of the limitations of the querying support in the Unicorn Workbench, as were identified in the previous section.

3.1   The Querying Architecture in the COG Project

In the COG project, a web client was created as a front-end application for the Unicorn semantic layer. The web client integrates the various disparate sources using the semantic back-bone provided by the Unicorn run-time API. Figure 4 shows the disparate data sources in the COG project that are integrated using the central ontology (called 'Information Model') in the Unicorn Workbench.

One of the goals in the COG project is to provide support for semantic platform-independent querying of the disparate data sources through the central ontological model.

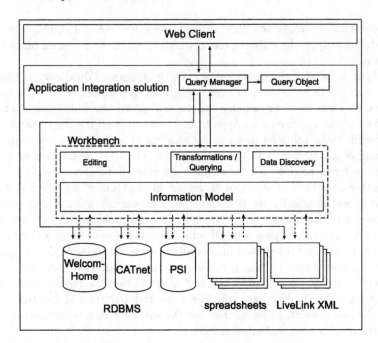

Fig. 4. COG Querying architecture

The COG architecture consists of the following major components:

Web Portal The Web portal is the front-end application for the user, where the user can perform different tasks related to both the management of tests to be performed on automobile prototypes and related to Data Discovery (using the ontology to find the location of data in the enterprise) and searching / browsing of the ontology.

Application Integration Solution This is a partly custom-built application for the COG project, which can be generalized for other applications. The Application Integration Solutions provides the run-time querying capabilities, interfacing between the Web portal, the Unicorn Workbench and the data sources.

Unicorn Workbench The Unicorn Workbench provides an API which can be used to retrieve queries and transformation stored in the Workbench and to retrieve information about the ontology and the mapping to the data sources (necessary for data discovery).

Data Sources The bottom layer consists of the actual data sources located throughout the enterprise. These can be arbitrary data sources ranging from Relational Databases to XML documents and Excel spreadsheets. The most important data sources for the COG project are the following:

    CATnet The CATnet database contains operational information about requests for tests on vehicle prototypes, as well as test execution information and test results

PSI The PSI database contains an organization of tests from the customer point-of-view and information about packages of tests. In the PSI system, a package of tests is created, before it is submitted to the CATnet system

WelcomHome The WelcomHome database contains project management information. This database contains, among other things, information about milestones achieved during different vehicle prototype development phases

OfficialMilestone The OfficialMilestone Excel spreadsheet contains information about official milestones, which are associated with phases in the prototype development

In the overall COG architecture (Figure 4), within the application integration layer, the Query Manager interacts with the Unicorn Workbench and with the individual data sources in order to automatically execute queries, created using the Information Model, on the disparate data sources. There are two active components in the query execution process. The Query Manager communicates with the Unicorn tool to retrieve the Query object for a specific query. This Query object translates the conceptual query from the Unicorn Workbench into the query language that is understood by the individual data source.

The querying process is depicted in figure 5. The web client sends a request to the Query Manager, which in turn retrieves the corresponding SQL query from the Unicorn Operational API, after which the Database System is contacted and the query is executed. The query results are then propagated back to the web client.

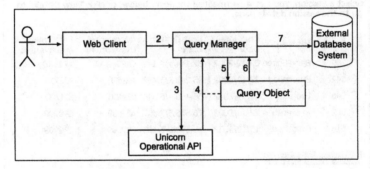

Fig. 5. The querying process in the COG architecture

The following steps are involved in the querying process:

1. The user selects the query to be executed along with its parameter values in the Web Client.
2. The Web Client identifies the query and sends the query name along with the parameter value to the Query Manager.
3. The Query Manager will use the Unicorn API to request the query.

4. The Unicorn API returns a Query Object, which represents the conceptual query.
5. The Query Manager sends the parameter values to the Query Object.
6. The Query Object returns the platform-native translation (typically SQL) of the conceptual query after having performed the parameter-value substitutions.
7. The query is sent to the database system, where it is execute. The results are returned, translated to a suitable format by the Query Manager, and ultimately displayed to the user by the Web Client.

We have shown in this section how the querying of databases works and what the role is of the Unicorn Workbench in the querying process. In the next section we clarify the querying architecture using an example from the user's point of view.

3.2   Querying in the COG Showcase

Two important tasks in which the COG application (or COG showcase) helps the user are (1) the selection of tests in order to see test results or in order to request the execution of test on a particular vehicle prototype and (2) the planning and monitoring of tests.

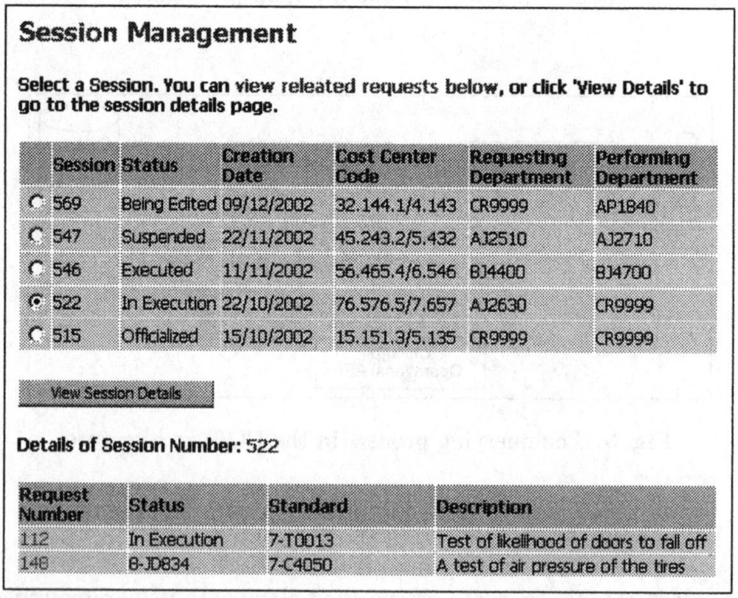

Session Management

Select a Session. You can view releated requests below, or click 'View Details' to go to the session details page.

Session	Status	Creation Date	Cost Center Code	Requesting Department	Performing Department
○ 569	Being Edited	09/12/2002	32.144.1/4.143	CR9999	AP1840
○ 547	Suspended	22/11/2002	45.243.2/5.432	AJ2510	AJ2710
○ 546	Executed	11/11/2002	56.465.4/6.546	BJ4400	BJ4700
● 522	In Execution	22/10/2002	76.576.5/7.657	AJ2630	CR9999
○ 515	Officialized	15/10/2002	15.151.3/5.135	CR9999	CR9999

View Session Details

Details of Session Number: 522

Request Number	Status	Standard	Description
112	In Execution	7-T0013	Test of likelihood of doors to fall off
148	8-JD834	7-C4050	A test of air pressure of the tires

Fig. 6. Example sessions in the session management section of the COG showcase

During the creation of test plans and the execution of test, two views are very important. First, there is the packet view, which is used to create packages of tests to be performed on a prototype. This view is used by the prototype manager to select a set of tests based on customer requirements. The second view is the session view (Figure 6), which is used by the testing manager, who configures testing sessions to be performed by specific testing laboratories. To summarize, a package is a set of tests from the customer requirement point-of-view and a session is a set of tests (Figure 8) to be performed by a specific laboratory, not specifically related to customer requirements. The COG architecture aids the user by integrating the data of the test packets (maintained in the PSI database) and the data of the testing sessions (maintained in the CATnet database).

We take the Session Management view (Figure 6) as an example of how queries are used in the COG showcase. Two queries are used to populate the general Session Management view: the query 'SessionListForSessionManagement', which retrieves the complete list of all sessions and the query 'RequestsForSession' (Figure 7), which is used to retrieve all requests belonging to a particular session. The function 'getNumberParameter(1)' (in the 'Where' clause of Figure 7) is used as a placeholder and is replaced at run-time with the actual session key.

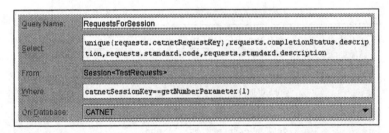

Fig. 7. The query 'RequestsForSession' retrieves all requests for a particular session

By clicking on the 'View Session Details' button, one ends up in the Session Details view (Figure 6), which is actually very interesting from a technical perspective. Three different data sources are queried in order to retrieve the information for the front-end application. The general data about sessions is stored in the CATnet database, while the information about the different project phases and the planned/actual start and finish dates is retrieved from the Excel spreadsheets and the WelcomHome database, respectively. Each of the sources has a different query in the Unicorn Workbench associated with it.

When the user selects a particular phase in the 'Phase' dropdown menu in Figure 8, a query is executed to retrieve the official milestones for that project phase. The query (Figure 9) is then executed on the 'OfficialMilestones' Excel spreadsheet in order to retrieve these milestones. Note that the query 'OfficialMilestonesForProjectPhase' contains the function 'getNumberParameter' in

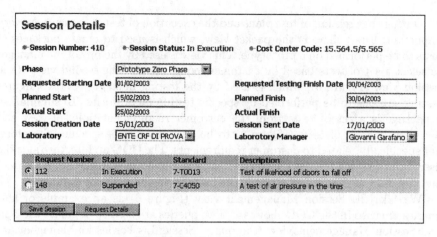

Fig. 8. Testing Session details

the 'Where' section. This function works as a place holder and is replaced at run-time by the COG architecture by the value associated with the project phase the user has selected in the dropdown menu.

Query Name:	OfficialMilestonesForProjectPhase
Select:	`activityCode`
From:	OfficialMilestone<ProjectManagement>

Where:	`((checkpoint.realNumberRepresentation >=`
	`getNumberParameter(1)) and`
	`(checkpoint.realNumberRepresentation <=`
	`getNumberParameter(2)))`

On Database:	Official Milestones ▼

Fig. 9. The query 'OfficialMilestonesForProjectPhase' retrieves the milestones for a particular project phase from the Excel spreadsheet

The COG run-time executes the composed query, consisting of the query retrieved from the Unicorn Workbench, where the placeholders have been replace by actual values, on the target platform; in this case an Excel spreadsheet. The answer to the query is a list of official milestones, which in turn form the input to another query, which is used to retrieve the earliest start and the latest finish date for this particular project phase. The official milestones form the input for the 'QueryMilestoneDates' query (Figure 10). Note that the query is issued on the same class in the ontology as the 'OfficialMilestonesForProjectPhase' query, but on a different underlying data source. This leads to the use of exactly the same property ('activityCode') being at the same time the output of the first query and the input of the second. The values retrieved using the 'QueryMilestoneDates' query are the Requested Starting Date and Requested Finish Date (as seen in Figure 8).

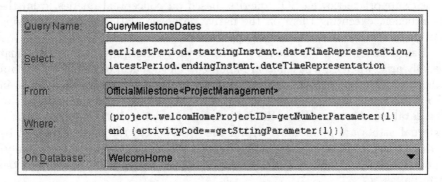

Fig. 10. The query 'QueryMilestoneDates' retrieves the start and end date for a particular milestone from the WelcomHome database

3.3 Overcoming the Limitations of the Unicorn Workbench in the COG Architecture

One limitation of the querying support of the Unicorn Workbench, as identified in section 2.3, is the fact that the Workbench can not execute queries and retrieve results. The role is taken over by the Query Manager component in the COG architecture, which executes the queries in the native data platforms and retrieves the results.

One of the major limitations in the querying support of the Unicorn Workbench, as identified in section 2.3, is the fact that it is not possible to query multiple data sources. As the example in the previous section showed, this is possible in the COG architecture, which can retrieve several queries from the Unicorn Workbench and execute them in the respective data platforms and show the query results to the user.

4 Conclusions

In this paper, we have evaluated the ontology querying capabilities in the Unicorn Workbench, as well as the possibilities of generating native queries on physical database schemas that have been mapped to the Information Model.

We have furthermore analyzed how this querying functionality is used in the COG architecture. We have seen how conceptual queries originating from the web front-end application are translated by the Unicorn Workbench into SQL queries that are ready to be executed on the native database platforms; how these queries are executed by the Query Component and how the results are returned to the front-end, which displays them to the user.

We have shown above how conceptual queries, created in the Unicorn Workbench, are used in an actual application. We presented the COG architecture, which support retrieving SQL queries, based on conceptual queries, from the Workbench, executing them on the native database platforms, and retrieving the query results for the front-end application.

Using the Unicorn Workbench to retrieve the queries prevents problems that usually arise when data schemas are updated. The applications using these data schemas will usually break and be rendered useless. By storing the queries in the Workbench, queries are maintained with the ontology and the mappings to the database schemas. When the Information Model and the mappings to the external assets are maintained within the Workbench, the maintainer will be warned when invalidating existing queries and will be inclined to (automatically) update these queries to reflect the changes in the Information Model and the external assets.

References

[1] Jos de Bruijn. Semantic integration of disparate data sources in the cog project. In *Proceedings of the 6th International Conference on Enterprise Information Systems (ICEIS2004)*, Porto, Portugal, 2004.

[2] Jos de Bruijn, Ying Ding, Sinuhé Arroyo, and Dieter Fensel. Semantic information integration in the cog project. COG Project White Paper. Available on http://www.cogproject.org/, 2004.

[3] R. Hull. Managing semantic heterogeneity in databases: A theoretical perspective. In *ACM Symposium on Principles of Database Systems*, pages 51–61, Tuscon, Arizona, USA, 1997.

[4] Z. Schreiber. Semantic information management: Solving the enterprise data problem. To be found on the http://www.unicorn.com/ website, 2003.

[5] Unicorn. *Unicorn™ Workbench v2.5 User Manual*. Unicorn, 2003.

Knowledge Discovery in an Agents Environment

Manjula Patel and Monica Duke

UKOLN, University of Bath, UK
{m.patel, m.duke}@ukoln.ac.uk,
http://www.ukoln.ac.uk/

Abstract. We describe work undertaken to investigate automated querying of simple forms of ontology by software agents to acquire the semantics of metadata terms. Individual terms as well as whole vocabularies can be investigated by agents through a software interface and by humans through an interactive web-based interface. The server supports discovery, sharing and re-use of vocabularies and specific terms, facilitating machine interpretation of semantics and convergence of ontologies in specific domains. Exposure, and hence alignment through ontological engineering should lead to an improvement in interoperability of systems in particular sectors such as education, cultural heritage and publishing.

1   Background and Motivation

Work in the area of metadata vocabulary repositories has been on-going at UKOLN[1] for some time. As part of the DESIRE[2] and SCHEMAS[3] projects we have been involved in building metadata vocabulary or ontology registries. The primary function of these registries was to provide a publication environment for the disclosure of customised metadata vocabularies also known as *application profiles*[4, 5]. While the DESIRE project had concentrated on a human interface for interrogating the registry, the SCHEMAS project took a machine-processible approach based on RDF Schemas(RDFS)[6]. This work was taken further in the Metadata for Education (MEG) Registry project[7], which was primarily concerned with the UK Education domain and development of the SCART tool[8].

Both the SCHEMAS and MEG registries aimed to provide an environment in which individual terms as well as whole vocabularies can be investigated for adaptations, local usages and relationships with other vocabularies. At present, standard or canonical vocabularies such as the Dublin Core[9] are readily accessible, but this is not the case for application profiles, which are a type of metadata vocabulary that draw on canonical vocabularies and customise them for local use. One major reason for a web-based service is to facilitate the harmonisation[10, 11] of vocabularies or ontologies within specific domains such as education, cultural heritage, publishing or rights management and thereby enhance the opportunity for interoperability of systems within such domains.

Another use for an ontology server is the automated querying of metadata vocabularies by agents for acquiring the semantics associated with metadata terms. This in turn facilitates the type of reasoning and inference required to

J. Davies et al. (Eds.): ESWS 2004, LNCS 3053, pp. 121–136, 2004.

fulfill automated service provision and composition in a dynamic environment, and thus help towards the goal of realising the Semantic Web[12, 13]. However, the article by Berners-Lee et al.[14], provides an indication of just how precisely information needs to be organised and engineered in order to facilitate automated reasoning, deduction and inference. The paper clearly indicates the extent to which software agents will be required to be able to query and process a variety of data with little or no human intervention. In particular it highlights the importance of the role that machine-readable data will play in the process of automated inferencing.

We begin with a discussion that relates ontologies and metadata vocabularies and goes on to consider the similarities between ontology servers and metadata vocabulary repositories. We then describe a metamodel for metadata vocabularies which is used as the internal model in our ontology server. The rest of the paper is taken up with describing the implementation, deployment and querying of the ontology server in the context of the Agentcities.NET network environment[15, 16].

2   Ontologies and Metadata Vocabularies

From an AI point of view, an ontology serves to define the concepts, terms and relationships used to describe and represent an area or domain of knowledge[17, 18, 19]. Ontologies aim to capture domain knowledge in a generic way; with differing levels of formality they provide a commonly agreed understanding of a domain, which may be reused and shared across applications and groups. They require a certain degree of ontological commitment for knowledge to be shared. There are several other definitions and typologies of ontology. Some definitions may follow from the way that ontologies are built and used; distinctions are made between lightweight and heavyweight ontologies, where taxonomies are considered to be one of the former, whereas the latter kind of ontology would include axioms or business rules. For example, Sowa[20] defines a terminological ontology as "an ontology whose categories need not be fully specified by axioms and definition"; WordNet [21] is an example of such an ontology. Other distinctions are based on the kind of languages used to implement an ontology, such that some ontologies are rigorously formal if they are defined in a language with formal semantics, theories and proofs (e.g. of soundness and completeness); others are highly informal being expressed only in natural language. Some ontologies, such as the Dublin Core, are interdisciplinary and are intended to be reusable across domains whilst the majority, such as the IEEE Learning Object Metadata[22] for the education domain, tend to be specific to one area.

Knowledge in ontologies is mainly formalized using five kinds of components: classes, relations, functions, axioms and instances. A more detailed description of these components is provided in the OntoWeb Technical Roadmap[23]. However, in this paper we are concerned with only a specific type of simple ontology, referred to as a metadata vocabulary or element set[3]. In the world of digital libraries, a metadata vocabulary or schema declares a set of concepts or terms and their associated definitions and relationships. The terms are often known as elements, attributes and qualifiers. The definitions of the terms provide the semantics which are ideally both human and machine readable. In effect a metadata vocabulary is a manifestation of an ontology, albeit a lightweight one. Such an ontology comprises classes, relations and instances. One particular type of vocabulary that we are working with is the *application profile*. This is a vocabulary which has been created or tailored for a specific use or application. In particular, an application profile has the following characteristics, it may:

- mix-and-match terms from multiple element sets
- specify dependencies (e.g. mandate schemes)
- adapt existing definitions for local purposes
- declare rules for content (e.g. usage guidelines)
- specify whether an element is mandatory, optional or repeatable

In our internal data model terms are defined in *element sets*, which can be viewed as standard or canonical vocabularies. In contrast, *application profiles* draw on terms which are defined in one or more element sets and customise them for use in a local application. Application profiles are not allowed to define new terms, consequently other application profiles are disallowed from drawing on terms from extant application profiles in order to avoid semantic drift. Semantic drift occurs when a term is successively modified to the extent that its semantics no longer correspond to the terms of the original definition.

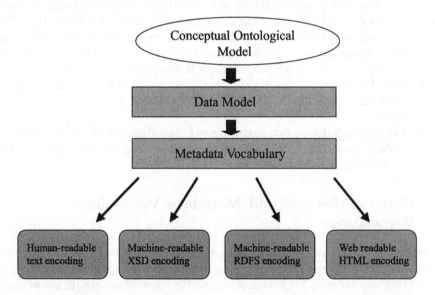

Fig. 1. Relation between Ontology, Data Model, Metadata Vocabulary and Bindings

Figure 1 shows the relationship between an abstract ontological model, an underlying data model or view onto the ontology model, and the metadata vocabulary that may be derived from the two. The metadata vocabulary can in turn be instantiated using differing encoding technologies or bindings such as XML or RDF Schemas, DAML or OWL.

3   Ontology Specification Languages

Semanticweb.org[24] provides a historical perspective on the representation of ontologies on the Web. The most influential over the past few years has been the Resource Description Framework (RDF)[25]. This is a general-purpose modeling framework for representing information on the Web. It consists of graph structures made up of object, predicate and subject triples. The RDF Schema specification (RDFS) [6] describes how to use RDF in order to describe RDF vocabularies. A major benefit of RDFS is that it provides for the expression of relationships between semantic terms. It is notable that RDF seems to be emerging as the lowest common denominator and a basis for many other ontology description languages.

More recently, the Web Ontology Language (OWL)[26] is being designed by the W3C Web Ontology Working Group[27] in order to provide a language which can be used by applications that need to process the content of information as opposed to just the syntax. OWL is a semantic markup language for publishing and sharing ontologies on the Web. It provides greater machine processibility of web content by supplementing RDFS with additional vocabulary terms for more accurate specification of relationships over and above that of subsumption. The OWL language is a revision of the DAML+OIL web ontology language, it incorporates experience from the design and application uses of DAML+OIL[28]. Different subsets of the OWL language are defined to suit different uses (OWL Lite, OWL DL and OWL Full). OWL has been designed for maximal compatibility with RDF and RDFS, an OWL ontology being represented as a set of RDF triples.

Whilst ontology description languages were in a state of flux, we chose to base our encodings on RDFS which is being used as the basis for more sophisticated specification languages such as OWL.

4   Ontology Servers and Metadata Vocabulary Repositories

A repository of metadata vocabularies enables individual terms as well as whole vocabularies to be investigated for adaptations, local usages and relationships with other vocabularies. Such data mining facilitates analysis of patterns of usage as well as the creation and inference of new information. Furthermore, these types of services are required as an essential part of ontological engineering procedures[29, 30] if there is to be any hope of convergence of domain level knowledge representation.

Our server has an architecture which can harvest distributed metadata vocabularies from their maintainers over the Web. In this manner authoritative control over particular vocabularies is devolved to their original developers and maintainers. Consequently, in contrast to other servers[31, 32, 33, 34, 35] we do not include the maintenance of individual ontologies, in terms of assertion and retraction of predicates, as a function of our server. In fact, our implementation has several commonalities with that of Pan et. al[36] in that both servers have been motivated by the need to publish and share ontologies. In addition, both servers make use of the more universal HTTP protocol for communication rather than OKBC[37] as recommended by the FIPA Ontology Service Specification[31].

A major area in which our implementation differs from that of Pan et. al., is in the sophistication of the internal data model. The choice of how to structure an ontology determines the types of information that a system can provide and infer. The meta-model we describe in section 5 enables a finer granularity of query which facilitates detailed analysis of the vocabularies registered in the server. The model is based on the types of information required by metadata vocabulary developers and implementers, based on the findings in the SCHEMAS project.

In response to queries, the server responds by providing term and vocabulary level definitions and usage information, along with contextual annotations. The repository, in effect functions as an indexing engine for dynamically updating, and serving up the semantics of metadata terms. The context for such a server is the notion of a Semantic Web where any person or organisation can declare a metadata vocabulary and assert a relationship between that vocabulary and any other vocabulary or term on the Web.

Other initiatives within the areas of ontology, ontology representation, storage and exchange have undertaken reviews of repositories of ontologies. The OntoWeb Technical RoadMap[23] lists some of the better known ones. The ontology repositories that are described include those in which ontologies are implemented in DAML, Ontolingua[33] and SHOE[38]. The DAML Repository[39] is a web-accessible catalogue of ontologies expressed in DAML. In addition, work in the area of developing knowledge bases of semantic terms is well established in the AI sector. A notable example is that of Lenat's Cyc[40].

One area in which UKOLN has been actively promoting harmonization is that of education in the UK. The Metadata for Education Group (MEG) was formed following a meeting of key UK stakeholders and serves as an open forum for debating the description and provision of educational resources at all educational levels across the UK. This group seeks to reach consensus on appropriate means by which to describe discrete learning objects in a manner suitable for implementation in a range of educational arenas. Preceding work undertaken in the DESIRE and SCHEMAS projects provided the basis for the MEG Registry Project, which adopted a slightly modified data model as described below. The aim of the MEG registry is to provide implementers of educational systems with a means to share information about their metadata vocabularies and to re-use existing schemas. The benefit being a saving in time and effort which would be spent in researching existing vocabularies and in re-inventing terms.

The Meg Registry is implemented as a server based on the RDF toolkit, Redland[41]. Information about the entities described in section 5 and their relationships, is stored and made available in machine-processible format as RDFS. The registry API has been developed in Perl and supports functions such as querying through an HTTP interface. In section 5 we provide an overview of the data model and definitions employed in the MEG Registry project since they have provided the framework for the work described in this paper.

5   A Meta-model for Metadata Vocabularies

Our ontology server is based on the following model of metadata vocabularies, i.e element sets and application profiles, additional details can be found in [8, 42, 43]:

Element Sets are owned and maintained by **Agencies**.
Element Sets are made up of **Elements**.
Element Usages may:
- introduce constraints on the value of an Element by associating it with one or more Encoding Schemes
- introduce constraints on the *obligation* to use an Element (e.g. make its use mandatory) or the *occurrence* of an **Element** (e.g. whether it is repeatable)
- *refine* the semantic definition of an **Element** to make it narrower or more specific to the application domain.

Encoding Schemes constrain the value space of **Elements**.
Application Profiles define a set of **Element Usages** of **Elements** drawn from one or more **Element Sets**.

The server holds information on each of the entities and their relationships:

- **Element Sets** (i.e. on the Element Sets as units, rather than on their constituent Elements), including information on their intended scope or area of use and their relationship to other Element Sets
- the **Elements** which make up those Element Sets, including information on the semantics of the Elements and their recommended usage, and any semantic relationships to other Elements in this or other vocabularies (e.g. the relationship described by the DC[9] concept of "element refinement" or by RDF Schema as a "sub-property" relation)
- **Application Profiles**, including information on their intended scope or area of use and their relationship to other Element Sets
- the **Usages of Elements** which make up Application Profiles, including the Element used, any prescription of Encoding Schemes, and other constraints on element use
- **Encoding Schemes**, which constrain the value space of Elements, including information on their intended scope or area of use; where an Encoding Scheme takes the form of an enumerated list, the **values** prescribed by that Encoding Scheme may be recorded
- the **Agencies** who own, create and maintain Element Sets, Application Profiles, and Encoding Schemes

6   Implementation of an Ontology Server

We have extended the work done in the MEG Registry project to deploy the registry within an agents environment, namely the Agentcities.NET network. The existing registry software stores information relating to metadata vocabularies and provides an interface for interacting with the repository of information. We have thus extended the interface to support interaction by agents.

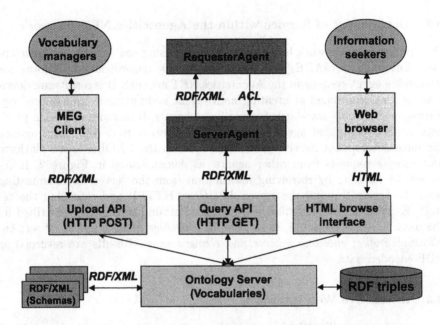

Fig. 2. Ontology Server Architecture (adapted from MEG Registry Architecture)

Figure 2 is an adapted diagram of the MEG Registry architecture, illustrating the architecture of the ontology server and its deployment in an agents environment. Below we discuss the processes, interfaces and protocols in more detail.

6.1   Ontology Acquisition, Server Population

The contents of the ontology server comprise metadata vocabularies also known as schemas or metadata element sets. As mentioned, the notion of element sets and application profiles has been used as the underlying data model for encoding the metadata vocabularies. The vocabularies are modelled within the server as outlined in section 5.

The server uses a harvesting paradigm to "pull in" vocabularies which have been encoded using RDFS with XML as the serialisation syntax. Population of the server is achieved by specifying a URI from which an RDFS encoding of a vocabulary is retrieved over HTTP and stored in a database. The advantage of using a harvesting paradigm is that maintenance and authority over an ontology is decentralised and devolved to those committed to its development (such authority is recorded as an "agency" in the metamodel as described in section 5). The server can be regularly updated in a similar manner to current search engines which crawl the Web in order to index Web pages.

6.2   Deployment of Service within the Agentcities.NET Network

Our implementation work has been carried out using the Java Agent Development Environment (JADE)[44]. JADE is one of the recommended platforms for developing agent systems in the Agentcities.NET network. It is a software development platform aimed at creating multi-agent systems and applications conforming to FIPA[45] standards for intelligent agents. It includes two main products, a FIPA-compliant agent platform and a package to develop Java agents. We have developed a *ServerAgent* which runs on the UKOLN agent platform and accepts requests from other agents, as demonstrated in Figure 2. It responds to requests by retrieving information from the server, communicating with the server through the server API (over HTTP), and returning the results. Exploration of vocabularies is organised around the entities described by the data model in section 5, these comprise: *agency*; *element*; *element set*; *application profile*; *encoding scheme* and *element usage*. Results are returned as RDF-encoded data.

6.3   Interactive Web Interface

For ease of accessibility, the knowledge base of semantic terms may be explored through an interactive web interface which caters for search, browse and navigation functions[46]. Metadata schema implementers have indicated that a service which allows for searching, browsing and navigation of vocabularies would play an essential role in developing new element sets, as well as serving in the harmonization of vocabularies for specific domains[3]. The screen shots in Figures 3 and 4 illustrate navigation using a web browser. Browsing a category (e.g. elements sets) reveals a list of all the resources of that class, with links to further details. When browsing a specific resource, the details from the RDF description of that resource are displayed, as well as links to related resources.

6.4   Machine Interface

We have developed a software interface to the server to allow agents to query and navigate metadata vocabularies. Below we describe the *ServerAgent* and two examples of requester agents. The *ServerAgent* can carry out search and browse requests on behalf of other agents, passing on the results from the server to the requester agents.

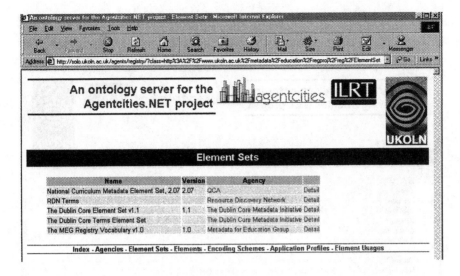

Fig. 3. Browsing the list of all element sets in the metadata vocabulary repository

Searches are carried out within a specific category, such as agency or element set. When the description found is that of an element, the description of the associated element set is also presented. Using the browse function, either a whole category can be explored, or a named resource from a category may be specified. The RDF descriptions for all the resources in a category, or for a single resource are returned respectively.

JADE conceptualises an agent as an independent and autonomous process that has an identity, possibly persistent, and that requires communication (e.g. collaboration or competition) with other agents in order to fulfill its tasks. This communication is implemented through asynchronous message passing and by using an Agent Communication Language (ACL) with a well-defined and commonly agreed semantics[44]. Queries to the *ServerAgent* are made using the FIPA ACL[45]. On receiving a request message, the *ServerAgent*:

- extracts components of the request (using an ontology)
- constructs a URL from the request
- connects to the server using the URL
- reads the response from the server
- places the response into a reply message

At present, the *ServerAgent* uses a simple behaviour model to deal with one request at a time, sending a reply before attending to the next request message in the queue.

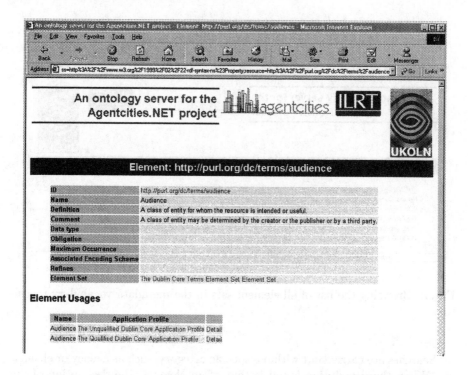

Fig. 4. Browsing the details of a specific vocabulary term or element

6.5   Server Ontology for Agent Communication

Agents implemented in JADE use ontologies to communicate requests to each other. We have therefore defined a simple ontology, (*ServerSearchOntology*) which is used to express requests to the *ServerAgent*. This ontology is at present intended to encapsulate the simple kinds of requests currently supported by the server. We envisage that additional types of queries will be required as the functionality of the server evolves.

The ontology consists of two *Action* concepts, *ReturnSearchResults* and *ReturnBrowseResults*. The *ReturnSearchResults* action emulates a search request through a web browser, while *ReturnBrowseResults* mimics the browsing action carried out through the web browser. The example below illustrates the use of the ontology and results returned from a search.

The search in the example finds two elements: the search term 'audience' is found within the useComment tag of the Mediator element, as well as the Audience element in the Dublin Core Metadata Element Set (as shown in the first two clips of RDF data). Both these elements are part of the Dublin Core Terms element set and the description for the element set is returned at the end, as shown in the third clip of RDF data.

```
(  (action
      (agent-identifier :name UKOLNServer@solo.ukoln.ac.uk:1099/JADE)
      (ReturnSearchResults
         (Search :Scope element :SearchTerm audience)
      )
   ) )
```

Example: A search for the term "audience" in the element category

```
<rdf:Description rdf:about="http://purl.org/dc/terms/mediator">
   <rdf:type rdf:resource="http://www.w3.org/1999/02/22-rdf-syntax-ns#Property"/>
   <rdfs:label>Mediator</rdfs:label>
   <rdfs:comment>A class of entity that mediates access to the resource
      and for whom the resource is intended or useful.</rdfs:comment>
   <reg:useComment>The audience for a resource in the
      education/training domain are of two basic classes:
      (1) an ultimate beneficiary of the resource (usually a
      student or trainee), and (2) frequently, an entity that
      mediates access to the resource (usually a teacher or trainer).
      The mediator element refinement represents the second of these
      two classes.</reg:useComment>
   <rdfs:subPropertyOf rdf:resource="http://purl.org/dc/terms/audience"/>
   <reg:isElementOf rdf:resource="http://www.ukoln.ac.uk/metadata/
      education/regproj/reg/elementSet/dcterms"/>
</rdf:Description>


<rdf:Description rdf:about="http://purl.org/dc/terms/audience">
   <rdf:type rdf:resource="http://www.w3.org/1999/02/22-rdf-syntax-ns#Property"/>
   <rdfs:label>Audience</rdfs:label>
   <rdfs:comment>A class of entity for whom the resource is intended
   or useful.</rdfs:comment>
   <reg:useComment>A class of entity may be determined by the creator
   or the publisher or by a third party.</reg:useComment>
   <reg:isElementOf rdf:resource="http://www.ukoln.ac.uk/metadata/education/
   regproj/reg/elementSet/dcterms"/>
</rdf:Description>


<rdf:Description rdf:about="http://www.ukoln.ac.uk/metadata/education/
   regproj/reg/elementSet/dcterms">
   <rdf:type rdf:resource="http://www.ukoln.ac.uk/metadata/education/
   regproj/reg/ElementSet"/>
   <dc:title>The Dublin Core Terms Element Set</dc:title>
   <dcterms:created>2000-07-11</dcterms:created>
   <reg:status>DCMI recommendation</reg:status>
   <dc:description> The Dublin Core metadata vocabulary is a simple
   vocabulary intended to facilitate discovery of resources.
   </dc:description>
   <reg:responsibleAgency rdf:resource="http://www.ukoln.ac.uk/metadata/
   education/regproj/reg/agency/dcmi"/>
   <reg:xmlNamespacePrefix>dcterms:</reg:xmlNamespacePrefix>
   <reg:specification rdf:resource="http://dublincore.org/usage/terms/
   terms-latest.html"/>
</rdf:Description>
```

6.6   Interrogating the ServerAgent

We have implemented two examples of *RequesterAgent*, both of which are driven
by a human user; they both make requests to the *ServerAgent*. These two agents
use the *ServerSearchOntology* to communicate requests to the *ServerAgent*, and
then display the response returned by the server. Results to queries consist simply of RDFS descriptions wrapped up in a standard agent response. Thus the
ServerSearchOntology is only used to communicate requests, not responses.

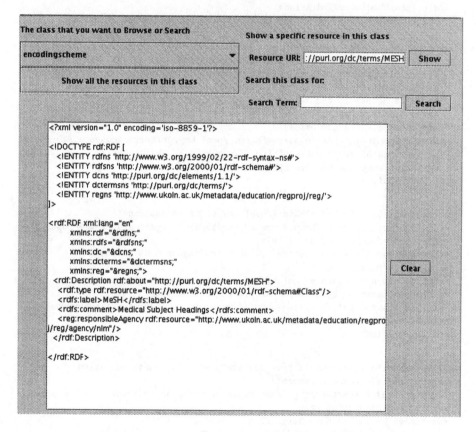

Fig. 5. Results are displayed in a window in the GUI

The GUI Agent This agent presents the user with a graphical interface. JADE
provides support for building interfaces for agents which need to interact with
users, and provides guidelines on how to implement agents that work within the
Java GUI concurrency model. An example of the results returned in the interface
is shown in Figure 5.

The Command Line Agent A second agent class, *ServerRequesterAgent*, has been provided to interact with the user through the command line. The agent prompts the user for input, establishing what kind of transaction the user is performing (browse or search) and its parameters: scope, search term or resource URI. A suitable request message is then built by the *ServerRequesterAgent* (using the *ServerSearchOntology*) and sent to the *ServerAgent*. The response from the *ServerAgent* is displayed to the user as an RDFS encoding as in the previous example.

7   Conclusions and Further Work

We have adapted software for a metadata vocabulary repository to serve as an ontology server which can be queried by agents on the Agentcities.NET network. The work presented has advanced the work begun in previous projects to investigate an approach based on automated querying and processing of simple ontologies by software agents as well as through human interaction.

The contents of the repository comprise metadata vocabularies which may be regarded as simple forms of ontology. It should be noted that the server accepts metadata vocabularies encoded in RDFS, and that the vocabularies need to adhere to the data model described in section 5, which is based on the notion of element sets and application profiles. Further discussions regarding issues relating to the model can be found in[43].

There are several avenues which would merit further investigation in the context of this work. Since the server was developed independently of the FIPA Ontology Service Specification, it will be interesting to see how effective the communication between FIPA agents and the server is and whether the information model we have used is adequate for semantic interpretation by heterogeneous agents.

Another interesting area which remains to be explored is that of performing inference, deduction and reasoning based on the knowledge base, as well as semantic search using a query language such as RDQL. The data model underlying RDF provides a simple, but flexible model through which a collection of vocabularies can be viewed and hence processed in a uniform manner. With this simple data model it is possible to merge and query RDF graphs to facilitate automated reasoning and inferencing [5].

As has already been mentioned, there is a need for a service which enables the publication and disclosure of the semantics that are being used in applications and web services. The advantages of providing a machine-processible format are numerous. An ontology server can be queried by software agents roaming the Web in order to retrieve semantics and thereby perform reasoning tasks which would aid automation of the Web and move it on to the next generation of development[13, 12].

Ontology servers are an essential part of the infrastructure required to enable the exchange and re-use of vocabularies as well as individual terms. Semantic interoperability requires domain-level concensus on the structure, concepts and terminology to be used in knowledge representation. An ontology server such as the one described goes a long way towards helping the necessarily human process of concensus building and ontological engineering within specific domains.

8 Acknowledgements

The work we have described was made possible by a deployment grant awarded to UKOLN under the European Commission funded 5th Framework IST project Agentcities.NET. The software used in this project for the ontology server was originally developed in the MEG Registry project funded by JISC and BECTa. Thanks to Pete Johnston and Owen Cliff for help in the realisation of this work. We would also like to thank the reviewers for their positive and constructive comments.

UKOLN is funded by Resource: The Council for Museums, Archives & Libraries, the Joint Information Systems Committee (JISC) of the Higher and Further Education Funding Councils, as well as by project funding from the JISC and the European Union. UKOLN also receives support from the University of Bath where it is based.

References

[1] : UKOLN metadata projects. (http://www.ukoln.ac.uk/metadata/, accessed 12/11/2003)

[2] Heery, R., Gardner, T., Day, M., Patel, M.: Desire metadata registry framework. http://www.desire.org/html/research/deliverables/D3.5/, accessed 12/11/2003 (2000)

[3] : SCHEMAS registry. (http://www.schemas-forum.org/registry/, accessed 12/11/2003)

[4] Heery, R., Patel, M.: Application profiles: mixing and matching metadata schemas. Ariadne (2000) http://www.ariadne.ac.uk/issue25/app-profiles/intro.html, accessed 12/11/2003.

[5] Baker, T., Dekkers, M., Heery, R., Patel, M., Salokhe, G.: What terms does your metadata use? application profiles as machine understandable narratives. Journal of Digital Information 2 (2001) http://jodi.ecs.soton.ac.uk/Articles/v02/i02/Baker/baker-final.pdf, accessed 25/11/2003.

[6] Brickley, D., Guha, R.: RDF vocabulary description language 1.0: RDF schema. (W3C Working Draft October 2003)

[7] : Metadata for education (MEG) registry project. (http://www.ukoln.ac.uk/metadata/education/regproj/, accessed 12/11/2003)

[8] Heery, R., Johnston, P., Beckett, D., Steer, D.: The MEG registry and SCART: complementary tools for creation, discovery and re-use of metadata schemas. In: Proceedings of the Dublin Core Conference. (2002) 125–132 http://www.bncf.net/dc2002/program/ft/paper14.pdf, accessed 12/11/2003.

[9] : ISO 15386: The dublin core metadata element set. (http://www.niso.org/international/SC4/sc4docs.html, accessed 12/11/2003)

[10] Patel, M.: Ontology harmonisation towards the semantic web. In: Proceedings of the International Semantic Web Conference. (2002) http://www.ukoln.ac.uk/ukoln/staff/m.patel/iswc2002/iswc-poster.pdf, accessed 10/11/2003.

[11] Holsapple, C.W., Joshi, K.D.: A collaborative approach to ontology design. Communications of the ACM **45** (2002) 42–47

[12] Gibbons, N., Harris, S., Shadbolt, N.: Agent based semantic web services. (In: Proceedings of the 12th World Wide Web Conference, Budapest, May 2003) http://www2003.org/cdrom/papers/refereed/p455/p455-gibbins.html, accessed 10/11/2003.

[13] Hendler, J.: Agents and the semantic web. IEEE Intelligent Systems **15** (2001) 30–37

[14] Berners-Lee, T., Hendler, J., Lassila, O.: The semantic web. Scientific American **284** (2001) 28–37

[15] : Agentcities.NET homepage. (http://www.agentcities.org/EUNET/, accessed 25/11/2003)

[16] Willmott, S., Dale, J., Burg, B., Charlton, C., O'Brien, P.: Agentcities: A worldwide open agent network. (AgentLink News 8, 13-15)

[17] Gruber, T.: What is an ontology? (http://www.ksl.standford.edu/kst/what-is-an-ontology.html, accessed 3/12/2003)

[18] Gruber, T.: The role of common ontology in achieving sharable, reusable knowledge bases. In: Principles of Knowledge Representation and Reasoning: Proceedings of the 2nd International Conference, Morgan Kaufmann (1991) 601–602

[19] Gruber, T.: Toward principles for the design of ontologies used for knowledge sharing. (Presented at the Padua workshop on Formal Ontology, March 1993)

[20] Sowa, J.: Building, sharing and merging ontologies. (Glossary) http://www.jfsowa.com/ontology/ontoshar.htm#s6, accessed 12/11/2003.

[21] Soergel, D.: Wordnet, book review. D-Lib Magazine (1998) http://www.dlib.org/dlib/october98/10bookreview.html, accessed 12/11/2003.

[22] : IEEE learning object metadata (IEEE LOM). (http://ltsc.ieee.org/wg12/, accessed 12/11/2003)

[23] : Ontoweb technical roadmap v 1.0. (http://babage.dia.fi.upm.es/ontoweb/wp1/OntoRoadMap/index.html, accessed 12/11/2003)

[24] : Semanticweb.org, markup languages and ontologies. (http://www.semanticweb.org/knowmarkup.html#ontologies, accessed 12/11/2003)

[25] Lassila, O., Swick, R.: Resource description framework (RDF) model and syntax specification. (W3C Recommendation 22 February 1999 http://www.w3.org/TR/1999/REC-rdf-syntax-19990222/, accessed 10/11/2003)

[26] McGuinness, D., van Harmelen, F.: Web ontology language overview. (W3C Candidate Recommendation 18 August 2003) http://www.w3.org/TR/2002/WD-owl-features-20020729/, accessed 10/11/2003.

[27] : W3C web ontology working group. (http://www.w3.org/2001/sw/WebOnt/, accessed 10/11/2003)

[28] : DAML+OIL (march 2001) reference description. (W3C Note 18, December 2001) http://www.w3.org/TR/daml+oil-reference, accessed 12/11/2003.

[29] Kim, H.: Predicting how ontologies for the semantic web will evolve. Communications of the ACM **45** (2002) 48–54

[30] Staab, S., Struder, R., Schum, H., Sure, Y.: Knowledge process and ontologies. IEEE Intelligent Systems **16** (2001) 26–35

[31] : FIPA ontology service specification. (http://www.fipa.org/specs/fipa00086/ accessed 04/03/2004)

[32] Suguri, H., Kodama, E., Mivazaki, M., Nunokawa, H.: Implementation of FIPA ontology service. In: Proceedings of the Workshop on Ontologies in Agent Systems, 5th International Conference on Autonomous Agents. (2001)

[33] Farquhar, A., Fikes, R., Rice, J.:   The ontolingua server: a tool for collaborative ontology construction.   In: Proceedings of Tenth Knowledge Acquisition for Knowledge-Based Systems Workshop.   (1996) http://ksi.cpsc.ucalgary.ca/KAW/KAW96/farquhar/farquharhtml,   accessed 22/12/2003.

[34] Li, Y., Thompson, S., Tan, Z., Giles, N., Gharib, H.: Beyond ontology construction; ontology services as online knowledge sharing communities. In: Proceedings International Semantic Web Conference, Springer-Verlag, Lecture Notes in Computer Science, 2870/2003 (2003) 469 – 483

[35] Volz, R., Oberle, D., Staab, S., Motik, B.: KAON server -a semantic web management system. In: Proceedings of the 12th WWW Conference, ACM Press (2003)

[36] Pan, J., Cranefield, S., Carter, D.: A lightweight ontology repository. In: Proceedings of the 2nd International Joint Conference on Autonomous Agents and Multiagent Systems, ACM Press (2003) 632–638

[37] Chaudri, V., Farquhar, A., Fikes, R., Karp, P., Rice, J.: Open knowledge base connectivity 2.0. (Technical Report KSL-98-06, Standford University 1998)

[38] Heflin, J., Hendler, J., Luke, S.: SHOE: A knowledge representation language for internet applications. Technical Report CS-TR-4078/UMIACS TR-99-71, University of Maryland (1999)

[39] : DAML ontology library.
(http://www.daml.org/ontologies/, accessed 12/11/2003)

[40] Lenat, D.: Cyc: A large-scale investment in knowledge infrastructure. Communications of the ACM **38** (1995) 33–38

[41] Beckett, D.: The design and implementation of the Redland RDF application framework. In: Proceedings of WWW10. (2001)
http://www10.org/cdrom/papers/frame.html, accessed 25/11/2003.

[42] Duke, M., Patel, M.: An ontology server for the agentcities.net project, october 2003. Technical report (2003)

[43] Heery, R., Johnston, P., Flp, C., Micsik, A.: Metadata schema registries in the partially semantic web: the cores experience. In: Proceedings of the Dublin Core Conference. (2003) http://www.siderean.com/dc2003/102_Paper29.pdf, accessed 10/11/2003.

[44] : Java agent development environment (JADE) homepage. (http://jade.cselt.it/, accessed 27/11/2003)

[45] : Foundation for intelligent physical agents (FIPA) homepage.
(http://www.fipa.org/, accessed 27/11/2003)

[46] : UKOLN ontology server for the Agentcities.NET network.
(http://agentcities.ukoln.ac.uk/server/, accessed 12/11/2003)

The HCONE Approach to Ontology Merging

Konstantinos Kotis, George A. Vouros

Dept. of Information & Communications Systems Engineering,
University of the Aegean,
Karlovassi, Samos,
83100, Greece
{kkot, georgev}@aegean.gr

Abstract. Existing efforts on ontology mapping, alignment and merging vary from methodological and theoretical frameworks, to methods and tools that support the semi-automatic coordination of ontologies. However, only latest research efforts "touch" on the *mapping /merging* of ontologies using the whole breadth of available knowledge. This paper aims to thoroughly describe the HCONE approach on ontology merging. The approach described is based on (a) capturing the intended informal interpretations of concepts by mapping them to WordNet senses using lexical semantic indexing, and (b) exploiting the formal semantics of concepts' definitions by means of description logics' reasoning services.

1 Introduction

Ontologies have been realized as the key technology to shaping and exploiting information for the effective management of knowledge and for the evolution of the Semantic Web and its applications. In such a distributed setting, ontologies establish a common vocabulary for community members to interlink, combine, and communicate knowledge shaped through practice and interaction, binding the knowledge processes of creating, importing, capturing, retrieving, and using knowledge. However, it seems that there will always be more than one ontology even for the same domain. In such a setting where different conceptualizations of the same domain exist, information services must effectively answer queries bridging the gaps between their formal ontologies and users' own conceptualizations. Towards this target, networks of semantically related information must be created at-request. Therefore, coordination (i.e. mapping, alignment, merging) of ontologies is a major challenge for bridging the gaps between agents (software and human) with different conceptualizations.

In [1] an extensive discussion about the way "semantics" are introduced, formalized and exploited in the semantic web, shows that coordination of ontologies using semantic knowledge can be achieved through several methods, depending on *where the semantics are* across the *semantic continuum*: From humans' minds, to their explicit but informal description, their formal description intended for human use, and finally, to their explicit and formal specification intended for machine utilization. The further we move along the continuum, from implicit to formal, explicit semantics, ambiguity is reduced and automated inference is made possible, regarding fully

J. Davies et al. (Eds.): ESWS 2004, LNCS 3053, pp. 137-151, 2004.

automated semantic interoperation and integration. Looking for methods that will fully automate the mapping, alignment and merging processes between ontologies, today we devise methods that are located in the middle of this continuum.

There are many works devoted to coordinating ontologies that exploit linguistic, structural, domain knowledge and matching heuristics. Recent approaches aim to exploit all these types of knowledge and further capture the intended meanings of terms by means of heuristic rules [2].

The HCONE [3] approach to merging ontologies exploits all the above-mentioned types of knowledge. In a greater extent than existing approaches to coordinating ontologies, this approach gives much emphasis on "uncovering" the intended informal interpretations of concepts specified in an ontology. Linguistic and structural knowledge about ontologies are exploited by the Latent Semantics Indexing method (LSI) for associating concepts to their informal, human-oriented intended interpretations realized by WordNet senses. Using concepts' intended semantics, the proposed method translates formal concept definitions to a common vocabulary and exploits the translated definitions by means of description logics' reasoning services. The goal is to validate the mapping between ontologies and find a minimum set of axioms for the merged ontology.

Our choice of description logics is motivated by the need to find the minimum set of axioms needed for merging, and to test the formal consistency of concepts' definitions by means of classification and subsumption reasoning services.

According to the suggested approach and with respect to the semantic continuum, humans are involved in the merging process in two stages: In capturing the intended semantics of terms by means of informal definitions (supported by LSI), and in clarifying relations between concepts in case such relations are not stated formally.

The paper is structured as follows: Section 2 formalizes the problem of semantically merging ontologies. Section 3 describes the HCONE approach to merging ontologies. Section 4 discusses the proposed approach, with remarks, insights on the relation of the proposed approach to other approaches, and future work.

2 The Problem Specification

In order to have a common reference to other approaches, we formulate the problem by means of definitions and terms used in [2].

An ontology is considered to be a pair O=(S, A), where S is the ontological signature describing the vocabulary (i.e. the terms that lexicalize concepts and relations between concepts) and A is a set of ontological axioms, restricting the intended interpretations of the terms included in the signature. In other words, A includes the formal definitions of concepts and relations that are lexicalized by natural language terms in S. This is a slight variation of the definition given in [2], where S is also equipped with a partial order based on the inclusion relation between concepts. In our definition, conforming to description logics' terminological axioms, inclusion relations are ontological axioms included in A. It must be noticed that in this paper we deal with inclusion and equivalence relations among concepts.

Ontology mapping from ontology $O_1 = (S_1, A_1)$ to $O_2 = (S_2, A_2)$ is considered to be a morphism $f:S_1 \rightarrow S_2$ of ontological signatures such that $A_2 \vDash f(A_1)$, i.e. all interpretations that satisfy O_2's axioms also satisfy O_1's translated axioms. Consider for instance the ontologies depicted in Figure 1.

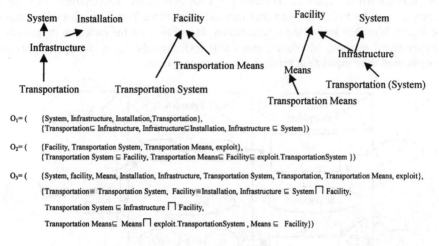

$O_1= ($ {System, Infrastructure, Installation, Transportation},
         {Transportation⊑ Infrastructure, Infrastructure⊑Installation, Infrastructure ⊑ System})

$O_2= ($ {Facility, Transportation System, Transportation Means, exploit},
         {Transportation System ⊑ Facility, Transportation Means⊑ Facility⊑ exploit.TransportationSystem })

$O_3= ($ {System, facility, Means, Installation, Infrastructure, Transportation System, Transportation, Transportation Means, exploit},
         {Transportation≡ Transportation System, Facility≡Installation, Infrastructure ⊑ System⊓ Facility,

         Transportation System ⊑ Infrastructure ⊓ Facility,

         Transportation Means⊑ Means⊓ exploit.TransportationSystem , Means ⊑ Facility})

Fig. 1. Example Ontologies

Given the morphism f such that $f(Infrastructure)=Facility$ and $f(Transportation)=Transportation\ System$, it is true that $A_2 \vDash \{f(Transportation) \sqsubseteq f(Infrastructure)\}$, therefore f is a mapping. Given the morphism f', such that $f'(Infrastructure)=Transportation\ System$ and $f'(Transportation)= Transportation\ Means$, it is not true that $A_2 \vDash \{f(Transportation) \sqsubseteq f(Infrastructure)\}$, therefore f' is not a mapping.

However, instead of a function, we may articulate a set of binary relations between the ontological signatures. Such relations can be the inclusion ($\sqsubseteq$) and the equivalence ($\equiv$) relation. For instance, given the ontologies in Figure 1, we can say that *Transportation≡Transportation System, Installation≡Facility* and *Infrastructure ⊑ Facility*. Then we have indicated an alignment of the two ontologies and we can merge them. Based on the alignment, the merged ontology will be ontology O_3 in Figure 1. It holds that $A_3 \vDash A_2$ and $A_3 \vDash A_1$.

Looking at Figure 1 in an other way, we can consider O_3 to be part of a larger intermediary ontology and define the alignment of ontologies O_1 and O_2 by means of morphisms $f_1 : S_1 \rightarrow S_3$ and $f_2 : S_2 \rightarrow S_3$. Then, the merging of the two ontologies [2] is the minimal union of ontological vocabularies and axioms with respect to the intermediate ontology where ontologies have been mapped.

Therefore, the ontologies merging problem (OMP) can be stated as follows: *Given two ontologies find an alignment between these two ontologies, and then, get the minimal union of their (translated) vocabularies and axioms with respect to their alignment.*

3 The HCONE Method to Solving the OMP

As it is shown in Figure 2, WordNet plays the role of an "intermediate" in order a morphism to be found. We consider that each sense in a WordNet synset describes a concept. WordNet senses are related among themselves via the inclusion (hyponym – hyperonym) relation. Moreover, terms that lexicalize the same concept (sense) are considered to be equivalent through the synonym relation.

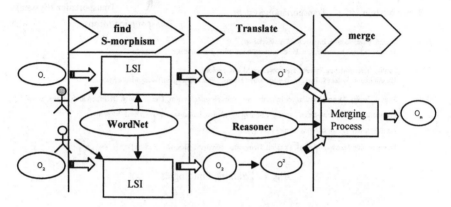

Fig. 2. The HCONE approach towards the OMP

It must be noticed that we do not consider WordNet to include any intermediate ontology, as this would be very restrictive for the specification of the original ontologies (i.e. the method would work only for those ontologies that preserve the inclusion relations among WordNet senses).

Therefore, we consider that there is an intermediate ontology "somewhere there" including a vocabulary with the lexicalizations of the specific senses of WordNet synsets we are interested on, and axioms that respect the set of axioms of the original ontologies. We will call this ontology *hidden intermediate*. It is important to notice that only part of this ontology will be uncovered through concept mappings: actually, the part that is needed for merging the source ontologies.

To find the mapping from each ontology to the hidden intermediate, we use a morphism (we call it *s-morphism*, symbolized by f_s), which is based on the lexical semantic indexing (LSI) method. Using the LSI method, each ontology concept is associated with a set of graded WordNet senses. For instance, the concept "facility" is associated with the five senses that WordNet assigns to the term "facility", whose meaning range from "something created to provide a service" to "a room equipped with washing and toilet facilities". The highest graded sense expresses the most possible informal meaning of the corresponding concept. This sense expresses the intended interpretation of the concept specification and can be further validated by a human. In case a human indicates an association to be the most preferable, then this sense is considered to capture the informal intended meaning of the formal ontology concept. Otherwise, the method considers the highest graded sense as the concept's intended interpretation. Given all the preferred associations from concepts to WordNet senses, we have captured the intended interpretation of ontology concepts.

Using the intended meanings of the formal concepts, we construct an ontology $O''=(S'', A'')$, $n=1,2$, where, S'' includes the lexicalizations of the senses associated to the concepts[1] of the ontology $O_n=(S_n, A_n)$, $n=1,2$, and A'' contain the translated inclusion and equivalence relations between the corresponding concepts. Then, it holds that $A'' \vDash f_s(A_n)$ and the ontology $O''=(S'', A'')$ with the corresponding associations from O_n to O'', is a model of $O_n=(S_n, A_n)$, $n=1,2....$ These associations define a mapping from O_n to O''.

Having found the mappings with the hidden intermediate ontology, the translated ontologies can be merged, taking into account the axioms A^1 and A^2 (which are the translated axioms of A_1 and A_2). The merging decisions are summarized in Table 1.

Table 1. HCONE-Merge Algorithm table summary

Concept & Role Names[2]	Concept Mapping to WordNet Senses[3]	Action
Match	No match	Rename concepts
Match	Match	Merge concept definitions
No match	Match	Merge concept definitions in a single concept named by the term lexicalizing their corresponding WordNet sense
No match	No match	Classify Concepts

3.1 Mapping and Merging through the Semantic Morphism (s-morphism)

To find the mapping from an ontology to the hidden intermediate, we use the semantic morphism (*s-morphism*, symbolized by *fs*), which, as already pointed, is based on the lexical semantic indexing (LSI) method.

LSI [5] is a vector space technique for information retrieval and indexing. It assumes that there is an underlying latent semantic structure that it estimates using statistical techniques. It takes a large matrix of term-document association data and constructs a semantic space. In our case the nXm space comprises the n more frequently occurred terms of the m WordNet senses the algorithm focuses on (later on we explain which senses constitute the focus of the algorithm). Lexical Semantic Analysis (LSA) allows the arrangement of the semantic space to reflect the major associative patterns in the data. As a result, terms that did not actually appear in a sense may still end up close to the sense, if this is consistent with the major patterns of association in the data [5]. Position in the space then serves as the new kind of semantic indexing. Therefore, it must be emphasized that although LSI exploits structural information of ontologies and WordNet, it ends up with semantic associations between terms.

Given an ontology concept, retrieval aims to locate a point in space that is close to the sense that expresses the intended meaning of this concept. The query to the retrieval mechanism is constructed by the concept names of all concepts in the vicinity of the given concept.

---

[1] Future work concerns mapping domain relations to WordNet senses as well.
[2] Match in this case means linguistic match of the concept names from the two ontologies.
[3] Match means that both concepts have been mapped to the same WordNet sense

To support this process, as already explained, we exploit the WordNet lexical database to match formal descriptions of concepts with word senses in WordNet. Using the lexicalizations of these senses, the ontology is translated to the hidden intermediate ontology. The steps of the algorithm for finding the semantic morphism are the following:

1. Choose a concept from the ontology. Let C be the concept name.
2. Get all WordNet senses S_1, S_2,...,S_m, lexicalized by C', where C' is a linguistic variation of C. These senses provide the *focus of the algorithm for C*.
3. Get the hyperonyms' and hyponyms' of all C' senses.
4. Build the *"semantic space"*: An nXm matrix that comprises the n more frequently occurred terms in the *vicinity* of the m WordNet senses found in step 2.
5. Build a query string using the terms in the *vicinity* of C.
6. Find the ranked associations between C and C' senses by running the Latent Semantics Analysis (LSA) function and consider the association with the highest grade. LSA uses the query terms for constructing the query string and computes a point in the semantic space constructed in step (4).

This algorithm is based on assumptions that influence the associations produced:

- Currently, concept names lemmatization and morphological analysis is not sophisticated. This implies that in case the algorithm does not find a lexical entry that matches a slight variation of the given concept name, then the user is being asked to provide a synonym term. However, in another line of research we produce methods for matching concept names based on a 'core set' of characters [4].

- Most compound terms have no senses in WordNet, thus we can only achieve an association for each component of the term (which is a partial indication of the intended meaning of the whole term). Currently, we consider that the compound term lexicalizes a concept that is related (via a generic relation *Relation*) to concepts that correspond to the single terms comprising the compound term. For instance, the concept lexicalized by "Transportation Means" is considered to be related to the concepts lexicalized by "Transportation" and "Means". It is assumed that humans shall clarify the type of relations that hold between concepts. Such a relation can be the inclusion, equivalence or any other domain relation. In general, in case a compound term C cannot be associated with a sense that expresses its exact meaning, then the term C is associated with concepts H_n, n=1,2... corresponding to the single words comprising it. Then, C is considered to be mapped in a virtual concept C_w of the intermediate ontology, while H_n are considered to be included in the ontological signature of the intermediate ontology and the axiom $C_w \sqsubseteq \sqcap_{Hn} \forall Relation.H_n$, n=1,2... is considered to be included in ontological axioms of the intermediate ontology. For instance, *"Transportation Means"* is considered to correspond to a virtual concept of the intermediate ontology, while the axiom *TransportationMeans $\sqsubseteq$ Relation.Transportation $\sqcap$ Relation.Means* is considered to be an axiom of this ontology. Given that *Means* subsumes *Transportation-*

Means, and the *Relation* to *Trasportation* is *function,* the axiom becomes *TransportationMeans ⊑ Means ⊓ function.Transportation.*

This treatment of compound terms is motivated by the need to reduce the problem of mapping these terms to the mapping of single terms. Then we can exploit the translated formal definitions of compound terms by means of description logics reasoning services for testing equivalence and subsumption relations between concepts definitions during ontologies alignment and merging.

– The performance of the algorithm is related to assumptions concerning the information that has to be used for the computation of the (a) "semantic space", and (b) query terms.

– The implementation of LSI that we are currently using, as it is pointed by the developers[4], works correctly when the nXm matrix corresponding to the semantic space has more than 4 and less than 100 WordNet senses. This case occurs frequently, but we resolve it by extending the vicinity of senses.

The semantic space is constructed by terms in the *vicinity* of the senses S_1, S_2,...S_m that are in focus of the algorithm for a concept C. Therefore, we have to decide what constitutes the *vicinity* of a sense for the calculation of the semantic space. In an analogous way we have to decide what constitutes the *vicinity* of an ontology concept for the calculation of the query string. The goal is to compute valid associations without distracting LSI with "noise" and by specifying vicinities in an application independed way.

Table 2. Algorithm's design assumptions (The switches with the asterisk are always activated)

Semantic Space Variations	☑ concept's name*	The term C' that corresponds to C. C' is a lexical entry in WordNet
	☑ concept's senses*	Terms that appear in C' WordNet senses
	☑ hyperonyms & hyponyms	Terms that constitute hyperonyms / hyponyms of each C' sense.
	☑ hyperonyms' / hyponyms' senses	Terms that appear in hyper(hyp)onyms of C' senses
Query Terms Variation	☑ primitive parents*	Concept's C primitive parents.
	☑ taxonomy parents	Concepts that subsume C and are immediate parents of C (subsumers of C).
	☑ children*	Concepts that are immediate children of C (subsumed by C)
	☑ related concepts	Concepts that are related to C via domain specific relations
	☑ WordNet Senses	The most frequent terms in WordNet senses that have been associated with the concepts in the vicinity of C.

[4] KnownSpace Hydrogen License: This product includes software developed by the Know Space Group for use in the KnownSpace Project (http://www.knownspace.org)

Towards this goal we have ran a set of experiments by activating / deactivating the "switches" shown in Table 2, thus specifying "vicinity" based on structural features of the ontology and WordNet.We have run experiments both in small (10 concepts) and large ontologies (100 concepts) for the transportation domain. The ontology presented in this paper comprises about 10 concepts. It must be noticed that using the proposed method, small ontologies are considered to be harder to be mapped since the available information for performing the semantic analysis is limited. By the term "small" ontologies" we denote ontologies for which the vicinity of ontology concepts includes a limited number of concepts for the construction of the query string. On the contrary, in "large" ontologies, the query string can include sufficient information for computing the intented sense of ontology concepts.

Furthermore, the small ontology allowed us to control and criticize the results. To perform our experiments we have distinguished several cases whose results have been measured by method's recall and precision. These cases correspond to different WordNet senses and concepts' vicinity definitions. Table3 shows two cases that resulted to high (balanced case) and quite low precision (all-activated case). Recall· in all these cases was constantly 90% due to one compound term that could only be partially associated to a WordNet sense. Similar results have been given by larger ontologies.

Table 3. A balanced combination of senses and concepts' vicinities (defined by the activated switches for the computation of the semantic space and queries, respectively) resulted to the highest precision percentage of 90%

		Variations of LSI algorithm – Design Implications		Precision
Balanced Case	Space Variations	☑ concept ☑ concept senses ☐ hyper(hyp)onyms ☐ hyper(hyp)onyms senses		90%
	Query Terms Variation	☑ primitive parents ☐ taxonomy parents ☑ children ☐ WordNet Senses ☑ related concepts		
All-activated Case	Space Variations	☑ concept ☑ concept senses ☑ hyper(hyp)onyms ☑ hyper(hyp)onyms senses		50%
	Query Terms Variation	☑ primitive parents ☑ taxonomy parents ☑ children ☑ WordNet Senses ☑ related concepts		

The balanced case corresponds to a "balanced amount" of information for computing the semantic space and for constructing the queries. The conjecture that LSI can be distracted in large semantic spaces by, what we may call, *semantic noise*, has been proved in test cases where the semantic space has been computed taking into account the WordNet senses of the hyperonyms and/or hyponyms of the senses in focus. By reducing the amount of information in the semantic space we actually achieved to get more hits. Experiments imply that to compute correct concept-senses associations, LSI must consider senses that are "close" to the meaning of the concepts in the hidden intermediate ontology, otherwise noise (or ellipsis of information) can seriously distract computations due to influences from other domains/conceptualizations. A similar case occurs when the query string includes terms that appear in the WordNet senses associated with the super-concepts and sub-concepts of an ontology concept. For this reason, the balanced case shown in Table 3 does not consider these WordNet senses. The balanced case has been specified manually, by the proper examination of experiments. In a latest work of ours, we are investigating techniques for automatically tuning the mechanism to maximize the precision.

Having found the associations between the ontology concepts and WordNet senses, the algorithm has found a semantic morphism between the original ontologies and the hidden intermediate ontology. The construction of the intermediate ontology with the minimal set of axioms results in ontologies' merging.

For instance, as it is shown in Figure 3, given the morphisms produced, it holds that:

- For ontology O_1

    $f_s(System) = System_1,$
    $f_s(Installation) = Facility_1,$
    $f_s(Infrastructure) = Infrastructure_1,$ and
    $f_s(Transportation) = TransportationSystem_1.$

- For ontology O_2

    $f_s(Facility) = Facility_1,$
    $f_s(Transportation System) = TransportationSystem_1,$ and
    $f_s(Transportation Means) = TransporationMeans_W$ *{virtual concept}*
    $f_s(Means) = Means_1$
    $f_s(Transportation) = Transportation_2$

The indices of the associated terms indicate the WordNet senses that provide the informal intended meanings of concepts. Notice that the intended interpretation of the concept Transportation in O_2 is different from the intended interpretation of the homonym concept in O_1.

Both ontologies are being translated using the corresponding WordNet senses' lexicalizations and are being merged. We must notice that the compound term *Transportation Means* has been related with the concept *Transportation* (the relation has been specified to be *function)* and with the concept *Means* (via the subsumption relation). This definition is in conjunction to the definition given in O_2, where Transportation Means are defined to be entities that exploit the Transportation System.

The new ontology will incorporate the mappings of the original concepts, the translated axioms of O_1 and O_2, modulo the axioms of the intermediate ontology.

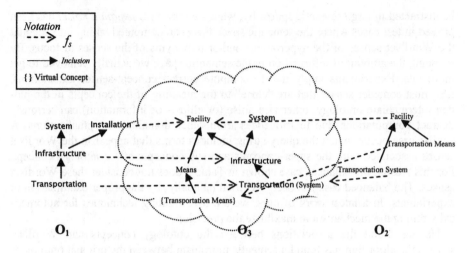

Fig. 3. S-morphism and the intermediate ontology

Therefore, the merged ontology is $O_m = (S_m, A_m)$, where:

$S_m = \{System, facility, Means, Installation, Infrastructure, Transportation System,$
$\quad Transportation, Transportation Means, exploit\},$
$A_m = \{Transportation \equiv TransportationSystem,$
$\quad Facility \equiv Installation, Infrastructure \sqsubseteq System \sqcap Facility,$
$\quad TransportationSystem \sqsubseteq Infrastructure Means \sqsubseteq Facility,$
$\quad TransportationMeans \sqsubseteq Means \sqcap function.Transportation\text{-}O2$
$\qquad\qquad\qquad\qquad\qquad \sqcap exploit.TransportationSystem \}$

It must be noticed that the concepts *Transportation* and *Transportation System* have the same intended interpretation, and therefore are considered equivalent. According to Table 1, the merging of their formal definitions results to:

$TransportationSystem \sqsubseteq Infrastructure \sqcap Facility$

However, the description logics classification mechanism considers the axiom *TransportationSystem $\sqsubseteq$ Facility* to be redundant. Therefore O_3 contains only the axiom *TransportationSystem $\sqsubseteq$ Infrastructure*. Doing so, the merged ontology contains only the minimal set of axioms resulting from original ontologies mapping.

Furthermore, according to Table 1, the concept Transportation of O_2 will be renamed to Transportation-O_2 since it corresponds to a sense that is different to the sense of the homonym concept Transportation in O_1. This latter concept, based on the morphism, has been renamed to TransportationSystem.

4   Concluding Remarks

As already explained in section 2, mapping between ontologies has a close relation to the merging of ontologies. Mapping may utilize a reference ontology but it can also be point-to-point (non mediated). In either case it must preserve the semantics of the mapped ontology. The merging process takes into account the mapping results [6] in order to resolve problems concerning name conflicts, taxonomy conflicts, etc between the merged ontologies.

To accomplish a mapping between two conceptual models, a matching algorithm is required which will eventually discover these mappings. *Matching* can be distinguished in syntactic, structural and semantic matching depending on the knowledge utilized and on the kind of the similarity relation used [7]. Syntactic matching involves the matching of ontology nodes' labels, estimating the similarity among nodes using syntactic similarity measures, as for instance in [8]. Minor name and structure variations can lead the matching result astray. On the other hand, structural matching involves matching the neighbourhoods of ontology nodes, providing evidence for the similarity of the nodes themselves. Semantic matching explores the mapping between the meanings of concept specifications exploiting domain knowledge as well. Semantic matching specifies a similarity relation in the form of a semantic relation between the intensions of concepts [9]. Semantic matching may also rely to additional information such as lexicons, thesaurus or reference ontologies incorporating semantic knowledge (mostly domain dependent) into the process.

Instance based approaches to mapping and merging ontologies, which contrast techniques for merging non-populated ontologies, exploit the set-theoretic semantics of concept definitions in order to uncover semantic relations among them. However, such approaches deal with specific (quite restricted) domains of discourse, rather than with the semantics of the statements themselves. Therefore, these approaches are useful in cases where information sources are rather stable (where the domain of discourse does not change frequently) or in cases where information is "representative" (e.g., as it is required in FCA-Merge) for the concepts specified.

There are a variety of research efforts towards coordinating ontologies. According to [10] and [11] there is not a "best tool" or method, since there is not always the case that it will fit every users' or applications' needs. To comment however on such efforts, we conjecture that several criteria could be considered such as:

a)   The kind of *mapping architecture* they provide:(i) point-to-point mapping or mediated mapping, (ii) top-down or bottom up mapping, considering techniques applied to the intensions of concepts (non-populated ontologies) or to the extensions of concepts (populated ontologies), respectively.

b)   The *kind of knowledge* (structural, lexical, domain) used for node matching, i.e. i) techniques that are based on the syntax of labels of nodes and to syntactic similarity measures, ii) techniques that are based on the semantic relations of concepts and to semantic similarity measures, and iii) techniques that rely on structural information about ontologies.

c)   The *type of result* corresponding algorithms produce: For instance, a mapping between two ontologies or/and a merged ontology

d) Additional information sources consulted during the mapping/merging process, for instance, thesaurus, lexicons.
e) The level of user involvement: How and when the user is involved in the process.

Table 4 summarises the existing efforts to ontologies' coordination using the above issues. A careful examination of the table shows that each effort focuses on certain important issues. The HCONE method to merging ontologies, borrowing from the results of the reported efforts, focuses on all of the issues mentioned above.

In particular, we have realised that efforts conforming to mediated mapping and merging [12][13] will possibly not work, since a reference ontology (that preserves the axioms of the source ontologies) may not be always available or may be hard to be constructed (especially in the "real world" of the SemanticWeb). On the other hand, point-to-point efforts are missing the valuable knowledge (structure and domain) that a reference ontology can provide in respect to the semantic similarity relations between concepts. The proposed HCONE merging process assumes that there is a hidden intermediate reference ontology that is build on the fly using WordNet senses, expressing the intended interpretations of ontologies' concepts, and user specified semantic relations among concepts.

Although bottom-up approaches [12], [13], [14] rely on strong assumptions concerning the population of ontologies, they have a higher grade of precision in their matching techniques since instances provide a better representation of concepts' intended meaning in a domain. However, using WordNet senses we provide an informal representation of concepts' intensions (i.e. of the conditions for an entity to belong in the denotation of a concept, rather than the entities themselves).

More importantly, we have identified that apart from [9], [15] all efforts do not consult significant domain knowledge. However, to make use of such knowledge, additional information must be specified in the ontology. WordNet is a potential source of such information [9]. However, utilizing this source implies that the domain ontologies must be consistent to the semantic relations between WordNet senses, which is a very restrictive (if not prohibiting) condition to the construction of source ontologies.

HCONE exploits WordNet, which is an external (to the source ontologies) natural language information source. The proposed HCONE method consults WordNet for lexical information, exploiting also structural information between senses in order to obtain interpretations of concepts (i.e. the informal human oriented semantics of defined terms). Other efforts such as [8], [14], [16] have used additional information sources but only [9] have used WordNet for lexical and domain knowledge.

A complete automated merging tool is not the aim of this research. Since we conjecture that in real environments such as the Semantic Web humans' intended interpretations of concepts must always be captured, the question is where to place this involvement. Existing efforts [12][15][14], place this involvement after the mapping between sources ontologies has been produced, as well as during, or at the end of the merging method. The user is usually asked to decide upon merging strategies or to guide the process in case of inconsistency. Some other efforts head towards automatic mapping techniques [9], [8], [13] but they have not shown that a consistent and automatic merging will follow.

Table 4. Issues concerning existing ontology mapping/merging tools

	Mapping Architecture	Kind of knowledge used	Type of result	N.L Information	User Involvement
ONIONS [12]	Mediated Bottom-up	Syntactic	Mapping & Merging	No	Semi-automatic
PROMPT [17]	Point-to-point Top-down	Syntactic	Merging	No	Semi-automatic
FCA-Merge [14]	Point-to-point Bottom-up	Syntactic	Merging	Natural Language Document	Semi-automatic
ONION [18]	Point-to-point Top-down	Syntactic	Mapping & Merging	No	Semi-automatic
MOMIS [16]	Point-to-point Top-down	Syntactic	Mapping (similarity between nodes) & Merging	Thesaurus	Semi-automatic
CUPID [8]	Point-to-point Top-down	Syntactic	Mapping (similarity between nodes)	Thesaurus	Automatic (schema matching)
IF-based [13]	Mediated Bottom-up	Syntactic	Mapping	No	Automatic (Not yet shown)
GLUE [15]	Point-to-point Top-down	Syntactic & Semantic (domain constraints)	Mapping (similarity between nodes)	No	Semi-automatic
CTX-Match [9]	Point-to-point Top-down	Syntactic & Semantic (semantic relations)	Mapping (semantic relations between nodes)	WordNet	Automatic (identify relations)

The HCONE approach places human involvement at the early stages of the mapping/merging process. If this involvement leads to capturing the intended interpretation of conceptualisations, then the rest is a consistent, error-free merging process, whose results are subject to further human evaluation.

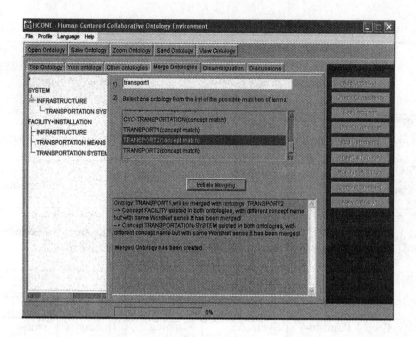

Fig. 4. HCONE-merge functionality. Merged concepts (e.g. FACILITY and INSTALLATION) are shown in the form Concept1+Concept2 (FACILITY+INSTALLATION) for presentation reasons

References

1. Uschold, M., Gruninger, M.: Creating Semantically Integrated Communities on the World Wide Web. Invited Talk, Semantic Web Workshop, WWW 2002 Conference, Honolulu, H1 (2002)
2. Kalfoglou, Y., Schorlemmer, M.: Ontology mapping: the state of the art. The Knowledge Engineering Review 18(1) (2003) 1–31
3. Kotis, K., Vouros, G.: Human-Centered Ontology Management with HCONE. In Proceedings of Ontologies and Distributed Systems Workshop, IJCAI-03 Conference, Acapulco, Mexico (2003)
4. Valarakos, A., Paliouras, G., Karkaletsis V., Vouros, G.: A name-Matching Algorithm for supporting Ontology Enrichment. In Proceedings of SETN'04, 3rd Hellenic Conference on Artificial Intelligence, Samos, Greece (2004)
5. Deerwester, S., Dumais, T. S., Furnas, W. G., Landauer, K. T., Harshman, R.: Indexing by Latent Semantic Analysis. Journal of the American Society of Information Science (1990)
6. Madhavan, J., Bern-stein, A. P., Domingos, P., Halevy, Y. A.: Representing and reasoning about mappings between domain models. In Proceedings of the 18th AAAI Canada (2002) 80–86
7. Giunchiglia F., Shvaiko, P.: Semantic Matching. In Proceedings of SemWeb-03 Conference, Workshop on Semantic Integration, Florida USA (2003)
8. Madhavan, J., Bern-stein, P. A., Rahm, E.: Generic schema matching with Cupid. VLDB Journal (2001) 49–58

9. Serafini, L., Bouquet, P., Magnini, B., Zanobini, S. : An Algorithm for Matching Contextualized Schemas via SAT. In Proceedings of CONTEX'03 (2003)
10. Uschold, M.: Where are the Semantics in the Semantic Web? AI Magazine, Vol. 24, No.3, Fall (2003)
11. Noy, F. N., Musen, A. M.: Evaluating Ontology-Mapping Tools: Requirements and Experience. In Proceedings of OntoWeb-SIG3 Workshop at the 13th International Conference on Knowledge Engineering and Knowledge Management, Siguenza, Spain, (2002) 1–14
12. Gangemi, A., Pisanelli, D. M., Steve, G.: An Overview of the ONIONS Project: Applying Ontologies to the Integration of Medical Terminologies. Data and Knowledge Engineering, Vol. 31 (1999) 183–220
13. Kalfoglou, Y., Schorlemmer, M.: Information-Flow-based Ontology Mapping. In Proceedings of the 1st International Conference on Ontologies, Databases and Application of Semantics, Irvine, CA, USA (2002)
14. Stumme, G., Mädche, A.: FCA-Merge: Bottom-Up Merging of Ontologies. In: B. Nebel (Ed.): Proceedings of 17th Intl. Joint Conference on Artificial Intelligence. Seattle, WA, USA (2001) 225-230
15. Doan, A., Madhavan, J., Domingos, P., Halvey, A.: Learning to map between ontologies on the semantic web. In Proceedings of 11th International WWW Conference, Hawaii (2002)
16. Beneventano, D., Bergamaschi, S., Guerra, F., Vincini, M.: The MOMIS approach to Information Integration. IEEE and AAAI International Conference on Enterprise Information Systems, Setúbal, Portugal, (2001)
17. Noy, F. N., Musen, A. M.: PROMPT: Algorithm and tool for automated ontology merging and alignment. In Proceedings of 7th National Conference on AI, Austin, TX (2000)
18. Mitra, P., Wiederhold, G., Decker, S.: A Scalable Framework for Interoperation of Information Sources. In Proceedings of the 1st International Semantic Web Working Symposium, Stanford University, Stanford, CA (2001)

Question Answering Towards Automatic Augmentations of Ontology Instances

Sanghee Kim, Paul Lewis, Kirk Martinez, and Simon Goodall

Intelligence, Agents, Multimedia Group, School of Electronics and Computer Science,
University of Southampton, U.K.
{sk,phl,km,sg02r}@ecs.soton.ac.uk

Abstract. Ontology instances are typically stored as triples which associate two named entities with a pre-defined relational description. Sometimes such triples can be incomplete in that one entity is known but the other entity is missing. The automatic discovery of the missing values is closely related to relation extraction systems that extract binary relations between two identified entities. Relation extraction systems rely on the availability of accurately named entities in that mislabelled entities can decrease the number of relations correctly identified. Although recent results demonstrate over 80% accuracy for recognising named entities, when input texts have less consistent patterns, the performance decreases rapidly. This paper presents OntotripleQA which is the application of question-answering techniques to relation extraction in order to reduce the reliance on the named entities and take into account other assessments when evaluating potential relations. Not only does this increase the number of relations extracted, but it also improves the accuracy of extracting relations by considering features which are not extractable with only comparisons of the named entities. A small dataset was collected to test the proposed approach and the experiment demonstrates that it is effective on sentences from Web documents with an accuracy of 68% on average.

Keywords: relation extraction, ontology population, information extraction, question answering systems

1   Introduction

The increasing interest in knowledge technologies and the semantic web is leading to a rapid development of ontologies describing many and diverse application domains. Ontologies are often defined as shared conceptualizations of a domain and consist of concepts, relations between them and instance information held as entity-relation-entity triples.

Relation extraction systems recognize pre-defined relation types between two identified entities from natural language sentences. They infer the types of relations to be extracted either from a relation entry template or an ontology. Both define which types of entities are associated with the relations so that once the entities are available, appropriate relations can be extracted. Relations describe features specific to the entities associated and typically link two entities. For example, consider 'painter' and

J. Davies et al. (Eds.): ESWS 2004, LNCS 3053, pp. 152-166, 2004.

'painting' entities. One of the properties attached to the 'painter' class is 'produced' that links to 'painting' specifying a semantic relationship between the two classes. Relation extraction is important for the task of automatically extracting missing values of instances in the ontology where the instance is represented as a binary relation (i.e. 'entity – relation – entity').

When organizations (e.g. museums or galleries) hold large quantities of information in the form of ontologies, missing values for some data can occur for a variety of reasons. For example, the data are distributed across different locations limiting accessibility. Expert intervention is required to extract the values or additional information sources (e.g. the Web) might be needed to obtain such information. Here, we focus on the third situation where the Web holds a vast amount of information, increasing opportunities for extracting such missing values. Figure 1 shows an example of how an automatic relation extraction system (such as OntotripleQA described in this paper) extracts the missing instances from the Web. It identifies "impressionists" as an answer to the missing entity in the relation "is_member_of" describing which group "Renoir Pierre-Auguste" was a member of.

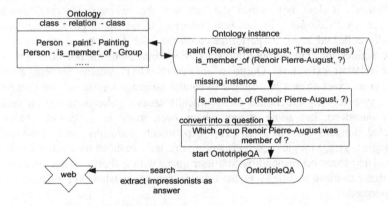

Fig.1. Showing how OntotripleQA accesses the Web to extract answers.

Search engines on the Web provide an interface where a user submits a query and receives a set of related documents. Although the search engines are efficient in retrieving documents sought-after, answering user queries with concise and accurate forms is not yet fully-fledged. That is, a user needs to sift through the retrieved documents in order to find answers to a question, e.g. '*where was Bill Gates born*?'. In fact, the answer is hidden in the sentences of '*Bill Gates was born on October 28, 1955. He and his two sisters grew up in Seattle*' and while it might be easy for a person to infer 'Bill' was born in 'Seattle', it is one of the tasks that the search engines are unable to handle at the moment.

One of the reasons why it is difficult to extract a concise answer with current search engines is the fact that that current Web annotations are too basic to enable the automatic extraction of answers sought-after and no explicit descriptions for the entities conveyed are available. Recent interest in the Semantic Web highlights the importance of providing expressive mark-up through which the meanings and roles of the words are defined. It is, in particular, important for sharing and communicating data between an information provider and a seeker over the Web. With pages conforming to the Semantic Web standards, it would be easier for the information seeker to extract answers of interest. However, in the absence or lack of semantic annotations on the Web, it is useful to provide semi or automatic tools for extracting the appropriate pieces of text in order to reduce the users' efforts. Research on issues such as information extraction, question answering, and techniques like natural language processing, machine learning and traditional information retrieval are closely related.

Information extraction (IE) systems aim to provide easy access to natural language documents by organising data into pre-defined named-entity types and relations. Many IE systems mainly focus on recognising named-entities and recent experimental results showed that performance can reach over an 80% F-measure (the harmonic mean of precision and recall values) [15]. Whereas some systems try to extract relations, the number of relation types is rather small or no relations are extracted [2]. For example, although GATE [7] can recognize "*French Museum*" as a type of "*organization*", it does not extract the fact that the "*French Museum*" holds a masterpiece by "*Courbet*". In addition, whereas IE shows high accuracy using specifically collected texts, its performance on the Web is poor and requires much complex engineering. This implies that some IE systems alone are not sufficient to be used for relation extraction. Question answering (QA) systems retrieve a short sentence or an exact answer in response to natural-language questions. Until recently, most QA systems only functioned on specifically created collections and on limited types of questions, but some attempts have been made to scale the system to unrestricted domains like the Web [12]. Experiments show that in comparison to search engines (e.g. Google), QA systems significantly reduced user effort to obtain answers. They focus on responding to a user query with a short passage or an exact answer that has close similarity to the relation extraction where the relation is the answer pursued.

Since QA takes natural-language questions as input, the question analysis that parses the query to identify core query terms, expected answer types, and any semantic and syntactic constraints on the answers is critical [18]. The outcome directly affects answer retrieval and extraction modules so that a highly accurate and efficient method is required. One challenge derives from the questions generally being too short to infer contexts and they have various types and topics, making it hard to predict regular patterns to classify them. Compared to QA, relation extraction (RE) systems infer the types of relations to be extracted either from a relation entry template or an ontology. Both define which types of entities are associated with the relations and the relations can be regarded as answers to the question constructed by using one of the associated entities. That is, relation extractions can be regarded as the QA task that finds answers (missing entities) to questions containing relation features and known entities. As such, the task of the relation extraction is repositioned as finding one entity name as an answer in a response to a question in which the other entity and the relation are implied. The types of the questions are mainly limited to description-oriented queries, although other types and more complex queries can occur.

Most QA systems use named-entity recognisers for evaluating whether or not the given piece of text is an answer candidate [22]. Other assessments such as semantic distance to the query or structural evidence are also considered, implying that even though entities matching answers are not available, it may still be possible to obtain the answers through other evaluations. QA systems aim at dealing with unlimited types of questions focused on how to make use of the terms in the questions for identifying answer clues and conditions upon which answer types are feasible. Their emphasis on answer selection and extraction is also useful for relation extraction as it leads them to be less dependent on named-entities.

This paper presents OntotripleQA, the application of QA techniques to the task of extracting ontological triples which are binary relations between two identified entities. The triples are instances in the ontology where one entity is available and the other is missing. OntotripleQA aims at improving relation extraction performance by incorporating techniques from general QA systems, especially those useful for dealing with Web pages where named entities are difficult to identify and where semantic variations among the pages are large. For example, 'date_of_death' that specifies the date when a person died can be extracted from the following sentences: *"On July 27, 1890 Van Gogh shot himself in the chest. He died two days later"* (source: http://www.euro-art-gallery.net/history/vangogh.htm), *"Vincent van Gogh died at 1:30 am. on 29 July 1890"* (source: http://www.vangoghgallery.com/misc/bio.htm). Obviously, "29 July 1890" is more easily extracted from the third sentence. Since most QA systems have only been tested within special collections and have not fully explored the use of Web documents, our focus is not to prove the usefulness of QA on Web pages; instead, OntotripleQA examines some components of QA from the perspective of reducing poor performance of relation identification when coping with unconstrained texts. In fact, the tasks, like a question analysis in QA, can be simplified since the ontology provides necessary information concerning the query classification and the questions are fixed, making it easier to constrain expected answer types.

This paper is organised as follows: in section 2, reviews of the state-of-the-art in research on QA, IE and RE are presented; section 3 describes OntotripleQA beginning with the details of RE in the context of the ontology and the introduction of the QA modules. Experimental results are presented in section 4 followed by conclusions and future work.

2   Related Work

There has not been much research concerned with relation extractions. It is one part of the tasks within the Message Understanding Conference (MUC) which focuses on various IE tasks. Aone et al. [3] presented a scalable relation extraction system by using NLP techniques and a pre-defined template for specifying rules. However, the provision of manually created rules for each relation type can be a difficult and tedious task when the number of relations is large and few regular patterns among the relations are observed.

Roth presented a probabilistic method for recognising both entities and relations together [19]. The method measures the inter-dependency between entities and relations and uses them to restrain the conditions under which entities are extractable given relations and vice versa. Local classifiers for separately identifying entities and relations are first calculated. Global inferences are derived from the local classifiers by taking the outputs in the form of conditional probabilities as inputs for determining the most appropriate types. An evaluation with test documents showed over 80% accuracy on entities and a minimum of 60% on relations. However, the computational resources for generating such probabilities are generally intractable.

OntotripleQA, to be described in this paper, uses an existing named-entity recogniser (GATE [7]) as well as a lexical database (WordNet [16]) for annotating an entity with pre-defined types. Similarly to the relation extraction, applying machine learning algorithms to induce entity recognition rules has been proposed. Freitag [8] uses SRV, a token-basis general-specific rule learning algorithm for information extraction from online texts. It makes use of grammatical inferences for generating pattern-based extraction rules appropriate for HTML structures. Its core token features are separated from domain-specific attributes making the SRV easy to apply to a new system. The evaluation shows lower performance of the multiple-value (e.g. project members) instantiations compared to that of single-value (e.g. project title) entities implying that the former is harder to extract. (LP)^2 is a supervised wrapper induction system that generalizes extraction rules based on a bottom-up approach [5]. The generalization starts with word string features suitable for highly structured texts and gradually adds linguistic attributes to induce more appropriate patterns. It uses shallow-level natural language processing, such as POS tagging, or case information ('lowercase'). The generated rules are corrected from mislabeled tags by inducing correct tag positions from a corpus provided. This correction step is one of contributions that enables (LP)^2 to show higher performance compared to other entity rule induction systems (e.g SRV).

QA systems in general follow three steps. Given a question, they start with the query analysis that classifies the question according to its answer types by taking into account terms in the question. The results of the analysis initiate retrieval of candidate answers by using various retrieval techniques. Systems then examine the retrieved documents in order to extract answers by using NLP techniques and named-entity techniques. Since QA systems in TREC (Text REtrieval Conference) can make use of examples used for previous TREC series, many systems examine the examples to create hand-crafted rules for question patterns with answers. For example, Hermjakob et al. [9] explored the idea of reducing the semantic gap between questions and answers by providing semantically interchangeable reformulations of the questions and assuming that searches for a correct answer which matches with any strings found in the reformulations. The paraphrasing includes syntactic as well as semantic variations, and on average, questions have about 3 variations.

Creating rules manually requires a large set of examples from which regular patterns are derived. It is difficult to construct such rules from the Web documents since structural and semantic variations among them are large. As such, scalability and domain-dependency can be problems when QA techniques are imported to new domains. In OntotripleQA, the question analysis is relatively simple as the types of questions and corresponding answers are pre-defined in the ontology. However, since it operates on the Web, document searching and answer selection might be harder compared to closed-domains, like newswires or newspapers.

TREC12 introduced two new requirements to the QA task that retrieves an exact answer and only one answer in response to a question [22]. Previous conferences allowed participant systems to retrieve five answer candidates and the answers could have 50 or 250 bytes length. Test datasets are collected from the articles from newswires or newspapers, and the Web is often used for two different purposes; it acts as an additional source of finding answers or the Web redundancy provides one way of validating candidate answers. Magniti et al. [14] identified that the main errors were attributed to the search and answer extraction components so they proposed an answer validation component that validates an answer based on the number of co-occurrences between a question and the answer by mining the Web or a large corpus. It involves a validation pattern, in which the question and answer keywords co-occur closely and uses a statistical count of Web search results and document analysis. Relational triples were exploited by Litkowski [13] in matching answers with the questions given by converting both of them into database-like formats.

3   OntotripleQA

OntotripleQA is the application of QA techniques to the task of extracting relational descriptions between two named entities from natural language sentences. The extracted relations are entered into the ontology after being verified by users. It uses the Apple Pie Parser [21] for syntactic analysis and parts of the semantic analysis tools used in the Artequakt project [10]. OntotripleQA is an improved version of Ontotriple produced by incorporating components used for QA into the steps where poor performance was observed [11]. It also improves some modules in favour of dealing with new entities which are not extractable by the entity recognizer employed.

3.1 An Overview of OntotripleQA

Figure 2 shows an overview of OntotripleQA. Given a missing value of an ontology instance, the corresponding question is constructed and is used for searching for answers with search engines. A set of documents are downloaded and examined in order to select the sentences which are assumed to be relevant to the question. The sentences are then analyzed and answer fragments are extracted from them. A scoring function is applied to the fragments in order to identify the most appropriate answers to the missing value.

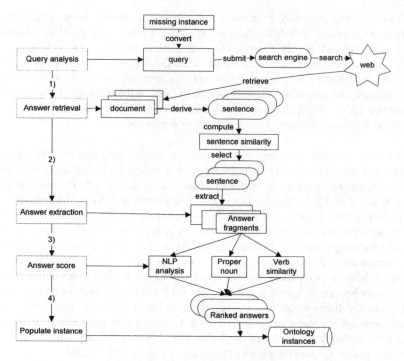

Fig.2. An overview of OntotripleQA

3.2 Relation Extraction

Information in an ontology is structured as 'class' and 'property', where the property is a binary link between two classes. For example, the relation 'produced' links the two entities, 'painter' and 'painting'. A relation (triple) is defined as a property having two entities as arguments, and it is the task of OntotripleQA to extract the missing values of the entities. Consider, the triple of 'place_of_birth'('Charles Anthony',?). OntotripleQA searches the Web to extract 'Paris' as an answer for the question about where 'Charles Anthony' was born. A corresponding question to each triple is created when the ontology is constructed. Since the triples in general can be translated into description-oriented questions, it is relatively straightforward. However, temporal features attached to the triples need to be considered. In particular, if 'Charles Anthony' is currently alive, the triple of 'name_of_group' (a group which a person is a member of) needs to be translated as both 'which group was 'Charles Anthony' a member of' and 'which group is 'Charles Anthony' a member of', whereas if he has died, only the latter is of use. Some triples depend on others in that the values of them are only available when the dependent triples are known. For example, 'date_of_ownership' is dependent on the 'name_of_owner' triple since it is reasonable to infer the first triple when we know who the owner is.

3.3 Query Analysis

Query analysis takes triples as input and transforms them into appropriate formats for the answer retrieval component. In Ontotriple, a query (i.e. artist's name and relation name) was submitted to search engines without any expansions (e.g. the additions of related terms) [11]. A central focus was given to interpret a given sentence with regard to its similarity to the target relation. Retrieved texts were then fully analysed with NLP techniques following syntactic, morphological, and named-entity analyses. Whereas this is simple to implement, some related documents might not be identified due to term difference to the query. This in particular affects the triples like "name_of_school" (i.e. institutions where a person studied) where the number of instances extracted is what matters. Based on the assumption that if a given query is converted into a format which resembles answer sentences it could maximize chances of extracting the missing triples, the transformed query is submitted to search engines to retrieve initial answer documents.

Typical QA systems manually define a table of expected answer types in response to query types. In OntotripleQA, the table is replaced with the ontology triples. We created the ontology based on the CIDOC CRM (Conceptual Reference Model) which defines artifacts and various concepts related to the cultural heritage domain [6]. Figure 3 shows a part of the ontology created. For example, a concept E84.Information_Carrier has two relations: P138F.represents and P52F.has_current_owner, where the former links to E21.Person, denoting a person depicted in an art object and the latter specifies a group of people (E74.Group) who owned the art object. The range and complexity of the ontology depend on the applications used or the roles for which the ontology is designed. For example, [17] conceptualizes not only hierarchical definitions but it also defines physical or geographical descriptions such as 'part-of' and 'is_part_of'. These descriptions are of use when comparing or merging two entities. In OntotripleQA, the ontology has direct access to an external lexical database (i.e. WordNet) to obtain such information. The direct access makes it easier for the ontology to get up-to-date information.

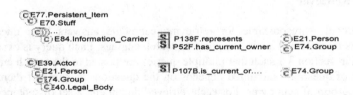

Fig. 3. A snapshot of the ontology created

Each question is expanded with additional synonyms obtained from the ontology and WordNet. One of the advantages of enriching the queries with terms which are deemed to occur in answer sentences is that not all the retrieved sentences are required to be analysed. That is, only sentences which are matched with the query terms are analysed. Currently, the query conversion and expansion are based on manually constructed rules:

- Convert question into a statement: we ignore auxiliary verb and substitute it with a main verb, e.g. "which school did Charles go to"=> Charles went to <Answer>

- Add synonyms based on WordNet: for each relation; a verb assumed to be representative is associated with a sense number as defined in WordNet. For example, "who is the owner of SunFlower" has 'own' verb with the sense 1, and it has synonyms of 'has' and 'possess' => <Answer> (own OR has OR possess) Sunflower.

- Add synonyms based on the ontology: 'own' verb asserts the state of having ownership according to WordNet definitions with no regard to how the ownership has been changed. It could be caused by purchasing, gift or transferring. In the ontology, however, this is fully described through the acquisition event which links an art object to an owner. WordNet specifies various ways of acquiring objects, e.g. buy, purchase, receive, and accept which are of use to expand the owner relation. For example, "who is the owner of SunFlower", is expanded <Answer> (purchased OR bought OR received OR inherited OR acquired OR got OR donated) Sunflower.

OntotripleQA refers to the ontology's hierarchical network when it needs to infer further information concerned with extracting the triples. For example, when it is not explicitly known if a given entity is of type "E74.Group" (any gathering of people), the sub-class "E40.Legal_Body" (any institution or a group of people) or the super-class "E21.Person can be alternatively used for matching the entity. Term difference between a class name in the ontology and a named-entity can occur since the ontology was based on the CRM which does not take into account terminologies used for the entity recognizer used. We refer to WordNet for matching the names in the ontology with the entities by looking up the class definitions. This process is not automatically performed yet since it is still difficult to convert the class definitions, including scope notes, into machine-readable formats without human intervention.

3.4 Answer Retrieval

Answer retrieval is responsible for retrieving candidate answers to a query by submitting its transformed query statement to search engines. Each query is expanded as described in section 3.3 such that multiple queries are posted to the search engines. The number of questions submitted depends on the questions as some of them may have a large group of synonyms. For each retrieved document, a set of sentences are derived. In order to select only the sentences which might contain answers to a given query, it is necessary to measure how well each sentence is related to the query. Similarity reflects the degree of term correlation, which quantifies the closeness of index terms that occur both in the query and in the sentence. It is computed by using the Cosine measurement [20] after converting the sentences into the revised TFIDF vector models adapted to a sentence-centric term-weighting method ($s\_term(s_i)$):

tf is the frequency of the term within the sentence (si), and idf is defined as

$\log(N/r)$ where, N is the total number of sentences in the retrieved documents, and r is the number of sentences in which the term occurs.

After ranking the sentences according to the similarity values, each sentence is examined to test whether it conforms to the ontological definitions (i.e. whether it contains the types of missing entities). The output of this module is a set of sentences which are assumed to contain the answers.

3.5 Answer Extraction and Answer Scoring

Answer extraction extracts answer fragments from the sentences selected in the answer retrieval module. Since most answers are in the form of a noun, some attention is given to proper nouns (e.g. person name or city name). Each fragment is categorized with the following criteria: 1) the location of the fragment in the sentence (i.e. after or before a main verb), 2) the availability of proper nouns, and 3) the similarity between a verb in the sentence in which the fragment is extracted and the verb associated with the relation.

A weighting is applied to the answer fragments in order to assign higher evaluation values to more reliable fragments. This is defined as:

$$w(f_{ij}) = \alpha * s\_term(s_i) + \beta * s\_nlp(s_i, f_j) + \gamma * s\_ne(f_j)$$

where, $w(f_{ij})$ is the weight of fragment (f_j) in the sentence (si), and $\alpha(0 \le \alpha \le 1), \beta(0 \le \beta \le 1), \gamma = (1-(\alpha+\beta))$ are confidence rates, and $s\_term(s_i)$ is derived using the method described in section 3.4. Also

$$s\_nlp(s_i, f_j) = vs(s_i) * loc(f_j)$$

where, $s\_nlp(s_i, f_j)$ is the similarity measured by NLP techniques, $vs(s_i)$ is the similarity between a verb in the sentence (si) and the verb associated with the relation sought-after, and $loc(f_j)$ specifies whether the answer fragment (f_j) is positioned after or before a main verb. If the two verbs are matched, $vs(s_i)$ is 1, otherwise the score is reduced (i.e. discount rate, $dc(vs(s_i))$ is 0.3). Similarly, if the fragment is followed by the main verb, and the answer is supposed to occur the right side of the verb, $loc(f_j)$ is 1, otherwise its value is reduced.

$$s\_ne(f_j) = \max(gate(f_j), wn(f_j), ps(f_j), gatewn(f_j))$$

where, $s\_ne(f_j)$ is the score assigned by considering the resources from which the fragment (f_j) is identified, i.e. the named entity recognizer (gate=0.6), WordNet (wn=0.4), part-of-speech tag (ps=0.2), or both by gate and wn (gatewn=0.8). A maximum value from among the four options is considered.

Counting the number of candidate answer occurrences aims to counteract the Web redundancy which implies that similar information is stated in a variety of ways and repeated in different documents such that a single instance of an answer may not provide sufficient justification of relevance. For example, without considering further context, the following both sentences are assumed to contain valid answers to the query of the date when "Vincent Willem van Gogh" was born: *"Vincent Willem van Gogh is born on March 30, 1853, in Zundert"*, *"Theo's son, Vincent Willem van Gogh, is born in January 1890"*. In fact, the answer is in the first sentence since "Gogh" in the second sentence refers to the nephew of "Vincent Willem van Gogh". Given a list of scored answers, similar answers are grouped together and the weighting is summarized over one distinctive answer.

4   Experimentation

This experiment tests the effectiveness of the proposed approach in extracting missing values of the ontology instances from the Web documents. It is evaluated with respect to its capability to correctly rank candidate answer relations such that the most appropriate relation can be extracted. The scoring function, as described in section 3.5, arranges the answers in the order of relevance to a given missing relation and the performance of OntotripleQA is measured by the proportion of the correctly first ranked relations to the total number of correct relations. The contribution of the paper is summarised thus. OntotripleQA is able to extract correct relations when no named entities are derivable by considering other clues related to the relations. It is efficient and fast since it filters out sentences which are evaluated to be less relevant to the query measured by a simple similarity method (i.e. Cosine similarity). In addition, OntotripleQA facilitates the retrieval of more relevant answers by using QA techniques such as the conversion of the missing relations into a query which resembles the statement from which the relations can be easily extracted.

4.1 Dataset

A total of 12 relations were tested with one artist name (i.e. 'Vincent Willem van Gogh') and the top 10 documents were retrieved and downloaded from the 'Google' search engine. As described in section 3.3, corresponding questions for each relation were constructed and expanded with synonyms according to WordNet and the ontology hierarchies. In addition, each question converted is formatted following the search syntax of 'Google'. For example, the submitted query to 'Google' for the "date_of_birth" is *Vincent Willem van Gogh +was born OR given_birth OR delivered*. Since the questions here were converted from the triples in the ontology specifications, most of them are fact-based and have short-length (i.e. four words on average). Table 1 shows the details of the dataset. For the relations concerning "school" and "work", multiple answers are expected since a person can attend or work in more than one place and for several organizations.

Table 1: The details of dataset

Relation	A converted question	An example of an answer
Date_of_birth	When was Vincent Willem van Gogh born	30 March 1853
Place_of_birth	Where was Vincent Willem van Gogh born	Groot-Zundert
Date_of_death	When did Vincent Willem van Gogh die	29 July 1890
Place_of_death	Where did Vincent Willem van Gogh die	Paris
Name_of_father	Who was Vincent Willem van Gogh's father	Theodorous van Gogh
Name_of_mother	Who was Vincent Willem van Gogh's mother	Anna Cornelia Carbentus
Name_of_school	What school did Vincent Willem van Gogh attend	Art academy
Date_of_school	When did Vincent Willem van Gogh attend school	1885
Place_of_school	Where did Vincent Willem van Gogh attend school	Antwerp
Name_of_work	What did Vincent Willem van Gogh work for	Art dealer, Goupil & Co
Date_of_work	When did Vincent Willem van Gogh work	1869
Place_of_work	Where did Vincent Willem van Gogh work	Hague

4.2. Results

Table 2 shows the experimental results. In order to examine the impact of various similarity factors on the scoring function, Table 2 also shows three different performance results. Performance A is set as: $\alpha = 0.3$, $\beta = 0.5$, $\gamma = 0.2$, $dc(vs) = 0.3$, $dc(loc) = 0.3$. For performance B, the settings are: $\alpha = 0.5$, $\beta = 0.3$, $\gamma = 0.2$, $dc(vs) = 0.7$, $dc(loc) = 0.7$. Performance C is set as: $\alpha = 0.3$, $\beta = 0.2$, $\gamma = 0.5$, $dc(vs) = 0.5$, $dc(loc) = 0.5$. In addition, the performance of a baseline which extracts relations by considering the similarity between a verb in a given sentence and the verb associated with the relation is given as in the baseline Ontotriple [11].

Table 2: The experimental results

Relation	Performance A	Performance B	Performance C	Baseline
Date_of_birth	100%	100%	100%	100%
Place_of_birth	100%	100%	100%	100%
Date_of_death	100%	50%	50%	100%
Place_of_death	50%	50%	100%	0
Name_of_father	50%	33%	33%	0
Name_of_mother	50%	33%	33%	0
Name_of_school	50%	33%	50%	50%
Date_of_school	100%	50%	100%	50%
Place_of_school	50%	50%	50%	50%
Name_of_work	66%	33%	33%	33%
Date_of_work	66%	33%	66%	33%
Place_of_work	33%	33%	33%	33%
Average	*68%*	*50%*	*62%*	*42%*

Overall, performance A obtained the highest accuracy as shown in table 2, although it did not correctly rank the answers in the first position for some relations. That is, it was only able to rank the right answer in the second position for the relations of "place_of_death", "name_of_father" and "name_of_mother" (i.e. 50%). We examined the Web pages retrieved in order to investigate why these relations were hard to extract and discovered that they were only mentioned in a small number of documents and the information was only indirectly implied. For example, only 2 among 10 pages mentioned the names of father and mother, and both of them stated the information in the sentence "*His father, Theodorus van Gogh, his mother, Anna Carbentus, and his brother all lived in Zundert*", in which it is rather difficult to extract "Theodorus van Gogh" as the father's name.

It is hard to derive any strong conclusions regarding how well the proposed approach could be applied to other domains since the tested dataset was small. However, close examination of the results reveals that some correct answers were not extractable by the entity recognizer since the recognizer has a limited coverage of entities. It implies that other assessments such as the location of the answer fragments in a given sentence would be of use when the recognizer fails to identify answers.

5   Conclusions and Future Work

We have presented an overview of OntotripleQA which is the application of question-answering techniques to the task of extracting ontological triples from Web documents. Triples are the relational descriptions between two identified entities, and incomplete triples can occur when one of the entities is missing. Relation extraction systems are dependent on the availability of correctly named entities in that mislabelled entities can decrease the number of relations correctly identified. This observation led us to take into account the techniques used by QA which in general take identified named entities as one of the assessments, implying that even though entities matching answers are not available, it is still possible to obtain the answers through other evaluations. The experimental results as described in section 4.2 demonstrated that OntotripleQA obtained on average 26% higher performance compared to that of the baseline approach.

OntotripleQA assumes the existence of pre-defined classifications for questions and the corresponding answer types since these can be inferred from the ontology. When a new triple is added, a question is created manually and it initiates OntotripleQA to look for answers. Compared to the questions explored in other QA systems, it only deals with fact-oriented question types since most triples in the ontology are the descriptions between two entities. Other types include definition (e.g. what are polymers?) or questions that ask for a list of items (e.g. Name 6 films in which Jude Law acted). Whether or not OntotripleQA needs to expand its coverage to deal with these types of questions depends on the ontology used. Whereas it was rather straightforward to convert the ontology triple into a natural language question, an automatic transformation would be advantageous and is necessary if the conversion relies on an end-user whose NLP expertise is low.

Verifying extracted answers before entering them into the ontology is necessary in order not to store false or unconfirmed data. Anyone can publish anything on the Web and no Web standards exist to ensure content accuracy. In addition, expert reviews for content justification are hardly available. As such, the quality of data varies significantly on the Web. Authority of information sources, for example, the idea that information from prestigious organisations is more reliable than that from a young child, can be used to help with such verification.

The investigation of inter-dependency between the triples is of interest for future study. If some triples tend to be extracted from the same sentences or from the same documents, we can assume that those triples have certain levels of association which OntotripleQA could make use of when it searches the Web.

Acknowledgement

The authors wish to thank the EU for support through the SCULPTEUR project under grant number IST-2001-35372. They are also grateful to their collaborators on the project for many useful discussions, use of data and valuable help and advice.

References

[1] Aitken, J. S.: Learning information extraction rules: An inductive logic programming approach. In Proc. of European Conf. on Artificial Intelligence ECAI France (2002) 335-359

[2] Aone, C., Halverson, L., Hampton, T., Ramos-Santacruz, M.: SRA: Description of the IE system used for MUC-7 MUC-7 (1998)

[3] Aone, C., Ramos-Santacruz, M.: REES: A Large-Scale Relation and Event Extraction System, In Proc. of the 6th Applied Natural Language Processing Conf. U.S.A (2000) 76-83

[4] Clarke, C.L.A., Cormack, G. V., Kemkes, G., Laszlo, M., Lynam, T. R., Terra, E. L., Tilker, P.L.: Statistical Selection of Exact Answers. In Proc. Text Retrieval Con. (TREC) (2002)

[5] Ciravegna, F.: Adaptive Information Extraction from Text by Rule Induction and Generalisation. In Proc. 17th Int. Joint Conf. on Artificial Intelligence Seattle (2001)

[6] Crofts, N., Doerr M., Gill, T: The CIDOC Conceptual Reference Model: A standard for communicating cultural contents. Technical papers from CIDOC CRM, available at http://cidoc.ics.forth.gr/docs/martin_a_2003_comm_cul_cont.htm (2003)

[7] Cunningham, H., Maynard, D., Bontcheva, K., and Tablan, V.: GATE: a framework and graphical development environment for robust NLP tools and applications. In Proc. of the 40th Anniversary Meeting of the Association for Computational Linguistics Philadelphia USA (2002) 168-175

[8] Freitag, D.: Information Extraction from HTML: Application of a General Machine Learning Approach. In Proc. of AAAI 98, (1998) 517-523

[9] Hermjakob, U., Echihabi, A., Marcu, D.: Natural Language based Reformulation Resource and Web Exploitation for Question Answering. In Proc. of the Text Retrieval Con. (TREC) (2002)

[10] Kim, S., Alani, H., Hall, W., Lewis, P.H., Millard, D.E., Shadbolt, N.R., Weal, M. W.: Artequakt: Generating Tailored Biographies with Automatically Annotated Fragments from the Web. In Proc. of the Workshop on the Semantic Authoring, Annotation & Knowledge Markup in the European Conf. on Artificial Intelligence France (2002) 1-6

[11] Kim, S., Lewis, P., Martinez, K.: The impact of enriching linguistic annotation on the performance of extracting relation triples. In Proc. of Conf. on Intelligent Text Processing and Computational Linguistics Korea (2004) 547-558

[12] Kwok, C. C., Etzioni, O., Weld, D. S.: Scaling Question Answering to the Web. In Proc. of the 10th Int. Conf. on World Wide Web (2001)

166   S. Kim et al.

[13] Litkowski, K.C.: Question-Answering Using Semantic Relation Triples. In Proc. of the 8th Text Retrieval Conf. (TREC-8) (1999) 349-356
[14] Magniti, B., Negri, M., Prevete, R., Tanev, H.: Mining Knowledge from Repeated Co-occurrences: DIOGENE. In Proc. of the Text Retrieval Con. (TREC) (2002)
[15] Marsh, E., Perzanowski, D.: MUC-7 Evaluation of IE Technology: Overview of Results, available at http://www.itl.nist.gov/iaui/894.02/related_projects/muc/index.html (1998)
[16] Miller, G.A., Beckwith, R. , Fellbaum, C., Gross, D. ., Miller, K.: Introduction to wordnet: An on-line lexical database. Technical report University of Princeton U.S.A. (1993)
[17] Nirenburg, S., McShane, M., Beale, S.: Enhancing Recall in Information Extraction through Ontological Semantics. In Proc. of Workshop on Ontologies and Information Extraction conjunction with The Semantic Web and Language Technology Romania (2003)
[18] Nyberg, E., Mitamura, T., Carbonnell, J., Callan, J., Collins-Thompson, K., Czuba, K., Duggan, K., Hiyakumoto, L., Hu, N., Huang, Y., Ko, J. et al.: The JAVELIN Question-Answering System at TREC Carnegie Mellon University In Proc. of the Text Retrieval Con. (TREC) (2002)
[19] Roth, D. , Yih, W. T.: Probabilistic reasoning for entity & relation recognition. In Proc. of the 19th Int. Conf. on Computational Intelligence (2002)
[20] Salton, G., Lesk, M. E.: Computer Evaluation of Indexing and Text Processing, Salton, G. (Ed.) In the Smart Retrieval System-Experiment in Automatic Document Processing Prentice-Hall (1971)
[21] Sekine, S., Grishman, R.: A corpus-based probabilistic grammar with only two non-terminals. In. Proc. of the 1st International Workshop on Multimedia annotation Japan (2001)
[22] Voorhess, E. M: Overview of the TREC 2002 Question Answering Track. In Proc. of the Text Retrieval Con. (TREC) (2002)

The SCAM Framework: Helping Semantic Web Applications to Store and Access Metadata

Matthias Palmér, Ambjörn Naeve, and Fredrik Paulsson

KMR group at CID/KTH (Royal Institute of Technology)
Lindstedtsvägen 5
100 44 Stockholm, Sweden
{matthias,amb,frepa}@nada.kth.se

Abstract. In this paper we discuss the design of the SCAM framework, which aims to simplify the storage and access of metadata for a variety of different applications that can be built on top of it. A basic design principle of SCAM is the aggregation of metadata into two kinds of sets of different granularity (SCAM records and SCAM contexts). These sets correspond to the typical access needs of an application with regard to metadata, and they constitute the foundation upon which access control is provided.

1 Introduction

The web of today is by far the largest source of information ever created by man. However, the information about this information, its metadata, is not well-structured, which leads to the well-known difficulties in finding what one is looking for. The semantic web is an international effort to improve this situation by providing machine-interpretable expressions for relations between and statements about a variety of resources.

However, the strength of the semantic web approach will not be fully apparent until all resource producers – large as well as small – will express information about these resources as a natural part of the creation process. In order for this to happen, they must be stimulated to supply the neccessary information, which requires not only good technology but also convenient and user-friendly metadata applications that cater to existing needs.

A necessary requirement for such applications is a good metadata storage system, where metadata is accessed, i.e. created, stored, retrieved and updated. The kind of access that is provided has an important impact on the simplicity and the efficiency of the application. Moreover, the kind of access that would be most helpful for an application depends on the choice and usage of metadata, which in turn is a consequence of the purpose of the application. Hence, when defining a framework that will support many different applications the granularity of access cannot be tied to a specific metadata standard.

There are many storage systems for semantic web metadata, for instance Sesame [11], RDFSuite [6] and Redland [9]. These systems [8] focus on supporting

J. Davies et al. (Eds.): ESWS 2004, LNCS 3053, pp. 167–181, 2004.

RDF Schema [10], on effective query capabilities, inference, as well as on how to store large quantities of metadata. However, as described in section 3.1 there are several aspects of metadata access that these systems do not address.

In this paper we describe the design of the *Standardized Contextualized Access to Metadata(SCAM)*[1] *framework* that provides a basis upon which different applications can be built [23]. The SCAM framework is developed as an open source project and it supports applications in storing and accessing metadata. The design of SCAM is derived mainly from the demands of applications such as archives and personal portfolios. Most prominently, SCAM provides access to sets of semantic web metadata, i.e. not to individual triples but to *sets* of triples. Like other storage systems, SCAM also provides search capabilities. To help applications protect the integrity of the metadata, basic access control is provided.

In Section 2, we briefly discuss the SCAM framework from a more technical perspective in order to provide a setting for the specific design issues discussed in this paper. In Section 3 we look at the basic system design of SCAM, starting by listing the requirements behind it. In Section 4, the issue of metametadata is treated. In Section 5, we present two specific applications that have been built upon SCAM and how they make use of the functionality. Finally, in Section 6 we provide a conclusion and future work.

2   The SCAM Framework

In this section we will see how the SCAM framework is implemented as a J2EE[2] application using the JBoss[3] platform. There is documentation on its homepage[4] where more technical details can be found. SCAM can be divided into the repository, the metadata storage and the middleware, where the application logic is placed.

2.1   Repository

The repository relies on Jena2 [3] as a triple store, which in turn connects to various Relational Database back-ends. The following five Enterprise Java Beans (EJB) provide all the functionality of the repository.

- **AdministerBean – supports the administration of SCAM.** Through this bean users, groups (see Section 3.5) and containers for metadata are administered.
- **StoreBean – supports the access to metadata sets.** The access to metadata records and containers of records are discussed in detail in Section 3.3 and 3.4.

---

[1] The previous full name of SCAM, *Standardized Content Archiving Management* wich occurs in previous publications, was changed since it was slightly misleading.

[2] Java 2 Platform, Enterprise Edition (J2EE).

[3] JBoss is an application server http://www.jboss.org/index.html

[4] http://scam.sourceforge.net

- **SearchBean – supports the querying of metadata sets** The query
  capabilities are discussed in Section 3.6.
- **ManifestBean – supports the organization of resources** Many applications need to provide hierarchical views of resources. We have chosen
  to implement support for a specific kind of organization, the metadata part
  of IMS Content Packaging [2], mainly because of its wide acceptance in the
  learning community. To be able to store the IMS content packaging metadata
  within SCAM, we have implemented a RDF-binding for it.
- **ContentBean – supports the storage of content** The ContentBean
  provides some useful functionality for handling content together with its associated metadata. With *content* we mean only those digital representations
  of resources that are administered within SCAM. Using the ContentBean, a
  simplified WebDAV [15] has been implemented, where the content resources
  are accessed in accordance with the IMS Content Packaging hierarchy described above.

2.2 Middleware

The main purpose of the middleware is to provide HTTP access to the repository.
In fact, it is suitable to consider SCAM as a Model View Controller (MVC) application framework [24], where the repository is the model and the middleware
provides the view and controller. The configurable controller that SCAM provides is somewhat similar to the Struts framework[5]. We are considering moving
towards a more widely spread solution such as Struts or more recent initiatives
such as JavaServer Faces[6]. The view has to be defined by individual applications that build on SCAM by using JavaServer Pages and Taglibs[7]. Some *utility*
taglibs are provided in order to simplify the management of metadata. One of
the utility taglibs is a *metadata form generator*. The forms can be configured to
be either presentations or editors for metadata – according to a specific application profile. This *configurable form system* is called SHAME[8], and is briefly
discussed in [13]. A more detailed report on the SHAME system is in progress.

Stand-alone applications work directly against the repository, and hence ignore the middleware altogether. Here we will not consider the middleware further. We refer to the SCAM homepage for its documentation.

3 Basic System Design

In this section we will discuss what constitutes the basic design of the framework, i.e. the management of metadata. This corresponds to AdministerBean,

---

[5] A framework for building java web applications can be found at
  http://jakarta.apache.org/struts
[6] http://java.sun.com/j2ee/javaserverfaces
[7] Taglibs are a part of the JavaServer Pages, which can be found at
  http://java.sun.com/products/jsp
[8] Standardized Hyper-Adaptable Metadata Editor

StoreBean and SearchBean in the repository part of SCAM. We will begin by listing the requirements. Each requirement will then be analyzed, together with the corresponding design decisions.

3.1 Functional Requirements

Since the SCAM system is a framework upon which several different types of applications can be built, the design should support, but not be limited to, individual applications. However, the requirements that motivate the design have been inspired by practical needs, most prominently by the needs of archiving and personal portfolio applications. In such applications many users express metadata around individual resources in a web-like environment. The metadata is then provided through various interfaces, typically via exploration or search. Furthermore, the metadata is allowed to change often, not only updated but entirely new metadata constructs are allowed to be added on the fly.

The six requirements below will be treated in the following subsections.

1. SCAM should be independent of application profiles, i.e. not be limited to a set of metadata elements adapted to the needs of a specific community.
2. SCAM should support the ability to work with metadata records, i.e. to work with metadata centered around individual resources.
3. SCAM should support the administration and separation of metadata between different contexts. Specifically, contexts should:
   (a) provide simple mechanisms for exchanging metadata with other systems, e.g. another SCAM system, another metadata management system, an external storage system.
   (b) allow the expression of different opinions that if kept together would be inconsistent.
4. SCAM should support access control of both metadata records and contexts.
5. SCAM should provide search capabilities of metadata records.
6. SCAM should provide support for vocabularies.

Before continuing let us consider some existing RDF stores with respect to these requirements. RDFSuite [6] fails to fulfill 1 (since it can only store statements if there is a schema), as well as 2, 3 and 4 (since there is only one RDF model to upload statements into), but it does manage 5. Redland [9], Sesame [11] and Jena[3] fulfill 1, 3, and 5 more or less directly. Since SCAM builds on Jena and fulfills 2, 4 and to some extent 6 via conventions and algorithms, SCAM could in principle be built on top of either Sesame or Redland. This would probably result in a similar amount of work.

3.2 Independence of Application Profiles

The concept of an application profile has been developed and clarified over time. We have chosen to follow the definition in [12]:

"An application profile is an assemblage of metadata elements selected from one or more metadata schemas and combined in a compound schema. Application profiles provide the means to express principles of modularity and extensibility. The purpose of an application profile is to adapt or combine existing schemas into a package that is tailored to the functional requirements of a particular application, while retaining interoperability with the original base schemas. Part of such an adaptation may include the elaboration of local metadata elements that have importance in a given community or organization, but which are not expected to be important in a wider context."

We think that the use of the expression "metadata schema" is somewhat too general for our discussion around application profiles. Therefore, from now on, we will use the more narrow expression *metadata standard*, which will refer only to metadata schemas with well defined sets of metadata elements – as introduced by specific standardization bodies. Two examples of metadata standards are Dublin Core [5] and IEEE/LOM [17]. An example of an application profile is CanCore [1], which uses metadata elements from the metadata standard IEEE/LOM.

Since the intention with SCAM is to be independent of application profiles, which may collect metadata elements from several metadata standards, we argue that SCAM should be independent of metadata standards as well. This is not only a technical consequence, but reflects our firm belief in the benefits of a multitude of independently developed metadata standards and application profiles covering different needs. It is not an option to wait for this diversity to be incorporated as extensions to one fundamental metadata standard. Hence, choosing any specific metadata standard today (or at any specific point in time) would limit the expressibility of the applications built upon SCAM.

In our design of SCAM, we have discarded the approach to support several metadata standards separately, and more specific application profiles on top of those, since this will either create numerous problems with incomplete metadata records or result in a "combinatorial explosion" of the many translations between them.

Instead we have chosen a solution offered by semantic web technology, more specifically by RDF(S) [16] [10], which provides a common meta-model, within which metadata elements – and hence metadata standards – can be expressed with well defined syntax and semantics. The choice of RDF is perhaps best motivated when it comes to defining application profiles in terms of combinations and reuse of bits and pieces from previously existing application profiles and metadata standards. This is supported by the fact that the RDF-bindings of major metadata standards – such as e.g. IEEE/LOM and Dublin Core – are specifically designed in order to allow such combinations and reuse of their constituent parts.

Today there already exists RDF bindings of Dublin Core and vCard and the RDF binding[20] of IEEE/LOM is nearly finished. These three metadata standards have provided the basic building blocks from which we have constructed the various application profiles on top of SCAM. When these "standard building blocks" have been unable to provide sufficient expressive power, we have invented new metadata constructs or – if possible – extended the existing ones via the RDF vocabulary description language (RDFS).

3.3   SCAM Records

We have defined SCAM records so they are suitable for managing the metadata of a single resource, independently of which application profile that is used. With "manage" we here mean create, update, store, retrieve or present an entire metadata record. A prerequisite requirement has been that the granularity of a SCAM record should be comparable to that of the document-centric approach for exchanging metadata records of a fixed application profile.

A SCAM record is defined to be the *anonymous closure* of a RDF graph computed from a given non-anonymous RDF resource. The anonymous closure is computed by following chains in the natural direction, from subject to object, of statements until a non-anonymous RDF resource or RDF Literal is found. Furthermore, each anonymous resource is not allowed to occur in more than one SCAM record. Any anonymous resource that fails to follow this requirement is duplicated when imported into SCAM. Within a RDF graph, a SCAM record is uniquely identified by the URI-reference of the non-anonymous RDF resource from which the anonymous closure is computed.

SCAM records coincide – except with respect to reifications – with Concise Bounded Resource Descriptions as defined in URIQA[9].

URIQA also defines a retrieval mechanism together for Concise Bounded Resource Descriptions, forcing them to always be retrieved from an authoritative server, i.e. the server specified by the host part of the resource's URI-reference. This approach does only allow one set of metadata for a specific resource, clearly conflicting with the idea of a metadata ecosystem as presented in [21]. Hence, even though we could implement the URIQA protocol on top of SCAM, this is not a preferred way to go, since it would only allow access to a subset of all SCAM records on a given server.

In fact we have chosen not to commit SCAM to a specific protocol for accessing SCAM records since there is no mature standards for this yet. We are keeping a close watch on initiatives such as URIQA, the RDF WebAPI in Joseki [4] and the metadata retrieval support in WebDAV [15].

These SCAM records have several useful properties:

1. In terms of RDF statements, SCAM records are always well-defined and disjoint, which avoids problems when updating, removing etc.
2. SCAM records connect the administration of metadata constructs with things that have a public identifier. This means that things that have no identifier cannot be administered on their own.
3. SCAM records with different identifiers can co-exist in the same RDF graph.
4. RDF query engines need not respect the borders of SCAM records, which allows more advanced queries.

---

[9] The URI Query Agent Model, see http://sw.nokia.com/uriqa/URIQA.html

5. SCAM records have a granularity for management that matches most application profiles, such as LOM, Dublin Core etc.

A drawback of SCAM records is that there are RDF graphs that aren't accessible or expressible. For example, a statement with an anonymous resource as subject that does not occur anywhere else and with a non-anonymous resource as object cannot be reached through SCAM records. There are also statements – potentially small graphs – that consist solely of anonymous RDF resources and RDF literals that simply have no natural connections to any SCAM records.

From a more practical perspective, statements that might be interesting to include in a SCAM record include anonymous reifications, as a way to express metametadata about individual statements. See Section 4 for a more thorough discussion of reifications and metametadata.

3.4   SCAM Contexts

When administrating a SCAM system, it is often not enough to work on the level of SCAM records, simply because they are of too small granularity. For example, many common administrative operations would involve hundreds or thousands of SCAM records. Hence, we introduce a *SCAM context* to denote a set of SCAM records that somehow belong together. Exactly which SCAM records that belong together depends on the application at hand.

Another requirement on SCAM is to allow several SCAM records for the same resource. We will call such SCAM records *siblings*. For example, an application serving many users may contain several different opinions about the same resource; opinions that will have to be kept separate if metametadata about their origin are to be preserved, e.g. access rights, author etc. To be able to refer to individual siblings, we need – apart from the resource – some kind of marker to distinguish them.

Now, with knowledge about SCAM records, siblings and SCAM contexts, let us take a closer look at how we actually store them as RDF graphs in SCAM. We have considered three basic approaches:

1. Keep all SCAM records together in one RDF graph and use some markers telling what SCAM contexts they belong to.
2. Keep all SCAM records belonging to the same SCAM context together in one RDF graph.
3. Keep every SCAM record in a separate RDF graph and use some marker to tell what SCAM contexts that the SCAM record belongs to.

The first approach is immediately disqualified since it does not allow siblings. The second approach allows siblings but forces them to be in separate SCAM context. Consequently, all SCAM records are uniquely identified within a SCAM context, no separate marker is needed. The last approach opens up for having several siblings within a single SCAM context. A separate marker is needed to distinguish siblings.

We have chosen the second approach, where SCAM contexts contain only one sibling for a single resource. This has the advantage of being simple and no extra marker is needed. See Figure 1 for a illustration of how SCAM contexts and SCAM records relate. On the other hand it is clear that this choice is a limitation on the use of siblings in SCAM contexts. However, without this limitation a SCAM context cannot always be collected into a single RDF graph. The reason is that if you want to preserve the integrity of siblings in a single RDF graph, triples have to be reified and be 'owned' by one or several SCAM contexts. To be 'owned' would have to be expressed on the reifications by some property that is yet to be invented. Hence, we would end up with a situation where import and export of metadata would either be *non standardized* – via ownership on reifications – or more *complicated* – several RDF graphs would represent a single SCAM context.

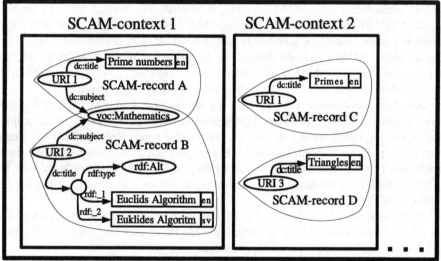

Fig. 1. A SCAM repository has SCAM contexts as separate RDF graphs, which are further divided via the anonymous closure algorithm into SCAM records. *SCAM records A* and *C* are siblings since they both express metadata for a resource identified via the URI reference *URI1*.

3.5   Access Control Lists

SCAM provides access control on all SCAM records. The access control is focused on the access to the metadata in the SCAM record and, if present, to the resources that are described therein. We use a form of Access Control Lists (ACL) for describing the rights. Our solution is inspired by – but not derived from – ACLs in file systems such as NTFS[10], AFS[11] etc. In the future we will take a closer look at the access control protocol specified by WebDAV [15] and initiatives for expressing ACLs in RDF such as W3C ACLs[12].

The basic functionality of an Access Control List is simple. It provides a list of *principals*, i.e. users or roles, paired with intended rights. For SCAM the access control list states the access rights and user privileges only in terms of right to read and/or write. Other rights might be considered, e.g. the right to lock, change metametadata etc. Due to performance and complexity reasons, in the current representation there is no negation of permissions.

Currently SCAM only supports groups for roles. The groups in SCAM can be defined by how they relate to the users:

1. Every user belongs to a set of groups.
2. Groups are defined by which users they contain, no empty groups are allowed, which means that you have to define some users before you introduce the groups they should belong to.
3. Groups cannot be defined in terms of other groups.

Even though SCAM currently is limited to groups, the representation of the ACLs could as well be used for expressing things like Role-Based Access Control (RBAC) as defined in [14]. See [7] for a comparison between RBAC and the more basic approach of ACLs that we have chosen for SCAM. RBAC was not chosen for SCAM, since it was deemed unnecessarily complicated for our current needs. More specifically:

1. It was required that access should be possible to grant to individual users without creating a role for every user.
2. It was not required to support the change between sessions of roles assigned to a user. For example, the ability of the same user to log in as an administrator or a regular user depending on the situation was not a requirement.

Another – somewhat independent – restriction is that a SCAM context must always be "owned" by a principal, i.e. a user or a group. A user will have all permissions on all SCAM records in a SCAM context, if either the user is the owner of that context, or the owner is a group and the user belongs to that group. Furthermore, there are two principals in SCAM who have special meaning, the "Administrator" and the "Guest". The group Administrator always overrides the access control, which means that all users in that group has the permission to perform "everything". A Guest is a fictional principal that is used by unauthenticated users. If the Guest is included in an ACL it means that everyone has the given permission.

Since the SCAM records are represented in RDF, we have chosen to express the ACLs in RDF as well. Figure 2 shows the RDF structure of an ACL in SCAM.

---

[10] NTFS is the Windows NT file system developed by Microsoft.
[11] Andrew File System is a distributed file system developed at Carnegie-Mellon University.
[12] http://www.w3.org/2001/04/20-ACLs

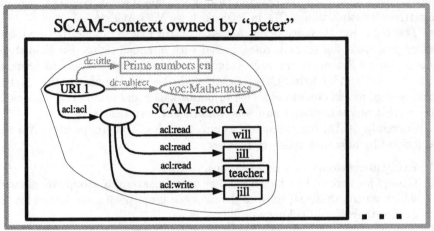

Fig. 2. A user named *peter* is the owner of the SCAM context and consequently has full access rights to the SCAM records within it. All the other principals e.g. *will, jill* and *teacher* have read-access, in addition *jill* also has write-access.

The ACL RDF graph is expressed via an *anonymous resource*, which allows it to be automatically included into the corresponding SCAM record. The semantics of pointing to the ACL directly from the resource is somewhat dubious (see our discussion on metametadata in Section 4).

3.6   Queries

In order to support queries against metadata, we had to make some "strategic decisions" concerning the following two questions:

1. Against what portions of metadata should the queries be allowed to execute?
2. What query languages and result types should be supported?

In response to the first question, we have chosen to allow queries to be executed against *one* SCAM context at a time – or *all* SCAM contexts *at once*. To search against several – but not all – SCAM contexts at once is not supported (due to technical limitations that we expect to be able to overcome soon). Another technical limitation has forced us to skip the check for access restrictions expressed in the ACLs when executing the search.

In response to the second question, we have chosen to support simple free-text search, RDQL [18] and QEL [22].

The two first query languages are motivated by the fact that typical applications provide two levels of search, first simple free-text search and second, a more advanced search on specific metadata elements. With free-text search we mean sub-string matching of literals – disregarding which metadata elements they belong to. Strictly speaking, free-text search does not require a special treatment, since it can be expressed in the other query languages, rather it is provided for simplicity and efficiency reasons. Until recently, advanced search has been achieved through the use of RDQL, a rather restricted SQL-like language that nevertheless is expressive enough to perform most simple tasks. The reason for supporting RDQL is because it is the query language supported by Jena2, which is the RDF API we have used internally. QEL is a very powerful datalog-like language that is part of the Edutella project [19] which aims to provide a peer to peer network where semantic web metadata can be searched for. The QEL language is quite powerful, it provides conjunction, disjunction, rules, outer join, built in predicates – linear and general recursion. The implementation that SCAM uses does not yet support linear and general recursion.

With support for QEL, metadata in individual SCAM repositories can be made searchable over Edutella and consequently discovered by people without previous knowledge of the systems location. We foresee that QEL will to some extent replace RDQL for doing local searches as well.

3.7 Support for Vocabularies

Most applications make use of vocabularies. In many cases queries and graphical user interfaces require the presence of such vocabularies in order to work as expected. The obvious design, to keep vocabularies together with other metadata, is seldom preferable since it complicates administration and update. SCAM contexts dedicated for managing one or several vocabularies is probably a better alternative. A necessary complication is that the query engines would somehow have to be aware of this. For expressing vocabularies, in most cases RDF Vocabulary Description Language (RDF Schema) is sufficient.

In order to understand class and property hierarchies, support for inference should be added. Currently we have satisfied such needs by forward chaining (i.e. calculating and storing implicit triples) in copies of SCAM contexts. The vocabularies have been merged into these copies, and all queries are then executed against them. This is a temporary design that we are investigating alternatives for.

4   Support for Metametadata

Metadata is data about data, consequently, metametadata is data about metadata. E.g. the date when a SCAM record was created or modified, access control lists controlling the access to a SCAM record or an entire SCAM context.

In RDF there is a basic mechanism for creating metametadata called *reification*. A reification is a resource that is treated as a placeholder for a statement. Statements around a reification are implicitly statements around the statement that has been reified. Furthermore, reified statements can be collected into collections, which provide handles for expressing statements on sets of other statements without repeating them. In principle, reification is very precise – since it allows you to express statements about any set of statements. Unfortunately, from a more practical perspective it is a rather clumsy mechanism, especially if the most common case is to express statements about all the statements in a RDF graph. (This adds at least 4 new statements for each statement to be reified).

In our case, we would like to express metametadata around all statements within every SCAM record. Currently, we express the metametadata directly on the resource identifying the SCAM record. We realize that the semantics of such statements may be wrong, and that they may conflict with the chosen application profile. Lets consider two problematic situations:

1. Metametadata such as the date when a SCAM record was created uses the Dublin-Core-created property directly attached on the resource. The semantics – as expressed by Dublin Core – says that the resource itself was created at the specific date, not – as we intended – the SCAM record.
2. Applications – building on SCAM – that manage both metadata and data, incorrectly let the ACLs apply to the data as well. Unfortunately, the current design of ACLs carries with it the natural interpretation that they should apply to the data (content) – and not to the metadata (SCAM record) as defined. Hence, the ACLs presently used for SCAM records are in the way for the data-access-controlling ACLs.

Both these situations could be remedied by defining new properties with the correct semantics. However, this would not allow reuse of existing standardized metadata elements on the metametadata level.

Instead, we are redesigning SCAM so that metametadata properties apply to an intermediate anonymous resource pointed to via a 'metametadata' property from the resource identifying the SCAM record. Consequently, ACLs can be provided on both the metadata and the resource (the latter only when the resource represents some content that is within the control of the SCAM content extension system). See Figure 3 for an illustration.

If there is a need to express metametadata at a higher granularity level, there are several possible solutions. For example, a specific SCAM context can be used in order to express metametadata on SCAM contexts.

At the other end of the scale, there might be a need for more fine-grained metametadata. It is quite easy to imagine scenarios where there is a need for metametadata on specific parts of the SCAM record. For example, the Dublin Core description property could in some situations need a date of modification or even a complete version history with information about who the changes was made by.

In this case the right way to go is probably to use reification directly since the alternative, to invent specific metadata constructs where metametadata is integrated with the metadata, has as a consequence that established metadata standards such as Dublin Core and IEEE / LOM cannot be used.

For this to be reasonably efficient, especially in combination with the special case of version history, there would have to exist specific support in SCAM, something that has yet to become a priority.

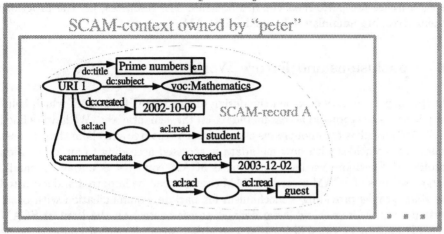

Fig. 3. The resource, which can be thought of as a file, has metadata that says that it is readable by all students, was created "2002-10-09", is about "mathematics" and has a title that reads "Prime numbers". The metametadata on the other hand says that the metadata was created "2003-12-02 and is readable by everyone.

5 Applications

There are currently about ten different applications that have been built upon SCAM[13]. For example, the *SCAM portfolio* provides storage of metadata on resources such as web resources, uploaded files, traditional books or abstract ideas. The resources can be organized into folders that can be shared with others. Just as SCAM itself, the SCAM portfolio is not bound to a specific application profile. Instead there is a configurable web user interface (SHAME) mentioned above, where editors, exploration view and query interface can be configured. The aim is to make this configuration so simple that the end-user could create new application profiles from a toolbox whenever new kinds of resources are encountered.

A SCAM application that has a fixed application profile is *the Digital Media Library*[14] *of The Swedish Educational Broadcasting Company (UR)*. The main goal is to give public access – via a web interface – to rich metadata for all resources that UR produces. These resources include TV and Radio programs, series of those, related resources such as teacher tutorials, web sites etc. The resources are expressed as application profiles, where standard metadata elements and vocabularies are used when possible. We have used, IEEE / LOM, Dublin Core, DC-terms, VCard plus some national vocabularies regarding educational material. The interface should provide rich search capabilities as well as possibil-

---

[13] For a more complete list see SCAM's homepage http://scam.sourceforge.net
[14] http://www.ur.se/mb

ities to find related resources via containments in series, explicitly given relations etc. Searches are performed via vocabularies. The resources, i.e. the programs themselves, are administered outside of SCAM.

6   Conclusions and Future Work

In this paper we have descibed the design of the SCAM framework which helps applications to store and access metadata on the semantic web. We have defined a SCAM record as the anonymous closure from a resource and claim that in most cases this coincides with how metadata is accessed according to an application profile. Furthermore we have introduced SCAM contexts as a way to handle large amounts of SCAM records. SCAM contexts can be imported and exported as RDF graphs providing a mechanism for backup, communication with other systems etc. Moreover, we have defined access control on the level of SCAM records and query capabilities that can either span all SCAM contexts or be limited to a single SCAM context. We have also seen how different applications can make use of the SCAM framework for different purposes.

Future work will include support for inference and special treatment of vocabularies / ontologies. We will include specific support for metametadata, which e.g. will change the way that ACLs are applied. The ACL model will be revised and extended with e.g. time aspects and authentication by formal deduction rules. Furthermore, we plan to do a quantitative investigation of SCAM's performance and storage capabilities.

7   Acknowledgements

We are indepted to Jan Danils and Jöran Stark for their programming efforts and to Mikael Nilsson for sharing his expertise on metadata standards. The SCAM project has several stakeholders, the support of which we gratefully acknowledge. Prominent among them are the Swedish National Agency for School Improvement, the Swedish Educational Broadcasting Company, the Swedish National Center for Flexible Learning,Uppsala Learning Lab and the Wallenberg Global Learning Network. The financial support from Vinnova is also gratefully acknowledged.

References

[1] Canadian Core Learning Resource Metadata Application Profile. http://www.cancore.org.
[2] IMS Content Packaging. http://www.imsproject.org/content/packaging.
[3] Jena - A Semantic Web Framework for Java. http://jena.sourceforge.net.
[4] RDF WebAPI. http://www.joseki.org/protocol.html.
[5] The Dublin Core Metadata Initiative. http://dublincore.org.

[6] S. Alexaki, V. Christophides, G. Karvounarakis, D. Plexousakis, and K. Tolle. The ICS-FORTH RDFSuite: Managing Voluminous RDF Description Bases. In *The Second International Workshop on the Semantic Web - SemWeb'2001.*

[7] B. Barkley. Comparing simple role based access control models and access control lists. In *Proceedings of the second ACM workshop on Role-Based Access Control*, pages 127–132, Fairfax, Virginia, United States, 1997.

[8] B. Beckett and J. Grant. Mapping Semantic Web Data with RDBMSes. http://www.w3.org/2001/sw/Europe/reports/scalable_rdbms_mapping_report.

[9] D. Beckett. The Design and Implementation of the Redland RDF Application Framework. In *Proceedings of the tenth World Wide Web Conference*, 2001.

[10] D. Brickley and R.V. Guha. RDF Vocabulary Description Language 1.0: RDF Schema. http://www.w3.org/TR/2002/WD-rdf-schema-20020430.

[11] J. Broekstra, A. Kampman, and F. van Harmelen. Sesame: A Generic Architecture for Storing and Querying RDF.

[12] E. Duval, W. Hodgins, S. Sutton, and S.L. Weibel. Metadata Principles and Practicalities. D-Lib Magazine Vol. 8 No. 4, April 2002.

[13] H. Eriksson. Query Management For The Semantic Web. http://kmr.nada.kth.se/papers/SemanticWeb/CID-216.pdf.

[14] D.F. Ferraiolo and D.R. Kuhn. Role Based Access Control. In *15th National Computer Security Conference*, 1992.

[15] Y. Goland, E. Whitehead, A. Faizi, S. Carter, and D. Jensen. HTTP Extensions for Distributed Authoring – WEBDAV, 1999.

[16] K. Graham and J. J. Carroll. Resource Description Framework (RDF):Concepts and Abstract Syntax. http://www.w3.org/TR/rdf-concepts.

[17] Learning Technology Standards Comittee of the IEEE:. DraftStandard for Learning Objects Metadata IEEEP1484.12.1/D6.4, June 2002.

[18] L. Miller, A. Seaborne, and A. Reggiori. Three Implementations of SquishQL, a Simple RDF Query Language. In *Proceedings of the First International Semantic Web Conference on The Semantic Web*, pages 423–435, 2002.

[19] W. Nejdl, B. Wolf, C. Qu, S. Decker, M. Sintek, A. Naeve, M. Nilsson, M. Palmér, and T. Risch. EDUTELLA: A P2P Networking Infrastructure Based on RDF. In *Proceedings of the 11th World Wide Web Conference*, 2002.

[20] M. Nilsson, M. Palmér, and J. Brase. The LOM RDF binding - principles and implementation. ARIADNE Conference 2003.

[21] M. Nilsson, M. Palmér, and A. Naeve. Semantic Web Meta-data for e-Learning - Some Architectural Guidelines. In *Proceedings of the 11th World Wide Web Conference*, 2002.

[22] M. Nilsson and W. Siberski. RDF Query Exchange Language (QEL) - concepts, semantics and RDF syntax. http://edutella.jxta.org/spec/qel.html, 2003.

[23] F. Paulsson and A. Naeve. Standardized Content Archive Management – SCAM. IEEE Learning Technology newsletter Vol 5, Issue 1, January 2003.

[24] Sun Microsystem Inc. *Web-Tier Application Framework Design.* 2002.

All URLs that are referenced in this paper have been accessed on 2004-01-12.

Publish/Subscribe for RDF-based P2P Networks

Paul-Alexandru Chirita[1], Stratos Idreos[2], Manolis Koubarakis[2], and Wolfgang Nejdl[1]

[1] L3S and University of Hannover
Deutscher Pavillon Expo Plaza 1
30539 Hannover, Germany
{chirita, nejdl}@learninglab.de
[2] Intelligent Systems Laboratory, Department of Electronic and Computer Engineering,
Technical University of Crete, 73100 Chania, Crete, Greece
{sidraios, manolis}@intelligence.tuc.gr

Abstract. Publish/subscribe systems are an alternative to query based systems in cases where the same information is asked for over and over, and where clients want to get updated answers for the same query over a period of time. Recent publish/subscribe systems such as P2P-DIET have introduced this paradigm in the P2P context. In this paper we built on the experience gained with P2P-DIET and the Edutella P2P infrastructure and present the first implementation of a P2P publish/subscribe system supporting metadata and a query language based on RDF. We define formally the basic concepts of our system and present detailed protocols for its operation. Our work utilizes the latest ideas in query processing for RDF data, P2P indexing and routing research.

1 Introduction

Consider a peer-to-peer network which manages metadata about publications, and a user of this network, Bob, who is interested in the new publications of some specific authors, e.g. Koubarakis and Nejdl. With conventional peer-to-peer file sharing networks like Gnutella or Kazaa, this is really difficult, because sending out queries which either include "Koubarakis" or "Nejdl" in the search string will return all publications from one these authors, and Bob has to filter out the new publications each time. With an RDF-based peer-to-peer network, this is a bit easier, because Bob can formulate a query, which includes a disjunction for the attribute "dc:creator" (i.e. dc:creator includes "Nejdl" or dc:creator includes "Koubarakis"), as well as a constraint on the date attribute (i.e. dc:date > 2003), which includes all necessary constraints in one query and will only return answers containing publications from 2004 on. Still, this is not quite what Bob wants, because if he uses this query now and then during 2004, he will get all 2004 publications each time.

What Bob really needs from his peer-to-peer file sharing network are publish/subscribe capabilities:

1. *Advertising*: Peers sends information about the content they will publish, for example a Hannover peer announces that it will make available all L3S publications, including publications from Nejdl, a Crete peer announces that it would do the same for Koubarakis' group.

J. Davies et al. (Eds.): ESWS 2004, LNCS 3053, pp. 182–197, 2004.
© Springer-Verlag Berlin Heidelberg 2004

2. *Subscribing*: Peers send subscriptions to the network, defining the kind of documents they want to retrieve. Bob's profile would then express his subscription for Nejdl and Koubarakis papers. The network should store these subscriptions near the peers which will provide these resources, in our case near the Hannover and the Crete peer.

3. *Notifying*: Peers notify the network whenever new resources become available. These resources should be forwarded to all peers whose subscription profiles match them, so Bob should regularily receive all new publications from Nejdl and Koubarakis.

In this paper we will describe how to provide publish/subscribe capabilities in an RDF-based peer-to-peer system, which manages arbitrary digital resources, identified by their URL and described by a set of RDF metadata. Our current application scenarios are distributed educational content repositories in the context of the EU/IST project ELENA [16], whose participants include e-learning and e-training companies, learning technology providers, and universities and research institutes (http://www.elena-project.org/), our second application scenario being digital library environments.

Section 2 specifies the formal framework for RDF based pub/sub systems, including the query language used to express subscriptions in our network. Section 3 discusses the most important design aspects and optimizations necessary to handle large numbers of subscriptions and notifications, building upon the Super-Peer architecture and HyperCuP protocol implemented in the Edutella system [10], as well as on index optimizations first explored in the RDF context in P2P-DIET [9]. Section 4 includes a short discussion of other important features of our system, and section 5 includes a survey of related work.

2 A Formalism for Pub/Sub Systems Based on RDF

In this section we formalize the basic concepts of pub/sub systems based on RDF: advertisements, subscriptions, and publications. We will need a *typed first-order language* $\mathcal{L}$. $\mathcal{L}$ is equivalent to a subset of the Query Exchange Language (QEL) but has a slightly different syntax that makes our presentation more formal. QEL is a Datalog-inspired RDF query language that is used in the Edutella P2P network [11].

The logical symbols of $\mathcal{L}$ include parentheses, a countably infinite set of variables (denoted by capital letters), the equality symbol = and the standard sentential connectives. The parameter (or non-logical) symbols of $\mathcal{L}$ include types, constants and predicates. $\mathcal{L}$ has four types: $\mathcal{U}$ (for *RDF resource identifiers* i.e., *URI references* or *URIrefs*), $\mathcal{S}$ (for RDF literals that are *strings*), $\mathcal{Z}$ (for RDF literals that are *integers*), and $\mathcal{UL}$ (for the union of RDF resource identifiers and RDF literals that are strings or integers). The predicates of our language are $<$ of type $(\mathcal{Z}, \mathcal{Z})$, $\sqsupseteq$ of type $(\mathcal{S}, \mathcal{S})$, and t of type $(\mathcal{U}, \mathcal{U}, \mathcal{UL})$. Predicate $<$ will be used to compare integers, predicate $\sqsupseteq$ (read "contains") will be used to compare strings and t (read "triple") will be used to represent *RDF triples*. Following the RDF jargon, in an expression $t(s, p, o)$, s will be called the *subject*, p the *predicate* and o the *object* of the triple.

The well-formed formulas of $\mathcal{L}$ (atomic or complex) can now be defined as usual. We can also define a semantics for $\mathcal{L}$ in the usual way. Due to space considerations, we omit the technical details.

The following definitions give the syntax of our subscription language.

Definition 1. *An* atomic constraint *is a formula of $\mathcal{L}$ in one of the following three forms: (a) $X = c$ where X is a variable and c is a constant of type $\mathcal{U}$, (b) $X \, r \, c$ where X is a variable of type $\mathcal{Z}$, c is a constant of type $\mathcal{Z}$ and r is one of the binary operators $=, <, \leq, >, \geq$, and (c) $X \sqsupseteq c$ where X is a variable and c is a constant, both of type $\mathcal{S}$. A* constraint *is a disjunction of conjunctions of atomic constraints (i.e., it is in DNF form).*

We can now define the notion of a *satisfiable* constraint as it is standard.

Definition 2. *A* query (subscription) *is a formula of the form*

$$X_1, \ldots, X_n : t(S, p_1, O_1) \wedge t(S, p_2, O_2) \wedge \cdots \wedge t(S, p_m, O_m) \wedge \phi$$

where S is a variable of type $\mathcal{U}$, $p_1, \ldots, p_m$ are constants of type $\mathcal{U}$, $O_1, \ldots, O_m$ are distinct variables of type $\mathcal{UL}$, $\{X_1, \ldots, X_n\} \subseteq \{S, O_1, \ldots, O_m\}$, and ϕ is a constraint involving a subset of the variables $S, O_1, \ldots, O_m$.

The above definition denotes the class of *single-resource multi-predicate* queries in QEL. This class of queries can be implemented efficiently (as we will show in Section 3) and contains many interesting queries for P2P file sharing systems based on RDF. It is easy to see that only *join* on S is allowed by the above class of queries (i.e., S is a subject *common to all* triples appearing in the subscription).

As it is standard in RDF literature, the triple notation utilizes *qualified names or QNames* to avoid having to write long formulas. A QName contains a prefix that has been assigned to a namespace URI, followed by a colon, and then a *local name*. In this paper, we will use the following prefixes in QNames:

```
@prefix dc:  <http://purl.org/dc/elements/1.1/>
@prefix rdf: <http://www.w3.org/1999/02/22-rdf-syntax-ns#>
@prefix isl: <http://www.intelligence.tuc.gr/publications/>
```

Example 1. The subscription "I am interested in articles authored by Nejdl or Koubarakis in 2004" can be expressed by the following subscription:[1]

```
X: t(X,<rdf:type>, <dc:article>) ∧ t(X,<dc:creator>,Y) ∧
   t(X,<dc:date>,D) ∧(Y ⊒ "Nejdl" ∨ Y ⊒ "Koubarakis") ∧ D=2004)
```

Queries(subscriptions) are evaluated over sets of RDF triples. If T is a set of RDF triples, then $ans(q, T)$ will denote the answer set of q when it is evaluated over T. This concept can be formally defined as for relational queries with constraints.

We can now define the concept of subscription subsumption that is heavily exploited in the architecture of Section 3.

---

[1] Sometimes we will abuse Definition 2 and write a constant o_i in the place of variable O_i to avoid an extra equality $O_i = o_i$ in ϕ.

Definition 3. *Let q_1, q_2 be subscriptions. We will say that q_1 subsumes q_2 iff for all sets of RDF triples T, $ans(q_2, T) \subseteq ans(q_1, T)$.*

We now define the concept of *publication*: the meta-data clients send to super-peers whenever they make available new content. Publications and subscriptions are matched at super-peers and appropriate subscribers are notified.

Definition 4. *A publication b is a pair (T, I) where T is a set of ground (i.e., with no variables) atomic formulas of $\mathcal{L}$ of the form $t(s, p, o)$ with the same constant s (i.e., a set of RDF triples with the same subject-URIref) and I is a client identifier. A publication $b = (T, I)$ matches a subscription q if $ans(q, T) \neq \emptyset$.*

Notice that because URIrefs are assumed to be *unique*, and subscriptions and publications obey Definitions 2 and 4, publication matching in the architecture of Section 3 takes place *locally* at each super-peer.

Example 2. The publication

```
({t(<isl:esws04.pdf>, <rdf:type>, <dc:article>),
  t(<isl:esws04.pdf>, <dc:creator>, "Koubarakis"),
  t(<isl:esws04.pdf>, <dc:date>,2004)}, C3)
```
matches the subscription of Example 1.

We now define three progressively more comprehensive kinds of advertisement. Advertisements formalize the notion of what clients or super-peers send to other nodes of the network to describe their content in a *high-level intentional* manner. Super-peers will match client subscriptions with advertisements to determine the routes that subscriptions will follow in the architecture of Section 3. This is formalized by the notion of "covers" below.

Definition 5. *A schema advertisement d is a pair (S, I) where S is a set of schemas (constants of type $\mathcal{U}$ i.e., URIrefs) and I is a super-peer id. If $d = (S, I)$ then the expression $schemas(d)$ will also be used to denote S. A schema advertisement d covers a subscription q if $schemas(q) \subseteq schemas(d)$.*

Example 3. The schema advertisement $(\{dc, lom\}, SP_1)$ covers the subscription of Example 1.

Definition 6. *A property advertisement d is a pair (P, I) where P is a set of properties (constants of type $\mathcal{U}$ i.e., URIrefs) and I is a super-peer identifier. If $d = (P, I)$ then the expression $properties(d)$ will also be used to denote P. A property advertisement d covers a subscription q if $properties(q) \subseteq properties(d)$.*

Example 4. The property advertisement $(\{<dc:subject>, <lom:context>\},$ $SP_6)$ covers the subscription of Example 1.

Definition 7. *A* property/value advertisement *d* *is a pair* $((P_1, V_1), \ldots, (P_k, V_k)), I)$ *where* $P_1, \ldots, P_k$ *are distinct properties (constants of type* $\mathcal{U}$ *i.e., URIrefs),* $V_1, \ldots, V_k$ *are sets of values for* $P_1, \ldots, P_k$ *(constants of type* $\mathcal{UL}$*) and I is a super-peer identifier.*

Definition 8. *Let q be a subscription of the form of Definition 2 and d be a property/value advertisement of the form of Definition 7. Let* $Y_1, \ldots, Y_k$ *(1 ≤ k ≤ m) be the variables among the objects* $o_1, \ldots, o_m$ *of the triples of q that correspond to the properties* $P_1, \ldots, P_k$ *of d. We will say that d* covers *a subscription q if there exist values* $v_1 \in V_1, \ldots, v_k \in V_k$ *such that the constraint* $\phi[Y_1 \leftarrow v_1, \ldots, Y_k \leftarrow v_k]$ *resulting from substituting variables* $Y_1, \ldots, Y_k$ *with constants* $v_1, \ldots, v_k$ *in* ϕ *is satisfiable.*

Example 5. The property/value advertisement

```
( (<dc:creator>, { W. Nejdl, P. Chirita}),
  (<dc:title>, {"Algorithms", "Data Structures"}),
  (<dc:year>, [2002, ∞]), SP₁ )
```

covers the subscription of Example 1. In the architecture of Section 3 this advertisement will be sent using the RDF file given in the appendix of this paper.

3   Processing Advertisements, Subscriptions, and Notifications

Efficiently processing advertisements, subscriptions and notifications is crucial for publish/subscribe services. After discussing our basic peer-to-peer topology based on the super-peer architecture described in [10], we will describe the optimizations necessary for processing advertisements, subscriptions and notifications in an efficient manner.

3.1   Basic Network Topology: Super-Peers and HyperCuP

Our publish/subscribe algorithm is designed for working with super-peer networks, i.e. peer-to-peer networks, where peers are connected to super-peers who are responsible for peer aggregation, routing and mediation.

Super-peer based infrastructures are usually based on a two-phase routing architecture, which routes queries and subscriptions first in the super-peer backbone and then distributes them to the peers connected to the super-peers. Super-peer based routing can be based on different kinds of indexing and routing tables, as discussed in [4, 10]. In the following sections we will also present indexing and routing mechanisms appropriate for publish/subscribe services. These will be based on two levels of indices, one storing information to route within the super-peer backbone, and the other handling the communication between a super-peer and the peers connected to it. These indices will draw upon our previous work for query routing, as discussed in [10], as well as further extensions and modifications necessary for publish/subscribe services.

Our super-peers are arranged in the HyperCuP topology, not only because this is the solution adapted in the Edutella infrastructure [11], but also because of its special characteristics regarding broadcasts and network partitioning. The HyperCuP algorithm

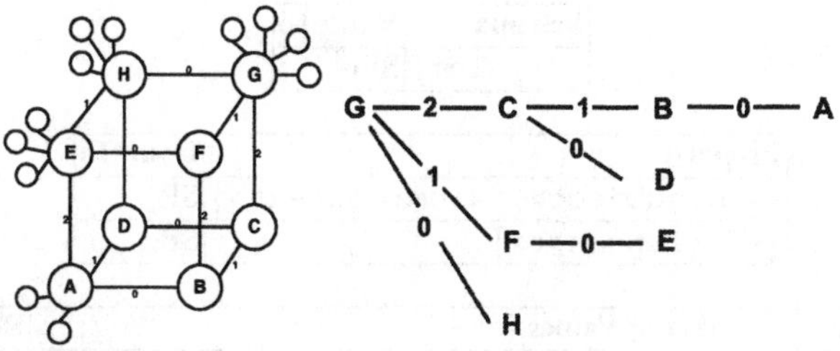

Fig. 1. HyperCuP Topology and Spanning Tree Example

described in [15] is capable of organizing super-peers of a P2P network into a recursive graph structure called hypercube that stems from the family of Cayley graphs. Super-peers join the network by asking any of the already integrated super-peers which then carries out the super-peer integration protocol. No central maintenance is necessary.

HyperCuP enables efficient and non-redundant query broadcasts. For broadcasts, each node can be seen as the root of a specific spanning tree through the P2P network, as shown in figure 1. The topology allows for log_2N path length and log_2N number of neighbors, where N is the total number of nodes in the network (i.e., the number of super-peers in this case). Peers connect to the super-peers in a star-like fashion, providing content and content metadata. Alternatives to this topology are possible provided that they guarantee the spanning tree characteristic of the super-peer backbone, which we exploit for maintaining our index structures.

3.2 Processing Advertisements

The first step in a publish/subscribe scenario is done by a client c which sends an advertisement a to its access point AP, announcing what kind of resources it will offer in the future. Access points use advertisements to construct *advertisement routing indices* that will be utilized when processing subscriptions (see Section 3.3 below). Advertisements are then selectively broadcast from AP to reach other access points of the network. The advertisement indices are updated upon each advertisement arrival on three levels (we use three separate indices): schema level, property (attribute) level, and property/value level. Table 1 shows examples for these indices.

Schema Index. We assume that different peers will support different RDF schemas and that these schemas can be uniquely identified (e.g. by an URI). The routing index contains the schema identifier, as well as the peers supporting this schema. Subscriptions are forwarded only to peers which support the schemas used in the subscription.

Property Index. Peers might choose to use only part of (one or more) schemas, i.e. certain properties/attributes, to describe their content. While this is unusual in conventional database systems, it is more often used for data stores using semi-structured data, and very common for RDF-based systems. In this index, super-peers use the properties (uniquely identified by name space / schema ID plus property name) or sets of properties to describe their peers. Sets of properties can also be useful to characterize subscriptions.

Schema	RouteTo
{dc, lom}	SP_1

Property	RouteTo
{<dc:subject>, <lom:context>}	SP_6
{<dc:language>}	SP_7

Property	Set of Values	RouteTo
<dc:creator>	{ W. Nejdl, P. Chirita }	SP_1
<dc:title>	{"Algorithms", "Data Structures" }	SP_1
<dc:year>	[2002, ∞]	SP_1
<dc:year>	[1990, 2000]	SP_2

Table 1. Advertisement Routing Indices Example: a) Schema Index; b) Property Index; c) Property/Value Index

Property/Value Index. For many properties it will be advantageous to create a value index to reduce network traffic. This case is identical to a classical database index with the exception that the index entries do not refer to the resource, but the super-peer / peer providing it.

We use two kinds of indices: super-peer/super-peer indices (handling communication in the super-peer backbone) and super-peer/peer indices (handling communication between a super-peer and all peers connected to it). Except for the functionality they employ, both indices use the same data structures, have the same update process, etc.

Update of Advertisement Indices. Index updates are triggered when a new peer registers, a peer leaves the system permanently or migrates to another access point, or the metadata information of a registered peer changes. Peers connecting to a super-peer have to register their metadata information at this super-peer thus providing the necessary schema information for constructing the SP/P and SP/SP advertisement indices. During registration, an XML registration message encapsulates a metadata-based description of the peer properties. A peer is assigned at least one schema (e.g., the dc or the lom element set) with a set of properties (possibly with additional information) or with information about specific property values.

If a peer leaves a super-peer all references to this peer have to be removed from the SP/P indices of the respective super-peer. The same applies if a peer fails to re-register periodically. In the case of a peer joining the network or re-registering, its respective metadata/schema information are matched against the SP/P entries of the respective super-peer. If the SP/P advertisement indices already contain the peers' metadata, only a reference to the peer is stored in them. Otherwise the respective metadata with references to the peer are added to the indices. The following algorithm formalizes this procedure:

We define S as a set of schema elements: $S = \{s_i \mid i = 1...n\}$. The super-peer SP_x already stores a set S_x of schema elements in its SP/P indices. The SP/P indices of a super-peer SP_x can be considered as a mapping $s_i \mapsto \{P_j \mid j = 1...m\}$. A new peer P_y registers at the super peer SP_x with a set S_y of schema elements.

1. If $S_y \subseteq S_x$, then add P_y to the list of peers at each $s_i \in S_y$

2. Else, if $S_y \setminus S_x = \{s_n, ..., s_m\} \neq \emptyset$, then update the SP/P indices by adding new rows $s_n \mapsto P_y, ..., s_m \mapsto P_y$.

Generally, upon receiving an advertisement, the access point (let's call it SP_a) will initiate a selective broadcasting process. After the advertisement has been received by another super-peer (say SP_i), it is matched against its advertisement indices and updated using the algorithm described above. When this operation does not result in any modification of the advertisement indices, no further broadcasting is necessary. So for example if a peer publishes something on Physics and the advertisement indices are already sending subscriptions on this topic towards this partition of the network, then there is no need to update these indices, nor any other indices further down the spanning tree of the super-peer network – they will also be pointing towards SP_a already.

3.3   Processing Subscriptions

When a client C posts a subscription q to its access point SP, which describes the resources C is interested in, SP introduces q into its *local subscription poset* and decides whether to further forward it in the network or not. A subscription poset is a hierarchical structure of subscriptions and captures the notion of subscription subsumption defined in Section 2. Figure 2 shows an example of a poset. The use of subscription posets in pub/sub systems was originally proposed in SIENA [2]. Like SIENA, our system utilizes the subscription poset to minimize network traffic: super-peers do not forward subscriptions which are subsumed by previous subscriptions.

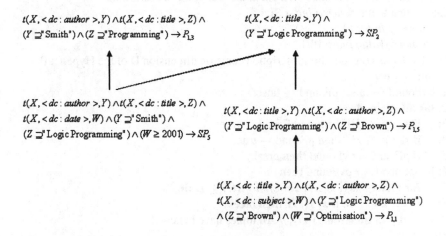

Fig. 2. Poset Example

As shown in the example, each super-peer will add to its local subscription poset information about where the subscription came from (either from one of the peers connected to it or from another super-peer). The addition of super-peer information in the poset reduces the overall network traffic and is therefore very important.

Once a super-peer has decided to send the subscription further, it will initiate a selective broadcast procedure (based on the HyperCuP protocol). Upon subscription receival, a super-peer will have to use its advertisement routing indices in order to decide whether to send it to its neighboring super-peers along the spanning tree or not. There are two criteria which need checked:

1. If the indices contain a super-peer that supports the targeted schema (or properties), but there is no information about the values it covers, then we route the subscription to the respective super-peer, using HyperCuP.[2]
2. If there is also information about the values it covers, then we check if the values are consistent with the constraints of the subscription. If yes, we route the subscription forward, otherwise, we don't.

We give a more formal description of this routing process in the algorithm below.

Algorithm 1. Routing subscriptions.

Let q be the subscription. Then, q is of the form:

$$t_1(x, < s_1 : p_1 >, a_1) \wedge \ldots \wedge t_m(x, < s_m : p_m >, a_m) \wedge C(a_{p1}) \wedge \ldots \wedge C(a_{pf})$$

s_i are (possibly) different schemas,

p_i are (possibly) different attributes,

a_i are either constants or variables; for all a_i which are variables we have some additional constraints on them at the end of the subscription.

Let us denote the *Schema Index* SI,

Property Index PI,

Property/Value Index PVI.

Finally, let us consider the subscription came on dimension D of the HyperCuP spanning tree.

```
1: pvFound ← false; pFound ← false;
2: for all s_i : p_i do
3:    if s_i : p_i ∈ PVI then pvFound ← true;
4:    if s_i : p_i ∈ PI then pFound ← true;
5:    if pFound ∧ pvFound then break;
6: if ¬pFound ∧ ¬pvFound then
7:    for all targets t_i ∈ SI, dimension(t_i) ≥ D do
8:       for all s_j do if s_j ∉ SI then break;
9:       if j=m then routeTo t_i; // All tuples have matched
10:   exit;
```

---

[2] The HyperCuP algorithm uses *dimensions* to avoid sending a message twice to the same peer/super-peer. Every broadcast message is sent only on higher dimensions than the dimension on which it was received. See [10] for more details.

11: **if** pFound $\wedge$ ¬pvFound **then**
12:     **for all** targets $t_i \in SI \cup PI, dimension(t_i) \geq D$ **do**
13:         **for all** $s_j : p_j$ **do if** $(s_j \notin SI) \wedge (s_j : p_j \notin PI)$ **then** break;
14:         **if** j=m **then** routeTo t_i;
15:     exit;
16: **for all** targets $t_i \in PVI, dimension(t_i) \geq D$ **do**
17:     **for all** $(s_j : p_j, a_j)$ **do**
18:         **if** $(s_j : p_j \subset l \in PVI) \wedge (a_j \not\subseteq l \in PVI)$ **then** break;
19:         **if** $(s_j : p_j \notin PVI) \wedge (s_j : p_j \notin PI \cup SI)$ **then** break;
20:     **if** j=m **then** routeTo t_i;

3.4 Processing Notifications

When a new notification arrives at the super-peer, it is first matched against the root subscriptions of its local subscription poset (see also figure 2). In case of a match with the subscription stored in a root node R, the notification is further matched against the children of R, which contain subscriptions refining the subscription from R. For each match, the notification is sent to a group of peers/super-peers (those where the subscription came from), thus following backwards the exact path of the subscription. The complete algorithm is depicted in the following lines.

Algorithm 2. Notification Processing.

Let P be the poset and n the notification.
1: **function** match (posetEntry pe, notification n)
2: **if** $n \supseteq pe$ **then**
3:     **for all** targets $t_i \in pe$ **do** routeTo t_i;
4:     **for all** children $c_i \in pe$ **do** match (c_i, n);
5: **end function**;
6:
7: **for all** roots $r_i \in P$ **do** match (r_i, n);

4 Handling Dynamicity in a P2P Pub/Sub Network

As peers dynamically join and leave the network, they may be offline when new resources arrive for them. These are lost if no special precautions are taken. In the following we discuss which measures are necessary to enable peers to receive notifications which arrive during off-line periods of these peers.

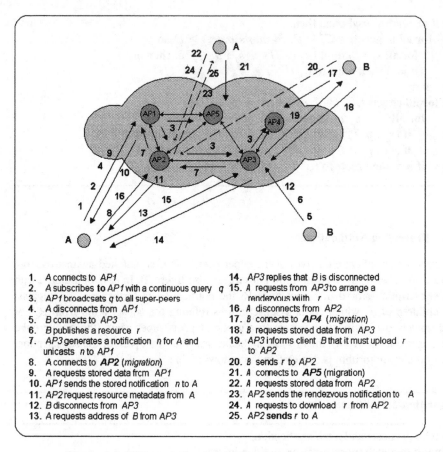

1. A connects to *AP1*
2. A subscribes to *AP1* with a continuous query *q*
3. *AP1* broadcsats *q* to all super-peers
4. A disconnects from *AP1*
5. B connects to *AP3*
6. B publishes a resource *r*
7. *AP3* generates a notification *n* for A and unicasts *n* to *AP1*
8. A connects to **AP2** (*migration*)
9. A requests stored data frcm *AP1*
10. *AP1* sends the stored notification *n* to A
11. *AP2* request resource metadata from A
12. B disconnects from *AP3*
13. A requests address of B from *AP3*
14. *AP3* replies that B is disconnected
15. A requests from *AP3* to arrange a rendezvous wiith *r*
16. A disconnects from *AP2*
17. B connects to **AP4** (*migration*)
18. B requests stored data from *AP3*
19. *AP3* i+forms client B that it must upload *r* to *AP2*
20. B sends *r* to *AP2*
21. A connects to **AP5** (migration)
22. A requests stored data from *AP2*
23. *AP2* sends the rendezvous notification to A
24. A requests to download *r* from *AP2*
25. *AP2* sends *r* to A

Fig. 3. An off-line notification, rendezvous and migration example

4.1   Offline Notifications and Rendezvous at Super-Peers

Whenever a client *A* disconnects from the network, its access point *AP keeps* the client's identification information and subscriptions for a specified period of time, and its indices will not reflect that *A* has left the network. This means that notifications for *A* will still arrive at *AP*, which has to store these and deliver them to *A* after he reconnects. A client may request a resource at the time that it receives a notification *n*, or later on, using a saved notification *n* on his local *notifications directory*.

Let us now consider the case when a client *A* requests a resource *r*, but the resource owner client *B* is not on-line. Client *A* requests the address of *B* from *AP2* (the access point of *B*). In such a case, client *A* may request a *rendezvous* with resource *r* from *AP2* with a message that contains the identifier of *A*, the identifier of *B*, the address of *AP* and the location of *r*. When client *B* reconnects, *AP2* informs *B* that it must upload resource *r* to *AP* as a *rendezvous file* for client *A*. Then, *B* uploads *r*. *AP* checks if *A* is on-line and if it is, *AP* forwards *r* to *A* or else *r* is stored in the *rendezvous directory* of *AP* and when *A* reconnects, it receives a rendezvous notification from *AP*.

The features of off-line notifications and rendezvous take place even if clients migrate to different access points. For example, let us assume that client *A* has migrated to *AP3*. The client program understands that it is connected to a different access point *AP3*, so it requests from *AP* any rendezvous or off-line notifications and informs *AP* that it is connected to a different access point. *A* receives the rendezvous and off-line notifications and updates the variable's *previous access point* with the address of *AP3*. Then, *AP* updates its SP/P and SP/SP indices. Finally, *A* sends to *AP3* its subscriptions and *AP3* updates its SP/P and SP/SP indices. A complete example is shown in Figure 3.

4.2 Peer Authentication

Typically, authentication of peers in a peer-to-peer network is not crucial, and peers connecting to the network identify themselves just using their IP-adresses. In a pub/sub environment, however, where we have to connect peers with their subscriptions and want to send them all notifications relevant for them, this leads to two problems:

– IP addresses of peers may change. Therefore the network will not be able to deliver any notifications, which might have been stored for a peer during his absence, after he reconnects with another IP address. Furthermore, all subscriptions stored in the network for this peer lose their relationship to this peer.
– Malicious peers can masquerade as other peers by using the IP address of a peer currently offline. They get all notifications for this peer, which are then lost to the original peer. Moreover they can change the original peer's subscriptions maliciously.

We therefore have to use suitable cryptography algorithms to provide unique identifiers for the peers in our network (see also the discussion in [7]).

When a new client x wants to register to the network, it generates a pair of keys (E_x, D_x) where E_x is the *public key* of x (or the *encryption key*) and D_x is the *private key* of x (or the *decryption key*) as in [13]. We assume that the client x has already found the IP address and public key of one of the super-peers s, through some secure means e.g., a secure web site. Then, x securely identifies the super-peer s and if this succeeds, it sends an encrypted message to s (secure identification and encryption are explained below). The message contains the public key, the IP address and port of x. The super-peer s decrypts the message and creates a *private unique identifier* and a *public unique identifier* for x by applying the cryptographically secure hash function SHA-1 to the concatenated values of current date and time, the IP address of s, the current IP address of x and a very large random number. The properties of the cryptographically secure hash function now guarantee that it is highly unlikely that a peer with exactly the same identifiers will enter the network. Then, s sends the identifiers to x with an encrypted message. From there on the private identifier is included to all messages from x to its access-point and in this way a super-peer knows who sends a message. The private identifier of a client is never included in messages that other clients will receive; instead the public identifier is used. To clarify the reason why we need both public and private identifiers we give the following example. When a client x receives a notification n, n contains the public identifier of the resource owner $x1$. When x is ready to download the resource, it communicates with the access-point of $x1$ and uses this public identifier to request the address of $x1$. If a client-peer knows the private identifier of x then it can authenticate itself as x, but if it knows the public identifier of x then it can only use it to request the address of x or set up a rendezvous with a resource owned by x. All the messages that a client-peer x sends to a super-peer and contain the private identifier of x are encrypted. In this way, no other client can read such a message and acquire the private identifier of x.

Secure identification of peers is carried out as in [7]. A peer A can securely identify another peer B by generating a random number r and send $E_B(r)$ to B. Peer B sends a reply message that contains the number $D_B(E_B(r))$. Then, peer A checks if $D_B(E_B(r)) = r$ in which case peer B is correctly identified. For example, in our system super-peers securely identify client-peers as described above before delivering a notification. In this case, the super-peer starts a communication session with a client-peer so it cannot be sure that the client-peer listens on the specific IP address.

When a client disconnects, its access point does not erase the public key or identifiers of; it only erases the private identifier from the active client list. Later on, when the client reconnects, it will identify itself using its private identifier and it will send to its access point, its new IP address. In case that the client migrates to a different access point, it will notify the previous one, so that it erases all information about the client. Then, the client securely identifies the new access point and sends a message to it that contains the public key, the public and the private identifiers and the new IP address of the client. All the above messages are encrypted since they contain the private identifier of the client.

5 Analysis of Other Publish/Subscribe Systems

In this section we review related research on pub/sub systems in the areas of distributed systems, networks and databases.

Most of the work on pub/sub in the database literature has its origins in the paper [5] by Franklin and Zdonik who coined the term *selective dissemination of information*. Other influential work was done in the context of SIFT [18] where publications are documents in free text form and queries are conjunctions of keywords. SIFT was the first system to emphasize query indexing as a means to achieve scalable filtering in pub/sub systems [17]. Since then work concentrated on query indexing for data models based on attribute-value pairs and query languages based on attributes with comparison operators. A most notable effort among these works is [1] because it goes beyond conjunctive queries – the standard class of queries considered by all other systems. More recent work has concentrated on publications that are XML documents and queries that are subsets of XPath or XQuery (e.g., Xtrie [3] and others).

In the area of distributed systems and networks various pub/sub systems with data models based on *channels*, *topics* and *attribute-value pairs* (exactly like the models of the database papers discussed above) have been developed over the years [2]. Systems based on attribute-value pairs are usually called *content-based* because their data models are flexible enough to express the content of messages in various applications. Work in this area has concentrated not only on filtering algorithms as in the database papers surveyed above, but also on distributed pub/sub architectures. SIENA [2] is probably the most well-known example of system to be developed in this area. SIENA uses a data model and language based on attribute-value pairs and demonstrates how to express notifications, subscriptions and advertisements in this language. From the point of view of this paper, a very important contribution of SIENA is the adoption of a *peer-to-peer* model of interaction among servers (super-peers in our terminology) and the exploitation of traditional network algorithms based on shortest paths and minimum-weight spanning trees for routing messages. SIENA servers additionally utilize partially ordered sets encoding subscription and advertisement subsumption to minimize network traffic. The core ideas of SIENA have recently been used by some of us in the pub/sub systems DIAS [8] and P2P-DIET (http://www.intelligence.tuc.gr/p2pdiet) [9]. DIAS and P2P-DIET offer data models inspired from Information Retrieval and, in contrast with SIENA, have also emphasized the use of sophisticated subscription indexing at each server to facilitate efficient forwarding of notifications. In summary, the approach of DIAS and P2P-DIET puts together the best ideas from the database and distributed systems tradition in a single unifying framework. Another important contribution of P2P-DIET is that it demonstrates how to support by very similar protocols the traditional *one-time* query scenarios of standard super-peer systems [19] and the pub/sub features of SIENA [9].

With the advent of distributed hash-tables (DHTs) such as CAN, CHORD and Pastry, a new wave of pub/sub systems based on DHTs has appeared. Scribe [14] is a topic-based publish/subscribe system based on Pastry. Hermes [12] is similar to Scribe because it uses the same underlying DHT (Pastry) but it allows more expressive subscriptions by supporting the notion of an event type with attributes. Each event type in Hermes is managed by an event broker which is a rendezvous node for subscriptions and publications related to this event. PeerCQ [6] is another notable pub/sub system implemented on top of a DHT infrastructure. The most important contribution of PeerCQ is that it takes into account peer heterogeneity and extends consistent hashing with simple load balancing techniques based on appropriate assignment of peer identifiers to network nodes.

6 Conclusions

Publish/subscribe capabilities are a necessary extension of the usual query answering capabilities in peer-to-peer networks, and enable us to efficiently handle the retrieval of answer to long-standing queries over a given period of time, even if peers connect to and disconnect from the network during this period.

In this paper we have discussed how to incorporate publish/subscribe capabilities in an RDF-based P2P network, specified a formal framework for this integration, including an appropriate subscription language, and described how to optimize the processing of subscriptions and notifications handling in this network.

Further work will include the full integration of these capabilities into our existing P2P prototypes Edutella and P2P-DIET, as well as further investigations for extending the query language in this paper with more expressive relational algebra and IR operators, while still maintaining efficient subscription/notification processing.

7 Acknowledgements

The work of Stratos Idreos and Manolis Koubarakis is supported by project Evergrow funded by the European Commission under the 6th Framework Programme (IST/FET, Contract No 001935).

References

[1] A. Campailla and S. Chaki and E. Clarke and S. Jha and H. Veith. Efficent filtering in publish-subscribe systems using binary decision diagrams. In *Proc. of 23rd International Conference on Software Engineering*, Toronto, Ontario, Canada, 2001.

[2] A. Carzaniga, D.-S. Rosenblum, and A.L Wolf. Design and evaluation of a wide-area event notification service. *ACM Transactions on Computer Systems*, 19(3):332–383, August 2001.

[3] C.-Y. Chan, P. Felber, M. Garofalakis, and R. Rastogi. Efficient Filtering of XML Documents with XPath Expressions. In *Proceedings of the 18th International Conference on Data Engineering*, pages 235–244, February 2002.

[4] A. Crespo and H. Garcia-Molina. Routing indices for peer-to-peer systems. In *Proceedings of the 22th International Conference on Distributed Computing Systems*, 2002.

[5] M.J. Franklin and S.B. Zdonik. "Data In Your Face": Push Technology in Perspective. In *Proceedings ACM SIGMOD International Conference on Management of Data*, 1998.

[6] B. Gedik and L. Liu. PeerCQ: A Decentralized and Self-Configuring Peer-to-Peer Information Monitoring System. In *Proceedings of the 23rd IEEE International Conference on Distributed Computer Systems*, May 2003.

[7] M. Hauswirth, A. Datta, and K. Aberer. Handling identity in peer-to-peer systems. Technical report, LSIR-EPFL.

[8] M. Koubarakis, T. Koutris, C. Tryfonopoulos, and P. Raftopoulou. Information alert in distributed digital libraries: Models, languages and architecture of dias. In *Proceedings of the 6th European Conference on Research and Advanced Technology for Digital Libraries*, 2002.

[9] M. Koubarakis, C. Tryfonopoulos, S. Idreos, and Y. Drougas. Selective Information Dissemination in P2P Networks: Problems and Solutions. *ACM SIGMOD Record, Special issue on Peer-to-Peer Data Management, K. Aberer (editor)*, 32(3), September 2003.

[10] W. Nejdl, M. Wolpers, W. Siberski, C. Schmitz, M. Schlosser, I. Brunkhorst, and A. Loser. Super-peer based routing and clustering strategies for rdf-based peer-to-peer networks. In *Proceedings of the 12th International World Wide Web Conference*, 2003.

[11] Wolfgang Nejdl, Boris Wolf, Changtao Qu, Stefan Decker, Michael Sintek, Ambjrn Naeve, Mikael Nilsson, Matthias Palmer, and Tore Risch. Edutella: A p2p networking infrastructure based on rdf. In *Proceedings of the 11th International World Wide Web Conference*, 2002.

[12] P.R. Pietzuch and J.M. Bacon. Hermes: A distributed event-based middleware architecture. In *Proceedings of the 1st International Workshop on Distributed Event-Based Systems (DEBS'02)*, July 2002.

[13] R.L. Rivest, A. Shamir, and L.M. Adleman. A method for obtaining digital signatures and public-key cryptosystems. *CACM*, 21(2):120–126, February 1978.

[14] A. Rowstron, A.-M. Kermarrec, M. Castro, and P. Druschel. Scribe: the design of a large-scale event notification infrastructure. In J. Crowcroft and M. Hofmann, editors, *3rd International COST264 Workshop*, 2001.

[15] Mario Schlosser, Michael Sintek, Stefan Decker, and Wolfgang Nejdl. HyperCuP – hyper-cubes, ontologies and efficient search on peer-to-peer networks. In *Proceedings of the 1st Workshop on Agents and P2P Computing, Bologna*, 2002.

[16] Bernd Simon, Zoltn Mikls, Wolfgang Nejdl, Michael Sintek, and Joaquin Salvachua. Smart space for learning: A mediation infrastructure for learning services. In *Proceedings of the Twelfth International Conference on World Wide Web*, Budapest, Hungary, May 2003.

[17] T.W. Yan and H. Garcia-Molina. Index structures for selective dissemination of information under the boolean model. *ACM Transactions on Database Systems*, 19(2):332–364, 1994.

[18] T.W. Yan and H. Garcia-Molina. The SIFT information dissemination system. *ACM Transactions on Database Systems*, 24(4):529–565, 1999.

[19] B. Yang and H. Garcia-Molina. Designing a super-peer network. In *Proceedings of the 19th International Conference on Data Engineering (ICDE 2003)*, March 5–8 2003.

Streaming OWL DL

Jeremy J. Carroll

Hewlett-Packard Labs,Bristol*

Abstract. A triple based approach to syntactically recognizing OWL DL files is described in detail. An incremental runtime refinement algorithm and two compile time algorithms are given. Many aspects of OWL DL syntax are addressed. These techniques are combined into a streaming OWL recogniser. This shows a threefold time and space improvement over abstract syntax tree based approaches.

1 Introduction

The syntactic relationship between OWL and RDF is complicated.

The Web Ontology Language (OWL) [5] defines three classes of documents: Lite, DL and Full. All RDF/XML documents are OWL Full documents. Some OWL Full documents are also OWL DL documents, and some OWL DL documents are also OWL Lite documents. The characterisation of OWL DL and OWL Lite is essentially *syntactic* in nature: it is defined by structural manipulation, rather than by semantic rules which give interpretation of structures.

The Jena OWL syntax checker is distinctive in that it depends on a transformation of the abstract syntax centred grammar from OWL Semantics and Abstract Syntax [7] (S&AS), into a triple centred approach. Earlier work [2] contrasts this with the more popular approach of direct implementation with OWL abstract syntax trees.

The core algorithm in this paper remembers as little as possible, processing one triple after another, and then forgetting it as quickly as possible. However, given that in an OWL DL file each URI ref can only be used in one way (e.g. as a class or as a datatype property, but not both), it is necessary to remember at least *which* way for each URI ref that has been processed. The final goal of the techniques in this paper is to get as close to that minimum as possible.

The level of detail in this paper is aimed at a (fairly small) audience of developers of OWL tools, particularly syntactic tools. A sufficiently motivated reader should be able to reimplement the checker using this paper, (the Jena source code is also available[1]). It is suggested that the more general reader should start with more introductory material such as Bechhofer [1], OWL Reference [5] (appendix E), OWL Semantics and Abstract Syntax [7] (sections 2 and 4), and Bechhofer and Carroll [2]. The OWL user who just wants to get straight to the point should skip to the results section 8 near the end of the paper.

---

* Jeremy Carroll is a visiting researcher at ISTI, CNR in Pisa, and thanks his host Oreste Signore. Thanks also to the anonymous referees for their exceptionally detailed comments.

[1] http://jena.sourceforge.net/

J. Davies et al. (Eds.): ESWS 2004, LNCS 3053, pp. 198–212, 2004.

The Jena OWL Syntax Checker is implemented in Java, with a Prolog precompiler. Given space constraints, this paper only partially addresses OWL Lite.

1.1 Checking or Parsing

The output of an OWL syntax checker, is as specified in [4], merely one word. For this basic functionality there is no requirement to ever build an abstract syntax tree (or anything like it). Most checkers deliver parse trees as well as separating OWL Lite and OWL DL from OWL Full. This is useful for reasoners based on the direct semantics in S&AS.

In other environments the parse tree is not necessarily relevant. Ontology editors may wish to inform the user when a file is not OWL DL. Systems with OWL Full (triple) based reasoners may wish to export OWL DL files. The one word result and any error messages is all that is required. Moreover, an efficient design for a recognizer can usually be extended to be a parser without grossly compromising its efficiency. Thus, this paper is focussed on the recognition problem.

2   OWL Syntax

The rules for OWL DL are defined constructively in S&AS. An abstract syntax is defined, that describes a set of parse trees. Each of these parse trees can then be converted into one or more RDF graphs using nondeterministic mapping rules.

An OWL syntax checker, has to, at least implicitly, do this process backwards - i.e. take an RDF graph, invert the mapping rules, and hence find a corresponding abstract syntax tree. If there is one, then the document is in OWL DL, otherwise it is in OWL Full.

Since the grammar transformations are programmatic formal manipulations, it helps if as many aspects of the grammar as possible are expressed in a uniform machine processable notation. This leads to a few differences with the grammar in S&AS which is targetted at the human reader.

2.1 The Abstract Syntax

The abstract syntax rules are described in section 2 of S&AS [7].

These are fairly conventional looking BNF [6] rules:

$\langle ontology \rangle$ ::= 'Ontology(' [$\langle ontologyID \rangle$] { $\langle directive \rangle$ } ')'

$\langle fact \rangle$ ::= $\langle individual \rangle$

$\langle individual \rangle$ ::= 'Individual(' [$\langle individualID \rangle$] ...
             { 'type(' $\langle type \rangle$ ')' } { $\langle value \rangle$ } ')'

The principle novelty is that these rules describe abstract syntax trees, and not a document. There is no intent that the terminal leaves of the tree be read off to form a text string. Thus the abstract syntax is a set of trees, defined by a BNF.

The trees defined by these rules are not quite the parse trees according to the BNF, but structural trees defined by the '(' and ')' in the terminals in the rules. A simple rule, like that for *fact*, is not made explicit in any corresponding abstract syntax tree.

Transitive Properties S&AS says:

> An individual-valued property is complex if 1/ it is specified as being functional
> or inverse-functional, 2/ there is some cardinality restriction that uses it, 3/ it
> has an inverse that is complex, or 4/ it has a super-property that is complex.
> Complex properties cannot be specified as being transitive.

We change the grammar to reflect this text by replacing the single category `in-dividualvaluedPropertyID` with two: `transPropID` and `complexPropID`. The first may be specified as transitive, or related to a transitive property, the second may be functional or inverse-functional or used in a cardinality restriction, or related to a complex property. All grammar rules involving `individualvaluedPropertyID` are duplicated (with one version for `transPropID` and the other for `complexPropID`) except those specifically excluded by the constraints. In particular the modified grammar permits a `complexPropID` to have a super property that is a `transPropID` but not vice-versa.

This change allows the techniques of this paper to cover this rule directly, and not require any special purpose code. This transformation of duplicating the appropriate grammar rules was performed by hand.

The Ontology Header S&AS says:

> An RDF graph is an OWL DL ontology in RDF graph form if it is equal ... to a
> result of the transformation to triples ... of *a collection of OWL DL ontologies
> and axioms and facts* in abstract syntax form that has a separated vocabulary.

To simplify the treatment of the emphasised text we modify the grammar such that any such collection of S&AS ontologies is equivalent to a single ontology in the modified grammar. This is done by having a new directive `header`, which the mapping rules treat like the `ontology` node in the S&AS grammar. Thus the `header` contains the annotations of the ontology, the imports directives etc. We permit zero or more of these `header`'s, which is equivalent to the S&AS approach of permitting zero or more ontology nodes and also additional axioms and facts.

⟨*header*⟩ ::= 'header (' [⟨*ontologyID*⟩], ⟨*ontologyPropertyValue*⟩, ⟨*annotation*⟩ ')'

2.2   The Mapping Rules

The mapping rules are described in section 4 of S&AS [7].

A simplified mapping rule looks like:

```
Individual( value( pID₁ v₁ )      ─:x→       _:x  T(pID₁) T(v₁) .
    ...value(  pIDₖ vₖ ))               ..._:x  T(pIDₖ) T(vₖ) .
```

This shows that an abstract syntax tree matching the left hand side, can be transformed into triples as given on the right hand side. The functor $T(\cdot)$ is used to show recursive application of the mapping rules. Such a recursive application returns a node to be used within the triples on the right hand side of the calling rule, (`_:x` in this case; the 'main node' in the terminology of S&AS).

The mappings of the substructures are shown on the right hand side in the *same order* as the abstract syntax tree on the left.

To make it easier to formally manipulate these rules, we make two key changes: the dots to indicate repetition are replaced by braces as in the abstract syntax; and the transformation is described using two functions rather than one. As well as a function of one argument that shows how a structure is transformed, we have an additional function with two arguments, one being a structure to be transformed the other being a node in the graph that is modified by this structure.

Thus the rule above is expressed, using two rules, in this way:

```
individual( i, {value} ) ->
    {x(x(i),value)};                                    x(i).
D+value( datatypePropertyID, dataLiteral ) ->
        t( D, x( datatypePropertyID ), x( dataLiteral ) ).
```

The final `x(i)`, in the first rule, indicates the main node; the variable `D` in the second rule indicates the first argument in the recursive call. Further `value` rules deal with `individualvaluedPropertyID`. Again this slight transformation of the mapping rules into a clearer form is done by hand.

A specific advantage of using braces for repetition, as oppposed to $d_1 \ldots d_n$, is that numeric constraints such as the phrase "With at least one type." used in a mapping rule can be expressed formally as:

```
..., type( description-1 ), {type( description-2 )}, ...
```

In this rule, as in others in S&AS, the same term (`description`) may occur more than once. These are distinguished by subscripts in S&AS, corresponding to the -1 and -2 above. There are a number of other minor variations, partly for historical reasons, partly reflecting the Prolog implementation.

3   Runtime Algorithm

3.1   An Example of the Approach

Suppose we are given the following three triples in order:

```
_:r owl:onProperty eg:p .
_:r owl:hasValue "a value" .
eg:p rdf:type owl:ObjectProperty .
```

When processing the first triple, we can conclude that it must have come from one of the mapping rules for restrictions, for example:

```
restriction( ID          _:x rdf:type owl:Restriction .
    allValuesFrom( --x-> _:x owl:onProperty T(ID).
        range ))           _:x owl:allValuesFrom T(range).
```

Thus `eg:p` must be either a datavaluedPropertyID[2] or an individualvaluedPropertyID, and `_:r` is the node corresponding to some restriction.

When we process the second triple, we already know that `_:r` is a restriction of some sort, and the additional triple tells us that it is a `value(·)` restriction. Moreover,

---

[2] The reader may need to refer to S&AS[7] during this section!

the literal object, tells us that this is a value restriction using the following mapping rule:

```
restriction( ID        _:x rdf:type owl:Restriction .
    value(        ⎯ˣ→ _:x owl:onProperty T(ID).
        value ))         _:x owl:hasValue T(value).
```

We note that for $T(value)$ to be a literal, then *value* must be *dataLiteral* and the following abstract syntax rule must have been used:

⟨*dataRestrictionComponent*⟩ ::= 'value(' ⟨*dataLiteral*⟩ ')'

This rule can only fire if *ID* is a *datavaluedPropertyID*.

Thus, the second triple tells us that _:r corresponds to a value restriction on a *datavaluedPropertyID*. If we now return to the first triple, given the new information about _:r we now know that eg:p is a *datavaluedPropertyID*.

Since the mapping rule only applies to abstract syntax constructs that come from OWL DL we know that the triples are not from an OWL Lite document.

There is nothing more that can be said about either the predicate or the object of either the first or second triples. Thus neither triple will make any further difference to the rest of the processing, and both could be discarded in an incremental recognizer. All that needs to be remembered is the classification of _:r and eg:p.

When we come to the third triple, we find a *datavaluedPropertyID* as the subject of an rdf:type triple, with an owl:ObjectProperty object. The mapping rules do not produce such triples, and so this is an error.

Processing the triples in reverse order, we would have concluded that eg:p was an *individualvaluedPropertyID*, (from the third triple), and found the error while processing the first triple, because the grammar does not generate owl:onProperty triples linking value restrictions on datavalued properties with *individualvaluedPropertyID*s.

3.2 Node Categorization

The example depended upon an analysis of whether eg:p was an *individualvaluedPropertyID* or a *datavaluedPropertyID*. and of what sort of restriction corresponded to _:r

We view this as a function from the nodes in the graph to a set of syntactic categories generated from the grammar. Each uriref node may be a builtin uriref, with its own syntactic category (such as owl:onProperty), or a user defined ID, such as a *classID*. Each blank node is introduced by one of the mapping rules. We hence have one or more[3] syntactic categories for each mapping rule that creates a blank node.

---

[3] Sometimes, the combination of the abstract syntax and the mapping rules, is such that the same mapping rule is used for two different abstract syntax constructs. The rule for the value restriction is one, which can be used for both literal values and object values. In such cases, we clone the mapping rule and have one for each abstract syntax construct, giving rise to two syntactic categories for blank nodes.

3.3   The Category Refinement Algorithm

The main goal of the algorithm is to determine which category each of the nodes is in.

To make the runtime algorithm simpler, the grammar (including the mapping rules) is precompiled into a grammar table of triples of syntactic categories.

Two of the entries in this table, relevant to the example are:

```
individualValuedProperty rdf:type owl:ObjectProperty .
literalValueRestriction owl:hasValue literal . (DL)
```

Some of the entries are annotated with actions, for example the second triple sets the DL (i.e. not Lite) flag.

Each step in the algorithm processes one triple.

The currently known possible categories for each of the three nodes are retrieved. Each combination of these is tested to see if it is in the grammar table. Such tests allows the elimination of some of the previous possible categories for each node. If all the possible categories are eliminated, then the graph did not conform to the syntax.

The algorithm incrementally defines a function C that assigns a set of categories to each node in the graph, using a set T' of triples that have already been processed. In this version T' remembers every triple, a *streaming* mode which can forget some of them is discussed in section 7.1.

1. For each blank node n in the graph, set $C(n)$ to the set of all blank categories.
2. For each builtin uriref n in the graph, set $C(n)$ to be $\{n\}$.
3. For other urirefs n in the graph, set $C(n)$ to be the set of all ID categories (classID etc).
4. For each node equivalent to "0"^xsd:int or "1"^xsd:int set $C(n)$ to $\{liteInteger\}$ (for use in cardinality restrictions).
5. For each other node equivalent to x^xsd:nonNegativeInteger set $C(n)$ to $\{dlInteger\}$.
6. For any typed literal node with user defined type set $C(n)$ to $\{uTypedLiteral\}$, and for the datatype URI dt set $C(dt)$ to $\{datatypeID\}$.
7. For each other[4] literal node set $C(n)$ to $\{literal\}$.
8. For each triple $t = < s, p, o >$ in the graph, *refine(t)*, where *refine* is defined as:
   (a) Set $S = C(s)$, $P = C(p)$, $O = C(o)$, to be the set of categories currently associated with the subject, predicate and object of t respectively.
   (b) Set $S' = \{s* \in S | \exists p* \in P, o* \in O$ with $< s*, p*, o* > \in Grammar\}$
   (c) If S' is empty then fail.
   (d) Set P' and O' similarly
   (e) If $S \neq S'$ update $C(s) := S'$ and for each $t' \in T'$ involving s, *refine(t')*
   (f) Similarly for P' and O'
   (g) If every match from S', P' O' in the grammar table is annotated with the same action, perform that action.
   (h) Add t to T'.
9. Check for missing triples.

---

[4] This rather *ad hoc* list of literal classifications reflects precisely the relevant division in OWL DL syntax. In particular, non-integer XSD literals, such as "1.3"^xsd:float, are treated the same as plain literals.

The actions in step 8g are discussed in more detail below. Other details, such as the final checks of step 9, and 'pseudocategories' are discussed in section 5.

3.4   The Actions

The actions used by the grammar are: the DL action, for triples which do not occur in Lite; an Object action when the object of this triple is a blank node which must not be the object of any other triple; and actions for when the subject of this triple corresponds to a construct with one or two components each reflected by exactly one triple in the graph, and this triple is such a component. These are divided into three cases: FirstOfOne (example owl:unionOf), FirstOfTwo (example owl:onProper-ty) and SecondOfTwo (example rdf:rest). For each of these, the runtime processing performs the action by remembering the triple as fulfilling the specified role and it is an error if some other triple plays the same role.

There could be further actions that construct an abstract tree if desired. These would construct part of the tree corresponding to the subject of the triple by adding an appropriate link to the part of the tree corresponding to the object of the triple.

4   The Precompiler

The first precompilation stage transforms the OWL DL grammar from being an abstract syntax with mapping rules based on S&AS[7] to a triple oriented form suitable for the refinement algorithm.

The input consists of: a list of the names of the syntactic categories for urirefs (e.g. classID); the abstract syntax (reformulated as in section 2.1); and the mapping rules (reformulated as in section 2.2). The output is as follows:

- A list of syntactic categories for nodes (86 categories: 42 for the keywords in OWL, such as rdf:type, 15 corresponding to the different uses of user defined urirefs, 24 for different usages of blank nodes, 5 artificial pseudocategories)
- Various groupings of these categories (e.g. all those categories that are involved with owl:disjointWith).
- A table of legal triples of syntactic categories, annotated with actions and a DL flag (2943 entries).
- Lookup functions that assign an initial set of syntactic categories to a node

The precompiler[5] is written in Prolog, and the grammar and mapping rules have been written in a Prolog form.

4.1   Detailed Account

The first step is to take the abstract syntax which, while Prolog readable, is still formatted principally for humans, and to preprocess to facilitate the later steps. An example of

---

[5] It is available in the Jena distribution in the tools directory, or from
http://cvs.sf.net/viewcvs.py/jena/jena2/tools/syntax-checker/.

the preprocessing is turning the structures on the right hand side of a grammar rule into a list of terminals and nonterminals.

The second step preprocesses the mapping rules. It makes explicit the implicit alignment between the optional or repeated elements on the left hand side and on the right.

The third step is to assign an initial syntactic category to each mapping rule that returns a main node. The main node is analysed as follows:

- User urirefs are each categorized as in the corresponding abstract syntax expression, e.g. a `classID`.
- When a built-in is known to have a corresponding abstract syntax category, such as the built-in class `owl:Thing` then it is categorized in that way.
- Literals are categorized as `liteInteger`, `dlInteger`, or `literal`.
- Blank nodes are categorized by examining the name of the abstract syntax structure being mapped. Blank nodes are categorized as `unnamedOntology`, `unnamedIndividual`, `restriction`, `description`, `dataRange`, `allDifferent`, or as a list node.
- The list nodes are categorized depending on the category of the first entry, giving `listOfDescription`, `listOfIndividualID`, and `listOfDataLiteral`.

This hard codes some knowledge of the grammar into the precompiler. The precompiler is hence *not* reusable for other similar grammars without significant work.

These rules also include some optimizations such as knowledge that a blank node arising from a `unionOf` construct and one arising from a `intersectionOf` can both be treated very similarly, and be given the same syntactic category, `description`. A less pragmatic approach would have insisted that the precompiler needed to observe this similarity, by some analysis of the grammar, rather than just know it.

The fourth step is where we initially form the triple table. Each triple on the RHS of a mapping rule is converted into one or more triples of categories. The same categorization rules as before are used. These rules are extended to cover recursive application of the mapping rules as in

```
individual( individualID, {annotation},
            {type( description )}, {value} ) ->
        {x(x(individualID),annotation)},
        {t(x(individualID),rdf:type,x(description))},
        {x(x(individualID),value)};
            x(individualID).
```

The triple on the RHS of this rule, includes a recursive application of the mapping rules to the description element. In order to work out the possible types of this element, we first have to use the abstract syntax production for `description` to nondeterministically expand the left hand side of the mapping rule. The `x(description)` may be of category `classID` with one abstract syntax expansion. It may be of category `restriction` with a different abstract syntax expansion, or it may be of category `description` with yet another abstract syntax expansion (e.g. as a `unionOf(·)`)

The triple table constructed in this way is modified to better reflect the constraints on restrictions. The approach taken considers restrictions on transitive properties, restrictions on complex properties and restrictions on datavalued properties as distinct syntactic categories. Each triple in the triple table is annotated by the id of the mapping rule from which it was generated. By looking at the `owl:onProperty` triple annotated with each id, the relationship between mapping rule id and the category of restriction is established.

The next steps prepare for the output of the triple table generated. These tend to be increasingly *ad hoc*, and they depend on specific knowledge of the grammar.

Various simplifications are applied. A straightforward one is to replace all occurrences of `owl:minCardinality` and `owl:maxCardinality` by `owl:cardinality`. These properties, while they have different semantics, have identical syntactic behaviour. Similarly `owl:someValuesFrom` and `owl:allValuesFrom` can be treated as a single term syntactically.

In order to interact with the actions part of the runtime algorithm (see section 3.3), triples with certain properties (such as `rdf:first`, `owl:oneOf`, `owl:someValues-From`) are annotated with the appropriate action. Triples could also be annotated with actions to build the abstract syntax tree corresponding to the left hand side of the mapping rule.

An analysis of the use of blank nodes in OWL DL, found in [2], gives the four following cases:

1. Be the subject or object of any number of `owl:equivalentClass` triples
2. Be the subject or object of any number of `owl:disjointWith` triples (in which case a further check must be applied)
3. Be the subject or object of an `rdfs:subClassOf` triple.
4. Be the object of some other triple.

To reflect this, the `description` category and the three `restriction` categories are multiplied out, one for each of the above cases. This multiplication has to be applied to the triples as well, so that a triple such as `restrictionOnTransProp owl:some-ValuesFrom description` is multiplied out to sixteen new triples.

The triple table and the other products of the precompiler are output as a Java file. This is then used in the second preparation phase, see section 6.

5   Missing Triples

The category refinement algorithm (section 3.3), and the triple table, address many errors. They detect conflicts between the vaocabulary usage in the triples in the graph and the rules of OWL DL. To fix such problems it would be necessary to remove some of the triples.

The actions also detect further errors caused by too many triples, such as a list node with two `rdf:rest` triples, or a blank node that is the object of more than one triple.

Some other errors cannot be detected in this way; but are characterized by a 'missing' triple. There is some set of triples that if added to the graph will make it an OWL DL graph. At the end of the category refinement algorithm step 9 checks for missing triples. This section describes that step.

5.1   Missing Components

Most blank node categories are expected to have one or two components. The two exceptions are those corresponding to individuals and ontologies.

The actions (see section 3.4) have to save these components anyway, in order to check that no component is specified in two different ways. Thus the check for missing triples simply inspects the record concerning each such blank node, and verifies that the appropriate number (one or two) of components have been found.

5.2   Example: Type Triples

Most nodes in OWL Lite and OWL DL need an explicit type triple in OWL Lite and OWL DL. Given the desire to *not* remember every triple, but to remember as little as possible, it makes sense to check whether each triple provides the type for its subject as it is processed in the category refinement algorithm.

Rather than extending the algorithm, we use the algorithm from section 3.3 unchanged, and extend the grammar to do this work for us. The extension consists of a new category, a 'pseudocategory' notype and new triples in the triple table that use that category. For clarity, we use two tables, the original table of triples, and an extension table of 'pseudotriples'. The category refinement algorithm uses the union of the two.

The pseudotriples permit notype to appear anywhere in any triple except as the subject of a triple with predicate rdf:type and object being one of the possible required types from OWL DL (only a few built-in RDF classes, such as rdf:Property are excluded). A sample piece of program logic implementing such a pseudotriple table is:

```
boolean pseudoTriple( int subjC, int predC, int objC ) {
   int numberOfNotype =
       ( subjC == Grammar.notype ? 1 : 0 )
    + ( predC == Grammar.notype ? 1 : 0 )
    + ( objC == Grammar.notype ? 1 : 0 );
   if ( numberOfNotype != 1 ) return false;
   if ( subjC == Grammar.notype
       && predC == Grammar.rdf_type
       && !excludedBuiltinClass( objC ) )
     return false;
   return true;
}
```

This functions acts as the pseudotriple table, in that a triple is in that virtual table if the function returns true; i.e. if it has exactly one notype category, and the triple is not a type triple for that category.

The check for missing triples then checks that every node has a required type by checking whether any node has category notype. If there is such a node, then it does not have a type triple and the input is in OWL Full.

5.3 Pseudotriples

Generalizing from the example, to check for missing triples, we try to utilize the category refinement algorithm as much as possible.

We introduce pseudocategories (five in all), and new virtual triples involving these. The virtual triples are implemented as a piece of Java code, extending the implementation for notype. By an appropriate choice of which pseudotriples are in the virtual table, global properties can be propogated through the node categories. Nodes with syntactic defects are marked as being in appropriate pseudocategories. As a triple is processed which addresses each defect then the node is no longer marked as in the corresponding pseudocategory.

The five pseudocategories are notype (see above), badRestriction (which deals with the specific difficulty of restrictions needing a type owl:Restriction and not only the optional owl:Class), orphan (see section 5.4), and cyclicFirst and cyclicRest (see section 5.5).

The final checks for missing triples are then optimised, particularly for not having to look back at the actual triples, by analysis of which nodes have which pseudocategories.

The use of pseudocategories also impacts the initial assignment of category sets to nodes. Most nodes are assigned most of the pseudocategories.

5.4 Orphans

In OWL DL every blank node corresponding to a list must be the object of some triple. In OWL Lite every blank node corresponding to a restriction must be the object of some triple. Such orphaned nodes are detected by having a pseudocategory orphan which is permitted in subject position with any predicate and object, but never in object position. The final checks simply look for nodes of this category.

5.5 Cyclicity Constraints

In OWL DL, directed cycles of blank nodes are typically prohibited.

Analysis of the grammar shows that a cycle which does not break any other rules is either a cycle of descriptions and restriction nodes, or a cycle of unnamed individuals, or a cyclic list-like structure (every edge in the cycle labelled with rdf:rest).

Each unnamed individual is the object of at most one triple. In any cycle of these, each is the object of exactly one triple, which must have a further cyclic blank node as subject. However, each may be the subject of arbitrary other triples. Thus, the refinement algorithm can help check for cycles by initially classifying each blank node as (potentially) cyclic, and pemitting a cylic node to be the subject of any pseudotriple, and the object of a pseudotriple whose subject is also (potentially) cyclic.

In a legal OWL DL file this still leaves some unnamed individuals which have to be checked at the end. This check consists of looking at the triple of which this node is an object (this triple has to be remembered anyway because it can occur twice, but no other triple with this node as object may occur). We then recursively follow that triple until we find an unnamed individual which is not the object of a triple (which is good), or we come back to the first node (which indicates OWL Full). The case in which following the triple leads to a uriref subject is not possible, since there is no such pseudotriple in the extended grammar, which has already been considered by the refinement algorithm.

Blank nodes corresponding to description and restrictions which are the subject or object of `owl:disjointWith` or `owl:equivalentClass` predicates may be in cycles. Each other description, restriction or list node is the subject of zero, one or two triples which may have a blank object. If the node is on a cycle then that cycle must use one or other of these triples. This is encoded in pseudotriples using two pseudocategories, effectively to be able to count up to two. Since we have already checked that each component of this node is specified, this means that we know that in the non-cyclic case we have found the one or two component triples with non-cyclic objects. Thus the final check is again a simple search for nodes with either of the two pseudocategories.

5.6 Disjoint

The hardest part is checking the constraint on `owl:disjointWith`. During the refinement algorithm each pair of nodes linked by `owl:disjointWith` is saved in a classical undirected graph G. The final check then verifies the following transitivity constraint on G, which is sufficient for there to be appropriate `owl:disjointWith` cliques:

$$\forall a, c \in V(G) \; \forall \text{ blank } b \in V(G), \{a, b\} \in E(G) \wedge \{b, c\} \in E(G) \Rightarrow \{a, c\} \in E(G)$$

Constructing this undirected graph is the major modification needed to the refinement algorithm, and points to additional syntactic costs associated with `owl:disjointWith`.

6   Precomputing the Lookup Table

Examination of the category refinement algorithm reveals a block that implements a pure function without side effects. This suggests a possible optimization of precomputing that pure function and just using a lookup table at runtime. The block in question is in the *refine* subroutine:

(a) Set $S = C(s)$, $P = C(p)$, $O = C(o)$, to be the set of categories currently associated with the subject, predicate and object of t respectively.
(b) Set $S' = \{s* \in S | \exists p* \in P, o* \in O \text{ with } < s*, p*, o* > \in Grammar\}$
(c) If S' is empty then fail.
(d) Set P' and O' similarly
(g) If every match from S', P' O' in the grammar table is annotated with the same action,

Precomputing this turns the triple table (including the pseudotriples) into a new form. The *Grammar* used in the algorithm in section 3.3 is a set of triples of categories. After precomputation we have a new grammar that is a set of triples of sets of categories. The rest of the algorithm remains unchanged.

However, this precomputation is non-trivial. Initial attempts failed because the powerset of the set of categories is simply too big (about 2^{80}).

The following approach combines a reachability analysis with the precomputation and hence is tractable.

1. Initialize a set RC of reachable sets of categories with all possible initial assignments of sets of categories to nodes, from the refinement algorithm.
2. Initialize a set RC' of recently added reachable sets to RC.
3. Initialize a set RC'' of new reachable sets to empty.
4. For each set in RC' and each pair of sets in RC form a triple of sets in any order,
   (a) Precompute the result of the pure function above.
   (b) If the result is fail then do nothing.
   (c) Otherwise add the result to the precomputation table being created.
   (d) For each of the sets of categories in the result (the subject, predicate and object values), if the set is not in RC add the set to RC''.
5. Set RC' to RC'', set RC to $RC \cup RC'$, set RC'' to empty.
6. If RC' is empty then finish, else repeat at step 4.

This algorithm runs in about ten minutes on unimpressive kit.

Moreover the resulting lookup table is small enough. There are 390 reachable sets of categories. The table has 193,420 entries, indexed by triples of sets of categories.

Hence, a triple fits in 32 bits, and the whole table (with a one byte action flag) can be stored in a sparse array of 1.7 MB.

Further space optimizations can be gained by making the table three dimensional. The object set of categories is used as a dense key. The next dimension is sparsely index by predicate, and the third dimension is sparsely indexed by subject. Further auxiliary tables permit reducing the necessary number of bits for the values in the table entry. These techniques, unsurprisingly, halve the space requirements.

Combining them with an intern function, storing identical integer arrays only once, provides a further ten fold improvement. The resulting table size is 145 KB, which compresses to 49 KB.

7   Streaming Mode Parsing

The refinement algorithm is presented as processing each triple in an RDF graph. By using this with a streaming RDF/XML parser [3], we can avoid actually creating the graph, but process each triple as the RDF/XML parser detects it.

7.1   Forgetting Triples

A streaming parser needs to forget things as quickly as possible.

The category refinement algorithm as in section 3.3 remembers every triple. To provide a streaming mode we need to forget something.

The precomputed lookup table from the previous section can be annotated with a flag of forgetting which is added to some entries. This triggers an action, if the flag is set, then the triple t is removed from the set of previously seen triples T'.

This flag is set in the table as follows. A triple $< s, p, o >$, can no longer impact the refinement algorithm once, every member of $C(s) \times C(p) \times C(o)$ is in the $Grammar$ of triples of categories. Thus any entry in the lookup table of sets of categories, whose value is such a triple, can have this flag set. In many cases, this permits a triple to never be remembered in T' but discarded immediatly.

7.2   Forgetting Blank Nodes

Each blank node has a significant amount of store associated with it. The triple of which it is an object (if any) has to be remembered, and the triples that are components of the restriction, description or list node must be remembered. Also the owl:disjointWith subgraph must be remembered.

However, a streaming RDF/XML parser can notify the invoker when blank nodes go out of scope. If a blank node does not have an explicit rdf:nodeID then once the XML element that contains that node has been processed, no further refence to the blank node is possible. Triples in one file cannot refer to blank nodes in another, so even the blank nodes with an explicit nodeID go out of scope after processing an owl:imports.

Most of the final checks concerning a blank node are for missing triples that involve that node. Once the node is out of scope, these checks can be executed immediatly. This allows the forgetting of most information about that node. Forgetting information about the cylicity and the owl:disjointWith subgraph is not quite as straightforward.

8   Results

To test the effectiveness of the approach we used a test data set consisting of all the OWL Test Cases [4]. The test data was read from a local disk.

To permit examination of the relative costs of different parts of the processing we ran the following software with each test file as input.

1. Xerces 2.6, to give XML parsing times.
2. ARP, from Jena 2.1, to give RDF/XML parsing times[6].
3. Jena 2.1, giving the time and memory needed for triple storage.
4. The Jena OWL syntax checker running from the in-memory copy of the RDF graph. The in-memory copy eliminates duplicate triples.
5. The streaming checker avoiding the in-memory copy. Duplicate triples are processed twice.
6. The streaming checker with the forgetting optimizations switched off.
7. The WonderWeb OWL DL Parser and species recognizer[7].
8. Pellet's OWL syntax checker[8]

The results are grouped by the number of triples in the input. For XML parsing and RDF/XML parsing, the action of OWL imports was simulated. The times are the average of ten runs (ignoring the first). The memory use was computed in a separate run, using frequent polling on another thread. The results were gathered using Java system functions rather than OS functions. The WonderWeb and Pellet times are for rough comparison purposes: it is misleading to directly compare the Jena checker which has just been optimised with the other checkers which are still early versions. Moreover, both WonderWeb and Pellet produce abstract syntax trees, which takes significantly more space, and some more time, than a recognizer.

[6] These tests reveal that ARP has a memory leak.
[7] http://sourceforge.net/projects/owlapi, CVS copy 10th Jan 2004.
[8] http://www.mindswap.org/2003/pellet/download/pellet-20031224

No. triples	0-40		40-80		80-120		120-200		400-600		600-1000		1000-1500		2900-3000	
Average	8		54		92		136		497		801		1180		2913	
No. tests	343		60		10		10		7		4		5		8	
	ms	KB	ms	KB	ms	KB	ms	KB	ms	KB	ms	KB	ms	KB	ms	KB
Xerces	2	19	3	21	3	22	3	22	6	21	10	22	13	22	40	48
ARP	2	22	5	24	8	24	10	24	29	26	58	97	86	261	276	541
Jena	3	23	7	31	12	50	14	63	67	215	117	249	179	493	503	1007
Jena Checker																
memory	4	30	10	61	15	85	21	108	99	478	163	750	245	922	746	2129
streaming	3	21	9	29	14	34	20	49	83	310	132	416	191	679	806	1361
unoptimised	3	18	10	28	14	46	20	62	87	324	143	548	213	757	856	1594
WonderWeb	17	59	56	212	83	453	114	478	381	1290	617	1744	785	2342	2075	5467
Pellet	55	192	190	600	265	617	349	625	1136	805	1760	897	2628	968	11767	1928

Table 1. Average Runtimes and Incremental Memory Use for the OWL Test Cases

Almost all the systems have near-linear time and space requirements, with the streaming checker being the best candidate for sublinear in space, and Pellet looking a little above linear. This suggests that we need bigger test files to examine the practical scalabity of the various software. The streaming checker is nevertheless the most efficient in terms of its incremental memory needs for the larger tests.

9   Conclusions

The techniques in this paper result in OWL syntax checkers that are significantly more efficient than ones based on a direct implementation of the abstract syntax. The results support the hypothesis that the streaming checker will scale better than the others, but are not sufficiently conclusive. Better tests are needed.

While these techniques do not currently deliver the abstract syntax tree, needed by some OWL reasoners, it is suggested (in section 3.4) that a simple extension could do so. Moreover, noting that actions are performed late in the algorithm, such an extension would have additional complexity which is linear in the size of the output tree.

References

[1] S. Bechhofer. Parsing OWL in RDF/XML. http://www.w3.org/TR/owl-parsing, 2004. W3C WG Note.
[2] S. Bechhofer and J. J. Carroll. Parsing OWL DL: Tress or Triples? In *WWW2004*, 2004.
[3] J. J. Carroll. CoParsing of RDF & XML. Technical Report HPL-2001-292, HP Labs, 2001.
[4] J. J. Carroll and J. D. Roo. Web Ontology Language (OWL) Test Cases. http://www.w3.org/TR/owl-test/, 2004.
[5] M. Dean and G. Schreiber. OWL Web Ontology Language Reference. http://www.w3.org/TR/owl-ref/, 2004.
[6] ISO/IEC. Information technology – Syntactic metalanguage – Extended BNF. Technical Report 14977:1996(E), ISO/IEC, 1996.
[7] P. F. Patel-Schneider, P. Hayes, and I. Horrocks. OWL Web Ontology Language Semantics and Abstract Syntax. http://www.w3.org/TR/owl-semantics/, 2004.

Mathematics on the (Semantic) NET*

Olga Caprotti[1], James H. Davenport[2], Mike Dewar[3], and Julian Padget[2]

[1] RISC-Linz, Johannes-Kepler Universiät, A4040 Linz, Austria
caprotti@risc.uni-linz.ac.at
[2] Department of Computer Science, University of Bath, Bath BA2 7AY, England
{jhd,jap}@cs.bath.ac.uk
[3] NAG Ltd., Wilkinson House, Jordan Hill Rd., Oxford OX2 8DR, United Kingdom
miked@nag.co.uk

Abstract. Although web service technology is becoming more prevalent the mechanisms for advertising and discovering web services are still at a rudimentary stage. WSDL provides information about service name and parameters for the purpose of invocation. UDDI provides a set of WSDL documents matching keywords in a query. The aim of the Mathematics On the NET (MONET) project is to deliver a proof-of-concept demonstration of a framework for mathematical web services which uses semantic web technologies to broker between user requirements and deployed services. This requires mechanisms for describing mathematical objects and properties so that a piece of software can evaluate the applicability of a particular service to a given problem. Thus we describe our Mathematical Service Description Language (MSDL), with its ontological grounding in OpenMath and outline its role in service brokerage and service composition within MONET. We believe similar issues arise in many other (scientific) domains, and the leverage obtained here, through the formal background of mathematics, suggests a road-map for the development of similar domain-specific service description languages.

1 Introduction

Much mathematical computation – and computational mathematics research – relies on a relatively small number of specialized libraries, mostly for numerical work, and an even smaller number of interactive systems supporting a mixture of numerical and symbolic mathematics (*e.g.* Matlab, Maple, Axiom, Reduce, Mathematica, Scilab, GAP, Magma). It is a natural reflection of the constructive nature of mathematics that new mathematical knowledge in these domains is often published in the form of packages that build on the functionality of one or more of these systems.

The potential user with a mathematical problem to solve is in much the same position as any other web user: they may know the information they need is out there, but tracking it down is difficult and is only the first step. Textual keyword-based searching is not always very discriminating and it requires expertise and judgement to determine whether a particular package discovered this way is actually applicable to the problem

---

* The MONET project (http://monet.nag.co.uk) is funded by the Commission of the European Communities Information Society program (project IST-2001-34145)

J. Davies et al. (Eds.): ESWS 2004, LNCS 3053, pp. 213–224, 2004.
© Springer-Verlag Berlin Heidelberg 2004

in hand. This can be hard work, involving reading and interpreting the documentation if present or the code if not. The user then has to deal with availability of the base system and the usual impedimenta of version incompatibilities and the like.

Virtually all the interactive sytems listed above offer some proprietory mechanism for linking to code written in another language, possibly running on another platform. A web-services based architecure might well offer advantages to package developers who could write one package accessible from multiple systems, and consequently to end-users who would have access to a much wide range of functionality from within the comfort of their favourite environment. However as software becomes more distributed so does the information describing its capabilities, and as the coupling between host environment and package becomes looser it becomes more difficult to re-use existing resources.

To deal with these issues the MONET project is using semantic web technologies to describe the mathematical capabilities of a piece of software and match it with a user's requirements. Although we are working in a web-services environment exactly the same approach could be used to advertise conventional pieces of software on a specialised portal. An overview of the MONET project appears in [1].

The MONET architecture (detailed in Figure 1) features the following components:

– Brokers that function as semantic search engines, accepting mathematical queries and returning either references to appropriate web services or answers to the client's problem, having invoked those services on his or her behalf.
– Brokers that are capable of (a) using mathematical reasoning services in order to re-formulate a query for which no direct service is found, so that it may be solved through the composition of several services; and (b) using specialist domain-specific services to investigate the mathematical properties of a problem, for example to determine the stiffness of a set of differential equations, to select the most appropriate service based on the particular algorithm it implements.
– Mathematical web services that permit a package to be published and deployed as a working service rather than as something that must be distributed and installed, avoiding the potential difficulties listed earlier

The contributions of the MONET project that we focus on in this paper are:

1. The extension of WSDL [16] by the Mathematical Service Description Language (MSDL) [4], which is how the mathematical semantic information about a service is defined and published.
2. The evolution of brokerage facilities based on the new Web Ontology Language (OWL) [17] and extending functionalities provided by UDDI [15].
3. The role of OpenMath [14] as a grounding ontology for queries, service descriptions and as a package-neutral mathematical content language.

The paper is structured as follows: the following three sections discuss OpenMath, MSDL, and how brokers fit into the MONET architecture. We then briefly look at some of the sample services that have been deployed and finish with a consideration of related and future work.

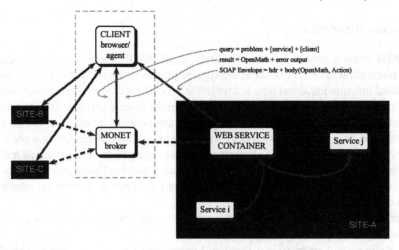

query = problem + [service] + [client]
result = OpenMath + error output
SOAP Envelope = hdr + body(OpenMath, Action)

Fig. 1. General Monet Architecture

2   OpenMath

OpenMath [14] is a mechanism for representing mathematical objects in an unambiguous way. Its XML representation can be transformed to MathML [18] for rendering in browsers. Unlike MathML, however, OpenMath does not rely on a fixed vocabulary: Content Dictionaries are used to assign informal and formal semantics to all the symbols used in the construction of an OpenMath object. Each Content Dictionary defines the symbols used to represent concepts arising in a particular area of mathematics and new Content Dictionarys can be constructed at any time.

The Content Dictionaries are public and represent the shared understanding between a number of OpenMath applications. Content Dictionaries fix the "meaning" of objects independently of the application and as such can be regarded as "micro-ontologies". The application receiving the object may then recognize whether or not, according to the semantics of the symbols defined in the Content Dictionaries, the object can be processed in any meaningful way.

Within MONET we use OpenMath as an exchange format to allow clients, brokers and services to exchange mathematical objects. However we also use the OpenMath symbols to represent concepts in MSDL and OWL as we shall describe later.

3   Describing a Service in Terms of Its Semantics — MSDL

Ontologies perform several roles within the MONET framework - they are used to describe queries from clients, problems, algorithms and services. The ontologies we describe below are in effect information models, when using them within the broker to perform serviced matching they are transformed to OWL. We chose OWL because it appears to be the emerging standard, however we could equally well have used a more mature technology such as DAML+OIL[9].

3.1 Service Description

In MONET terms a service is defined entirely by its MSDL document. This contains both mathematical information about the type of problems the service solves, as well as logistical information about how to invoke the service, its cost etc. In practice, many aspects of a service description can be shared among several services (for instance, information concerning hardware in the case of many services being deployed on the same host) and only the relatively small part associated with the semantics of a particular service actually varies. An XSD schema for this language has been produced and is available from http://monet.nag.co.uk/. A Mathematical Service Description consists of the following (note that the MSDL provides an extended service description intended to wrap around WSDL [16]):

Classification: specification about what functionality the service offers. This consists of some or all of the following components:
- Reference to an entry in a Problem Library (see Section 3.2 below). This describes the type of problem a service solves by specifying inputs, outputs, pre- and post-conditions, as well as optional information such as bibliographic entries, pointers to equivalent problem descriptions in taxonomies etc.
- Reference to taxonomies describing mathematical problems. This is the easiest way to describe what a service does since it defines, in effect. a shorthand notation for entries in the Problem Description Library. In MONET we are using an extended version of the Guide to Available Mathematical Software (GAMS) [11], produced by the National Institute of Science and Technology. The extension is necessary because GAMS is not sufficiently fine-grained in certain areas (symbolic computation and statistics in particular). It is expected that the deployer would choose which node(s) in the taxonomy – and which taxonomy – best matches their proposed service by looking up a published list. Taxonomic references may also occur within the Algorithm Reference element as shown below.
- Supported data formats. This describes the language which a client can use to interact with the service and can be very general (for example LaTeX) or very specific (for example a list of OpenMath Content Dictionaries as described in Section 2. The input and output formats may be different, e.g. for an OpenMath to LaTeX translation service.
- Supported Directives. These are verbs used to describe the type of action a service performs for example *solve*, *prove* and *decide*. The service deployer would be expected to choose from a fixed list of directives.

The MSDL snippet shown in Figure 2 classifies an evaluation service performing numerical integration by reference to routines listed in the H2a1a1 category in the GAMS classification, namely *Automatic 1-D finite interval quadrature (user need only specify required accuracy), integrand available via user-defined procedure*

Implementation Details: information about the particular service. This may include some or all of the following:
- A reference to an entry in an Algorithm Library.
- Information about the software used to construct the service.
- Information about the hardware platform on which the service runs.

```
<monet:classification>
  <monet:directive-type
    href="http://monet.nag.co.uk/owl#evaluate"/>
  <monet:taxonomy
    taxonomy="http://gams.nist.gov/" code="GamsH2a1a1"/>
</monet:classification>
```

Fig. 2. Service classification example

- Algorithmic Properties: extra features of the algorithm which allow the client to control the way it works (e.g. a limit on the number of iterations) or extra information about the result (e.g. the accuracy of the solution). In the case of an algorithm implementing quadrature rules, it may be it allows a user to choose the number of abscissae at which the integrand will be evaluated. This is a parameter which does not appear in the problem description and so is encoded as an algorithmic property.
- Descriptions of actions needed to solve a problem. These are used in the case where a service requires several steps to perform a computation and could be such actions as *initialise, execute, finalise*. These actions are also included in the Service Binding description below, where they are mapped into concrete operations.

It should be noted that none of the Classification or Implementation details are mandatory.

Service Interface Description: This describes the iunterface exposed by the service and is typically a WSDL document.

Service Binding Description: This is a mapping from abstract problem components and actions to elements of the service interface. This allows the service to be invoked automatically from an abstract query.

Broker Interface: This is the API exposed to the broker by the service allowing it to generate service instances, perform housekeeping actions etc. Typically, this is a service URI and an interface description.

The purpose of the MSDL document is to provide a client with information about how to connect to/invoke a particular service, and also for the broker to match a client's query to a service which could solve it. The Problem and Algorithm Libraries are key components in the MONET architecture: they store descriptions that can be shared among services and provide the actual semantics of mathematical services.

3.2 Mathematical Problem Description

The Mathematical problem description is a very important part of the service description as it can be used by the broker when choosing an appropriate service, and by the client to decide which types of input arguments the service takes. Consequently it is important for the person deploying a package to provide a problem description in terms of inputs, output, pre- and post-conditions. The mathematical concepts and expressions in problem descriptions are written in OpenMath, however any other semantic encoding of mathematics could be used. The key points are that each input and output object in the problem is given a unique name and that the description has a URI to allow service descriptions and queries to refer to it. The pre- and post-conditions are currently just used to disambiguate one problem from another — however, we envision the possibility of reasoning about relationships among problems by using them. An example of a problem description (with the XML suppressed for readability) for a numerical integration service appears in Figure 3, where there are five input elements, of which the first is a function over the reals, the subject of the integration operation, a and b are the start and finish of the integration region, x is the name of the parameter of the function and e is the tolerance for the accuracy of the computation.

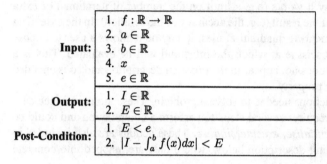

Fig. 3. A problem description for definite integration

3.3   Algorithm Description

The MSDL schema [13] states that an algorithm description has to refer to the problem it solves and must have a name by which it can be referred to. It may also include taxonomic, complexity and bibliographic information. Below is an example which includes two bibliographic references and a taxonomic reference.

```
<monet:implementation>
  <monet:algorithm
    name="Gauss Legendre N-point Quadrature"
    href="http://www.cs.bath.ac.uk/~mapma/Monet/num_int_problem_desc.xml">
    <monet:taxonomy taxonomy="http://gams.nist.gov" code="GamsH2a1a1"/>
    <monet:bibliography
      name="Introduction to Numerical Analysis"
      href="http://www.ams.org/msnpdf/a0075670.pdf"/>
    <monet:bibliography
      name="Numerical Recipes:The Art of Scientific Computing"
      href="http://www.ams.org/msnmain?co3=AND&dr=all&fmt=doc&fn
        =105&id=98a_65001d&l=100&pg3=TI&pg4=ET&r=1&s3=numeri
        cal%20recipes%3A%20the%20art%20of%20scientific%20com
        puting&s4=Books"/>
  </monet:algorithm>
</monet:implementation>
```

3.4   Errors and Explanation

When errors or exceptions occur during the execution of a service by the broker on behalf of a client, they need to be reported back to the client in a meaningful way. Since in general the broker executes not only a single service but a plan involving possibly several services, error tracing has to take into account the flow of data between services. Moreover, since one service may invoke another one with data which is not obviously part of the client's initial problem specification, the context in which an error occurs is quite important.

At the client end, both as a means of conveying error information and of describing where and possibly why something went wrong, or a justification of the solution the broker proposes, we have developed an initial version of an Explanation Ontology [6]. As with the Problem Description Ontology [5] that does not itself describe problems, but rather provides a meta-structure in which to state the nature and existence of problems, so the Explanation Ontology does not provide explanations, but rather provides a meta-structure in which to state the nature and existence of explanations. As such it provides a framework for the production of non-result output. This will then allow clients invoking the service to track how the invocation was handled so as to understand any errors or unsatisfactory results.

There is obviously an overlap between the task the explanation ontology is designed to perform, and workflow languages. However while a workflow language is designed to model a process before it is carried out, we would like to record details of an instance of a process *as it happens*. The strategy we have chosen is to view the explanation ontology as a set of annotations which can be used to decorate a workflow document. At present, we are using BPEL4WS [3] for the orchestration of multiple services, and fortunately this is extensible in the sense that elements from other namespaces can appear as children of the elements they describe.

This is quite an extensive issue and although important, not central to the focus of this paper, the interested reader is referred to [6].

4   Brokering Mathematical Services

The focus of this section is on how the brokerage requirements are reflected in the structure and content of MSDL and how this experience might be of benefit in similar domains. The MONET brokerage mechanisms are covered in detail in [2] and [19].

The broker is expected to operate in a number of roles in order to process mathematical queries and discover services registered by MSDL descriptions.

A client may send a query to a broker which describes the problem it wishes to solve in any number of ways. It might simply identify the mathematical problem and provide some data values, it might provide an OpenMath representation of the problem and expect the broker to work out what the problem is, or it might provide a fragment of MSDL which represents a template for the service required. This last is a particularly powerful mechanism since it allows a wide variety of queries to be specified, such as for example:
- Which services are implemented with NAG software?
- Which services implement the FGLM algorithm?
- Which services implement the algorithm described in the paper with MathSciNet index number MR0386254?

- Which services solve multi-dimensional quadrature problems and accept their input in the Maple language?
- Which services for solving sparse linear systems are running on SMP machines?
- ...

The broker has an extensive OWL ontology which it uses for service matching — in particular it is able to relate concepts such as problem and taxonomy classes to the particular OpenMath symbols used to express a mathematical problem. This allows the broker to understand that a query such as that shown in Figure 4 is actually a request to solve a 1-dimensional quadrature problem.

```
<monet:query id="quad-query"
  xmlns:monet="http://monet.nag.co.uk/monet/ns"
  xmlns:om="http://www.openmath.org/OpenMath">

  <monet:problem >
    <monet:header/>
    <monet:body>
      <monet:output name="I">
        <monet:value>
          <om:OMOBJ>
            <om:OMA>
              <om:OMS name="defint" cd="calculus1"/>
              <om:OMA>
                <om:OMS name="interval" cd="interval1"/>
                <om:OMF dec="0.0"/>
                <om:OMF dec="1.0"/>
              </om:OMA>
              <om:OMBIND>
                <om:OMS name="lambda" cd="fns1"/>
                <om:OMBVAR>
                  <om:OMV name="x"/>
                </om:OMBVAR>
                <om:OMA>
                  <om:OMS name="sin" cd="transc1"/>
                  <om:OMV name="x"/>
                </om:OMA>
              </om:OMBIND>
            </om:OMA>
          </om:OMOBJ>
        </monet:value>
      </monet:output>
    </monet:body>
  </monet:problem>
</monet:query>
```

Fig. 4. A Simple Query

The broker constructs an OWL expression describing the characteristics of the service which the client would like to access. It then tries to match these characteristics to the services which have registered with it, taking account of the hierarchies and relationships expressed in the OWL ontology.

5   Example Services

Services are typically deployed by means of AXIS [12] and invoked through Apache and Tomcat. We noted earlier that the content language for service communications is

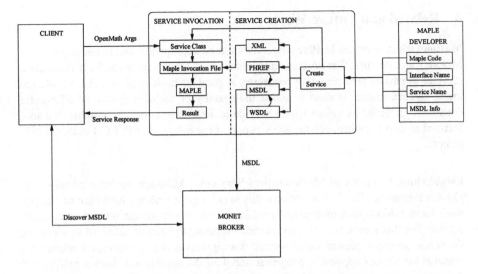

Fig. 5. Architecture of the Maple Wrapper Service

OpenMath, but mathematical software typically has its own (user-friendly?) input syntax, so we have the concept of phrase-books that are used to translate in each direction between network and applications syntax. Services are currently deployed at several of the partners' sites:

Bath: provides a number of specific Maple applications, such as root-finding and integration, but also a generic Maple service generator through which a client (user or program) can provide the elements of a service description (see Section 3) and the Maple application code implementing the service. The Maple wrapper service then creates a MSDL document, publishes it and deploys the service on the server (see Figure 5). A similar REDUCE service may be deployed in the near future.

NAG: provides a number of NAG numerical routines as individual services, along with their MSDL descriptions.

UWO: like Bath, provides a Maple service generator externally similar to Bath's, but which differs in respect of some internal technical details

Bath's Maple Wrapper service is available[4] and from this page a client can add, remove, update, list and invoke Maple services. When adding a Maple service the client is prompted to submit details such as service name and Maple code. The client must also specify the number of inputs, outputs, post-conditions and pre-conditions, and is then prompted to enter descriptions of these in OpenMath. When invoking a Maple service through the Maple Wrapper service, a client fills out fields providing the service name and input arguments in OpenMath.

---

[4] http://agentcities.cs.bath.ac.uk:8090/axis/SMaple/services/index.jsp

6   Related and Future Work

Mathematical Services in Planning: It would be appropriate, and is envisaged in the MONET architecture, that brokers and planners could themselves invoke mathematical services as part of their planning processes. A good example is given in [7, 8], where a linear algebra routine is used to assess the sparsity or not of a system of differential equations, in order to assess which service to invoke to solve the system. We look forward to incorporating such facilities as part of the follow-on EPSRC-funded GENSS project.

Establishing Corpora of Mathematical Services: Although we have talked of deployers preparing MSDL descriptions, this may be quite tedious, furthermore one person's service description may be quite unlike another's even though written for a similar service. For this reason we have just started exploring the classification of services and the semi-automatic generation of service descriptions using conventional information retrieval techniques applied to programs and their documentation. Such a facility will draw on much previous work in information retrieval, classification and machine learning. The describer service developed in myGrid [10] which is a web service front end to a RDF database appears to offer a good basis for the representation and management of this service classification data.

7   Conclusion

We have described the role of an extended form of service description language in delivering mathematical services, which provides semantic information using a combination of input/output and pre-/post-condition constraints grounded in the OpenMath ontology. This richer form of service description in turn enables more effective service discovery and identification than is feasible through UDDI and its developments, moving away from passive directories to active brokerage that may reason about the problem in question.

By taking the well-formalized domain of computational mathematics, significantly assisted by the existence of the OpenMath content dictionaries, it has been possible to focus on developing end-to-end demonstrations of service definition, construction, deployment and discovery with relatively little debate. It is hoped this experience may now be spread into neighbouring disciplines that have a heavy reliance on mathematics, such as physics and engineering, to support e-Science in particular and wider experimentation with web services in general.

Acknowledgements

The authors would like to acknowledge the partners in the MONET project: NAG Ltd., Stilo Ltd., University of Eindhoven, Université de Nice/INRIA Sophia Antipolis, University of Bath, University of Manchester, University of Western Ontario and also thank the Commission of the European Communities for funding this work (project IST-2001-34145).

References

[1] Marc-Laurent Aird, Walter Barbera Medina, and Julian Padget. Monet: service discovery and composition for mathematical problems. In Omer Rana and Sven Graupner, editors, *Proceedings of IEEE workshop on Agent-based Cluster and Grid Computing (at CC-Grid 2003)*, pages 678–687. IEEE Computer Society, IEEE Computer Society Press, May 2003. ISBN 0-7695-1919-9. Invited paper. Also available from the MONET project website: http://monet.nag.co.uk.

[2] Marc-Laurent Aird, Walter Barbera Medina, and Julian Padget. Brokerage for Mathematical Services in MONET. In Laurence Cavedon, editor, *Collected papers from Web Services and Agent Based Systems workshop (AAMAS'03)*. Kluwer, 2004. revised, extended version of [?]; in press.

[3] Tony Andrews, Francisco Curbera, Hitesh Dholakia, Yaron Goland, Johannes Klein, Frank Leymann, Kevin Liu, Dieter Roller, Doug Smith, Satish Thatte, Ivana Trickovic, and Sanjiva Weerawarana. Specification: Business Process Execution Language for Web Services Version 1.1. Report, IBM, May 2003.

[4] S. Buswell, O. Caprotti, and M. Dewar. Mathematical Service Description Language: Initial Draft. Technical report, Technical Report Deliverable, The MONET Consortium, March 2003. Available from http://monet.nag.co.uk.

[5] O. Caprotti, D. Carlisle, A.M. Cohen, and M. Dewar. Mathematical Problem Ontology. Technical report, Technical Report Deliverable, The MONET Consortium, March 2003. Available from http://monet.nag.co.uk.

[6] J.H Davenport. Mathematical Explanation Ontology: Draft. Technical report, Technical Report Deliverable, The MONET Consortium, March 2003. Available from http://monet.nag.co.uk.

[7] B.J. Dupée. Measuring the Likely Effectiveness of Strategies. In J. Calmet, J.A. Campbell, and J. Pfalzgraf, editors, *Proceedings Artificial Intelligence and Symbolic Computation 3*, pages 191–196, 1996.

[8] B.J. Dupée and J.H. Davenport. An Intelligent Interface to Numerical Routines. In J. Calmet and J. Limoncelli, editors, *Proceedings DISCO '96*, pages 252–262, 1996.

[9] I. Horrocks, F. van Harmelen, T. Berners-Lee, and D. Brickley. DAML Joint Committee, March 2001. Available from http://www.daml.org/2001/03/daml+oil-index.html.

[10] Luc Moreau, Simon Miles, Carole Goble, Mark Greenwood, Vijay Dialani, Matthew Addis, Nedim Alpdemir, Rich Cawley, David De Roure, Justin Ferris, Rob Gaizauskas, Kevin Glover, Chris Greenhalgh, Peter Li, Xiaojian Liu, Phillip Lord, Michael Luck, Darren Marvin, Tom Oinn, Norman Paton, Stephen Pettifer, Milena V Radenkovic, Angus Roberts, Alan Robinson, Tom Rodden, Martin Senger, Nick Sharman, Robert Stevens, Brian Warboys, Anil Wipat, and Chris Wroe. On the Use of Agents in a BioInformatics Grid. In Sangsan Lee, Satoshi Sekguchi, Satoshi Matsuoka, and Mitsuhisa Sato, editors, *Proceedings of the Third IEEE/ACM CCGRID'2003 Workshop on Agent Based Cluster and Grid Computing*, pages 653–661, Tokyo, Japan, May 2003.

[11] National Institute for Standards. GAMS Guide to Available Mathematical Software. http://gams.nist.gov/, February 2003.

[12] The Apache Project. Jakarta Home Page. http://jakarta.apache.org. Last accessed January 2004.

[13] The MONET Project. An XSD scheme for Mathematical Services Decsription. http://monet.nag.co.uk/cocoon/monet/publicdocs/index.html.

[14] The OpenMath Society. OpenMath website. http://www.openmath.org, February 2003.

[15] UDDI consortium. UDDI Technical White Paper. http://www.uddi.org/pubs/Iru_UDDI_Technical_White_Paper.pdf, September 2000. Last accessed January 2004.

[16] W3C. *Web Services Description Language (WSDL) Version 1.2 W3C Working Draft*. W3C, 2002-2003. Available from http://www.w3.org/TR/wsdl12.

[17] W3C OWL Working Group. OWL-Web Ontology Language. W3C Working Draft 21 February 2003, April 2003. Available from http://www.w3.org/TR/owl-ref.

[18] World Wide Web Consortium (W3C). Mathematical Markup Language (MathML) Version 2.0 (Second Edition). http://www.w3.org/TR/MathML2/.

[19] Y.Chicha and M.Gaetano. Tbd. Technical report, Implementation Report, The MONET Consortium, February 2003. Available from http://monet.nag.co.uk.

Approaches to Semantic Web Services:
an Overview and Comparisons

Liliana Cabral[1], John Domingue[1], Enrico Motta[1],
Terry Payne[2] and Farshad Hakimpour[1]

[1] Knowledge Media Institute, The Open University, Milton Keynes, UK
{L.S.Cabral, J.B.Domingue, E.Motta, F.Hakimpour}@open.ac.uk
[2] IAM, University of Southampton, Southampton, UK
trp.@ecs.soton.ac.uk

Abstract. The next Web generation promises to deliver Semantic Web Services (SWS); services that are self-described and amenable to automated discovery, composition and invocation. A prerequisite to this, however, is the emergence and evolution of the Semantic Web, which provides the infrastructure for the semantic interoperability of Web Services. Web Services will be augmented with rich formal descriptions of their capabilities, such that they can be utilized by applications or other services without human assistance or highly constrained agreements on interfaces or protocols. Thus, Semantic Web Services have the potential to change the way knowledge and business services are consumed and provided on the Web. In this paper, we survey the state of the art of current enabling technologies for Semantic Web Services. In addition, we characterize the infrastructure of Semantic Web Services along three orthogonal dimensions: *activities, architecture and service ontology*. Further, we examine and contrast three current approaches to SWS according to the proposed dimensions.

1 Introduction

In recent years, distributed programming paradigms have emerged, that allow generic software components to be developed and shared. Whilst early versions were little more than shared libraries of functions with little user documentation and unpredictable side effects, it wasn't until the advent of object-oriented programming and architectures such as CORBA, that self contained components could be reliably defined, documented and shared within a distributed environment. Although ideal for some enterprise integration and eCommerce, it has only been with the adoption of XML as a common data syntax that the underlying principals have gained wide scale adoption, through the definition of Web Service standards. Web services are well defined, reusable, software components that perform specific, encapsulated tasks via standardized Web-oriented mechanisms. They can be discovered, invoked, and the composition of several services can be choreographed, using well defined workflow modeling frameworks.

Whilst promising to revolutionize eCommerce and enterprise-wide integration, current standard technologies for Web services (e.g. WSDL [6]) provide only syntac-

J. Davies et al. (Eds.): ESWS 2004, LNCS 3053, pp. 225-239, 2004.

tic-level descriptions of their functionalities, without any formal definition to what the syntactic definitions might mean. In many cases, Web services offer little more than a formally defined invocation interface, with some human oriented metadata that describes what the service does, and which organization developed it (e.g. through UDDI descriptions). Applications may invoke Web services using a common, extendable communication framework (e.g. SOAP). However, the lack of machine readable semantics necessitates human intervention for automated service discovery and composition within open systems, thus hampering their usage in complex business contexts.

Semantic Web Services (SWS) relax this restriction by augmenting Web services with rich formal descriptions of their capabilities, thus facilitating automated composition, discovery, dynamic binding, and invocation of services within an open environment A prerequisite to this, however, is the emergence and evolution of the Semantic Web, which provides the infrastructure for the semantic interoperability of Web Services. Web Services will be augmented with rich formal descriptions of their capabilities, such that they can be utilized by applications or other services without human assistance or highly constrained agreements on interfaces or protocols. Thus, Semantic Web Services have the potential to change the way knowledge and business services are consumed and provided on the Web.

Current efforts in developing Semantic Web Service infrastructures can be characterized along three orthogonal dimensions: *usage activities, architecture and service ontology*. Usage activities define the functional requirements, which a framework for Semantic Web Services ought to support. The architecture of SWS describes the components needed for accomplishing the activities defined for SWS, whereas the service ontology aggregates all concept models related to the description of a Semantic Web Service.

In this paper we survey the state of the art of current enabling technologies for Semantic Web Services. Further, we examine and contrast three current approaches to SWS according to the proposed dimensions. The rest of the paper is structured as follows: in section 2 we provide a general overview of Web services; in section 3 we provide an overview of the Semantic Web and in particular of those aspects which allow the specification of semantic description for Web services. In section 4 we describe Semantic Web Services according to the dimensions introduced earlier. Sections 5-7 describe the main existing approaches to delivering SWS. Finally we compare and discuss the main differences among the approaches presented.

2 Web Services

Web Services are changing the way applications communicate with each other on the Web. They promise to integrate business operations, reduce the time and cost of Web application development and maintenance as well as promote reuse of code over the World Wide Web. By allowing functionality to be encapsulated and defined in a reusable standardized format, Web services have enabled businesses to share (or trade) functionality with arbitrary numbers of partners, without having to pre-negotiate communication mechanisms or syntax representations. The advent of discovery has enabled vendors to search for Web services, which can then be invoked as necessary.

For example, a book-selling company may look for shipping services, which they may later invoke to ensure that books are delivered to the customers. This flexibility is achieved through a set of well-defined standards that define syntax, communication protocol, and invocation signatures, which allow programs implemented on diverse, heterogeneous platforms to interoperate over the internet.

A Web Service is a software program identified by an URI, which can be accessed via the internet through its exposed interface. The interface description declares the operations which can be performed by the service, the types of messages being exchanged during the interaction with the service, and the physical location of ports, where information should be exchanged. For example, a Web service for calculating the exchange rate between two money currencies can declare the operation *getExchangeRate* with two inputs of type string (for source and target currencies) and an output of type float (for the resulting rate). A binding then defines the machine and ports where messages should be sent. Although there can be many ways of implementing Web services, we basically assume that they are deployed in Web servers such that they can be invoked by any Web application or Web agent independently of their implementations. In addition Web services can invoke other Web services.

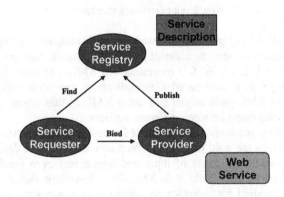

Fig. 1. Web Service usage scenario.

The common usage scenario for Web services (fig. 1) can be defined by three phases; *Publish, Find,* and *Bind;* and three entities: the service requester, which invokes services; the service provider which responds to requests; and the registry where services can be published or advertised. A service provider *publishes* a description of a service it provides to a service registry. This description (or *advertisement*) includes a profile on the provider of the service (e.g. company name and address); a profile about the service itself (e.g. name, category); and the URL of its service interface definition (i.e. WSDL description).

When a developer realizes a need for a new service, he *finds* the desired service either by constructing a query, or browsing the registry. The developer then interprets the meaning of the interface description (typically through the use of meaningful label or variable names, comments, or additional documentation) and *binds* to (i.e. includes a call to invoke) the discovered service within the application they are developing. This application is known as the *service requester.* At this point, the service requester can automatically invoke the discovered service (provided by the service provider) using Web service communication protocols (i.e. SOAP).

Key to the interoperation of Web services is an adoption of a set of enabling standard protocols. Several XML-based standards (fig. 2) have been proposed to support the usage scenario previously described.

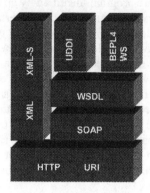

Fig. 2. Web Services enabling standards

XML schema (XML-S) [2] provides the underlying framework for both defining the Web Services Standards, and variables/objects/data types etc that are exchanged between services. SOAP [27] is W3C's recommended XML-data transport protocol, used for data exchange over web-based communications protocols (http). SOAP messages can carry an XML payload defined using XML-S, thus ensuring a consistent interpretation of data items between different services.

WSDL [6] is the W3C recommended language for describing the service interface. Two levels of abstraction are used to describe Web services; the first defines atomic method calls, or *operations*, in terms of input and output *messages* (each of which contain one or more parameters defined in XML-S). Operations define the way in which messages are handled e.g. whether an operation is a *one-way operation, request-response, solicit-response* or *notification*. The second abstraction maps operations and associated messages to physical endpoints, in terms of *ports* and *bindings*. Ports declare the operations available with corresponding inputs and outputs. The bindings declare the transport mechanism (usually SOAP) being used by each operation. WSDL also specifies one or more network locations or endpoints at which the service can be invoked.

As services become available, they may be registered with a UDDI registry [26] which can subsequently be browsed and queried by other users, services and applications. UDDI web service discovery is typically human oriented, based upon yellow or white-page queries (i.e. metadata descriptions of service types, or information about the service providers). UDDI service registrations may also include references to WSDL descriptions, which may facilitate limited automation of discovery and invocation. However, as no explicit semantic information is normally defined, automated comprehension of the WSDL description is limited to cases where the provider and requester assume pre-agreed ontologies, protocols and shared knowledge about operations.

A service might be defined as a workflow describing the choreography of several operations. Such a workflow may determine: the order of operation execution; what operations may be executed concurrently; and alternative execution pathways (if conditional operators are included in the workflow modeling language). Conversely, workflows are required to orchestrate the execution of several simple services that may be composed together for forming a more complex service. Various choreography and orchestration languages have been proposed such as BPEL4WS [5], and are currently being evaluated by various industry standardization bodies.

3 The Semantic Web

The Semantic Web is a vision of a Web of meaningful contents and services, which can be interpreted by computer programs (see for example [1]). It can also be seen as a vast source of information, which can be modelled with the purpose of sharing and reusing knowledge. Semantic Web users will be able to do more accurate searches of the information and the services they need from the tools provided.

The Semantic Web provides the necessary infrastructure for publishing and resolving ontological descriptions of terms and concepts. In addition, it provides the necessary techniques for reasoning about these concepts, as well as resolving and mapping between ontologies, thus enabling semantic interoperability of Web Services through the identification (and mapping) of semantically similar concepts.

Fig. 3. Semantic Web Enabling standards

Ontologies have been developed within the Knowledge Modelling research community [11] in order to facilitate knowledge sharing and reuse. They provide greater expressiveness when modelling domain knowledge and can be used to communicate this knowledge between people and heterogeneous and distributed application systems.

As with Web Services, Semantic Web enabling standards fit into a set of layered specifications (fig. 3) built on the foundation of URIs and XML Schema. The current components of the Semantic Web framework are RDF [13], RDF Schema (RDF-S)

[3] and the Web Ontology Language – OWL [4]. These standards build up a rich set of constructs for describing the semantics of online information sources.

RDF is a XML-based standard from W3C for describing resources on the Web. RDF introduces a little semantics to XML data by allowing the representation of objects and their relations through properties. RDF-Schema is a simple type system, which provides information (metadata) for the interpretation of the statements given in RDF data. The Web Ontology language – OWL will facilitate greater machine interpretability of Web content than RDF and RDF Schema by providing a much richer set of constructs for specifying classes and relations. OWL has evolved from existing ontologies languages and specifically from DAML+OIL [12].

4 Semantic Web Services

Semantic descriptions of Web services are necessary in order to enable their automatic discovery, composition and execution across heterogeneous users and domains. Existing technologies for Web services only provide descriptions at the syntactic level, making it difficult for requesters and providers to interpret or represent nontrivial statements such as the meaning of inputs and outputs or applicable constraints. This limitation may be relaxed by providing a rich set of semantic annotations that augment the service description. A Semantic Web Service is defined through a service ontology, which enables machine interpretability of its capabilities as well as integration with domain knowledge.

The deployment of Semantic Web Services will rely on the further development and combination of Web Services and Semantic Web enabling technologies. There exist several initiatives (e.g. http://dip.semanticweb.org or http://www.swsi.org) taking place in industry and academia, which are investigating solutions for the main issues regarding the infrastructure for SWS.

Semantic Web Service infrastructures can be characterized along three orthogonal dimensions (fig. 4): *usage activities, architecture and service ontology*. These dimensions relate to the requirements for SWS at business, physical and conceptual levels. Usage activities define the functional requirements, which a framework for Semantic Web Services ought to support. The architecture of SWS defines the components needed for accomplishing these activities. The service ontology aggregates all concept models related to the description of a Semantic Web Service, and constitutes the knowledge-level model of the information describing and supporting the usage of the service.

From the usage activities perspective, SWS are seen as objects within a business application execution scenario. The activities required for running an application using SWS include: publishing, discovery, selection, composition, invocation, deployment and ontology management, as described next.

The publishing or advertisement of SWS will allow agents or applications to discover services based on its goals and capabilities. A semantic registry is used for registering instances of the service ontology for individual services. The service ontology distinguishes between information which is used for matching during discovery and that used during service invocation. In addition, domain knowledge should also be published or linked to the service ontology.

The discovery of services consists of a semantic matching between the description of a service request and the description of published service. Queries involving the service name, input, output, preconditions and other attributes can be constructed and used for searching the semantic registry. The matching can also be done at the level of tasks or goals to be achieved, followed by a selection of services which solves the task. The degree of matching can be based on some criteria, such as the inheritance relationship of types. For example, an input of type Professor of a provided service can be said to match an input of type Academic of a requested service.

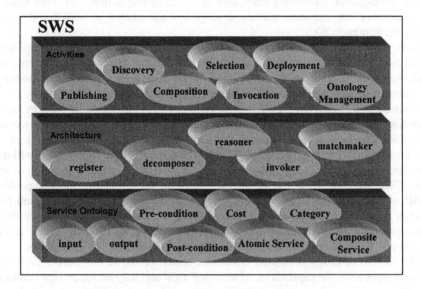

Fig. 4. Semantic Web Services infrastructure dimensions.

A selection of services is required if there is more than one service matching the request. Non-functional attributes such as cost or quality can be used for choosing one service. In a more specialized or agent-based type of interaction a negotiation process can be started between a requester and a provider, but that requires that the services themselves be knowledge-based. In general, a broker would check that the pre-conditions of tasks and services are satisfied and prove that the services post-conditions and effects imply goal accomplishment. An explanation of the decision-making process should also be provided.

Composition or choreography allows SWS to be defined in terms of other simpler services. A workflow expressing the composition of atomic services can be defined in the service ontology by using appropriate control constructs. This description would be grounded on a syntactic description such as BEPL4WS [5]. Dynamic composition is also being considered as an approach during service request in which the atomic services required to solve a request are located and composed on the fly. That requires an invoker which matches the outputs of atomic services against the input of the re-quested service.

The invocation of SWS involves a number of steps, once the required inputs have been provided by the service requester. First, the service and domain ontologies associated with the service must be instantiated. Second, the inputs must be validated against the ontology types. Finally the service can be invoked or a workflow executed through the grounding provided. Monitoring the status of the decomposition process and notifying the requester in case of exceptions is also important.

The deployment of a Web service by a provider is independent of the publishing of its semantic description since the same Web service can have serve multiple purposes. But, the SWS infrastructure can provide a facility for the instant deployment of code for a given semantic description.

The management of service ontologies is a cornerstone activity for SWS since it will guarantee that semantic service descriptions are created, accessed and reused within the Semantic Web.

From the architecture perspective (fig. 4), SWS are defined by a set of components which realize the activities above, with underlying security and trust mechanisms. The components gathered from the discussion above include: a register, a reasoner, a matchmaker, a decomposer and an invoker.

The reasoner is used during all activities and provides the reasoning support for interpreting the semantic descriptions and queries. The register provides the mechanisms for publishing and locating services in a semantic registry as well as functionalities for creating and editing service descriptions. The matchmaker will mediate between the requester and the register during the discovery and selection of services. The decomposer is the component required for executing the composition model of composed services. The invoker will mediate between requester and provider or decomposer and provider when invoking services. These components are illustrative of the required roles in the SWS architecture for the discussion here as they can have different names and a complexity of their own in different approaches.

The service ontology is another dimension under which we can define SWS (fig. 4), for it represents the capabilities of a service itself and the restrictions applied to its use. The service ontology essentially integrates at the knowledge-level the information which has been defined by Web services standards, such as UDDI and WSDL with related domain knowledge. This would include: functional capabilities such as inputs, output, pre-conditions and post-conditions; non-functional capabilities such as category, cost and quality of service; provider related information, such as company name and address; task or goal-related information; and domain knowledge defining, for instance, the type of the inputs of the service. This information can, in fact be divided in several ontologies. However, the service ontology used for describing SWS will rely on the expressivity and inference power of the underlying ontology language supported by the Semantic Web.

Three main approaches have been driving the development of Semantic Web Service frameworks: IRS-II [17], OWL-S [19] and WSMF [9]. IRS-II (Internet Reasoning Service) is a knowledge-based approach to SWS, which evolved from research on reusable knowledge components [16]. OWL-S is an agent-oriented approach to SWS, providing fundamentally an ontology for describing Web service capabilities. WSMF (Web Service modeling framework) is a business-oriented approach to SWS, focusing on a set of e-commerce requirements for Web Services including trust and security. The following sections describe these approaches in more detail.

5 IRS Approach

The Internet Reasoning Service - IRS-II [17] is a Semantic Web Services framework, which allows applications to semantically describe and execute Web services.

IRS-II is based on the UPML (Unified Problem Solving Method Development Language) framework [18], which distinguishes between the following categories of components specified by means of an appropriate ontology:

- *Domain models.* These describe the domain of an application (e.g. vehicles, a medical disease).

- *Task models.* These provide a generic description of the task to be solved, specifying the input and output types, the goal to be achieved and applicable preconditions.

- *Problem Solving Methods (PSMs).* These provide abstract, implementation-independent descriptions of reasoning processes which can be applied to solve tasks in a specific domain.

- *Bridges.* These specify mappings between the different model components within an application.

The main components of the IRS-II architecture are the IRS-II Server, the IRS-II Publisher and the IRS-II Client, which communicate through the SOAP protocol. The IRS-II server holds descriptions of Semantic Web Services at two different levels. A knowledge level description is stored using the UPML framework of tasks, PSMs and domain models. These are currently represented internally in OCML [16], an Onto-lingua-derived language which provides both the expressive power to express task specifications and service competencies, as well as the operational support to reason about these. In addition, IRS-II has a special-purpose mapping mechanism to ground competence specifications to specific Web services.

The IRS-II Publisher plays two roles in the IRS-II architecture. Firstly, it links Web services to their semantic descriptions within the IRS-II server. Note that each PSM is associated with exactly one Web service although a Web service may map onto more than one PSM since a single piece of code may serve more than one function. Secondly, the publisher automatically generates a wrapper which turns the code into a Web service. Once this code is published within the IRS-II it appears as a standard message-based Web service, that is, a Web service endpoint is automatically generated. There can be more than one type of Publisher or publishing platform, depending on the implementation of the service. This design option allows for the instant deployment of code during publishing as explained before and mediation between the server and the actual service (code) during invocation.

A key feature of IRS-II is that Web service invocation is capability driven. The IRS-II supports this by providing a task centric invocation mechanism. An IRS-II user simply asks for a task to be achieved and the IRS-II broker locates an appropriate PSM and then invokes the corresponding Web service.

IRS-II was designed for ease of use. Developers can interact with IRS-II through the IRS-II browser, which facilitates navigation of knowledge models registered in IRS-II as well as the editing of service descriptions, the publishing and the invocation of individual services. Application programs can be integrated with IRS-II by using the Java API. These programs can then combine tasks that can be achieved within an application scenario.

6 OWL-S Approach

OWL-S (previously DAML-S [9]) consists of a set of ontologies designed for describing and reasoning over service descriptions. OWL-S approach originated from an AI background and has previously been used to describe agent functionality within several Multi-Agent Systems as well as with a variety of planners to solve higher level goals.

OWL-S combines the expressivity of description logics (in this case OWL) and the pragmatism found in the emerging Web Services Standards, to describe services that can be expressed semantically, and yet grounded within a well defined data typing formalism. It consists of three main upper ontologies: the Profile, Process Model and Grounding. The Profile is used to describe services for the purposes of discovery; service descriptions (and queries) are constructed from a description of functional properties (i.e. inputs, outputs, preconditions, and effects - IOPEs), and non-functional properties (human oriented properties such as service name, etc, and parameters for defining additional meta data about the service itself, such as concept type or quality of service). In addition, the profile class can be subclassed and specialized, thus supporting the creation of profile taxonomies which subsequently describe different classes of services.

OWL-S process models describe the composition or orchestration of one or more services in terms of their constituent processes. This is used both for reasoning about possible compositions (such as validating a possible composition, determining if a model is executable given a specific context, etc) and controlling the enactment/invocation of a service. Three process classes have been defined: the composite, simple and atomic process. The atomic process is a single, black-box process description with exposed IOPEs. Inputs and outputs relate to data channels, where data flows between processes. Preconditions specify facts of the world that must be asserted in order for an agent to execute a service. Effects characterize facts that become asserted given a successful execution of the service, such as the physical side-effects that the execution the service has on the physical world. Simple processes provide a means of describing service or process abstractions – such elements have no specific binding to a physical service, and thus have to be realized by an atomic process (e.g. through service discovery and dynamic binding at run-time), or expanded into a composite process. Composite processes are hierarchically defined workflows, consisting of atomic, simple and other composite processes. These process workflows are constructed using a number of different composition constructs, including: Sequence, Unordered, Choice, If-then-else, Iterate, Repeat-until, Repeat-while, Split, and Split+join.

The profile and process models provide semantic frameworks whereby services can be discovered and invoked, based upon conceptual descriptions defined within Semantic Web (i.e. OWL) ontologies. The grounding provides a pragmatic binding between this concept space and the physical data/machine/port space, thus facilitating service execution. The process model is mapped to a WSDL description of the service, through a thin grounding. Each atomic process is mapped to a WSDL operation, and the OWL-S properties used to represent inputs and outputs are grounded in terms of XML data types. Additional properties pertaining to the binding of the service are also provided (i.e. the IP address of the machine hosting the service, and the ports used to expose the service).

7 WSMF Approach

The Web Service Modeling Framework (WSMF) [9] provides a model for describing the various aspects related to Web services. Its main goal is to fully enable e-commerce by applying Semantic Web technology to Web services. WSMF is the product of research on modelling of reusable knowledge components [10].

WSMF is centered on two complementary principles: a strong de-coupling of the various components that realize an e-commerce application; and a strong mediation service enabling Web services to communicate in a scalable manner. Mediation is applied at several levels: mediation of data structures; mediation of business logics; mediation of message exchange protocols; and mediation of dynamic service invocation.

WSMF consists of four main elements: ontologies that provide the terminology used by other elements; goal repositories that define the problems that should be solved by Web services; Web services descriptions that define various aspects of a Web service; and mediators which bypass interoperability problems.

WSMF implementation has been assigned to two main projects: Semantic Web enabled Web Services (SWWS) [25]; and WSMO (Web Service Modelling Ontology) [28]. SWWS will provide a description framework, a discovery framework and a mediation platform for Web Services, according to a conceptual architecture. WSMO will refine WSMF and develop a formal service ontology and language for SWS.

WSMO service ontology includes definitions for goals, mediators and web services. A web service consists of a capability and an interface. The underlying representation language for WSMO is F-logic. The rationale for the choice of F-logic is that it is a full first order logic language that provides second order syntax while staying in the first order logic semantics, and has a minimal model semantics. The main characterizing feature of the WSMO architecture is that the goal, web service and ontology components are linked by four types of mediators as follows:

- OO mediators link ontologies to ontologies,
- WW mediators link web services to web services,
- WG mediators link web services to goals, and finally,
- GG mediators link goals to goals.

Since within WSMO all interoperability aspects are concentrated in mediators the provision of different classes of mediators based on the types of components connected facilitates a clean separation of the different mediation functionalities required when creating WSMO based applications.

8 SWS Approaches Comparison

This comparison discusses the delivered results of IRS-II, OWL-S and WSMF (SWWS) as they represent the main approaches driving the implementation of Semantic Web Service components. The following table shows the high-level elements of each approach as implemented by the time of this writing fitting into the previously discussed dimensions of SWS, including the application tools provided as well.

Table 1. Delivered components of current SWS approaches

	IRS-II	OWL-S	WSMF
SWS Activities	Publishing Selection Task Achievement	Composition Discovery Invocation	Discovery
Architecture	Server Publisher Client	Daml-s Virtual Machine Matchmaker	Service Registry Profile Crawler
Service Ontology	Task/PSM Ontology	OWL-S	WSMO
Application tools	IRS Browser and Editor; Publisher; Java API	WSDL2DAML-S	Query interface

The IRS-II approach has concentrated efforts in delivering an infrastructure that users can easily use from the stage where they have some service code available, to the semantic markup and publishing of this code, to the invocation of this code through task achievement. Because services are considered atomic in IRS-II, there is no semantic description of composed services, although a PSM can embody a control flow for subtasks. Also, a selection of services is performed for finding which PSMs can solve the task requested.

The service ontology of IRS-II consists of a Task ontology and a PSM ontology, which separate the description of what a service does from the parameters and constraints of a particular implementation. Additionally, the task ontology can also include a domain ontology. In IRS, service constraints (e.g. pre-conditions and post-conditions) must be expressed in OCML but an OWL-to-OCML parser has recently been completed. An import/export mechanism for OWL-S service descriptions, which includes the adoption of the properties of the OWL-S Profile is being implemented as well.

The main contribution of the OWL-S approach is its service ontology, which builds on the Semantic Web stack of standards. OWL-S models capabilities required for Web services to the extent of grounding, which maps to WSDL descriptions. Additionally, the Daml consortium has put a lot of effort in representing the interactions among Web Services through the process model of the OWL-S service ontology.

Since the OWL-S service ontology is public and does not prescribe a framework implementation it has been used as the starting point of individual efforts towards SWS, for example [15]. Nevertheless, the DAML consortium has implemented some components of an architecture based on the DAML inference engine [20] [21]. The invocation activity of OWL-S involves a decomposition of the process model. The discovery activity demonstrated in [22] relies on the extension of UDDI registry.

The WSMF approach, although delivering a conceptual framework, invested considerable effort in bringing business requirements into account when proposing a conceptual architecture. Some of the outcomes are still in the form of more detailed specifications. In particular, a service registry has been proposed for which a high-level query language is defined according to the service ontology [25]. WSMO distinguished characteristic is the inclusion of mediators in the ontology specification.

In common with IRS-II, the WSMF approach builds on the UPML framework, taking advantage of the separation of tasks (goals) specifications from the service specifications.

9 Discussion and Conclusions

A complete solution for delivering Semantic Web Services is on the way. Although the vision for SWS has been set and many partial solution cases demonstrated (see for example ISWC 2003) for solving particular issues, only now is the area as a whole taking shape. This is evidenced by the fast-paced evolution of the underlying standards and technologies and the proof-of-concept stage of research in the area.

The state of the art of SWS shows that technologies will shape towards accepted enabling standards for Web Services and the Semantic Web. In particular, IRS-II, OWL-S and WSMF promise inter-compatibility in terms of OWL-based service descriptions and WSDL-based grounding.

However, an assessment of the delivered results of IRS-II, OWL-S and WSMF approaches show that Semantic Web Services are far from mature. While they represent different development approaches converging to the same objective, they provide different reasoning support, which are based on different logic and ontology frameworks. Furthermore, they emphasize different ontology-based service capabilities and activities according to the orientation of their approaches.

None of the approaches described provide a complete solution according to the dimensions illustrated, but interestingly enough they show complementary strengths. For example, IRS-II has strong user and application integration support while OWL-S provides a rich XML-based service-ontology. WSMF has a comprehensive conceptual architecture, which covers requirements of one of the most demanding web-based application area, namely e-commerce. These requirements reflect the way business clients buy and sell services.

Summarizing, Semantic Web Services are an emerging area of research and currently all the supporting technologies are still far from the final product. There are technologies available for creating distributed applications which rely on the execution of Web services deployed on the WWW, however, these technologies require a human user in the loop for selecting services available in registries. Semantic Web technology can be utilised to do the markup and reasoning of Web service capabilities.

We have described the current main approaches to Semantic Web Services: IRS-II, OWL-S and WSMF. These approaches are complementary in many ways and can be compared according to different dimensions of SWS.

Nevertheless, there are still a number of issues concerning Semantic Web Services being investigated in a number of initiatives. These issues range from service composition to service trust and will have the attention of industry and academia for the next few years.

References

1. Berners-Lee, T. Hendler, J., Lassila, O.: The Semantic Web. Scientific American, Vol. 284 (4). (2001) 34-43
2. Biron, P. V., Malhotra, A. (eds.): XML Schema Part 2: Datatypes, W3C Recommendation, 2 May 2001. http://www.w3.org/TR/xmlschema-2/. (2001)
3. Brickley D., Guha R.V. (eds.): RDF Vocabulary Description Language 1.0: RDF Schema, W3C Proposed Recommendation (work in progress). http://www.w3.org/TR/rdf-schema/. (2003)
4. Bechhofer, S., Dean, M., Van Harmelen, F., Hendler, J., Horrocks, I., McGuinness, D., Patel-Schneider, P., Schreiber, G., Stein, L.: OWL Web Ontology Language Reference, W3C Proposed Recommendation (work in progress). http://www.w3.org/TR/owl-ref/. (2003)
5. BPEL4WS Consortium. Business Process Execution Language for Web Services. http://www.ibm.com/developerworks/library/ws-bpel
6. Christensen, E. Curbera, F., Meredith, G., Weerawarana, S. Web Services Description Language (WSDL), W3C Note 15. http://www.w3.org/TR/wsdl. (2001)
7. Christoph, B., Fensel, D., Maedche, A.: A Conceptual Architecture for Semantic Web Enabled Web Services. . http://swws.semanticweb.org/public_doc/D2.1.pdf. (2003)
8. DAML-S Coalition: DAML-S 0.9 Draft Release. http://www.daml.org/services/daml-s/0.9/. (2003)
9. Fensel, D., Bussler, C. The Web Service Modeling Framework WSMF. Eletronic Commerce: Research and Applications. Vol. 1. (2002). 113-137
10. Fensel, D. and Motta, E.: Structured Development of Problem Solving Methods. IEEE Transactions on Knowledge and Data Engineering, Vol. 13(6). (2001). 913-932.
11. Gruber, T. R. A Translation Approach to Portable Ontology Specifications. Knowledge Acquisition, 5(2). (1993)
12. Joint US/EU ad hoc Committee. Reference Description of the DAML-OIL Ontology Markup Language. http://www.daml.org/2001/03/reference. (2001)
13. Klyne, G., D., Carroll, J.J. (eds.): Resource Description Framework (RDF): Concepts and Abstract Syntax. W3C Proposed Recommendation (work in progress). http://www.w3.org/TR/rdf-concepts/. (2003)
14. Mandell, D., McIlraith, S. Grounding the Semantic Web: A Bottom-up Approach to Automating Web Service Discovery, Customization and Semantic Translation. In Workshop on E-Services and the Semantic Web (ESSW03) in conjunction with WWW03.
15. McIlraith, S., Son, T. C., Zeng, H. Semantic Web Services. IEEE Intelligent Systems, Vol. 16(2). (2001) 46-53.
16. Motta E.. Reusable Components for Knowledge Modelling. IOS Press, Amsterdam, The Netherlands. (1999)

17. Motta, E., Domingue, J., Cabral, L., Gaspari, M.: IRS-II: A Framework and Infrastructure for Semantic Web Services. In: Fensel, D., Sycara, K., Mylopoulos, J. (volume eds.): The SemanticWeb - ISWC 2003. Lecture Notes in Computer Science, Vol. 2870. Springer-Verlag, Heidelberg (2003) 306–318

18. Omelayenko, B., Crubezy, M., Fensel, D., Benjamins, R., Wielinga, B., Motta, E., Musen, M., Ding, Y..: UPML: The language and Tool Support for Makiing the Semantic Web Alive. In: Fensel, D. et al. (eds.): Spinning the Semantic Web: Bringing the WWW to its Full Potential. MIT Press (2003) 141–170

19. OWL-S Coalition: OWL-S 1.0 Release. http://www.daml.org/services/owl-s/1.0/. (2003)

20. Paolucci, M., Sycara, K. and Kawamura, T.: Delivering Semantic Web Services. Tech. report CMU-RI-TR-02-32, Robotics Institute, Carnegie Mellon University, May, 2003

21. Paolucci, M., Ankolekar, A., et al.: The Daml-S Virtual Machine. In: Fensel, D., Sycara, K., Mylopoulos, J. (volume eds.): The Semantic Web - ISWC 2003 Proceedings. Lecture Notes in Computer Science, Vol. 2870. Springer-Verlag, Heidelberg (2003) 290-305

22. Paolucci, M., Kawamura, T., Payne, T., Sycara, K.: Semantic Matching of Web Services Capabilities. In: Horrocks, I. Handler, J. (eds.): The Semantic Web - ISWC 2002 Proceedings. Lecture Notes in Computer Science, Vol. 2342. Springer-Verlag, Heidelberg (2002) 333-347

23. Sirin, E., Hendler, J. and Parsia, B. Semi-automatic Composition of Web Services using Semantic Descriptions. In: Web Services: Modeling, Architecture and Infrastructure workshop in conjunction with ICEIS2003. (2003).

24. Wu, D., Parsia, B., et al: Automating DAML-S Web Services Composition Using SHOP2. In: Fensel, D., Sycara, K., Mylopoulos, J. (volume eds.): The SemanticWeb - ISWC 2003. Lecture Notes in Computer Science, Vol. 2870. Springer-Verlag, Heidelberg (2003) 195-210

25. SWWS Consortium. Report on Development of Web Service Discovery Framework. October 2003. http://swws.semanticweb.org/public_doc/D3.1.pdf

26. UDDI Consortium. UDDI Specification. http://www.uddi.org/specification.html (2000)

27. W3C. SOAP 1.2, W3C Recommendation. http://www.w3.org/TR/soap12-part0/ (2003)

28. WSMO Working Group. Web Service Modelling Ontology Project. DERI Working Drafts. http://www.nextwebgeneration.org/projects/wsmo/ (2004)

OWL-S Semantics of Security Web Services: a Case Study

Grit Denker*, Son Nguyen, and Andrew Ton

SRI International, Menlo Park, California, USA
denker@csl.sri.com

Abstract. The power of Web services (WS) technology lies in the fact that it takes integration to a new level. With the increasing amount of services available on the Web, solutions are needed that address security concerns of distributed Web service applications such as end-to-end service requirements for authentication, authorization, data integrity and confidentiality, and non-repudiation in the context of dynamic WS applications. Semantic Web technology and Semantic Web services (SWSs) promise to provide solutions to the challenges of dynamically composed service-based applications. We investigate the use of semantic annotations for security WS that can be used by matchmakers or composition tools to achieve security goals. In the long-term we aim at establishing a security framework for SWS applications that include security services, authentication and authorization protocols, and techniques to exchange and negotiate policies. In this paper, we report on the first step toward this larger vision: specification, design, and deployment of semantically well-defined security services.

1 Introduction

Web services (WS) are celebrated as the next generation of Web technologies that will dramatically increase integration and interoperability among distributed applications. One crucial aspect is the *dynamic nature* of many WS-based transactions where service requesters and service providers interact to achieve goals. In this dynamic context, applications are created on-the-fly by discovering, selecting, and composing appropriate WSs.

Given that many of today's WS applications are concerned with financial or personal data, one of the main barriers to overcome is the provision of appropriate security measures including means to address privacy concerns, protect confidential data, and reliably establish authenticated and trusted connections between entities that want to share business, collaborate on research projects, or enter into other kinds of mutual contracts. In the course of dynamically establishing distributed, complex WS applications, various security-related tasks must be completed. Clients need to be authenticated to services and vice versa, and credentials need to be exchanged to authorize the use of the services. Payment methods and privacy policies must be negotiated until a contract is established

* Supported by the Defense Advanced Research Projects Agency through the Air Force Research Laboratory under Contract F30602-00-C-0168 to SRI.

J. Davies et al. (Eds.): ESWS 2004, LNCS 3053, pp. 240–253, 2004.

that is to everyone's satisfaction. Protocols are needed to establish trust among clients and services (in a client-server model) or among services that work together to accomplish a complex task (in a server-server model).

Generally, distribued WS applications connect independently controlled domains, across application and organizational boundaries, and issues related to service protection and security, reliability of results, or validity of source and cost become important. Standard security requirements include authentication, authorization, data integrity and confidentiality, and non-repudiation. Instead of implementing new security mechanisms for each WS application, we propose security capabilities that can be reused to meet the security needs of various applications. We use standard cryptographic techniques such as encryption and digital signatures to provide basic security building blocks that can be used in combination with other services to provide functionality sought after by users in application scenarios in which security is one of the concerns.

Our approach is to define *semantically meaningful, declarative, machine-processable descriptions of security capabilities in form of WSs*. For the future we envision that in the dynamic process of generating a composed WS application appropriate tools, such as service matchmakers, can discover these semantically well-defined, high-level security WSs and use them to satisfy the security needs of service requesters and providers. In our opinion, engineers and application experts should not be forced to be information security specialists in order to build WS application. We rather envision a technology that will support them by making the greatest possible use of existing technology to meet the needs of emerging applications. In this paper, we address the first step of this vision. We report on our experience in semantically specifying and deploying various security services.

We use Semantic Web technology to model the capabilities of security WSs. Semantic Web is the next generation of the World Wide Web that envisions all Web data to be annotated in a machine-readable and machine-comprehensible way (see http://www.w3c.org). This allows machines to process and exchange information over the Internet more effectively and more meaningfully than today's XML-based approaches to interoperability allow. This way, Semantic Web technology promises to provide solutions to the challenges of dynamic discovery, selection, composition, invocation, and runtime monitoring of Web applications. WSs annotated with meta-data are commonly referred to as Semantic Web services (SWS). SWSs were invented as an extension of WSs that are already widely in use.

Our work is done in the context of the DARPA Agent Markup Language (DAML) project, a project that promotes the vision of the Semantic Web and SWS. The definition of the Web Ontology Language (OWL), currently in the standardization phase at W3C, was one of the major achievements supported by DAML. One of the applications of OWL resulted in specifying a sublanguage of OWL, called *OWL-S*, for Semantic WSs. Given this background, the security services proposed in this paper are annotated in OWL-S. Our services are among very few existing OWL-S services that have not only been rigorously specified but also realized and deployed. We report on the design, annotation, implementation and deployment of those services.

The remainder of this paper is organized as follows. In Section 2 we briefly introduce OWL-S and basic security notations. We also discuss related work. Section 3 introduces the services that we have implemented so far. We describe the architecture common to all security services and software components used in our project. One of the security services, an XML signature service, is discussed in more detail in Section 4. We present which WS development environments we investigated and discuss advantages and disadvantages of those environments. We will provide OWL-S markup and details about the implementation (including code samples) of the XML signature service. Section 5 discusses how we envision the basic security services to be used in complex SWS applications and points out directions of future work.

2 Background and Related Work

We briefly discuss OWL-S—a service ontology which is the basis of our work— and security notations used in the remainder of the paper, followed by an overview of related work.

2.1 Background

Our work is built on OWL-S (see http://www.daml.org/services/owl-s/1.0/), an OWL-based ontology for semantic markup of WSs and supporting tools and agent technology to enable automation of SWSs. OWL-S is grounded on previous work in open Multi-Agent systems and WSs [1, 2, 3, 4, 5] that identified the main features of WSs operating in an open environment such as the Web. Specifically, OWL-S describes a WS at three levels of abstraction: capability, process, and invocation. The top-level class of an OWL-S description is Service. A service presents a ServiceProfile (*what it does*, i.e., capabilities), is described by a ServiceModel (*how it works*, i.e., process), and supports ServiceGroundings (*how it is used*, i.e., invocation). More detailed information about the OWL-S ontologies will be given in the course of presenting the security service in OWL-S in Section 4.

In this paper we will refer to various well-known security notations that we briefly overview here to establish a common ground. In many applications it is crucial that information that is retrieved can be trusted wrt its integrity. That means that a requesting client would like to get assurance that the content of the Web page or message that is being retrieved is in fact what the purported author of the Web page intended to state. There exist several cryptographic techniques that assure data integrity wrt malicious behavior that deliberately alters data. Such errors can be detected using message authentication codes (MACs) or digital signatures on hash values. Another important aspect is confidentiality of data. This is often achieved by using encryption. Underlying key infrastructures necessary for performing encryption and digital signatures are either *public key infrastructures*—also called *asymmetric key infrastructures*—or *symmetric key infrastructures*—also called *shared key infrastructures*. Symmetric keys are meant to be kept secret between the entities that use the key to encrypt or sign data. Since a symmetric key is its own inverse, only one key is needed for encryption and decryption. Public key infrastructures have pairs of (private,public) keys, being inverses of each other. The private key is supposed to be secret to the owner of the key, and the public key is made publicly available. The secret key is used for digital signatures, and the public key can be used for encryption, transforming the plaintext into a cyphertext from which the plaintext can be obtained only by those entities that possess the corresponding secret key to decrypt it.

2.2   Related Work

Related work stems from the areas of trust and privacy policies for the Semantic Web, security for WSs, and (semantic) WS compositions.

Rei [6, 7], KAoS [8, 9], Security Policy Language [10], and Ponder [11] are languages for high-level, security-related policy specification. We envision that the security services proposed in this paper will be used as one concrete realization of some of the authentication and privacy policies stated in Rei or KAoS. Some work in this direction is under development as a collaboration between IHMC, SRI, and UMBC. An approach to combining cryptographically-based techniques with trust in social networks by using ontological trust specifications has been proposed in [12]. The work by Sadeh and Gandon on semantic e-wallet [13] focusses on privacy issues. It provides means to capture a user's operating context at a semantic level and rules to specify when access to this context is granted. It would be interesting to investigate how this work can be combined with our approach. If a requesting entity is granted access to a user's private information, it may be preferable to send this information in a confidential way. This is where our security services could prove useful. Other Semantic Web-inspired work on assessments about information resources based on individual feedback can be found in [14].

Lately there has been a significant body of standardization efforts for XML-based security (e.g., WS Security [15], XML encryption and digital signature [16, 17] SAML [18], and the Security Specifications of the Liberty Alliance Project [19]). The standards support low-level security or policy markups that concern formats of credentials or supported character sets for encoding. This work is not intended to define the semantics of a security service. It is rather meant to describe low-level implementation security details of WSs.

For WS composition there exist standardization efforts (cf. WSCI http://www.w3.org/TR/wsci/ or OASIS Web Services Composite Application Framework) as well as work that aims to take advantage of semantically rich service markup (for example [20] and [21]). The latter work is relevant for our future work when we need to compose security services with other services to satisfy complex application goals.

3   Semantic Security Web Services: an Overview

We aim to provide a security framework that supports establishing trust between clients and WSs (or among WSs) for the purpose of achieving the goals
of a complex application. Our first steps toward this vision are the design and
implementation of security services that are the basic building blocks for such a
framework. The security services implement clearly defined functionality, such
as signing or verifying XML signatures or encryption and decryption of messages
and files. Security services can be combined to achieve more complex security
mechanisms, such as authentication of individuals intending to form a group
that shares a key for confidential communication.

3.1   Development and Architecture

The security services provided are deployed in an environment that makes use
of various publicly available software modules. An overview of the architecture
is illustrated in Figure 1.

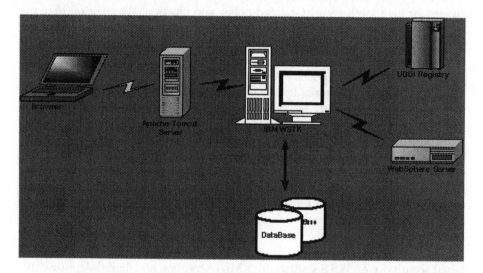

Fig. 1. Web Service Architecture

The Apache Tomcat Web server is used to host Web applications that
represent the presentation layer. The applications include html, jsp, and
servlets for GUIs. The user interacts with the presentation layer to exchange information. WSTK is a WSs toolkit provided by IBM that supports developing WSs with a product-level development environment (see
http://alphaworks.ibm.com/tech/webservicetoolkit). The WSTK hosts applications that represent the business logic layer. Actual transactions such as processing data, encrypting, decrypting, and accessing the database are executed here.

In other words, all services hosted by WSTK are carried out in the background in the business layer. These two layers constitute a two-tier architecture that is appropriate because of the comparable small size of our project and it gives us sufficient flexibility and independence between the two layers in developing WSs. The main reason for choosing Apache Tomcat and WSTK servers is that these servers do not require licenses. On the other hand, they have some restrictions that do not allow us to develop the project in a multiple-tier architecture model. Other commercial development environments such as BEA WebLogic, Websphere, and .NET offer more flexibilities to develop WSs, but developers are required to have licenses.

We provide OWL-S annotation of our security services. These annotations are developed by hand and have been validated using BBN's online OWL validator (see http://owl.bbn.com/validator). Validating our ontologies with this toolkit results in some warnings. These warnings are not caused by problems in the ontologies; rather, they are due to current restrictions in the validator. All warnings reported are due to missing reasoning about a somewhat complex inheritance relationship in ontologies that is not yet performed by the validator. We reported our findings to Mike Dean (BBN), one of the implementors of the validator, and he confirmed that the current validator is not yet capable of performing the necessary reasoning steps.

3.2 Deployed Security Services

We present several basic security services that we designed, implemented, and deployed using the above-described approach. The following four services have been implemented so far:
1. Login service for authentication
2. X.509 certificate generation
3. Signing and verifying SOAP and XML messages
4. Encryption and decryption of text messages and files

In the following we give brief descriptions of each of the services. We then outline how we intend to apply these services in a larger context to establish a security framework for SWS applications. More details on the design, realization, and deployment of one of the services, namely the service for signing and verifying SOAP or XML messages, is presented in the Section 4.

Login Service. The login service realizes a simple authentication policy. A new user registers with the service by providing that user's first name, last name, user name, a password, and email address. A public key pair is generated for each user at registration time, and it is stored in a database. In this way, the same public/private key pair can be loaded after login from the database when other cryptographic services are requested by the user.

X.509 Certificate Generation Service. The X.509 certificate generation WS has the capability to generate a keystore. X.509 certificates are structured data types that contain the name and public key of the user to which the certificate is issued.

For the moment, our certificate generation service creates only self-signed X.509 certificates. In the future we will explore certificate chain generation rooted in certificates signed by a certificate authority. Certificates are stored together with the corresponding private key in the keystore. A client can request an X.509 certificate and the private key from the service provider. We used a capability from Bouncy Castle (bcprov-jdk14.119.jar) to support different key pair generation algorithms such RSA and DSA.

SOAP/XML Signature and Verification Service. We implemented a security WS that provides SOAP and XML signing and verifying. Input parameter to this service are the XML file containing the SOAP message and a keystore filename and the output is an XML file that contains a signed SOAP message. The verification service requires an XML file that contains a signed SOAP message as an input parameter. The output is a status message that indicates whether the signature is valid or invalid. We used the Apache XML Security 1.0 package to implement the security service.

Encryption/Decryption Service. We provided a service that supports encryption of messages, text files, or XML documents. The service can also perform decryption on these three input types. We describe the functionality of this service for XML documents.

The user specifies the XML document to be encrypted and chooses among three options: (a) encrypting the whole XML document, (b) encrypting an element of the XML document, or (c) encrypting the content of an element in the XML document. The WS gets the name of the element that is to be encrypted (in case of option b or c), the name of the encryption algorithm (transparent to the user since it is chosen by our implementation), the encrypted symmetric key, the XML document, and an indication of which option (element, element content, or document) was chosen by the client. At the server side a symmetric key is created and encrypted with the public key of the user. The XML document or element is encrypted with the symmetric key. The encrypted symmetric key and the name of the encryption algorithm are also included in the output that contains the encrypted XML document. The output document is sent back to the client.

In the decryption of an XML document specified by a client, the secret key that was previously created, encrypted with the user's password, and stored, is loaded and decrypted with the user's password before it is sent along with the XML document to the WS. On the server side the encrypted symmetric key, key name, and encryption method are obtained from the XML document. The symmetric key is decrypted with the secret key, and the resulting encryption key is used to decrypt the encrypted part of the XML document. The output file is sent back to the client side.

4   XML Signature Web Service

Our security services will not be useful as stand-alone applications. They become meaningful if they are semantically annotated in ways that tools can detect, select, and invoke them in order to fulfill security policies of requester or providers participating in WS applications. We propose semantic annotation for security services to make them amenable for tools performing analysis and composition of services.

In taking a closer look at the XML signature service, we begin with the OWL-S markup of this service. Then we present details about the implementation.

4.1   OWL-S Ontologies

The complete OWL-S ontologies for the XML signature service can be found at http://www.csl.sri.com/users/denker/owl-sec/SecurityServices/SignatureService/.

The service ontology (SignatureService.owl) defines two services: a signing service and a verification service. References to the profile, process, and grounding specifications of each service are given. We present only parts of the ontologies for the signing service.

```
<service:Service rdf:ID="SigningService">
  <service:presents rdf:resource="&sign_profile;#Profile_Sign"/>
  <service:describedBy rdf:resource="&sign_process;#Process_Sign"/>
  <service:supports rdf:resource="&sign_grounding;#Grounding_Sign"/>
</service:Service>
```

In the profile (SignatureProfile.owl) we refer to input, output, precondition, and effect (IOPE) parameters of the service that are defined in more detail in the process model.

```
<profile:Profile rdf:ID="Profile_Sign">
  <!-- Function:  DataHandler sign(DataHandler soapHandler,
                                   DataHandler keystoreHandler) -->
  <profile:hasInput rdf:resource="&sign_process;#Signature_sign_in0_IN"/>
  <profile:hasInput rdf:resource="&sign_process;#Signature_sign_in1_IN"/>
  <profile:hasOutput rdf:resource="&sign_process;#Signature_sign_return_OUT"/>
</profile:Profile>
```

Inputs and outputs for the atomic processes are defined in the process ontology (SignatureProcess.owl).

```
<process:Input rdf:ID="Signature_sign_in0_IN">
  <process:parameterType rdf:resource="#DataHandler"/>
</process:Input>
<process:UnConditionalOutput rdf:ID="Signature_sign_return_OUT">
  <process:parameterType rdf:resource="#DataHandler"/>
</process:UnConditionalOutput>
```

The WSDL grounding for both services is defined in SignatureGrounding.owl. The grounding refers to the corresponding WSDL operation that is implemented and locates the port to be used. Moreover, for each WSDL message a mapping between inputs and outputs of the WSDL message and the process description is given. We illustrate only part of mapping for the signRequest message.

```
<grounding:WsdlAtomicProcessGrounding rdf:ID="WSDLGrounding_Signature_sign">
  <grounding:owlsProcess rdf:resource="&sign_process;#Signature_sign"/>

  <!-- refer to corresponding WSDL operation and port -->
  <grounding:wsdlOperation>
    <grounding:WsdlOperationRef>
      <grounding:portType>
        <xsd:anyURI rdf:value="&sign_wsdl;#SOAPSignature"/>
      </grounding:portType>
      <grounding:operation>
        <xsd:anyURI rdf:value="&sign_wsdl;#sign"/>
      </grounding:operation>
    </grounding:WsdlOperationRef>
  </grounding:wsdlOperation>

  <grounding:wsdlInputs rdf:parseType="Collection">
    <grounding:WsdlInputMessageMap>
      <grounding:owlsParameter
                  rdf:resource="&sign_process;#Signature_sign_inO_IN"/>
      <grounding:wsdlMessagePart>
        <xsd:anyURI rdf:value="&sign_wsdl;#inO"/>
      </grounding:wsdlMessagePart>
    </grounding:WsdlInputMessageMap>
  </grounding:wsdlInputs>

</grounding:WsdlAtomicProcessGrounding>
```

Two WSDL files are generated by the WSTK development environment: an interface file (Sign_Intf.wsdl) and an implementation file (Sig_Impl.wsdl). The implementation file defines the physical address of the WSDL service:

```
<wsdl:service name="SOAPSignatureService">
  <wsdl:port name="sign_port" binding="intf:sign_portSoapBinding">
    <wsdlsoap:address
  location="http://stick.csl.sri.com:8080/SOAPSignature/services/sign_port"/>
  </wsdl:port>
</wsdl:service>
```

The interface file is further annotated with links into the OWL-S grounding ontology of our service. The input and output parameters of WSDL messages are associated to the appropriate OWL parameters, and WSDL operations are linked to OWL-S processes.

```
<wsdl:message name="signRequest">
  <wsdl:part name="inO" type="tns1:DataHandler"
    grounding:owlsParameter="&sign_process;#Signature_sign_inO_IN"/>
  <wsdl:part name="in1" type="tns1:DataHandler"
    grounding:owlsParameter="&sign_process;#Signature_sign_in1_IN"/>
</wsdl:message>

<wsdl:portType name="SOAPSignature">
  <wsdl:operation name="sign" parameterOrder="inO in1"
    grounding:owlsProcess="&sign_process;#Signature_sign">
  </wsdl:operation>
</wsdl:portType>
```

4.2   Implementation and Deployment

We looked into several WS development environments, including .Net from Microsoft and J2EE Web Services from Sun. Though .Net Visual Studio provides a better development environment with a lot of visualization features, we chose J2EE over .Net for the following reasons.

J2EE is a cross-platform technology, whereas .Net is a Windows-based platform. J2EE is more portable since the Java Runtime Environment (JRE) is available on Windows, Unix, Linux, and so on. Therefore, J2EE can run virtually on any hardware and operating platform.

With J2EE existing Java classes and (Enterprise) Java beans can be supported as WSs without any, or with little, change to their code. In the .Net environment, on the other hand, one needs to make more changes to existing applications to transform them into WSs.

Finally, there is no licensing issue with J2EE because of the wealth of WSs toolkits available for developers to use. Some of these toolkits provide WS hosting, for example, IBM WSTK and ETTK with built-in basic components of Web Sphere for testing.

Clients or servers can easily invoke our security services through the Java architecture for XML-RPC (JAX-RPC). JAX-RPC enables the service provider (server) to define its services by using standard APIs and to describe its services using WSDL. On the client side, it enables the client to consume the service by using a set of standard APIs. JAX-RPC provides a type-mapping system to map XML types (simple types and complex types) to Java types and WSDL types to Java types.

The signature service on the provider side is defined as follows:

```
/**
     input:  XML filename
     output:  a signed XML filename
 **/
public DataHandler sign(DataHandler soapHandler, DataHandler keystoreHandler)
{
    // initialize the Apache XML Security library
    org.apache.xml.security.Init.init();
    ...
    // load keystore and get private key from keystore
    KeyStore ks = KeyStore.getInstance(keystoreType);
    FileInputStream fis = new FileInputStream(keystoreFile);
    ks.load(fis, keystorePass.toCharArray());
    PrivateKey privateKey = (PrivateKey) ks.getKey(privateKeyAlias,
                                    privateKeyPass.toCharArray());
    ...
    // create <Signature> Element using DSA Algorithm
    // add empty <SignedInfo> Element in the XML document
    XMLSignature sig = new XMLSignature(doc,"",XMLSignature.ALGO_ID_SIGNATURE_DSA);
    headerElement.appendChild(sig.getElement());
    ...
    // add certificate and public key information from the keystore
    // needed later for verification of signature
    X509Certificate cert = (X509Certificate) ks.getCertificate(certificateAlias);
    sig.addKeyInfo(cert);
    sig.addKeyInfo(cert.getPublicKey());
    ...
    //sign the document with author?s private key
    sig.sign(privateKey);
    ...
}
```

On the client side the service is invoked using the service provider's WSDL description.

```
/**
    input:  keystore filename and XML filename
    output: a link where user can view/download the file
**/

public  String signSOAP() throws Exception
{
    ...
    String serviceName = "SOAPSignatureService"; // found in wsdl service file
    String servicePortName  = "sign_port"; // see WSDL service file
    String namespace = "http://SOAPSignature";
    QName   serviceQN = new QName( namespace, serviceName);
    QName   portQN    = new QName( namespace, servicePortName);
    String operation1Name = "sign";
    ...
    // create a soap binding to the service name
    Call call = (Call) service.createCall(portQN, operation1Name);
    ...
    // Invoke the service by sending keystore and XML file
    // to the service provider using DataHandler
    // service provider uses this info to sign document
    DataHandler signedSoapFileHandler = (DataHandler)call.invoke(new Object[]
                                        {soapFileHandler, keyStoreHandler});   ...
    // receive file from service provider
    // return the full pathname of the signed XML file
    ...
    signedSoapFileHandler.writeTo(signedFos);
    signedFos.close();
    signResult = SOAP_RECEIVED_FILENAME;
}
```

5   Future Work: an SWS Security Framework

We have presented semantic security services specified in OWL-S and deployed using the WSTK WS toolkit. Our security services will not be useful as stand-alone applications. Their full impact will be in the context of complex SWS applications where the security services are basic building blocks to establish trusted environments for online transactions. To achieve an SWS security framework, supporting services and protocols need to be semantically annotated to make them amenable for tools performing analysis and composition of services.

OWL-S descriptions of our security services can be used to choose among the security capabilities in order to satisfy the needs of an application. Our security services have well-defined, restricted functionality that is described with the help of OWL-S annotations. This meta-information will be useful when it comes to service selection and composition. Tools capable of processing OWL-S descriptions could reason about the compatibility of WSs and compose complex work flows from basic services. Such tools are yet to be implemented in a satisfactory manner. Nevertheless, as referenced in Section 2, theory and praxis of WS composition and choreography is the subject of current research. We intend to apply the results to security service composition.

More work is needed for an SWS security framework besides providing deployed, publicly available security services with formally well defined OWL-S interfaces. A workable environment will deploy various conversation, authentication, or interaction protocols to establish and exchange keys or policies and agree on contracts. These protocols are subject to a variety of impersonation attacks. Cryptographic protocols have been proposed to avoid such attacks and provably achieve the goals of a protocol. For example, in order to authenticate the identity of the communicating party during an online transaction, a cryptographic protocol could be used that follows a sequence of message exchanges at the end of which the parties trust the authenticity of each other (e.g., NSPK [22] to name one of the more famous ones). Other cryptographic protocols are available for contract signing and fair exchange (e.g., [23, 24, 25]), asserting that agents commit to certain actions. These protocols use cryptographic mechanisms and as a first step we intend to use our security services to perform protocol tasks.

In the long run, we are interested in putting these protocols in the context of policy specification and enforcement. Cryptographic protocols usually satisfy policies such as authentication. Research in cryptographic protocols has mainly been concerned with analyzing the sequence of messages exchanged in protocol to determine protocol vulnerabilities. The focus is on a layer of trust that is based on cryptographic mechanisms such as fresh nonces and uncompromised keys. We propose to focus on the *trust and policy assertions* that are the result of successfully terminating a protocol. We propose to investigate the relation between various cryptographic protocols and higher-level policies and provide policy annotations for these protocols. One technical challenge is to identify smallest units of protocols that, together with assertions, guarantee a certain policy. We will investigate some well-known authentication, contract signing, and e-commerce protocols, in order to establish the relation between policies and (sub)protocols. The work in [26] will be useful as it defines basic security components. Similar to our proposal to enrich cryptographic protocols with policy statements, Guttman et al. [27] propose rely-guarantee formulas as part of protocol description. Contrary to their formalization, which is done in the strand space framework for protocol analysis, we will focus on protocol policy markup in ontology-based languages.

References

[1] Sycara, K., Ju, J., Klusch, M., Widoff, S.: Dynamic service matchmaking among agents in open information environments. ACM SIGMOD Record, Special Issue on the Semantic Interoperability in Global Information Systems (1999)

[2] Denker, G., Hobbs, J., Martin, D., Narayanan, S., Waldinger, R.: Accessing information and services on the DAML-enabled Web. In Decker, S., Fensel, D., Seth, A., Staab, S., eds.: 2nd. Intern. Workshop on the Semantic Web SemWeb'2001, Workshop at WWW10, Hong Kong, China. (2001) http://sunsite.informatik.rwth-aachen.de/Publications/CEUR-WS/Vol-40/.

[3] McIlraith, S., Song, T., Zeng, H.: Mobilizing the Semantic Web with DAML-enabled Web services. In Decker, S., Fensel, D., Seth, A., Staab, S., eds.: 2nd. Intern. Workshop on the Semantic Web SemWeb'2001, Workshop at WWW10, Hongkong, China. (2001) http://sunsite.informatik.rwth-aachen.de/Publications/CEUR-WS/Vol-40/.

[4] McIlraith, S., Song, T., Zeng, H.: Semantic Web services. IEEE Intelligent Systems, Special Issue on the Semantic Web 16 (2001) 46–53

[5] Hendler, J.: Agents on the Web. IEEE Intelligent Systems, Special Issue on the Semantic Web **16** (2001) 30–37

[6] Kagal, L.: Rei : A Policy Language for the Me-Centric Project. HP Labs Technical Report (2002)

[7] Kagal, L., Finin, T., Joshi, A.: A policy language for pervasive systems. In: Fourth IEEE International Workshop on Policies for Distributed Systems and Networks. (2003)

[8] Uszok, A., Bradshaw, J., Jeffers, R., Suri, N., Hayes, P., Breedy, M., Bunch, L., Johnson, M., Kulkarni, S., Lott, J.: KAoS policy and domain services: Toward a description-logic approach to policy representation, deconfliction and enforcement. In: IEEE Workshop on Policy 2003. (2003) 93–96

[9] Bradshaw, J., Uszok, A., Jeffers, R., Suri, N., Hayes, P., Burstein, M., Acquisiti, A., Benyo, B., Breedy, M., Carvalho, M., Diller, D., Johnson, M., Kulkarni, S., Lott, J., Sierhuis, M., Hoof, R.V.: Representation and Reasoning for DAML-Based Policy and Domain Services in KAoS and Nomads. In: *Submitted to* AAMAS'03, July 14-18, 2003, Melbourne, Australia. (2003)

[10] Ribeiro, C.N., Zuquete, A., Ferreira, P., Guedes, P.: SPL: An access control language for security policies with complex constraints. In: Network and Distributed System Security Symposium (NDSS'01). (2001)

[11] Damianou, N., Dulay, N., Lupu, E., Sloman, M.: The ponder policy specification language. Lecture Notes in Computer Science **1995** (2001)

[12] Golbeck, J., Parsia, B., Hendler, J.: Inferring reputation on the Semantic Web (2004) http://www.mindswap.org/papers/GolbeckWWW04.pdf.

[13] Gandon, F., Sadeh, N.: A semantic e-wallet to reconcile privacy and context awareness. [28] 385–401 LNCS 2870.

[14] Gil, Y., Ratnakar, V.: Trusting information sources one citizen at a time. In Fensel, D., Sycara, K., Mylopoulos, J., eds.: Proc. 1st Intern. Semantic Web Conference (ISWC 2002), Sardinia, Italy, June 2002, Springer (2002) LNCS.

[15] Atkinson, B., Della-Libera, G., Hada, S., Hondo, M., Hallam-Baker, P., Klein, J., LaMacchia, B., Leach, P., Manferdelli, J., Maruyama, H., Nadalin, A., Nagaratnam, N., Prfullchandra, H., Shewchuk, J., Simon, D.: Web services security (WS-Security) (2002) http://www-106.ibm.com/developerworks/webservices/library/ws-secure/.

[16] IETF and W3C Working Group: XML encryption. http://www.w3.org/Encryption/2001/ (2001)

[17] IETF and W3C Working Group: XML signature. http://www.w3.org/Signature/ (2003)

[18] (SSTC), O.S.S.T.: Security assertion markup language (SAML) - core assertion architecture. http://www.oasis-open.org/committees/security/docs/draft-sstc-core-19.p% df (2001)

[19] : (Liberty alliance project specifications) http://www.projectliberty.org/specs/.

[20] Wu, D., Parsia, B., Sirin, E., Hendler, J., Nau, D.: Automating DAML-S Web services composition using SHOP2. [28] 195–210 LNCS 2870.

[21] Chen, L., Shadbold, N., Goble, C., Tao, F., Cox, S., Puleston, C., Smart, P.: Towards a knowledge-based approach to semantic service composition. [28] 319–334 LNCS 2870.

[22] Needham, R., Schroeder, M.: Using encryption for authentication in large networks of computers. Communications of the ACM **21** (1978) 993–998

[23] Even, S., Goldreich, O., Lempel, A.: A randomized protocol for signing contracts. Communications of the ACM **28** (1985) 637–647

[24] Bao, F., Deng, R., Mao, W.: Efficient and practical fair exchange protocols with off-line TTP. In: Proc. 19th IEEE Computer Society Symposium on Research in Securiyt and Privacy, IEEE (1998)
[25] Franklin, M.K., Reiter, M.K.: Fair exchange with a semi-trusted third party (extended abstract). In: ACM Conference on Computer and Communications Security. (1997) 1–5
[26] Datta, A., Derek, A., Mitchell, J., Pavlovic, D.: A derivation system for security protocol and its logical formalization. In: Proc. IEEE Computer Security Foundations Workshop, Asilomar, CA, 30 June - 2 July, 2003. (2003) 109–125
[27] Guttman, J., Thayer, F., Carlson, J., Herzog, J., Ramsdell, J., Sniffen, B.: Trust management in strand spaces: A rely-guarantee method. In: European Symposium on Programming (ESOP 2004), Barcelona, Spain, March 29-April 2, 2004. (2004)
[28] Fensel, D., Sycara, K., Mylopoulos, J., eds.: Proc. 2nd Intern. Semantic Web Conference (ISWC 2003), Sanibel Island, FL, October 2003. In Fensel, D., Sycara, K., Mylopoulos, J., eds.: Proc. 2nd Intern. Semantic Web Conference (ISWC 2003), Sanibel Island, FL, October 2003, Springer (2003) LNCS 2870.

Directory Services for Incremental Service Integration

Ion Constantinescu, Walter Binder, and Boi Faltings

Artificial Intelligence Laboratory
Swiss Federal Institute of Technology,
IN (Ecublens), CH–1015 Lausanne, Switzerland.
{ion.constantinescu,walter.binder,boi.faltings}@epfl.ch

Abstract. In an open environment populated by heterogeneous information services integration will be a major challenge. Even if the problem is similar to planning in some aspects, the number and the difference in specificity of services makes existing techniques not suitable and requires a different approach. Our solution is to incrementally solve integration problems by using an interplay between service discovery and integration alongside with a technique for composing specific partially matching services into more generic constructs. In this paper we present a directory system and a number of mechanisms designed to support incremental integration algorithms with partial matches for large numbers of service descriptions. We also report experiments on randomly generated composition problems that show that using partial matches can decrease the failure rate of the integration algorithm using only complete matches by up to **7 times** with no increase in the number of directory accesses required.[1]

1 Introduction

In a future service-oriented Internet service discovery, integration, and orchestration will be major building blocks. So far most research has been oriented towards service discovery and orchestration. Seminal work exists for service composition (e.g., [11] and [13]) which is now increasingly the focus of attention.

Earlier work on service integration has viewed service composition as a planning problem (e.g., [23]), where the service descriptions represent the planning operators, and applied traditional planning algorithms. Still the current and future state of affairs regarding web services will be quite different since due to the large number of services and to the loose coupling between service providers and consumers we expect that services will be indexed in directories. Consequently, planning algorithms will have to be adapted to a situation where operators are not known a priori, but have to be retrieved through queries to these directories.

Our approach to automated service composition is based on matching input and output parameters of services using type information in order to constrain the ways that services may be composed.

---

[1] The work presented in this paper was partly carried out in the framework of the EPFL Center for Global Computing and was supported by the Swiss National Science Foundation as part of the project MAGIC (FNRS-68155), as well as by the Swiss National Funding Agency OFES as part of the European projects KnowledgeWeb (FP6-507482) and DIP (FP6-507483).

J. Davies et al. (Eds.): ESWS 2004, LNCS 3053, pp. 254–268, 2004.

Consider the example (Fig. 1 (a)) of a personal agent that has the task of booking for its user tickets to a good movie and to find also directions for the user to reach the cinema, directions in the user's language. For this purpose the agent has to compose the following types of services: cinema services (show information and ticket booking), movie recommendation services, payment services, and geographical information services (GIS).

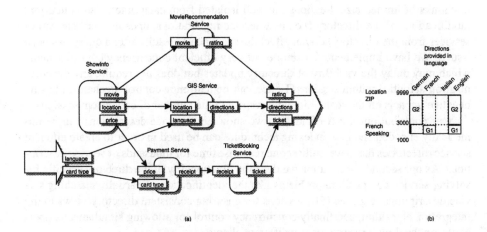

Fig. 1. Composition example: going out for a movie.

However, frequently a certain service cannot be applied because it requires a parameter to be within a certain range that is smaller than that of the possible inputs. Existing service composition algorithms will not be able to make use of such a service, even though a collection of distinct services may be able to handle the full range of the available inputs.

In the evening organizer example this could be the case of the GIS service. We presume a domain for Swiss GIS services which defines zip codes between 1000–9999 and is able to give directions in german, french, italian, and english language. In our setup we assume the existence of two GIS providers: G1 that is able to give directions in french and english for the french speaking part of Switzerland and G2 that is able to give directions in german and english for the rest. In this case requests for directions in english could be handled by a single service only if the zip codes are restricted to particular ranges: either between 1000 and 2999 (for G1) or between 3000 and 9999 (for G2).

Our approach (see Section 3) allows for *partially matching* types and handles them by computing and introducing software switches in the integration plan. In our example (Fig. 1 (b)) this could be done by composing together G1 and G2 using a software switch that will decide based on the runtime value of the zip code input parameter which of the two services to use. The value of composing partially matching services is evident as the composed service will work in more cases than any of G1 or G2. This is confirmed also by experimental results carried for two domains (see Section 5) which show that using *partial matches* allows to decrease the failure rate of the integration algorithm that uses only *complete matches* by up to **7 times**.

We have developed a directory service with specific features to ease service composition. Queries may not only search for complete matches, but may also retrieve partially matching directory entries. As the number of (partially) matching entries may be large, the directory supports incremental retrieval of the results of a query. This is achieved through sessions, during which a client issues queries and retrieves the results in chunks of limited size. Sessions are well isolated from each other, also concurrent modifications of the directory (i.e., new service registrations, updates, and removal of services from the directory) do not affect the sequence of results after a query has been issued. We have implemented a simple but very efficient concurrency control scheme which may delay the visibility of directory updates but does not require any synchronization activities within sessions. Hence, our concurrency control mechanism has no negative impacts on the scalability with respect to the number of concurrent sessions.

Our contributions are twofold: first we show how service descriptions can be numerically encoded and how indexing techniques can be used in order to create efficient service directories that have millisecond response time for thousands of service descriptions. As our second contribution we describe functionality of the directory specific for solving service composition problems like the identification of partially matching service descriptions (e.g., see [6]), sessions for ensuring consistent directory views to the integration algorithm, and finally concurrency control for allowing simultaneous operations on the directory structure by different clients.

This paper is structured as follows: next in Section 2 we show how service descriptions can be numerically encoded as sets of intervals and we described in more details the assumed semantics for service descriptions and integration queries. In Section 3 we present how an index structure for multidimensional data can be exploited such that numerically encoded service descriptions are efficiently retrieved using queries for complete and partial type matches. In Section 4 we introduce some extensions of the directory system specific to service composition that enable consistent views of the directory for the client during the integration process, the retrieval at each integration step of only services that are unknown and concurrency control between different clients. In Section 5 we present some experimental results on randomly generated problems. In Section 6 we review some existing directory systems. Finally, Section 7 concludes the paper.

2   Numerically Encoding Services and Queries

Service descriptions are a key element for service discovery and service composition and should enable automated interactions between applications. Currently, different overlapping formalisms are proposed (e.g., [21], [19], [7], [8]) and any single choice could be quite controversial due to the trade-off between expressiveness and tractability specific to any of the aforementioned formalisms.

In this paper, we will partially build on existing developments, such as [21], [1], and [7], by considering a simple table-based formalism where each service is described through a set of tuples mapping service parameters (unique names of inputs or outputs) to parameter types (the spaces of possible values for a given parameter). Parameter types can be expressed either as sets of intervals of basic data types (e.g., date/time, integers, floating-points) or as classes of individuals.

Class parameter types can be defined through a descriptive language like XML Schema [22] or the Ontology Web Language [20]. From the descriptions we can then derive either directly or by using a description logic classifier a directed graph (DG) of simple is-a relations (e.g., the is-a directed acyclic graph (DAG) for types of cuisine in Fig. 2 (a) derived from the ontology above).

For efficiency reasons, we represent the DG numerically. We assume that each class will be represented as a set of intervals. Then we encode each parent-child relation by sub-dividing each of the intervals of the parent (e.g., in Fig. 2 (b) Mediteraneean is sub-divided for encoding Italian and French cuisine); in the case of multiple parents the child class will then be represented by the union of the sub-intervals resulting from the encoding of each of the parent-child relations (e.g., the FrancoAsianFusion in Fig. 2 is represented through sub-intervals of the Asian and French concepts).

Since for a given domain we can have several parameters represented by intervals, the space of all possible parameter values can be represented as a rectangular hyper-space, with a dimension for each parameter.

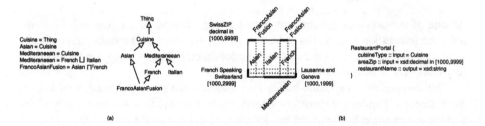

Fig. 2. An example domain: a restaurant recommendation portal.

Let's consider as an example (see Fig. 2 (b)) a restaurant recommendation portal that takes the user preference for a cuisine type and the Swiss zip-code (four digit numbers between 1000 and 9999) of the area of interest and will return a string containing a recommended restaurant located in a given area.

In this example the service will accept for the cuisineType parameter any of the keywords $Mediteraneean$, $Asian$, $French$, $Italian$, or $FrancoAsionFusion$ and for the $areaZip$ any decimal between 1000 and 9999 representing the location of the area of interest.

We assume that input and output parameters of service descriptions have the following semantics:

- In order for the service to be invokable, a value must be known for each of the service input parameters and it has to be consistent with the respective parameter type. For primitive data types the invocation value must be in the range of allowed values

or in the case of classes the invocation value must be subsumed by the parameter type.
- Upon successful invocation the service will provide a value for each of the output parameters and each of these values will be consistent with the respective parameter type.

Service composition queries are represented in a similar manner but have different semantics:

- The query inputs are the parameters available to the integration (e.g., provided by the user). Each of these input parameters may be either a concrete value of a given type, or just the type information. In the second case the integration solution has to be able to handle all the possible values for the given input parameter type.
- The query outputs are the parameters that a successful integration must provide and the parameter types define what ranges of values can be handled. The integration solution must be able to provide a value for each of the parameters in the problem output and the value must be in the range defined by the respective problem output parameter type.

3   Service Composition with Directories

As one of our previous assumptions is that a large number of services will be available, the integration process has to be able to discover relevant services incrementally through queries to the service directory. Interleaving the integration process with directory discovery is another novelty of our approach.

Our composition algorithm builds on forward chaining, a technique well known for planning [3] and more recently for service integration [18]. Most previous work on service composition has required an explicit specification of the control flow between basic services in order to provide value-added services.

For instance, in the eFlow system [5], a composite service is modelled as a graph that defines the order of execution of different processes. The Self-Serv framework [2] uses a subset of statecharts to describe the control flow within a composite service. The Business Process Execution Language for Web Services (BPEL4WS) [4] addresses compositions where the control flow of the process and the bindings between services are known in advance. In service composition using Golog [14], logical inferencing techniques are applied to pre-defined plan templates.

More recently, planning techniques have been applied to the service integration problem [16, 23, 24]. Such an approach does not require a pre-defined process model of the composite service, but returns a possible control flow as a result.

Other approaches to planning, such as planning as model checking [9], are being considered for web service composition and would allow more complex constructions such as loops.

Informally, the idea of composition with forward chaining is to iteratively apply a possible service S to a set of input parameters provided by a query Q (i.e., all inputs required by S have to be available). If applying S does not solve the problem (i.e., still not all the outputs required by the query Q are available) then a new query Q' can be computed from Q and S and the whole process is iterated. This part of our framework corresponds to the planning techniques currently used for service composition [18].

We will make the following assumptions regarding the service composition process:

- any service input or output in the composition will be assigned exactly *one semantic description* (through the name of the parameter) at the moment of its introduction (when provided either as a problem input or as a service output). Also we assume that the semantic definition of the parameter will not change for the rest of the composition independently of other services applied later to the parameter. Please note that the application of subsequent services could still cast the parameter to other different parameter types.
- during integration the view that the algorithm has of the directory will not change. This is similar to the isolation property of transactional systems.

3.1 Directories of Web Services

Currently UDDI is the state of the art for directories of web services (see Section 6 for an overview of other service directory systems). The standard is clear in terms of data models and query API, but suffers from the fact that it considers service descriptions to be completely opaque.

A more complex method for discovering relevant services from a directory of advertisements is matchmaking. In this case the directory query (requested capabilities) is formulated in the form of a service description template that presents all the features of interest. This template is then compared with all the entries in the directory and the results that have features compatible with the features of interest are returned. A good amount of work exists in the area of matchmaking including LARKS [17], and the newer efforts geared towards DAML-S [15]. Other approaches include the Ariadne mediator [11].

3.2 Match Types

We consider four match relations between a query Q and a service S, (see example for inputs in Fig. 3).

- **Exact** - S is an exact match of Q.
- **PlugIn** - S is a plug-in match for Q, if S could be always used instead of Q.
- **Subsumes** - Q contains S. In this case Q could be used under the condition that it satisfies some additional constraints such that it is specific enough for S.
- **Overlap** - Q and S have a given intersection. In this case, runtime constraints both over Q and S have to be taken into account.

It has to be noticed that the following implications hold for any match between query and service descriptions Q and S: $\text{Exact}(Q,S) \Rightarrow \text{PlugIn}(Q,S)$ and $\text{Exact}(Q,S) \vee \text{PlugIn}(Q,S) \vee \text{Subsumes}(Q,S) \Rightarrow \text{Overlap}(Q,S)$. Given also that a **Subsumes** match requires the specification of supplementary constraints we can

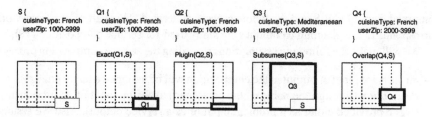

Fig. 3. Match types of inputs of query Q and service S by "precision": **Exact, PlugIn, Subsumes, Overlap.**

order the types of match by "precision" as following: **Exact, PlugIn, Subsumes, Overlap.** We consider **Subsumes** and **Overlap** as "partial" matches. The first three relations have been previously identified by Paolucci in [15].

Determining one match relation between a query description and a service description requires that subsequent relations are determined between all the inputs of the query Q and service S and between the outputs of the service S and query Q (note the reversed order of query and services in the match for outputs). Our approach is more complex than the one of Paolluci in that we take also into account the relations between the properties that introduce different inputs or outputs (equivalent to parameter names). This is important for disambiguating services with equivalent signatures (e.g., we can disambiguate two services that have two string outputs by knowing the names of the respective parameters).

In the example below, we show how the match relation is determined between the inputs available from the queries Q1, Q2, Q3, Q4 and the inputs required by service S.

3.3 Multidimensional Access Methods - GiST

The need for efficient discovery and matchmaking leads to a need for search structures and indexes for directories. We consider numerically encoded service descriptions as multidimensional data and we use in the directory techniques related to the indexing of such kind of information. This approach leads to local response times in the order of milliseconds for directories containing tens of thousands (10^4) of service descriptions.

The indexing technique that we use is based on the Generalised Search Tree (GiST), proposed as a unifying framework by Hellerstein [10]. The design principle of GiST arises from the observation that search trees used in databases are balanced trees with a high fanout in which the internal nodes are used as a directory and the leaf nodes point to the actual data. Each internal node holds a key in the form of a predicate P and can hold at the most a predetermined number of pointers to other nodes (usually a function of system and hardware constraints, e.g., filesystem page size). To search for records that satisfy a query predicate Q, the paths of the tree that have keys P that satisfy Q are followed.

4   Service Integration Sessions and Concurrency Control

As directory queries may retrieve large numbers of matching entries (especially when partial matches are taken into consideration), it is important to support incremental access to the results of a query in order to avoid wasting network bandwidth. Our directory service offers *sessions* which allow a user to issue a query to the directory and to retrieve the results one by one (or in chunks of limited size).

The session guarantees a consistent view of the result set, i.e., the directory structure and contents as seen by a session does not change. Concurrent updates (service registration, update, and removal) do not affect the sequence of query results returned within a session; sessions are isolated from concurrent modifications.

Previous research work has addressed concurrency control in generalised search trees [12]. However, these concurrency control mechanisms only synchronize individual operations in the tree, whereas our directory supports long-lasting sessions during which certain parts of the tree structure must not be altered. This implies that insertion and deletion operations may not be performed concurrently with query sessions, as these operations may significantly change the structure of the tree (splitting or joining of nodes, balancing the tree, etc.).

The following assumptions underly the design of our concurrency control mechanism:

1. Read accesses (i.e., queries within sessions and the incremental retrieval of the results) will be much more frequent than updates.
2. High concurrency for read accesses (e.g., 10^4 concurrent sessions).
3. Read accesses shall not be delayed.
4. Updates may become visible with a significant delayed, but feedback concerning the update (success/failure) shall be returned immediately.
5. The duration of a session may be limited (timeout).

A simple solution would be to create a private copy of the result set of each query. However, as we want to support a high number of concurrent sessions, such an approach is inefficient, because it wastes memory and processing resources to copy the relevant data. Hence, such a solution may not scale well and is not in accord with our first two assumptions.

Another solution would be to support transactions. However, this seems to be too heavy weight. The directory shall be optimized for the common case, i.e., for read accesses (first assumption). This distinguishes directory services from general-purpose databases.

Concurrency protocols based on locking techniques are not in accord with these assumptions either. Because of assumption 3, sessions shall not have to wait for concurrent updates.

In order to meet the assumptions above, we have designed a mechanism which guarantees that sessions operate on read-only data structures that are not subject to changes. In our approach the in-memory structure of the directory tree (i.e., the directory index) is replicated up to 3 times, while the actual service descriptions are shared between the replicated trees.

When the directory service is started, the persistent representation of the directory tree is loaded into memory. This master copy of the directory tree is always kept up to date, i.e., updates are immediately applied to that master copy and are made persistent, too. Upon start of the directory service, a read-only copy of the in-memory master copy is allocated. Session operate only on this read-only copy. Hence, session management is trivial, there is no synchronization needed. Periodically, the master copy is duplicated to create a new read-only copy. Afterwards, new sessions are redirected to the new read-only copy. The old read-only copy is freed when the last session operating on it completes (either by an explicit session termination by the client or by a timeout).

We require the session timeout to be smaller than the update frequency of the read-only copy (the duplication frequency of the master copy). This condition ensures that there will be at most 3 copies of the in-memory representation of the directory at the same time: The master where updates are immediately applied (but which is not yet visible to sessions), as well as the previous 2 read-only copies used for sessions. when a new read-only copy is created, the old copy will remain active until the last session operating on it terminates; this time span is bounded by the session timeout.

In our approach only updates to the master copy are synchronized. Updates are immediately applied to the master copy (yielding immediate feedback to the client requesting an update). Only during copying the directory is blocked for further updates. In accord with the third assumption, the creation of sessions requires no synchronization.

5   Evaluation and Assessment

This section first presents two domains used by our service integration testbed: one more concrete and another that provides more symmetry. A discussion of the results concludes this section.

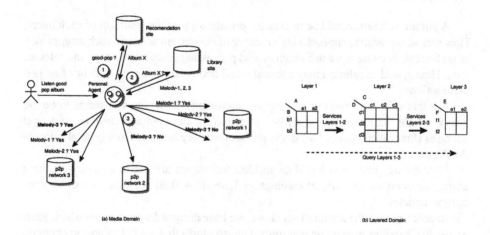

(a) Media Domain   (b) Layered Domain

Fig. 4. Testbed domains.

5.1   The Media Domain

For experimental purposes we have considered the following scenario (see Fig. 4 (a)): a personal agent (PA) is delegated the task to find a music provider for an album of good pop music. Since its user doesn't like to listen only to spare melodies we assume all-or-nothing semantics: only if all the melodies of a given album can be found then this is a solution. Otherwise another album has to be selected.

First the PA has to determine what is currently considered as good pop and uses a recommendation site (e.g., billboard.com) to find Album X as a first option. Then the PA has to use a library site (e.g., cdcovers.cc) to determine which are the melodies in Album X - let's presume that they are Melody-1, Melody-2 and Melody-3. Then finally the PA searches different p2p networks for providers that have different melodies from the album.

In this context partial type matches are used for selecting peers that can provide (cover) a sub-set of the melodies of an album. Then by computing the software switch we select those peers that together can provide all the melodies from the album.

Since for solving the integration we need at least a recommendation, an album description and a provider for the melodies the minimum number of required directory accesses for any integration in this domain is 3.

5.2   The Layered Domain

We have defined also a more abstract domain (see Fig. 4 (b)) where we consider a number of layers that define sets of parameter names. Services are defined as transformations between parameters in adjacent layers and problems are defined between parameters of the first and last layer. For example, a possible service between layers 1-2 with the parameters A, B could have as input the types A=a1, B=b1,b2 and for the output parameters C and D could have as types C=c2, c3 and D=d1, d2. A query could for the input parameters A, B the types A=a1,a2, B=b2 and for the output parameters E,F the type E=e1, F=f2.

For the purpose of our experiments, we have created environments with 3 layers for which the minimum number of required directory accesses for any integration is 2. Each of the layers defines two parameters with 11 possible subtypes for layers 1 and 3 and 63 possible overlapping subtypes for layer 2; between each two layers (1-2 or 2-3) there are 480249 possible services.

It has to be noted that in contrast with the media domain there is a symmetry regarding inputs and outputs in the configuration used for the layered domain.

5.3   Evaluation of Experimental Results

For both domains, we have randomly generated services and problems. For each specific type of services (e.g., album recommendation, album description, melody provider or service layer1-2, service layer2-3) or for queries (e.g., find good pop album in mp3 format or find a service that transforms an input in layer1 to an output in layer3) we had a pre-determined set of parameters. For actually generating the descriptions (service or

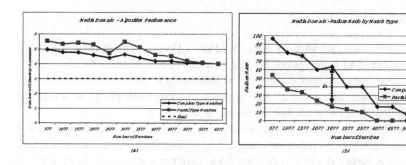

Fig. 5. The media domain.

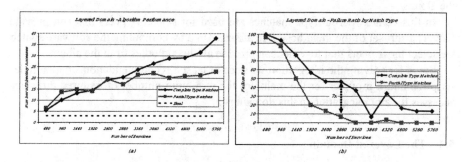

Fig. 6. The layered domain.

query) we randomly picked for any of the pre-determined parameters a random sub-type from a set of possible types.

We then solved the queries using first an algorithm that handles only *complete* type matches and then an algorithm that handles *partial* type matches (and obviously includes *complete* matches). We have measured the number of directory accesses and the failure ratio of the integration algorithms.

Fig. 5 (a) and Fig. 6 (a) show the average number of directory accesses for the algorithm using *complete* type matching versus the average number of directory accesses for the algorithm also using *partial* type matching.

Regarding performance, the first conclusion is that both algorithms scale well, as there is at most a slow increase in the number of directory accesses as the number of services in the directory grows. For the media domain the number of accesses actually decreases.

As expected, the algorithm using partial matches performs comparable with the one using complete matches. As it results from the experimental data for both domains the overhead induced by the usage of partial matches is not very significant and decreases as the directory gets saturated with services. This is probably due to the fact that having more choices makes the coverage problem intrinsic to the partial algorithm easier. More than that in the layered domain from some point the partial algorithm even performs better that the complete one (Fig. 6 (a) after 3000 services).

The most important result concerns the number of extra problems that can be solved by using partial matches and can be seen in Fig. 5 (b) and Fig. 6 (b). The graph show that the failure rate in the case of using only *complete matches is much bigger than the failure rate when* partial matches are used: **4 times** in the case of the Media domain and up to **7 times** in the case of the Layered domain. This shows that using partial matches opens the door for solving many problems that were unsolvable by the complete type matching algorithm.

6   Background and Related Work

In this section we will review a number of existing directory systems. As we will see next only some of the presented systems fullfill particular requirements of service integration like incremental access (UDDI, LDAP, CosTrader) and partial matches (LDAP, CoSTrader) but there is none that fulfills requirements that are more specific to service integration like the retrieval of only unkown services or maintaining the same view during the integration episode, issues that we address in our system trough the session mechanism.

6.1   UDDI

The Universal Description, Discovery and Integration (UDDI [19]) is an industrial effort to create an open specification for directories of service descriptions. It builds on existing technology standardized by the World Wide Web Consortium (http://www.w3c.org) like the eXtensible Markup Language (XML), the Simple Object Access Protocol (SOAP) and the Web Services Description Language (WSDL).

UDDI v.3 specifies a data model with four levels: business entities which provide services, for which bindings are described in terms of tModels. Note that there is a complete containment for the first three levels (business, service, binding) but not for the fourth - tModel - which is linked in by reference. This data model can be managed through an API covering methods for inquiry, publication, security, custody, subscription and value sets.

6.2   X.500 and LDAP

The X.500 directory service is a global directory service. Its components cooperate to manage information about objects such as countries, organizations, people, machines, and so on in a worldwide scope. It provides the capability to look up information by name (a white-pages service) and to browse and search for information (a yellow-pages service).

The information is held in a directory information base (DIB). Entries in the DIB are arranged in a tree structure called the directory information tree (DIT). Each entry is a named object and consists of a set of attributes.

The Lightweight Directory Access Protocol (LDAP) is a network protocol for accessing directories, based on X.500 which uses an internet transport protocol.

6.3   COrba Services: COS Naming and COS Trader

COS Naming and COS Trade are two services standardized by the Object Management Group OMG.

The COS Naming service provides a white-pages service through which most clients of an ORB-based system locate objects that they intend to use (make requests of). Given an initial naming context, clients navigate naming contexts retrieving lists of the names bound to that context.

The COS Trader is a yellow-page service that facilitates the offering and the discovery of instances of services of particular types. Advertising a capability or offering a service is called export. Matching against needs or discovering services is called import. Export and import facilitate dynamic discovery of, and late binding to, services.

Importers use a service type and a constraint to select the set of service offers in which they have an interest. The constraint is a well formed expression conforming to a constraint language. The operators of the language are comparison, boolean connective, set inclusion, substring, arithmetic operators, property existence. Then the result set is ordered using preferences before being returned to the importer. The ordering preference can be specified as either the maximization of minimization of a numeric expression, as the services that fulfill a given boolean constraint, as a random pick of the matching services or by default just as they are ordered by the trader.

When querying the trader results can be returned in chunks of a given size, specified by the importer.

6.4   FIPA Directories: AMS and DF

The FIPA management specification defines two kind of directories: the Agent Management System (white pages) and the Directory Facilitator (yellow pages). Both directories can be queried using a projection mechanism where a template of the objects of interest can be specified.

AMS entries define agent identification information, the state of the agent (active, suspended, etc.) and the ownership of the agent.

As specific functionality the AMS can be specified as transport resolver for given agent identifier entries. Upon submitting a search operation with an agent identifier without transport information the AMS will return another version of the agent identifier that will include transport details. Finally the AMS also is able to provides metadata regarding the current platform like name, transport addresses and platform-level services.

DF entries are more expressive: each entry defines one or more services provided by a given agent. Each service is describe trough the accepted content languages, ontologies and protocols. DF entries can be published on a leasing basis such that once a service provider fails to renew it's lease the entry will be removed from the DF. DFs can be federated and searched recursively. The search is controlled by simple parameters like search depth and maximum number of results. The results of the search are returned all at the time, in the internal order decided by the queried DF.

6.5   JINI Registrars

The JINI infrastructure provides object matching capabilities trough distribute directories named registrars. Service providers advertise their capabilities by leasing the publication of an advertisement entry to a previously discovered registrar. When the service provider fails to renew the lease it's advertisement is remove from the registry. Service consumers search the registrar by specifying entry templates.

Match operations use entry objects of a given type, whose fields can either have values (references to objects) or wildcards (null references). When considering a template T as a potential match against an entry E, fields with values in T must be matched exactly by the value in the same field of E. Wildcards in T match any value in the same field of E.

The results of the search are returned all at the time, in the internal order of the registrar.

7   Conclusions

In this paper we have looked at aspects specific to service integration in large open environments like the interplay between massive discovery and composition using partially matching services. We have described a service directory system and mechanisms specifically designed to meet the requirements of the assumed environment: numerically encoding of service descriptions, the use of indexing techniques that allow the efficient retrieval of matching services including the partially matching ones and finally a specific scheme for enabling service integration sessions. Sessions provide a constant view of the directory during the integration episode, the retrieval at each integration step of only unknown service descriptions and consistent concurrent accesses to the directory between different clients. We presented some experimental results on randomly generated problems that show mainly that the implemented system scales well and is able to deal with large numbers of services and also that partial matches bring significant gains in the range of problems that can be solved. Finally we have reviewed a number of existing directory systems that fulfills some but not all of the specific requirements for service integration. In particular by using sessions our system is able to provide unique features specific to service integration like consistent views during integration episodes and the retrieval at each step of only unknown services descriptions.

References

[1] D.-S. C. A. Ankolekar, M. Burstein, J. R. Hobbs, O. Lassila, D. Martin, D. McDermott, S. A. McIlraith, S. Narayanan, M. Paolucci, T. Payne, and K. Sycara. DAML-S: Web service description for the Semantic Web. *Lecture Notes in Computer Science*, 2342, 2002.
[2] B. Benatallah, Q. Z. Sheng, and M. Dumas. The self-serv environment for web services composition. *IEEE Internet Computing*, 7(1):40–48, 2003.
[3] A. L. Blum and M. L. Furst. Fast planning through planning graph analysis. *Artificial Intelligence*, 90(1–2):281–300, 1997.
[4] BPEL4WS. Business process execution language for web services version 1.1, http://www.ibm.com/developerworks/library/ws-bpel/.

[5] F. Casati, S. Ilnicki, L. Jin, V. Krishnamoorthy, and M.-C. Shan. Adaptive and dynamic service composition in eflow. Technical Report HPL-2000-39, Hewlett Packard Laboratories, Apr. 06 2000.

[6] I. Constantinescu and B. Faltings. Efficient matchmaking and directory services. In *The 2003 IEEE/WIC International Conference on Web Intelligence*, 2003.

[7] DAML-S. DAML Services, http://www.daml.org/services.

[8] FIPA. Foundation for Intelligent Physical Agents Web Site, http://www.fipa.org/.

[9] F. Giunchiglia and P. Traverso. Planning as model checking. In *European Conference on Planning*, pages 1–20, 1999.

[10] J. M. Hellerstein, J. F. Naughton, and A. Pfeffer. Generalized search trees for database systems. In U. Dayal, P. M. D. Gray, and S. Nishio, editors, *Proc. 21st Int. Conf. Very Large Data Bases, VLDB*, pages 562–573. Morgan Kaufmann, 11–15 1995.

[11] C. A. Knoblock, S. Minton, J. L. Ambite, N. Ashish, I. Muslea, A. Philpot, and S. Tejada. The Ariadne Approach to Web-Based Information Integration. *International Journal of Cooperative Information Systems*, 10(1-2):145–169, 2001.

[12] M. Kornacker, C. Mohan, and J. M. Hellerstein. Concurrency and recovery in generalized search trees. In J. M. Peckman, editor, *Proceedings, ACM SIGMOD International Conference on Management of Data: SIGMOD 1997: May 13–15, 1997, Tucson, Arizona, USA*, volume 26(2) of *SIGMOD Record (ACM Special Interest Group on Management of Data)*, pages 62–72, New York, NY 10036, USA, 1997. ACM Press.

[13] S. McIlraith, T. Son, and H. Zeng. Mobilizing the semantic web with daml-enabled web services. In *Proc. Second International Workshop on the Semantic Web (SemWeb-2001)*, Hongkong, China, May 2001.

[14] S. A. McIlraith and T. C. Son. Adapting golog for composition of semantic web services. In D. Fensel, F. Giunchiglia, D. McGuinness, and M.-A. Williams, editors, *Proceedings of the 8th International Conference on Principles and Knowledge Representation and Reasoning (KR-02)*, pages 482–496, San Francisco, CA, Apr. 22–25 2002. Morgan Kaufmann Publishers.

[15] M. Paolucci, T. Kawamura, T. R. Payne, and K. Sycara. Semantic matching of web services capabilities. In *Proceedings of the 1st International Semantic Web Conference (ISWC)*, 2002.

[16] B. Srivastav. Automatic web services composition using planning. In *International Conference on Knowledge Based Computer Systems (KBCS-2002)*, 2002.

[17] K. Sycara, J. Lu, M. Klusch, and S. Widoff. Matchmaking among heterogeneous agents on the internet. In *Proceedings of the 1999 AAAI Spring Symposium on Intelligent Agents in Cyberspace*, Stanford University, USA, March 1999.

[18] S. Thakkar, C. A. Knoblock, J. L. Ambite, and C. Shahabi. Dynamically composing web services from on-line sources. In *Proceeding of the AAAI-2002 Workshop on Intelligent Service Integration*, pages 1–7, Edmonton, Alberta, Canada, July 2002.

[19] UDDI. Universal Description, Discovery and Integration Web Site, http://www.uddi.org/.

[20] W3C. OWL web ontology language 1.0 reference, http://www.w3.org/tr/owl-ref/.

[21] W3C. Web services description language (wsdl) version 1.2, http://www.w3.org/tr/wsdl12.

[22] W3C. XML Schema, http://www.w3.org/xml/schema.

[23] Wu, Dan and Parsia, Bijan and Sirin, Evren and Hendler, James and Nau, Dana. Automating DAML-S Web Services Composition Using SHOP2. In *Proceedings of 2nd International Semantic Web Conference (ISWC2003)*, Sanibel Island, Florida, October 2003.

[24] J. Yang and M. P. Papazoglou. Web component: A substrate for Web service reuse and composition. *Lecture Notes in Computer Science*, 2348, 2002.

A Framework for Automated Service Composition in Service-Oriented Architectures

Shalil Majithia, David W. Walker, and W.A. Gray

Cardiff School of Computer Science, Cardiff University,
Queens Building, Newport Road, Cardiff, UK
{shalil.majithia, david.w.walker, w.a.gray}@cs.cardiff.ac.uk

Abstract. Automated service composition refers to automating the entire process of composing a workflow. This involves automating the discovery and selection of the service, ensuring semantic and data type compatibility. We present a framework to facilitate automated service composition in Service-Oriented Architectures using Semantic Web technologies. The main objective of the framework is to support the discovery, selection, and composition of semantically-described heterogeneous services. Our framework has three main features which distinguish it from other work in this area. First, we propose a dynamic, adaptive, and highly fault-tolerant service discovery and composition algorithm. Second, we distinguish between different levels of granularity of loosely coupled workflows. Finally, our framework allows the user to specify and refine a high-level objective. In this paper, we describe the main components of our framework and describe a scenario in the genealogy domain.

1 Introduction

Service-Oriented Architecture (SOA) is emerging as an important paradigm for distributed computing [1, 2]. SOAs have been defined as 'a set of independently running services loosely bound to each other via event-driven messages.' [32]. A SOA consists of three primary components: the service provider provides the service, the service requester is the client that requires a service to be performed and the service agency provides registration and discovery services. It is argued that services will be composed as part of workflows to build complex applications to achieve client problem requirements [3, 4]. Current workflow composition techniques [12, 13, 14, 15] require the user to deal with the complexity of locating services, ensuring matching data types, and invoking each service. This implies a need for an automated approach to workflow composition. Automating the composition process involves automating the discovery and selection of the right service, ensuring semantic and data type compatibility, invoking each constituent service, coordinating data transfer and so on. The use of Semantic Web technologies to facilitate this automation has been researched recently [4, 5, 6, 7, 8, 9, 10, 17, 18, 31]. The Semantic Web [22] involves the explicit representation of the semantics underlying the data or services. A crucial component of the Semantic Web is the use of a common vocabulary i.e. ontologies.

J. Davies et al. (Eds.): ESWS 2004, LNCS 3053, pp. 269–283, 2004.

An ontology formally defines a common set of terms that are used to describe and represent a domain. The application of Semantic Web technologies in SOAs provides a powerful way of looking at distributed systems by making semantic discovery and invocation possible. Specifically, they allow explicit declarative representation of all material aspects of services. This allows the services to be discovered, selected, invoked, substituted and composed dynamically. By facilitating the automated composition of services, users can:

- Focus on the conceptual basis of their experiments rather than understand the low level details of constructing workflows.
- Easily create complex workflows, which may be composed of thousands of services.
- Easily and transparently create workflows with varying levels of granularity.
- Easily share workflows with colleagues.
- Generate high quality fault-tolerant workflows.

In this paper, we present a framework to automate the composition of complex workflows. The core of our approach is the use of Semantic Web technologies in SOAs. The framework presented in this paper has a number of important features. First, we distinguish between different levels of granularity of loosely coupled workflow representations. Second, the framework uses a dynamic fault-tolerant composition algorithm which adapts to the available resources. Third, the framework allows the user to specify and refine a high level objective. As a consequence, we propose that our framework:

- has a higher probability of successfully generating executable workflows compared to any existing similar algorithms.
- allows users to share workflows with different levels of granularity.
- allows users to specify and refine high level objectives.
- is domain independent.

The remainder of this paper is structured as follows. First we review related research in the area of workflow composition (Section 2). Second, we present an overview of the framework (Section 3). Third, we examine the main components of the framework (Sections 4 - 7). Fourth, we present an example application and the status of the implementation (Section 8). Finally, we conclude by discussing future directions.

2   Related Work

Composition in Service-Oriented Architectures has been the focus of much research recently, although the composition problem has been actively investigated in the database and agent communities [23, 24, 25, 26]. Service composition is an active field of research and we review the major frameworks that are most closely related to our research.

Service composition can be broadly classified into three categories: manual, semi-automated and automated composition. Manual composition frameworks

[12, 13, 15, 27] expect the user to generate workflow scripts either graphically or through a text editor, which are then submitted to a workflow execution engine. Triana [12, 13] provides a graphical user interface, allowing the user to select the service required from a toolbox and "drag-and-drop" onto a canvas. The services are retrieved from UDDI using a simple keyword search. Additionally, Triana allows the composition of services with locally available tools. The composed graph can then be distributed over a P2P or Grid network for execution. BPWS4J [15] provides an Eclipse plug-in to allow the user to compose a graph at the XML level. This composed graph, along with a WSDL document for the composite service, is submitted to the execution engine. Self-Serve [27] allows the user to build the workflow by locating the services required by using the service builder. The service builder interacts with UDDI to retrieve service meta-data. The composed graph, an annotated state chart, is then executed using a P2P based execution model. An interesting feature of this system is the use of a service container that aggregates services offering the same functionality. At run time, the service container selects the actual service based on membership modes and a scoring service. These systems have several drawbacks. First, the discovery and selection of services is un-scalable as the number of services increases. Second, they require the user to have low-level knowledge, e.g. in the case of BPWS4J, the user is expected to set up a workflow at the XML level. Although Triana provides a graphical drag and drop interface, this is not feasible for a large workflow. Third, if the service is no longer available, the execution will fail, although in the case of Self-Serve, the service container would probably substitute another functionally-equivalent service. Also, recent research [19] has 'extended' BPWS4J to allow runtime selection and substitution of services.

Semi-automated composition techniques [4, 6, 17, 31] are a step forward in the sense that they make 'semantic suggestions' for service selection during the composition process; the user still needs to select the service required from a shortlist of the appropriate services and link them up in the order desired. Sirin et. al. [17] propose a system that provides service choices which are semantically compatible at each stage. The generated workflow is then executed. Cardoso and Sheth [4] propose a framework which provides assistance to the user by recommending a service meeting the user's needs. This is done by matching the user-specified Service Template (ST) with the Service Object (SO). Chen et. al. [6] outline a knowledge-based framework which provides advice as the user constructs a workflow. The system allows the user to store workflows, hence facilitating reuse. Although these systems solve some of the problems of manual composition frameworks, they are still un-scalable as the filtering process may provide numerous services for the user to select from. Additionally, there are few, if any, fault-handling mechanisms built into these systems. For example in Cardoso and Sheth, if a ST fails to match an SO, composition will fail. Similarly in Sirin et. al., and Chen et. al., the composed workflow is sent to the enactment engine for execution. At this stage, if a service is not available, execution will fail. Finally, except for Chen et al., there is no support for generating workflows of differing levels of granularity.

Automated composition techniques [7, 8, 9, 10, 11, 18, 33, 34, 35, 36, 37] automate the entire composition process by using AI planning or similar technology. McIlraith and Son [10] address the automated composition problem by proposing an agent-based Web services composition framework which uses generic procedures and semantically marked up services to guide composition. The Agent Broker acts as a gateway to Web services and is responsible for selecting and invoking the services. The framework assumes the existence of a generic procedure. In the absence of one, composition cannot proceed. Additionally, if the Agent Broker cannot match a service, execution will fail. The SWORD toolkit [11] automates service composition by using rule-based service descriptions. The user specifies the initial and final state facts. Based on this, the planner attempts to put together a chain of services that can satisfy these requirements. The user is expected to be able to specify the state facts. More importantly, there is no automated service discovery mechanism built in. As a result, composition will fail if the service required cannot be found. Also, composition is based on specific implementations of services; this makes it difficult to share workflows as the service may no longer be available.

An important component of automated composition is the discovery of the services required. Research in this area has focused on the use of DAML-S to describe service capabilities. A matchmaker engine then compares the DAML-S description of the service requested with those of the services advertised [20, 21]. This work is extended by Sycara et. al. [16] to propose a preliminary composition framework based on AI planning technology, the DAML-S Matchmaker and the DAML-S Virtual Machine. The framework does not incorporate the use of a workflow repository. Hence, a workflow has to be recomputed each time a request is received. Also, the framework does not distinguish between executable and non-executable workflows; all workflows are based on implemented services available. As a result, the workflows are not reusable or cannot be shared as there is no guarantee that any component service will be available in the future. Sheshagiri et. al. [8] propose a framework with two key features: use of DAML-S to describe service capabilities and a planner to generate simple workflow graphs using a backward chaining algorithm. A very similar framework is proposed by Wu et al., [7] that uses SHOP2, an HTN planning system, to generate workflows. The Pegasus project [9, 33, 34, 35, 36, 37] proposes two workflow generation systems. The Concrete Workflow Generator (CWG) maps an abstract workflow onto an executable workflow. The second system (ACWG) uses AI planning technology to generate workflows in Grid environments. An interesting feature of this work is the distinction between abstract and concrete workflows. These frameworks suffer from the same drawbacks: there is no fault handling mechanism - if a service implementation is not available, execution will fail. Additionally, the frameworks proposed do not include a workflow repository which would make it possible to reuse previously constructed workflows. Further, there is no distinction between abstract and concrete workflows. This makes it difficult to share workflows. Although the Pegasus system does make this distinction, it does not provide mechanisms to expose the abstract and the concrete workflows as services. Finally, Koehler and Srivastava [29] point out several problems with current AI planning technology when applied to the service composition problem.

Laukkanen and Helin [28] put forward a model which includes simple fault-handling mechanisms. The model assumes that a workflow already exists in a repository and the user selects the workflow required. This workflow is then validated to ensure that all the participating services are available. If a service is not available, a matchmaker is used to retrieve similar services. Interestingly, if a single alternative cannot be found, the composer agent attempts to put together a simple chain of service which can provide the functionality. The workflow is then rewritten to include these new services and their network locations and sent to the execution engine. The drawbacks of this model are as follows: First, the model assumes a workflow is available. There is no mechanism for the user to create one. This is a severe drawback as it completely side-steps the issue of composition. Second, workflows are stored with the network locations of the services encoded within the workflow. This means that when a workflow is reused and all the participating services are available, there is no option for the user to select alternative implementations of the service based on changed optimization criteria. The IRS-II [18] framework provides an infrastructure which can be used to publish, compose and execute Semantic Web services. The system distinguishes between a task (generic description of the task to be solved) and a Problem Solving Method (an abstract, implementation-independent description of how to accomplish a task). A task may correspond to several PSMs. The user selects a task to be performed. A broker locates an appropriate PSM (which can satisfy the task) and then invokes the corresponding services. Although the system proposes an interesting distinction between a task and a PSM, this increase in the number of artifacts required merely enhances the probability that workflow composition will fail. First, a service developer has to manually associate a PSM to a service. This becomes un-scalable as the number of PSMs and services increase. Second, composition and/or execution will fail if a task, PSM or a service is not available. There appear to be no fault-handling mechanisms to tackle such a scenario.

The WebDG [30] framework proposes an approach for the automatic composition of Web services in four phases: specification, matchmaking, selection and generation. A high level description of the desired composition is generated in the specification phase. This high-level specification is in XML format and is translated into several composition plans by using composability rules in the matchmaking phase. In the selection phase, the user selects a desired plan based on QoC (Quality of Composition) parameters defined in his/her profile. Finally, a detailed description of the composite service is generated in the generation phase. While demonstrating several novel techniques, the framework suffers from several weaknesses. First, the user is expected to provide a high level specification in XML format. It is unrealistic to assume nave users to have knowledge of low-level programming. Second, the frame-work does not distinguish between executable and non-executable workflows; this would make it easier to store, reuse and share workflows. Third, if a service is not available, execution will fail. Finally, although the user can control the number of plans generated, the generation of several plans is inefficient and resource expensive.

In this section, we reviewed briefly several service composition frameworks. We identified gaps in existing systems; lack of a dynamic fault-tolerant composition algorithm, and non-distinction between different abstract levels of workflows.

3   Requirements and Overview of the Framework

In this section, we outline the general requirements for the framework and present the proposed architecture.

3.1   Requirements

In order to successfully generate workflows, an automated service composition framework must adhere to certain basic requirements.

- High degree of fault-tolerance: The framework must be able to handle common fault scenarios. There is no guarantee in a SOA that a particular service will be available at a particular time. Additionally, a service interaction may fail due to missing messages or not producing the intended result. In this case, there should be intelligent mechanisms to discover and invoke another service, or compose services which provide the same functionality. Similarly, in case a rulebase is not available for a particular objective, there must be mechanisms to chain services to achieve the objective.
- Workflow granularity: The framework should support mechanisms to allow users to generate workflows of varying levels of granularity. For example, abstract and concrete workflows. Abstract workflows specify the workflow without referring to any specific service implementation. Hence all services are referred to by their logical names. A concrete workflow specifies the actual names and network locations of the services participating in the workflow. An abstract workflow allows users to share workflows without reference to any specific service implementation. This is particularly useful as there is no guarantee of the availability of any service in a SOA. On the other hand, a concrete workflow could be useful for provenance purposes. Additionally, workflows of differing levels of granularity should be loosely coupled, i.e. with minimum interdependence.
- Specify and refine high-level objectives: The framework should support mechanisms to allow users to specify and dynamically refine a high-level objective which is then translated into a workflow. It should be possible to carry out "what-if" analysis in an efficient manner with only the changed sub-graphs being recomposed.
- User-specified optimization criteria: The framework should provide a mechanism which allows users to specify the workflow composition/execution optimization criteria. For example, the user may want to minimize the total runtime of the workflow or minimise the use of expensive resources.

- Scalable: The framework should be scalable to a large number of services.
- Domain independent: The framework should be as generic as possible in order to allow its use within any domain.

Based on our review of the related work and these requirements we identify the need for an holistic autonomic approach to service composition. Our proposed framework meets these requirements by providing the following:

- Support for dynamic fault-tolerant, adaptive service discovery and composition mechanism. We restrict the scope of fault to mean the non-availability of a service.
- Support for generating, storing, and reusing workflows with differing levels of granularity.
- Support for specification and refinement of high-level user objectives.
- Domain independence.

3.2 Framework Overview

The framework architecture is shown in Fig. 1. Everything is a service. Services are de-scribed and invoked based on their descriptions. The key bootstrap operation is the location of the Workflow Manager Service (WFMS). The WFMS puts together the framework required based on available services and user-specified preferences. The framework consists of two core and five supporting services: Abstract Workflow Composer (AWFC), Concrete Workflow Composer (CWFC), Reasoning Service (RS), Matchmaker Service (MMS), Abstract Workflow Repository (AWFR), Concrete Workflow Repository (CWFR) and the Rulebase (RB). The WFMS coordinates the entire process and manages the flow of messages between the components. The AWFC is a service which accepts an incoming user-specified high-level goal and transforms this into an abstract workflow. At this level, all tasks and their inputs and outputs are referred to by their logical names. The AWFC will typically query the AWFR to ascertain if the same request has been processed previously. If so, the abstract workflow will be returned to the Manager Service. If not, a request will be made to the Reasoning Service to retrieve a process template from the Rulebase which can satisfy the request. If a process template is not available, an attempt will be made to retrieve a combination of tasks that provide the same functionality based on the inputs, outputs, preconditions and effects. The same process will apply to all constituent services. An abstract workflow is generated and returned to the Manager Service. The CWFC Service accepts an abstract workflow and attempts to match the individual tasks with available instances of actually deployed services. If the matching process is successful, an executable graph is generated and returned to the Manager Service. If not, a request will be made to the Reasoning Service and the Matchmaker Service to retrieve a combination of services that can provide the required functionality. The AWFR and CWFR Services are domain specific services which wrap and provide access to the workflow repositories. The repositories store abstract and concrete workflows respectively. Sections 4 to 7 describe each of these components in more detail.

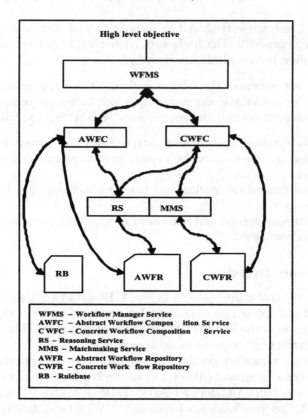

Fig. 1. The Framework Architecture.

4   Abstract Workflow Composition

As introduced above, the AWFC Service generates an abstract workflow from
a high-level objective. The AWFC uses a dynamic adaptable algorithm (Fig. 2)
which tries to build an abstract workflow by using at least three different sources
of information.

- AWF Repository. The AWF Repository stores semantically annotated descriptions of services and workflows. The AWFC queries the AWFR Service
  to ascertain if the same workflow has been processed previously. This is done
  by semantically matching the workflow name by referring to an ontology. If
  a match is found, the AWF is returned.
- Rulebase. If no match is found, the AWFC queries a rule base to retrieve
  a rule which can provide the template to achieve this goal. Given this rule,
  the AWFC again queries the AWFR, but this time an attempt is made to
  semantically match the inputs and outputs required to those of the abstract
  workflows in the repository. If an AWF is matched, this is returned. If the

matching does not succeed, the AWFC analyzes and splits the rule into component rules. This is done recursively until an atomic rule is reached. The AWFC will then query the AWFR to ascertain if any AWFs match the rule.

- Chaining Services. The AWFC uses the Reasoning Service (see Section 6) to create a chain of services that when put together can fulfil the user objective.

```
AWFC(name){
    retrieveFromAWFR(name);
    if (!found) {
        retrieve rule from rulebase;
        retrieveFromAWFR(input,output);
        if (!found) {
            split rule into smallest rule;
            for (each rule) {
                get rule output;
                get rule input;
                retrieveFromAWFR(input,output);
                if (!found) {
                    chain services(input,output);
                }
                concatenate;
            }
        }
    }
    return AWF
}
```

Fig. 2. AWFC algorithm

5   Concrete Workflow Composition

The CWFC uses a dynamic adaptable algorithm (Fig. 3) to match each service in the abstract workflow with an instance of an executable service available on the network at that time. It does this in two different ways:

- Matchmaking: Each abstract service is passed to the Matchmaker Service (see Section 7) which then attempts to retrieve a semantically matching service available on the network. Depending on the degree of the match, the CWFC Service may accept the service. The degree of match may vary from exact to plug-in.
- Chaining Services: The CWFC uses the Reasoning Service (see Section 6) to chain together services which can provide the same functionality.

It is possible that a service implementation may not be available. In this case, the AWFC is invoked through the WFMS, and asked to provide alternative AWFs for that particular sub-graph. This provides a high degree of fault tolerance.

```
CWFC(awf) {
   concrete service = matchmaker(service);
   if (!found){
      concrete Service = chain service(service);
   }
   return concrete service;
}
```

Fig. 3. CWFC algorithm

6   Reasoning Service

The Reasoning Service provides support to the two core composer services. Specifically, this service provides a back-tracking algorithm (Fig. 4) to produce a chain of services which can provide the output required using the given input. More specifically, the following steps are performed:

- For each service available, find a service that matches the output of the service requested. Let one such service be Sn.
- Ascertain the input of Sn. Find a service that can generate the input for Sn. Let this service be Sn-1.
- This process is iterated until the input of the service Sn-x matches the input of the service requested.
- Formulate the workflow which specifies the order of execution of the components S1 to Sn.

An interesting feature of our chaining algorithm is that it uses the Matchmaking Service to match the inputs and outputs of the services. As a result, it is not essential that matching be exact; plug-in matches are acceptable. This makes our chaining algorithm more robust and with a higher rate of success than similar other algorithms.

7   Matchmaking Service

The Matchmaking Service (MMS) provides an intelligent matchmaking mechanism. Its core functionality is to match two services based on the inputs, outputs, pre-conditions and effects (IOPEs). The Matchmaking Service is used by the

```
chain services(input, output){
   for(each service){
      get service output;
      if (service output = =output){
         get service input;
         graph = graph + chain services (input, service input);
      }
   }
   return graph;
}
```

Fig. 4. Chain Service Algorithm

Reasoning Service to match inputs and outputs of the service that it is chaining. Additionally, the MMS is used by the CWFC Service to match abstract services to concrete services. Our algorithm is based on that proposed by Paolucci et. al. [20]. However, we have modified this algorithm in two ways. First, it is not necessary to match all the outputs/inputs of the service requested with all the outputs/inputs of the service available. We only require that all the inputs/outputs of the service requested be matched to all or some of the inputs/outputs of the service available. This makes it possible to match services that would otherwise be rejected. Second, only exact and plug-in matches are calculated as there is no guarantee that a subsumes match would be able to provide the required functionality. As a consequence, we would expect the algorithm to be more suitable and efficient for use in automated composition frameworks.

8   An Example Application

In this section, we first describe the implementation of our framework. We then illustrate our approach by using a scenario from the genealogy domain.

All the main components are implemented as Web services using the Axis server to expose them. We use existing Semantic Web tools, like RDF, OWL-S, and reasoning mechanisms to provide the basic representation and reasoning technology. Services are described using DAML-S. The Reasoning and Matchmaking Services use DQL/JTP server to carry our subsumption reasoning. The repositories are currently implemented as flat files containing the DAML-S profiles and process models. The WFMS forms the core of the framework. It locates and coordinates all the other components required to form the framework. The AWFC Service generates an abstract workflow in BPEL4WS format. This document contains no network locations. This abstract workflow is passed to the CWFC Service, which then matches all the services taking part in the workflow with available implementations. Finally, a BPEL4WS document containing the network addressees of all the tasks is generated and this can now be submitted to any BPEL4WS engine for execution.

To illustrate the main features of our framework, we present the following scenario. A typical query in the genealogy domain is to locate a relative, say all cousins of a specified person, X. This can be stated as: I need a workflow to find all the cousins of X. To satisfy this query, either a previous workflow or a rule is available. In this case, a possible rule could be:

```
Cousins (X):= Exclude {Grandchildren [Grandparents (X)], Children
[Parents (X)]} Input: Name Output: Cousins
```

The Cousin rule may be split into 3 parts as follows in case an abstract workflow can-not be generated at this stage:

- Part1: Ascertain Grandchildren[Grandparents(X)]
- Part2: Ascertain Children[Parents(X)]
- Part3: Input the results from the above 2 into the Exclude Service.

If necessary, these may be still be further broken down into smaller units. For example the Grandparents rule may be split into:

```
Grandparents (X):= Parents [Parents (X)] Input: Name Output:
Grandparents
```

An example of the FindParents rule is shown in Fig. 5. Once the abstract workflow is generated, it is passed on to the CWFC Service. If the CWFC Service is unable to locate any suitable matches for any of these services, it will request the AWFC to propose alternatives. The CWFC Service will finally generate a BPEL4WS graph with binding information. The prototype application has been built and is currently under evaluation.

9   Conclusion

In this paper, we propose a framework to facilitate automated composition of services in a SOA made up of a Manager Service and other supporting services, including an abstract and a concrete workflow generator. We have described these components in detail and outlined their interactions. We have also described our prototype implementation and its use within the genealogy domain. The important features of our approach are: a highly dynamic and fault-tolerant workflow generation algorithm, distinction between different levels of granularity of the workflow in order to allow reuse and sharing, and the specification and refinement of high-level user objectives. These features ensure that our framework has a higher possibility of successfully generating executable workflows compared to existing similar algorithms. Further, the generic nature of our framework makes it possible to be used across a wide range of application domains. Future work involves the use our model in other application domains. We also plan to integrate user-specified optimization criteria to guide the generation of workflow. Finally, we intend to integrate the generation of provenance data within this framework.

A Framework for Automated Service Composition   281

```
<owl:Class rdf:about="#FindParents">
  <owl:subClassOf>
    <owl:Restriction>
      <owl:onProperty rdf:resource="&process;#composedOf"/>
      <owl:allValuesFrom>
        <owl:Class>
          <owl:intersectionOf rdf:parseType="Collection">
            <owl:Class rdf:about="&process;#Sequence"/>
            <owl:Restriction>
              <owl:onProperty rdf:resource="&process;#components"/>
              <owl:allValuesFrom>
                <owl:Class>
                  <process:listOfInstancesOf rdf:parseType="Collection">
                    <owl:Class rdf:about="#FindChildIn"/>
                    <owl:Class rdf:about="#FindSpouseIn"/>
                  </process:listOfInstancesOf>
                </owl:Class>
              </owl:allValuesFrom>
            </owl:Restriction>
          </owl:intersectionOf>
        </owl:Class>
      </owl:allValuesFrom>
    </owl:Restriction>
  </owl:subClassOf>
</owl:Class>
<!--io for FindParents-->
<rdf:Property rdf:ID="parentsIn">
  <owl:subPropertyOf rdf:resource="&process;#input"/>
  <owl:domain rdf:resource="#FindParents"/>
  <owl:range rdf:resource="&concepts;#Person"/>
</rdf:Property>
<rdf:Property rdf:ID="parentsOut">
  <owl:subPropertyOf rdf:resource="&process;#output"/>
  <owl:domain rdf:resource="#FindParents"/>
  <owl:range rdf:resource="&concepts;#Parents"/>
</rdf:Property>
```

Fig. 5. The FindParents Rule.

References

[1] Casati, F., Shan, M., and Georgakopoulos, D. 2001. E-Services - Guest editorial. The VLDB Journal. 10(1):1.
[2] Tsalgatidou, A and Pilioura, T. 2002. An Overview of Standards and Related Technology in Web services. Distributed and Parallel Databases. 12(3).
[3] Fensel, D., Bussler, C., Ding, Y., and Omelayenko, B. 2002. The Web Service Modeling Framework WSMF. Electronic Commerce Research and Applications.1(2).
[4] Cardoso, J. and Sheth, A. 2002. Semantic e-Workflow Composition. Technical Report, LSDIS Lab, Computer Science, University of Georgia.
[5] Paolucci, M., Sycara, K., and Takahiro Kawamura. 2003. Delivering Semantic Web Services. In Proc. Of the Twelfth World Wide Web Conference.
[6] Chen, L, Shadbolt, N.R, Goble, C, Tao, F., Cox, S.J., Puleston, C., and Smart, P. 2003. Towards a Knowledge-based Approach to Semantic Service Composition. 2nd International Semantic Web Conference
[7] Wu, D., Sirin, E., Hendler, J., Nau, D., and Parsia, B. 2003. Automatic Web Services Composition Using SHOP2. Twelfth World Wide Web Conference.
[8] Sheshagiri, M.,desJardins, M., and Finin, T. 2003. A Planner for Composing Service Described in DAML-S. Workshop on Planning for Web Services, International Conference on Automated Planning and Scheduling.

[9] Deelman, E., J. Blythe, Y. Gil, C. Kesselman, G. Mehta, K. Vahi, K. Blackburn, A. Lazzarini, A. Arbree, Cavanaugh, R. and Koranda, S. Mapping Abstract Complex Workflows onto Grid Environments. Journal of Grid Computing. Vol. 1, 2003

[10] McIlraith, S. and Son, T.C. 2002. Adapting golog for composition of semantic web services. In Proc. of the 8th International Conference on Knowledge Representation and Reasoning (KR '02), Toulouse, France.

[11] Ponnekanti, S. R., and Fox, A. 2002. SWORD: A Developer Toolkit for Web Service Composition. In Proc. Of the Eleventh International World Wide Web Conference, Honolulu.

[12] Taylor, I., Shields, M., Wang, I., and Philp, R: Grid Enabling Applications Using Triana, Workshop on Grid Applications and Programming Tools, June 25, 2003, Seattle. In conjunction with GGF8

[13] Taylor, I., Shields, M., Wang, I., and Philp, R: Distributed P2P Computing within Triana: A Galaxy Visualization Test Case. To be published in the IPDPS 2003 Conference, April 2003

[14] Mayer, A., McGough, S., Furmento, N., Lee, W., Newhouse,S., and Darlington, J: ICENI Dataflow and Workflow: Composition and Scheduling in Space and Time In UK e-Science All Hands Meeting, p. 627-634, Nottingham, UK, Sep. 2003

[15] IBM   Alphaworks,   BPWS4J,   http://www.alphaworks.ibm.com/tech/bpws4j [12.01.2004]

[16] Sycara, K., Paolucci, M., Ankolekar, A., and Srinivasan, N.: Automated Discovery, Interaction and Composition of Semantic Web Services, Journal of Web Semantics, Volume 1, Issue 1, December 2003

[17] Sirin, E., Hendler, J., and Parsia, B: Semi-automatic composition of web services using semantic descriptions. In Web Services: Modeling, Architecture and Infrastructure Workshop in conjunction with ICEIS 2003

[18] Motta, E., Domingue, J., Cabral, L. and Gaspari, M: IRS-II: A Framework and Infrastructure for Semantic Web Services. 2nd International Semantic Web Conference (ISWC2003) 20-23 October 2003, Sundial Resort, Sanibel Island, Florida, USA

[19] Mandell, D.J., and McIlraith, S.A: A Bottom-Up Approach to Automating Web Service Discovery, Customization, and Semantic Translation. In The Proceedings of the Twelfth International World Wide Web Conference Workshop on E-Services and the Semantic Web (ESSW '03). Budapest, 2003.

[20] Paolucci, M., Kawamura, T., Payne, T., Sycara, K: Semantic Matching of Web Services Capabilities. Proceedings of the 1st International Semantic Web Conference (ISWC), pp. 333-347, 2002.

[21] Lei Li and Ian Horrocks. A software framework for matchmaking based on semantic web technology. In Proc. of the Twelfth International World Wide Web Conference (WWW 2003), pages 331-339. ACM, 2003.

[22] Berners-Lee, T., Hendler, J., Lassila, O. The Semantic Web, Scientific American, May, 2001.

[23] Parent, C. and Spaccapietra, S: Issues and Approaches of Database Integration. Communications of the ACM 41(5): 166-178.

[24] Kashyap, V. and A. Sheth: Semantic Heterogeneity in Global Information Systems: The Role of Metadata, Context and Ontologies, Academic Press.

[25] Preece, A.D., K.Y. Hui, Gray, W.A., Marti, P., Bench-Capon, T.J.M., Jones, D.M., and Cui, Z: The KRAFT Architecture for Knowledge Fusion and Transformation. 19th SGES International Conference on Knowledge-based Systesm and Applied Artificial Intelligence (ES'99) , Springer, Berlin

[26] Bayardo, R.J., W. Bohrer, R. Brice, A. Cichocki, J. Fowler, A. Helal, V. Kashyap, T. Ksiezyk, G. Martin, M. Nodine, M. Rashid, M. Rusinkiewicz, R. Shea, C. Unnikrishnan, A. Unruh and D. Woelk: InfoSleuth: Agent-Based Semantic Integration of Information in Open and Dynamic Environments. Proceedings of the ACM SIGMOD International Conference on Management of Data, ACM Press, New York. pp. 195-206.

[27] Benatallah, B., Sheng, Q.Z., and Dumas, M.: The Self-Serv Environment for Web Services Composition, Jan/Feb, 2003, IEEE Internet Computing. Vol 7 No 1. pp 40-48.

[28] Laukkanen, M., and Helin, H: Composing Workflows of Semantic Web Services.In AAMAS Workshop on Web Services and Agent-Based Engineering, 2003.

[29] Koehler, J., and Srivastava, B: Web Service Composition: Current Solutions and Open Problems. ICAPS 2003 Workshop on Planning for Web Services, pages 28 - 35.

[30] Medjahed, B., Bouguettaya, A., and Elmagarmid A: Composing Web Services on the Semantic Web. The VLDB Journal, Special Issue on the Semantic Web, Volume 12, Number 4, November 2003.

[31] Stevens, R.D., Robinson, A.J., and Goble, C.A: myGrid: Personalised Bioinformatics on the Information Grid. Bioinformatics Vol. 19 Suppl. 1 2003, (Eleventh International Conference on Intelligent Systems for Molecular Biology)

[32] Business Integration, http://www.bijonline.com/default.asp [12.01.2004]

[33] Blythe, J., Deelman, E., Gil, Y., and Kesselman C: Transparent Grid Computing: a Knowledge-Based Approach. 15th Innovative Applications of Artificial Intelligence Conference (IAAI 2003), 2003.

[34] Blythe, J., Deelman, E., Gil, Y., Kesselman, C., Agarwal, A., Mehta, G., and Vahi, K: The Role of Planning in Grid Computing, 13th International Conference on Automated Planning and Scheduling, 2003.

[35] Blythe, J., Deelman, E., and Gil, Y: Planning for workflow construction and maintenance on the Grid. ICAPS 2003 Workshop on Planning for Web Services.

[36] Deelman, E., Blythe, J., Gil, Y., and Kesselman, C: Pegasus: Planning for Execution in Grids., GriPhyN technical report 2002-20, 2002

[37] Deelman, E., Blythe, J., Gil, Y., Kesselman C., Mehta, G., Vahi, K., Koranda, S., Lazzarini, A., Papa, M.A: From Metadata to Execution on the Grid Pegasus and the Pulsar Search. , GriPhyN technical report 2003-15

Reusing Petri Nets Through the Semantic Web

Dragan Gašević, Vladan Devedžić

FON – School of Business Administration, University of Belgrade, POB 52, Jove Ilića 154,
11000 Belgrade, Serbia and Montenegro
gasevic@yahoo.com, devedzic@galeb.etf.bg.ac.yu
http://goodoldai.org.yu

Abstract. The paper presents the Petri net ontology that should enable sharing Petri nets on the Semantic Web. Previous work on formal methods for representing Petri nets mainly defines tool-specific Petri net descriptions (i.e. metamodels) or formats for Petri net model interchange (i.e. syntax). However, such efforts do not provide a suitable model description for using Petri nets on the Semantic Web. This paper uses the Petri net UML model as a starting point for implementing the Petri net ontology. The UML model is then refined using the Protégé ontology development tool and the Ontology UML profile. Resulting Petri net models are represented on the Semantic Web is using XML-based ontology representation languages, Resource Description Framework (RDF) and Web Ontology Language (OWL). We implemented a Petri net software tool as well as tools for the Petri net Semantic Web infrastructure.

1 Introduction

The main idea of this paper is to propose a suitable way for Petri nets [1] to be used on the Semantic Web, i.e. to enable full semantic interoperability of Petri net models. Currently, Petri net interoperability is possible at the level of syntax for model sharing. It was first introduced in [2], where the authors said that it would be very useful if Petri net researchers could share their Petri net model descriptions. That way more software tools could be used for analyzing the same model. So far, all Petri net interchange attempts have been mainly tool-specific, but with very low (or without any) general acceptance. The *Petri Net Markup Language* (PNML) [3] is a recent Petri net community effort that tries to provide XML-based model sharing. PNML tends to be a part of the future ISO/IEC High-level Petri net standard [4]. A particularly important advantage of this approach is that XML documents can be easily transformed using *eXtensible Stylesheet Language Transformations* (XSLT) into other formats (that need not necessarily be XML-based).

A suitable way to represent Petri nets is needed in order to reuse them more effectively on the Semantic Web. It requires defining the *Petri net ontology* for semantic description of Petri net concepts and their relationships. The Petri net ontology enables describing a Petri net using Semantic Web languages (e.g. RDFS, and OWL) [5] [6]. Petri nets described that way can be inserted into other, non-Petri net XML-based formats, such as *Scalable Vector Graphics* (SVG, the XML-based WWW Consortium (W3C) standard for 2D vector graphics) [7]), which makes

J. Davies et al. (Eds.): ESWS 2004, LNCS 3053, pp. 284–298, 2004.

possible to reconstruct Petri net models using metadata and annotations according to the Petri net ontology. We defined the Petri net ontology using experience from previous Petri net formal descriptions (metamodel, ontologies, and syntax). They indicate very useful directions for selecting key Petri net concepts and specifying their mutual relations. The PNML is of primary importance here – it is closely related to the Petri net ontology. Actually, it is a medium (syntax) for semantics. We additionally empowered the PNML usability by defining mappings to/from the Semantic Web languages (i.e. RDFS and OWL).

The next section describes main sources for defining Petri net ontology. We concentrate on Petri net syntax because most work has been done in solving this problem (we specifically discuss the PNML). Section three enumerates advantages of the Petri net ontology, and gives guidelines for its construction. Section four outlines development of the Petri net ontology – its initial design and implementation using UML and Protégé [8] (i.e., RDF Schema (RDFS)-based implementation), whereas Section five extends the ontology using an OWL-based UML profile in order to support diversity of Petri net dialects. In Section six, we present the tool we implemented to support the Petri net ontology, as well as an ontology-driven infrastructure for sharing Petri nets using PNML, XSLT, and RDF. This work is a part of the effort of the Good Old AI research group (http://goodoldai.org.yu) in developing its platform for building intelligent systems, called AIR.

2 Sources for Petri Net Ontology

This section analyzes present Petri net: specifications, metamodels, ontologies, and syntax. Our main goal is to identify how each of these formal Petri net definitions can contribute to Petri net ontology. In Figure 1 we show relations between Petri net ontology (we are developing) and existing Petri net definitions. Also, this figure shows what we can use from all these sources to define the ontology.

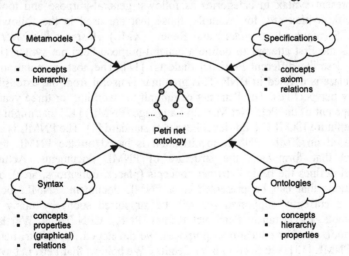

Fig. 1. Petri net ontology and elements that can be used from present formal ways for representing Petri nets

Specifications. We assume formal mathematical definitions as well as Petri net standards as Petri net specifications. Currently, there are many Petri net mathematical definitions for different Petri net dialects [1] [9]. On the other hand, there is an initiative to adopt ISO/IEC High-level Petri net standard [4]. We believe that from specifications we can obtain concepts of Petri net domain, axiom, and relations between Petri net concepts.

Metamodels. Some authors believe that metamodel is closely related to ontology. Accordingly, an illustrative and very comprehensive Petri net metamodel is proposed by Breton & Bézivin [10]. Their starting point is that a metamodel defines a set of concepts and relations, i.e. the terminology and a set of additional constraints (assertions).Note that this proposal is very important for development of Petri net tools. However, it does not show how Petri nets can be used on the Semantic Web with non-Petri net tool (i.e. annotation), and hence how Petri nets are mapped into Semantic Web language (e.g. RDF(S)). On the other hand, we can obtain useful guidelines how to develop taxonomy (hierarchy) of Petri net concepts.

Ontologies. So far, only one Petri net ontology has been developed. Perleg and her colleagues developed a Petri net ontology using Protégé and a specific graphical user interface (GUI) that extends the standard GUI of the Protégé tool. Actually, this GUI provides graphical tools for all Petri net concepts (Places, Transitions, and Arcs). In addition, the Petri net ontology is represented in RDFS, and concrete Petri net models are represented in RDF. This solution gives a solid starting point for defining the Petri net ontology. However, it has serious limitations. It covers only Time Petri nets, and no other kinds of Petri nets. It neither defines Petri net structuring mechanisms, nor provides precise constraints (e.g. types of an arc's source and target nodes that can be done using Protégé Axiom Language (PAL) constraints). Finally, it does not enable using other ontology languages for representing the Petri net ontology (e.g. DAML or OWL). This ontology can give us guidelines how to define conceptualization, properties, and taxonomy of the Petri net ontology

Syntax. A lot of work has been done in defining and using Petri net syntax. We can classify present syntax in categories as follows: general-purpose and tool-specific. Tool-specific syntax are, for example, those that are used in the following tools: DaNAMiCS (regular text syntax) and Renew (XML). *Abstract Petri Net Notation* (APNN) is the first attempt to define a general-purpose Petri net syntax (i.e., it has ability to describe different Petri net dialects) [11]. The abstract notation for each Petri net class is defined in BNF. This grammar is useful from the extensibility and modularity perspectives. The Petri net community is working for three years already on development of the Petri Net Markup Language (PNML) [12] that might become a part of the future ISO/IEC High-level Petri nets standard [4]. The PNML is a proposal that is based on XML. PNML specification is based on the PNML technology metamodel that formulates the structure of PNML documents. Actually, this metamodel defines the basic Petri net concepts (places, transitions, arcs), as well as their relations that can be presented in a PNML document. PNML, being more matured, is currently supported (or will be supported soon) by many Petri net software tools, for instance: Petri Net Kernel (PNK), CPN Tools, Worflan, PIPE, PEP, VIPtool, etc. For educational purposes, we developed *P3*, a Petri net tool that supports PNML [13] (see Section 6 for details). We believe that Petri net syntax give main contribution for Petri net ontology with: concepts, properties and their relations.

3 The Petri Net Ontology Guidelines

As we have seen so far, Petri net formats use different concepts for defining its syntax. Some of these syntax-based approaches actually have problems with syntax validation. For instance, it is very difficult to validate a text-based document (i.e. DaNAMiCS) without a special-purpose software for checking the corresponding format. A slightly better solution is to use DTD for XML definition as the Renew does. But, DTD does not support inheritance, does not have datatype checking (for the primary semantics checking), does not support defining specific formats, and what is more a DTD document has non-XML structure. The W3C XML Schema overcomes most DTD's problems. However, XML Schema has no full support for describing semantics [14]. In fact, XML Schema is only a way for defining syntax. Furthermore, if we want to share Petri net models not only with Petri net tools on the Semantic Web, we must have a formal way for representing Petri net semantics since we can not expect that a non-Petri net tool performs semantic validation.

We believe that the concept of ontology can be used for formal description of Petri net semantics. In this paper, domain ontology is understood as a formal way for representing shared conceptualization in some domain [15]. Ontology has formal mechanisms to represent concepts, concept properties, and relations between concepts in the domain of discourse. With the Petri net ontology, we can overcome validation problems that we have already noticed. However, the Petri net ontology does not exclude current Petri net formats (especially PNML). Ontology has relations to syntax, in the sense that syntax should enable ontological knowledge sharing [16]. With the Petri net ontology, we can use ontology development tools for validation of Petri net models (e.g. Protégé). Also, having the Petri net ontology one can use Semantic Web languages for representing Petri net models (e.g. RDF, RDF Schema – RDF, DAML+OIL, OWL, etc.) [5]. Thus, we show how PNML can be used as a guideline for the Petri net ontology.

Accordingly, we think that Petri net ontology should have common part that contains concepts common for all Petri net dialects. Afterward, this common part will be specialized for concrete Petri net dialect. Actually, this is the same principle that uses PNML [3]. In Figure 2 we show common part of Petri net ontology that we call Core Petri net ontology. The Core Petri net ontology is extracted from the analyzed ontology sources.

We introduced some concepts that do not really exist in Petri net models in order to obtain more suitable concept hierarchy in the core ontology. We call these concepts synthetic concepts. Overview of these concepts is given in Table 1. In the next section we define the Petri net ontology using UML and Protégé ontology development tool.

Table 1. Overview of the synthetic concepts in the Core Petri net ontology – generalizations of concepts from Fig. 2

Synthetic concept	Generalize concepts
Node reference	place reference, transition reference
Node	place, transition, node reference
Structural element	page, module instance
Model element	structural element, arc, node

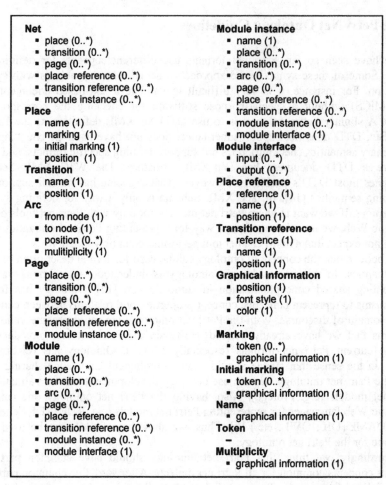

Fig. 2. Conceptualization of the Core Petri net ontology: key concepts, their mutual relations, and cardinality

4 The Petri Net Ontology – Initial Implementation

In order to develop the Petri net ontology, we decided to use UML [17]. UML was suitable because it is a generally accepted and standardised tool for analysis and modeling in software engineering. We were also able to employ UML-based Petri net descriptions existing within the PNML definition [3]. However, neither UML tools nor the UML itself are intended to be used for ontology development. Thus, in order to achieve more precise Petri net definition than a UML model provides, it is necessary to use an ontology development tool. We decided to use Protégé 2000 [8] since it is a popular tool for ontology development and can import UML models. This is enabled by Protégé's UML backend that imports UML models (represented in *XML Metadata Interchange* (*XMI*) format) into a Protégé ontology.

4.1 The Underlying Idea

The hierarchy of core concepts of the Petri net ontology is shown in Figure 3. In our design of the Petri net ontology, there is a single root element that we call *ModelElement*. This element is the parent for all elements of Petri net structure. The name of this class is *ModelElement* because the UML metamodel uses the same name for its root class [18]. A Petri net (the *Net* class) can contain many different *ModelElements*. *ModelElement* and *Net* have the ID attribute (unique identifier) of String type, and *Net* has also an attribute that describes the type of the Petri net. It is in accordance with PNML. The three main Petri net concepts (place, transition, and arc) define the structure of a Petri net, and they are represented in Figure 3 with the corresponding classes (*Place, Transition, and Arc*). Places and transitions are kinds of nodes (*Node*). In some Petri nets, an arc connects two nodes of different kinds. However, it is important to say that this is not a general the Petri net ontology statement, since there are Petri net dialects where an arc can connect, for instance, two transitions. Hence we did not include this statement in the core Petri net ontology, but it should be defined in ontology extensions for different Petri net dialects.

The *Node* class is introduced in the ontology in order to have a common way to reference both places and transitions. In order to make Petri net models easy to maintain, different concepts for structuring can be used. In the Petri net ontology, we have the class *StructuralElement*. This class is inherited from *ModelElement*, and we inherit from this class all classes that represent structuring mechanisms. We have decided to support two common mechanisms: pages (the *Page* class), and modules (the *Module* class). A *Page* may consist of other Petri net *ModelElements* – it may even consist of other pages. A *NodeReference*, which can be either a *TransitionReference* or a *PlaceReference*, represents an appearance of a node. Here, there are also constraints: a *TransitionReference* can refer to either a *Transition* or another *TransitionReference*, while a *PlaceReference* can refer to either a *Place* or another *PlaceReference*. We show these constraints using OCL in Figure 3. These constraints also affect the OCL constraint for arcs that we have already described, but we do not show their interaction due to the limited size of this paper. Unlike the OCL statement for arcs, this statement can be applied on all Petri net dialects.

The second kind of structuring mechanisms are modules. A *Module* consists of *ModelElements*, and it can be instantiated (much like an object is instantiated from a class in the object-oriented paradigm). Accordingly, *Module* is a metaclass (the stereotype in Figure 3), and *ModuleInstance* depends on *Module* (that shows a stereotyped *instanceOf* dependency from *ModuleInstance* to *Module*).

In Petri nets, an additional property (or feature) can be attached to almost every core Petri net element (e.g. name, multiplicity, etc.). Thus, we have included in the Petri net ontology a description of features and in Figure 4 we shortly depict how these features have been added. The root class for all features is *Feature*. This is also similar to the UML metamodel. The Petri net ontology follows the PNML's classification of features: those that contain graphical information (annotation) and those that do not have them (attribute). In the Petri net ontology every feature directly inherited from *Feature* class is an attribute (e.g. *ArcType*), whereas *GraphicalFeature* class represents annotations. *GraphicalFeature* has graphical information that can consist of, for instance, position (the *Position* class and its children *Absolute Position* and *Relative Position*). Examples of graphical features are: *Multiplicity, Name,*

InitialMarking, and *Marking*. It is interesting to notice that marking and initial marking consist of tokens (the *Token* class). In order to support token colors, the *Token* class is abstract. In Figure 4 we show a case when there are no colors attached to tokens; instead, we just take into account the number of tokens (*IntegerToken*).

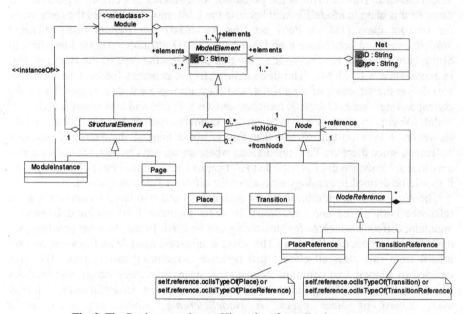

Fig. 3. The Petri net ontology – Hierarchy of core Petri net concepts

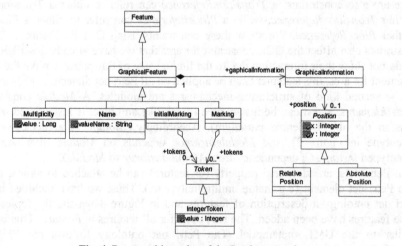

Fig. 4. Property hierarchy of the Petri net ontology

Attaching a new feature to a Petri net class requires just adding an association between a class and a feature. A UML description is a convenient way for representing the Petri net semantics. Also, this Petri net ontology can be used as a Petri net metamodel in future Petri net implementations that can take advantage of the

MDA concept and repository-based software development [19]. However, it does not let us semantically validate Petri net models. For example, we cannot use OCL statements to perform this task. In addition, UML attributes and ontology properties are semantically different concepts. Unlike a UML's attribute, ontology property is a first-class concept that can exist independently of any ontology class [20].

There are to ways to further refine the Petri net ontology. The first one is to use a UML profile [17] for UML-based ontology development. The second one recommends using standard ontology development tools. We decided to use: 1. Protégé 2000, since it provides all the necessary ontology development features (constraints and support for ontology languages), but it also has the ability to use the UML models we have shown; 2. The Ontology UML profile [21] that is based on OWL.

4.2 The Petri Net Ontology Implementation Using Protégé 2000

We can precisely define the Petri net ontology in Protégé 2000. We can differ between a class and a metaclass (e.g. *Module* – a metaclass, *ModuleInstance* – a class), we can use different Semantic Web languages provided through Protégé's backends (RDF(S), OWL, DAML+OIL) to represent the Petri net ontology, and we can specify the constraints that we defined in the UML model using OCL (e.g. PAL). We can then validate all ontology instances using these constraints, and detect if there is any instance that does not conform to some of the constraints.

After the initial UML design of the Petri net ontology, it was imported into the Protégé using Protégé's UML backend (http://protege.standford.edu/plugin/uml). This plug-in has the ability to read an XML format (i.e., XMI) for representing UML models. The main shortcoming of this UML backend is that it is unable to map UML class associations. Thus we had to add manually all the slots that are represented in UML as association ends. A snapshot of the Petri net ontology after we imported it and inserted all slots (i.e., association ends) in Protégé is shown in Figure 5.

Of course, Protégé does not have the ability to transform OCL constraints into PAL constraints. Thus we have also manually reconstructed all OCL-defined constraints from the UML model of the Petri net ontology into a set of corresponding PAL constraints.

Using Protégé we generated the RDFS that describes the Petri net ontology. One can use it for reasoning about a document that contains a Petri net model. Figure 6 shows an excerpt of this RDFS. This figure depicts how RDFS defines the classes for *ModelElement, Node, Transition, Place, Arc,* and *ArcType*. Also, this figure shows how RDFS defines *Feature*, as well as how *name* feature is defined and attached to classes that should have this property.

Since Protégé supports more concepts for ontology definition than RDFS does, one can notice some extensions of RDFS in Figure 6. These Protégé extensions are manifested by namespace a. For example, they are used to define cardinality (a:maxCardinality, a:minCardinality), to refer to a PAL constraint (a:slot_constraints), etc. Of course, this is neither a limitation of the Petri net ontology nor of the Protégé tool, but of RDFS itself. Most of such limitations are overcome in the forthcoming OWL [6], but this discussion is beyond the scope of this paper.

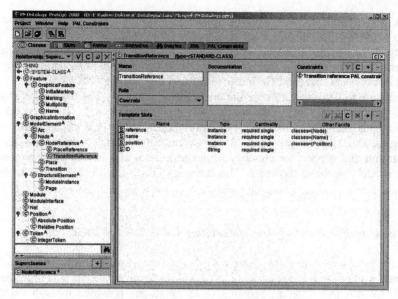

Fig. 5. The Petri net ontology in Protégé 2000

```
<rdf:RDF xmlns:rdf="&rdf;" xmlns:a="&a;" xmlns:rdfs="&rdfs;">
    <!-- ... -->
    <rdfs:Class rdf:about="ModelElement" a:role="abstract"
        rdfs:label="ModelElement">
        <rdfs:subClassOf rdf:resource="&rdfs;Resource"/>
    </rdfs:Class>
    <rdfs:Class rdf:about="Node" a:role="abstract" rdfs:label="Node">
        <rdfs:subClassOf rdf:resource="ModelElement"/>
    </rdfs:Class>
    <rdfs:Class rdf:about="Place" rdfs:label="Place">
        <rdfs:subClassOf rdf:resource="Node"/>
    </rdfs:Class>
    <rdfs:Class rdf:about="PlaceReference" rdfs:label="PlaceReference">
        <rdfs:subClassOf rdf:resource="NodeReference"/>
        <a:_slot_constraints rdf:resource="PN Ontology_00023"/>
    </rdfs:Class>
    <rdfs:Class rdf:about="Feature" rdfs:label="Feature">
        <rdfs:subClassOf rdf:resource="&rdfs;Resource"/>
    </rdfs:Class>
    <!-- ... -->
    <rdf:Property rdf:about="name" a:maxCardinality="1"
        a:minCardinality="1" rdfs:label="name">
        <rdfs:range rdf:resource="Name"/>
        <rdfs:domain rdf:resource="Node"/>
        <rdfs:domain rdf:resource="Place"/>
        <rdfs:domain rdf:resource="PlaceReference"/>
        <rdfs:domain rdf:resource="Transition"/>
        <rdfs:domain rdf:resource="TransitionReference"/>
    </rdf:Property>
    <!-- ... -->
</rdf:RDF>
```

Fig. 6. A part of the RDF Schema of the Petri net ontology

On the other hand, one can see that the RDFS/Protégé Petri net ontology does not take into account Petri net dialects. In this version of the Petri net ontology we can add Petri net dialect-specific properties or constraints, but we have no ability to distinguish between the core concepts form the Petri net ontology and concepts Petri net dialect-specific concepts. One possible solution is to use XML/RDF namespace mechanism. But, this solution is also limited to use in Protégé. We need a better way to represent ontology modularization. Accordingly, we decided to use OWL and an OWL-based UML profile in order to overcome these Petri net ontology limitations.

5 OWL-based Petri Net Ontology

For ontology development we use the Ontology UML profile (OUP) (see [21] for details) that is based on the forthcoming ontology language OWL [6]. The OUP provides stereotypes and tagged values for full ontology development. OUP models can be (automatically) transformed into OWL ontologies (e.g., using XSLT) [22]. Using the OUP, one can represent relations between the core concepts of the Petri net ontology and the specifics of a Petri net dialect. For that purposes we suggest using the OUP's package mechanism. In the OUP, we attach <<ontology>> to a package. That means the package is an ontology. Accordingly, we can put all core concepts of the Petri net ontology in an <<ontology>> package. If we extend the Petri net ontology with concepts of a Petri net dialect we only need to create a new <<ontology>> that would be related with the core <<ontology>> through the <<include>> dependency. In Figure 7 we illustrate this extension principle.

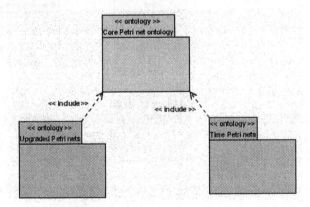

Fig. 7. Extension mechanism of the Petri net ontology: support for Petri net dialects

This example depicts how we extend the Core Petri net ontology (<<ontology>> *Petri net core*) with concepts of Upgraded and Time Petri nets (e.g. we attach new properties to the core classes for a Petri net dialect). An additional advantage of this approach is that we have the ability to merge concepts from a number of ontologies (i.e., <<ontology>> packages). As a result we obtain one ontology definition, for instance, in OWL (by applying XSLT). Comparing with the current PNML proposal for the Petri Net Definition Types [3] one can see that this approach improves the maintainability of Petri net concepts, and better supports reusability of the Petri net ontology concepts. So far, we have defined the Petri net ontology extensions for: P/T nets, Time Petri nets, and Upgraded Petri nets.

The Core Petri net hierarchy, which is shown in Figure 3, is the same for the Petri net ontology represented in the OUP. Actually, there is a difference with regard to both associations and attributes in the model from Figure 3, since ontology development understands property as a fist-class concept. Thus, it is necessary to transform all association between classes as well as all class attributes into the OUP property stereotypes (<<DataTypeProperty>> and <<ObjectProperty>>). Note that in the OUP Petri net ontology we do not need the *Feature* class since property is the first class in ontology development. Accordingly, we have <<ObjectProperty>> and <<DatatypeProperty>> that represent properties in the Petri net ontology. On the other hand, we want to provide support for graphical features (*GraphicalFeature*). Figure 8 gives an example of the <<ObjectProperty>> *name* that has already been declared as a graphical feature. In this case, the *name* property has as its range (through the <<range>> association) the *NameDescriptor* <<OntClass>>. However, this class is inherited from the *GraphicalFeature*. *GraphicalFeature* is introduced in the Petri net ontology to be the root class for all the classes that constitute the range for a graphical feature. Similarly, we define other graphical features (e.g. marking). In addition, the *name* property has domain (the <<domain>> association): *Net* and *Node*.

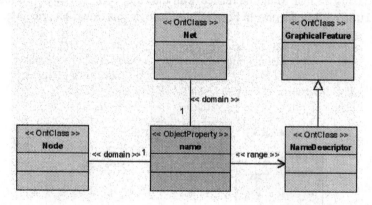

Fig. 8. An example of a graphical feature defined in the Ontology UML profile: name object property

Figure 9 shows an excerpt of the Petri net ontology in OWL. It was generated using an XSLT for transformation from the OUP ontology (i.e., XMI) to OWL [22]. The figure illustrates a part of the OWL *TransitionReference* restriction on the *reference* property. This restriction states that *TransitionReference*'s property *reference* must take all values from (*allValuesFrom*) the following classes: *Transition and TransitionReference*. It is important to note that in the OWL ontology logical expressions take an XML form (e.g. the *TransitionReference* restriction), unlike the Protégé PAL constraints that are written in a Lisp-like form. It is more convenient to parse an ontology statement represented in an XML format using standard XML parser, as well as transform it using the XSLT mechanism.

```
<owl:Class rdf:ID="TransitionReference">
    <rdfs:subClassOf rdf:resource="#NodeReference"/>
    <rdfs:subClassOf>
        <owl:Restriction>
            <owl:onProperty rdf:resource="#reference"/>
            <owl:allValuesFrom>
                <owl:Class>
                    <owl:unionOf rdf:parseType="Collection">
                        <owl:Class rdf:about="#Place"/>
                        <owl:Class rdf:about="#TransitionReference"/>
                    </owl:unionOf>
                </owl:Class>
            </owl:allValuesFrom>
        </owl:Restriction>
    </rdfs:subClassOf>
</owl:Class>
```

Fig. 9. A part the Petri net ontology in OWL: the TransitionReference class restriction from Fig. 3 expresed in OCL. This is also transformed in PAL contaraint in Section 4

6 Tools for the Petri Net Ontology

In order to show practical tool support for the Petri net ontology, we overview the P3 tool. This tool has been initially developed for Petri net teaching [13], but we extended it, and thus it can be used in conjunction with the Petri net ontology. Being based on the PNML concepts, P3 is compatible with PNML. The P3 tool supports P/T nets and Upgraded Petri nets. A P3 screenshot is shown in Figure 10a. The P3's architecture is shown in Figure 10b. The Petri net class organization is shown on the left in Figure 10b, whereas the supported formats are on the right side.

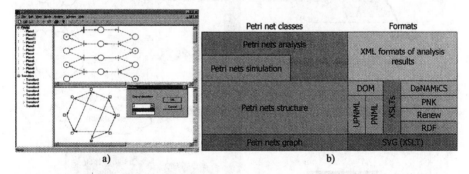

Fig. 10. P3, ontology-based Petri net tool: a) P3 screenshot; b) P3 architecture: class organization and supported XML formats

The formats supported by P3 are the main point of interest for the Petri net ontology. The P3's model sharing mechanism is based on using PNML. All other formats are implemented in P3 using XSLT (from the PNML). Accordingly, P3 can export to the following Petri net tool formats: *DaNAMiCS* – a tool that uses an ordinary text format, *Renew* – a tool that uses another XML-based format; *Petri Net Kernel* – a tool that uses PNML, but since there are some differences between this

PNML application and the P3's PNML, we had to implement an XSLT; *PIPE* – a tool that uses PNML (no need XSLT).

P3 tool has the ability to generate RDF description of a Petri net. This P3's feature is also implemented using XSLT. The generated RDF is in accordance with the Petri net ontology (in its RDFS form). We also implemented the XSLT for the opposite direction, i.e. to transform RDF into PNML, and hence we can analyze RDF-defined Petri nets using standard Petri net tools. P3 implements conversion of the PNML Petri net model description to SVG. Since this format can be viewed in standard Web browsers, it is suitable for creating, for instance, Web-based Petri net teaching materials. Learning objects, created in this way, have their underlying semantics described in RDF form, and can be transformed into PNML as well as analyzed with standard Petri net tools. P3 provides two kinds of RDF annotations [23] for SVG:

1. As embedded metadata – an RDF description is incorporated in SVG documents. The standard SVG has the `metadata` tag as an envelope for metadata.
2. As remote metadata – an RDF description is in a separated document.

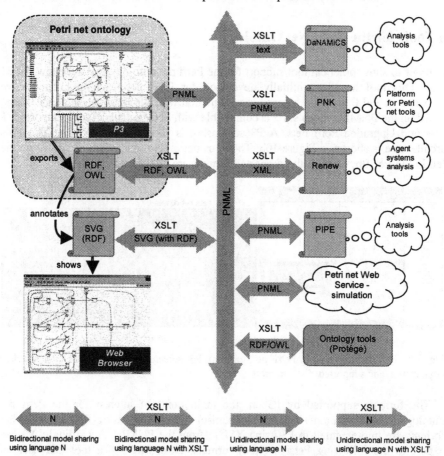

Fig. 11. Petri net infrastructure for the Semantic Web (that uses "PNML-based bus" for model sharing): the Petri net ontology, current Petri net tools, P3 tool, Web-based applications, Petri net Web Service, and ontology tools for validation of Petri net documents using the ontology

Although P3 uses RDF, it does not mean that we have abandoned PNML. On the contrary, since we implemented an XSLT (from RDF to PNML), we continued using PNML. Actually, we enhanced PNML because one can use P3 to convert a PNML model to RDF, and then the Petri net model can be validated against the Petri net ontology. That way, we achieved a semantic validation of Petri net models. Of course, PNML is very useful since it contains well-defined concepts for Petri net models interchange and it is now used by many Petri net tools. Furthermore, since we implemented the XSLTs from PNML to Petri net formats of other Petri net tools, we can also employ PNML's analysis capabilities.

In Figure 11 we show the Semantic Web infrastructure for Petri nets, which is now implemented. This infrastructure summarizes all major features of P3. The central part of this infrastructure is PNML, since it would be (probably) a part of the future High-level Petri net standard [4]. P3 can be linked with other Petri net tools though PNML (e.g., with PIPE), or by using additional XSLTs on PNML models (DaNAMiCS, Renew, and PNK). Also, P3 has XSLTs for conversions between PNML and RDF in both directions. Besides, P3 generates SVG by using XSLT form PNML to SVG. An XSLT is developed to generate the RDF-annotated SVG from the PNML. We have also developed the XSLT that transforms RDF-annotated SVG documents to PNML. This XSLT is based on the XSLT form RDF to PNML. Hence we have XSLTs for conversions between PNML and SVG in both directions.

7 Conclusions

The main idea of this paper is that the Petri net ontology should provide the necessary Petri net infrastructure for the Semantic Web. The infrastructure understands Petri nets sharing using XML-based ontology languages (i.e., RDFS and OWL). The Petri net ontology and Semantic Web languages do not abandon the PNML. On the contrary, we presented the "PNML-based bus" that takes advantage of the PNML together with the Petri net ontology. That way, we can exploit potentials of current Petri net tools in the context of the Semantic Web. We also presented P3, the Petri net tool that creates ontology-based Petri net models. Its abbreviated version, its technical description, as well as a few developed XSLTs can be downloaded from http://www15.brinkster.com/p3net.

The paper gives guidelines for putting Petri nets on the Semantic Web. It also shows complementary features of the Petri net syntax and semantics by the example of the PNML and the Petri net ontology. The example of RDF-based annotation of SVG documents indicates how to annotate other XML formats (e.g., Web Service Description Language – WSDL). This opens the door to incorporating "Petri net-driven intelligence" into Web-based applications (e.g., Web Service composition, Web Service analysis and simulation [24]).

In the future, the P3 tool will support OWL-based annotation of SVG documents with Petri net graphs. Furthermore, we will use this annotation principle to develop a Petri net Web-based learning environment, as well as to create Learning Object Metadata (LOM) repositories of Petri net models.

References

1. Peterson, J.: Petri net theory and the modeling of systems, Prentice Hall, Englewood Cliffs, New Jersey, USA (1981)
2. Berthelot, G. et al: A syntax for the description of Petri Nets, Petri Net Newsletter, No. 29 (1988) 4-15
3. Billington, J., et al: The Petri Net Markup Language: Concepts, Technology, and Tools, In Proceedings of the 24th International Conference on Applications and Theory of Petri Nets, Eindhoven, The Netherlands (2003) 483-505
4. (2002). ISO/IEC/JTC1/SC7 WG19, New proposal for a standard on Petri net techniques [Online]. Available: http://www.daimi.au.dk/PetriNets/standardisation/
5. Gómez-Pérez, A., Corcho, O.: Ontology Languages for the Semantic Web, IEEE Intelligent Systems, Vol. 17, No.1 (2002) 54-60
6. Bechhofer, S., et al: OWL Web Ontology Language Reference, W3C Recommendation., http://www.w3.org/TR/2004/REC-owl-ref-20040210 (2004)
7. D. Jackson, ed: Scalable Vector Graphics (SVG) Specification v1.2, W3C Working Draft, http://www.w3.org/TR/2003/WD-SVG12-20030715/ (2003)
8. Noy, N. F., et al: Creating Semantic Web Contents with Protégé-2000, IEEE Intelligent Systems, Vol. 16, No. 2 (2001) 60-71
9. Murata, T.: Petri nets: Properties, analysis and applications, Proceedings of the IEEE, Vol. 77, No. 4 (1989) 541-580
10. Breton, E., Bézivin, J.: Towards an Understanding of Model Executability, In Proc. of the Int. Conf. on Formal Ont. in Information Sys., Ogunquit, Maine, USA (2001) 70-80
11. Bause, F. et al: Abstract Petri Net Notation, Petri Net Newsletter, No. 49 (1995) 9-27
12. Weber, M., Kindler, E.: The Petri Net Markup Language, Petri Net Technology for Communication Based Systems, LNCS Vol. 2472, Springer-Verlag, Berlin Heidelberg New York (2003) forthcoming
13. Gašević, D., Devedžić, V.: Software support for teaching Petri nets: P3, In Proceedings of the 3rd IEEE International Conference on Advanced Learning Technologies, Athens, Greece (2003) 300-301
14. Klein, M.: XML, RDF, and Relatives, IEEE Intelligent Systems, Vol. 16, No. 2 (2001) 26-28
15. Gruber, T.: A translation approach to portable ontology specifications, Knowledge Acquisition, Vol. 5, No.2 (1993) 199-220
16. Chandrasekaran, B., et al: What Are Ontologies, and Why Do We Need Them?, IEEE Intelligent Systems, Vol. 14, No. 1 (1999) 20-26
17. Kogut, P., et al: UML for Ontology Development, The Knowledge Engineering Review, Vol. 17, No. 1 (2002) 61-64.
18. OMG Unified Modeling Language Specification v1.5, OMG document formal/03-03-01, http://www.omg.org/cgi-bin/apps/doc?formal/03-03-01.zip (2003)
19. Bock, C.: UML without Pictures, IEEE Software, Vol. 20, No. 5 (2003) 33-35
20. Baclawski, K., et al: Extending the Unified Modeling Language for ontology development, Int. J. Software and Systems Modeling, Vol. 1, No. 2, (2002) 142-156
21. Djurić, D., et al: Ontology Modeling and MDA, Journal on Object Technology, Vol. 4, No. 1, 2005, forthcoming.
22. Gašević, D., et al: Converting UML to OWL ontologies, 13th International WWW Conference, NY, USA (2004) forthcoming.
23. Handschuh, S., et al: Annotation for the Deep Web, IEEE Intelligent Systems, Vol. 18, No. 5 (2003) 42-48
24. Narayanan, S., McIlraith, S.: Analysis and Simulation of Web Services, Computer Networks: Int'l Journal of Computer and Telecommunications Networking, Vol. 42, No. 5 (2003) 675-693.

Methods for Porting Resources to the Semantic Web

Bob Wielinga[1], Jan Wielemaker[1], Guus Schreiber[2], and Mark van Assem[2]

[1] University of Amsterdam
Social Science Informatics (SWI)
Roetersstraat 15, 1018 WB Amsterdam, The Netherlands
{wielinga,jan}@swi.psy.uva.nl
[2] Vrije Universiteit Amsterdam
Department of Computer Science
De Boelelaan 1081a, 1081 HV Amsterdam, The Netherlands
{schreiber,mark}@cs.vu.nl

Abstract. Ontologies will play a central role in the development of the Semantic Web. It is unrealistic to assume that such ontologies will be developed from scratch. Rather, we assume that existing resources such as thesauri and lexical data bases will be reused in the development of ontologies for the Semantic Web. In this paper we describe a method for converting existing source material to a representation that is compatible with Semantic Web languages such as RDF(S) and OWL. The method is illustrated with three case studies: converting WordNet, AAT and MeSH to RDF(S) and OWL.

1 Introduction

Semantic Web applications will require multiple large ontologies for indexing and querying [5]. Developing such ontologies is a time consuming and costly process, so we assume that in general these ontologies will not be developed from scratch. Rather, existing resources such as thesauri, lexical data bases or ontologies published in a proprietary format will be used as sources for development of ontologies for the Semantic Web. In this paper we describe a method for converting existing source material to a representation that is compatible with semantic web languages such as RDF(S) and OWL.

The problem that we address in this paper is: how can existing resources be converted to representations that can be understood by Semantic Web applications without altering the original material, and at the same time assign semantics to these representations that is (presumed to be) compatible with the intended semantics of the source. An important corollary of this problem statement is that the transformation process from source material to Semantic Web ontology is transparent and traceable. Users of ontologies created through conversion processes will need to be aware of the interpretative steps that have taken place in the transformation process and may want to influence that process according to their own insights and requirements. So, although the conversion

J. Davies et al. (Eds.): ESWS 2004, LNCS 3053, pp. 299–311, 2004.

of a single source to Semantic Web standards may not be a very difficult task, the underlying principles and methods are of great importance to the Semantic Web enterprise.

This paper is organised as follows. In Sect. 2 we describe the general requirements and methods for converting existing materials. Section 3 to Section 5 discuss three case studies that demonstrate various applications of the method. Finally, Section 6 provides a discussion and conclusions.

2   General Method

The method for converting source material to ontologies is based on the general principle of fully automatic transformation of the source material in a number of steps. The first step (step 1a) in the conversion process is a structure-preserving syntactic translation from the source format to RDF(S). We assume that a data model of some sort is available of the source. This can be a conceptual model described in textual form, a template record structure, an XML DTD or a proper data model for example represented in UML. From the data model an RDF(S) schema is derived, where classes with properties are defined. It is recommended that naming conventions are preserved, with an exception for abbreviations which should be expanded. For example, the abbreviation "BT" for broader term, used in many thesauri, should be mapped to an RDF(S) property "broaderTerm". When the source is represented in XML some elements do not have to be represented as classes when they only serve as placeholders. For example the element "TermList" used in MeSH (see Section 5), can be directly mapped to the property "hasTerm" since RDF(S) properties can have multiple values.

Two complications may arise in the creation of the RDF schema. A first problem may occur when an XML DTD enforces a strict sequence through comma-separated element definitions. Only when the order is interpreted to be relevant the RDF list construct should be used, which can make the RDF representation somewhat complicated, since the representation of ordered relations as RDF lists requires special interpretation machinery. In general this should be avoided where possible. Although for example, the MeSH DTD states that a DescriptorRecord always has its children elements in strict order (comma), this is probably not required. Therefore, it is possible to translate DescriptorRecords by translating each child element and linking them to the Descriptor using properties.

A second complication may occur when data elements have internal substructures. For example, many dictionaries give multiple meanings under one headword, usually indicated by number codes. In such cases it has to be decided whether each subentry should be mapped onto a separate class or whether the subentries can be mapped to properties.

When an RDF(S) schema is established the data elements from the source can be translated to instances of the schema. In this structural translation step no information is lost or added, it concerns just a translation between the original format and RDF(S).

The next step (step 1b) in the conversion process concerns the *explication* of information that is implicit in the original data format but that is intended by the conceptual model. Examples of cases where explication can be applied are given below.

- Thesauri with an origin in the bibliographic sciences are often structured as a set of records, with fields for hierarchical relations. An example is MeSH, which has Descriptors with TreeNumbers. These TreeNumbers can be used to create (and are intended to signify) a hierarchy, e.g. by adding a subTree relation between Descriptors.

- Attributes in records often have terms as value, rather than unique identifiers. These terms have to be mapped to an XML namespace with a unique identifier.

- Some entries can play a special role. For example in AAT, some terms are "GuideTerms" that function as a structuring device in the hierarchy, but which are not supposed to be used for indexing. In AAT these terms are identified by enclosing them in brackets (<>). The special role of such entries can be made explicit by defining them as instances of a special class in the data model (e.g. "GuideTerm" as a subclass of "Term"). In this way the original intention of the conceptual model is preserved and made explicit.

The first two translation steps together form a syntactic conversion stage. A second stage in the conversion process concerns a semantic transformation. In the first step of the semantic conversion (step 2a) the RDF(S) instances generated in the syntactic stage are augmented according to the intended semantics of the source conceptual model. Many thesauri and lexical data bases intend their entries to be interpreted as a hierarchy of concepts. If the properties "broaderTerm" and "narrowerTerm" are used to represent the hierarchical relation they can be defined in OWL as inverse property of each other and as transitive properties.

In the second step (step 2b) of the semantic conversion the instances of the first stage are reinterpreted in terms of the RDFS or OWL semantics. For example the hierarchical relations of the thesaurus can be interpreted as RDF(S) "subClassOf" relations. This step adds semantics to the ontology (such as inheritance) which may or may not have been intended by the creators of the source. A standard way to achieve this reinterpretation is to make the classes in the syntactic schema subclasses of class Class (i.e. meta-classes) and making the hierarchical relations such as "subtreeOf" in MeSH and "broaderTerm" in other thesauri, a subproperty of "subClassOf". This creates an interpretation of the source as a proper subclass hierarchy. Other properties can also be mapped onto RDF(S) and OWL properties. For example a property such as "relatedTerm" which is present in many thesauri can be mapped onto "seeAlso" in RDFS/OWL.

Figure 1 summarizes the steps described above.

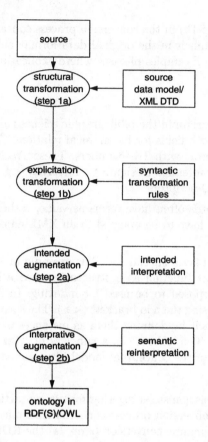

Fig. 1. Schematic representation of the conversion steps

3   Case 1: Wordnet

WordNet [1] is a large lexical data base, originally developed for linguistic purposes, but now an important resource for research on the Semantic Web. Step 1a of the conversion of WordNet to an RDF representation was performed by Decker and Melnik[3]. Their RDF Schema for WordNet defines classes and properties for the data model of WordNet. This means that WordNet *synsets* (the basic WordNet concepts) are represented as instances of the class LexicalConcept and that the WordNet hyponym relations (the subclass relations in Word-Net) are represented as tuples of the hyponymOf relation between instances of wns:LexicalConcept. The data model and source representation of WordNet is quite explicit and clean, so step 1b is not required in this case. In step 2a additional properties of the representation could be defined. For example, the WordNet relation wn:similarTo could be asserted to be a subproperty of the

---

[3] http://www.semanticweb.org/library/

OWL `owl:SymmetricProperty`. In our present implementation this step has not been performed.

The RDF(S) representation leads to a representational mismatch, as we are unable to treat WordNet concepts as classes and WordNet hyponym relations as subclass relations. This problem can be resolved by performing step 2b of the conversion process using RDFS meta-modeling primitives. Consider the following two RDFS descriptions:

```
<rdf:Description rdf:about="&wns;LexicalConcept">
  <rdfs:subClassOf rdf:resource="&rdfs;Class"/>
</rdf:Description>

<rdf:Description rdf:about="&wns;hyponymOf">
  <rdfs:subPropertyOf rdf:resource="&rdfs;subClassOf"/>
</rdf:Description>
```

The first statement specifies that the class `LexicalConcept` is a subclass of the built-in RDFS meta-class `Class`, the instances of which are classes. This means that now all instances of `LexicalConcept` are also classes. In a similar vein, the second statement defines that the WordNet property `hyponymOf` is a subproperty of the RDFS `subClassOf` property. This enables us to interpret the instances of `hyponymOf` as subclass links.

We expect representational mismatches to occur frequently in any realistic Semantic Web setting. RDF(S) mechanisms similar to the ones above can be employed to handle this. However, this poses the requirement on the toolkit that the infrastructure is able to interpret subtypes of `rdfs:Class` and `rdfs:subPropertyOf`. In particular the latter was important for our applications, e.g., to be able to reason with WordNet hyponym relations as subclass relations and to visualize WordNet as a class hierarchy.

4   Case 2: AAT

The Art and Architecture Thesaurus (AAT[4] [4]) was developed by the Getty[5] foundation as a vehicle for indexing catalogues of art objects. Originally set up as a monolingual thesaurus in English, it is now also (partially) available in other languages, such as Dutch, Spanish and French. The AAT is widely used in musea and other cultural heritage institutions for cataloguing art collections. The AAT was developed according to the ISO standard for the definition of monolingual (ISO2788) and multilingual thesauri (ISO5964). These standards prescribe a data model which basically is a record structure with a number of attributes and three relations: hierarchical relation (broader/narrower term), equivalence of terms (synonyms and lexical variants) and an associative relation (related term).

---

[4] ©2003, The J. Paul Getty Trust. All rights reserved.
[5] http://www.getty.edu/

```
LEN 513
STATUS  n
IDNO    255420
DATCHG  19950712
DATENT  19950407
CN  B.BM.CFS.AFU.ATG.RIQ.KKK.AHS
TERM    allergies
ALT ALTERNATE: allergy
BT  disease
SN  SCOPE NOTE: Abnormal reactions of the body produced by a
        sensitizing dosage of or exposure to some foreign material.
HN  April 1995 descriptor added.
SOURCE  allergies (CCE; ROOT)
SOURCE  allergy (CAND; MESH; OED2; RHUND2; W)
SOURCE  allergic diseases (NASATH)
SOURCE  allergy and immunology (MESH)
SOURCE  hypersensitivity (MESH)
LINK    allergy
```

Fig. 2. Example of the original AAT record representing the concept "allergies"

Fig. 2 shows an example of the AAT record representation of the concept "allergies". The record template of the AAT records is described in [6]. The field "IDNO" refers to a unique identifier of the entry. The "CN" field contains a code that determines the position of the term in the hierarchy. "TERM" and "ALT" contain the preferred term and alternative terms respectively. Besides "ALT", AAT uses also the fields "UF", "UK", "UKALT" and "UKUF" to indicate synonyms and alternative spellings. These fields represent the equivalence relation of the ISO standard, but are not always applied consistently. "BT" refers to the broader term in the hierarchy. The "SN" field contains the scope note, a natural language description of the term. The example does not show the "RT" field which is used to represent related terms.

In step 1a of the conversion method the AAT record structure was converted by a simple Prolog program to the (partial) RDF(S) representation shown in Fig. 3. The mapping of the fields of the AAT record to an instance of the class AATTerm is generally straightforward. However, the coding of the broaderTerm field requires step 1b to convert the value of the record field BT, which is a term, to a unique reference (an IDNO to a concept). The mapping between the broader term and the identification number is simple in AAT since preferred terms are unique in AAT. An alternative way of determining the position of the entry in the hierarchy would be to use the value of the "CN" field (see also Sect. 5).

---

[6] http://www.getty.edu/research/conducting_research/vocabularies/aat/AAT-Users-Manual.pdf

```
<aat:AATTerm rdf:about="&aat;255420">
  <aat:term>allergies</aat:term>
  <aat:alternate>allergy</aat:alternate>
  <aat:scopeNote>Abnormal reactions of the body produced by a
  sensitizing dosage of or exposure to some foreign material.
  </aat:scopeNote>
  <aat:broaderTerm rdf:resource="&aat;55130"/>
  <aat:source>allergy and immunology (MESH)</aat:source>
  <aat:source>hypersensitivity (MESH)</aat:source>
</aat:AATTerm>
```

Fig. 3. RDF(S) representation of (part of) the AAT record "allergies"

Step 2a of the conversion procedure could involve the definition of certain relations between properties in a similar way as described in Sect. 3. In our current implementation this has not been done.

The representation as instances of the class AATTerm has only a limited meaning to RDF(S) knowledgeable applications. In order to add subclass semantics to the instance representation (step 2b), we can make AATTerm a meta-class and define the properties of the AAT record as subproperties of RDF(S) properties rdfs:subClassOf, rdf:label and rdf:comment, as is shown in Fig. 4.

These meta-definitions allow the reinterpretation of the thesaurus entries as RDF(S) classes (i.e. instances of the meta-class AATTerm) and give the AAT properties a meaning which is interpretable within the semantics of RDF(S). For example the property "broaderTerm" is interpreted as a specialisation of the RDFS subClassOf relation resulting in a proper class hierarchy.

Since many thesauri are based on the same ISO2788 data model, the procedure described above can be applied in many cases. For example other resources of the Getty Foundation such as the ULAN [7] thesaurus of artist names and the thesaurus of geographical names TGN [6] which are available in record format can be easily converted to ontologies in a similar way as the AAT thesaurus.

5   Case 3: MeSH

The National Library of Medicine publishes the MeSH (Medical Subject Headings) thesaurus which provides a controlled vocabulary for indexing bio-medical literature. MeSH is available in a number of formats, including an XML format[7] [3]. Although we are aware of the fact that MeSH was not intended to be used as an ontology, we will demonstrate the conversion procedures using the XML representation of MeSH, since it reveals some important issues.

A simplified version of the MeSH data model is shown in Fig. 5. An entry in MeSH is represented by a *descriptor* record that has a Unique Identifier, a Name, an optional Annotation and one or more TreeNumbers. The TreeNumber

---

[7] http://www.nlm.nih.gov/mesh/xmlmesh.html

```
<rdfs:Class rdf:about="&aat;AATTerm">
  <rdfs:subClassOf rdf:resource="&rdfs;Class"/>
</rdfs:Class>

<rdf:Property rdf:about="&aat;broaderTerm">
  <rdfs:label>broader term</rdfs:label>
  <rdfs:domain rdf:resource="&aat;AATTerm"/>
  <rdfs:range rdf:resource="&aat;AATTerm"/>
  <owl:inverseOf rdf:resource="&aat;narrowerTerm"/>
  <rdfs:subPropertyOf rdf:resource="&rdfs;subClassOf"/>
</rdf:Property>

<rdf:Property rdf:about="&aat;term">
  <rdfs:label>preferred term</rdfs:label>
  <rdfs:domain rdf:resource="&aat;AATTerm"/>
  <rdfs:range rdf:resource="&rdfs;Literal"/>
  <rdfs:subPropertyOf rdf:resource="&rdfs;label"/>
</rdf:Property>

<rdf:Property rdf:about="&aat;alternate">
  <rdfs:label>synonym</rdfs:label>
  <rdfs:domain rdf:resource="&aat;AATTerm"/>
  <rdfs:range rdf:resource="&rdfs;Literal"/>
  <rdfs:subPropertyOf rdf:resource="&rdfs;label"/>
</rdf:Property>

<rdf:Property rdf:about="&aat;scopeNote">
  <rdfs:label>scopenote</rdfs:label>
  <rdfs:domain rdf:resource="&aat;AATTerm"/>
  <rdfs:range rdf:resource="&rdfs;Literal"/>
  <rdfs:subPropertyOf rdf:resource="&rdfs;comment"/>
</rdf:Property>
```

Fig. 4. Definitions of the AATTerm and its properties

is a code that determines the position in the hierarchy of descriptors. Associated with a descriptor are one or more *concepts*. Concepts are used to represent sets of synonymous terms and scope notes. Concepts can have relations [2].

Fig. 6 shows an example of the XML representation of a descriptor record. The full XML representation of the MeSH descriptors is a large document (233 MB) so a streaming XML parser [8] is used to process the original data.

The first syntactic transformation from XML to RDF(S) (step 1a) involves the translation of the XML serialisation of the instances of the data model to instances of RDFS classes. Part of the RDF(S) schema used is shown in Fig. 7. Descriptors and concepts are modelled as instances of the classes Descriptor and Concept with attributes that correspond to the XML subelements. Since RDF(S) properties can have multiple values, the notions of ConceptList and TermList

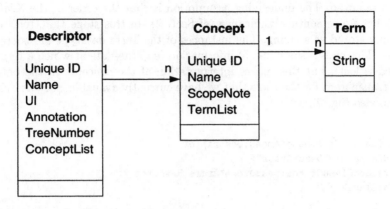

Fig. 5. The (simplified) data model of MeSH

```
<DescriptorRecord ...>                              <!-- Descriptor    -->
    <DescriptorUI>D000005</DescriptorUI>
    <DescriptorName><String>Abdomen</String></DescriptorName>
    <Annotation> region & abdominal organs...
    </Annotation>
    <ConceptList>

        <Concept PreferredConceptYN="Y">            <!-- Concept       -->
            <ConceptUI>M0000005</ConceptUI>
            <ConceptName><String>Abdomen</String></ConceptName>
            <ScopeNote> That portion of the body that lies
            between the thorax and the pelvis.</ScopeNote>
            <TermList>

                <Term ... PrintFlagYN="Y" ... >     <!-- Term          -->
                    <TermUI>T000012</TermUI>
                    <String>Abdomen</String>        <!-- String = the term itself -->
                    <DateCreated>
                        <Year>1999</Year>
                        <Month>01</Month>
                        <Day>01</Day>
                    </DateCreated>
                </Term>
                <Term  IsPermutedTermYN="Y"  LexicalTag="NON">
                    <TermUI>T000012</TermUI>
                    <String>Abdomens</String>
                </Term>
            <TermList>
        </Concept>
    </ConceptList>
</DescriptorRecord>
```

Fig. 6. Example MeSH descriptor record in XML

can be removed. The underlying assumption is that the order of the XML elements has no semantic significance (cf Sect. 2). In this stage the TreeNumber is simply stored as a string. The instances of the Term datatype are coerced to strings. This causes some loss of information (e.g. the date at which a term was created is lost), but this makes interpretation of the concepts in the ontology more transparent for the tools that we have currently available, such as Triple20 [9] (see also Fig. 9).

```
<rdfs:Class rdf:about="&mesh;Descriptor"
    rdfs:label="Descriptor">
  <rdfs:subClassOf rdf:resource="&rdfs;Resource"/>
</rdfs:Class>

<rdfs:Class rdf:about="&mesh;Concept"
    rdfs:label="Concept">
  <rdfs:subClassOf rdf:resource="&mesh;mesh_root"/>
</rdfs:Class>

<rdf:Property rdf:about="&mesh;HasConcept"
    rdfs:label="HasConcept">
  <rdfs:domain rdf:resource="&mesh;Descriptor"/>
  <rdfs:range rdf:resource="&mesh;Concept"/>
</rdf:Property>

<rdf:Property rdf:about="&mesh;TreeNumber"
    rdfs:label="TreeNumber">
  <rdfs:domain rdf:resource="&mesh;Descriptor"/>
  <rdfs:range rdf:resource="&rdfs;Literal"/>
</rdf:Property>

<rdf:Property rdf:about="&mesh;PharmacologicalAction"
    rdfs:label="PharmacologicalAction">
  <rdfs:domain rdf:resource="&mesh;Concept"/>
  <rdfs:range rdf:resource="&mesh;Descriptor"/>
</rdf:Property>
```

Fig. 7. Part of the RDF(S) schema for MeSH

In the second syntactic step (step 1a) the hierarchical relations that are implicit in the TreeNumbers are made explicit and modelled as a subTreeOf relation. In step 2b of the conversion of MeSH the same mechanism of meta-modeling is used as for WordNet and AAT.

```
<rdf:Description rdf:about="&mesh;Descriptor">
  <rdfs:subClassOf rdf:resource="&rdfs;Class"/>
</rdf:Description>

<rdf:Property rdf:about="&mesh;subTreeOf"
    rdfs:label="subTreeOf">
  <rdfs:domain rdf:resource="&mesh;Concept"/>
  <rdfs:range rdf:resource="&mesh;Concept"/>
  <rdfs:subPropertyOf rdf:resource="&rdfs;subClassOf"/>
</rdf:Property>

<rdf:Property rdf:about="&mesh;ConceptTerm"
    rdfs:label="ConceptTerm">
  <rdfs:domain rdf:resource="&mesh;Concept"/>
  <rdfs:range rdf:resource="&rdfs;Literal"/>
  <rdfs:subPropertyOf rdf:resource="&rdfs;label"/>
</rdf:Property>

<rdf:Description rdf:about="&mesh;DescriptorName">
  <rdfs:subPropertyOf rdf:resource="&rdfs;label"/>
</rdf:Description>

<rdf:Description rdf:about="&mesh;ConceptName">
  <rdfs:subPropertyOf rdf:resource="&rdfs;label"/>
</rdf:Description>

<rdf:Description rdf:about="&mesh;ScopeNote">
  <rdfs:subPropertyOf rdf:resource="&rdfs;comment"/>
</rdf:Description>
```

Fig. 8. The meta-schema definition of the MeSH ontology

6   Discussion and Conclusions

Ontologies are essential vehicles for the Semantic Web. Since RDF(S) and more recently OWL have become standard representation languages for ontologies the time has come to make the large variety of existing resources available for Semantic Web applications. The DAML repository of ontologies[8] is a first step towards this goal. However, the assumptions and methods that were used in creating the ontologies in this repository do not appear to be documented. The method presented in this paper supports the conversion of existing resources in such a way that the transformation steps can be made explicit and traceable. In addition, the method does not involve any changes in the original source material, the process consists just of mechanical transformation steps. This has the advantage that when new versions of the source material become available

---

[8] http://www.daml.org/ontologies

310   B. Wielinga et al.

the conversion process can easily be repeated. The separation of the conversion process in syntactic and semantic steps allows for a gradual transition from a straightforward translation of the source to a semantic interpretation and augmentation of the source material. This has the advantage that a user can decide what transformations are acceptable for his or her purposes.

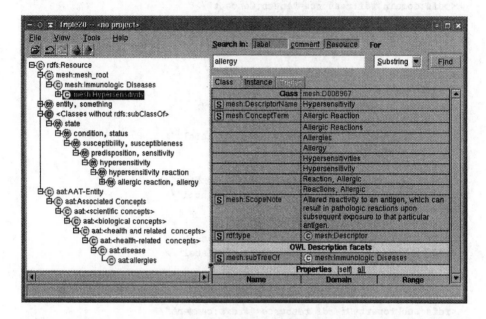

Fig. 9. Different representations of the concept "allergy" derived from three sources

Although the case studies described above are simplifications of the conversion process needed for a full mapping of the AAT and MeSH, they illustrate the principles of the method. An additional advantage of the methods is that the resulting ontologies can easily be compared using Semantic Web tools. Figure 9 shows a screenshot of the Triple20 ontology editor [9], [10] where an example concept ("allergy") is shown as it is represented in WordNet, AAT and MeSH. The uniform representation of the ontologies allows a comparative analysis of the different choices that were made in the different ontologies. A next step would be the mapping of equivalent or similar concepts from different ontologies. No doubt, such mappings will play an important role in future Semantic Web applications.

Acknowledgements

This work was partly supported by the IST project IST-2002-507967 "HOPS" and the CHIME project, part of the NWO ToKeN2000 programme.

References

[1] G. Miller. WordNet: A lexical database for english. *Comm. ACM*, 38(11), November 1995.

[2] Stuart J. Nelson, Douglas Johnston, and Betsy L. Humphreys. *Relationships in Medical Subject Headings (MeSH)*, volume 2 of *Information Science and Knowledge Management*, chapter 11. Kluwer Academic Publishers, October 2001.

[3] U.S. National Library of Medicine. Introduction to MeSH in XML format, November 2001.

[4] T. Peterson. *Introduction to the Art and Architecture Thesaurus*. Oxford University Press, 1994. See also: http://www.getty.edu/research/tools/vocabulary/aat/.

[5] A. Th. Schreiber, B. Dubbeldam, J. Wielemaker, and B. J. Wielinga. Ontology-based photo annotation. *IEEE Intelligent Systems*, 16(3):66–74, May/June 2001.

[6] TGN: Thesaurus of Geographical Names. The Getty Foundation. URL: http://www.getty.edu/research/tools/vocabulary/tgn/, 2000.

[7] ULAN: Union List of Artist Names. The Getty Foundation. URL: http://www.getty.edu/research/tools/vocabulary/ulan/, 2000.

[8] J. Wielemaker. *SWI-Prolog SGML/XML parser*. SWI, University of Amsterdam, Roetersstraat 15, 1018 WB Amsterdam, The Netherlands, 2002. URL: http://www.swi-prolog.org/packages/sgml2pl.html.

[9] J. Wielemaker. *Triple20 – An RDF/RDFS/OWL visualisation and editing tool*. SWI, University of Amsterdam, Roetersstraat 15, 1018 WB Amsterdam, The Netherlands, 2003. URL: http://www.swi-prolog.org/packages/Triple20.html.

[10] Jan Wielemaker, Guus Schreiber, and Bob Wielinga. Prolog-based infrastructure for RDF: Scalability and performance. In J. Mylopoulos D. Fensel, K. Sycara, editor, *The Semantic Web-ISWC2003*, pages 644–658, Berlin Heidelberg, 2003. Springer. LNCS 2870.

Learning to Harvest Information for the Semantic Web

Fabio Ciravegna, Sam Chapman, Alexiei Dingli, and Yorick Wilks

Department of Computer Science, University of Sheffield
Regent Court, 211 Portobello Street, S1 4DP Sheffield, UK
N.Surname@dcs.shef.ac.uk
http://nlp.shef.ac.uk/wig/

Abstract. In this paper we describe a methodology for harvesting information from large distributed repositories (e.g. large Web sites) with minimum user intervention. The methodology is based on a combination of information extraction, information integration and machine learning techniques. Learning is seeded by extracting information from structured sources (e.g. databases and digital libraries) or a user-defined lexicon. Retrieved information is then used to partially annotate documents. Annotated documents are used to bootstrap learning for simple Information Extraction (IE) methodologies, which in turn will produce more annotation to annotate more documents that will be used to train more complex IE engines and so on. In this paper we describe the methodology and its implementation in the Armadillo system, compare it with the current state of the art, and describe the details of an implemented application. Finally we draw some conclusions and highlight some challenges and future work.

1 Introduction

The Semantic Web (SW) needs semantically-based document annotation to both enable better document retrieval and empower semantically-aware agents. Most of the current technology is based on human centered annotation, very often completely manual. The large majority of SW annotation tools address the problem of single document annotation. Systems like COHSE [7], Ontomat [8] and MnM [14], all require presenting a document to a user in order to produce annotation either in a manual or a (semi-)automatic way. Annotations can span from annotating portions of documents with concept labels, to identifying instances or concept mentions, to connect sparse information (e.g. a telephone number and its owner. The process involves an important and knowledge intensive role for the human user. Annotation is meant mainly to be statically associated to the documents. Static annotation can: (1) be incomplete or incorrect when the creator is not skilled enough; (2) become obsolete, i.e. not be aligned with page updates; (3) be devious, e.g. for spamming or dishonest purposes; professional spammers could use manual annotation very effectively for their own purposes.

For these reasons, we believe that the Semantic Web needs automatic methods for (nearly) completely automatic page annotation. In this way, the initial

J. Davies et al. (Eds.): ESWS 2004, LNCS 3053, pp. 312–326, 2004.

annotation associated to a document will lose its importance because at any time it will be possible to automatically reannotate the document. Systems like SemTag [4] are a first step in that direction. SemTag addresses the problem of annotating large document repositories (e.g. the Web) for retrieval purposes, using very large ontologies. Its task is annotating portion of documents with instance labels. The system can be seen as an extension of a search engine. The process is entirely automatic and the methodology is largely ontology/application independent. The kind of annotation produced is quite shallow when compared to the classic one introduced for the SW: for example there is no attempt to discover relations among entities. AeroDaml [9] is an information extraction system aimed at generating draft annotation to be refined by a user in a similar way to nowadays' automated translation services. The kind of annotation produced is more sophisticated than SemTag's (e.g. it is also able to recognize relations among concepts), but, in order to cover new domains, it requires the development of application/domain specific linguistic knowledge bases (an IE expert is required). The harvester of the AKT triple store[1] is able to build large knowledge bases of facts for a specific application. Here the aim is both large scale and deep ontology-based annotation. The process requires writing a large number of wrappers for information sources using Dome, a visual language which focuses on manipulation of tree-structured data [11]. Porting requires a great deal of manual programming. Extraction is limited to highly regular and structured pages selected by the designer. Maintenance is complex because - as well known in the wrapper community - when pages changes their format, it is necessary to re-program the wrapper [10]. The approach is not applicable to irregular pages or free text documents. The manual approach makes using very large ontologies (like in SemTag) very difficult.

In this paper we propose a methodology for document annotation that was inspired by the latter methodology, but (1) it does not require human intervention for programming wrappers (2) it is not limited to highly regular documents and (3) it is largely unsupervised. The methodology is based on adaptive information extraction and integration, it is implemented in Armadillo, a tool able to harvest domain information from large repositories. In the rest of the paper we describe and discuss the methodology, present experimental results on a specific domain and compare Armadillo with the current state of the art. Finally we outline some challenges that the methodology highlights.

2   Armadillo

Armadillo is a system for producing automatic domain-specific annotation on large repositories in a largely unsupervised way. It annotates by extracting information from different sources and integrating the retrieved knowledge into a repository. The repository can be used both to access the extracted information and to annotate the pages where the information was identified. Also the link

---

[1] http://triplestore.aktors.org/SemanticWebChallenge/

```
Input:
      •an Ontology;
      •an Initial Lexicon;
      •a Repository of Documents;
Output: A set of triples representing the extracted information
        and to be used to annotate documents
do {
      ▪ spot information using the lexicon
      ▪ seek for confirmation of the identified information
      ▪ extend lexicon using adaptive information extraction
        and seek confirmation of the newly extracted information
      } while a stable set of information is found(e.g. the base
                does not grow anymore)
  • Integrate Information from different documents
  • Store information in repository
```

Fig. 1. The Armadillo's main algorithm

with the pages can be used by a user to verify the correctness and the provenance of the information. Armadillo's approach is illustrated in Figure 1. In the
first step in the loop, possible annotations from a document are identified using an existing lexicon (e.g. the one associated to the ontology). These are just
potential annotations and must be confirmed using some strategies (e.g. disam-
biguation or multiple evidence). Then other annotations not provided by the
lexicon are identified e.g. by learning from the context in which the known ones
were identified. All new annotations must be confirmed and can be used to learn
some new ones as well. They will then become part of the lexicon. Finally all
annotations are integrated (e.g. some entities are merged) and stored into a data
base. Armadillo employs the following methodologies:

- Adaptive Information Extraction from texts (IE): used for spotting information and to further learning new instances.
- Information Integration (II): used to (1) discover an initial set of information
  to be used to seed learning for IE and (2) to confirm the newly acquired
  (extracted) information, e.g. using multiple evidence from different sources.
  For example, a new piece of information is confirmed if it is found in different
  (linguistic or semantic) contexts.
- Web Services: the architecture is based on the concept of "services". Each
  service is associated to some part of the ontology (e.g. a set of concepts
  and/or relations) and works in an independent way. Each service can use
  other services (including external ones) for performing some sub-tasks. For
  example a service for recognizing researchers names in a University Web Site
  will use a Named Entity Recognition system as a sub-service that will recog-
  nise potential names (i.e. generic people's names) to be confirmed using some

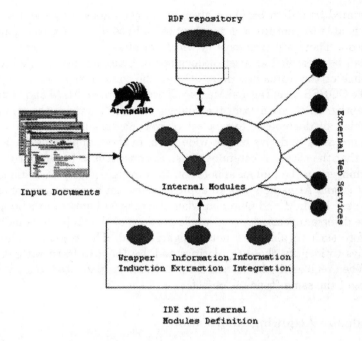

Fig. 2. The Armadillo Architecture

internal strategies as real researchers names (e.g. as opposed to secretaries' names).
- RDF repository: where the extracted information is stored and the link with the pages is maintained.

A development environment allows to define architectures for new applications. Porting to new applications does not require knowledge of IE. All the methods used tend to be domain independent and are based on generic strategies to be composed for the specific case at hand. The only domain dependent parts are: the initial lexicon, the ontology and the way the confirmation strategies are designed/composed.

2.1 Extracting Information

Most of the current tools (e.g. COHSE and SemTag) provide annotation using a static lexicon where the lexicalization of objects in the ontology is contained. The lexicon does not increase while the computation goes on, unless the user adds terms to it. Armadillo continually and automatically expands the initial lexicon by learning to recognize regularities in the repository. As a matter of fact, Web resources (and in general all repositories) have a specific bias, i.e. there are a number of regularities, either internal to a single document or across a set of documents [13]. Regularities can either be very strong (e.g. in case of pages generated by a data base), or given by a style imposed by the designers. Armadillo is able to capture such regularities and use it to learn to expand its initial lexicon. There are two ways in which an object (e.g., an instance of a concept) can be identified in a set of documents. Using its internal description (e.g. its name or the words describing it) and the context in which it appears. Systems like COHSE, SemTag and Magpie [6] use the former. MnM and Ontomat [8] use adaptive IE to learn from the context as well. They use the regularity in a collection of documents (e.g. a set of web pages about a specific topic from the same site) to derive corpus-wide rules. In those approaches, it is very important that the corpus is carefully chosen as consistent in its regularity. This allows learning from the human annotation to converge quickly to a stable and effective situation. Armadillo uses an approach that can be seen as an extension of the one used in MnM and Ontomat where there is no human in the loop and where large diverse repositories (e.g. whole portions of the Web) are annotated, and therefore such regularity is not straightforward. The system has to find its own ways to identify those regularities and use them to learn without user support. When regularities in the context are found, they are used to learn other occurrences of the same (type of) object.

2.2   Gradually Acquiring Information

Armadillo exploits a key feature of the Web: the *redundancy* of information. Redundancy is given by the presence of multiple citations of the same information in different contexts and in different superficial formats. Redundancy is currently used for improving question answering systems [5]. When known information is present in different sources, it is possible to use its multiple occurrences to bootstrap recognizers that, when generalized, will retrieve other pieces of information, producing in turn more (generic) recognizers [1]. Armadillo uses redundancy in order to bootstrap learning beyond the initial user lexicon (if any) and even to acquire the initial lexicon. In particular, information can be present in different formats on the Web: in documents, in repositories (e.g. databases or digital libraries), via agents able to integrate different information sources, etc. From them or their output, it is possible to extract information with different degrees of reliability. Systems such as databases contain structured data that can be queried either via APIs or web front ends (getting HTML output). In the latter case, wrappers can be induced to extract information. Wrapper Induction methodologies are able to model rigidly structured Web pages such as those produced by databases [10]. When the information is contained in textual documents, extracting information requires more sophisticated methodologies. Wrapper induction systems have been extended to cope with less rigidly structured pages, free texts and even a mixture of them [2]. There is an increasing degree of complexity in the extraction task mentioned above. As complexity increases more training data is required. Wrappers can be trained with a handful of examples whereas full IE systems may require millions of words.

All the IE process in Armadillo is based on integrating information from different sources to provide annotations which will bootstrap learning, which in turn will provide more annotation and so on. The process starts with simple methodologies which require limited annotation, to produce further annotation to train more complex modules. The ontology provides the mean for integrating information extracted from different sources. For example simple wrappers can be used to extract information from a web page produced by databases containing papers from computer science departments. In order to avoid wrapping each database separately (i.e., providing examples of annotated input/output for each of them), Armadillo uses information from a database already wrapped in order to provide automatic annotation of examples for the other ones as proposed in [13]. For example, if the goal is to extract bibliographic information about the Computer Science field, it is possible to use Citeseer (www.citeseer.com), a large (and largely incomplete) database to learn how to query and understand another service, e.g. the NLDB bibliography at Unitrier (http://www.informatik.uni-trier.de/~ ley/db/). This can be done by querying Citeseer and the NLDB using the same terms, and producing two parallel pages of results. The one from Citeseer will have a known format and the information can be easily extracted using a predefined wrapper. Then, some of the information contained in the NLDB output page can be automatically annotated (e.g. for the paper title generally it is necessary just an intelligent string matching). Using the annotated examples it is possible to induce wrappers that, given the high regularity of the information in the NLDB page, will be able to extract papers also from the latter. Considering that training a wrapper generally requires just a handful of examples, it is possible to focus only on those examples where the match is very clear and reliable, discarding others that are more questionable, therefore producing a highly reliable wrapper. Facilities for defining wrappers are provided in our architecture by Amilcare (nlp.shef.ac.uk/amilcare/), an adaptive IE system based on a wrapper induction methodology able to cope with a whole range of documents from rigidly structured documents to free texts [3].

2.3 Web Services

Each task in Armadillo (e.g. discovering all the papers written by an author) is performed by a server which in turn will use other servers for implementing some parts (subtask) of it. Each server exposes a declaration of input and output, plus a set of working parameters. Servers are reusable in different contexts and applications. For example one server could return all papers written by a person by accessing Citeseer. Another one will do the same on another digital library. Another one will use the papers extracted by the other two in order to discover pages where they are cited and to bootstrap learning. Another one will invoke these servers and integrate the evidence returned by each of them and decide if there is evidence enough to conclude that some newly discovered candidate strings represent a real new object or maybe just a variant version of a known name. All the servers are defined in a resource pool and can be used in a user-defined architecture to perform some specific tasks. New servers can be defined and added to the pool by wrapping them in a standard format. The defined architecture works as a "Glass Box". All the steps performed by the system are shown to the user together with their input and output. The user can check the intermediate results and manually modify their output, or change their strategy (if possible, such as in the case of modules who integrate information). For example if a piece of information is missed by the system, it can be manually added by the user. The modules working on the output of that module will then be re-run and further information will hopefully be retrieved. In this way the user is able both to check the results of each step and to improve the results of the system by manually providing some contributions (additions, corrections, deletion).

2.4   The Triple Store

Facts extracted from the Web are stored in an RDF store in the form of triples which define relations in the form "Subject - Verb - Object", where the subject and object are elemenets and the verb details the relation between them. For each element in the triples, the following information is stored: the string (e.g. J. Smith), the position where it was found (e.g. the document URL and its offset) and the concept, instance or relation represented. The triples can be used to derive also aliases for the same object, i.e. a lexicon ("J. Smith" at $< www\_address_1 >$: $33 : 44$ and "John Smith" at $< www\_address_2 >$: $21 : 35$), and to recover dispersed information (e.g. the person JSMITH45 has names "J. Smith" at $< www\_address_1 >$: $33 : 44$ and "John Smith" at $< www\_address_2 >$: $21 : 35$ and telephone number "+44.12.12.12.12 at $< www\_address_3 >$: $10 : 12$, homepage at $< www\_address_4 >$). The triple store constitutes the resource used by the different services to communicate. Each server stores the extracted information in the form of signed triples. The other services will extract them and elaborate the information to store further information (or to confirm the existing one). Each piece of information is tagged with its provenance both in terms of source document and in terms of extraction method, i.e. the service or agent that has retrieved it. The provenance is used to assign reliability to the information itself: the more the information is confirmed, the more reliable it is considered.

2.5   Confirming Information

A crucial issue in the cycle of seeding and learning is the quality of the information used to seed. Wrong selections can make the method diverge and produce spurious information. When a piece of information is acquired (e.g. a new paper is assigned to a specific author in the CS task mentioned in section 3), Armadillo requires confirmation by different sources before it can be used for futher seeding of learning. Again, using the redundancy of the Web, we expect that the same piece of information is repeated somewhere in a different forms and the system to find it. The strategy for evidence gathering is application dependent. Users have to identify task specific strategies. Such strategies can be defined declaratively in Armadillo by posing requirements on the provenance of the information in terms of methods of extraction and sources (including the number of times the information was confirmed in the different sources).

The next section describes how Armadillo was used in a specific application.

3 Armadillo in Action

Armadillo has been applied so far to three tasks: the CS website harvesting task, the Art Domain task and the discovery of geographical information[2]. Here we describe Armadillo's application to mining websites of Computer Science Departments, an extension of its original task in the AKTive Space application that won the 2003 Semantic Web Challenge[3]. Armadillo's task is to discover who works for a specific department (name, position, homepage, email address, telephone number) and to extract for each person some personal data and a list of published papers larger than the one provided by services such as Citeseer.

3.1 Finding People Names

The goal of this subtask is to discover the names of all the people who work in the specific department. This task is more complex than a generic Named Entity Recognition because many non researchers' names are cited in a site, e.g. those of undergraduate students, clerics, secretaries, etc, as well as names of researchers from other sites that e.g. participate in common projects or have co-authored papers with members of staff. Organizing the extraction around a generic Named Entity Recognizer (NER) is the most natural option. This does not finish the job, though, because a NER recognizes ALL the people's names in the site, without discriminating between relevant and irrelevant. Moreover classic NERs tend to be quite slow if launched on large sites and can be quite imprecise on Web pages, as they are generally defined for newspaper-like articles. A two-step strategy is used here instead: initially a short list of highly reliable seed names are discovered; this constitute the initial lexicon. Such lexicon could also be provided by an existing list. Here we suppose such list does not exist. Then these seeds are used to bootstrap learning for finding further names.

Finding Seed Names. To find seed names, a number of weak strategies are combined that integrate information from different sources. First of all the web site is crawled looking for strings that are potential names of people (e.g. using a gazetteer of first names and a regular expression such as $<$first-name$<^+$(capitalized word)$^+$.). Then the following web services are queried:

- Citeseer (www.citeseer.com): Input: the potential name; Output: a list of papers and a URL for homepage (if any);
- The CS bibliography at Unitrier (http://www.informatik.uni-trier.de/$\sim$ley/db/): Input: the potential name: Output: a list of papers (if any);

---

[2] http://www.dcs.shef.ac.uk/~sam/results/index.html
[3] http://challenge.semanticweb.org/)

- HomePageSearch (http://hpsearch.uni-trier.de/): Input: the potential name; Output: a URL for homepage (if any);
- Annie (www.gate.ac.uk): Input: the potential name and the text surrounding it; Output: True/False;
- Google (www.google.co.uk) Input: the potential name and the URL of the site in order to restrict search; Output: Relevant Pages that are hopefully homepages;

The digital libraries (Citeseer and Unitrier) are used as first filters to determine if a string is a name of a known researcher. If they return reasonable results for a specific string (i.e. not too few and not too many), this name is further processed, otherwise it is discarded. A string is a potentially valid name if the digital libraries return a reasonable number of papers (between 5 and 50 in our experiments). Results not in line with the reasonability criteria are discarded as inappropriate seeds. This is to discard potential anomalies such as ambiguous names (e.g. Citeseer returns more than 10,000 papers for the term "Smith"; this cannot be a single researcher) and invalid names (e.g. the words "Fortune Teller" do not return any paper). We tend to use quite restrictive criteria for keeping reliability high (i.e. it is very possible that a person writes some 100 papers, but that amount could also hide name ambiguity. The results of the digital libraries are integrated with those of the classic Named Entity Recognizer run on a window of words around the candidates (so to avoid the problem of slow processing). At this point a number of names are available that fall in three potential types: (1) correct (they are people working for the department); (2) wrong (they are not people: they are false positives); (3) people who do not work at the site but that are cited because, for example, they have coauthored papers with some of the researchers of the department. For this reason, Citeseer, Google and HomepageSearch are used to look for a personal web page in the site. If such a page is not found, the names are discarded. From the results, personal web pages are recognized with simple heuristics such as looking for the name in the title or in "<H1>" tags. The process mentioned above is meant to determine a small, highly reliable list of seed names to enable learning. Each of the strategies is, per se, weak, as they all report high recall, low precision. Their combination is good enough to produce data with high accuracy.

Learning Further Names. All the occurrences of seed names are then annotated on the site's documents and learning is initiated only on documents where a reasonable quantity of known names are organized in structures such as lists and tables. Such structures generally have an intrinsic semantic: lists generally contain elements of the same type (e.g. names of people), while the semantics in tables is generally related to the position either in rows or columns (e.g. all the elements of the first column are people, the second column represents addresses, etc.). When some seeds (at least four or five in our case) are identified in a list or specific portions of a table, we train a classifier able to relate a large part of these examples, for example using linguistic and/or formatting criteria (e.g. relevant names are always the first element in each row). If we succeed, we are able to reliably recognize other names in the structure. Every department generally has one or more pages listing their staff in some kind of lists. These are the lists that we are mainly looking for, but also tables assigning supervisors and students are useful, provided that students and teachers can be discriminated. Each time new examples are identified, the site is further annotated and more patterns can potentially be learnt. New names can be cross-checked on the resources used to identify the seed list: we have now more evidence that these names are real names. In our experiments this is enough to discover a large part of the staff of an average CS website with very limited noise, even using a very strict strategy of multiple cross-evidence. We are currently using combinations of the following evidence to accept a learnt name: (1) the name was recognized as seed; (2) the name is included in an HTML structure where other known occurrences are found (3) there is an hyperlink internal to the site that wraps the whole name; (4) there is evidence from generic patterns (as derived by recognizing people on other sites) that this is a person. The latter strategy was inspired by [12].

Evaluation. The CS task effectiveness was evaluated on a number of sites. Here we report results from an evaluation done on both a specific web site (the Computer Science Department site of the University of Sheffield, www.dcs.shef.ac.uk) and by pointing the system to some pages containing interesting infromation for the task, but distributed in random sites (the latter task is equivalent to applying Armadillo on the results of a document classifier providing interesting pages). Results on other sites are qualitatively largely equivalent. On the Sheffield department's website, the system initially discovers 51 seed names of people (either academics, researchers or PhD students) integrating information from Citeseer and NLDB. Of them, 48 are correct and 3 wrong. These names are used to the seed learning. Learning allows to discover other 57 names, 48 correct, 6 wrong. This increases the overall recall from 37% to 84% with a very limited loss in precision (see Table 1). Results obtained on the set of pages from random sites are in Table 2. In this experiments we checked Armadillo's ability to improve results in case the II step returned high recall. The AKT triple store was used as a source of information in addition to Citeseer and UniTrier. The gain in using the IE-based extraction is still considerable (recall grows from 73 to 85).

3.2 Discovering Papers Citations

Discovering what papers are written by what members of the departmental staff is a very difficult task. It requires recognizing the paper title and the authors, and then relating the authors to the people identified in the previous step. Authors are names in particular positions and in particular contexts: they must not be confused with editors of collections in which the paper can be published, nor they must be confused with other names mentioned in the surrounding text. A title is generally a random sequence of words (e.g. the tile of [5]) and cannot be characterized in any way (i.e. we cannot write generic patterns for identifying candidate strings as we did for people). Moreover paper titles must not be confused with titles of collections in which they are published. CS department sites

	Possible	Actual	Correct	Wrong	Missing	Precision	Recall	F-Measure
Seed discovery	129	51	48	3	0	94	37	51
Adaptive IE	129	108	99	9	30	92	84	87

Table 1. Results in Discovering People and Associated homepage. First line: accuracy reached using Information Integration only (Citeseer+Google, etc.); second line: accuracy using adaptive IE. Possible represents the number of people working for the department, Actual the number of people returned by the systems. Actual results are divided into Correct, Wrong and Missing.

	Possible	Actual	Correct	Wrong	Missing	Precision	Recall	F-Measure
Seed Discovery	331	243	242	1	89	99.59	73.11	84.32
Adaptive IE	331	288	284	4	47	98.61	85.80	91.76

Table 2. The results of discovering names of peoples working at some random sites.

typically contain lists of publications for the department as a whole or personal ones for each member of staff. Moreover papers are co-authored, so it is very possible that each paper is cited more than one time within a specific site. In rare cases personal lists of papers are produced using a departmental database (i.e. all the publication pages are formatted in the same way), but in most cases each person writes the list using a personal format; very often the style is quite irregular as the list is compiled manually over time. This is a typical case in which the classic methodology of manually annotating some examples for each page for each member of staff is unfeasible, due to the large number of different pages. Also irregularities in style produce noisy data and classic wrappers are not able to cope with noise. A generic methodology is needed that does not require any manual annotation.

In order to bootstrap learning we query the digital libraries (Citeseer and UniTrier) using staff names as keywords. The output for each name is hopefully a list of papers. Such lists will be incomplete because the digital libraries are largely incomplete. The titles in the list are then used to query a search engine to retrieve pages containing multiple paper citations. We focus on lists and tables where at least four papers are found. We use titles because they tend to be unique identifier. We are looking for seed examples, so we can discard titles which report too many hits (so to avoid titles which are very common strings such as "Lost"). As for discovering new papers, the seed examples are annotated and page-specific patterns are induced. We favour examples contained in structures such as lists and tables for which we have multiple evidence. Please note however that the structure of the citation is often not very structured internally. For example:

	Possible	Actual	Correct	Wrong	Missing	Precision	Recall	F-Measure
Seed Discovery	320	151	152	1	168	99	47	64
Adaptive IE	320	217	214	3	103	99	67	80

Table 3. Paper title harvesting for 7 random people.

```
<li> Fabio Ciravegna, Alexiei Dingli, Daniela Petrelli and Yorick Wilks:<br>
User-System Cooperation in Document Annotation based on Information Extraction
<br> in Asuncion Gomez-Perez, V. Richard Benjamins (eds.): Knowledge
Engineering and Knowledge Management (Ontologies and the Semantic Web),
<br> Lecture Notes in Artificial Intelligence 2473, Springer Verlag <br></li>
```

Simple wrappers would be ineffective, as there is no way to discriminate - for example - between authors and editors and title of paper and title of collection when relying on the HTML structure only. More sophisticated wrapper induction systems are needed, as that provided by Amilcare, which uses both html structure and (para-)linguistic information [3]. Using a cycle of annotation/learning/annotation we are able to discover a large number of new papers. Note that every time co-authorship among people is discovered on a publication page of one author, the paper is retained for annotation of the publication pages of the other authors (i.e. the redundancy is exploited again).

Evaluation. Discovering papers is a very complex task. We performed a task of associating papers to people discovered during the previous step. A paper was considered correctly assigned to a person if it was authored by the person **and** the title was 100% correct. We did not use reseeding in the experiment, i.e. if a paper was coauthored by two researchers, the information returned for one person was not used to further annotate the publication pages for the second person. In this sense the redundancy of information was not fully exploited. Checking correctness of papers for a hundred people is very labor intensive, therefore we randomly checked the papers extracted for 7 staff members for which the seed papers exceeded 6 examples; results are shown in Table 3. The use of IE increases significantly the overall recall rate which grows from 47 for seeds and 67 for IE-based, precision 99 and 98 and F-measure 64 and 80 respectively.

4 Conclusions

In this paper we have described a methodology to extract information from large repositories (e.g. large Web sites) with minimum user intervention. Extracted information can then be used for document annotation. Information is initially extracted by starting from highly reliable/easy-to-mine sources such as databases and digital libraries and is then used to bootstrap more complex modules such as wrappers for extracting information from highly regular Web pages. Information extracted by the wrappers is then used to train more sophisticated

IE engines. All the training corpora for the IE engines are produced automatically. Experiments show that the methodology can produce high quality results. The user intervention is limited to providing an initial URL and to add information missed by the different modules when the computation is finished. No preliminary manual annotation is required. The information added or deleted by the user can then be reused for restarting learning and therefore getting more information (recall) and/or more precision. The type of user needed is a person able to understand the annotation task. No skills in IE are needed. The natural application of such methodology is the Web, but large companies' repositories are also an option. In this paper we have focused on the use of the technology for mining web sites, an issue that can become very relevant for the Semantic Web, especially because annotation is provided largely without user intervention. It could potentially provide a partial solution to the outstanding problem of who is providing semantic annotation for the SW. It can potentially be used either by search engines associated to services/ontologies to automatically annotate/index/retrieve relevant documents or by specific users to retrieve needed information on the fly by composing an architecture.

Armadillo has been fully integrated into the AKT triple store and it is constantly providing new triples to it. Its contribution to the architecture is the ability to reindex the pages when they change format (in the classic architecture this step would require manually reprogramming of the wrapper) and the abillity to extract information from sources that are not highly structured and regular as possible to Dome [11]. Armadillo is compatible with SW tools like COHSE, Magpie, MnM, Ontomat, etc. In COHSE and Magpie it could provide a way to (1) extend the automatic annotation step beyond the connection between simple terms and concepts descriptions stored in a lexicon. It could allow to move towards relation identification. Moreover it couls provide automatic extension of the initial lexicon. In MnM and Ontomat, Armadillo could provide a way to converge more rapidly towards an effective annotation service. As a matter of fact, learning in those tools is limited to the documents already annotated by the user and to the use of an initial lexicon. Armadillo could provide a way to integrate information from external repositories in the corpus (e.g. digital libraries) to learn in an unsupervised way, from example from regularities found in documents not annotated.

From the IE point of view there are a number of challenges in learning from automatic annotation, instead of using human annotation. On the one hand not all the annotation is reliable: the use of multiple strategies and combined evidence reduces the problem, but still there is a strong need for methodologies robust with respect to noise. On the other hand, many IE systems are able to learn from completely annotated documents only, so that all the annotated strings are considered positive examples and the rest of the text is used as a set of counterexamples. In our cycle of seed and learn, we generally produce partially annotated documents. This means that the system is presented with positive examples, but the rest of the texts can never be considered as a set of negative examples, because unannotated portions of text can contain instances that the system has to discover, not counterexamples. This is a challenge for the learner. At the moment we present the learner with just the annotated portion of the text plus a windows of words of context, not with the whole document. This is enough to have the system learning correctly: the unannotated examples that become negative examples entering the training corpus is generally low enough to avoid problems. In the future we will have to focus on using machine learning methodologies that are able to learn from scattered annotation.

Many of the classic problems of integrating information are to be coped with in Armadillo. Information can be represented in different ways, in different sources from both a syntactic and a semantic point of view. The syntactic variation is coped with in the definition architecture definition step: when two modules are connected, a canonical form of the information is defined in the ontology, e.g. the classic problem of recognising film titles as "The big chill" and "Big chill, the" can be addressed. More complex tasks are to be addressed, though. In the art domain it is quite common to report the title of an art work in different languages. For example a number of Cezanne's paintings can be referred in different web sites as both "Apples and Oranges" and "Aepfel mit Orangen" (same title but in German), Michelangelo's can be referred as "The Last Judgment" or "Il Giudizio Universale" (in Italian). Relating them can be very difficult, even for a human, without looking at the actual artwork. Also, a person name can be cited in different ways in different documents: N. Weaver, Nick Weaver and Nicholas Weaver are potential variation of the same name. But do they identify the same person as well? This is the problem of intra- and inter-document coreference resolution well known in Natural Language Processing. In many applications it is possible to identify some simple heuristics to cope with this problem. For example in mining one specific CS websites, N. Weaver, Nick Weaver and Nicholas Weaver are most of the times the same person, therefore it is possible to hypothesize coreference. Another potential problem concerns ambiguity in the external resources (e.g. in the digital libraries). When querying with very common names (e.g. "John Smith") papers by different people are mixed. This is not a problem in Armadillo because the information returned is used to annotate the site in order to both seed more learning and to look for multiple confirmation. Papers from people from other departments or universities will not introduce any annotations and therefore will not be accepted. The same applies in case multiple homepages are returned: if some of them do not have an address local to the current site, they are not used.

Acknowledgements

This work was carried out within the AKT project (www.aktors.org), sponsored by the UK Engineering and Physical Sciences Research Council (grant GR/N15764/01), and the Dot.Kom project (www.dot-kom.org), sponsored by the EU IST asp part of Framework V (grant IST-2001-34038).

References

[1] Sergey Brin. Extracting patterns and relations from the world wide web. In *WebDB Workshop at 6th International Conference on Extending Database Technology, EDBT'98*, 1998.

[2] Fabio Ciravegna. Adaptive information extraction from text by rule induction and generalisation. In *Proceedings of 17th International Joint Conference on Artificial Intelligence (IJCAI)*, 2001. Seattle.

[3] Fabio Ciravegna. Designing adaptive information extraction for the Semantic Web in Amilcare. In S. Handschuh and S. Staab, editors, *Annotation for the Semantic Web*, Frontiers in Artificial Intelligence and Applications. IOS Press, 2003.

[4] S. Dill, N. Eiron, D. Gibson, D. Gruhl, R. Guha, A. Jhingran, T. Kanungo, S. Rajagopalan, A. Tomkins, J. A. Tomlin, and J. Y. Zien. SemTag and Seeker: Bootstrapping the semantic web via automated semantic annotation. In *Proceedings of the World Wide Web Conference 2003*, 2003.

[5] Susan Dumais, Michele Banko, Eric Brill, Jimmy Lin, and Andrew Ng. Web question answering: Is more always better? In *Proceedings of the 25th Annual International ACM SIGIR Conference on Research and Development in Information Retrieval (SIGIR 2002)*, Tampere, Finland, 2002.

[6] Martin Dzbor, John B. Domingue, and Enrico Motta. Magpie - towards a semantic web browser. In *Proceedings of the 2nd Intl. Semantic Web Conference*, October 2003. Sanibel Island, Forida.

[7] C. Goble, S. Bechhofer, L. Carr, D. De Roure, and W. Hall. Conceptual Open Hypermedia = The Semantic Web? In *The Second International Workshop on the Semantic Web*, pages 44–50, Hong Kong, May 2001.

[8] S. Handschuh, S. Staab, and F. Ciravegna. S-CREAM - Semi-automatic CREAtion of Metadata. In *Proceedings of the 13th International Conference on Knowledge Engineering and Knowledge Management, EKAW02*. Springer Verlag, 2002.

[9] P. Kogut and W. Holmes. Applying information extraction to generate daml annotations from web pages. In *Proceedings of the K-CAP 2001 Workshop Knowledge Markup & Semantic Annotation*, 2001. Victoria B.C., Canada.

[10] N. Kushmerick, D. Weld, and R. Doorenbos. Wrapper induction for information extraction. In *Proceedings of the International Joint Conference on Artificial Intelligence (IJCAI), 1997.*, 1997.

[11] Thomas Leonard and Hugh Glaser. Large scale acquisition and maintenance from the web without source access. In Siegfried Handschuh, Rose Dieng-Kuntz, and Steffen Staab, editors, *Proceedings Workshop 4, Knowledge Markup and Semantic Annotation, K-CAP 2001*, 2001.

[12] Tom Mitchell. Extracting targeted data from the web. In *Proceedings of the seventh ACM SIGKDD international conference on Knowledge discovery and data mining*, San Francisco, California, 2001.

[13] M. Perkowitz and O. Etzioni. Category translation: Learning to understand information on the internet. In *International Joint Conference on Artificial Intelligence, IJCAI-95*, pages 930–938, Montreal, Canada, 1995.

[14] M. Vargas-Vera, Enrico Motta, J. Domingue, M. Lanzoni, A. Stutt, and F. Ciravegna. MnM: Ontology driven semi-automatic or automatic support for semantic markup. In *Proc. of the 13th International Conference on Knowledge Engineering and Knowledge Management, EKAW02*. Springer Verlag, 2002.

Reverse Engineering of Relational Databases to Ontologies

Irina Astrova

Tallinn University of Technology, Ehitajate tee 5
19086 Tallinn, Estonia
irina.astrova@cellnetwork.com

Abstract. A majority of the work on reverse engineering has been done on extracting entity-relationship and object models from relational databases. There exist only a few approaches that consider ontologies, as the target for reverse engineering. Moreover, the existing approaches can extract only a small subset of semantics embedded within a relational database, or they can require much user interaction for semantic annotation. In our opinion, the potential source of these problems lies in that the primary focus has been on analyzing key correlation. Data and attribute correlations are considered rarely and thus, have received little or no analysis. As an attempt to resolve the problems, we propose a novel approach, which is based on an analysis of key, data and attribute correlations, as well as their combination. Our approach can be applied to migrating data-intensive Web pages, which are usually based on relational databases, into the ontology-based Semantic Web.

1 Introduction

With the development of Web technology, data-intensive Web pages, which are usually based on relational databases, are seeking ways to migrate to the ontology-based Semantic Web. However, a majority of the work on reverse engineering has been done on extracting entity-relationship and object models from relational databases. There exist only a few approaches (e.g. [1, 2]) that consider ontologies, as the target for reverse engineering.

Reverse engineering is defined as a process of analyzing a "legacy" system to identify all the system's components and the relationships between them [3]. However, the existing approaches can:

- Extract only a small subset of semantics embedded within a relational database, or
- Require much user interaction for semantic annotation, thus giving less opportunity for automation.

In our opinion, the potential source of these problems lies in that the primary focus has been on analyzing key correlation. Data and attribute correlations are considered rarely and thus, have received little or no analysis. As an attempt to resolve the problems, we propose a novel approach, which is based on an analysis of key, data and attribute correlations, as well as their combination.

J. Davies et al. (Eds.): ESWS 2004, LNCS 3053, pp. 327–341, 2004.

2 Motivation

The motivation for our approach is to migrate from data-intensive Web pages into the Semantic Web.

The current Web has been moving away from static fixed Web pages to those that are dynamically-generated at the time of user requests. The latter are called *data-intensive Web pages* [4] and usually based on relational databases.

Data-intensive Web pages have a number of benefits; for example, an automated update of the Web content [5]. However, they suffer from two main problems. First, data-intensive Web pages form an "invisible" Web, because search engines cannot index them [6, 7]. Second, the Web content is not machine-understandable, because information is presented in HTML and thus, suitable for human consumption only.

The *Semantic Web* [8] is an extension of the current Web, where information is given a well-defined meaning, thus allowing machines and users to work in cooperation. The Semantic Web is based on ontologies. An ontology is a common shared conceptualization between members of a community of interest, which help them exchange information [9].

Since information is suitable for both machine and human consumption, the Semantic Web is a solution to the second problem of data-intensive Web pages. However, the question is how to migrate from data-intensive Web pages into the Semantic Web and thus, to make the Web content machine-understandable. The best approach seems to rely on reverse engineering [1], rather than on semantic annotation [10], which is time-consuming and error-prone.

3 Relational Database Vs. Ontology

We assume the existence of a relational database (defined by a relational database schema) that requires reverse engineering to an ontology. The ontology differs from the relational database schema in that:

- In the type system, there are no basic types; everything is a *concept*
- In the concept, there are no attributes and relationships; everything is a *property*[1]
- Concepts and properties can be organized into *inheritance hierarchies*.

Before going into detail of reverse engineering, we give a formal description of: relational database schema, ontology, and relationship between the two.

Relational database schema. This is the source for reverse engineering. A relational database schema consists of: a set of relations R, a set of attributes A_R, a set of basic types T_R, a function *attr*: $R \rightarrow 2^{A_R}$ that returns attributes of relations, a function *type*: $A_R \rightarrow T_R$ that returns types of attributes and a function *key*: $R \rightarrow 2^{A_R}$ that returns primary keys of relations [11]. We use the SQL language [12] to express semantics of the relational database schema.

---

[1] Only binary relationships can be represented through properties; ternary or higher degree relationships get their own concepts.

Figure 1 gives an example of relational database schema, which defines a relation Employee that has an attribute employeeID of basic type INTEGER.

```
CREATE TABLE Employee(
 employeeID INTEGER PRIMARY KEY)
```

Figure 1. A relational database schema

Ontology. This is the target for reverse engineering. An ontology consists of: a set of concepts C, a set of properties P_C, a concept inheritance hierarchy: $H_C \subseteq C \times C$, a set of axioms A_C, a function *dom:* $P_C \rightarrow C$ that returns domains of properties and a function *range:* $P_C \rightarrow C$ that returns ranges of properties [1]. We use the Frame Logic language [13] to express semantics of the ontology[2].

Figure 2 gives an example of ontology, which defines a concept Employee that has a property employeeID of domain Employee and range INTEGER. Employee is defined as a sub-concept of Object.

```
Employee::Object.
Employee[
 employeeID =>> INTEGER].
```

Figure 2. An ontology

Relationship between the two. We describe how a relational database schema is related to an ontology using: a function *rel:* $C \rightarrow R$ that returns relations from which concepts have been derived and a function *tt:* $T_R \rightarrow C$ that translates basic types into concepts.

4 Reverse Engineering

Reverse engineering is made up of two processes: (1) schema transformation, and (2) data migration [11].

4.1 Schema Transformation

The *schema transformation* process concerns the mapping of a relational database into an ontology. Two phases of this process are to:

- Analyze information such as key, data and attribute correlations to extract a conceptual schema, which expresses semantics about the relational database, and
- Transform this schema into a (semantically equivalent) ontology.

The process uses a relational database in third normal form (3NF) as the main input. It goes through five steps: (1) classification of relations, (2) mapping relations, (3) mapping attributes, (4) mapping relationships, and (5) mapping constraints.

---

[2] An ontology expressed in Frame Logic can then be translated into RDF statements [14].

4.1.1 Classification of Relations

Relations can be classified into one of the three categories: base, dependent and composite relations.

Base relations. If a relation is independent of any other relation in a relational database schema, it is a base relation. Formally, a relation r∈R is a *base relation*, if ¬∃r₁∈R such that $K_1 \subset K$, where $K=$ key(r) and $K_1=$ key(r₁).

In Figure 3, Department is a base relation, as it has no foreign key. Employee is also a base relation, as an attribute departmentID – a foreign key to Department – is not part of its primary key.

```
CREATE TABLE Department(
 departmentID INTEGER PRIMARY KEY)
CREATE TABLE Employee(
 employeeID INTEGER PRIMARY KEY,
 departmentID INTEGER REFERENCES Department)
```

Figure 3. Base relations

Dependent relations. If a primary key of a relation depends on another relation's primary key, it is a dependent relation. Formally, a relation r∈R is a *dependent relation*, if ∃r₁, r₂ ... rₙ∈R such that $K_1 \subseteq K_2 ... \subseteq K_n \subseteq K$, where $K=$ key(r), $K_i=$ key(rᵢ), i∈{1... n} and n≥1.

In Figure 4, Identification is a dependent relation, as it gets Employee's employeeID that is part of its primary key.

```
CREATE TABLE Employee(
 employeeID INTEGER PRIMARY KEY,
 departmentID INTEGER REFERENCES Department)
CREATE TABLE Identification(
 identificationID INTEGER,
 employeeID INTEGER REFERENCES Employee,
 CONSTRAINT Identification_PK PRIMARY KEY(identificationID,
employeeID))
```

Figure 4. Dependent relations

Composite relations. All other relations fall into this category. Formally, a *composite relation* is a relation that is neither base nor dependent.

In Figure 5, Assignment is a composite relation, as its primary key is composed of primary keys of Employee and Project.

Because both dependent and composite relations require a composite key (the key that has more than one attribute in it), sometimes it may be difficult to distinguish between them. In Figure 6, Passport "looks" like a composite relation, as its primary key is composed of primary keys of Employee and Identification: key(Passport)=key(Employee)∪key(Identification). However, it is a nesting of keys: key(Employee)⊆key(Identification)⊆key(Passport) that classifies Passport as a dependent relation, as opposed to it being a composite relation.

```
CREATE TABLE Employee(
 employeeID INTEGER PRIMARY KEY)
CREATE TABLE Project(
 projectID INTEGER PRIMARY KEY)
CREATE TABLE Assignment(
 employeeID INTEGER REFERENCES Employee,
 projectID INTEGER REFERENCES Project,
 CONSTRAINT Assignment_PK PRIMARY KEY(employeeID, projectID))
```

Figure 5. Composite relations

```
CREATE TABLE Employee(
 employeeID INTEGER PRIMARY KEY)
CREATE TABLE Identification(
 identificationID INTEGER,
 employeeID INTEGER REFERENCES Employee,
 CONSTRAINT Identification_PK PRIMARY KEY(identificationID,
employeeID))
 CREATE TABLE Passport(
 employeeID INTEGER REFERENCES Employee,
 identificationID INTEGER REFERENCES Identification,
 CONSTRAINT Passport_PK PRIMARY KEY(employeeID, identifica-
tionID))
```

Figure 6. Dependent vs. composite relations

4.1.2 Mapping Relations

Mapping relations is straightforward and usually poses no difficulties in the schema transformation process, as each relation becomes a concept, with the exception of composite relations. A composite relation is difficult to map, because depending on its structure, it can correspond to a concept or property[3].

In Figure 7, we create a concept for each base relation: Employee and Project. Within each concept, we create a property to map a binary relationship: an employee *is assigned to* a project. That relationship is represented through a composite relation Assignment, which consists entirely of primary keys of the two associated relations: Employee and Project.

In Figure 8, not only does a composite relation Assignment comprise primary keys of the two associated relations, but it also contains the date, when an employee started to work on a project. Therefore, we create a concept for Assignment that acts as a binary relationship between Employee and Project, but yet has a property startDate.

---

[3] A composite relation can also map to an inheritance relationship (namely, a multiple inheritance), when all its attributes are primary/foreign keys. But as there is no really good way to represent a multiple inheritance in a relational database schema, a composite relation will map to a property or concept. The user can then replace that property or concept with a multiple inheritance.

```
CREATE TABLE Employee(
 employeeID INTEGER PRIMARY KEY)
CREATE TABLE Project(
 projectID INTEGER PRIMARY KEY)
CREATE TABLE Assignment(
 employeeID INTEGER REFERENCES Employee,
 projectID INTEGER REFERENCES Project,
 CONSTRAINT Assignment_PK PRIMARY KEY(employeeID, projectID))
                              ↓
Employee::Object.
Project::Object.
Employee[
 employeeID =>> INTEGER,
 projectID =>> Project].
Project[
 projectID =>> INTEGER,
 employeeID =>> Employee].
```

Figure 7. Mapping relations and binary relationships

```
CREATE TABLE Assignment(
 employeeID INTEGER REFERENCES Employee,
 projectID INTEGER REFERENCES Project,
 startDate DATE,
 CONSTRAINT Assignment_PK PRIMARY KEY(employeeID, projectID))
                              ↓
Assignment::Object.
Assignment[
 employeeID =>> Employee,
 projectID =>> Project,
 startDate =>> DATE].
```

Figure 8. Mapping binary relationships with attributes

In Figure 9, a composite relation Uses represents a ternary relationship between three relations: Employee, Skill, and Project; i.e. an employee *uses* a skill on a project. Since only a binary relationship can be represented through properties, we create a concept for Uses.

```
CREATE TABLE Uses(
 employeeID INTEGER REFERENCES Employee,
 skillID INTEGER REFERENCES Skill,
 projectID INTEGER REFERENCES Project,
 CONSTRAINT Uses_PK PRIMARY KEY(employeeID, skillID, projec-
tID))
                              ↓
Uses::Object.
Uses[
 employeeID =>> Employee,
 skillID =>> Skill,
 projectID =>> Project].
```

Figure 9. Mapping ternary relationships

4.1.3 Mapping Attributes

Each attribute in a relation becomes a property in a concept, with the exception of foreign keys and primary/foreign keys. A foreign key and primary/foreign key are ignored, as they represent relationships.

In Figure 10, we add a property `employeeID` to a concept `Employee`.

```
CREATE TABLE Employee(
  employeeID INTEGER PRIMARY KEY)
                        ↓
Employee[
  employeeID =>> INTEGER].
```

Figure 10. Mapping attributes

4.1.4 Mapping Relationships

In a relational database schema, relationships are represented through foreign keys and primary/foreign keys[4]. A foreign key and primary/foreign key can correspond to a concept, property or an inheritance relationship, depending on the types of key, data and attribute correlations.

4.1.4.1 Key, Data and Attribute Correlations

Formally, given two relations $r_1 \in R$ and $r_2 \in R$:

- The types of *key correlation* are: key equality ($K_1=K_2$), key inclusion ($K_1 \subset K_2$), key overlap ($K_1 \cap K_2 \neq \varnothing$, $K_1-K_2 \neq \varnothing$, $K_2-K_1 \neq \varnothing$) and key disjointedness ($K_1 \cap K_2 = \varnothing$)
- The types of *data correlation* are: data equality ($r_1[K_1]=r_2[K_2]$), data inclusion ($r_1[K_1] \subset r_2[K_2]$), data overlap ($r_1[K_1] \cap r_2[K_2] \neq \varnothing$, $r_1[K_1]-r_2[K_2] \neq \varnothing$, $r_2[K_2]-r_1[K_1] \neq \varnothing$) and data disjointedness ($r_1[K_1] \cap r_2[K_2] = \varnothing$)
- The types of (non-key) *attribute correlation* are: attribute equality ($A_1=A_2$), attribute inclusion ($A_1 \subset A_2$), attribute overlap ($A_1 \cap A_2 \neq \varnothing$, $A_1-A_2 \neq \varnothing$, $A_2-A_1 \neq \varnothing$) and attribute disjointedness ($A_1 \cap A_2 = \varnothing$),
  where $K_1=key(r_1)$, $K_2=key(r_2)$, $r_1[K_1]=\pi_{K1}(r_1)$, $r_2[K_2]=\pi_{K2}(r_2)$, $A_1=attr(r_1)-K_1$ and $A_2=attr(r_2)-K_2$.

4.1.4.2 Analysis Key Correlation

To map relationships, we start with analyzing key correlation. For example, consider a relationship between `Project` and `Task` in Figure 11, when **key disjointedness** holds on it. That relationship associates two relations, which are independent of each other. Because the relationship is binary, we map it to properties.

4.1.4.3 Analysis of Data and Attribute Correlations

In mapping relationships, while the analysis of key correlation is crucial for deriving semantics from a relational database, data and attribute correlations are also important to analyze. The importance of this analysis is best explained by example.

---

[4] Relationships can also be represented through composite relations, but we have already handled them in the early step of mapping (see Section 4.1.2).

```
CREATE TABLE Project(
 projectID INTEGER PRIMARY KEY)
CREATE TABLE Task(
 projectID INTEGER REFERENCES Project,
 taskID INTEGER PRIMARY KEY)
                                    ↓
Project[
 projectID =>> INTEGER,
 taskID =>> Task].
Task[
 taskID =>> INTEGER,
 projectID =>> Project].
```

Figure 11. Key disjointedness

First, consider a relationship between SoftwareProject and Project in Figure 12, when **key equality**, **data equality** and **attribute disjointedness** hold on it. This is an example of vertical partitioning, where attributes of a single (logical) relation have been split into two relations, having the same primary key. Therefore, we combine SoftwareProject and Project into a single concept, say SoftwareProject, whose properties are the union of the attributes of the two relations.

```
CREATE TABLE Project(
 projectID INTEGER PRIMARY KEY,
 budget FLOAT,
 dueDate DATE)
CREATE TABLE SoftwareProject(
 projectID INTEGER PRIMARY KEY,
 language VARCHAR)
                                    ↓
SoftwareProject[
 projectID =>> INTEGER,
 budget =>> FLOAT,
 dueDate =>> DATE,
 language =>> STRING].
```

Figure 12. Key equality, data equality and attribute disjointedness

Second, consider a relationship between SoftwareProject and Project in Figure 13, when **key equality**, **data disjointedness** and **attribute equality** hold on it. This is, again, an example of optimization structure; but horizontal partitioning, where data of a single (logical) relation have been split into two relations, having the same attributes. Therefore, we combine SoftwareProject and Project into a single concept, say SoftwareProject, whose instances are the union of the data of the two relations.

Third, consider a relationship between SoftwareProject and Project in Figure 14, when **key equality** and **data inclusion** hold on it. That relationship maps to a single inheritance, as all data of SoftwareProject are also included in Project; i.e. a software project is a project. But the converse is not true, as some projects can be hardware projects, for example.

```
CREATE TABLE Project(
 projectID INTEGER PRIMARY KEY,
 budget FLOAT,
 dueDate DATE,
 language VARCHAR)
CREATE TABLE SoftwareProject(
 projectID INTEGER PRIMARY KEY,
 budget FLOAT,
 dueDate DATE,
 language VARCHAR)
```

↓

```
SoftwareProject[
 projectID =>> INTEGER,
 budget =>> FLOAT,
 dueDate =>> DATE,
 language =>> STRING].
```

Figure 13. Key equality, data disjointedness and attribute equality

```
CREATE TABLE Project(
 projectID INTEGER PRIMARY KEY,
 budget FLOAT,
 dueDate DATE)
CREATE TABLE SoftwareProject(
 projectID INTEGER PRIMARY KEY REFERENCES Project,
 language VARCHAR)
```

↓

```
Project[
 projectID =>> INTEGER,
 budget =>> FLOAT,
 dueDate =>> DATE].
SoftwareProject::Project[
 language =>> STRING].
```

Figure 14. Key equality and data inclusion

Fourth, consider a relationship between SoftwareProject and Hardware-Project in Figure 15, when **key equality, data overlap** and **attribute disjointedness** hold on it. This is an example of a multiple inheritance, as some data are common to both relations. Therefore, we "discover" a new concept, say HardwareSoftwareProject, which has inheritance relationships to both SoftwareProject and HardwareProject.

Fifth, consider a relationship between SoftwareProject and Hardware-Project in Figure 16, when **key equality, data disjointedness** and **attribute overlap** hold on it. This example illustrates a single inheritance. Because some attributes are common to both relations, we can see that SoftwareProject and HardwareProject are part of the inheritance hierarchy; but there is no relation corresponding to their super-concept. Therefore, we "discover" a new concept, say Project, which both SoftwareProject and HardwareProject inherit from.

```
CREATE TABLE HardwareProject(
 projectID INTEGER PRIMARY KEY,
 supplier VARCHAR)
CREATE TABLE SoftwareProject(
 projectID INTEGER PRIMARY KEY,
 language VARCHAR)
```

↓

```
HardwareProject::Project[
 projectID =>> INTEGER,
 supplier =>> STRING].
SoftwareProject::Project[
 projectID =>> INTEGER,
 language =>> STRING].
HardwareSoftwareProject::Object.
HardwareSoftwareProject::HardwareProject.
HardwareSoftwareProject::SoftwareProject.
```

Figure 15. Key equality, data overlap and attribute disjointedness

```
CREATE TABLE HardwareProject(
 projectID INTEGER PRIMARY KEY,
 budget FLOAT,
 dueDate DATE,
 supplier VARCHAR)
CREATE TABLE SoftwareProject(
 projectID INTEGER PRIMARY KEY,
 budget FLOAT,
 dueDate DATE,
 language VARCHAR)
```

↓

```
Project::Object.
Project[
 projectID =>> INTEGER,
 budget =>> FLOAT,
 dueDate =>> DATE].
HardwareProject::Project[
 supplier =>> STRING].
SoftwareProject::Project[
 language =>> STRING].
```

Figure 16. Key equality, data disjointedness and attribute overlap

Sixth, consider what a relationship between SoftwareProject and Hard-wareProject in Figure 17 might look like, if **key equality, data overlap** and **attribute overlap** held on it. Because some data and attributes are common to both relations, this is an example of the "diamond-shaped" inheritance hierarchy, in which a concept has inheritance relationships to two super-concepts and the two super-concepts refer in turn to a common super-concept.

Finally, consider a relationship between Project and Employee in Figure 18, when **key overlap** and **data equality** (or **data inclusion**) hold on it. Because all the information about departments in Project is also included in Employee, a closer examination of that relationship reveals that a relation Department is missing. Therefore, we "retrieve" Department and add properties to it for each concept, participating in the relationship. That is, Project and Employee are indirectly related to each other through Department. (E.g. an employee is assigned to a project controlled by a department he or she belongs to.)

```
CREATE TABLE HardwareProject(
 projectID INTEGER PRIMARY KEY,
 budget FLOAT,
 dueDate DATE,
 supplier VARCHAR)
CREATE TABLE SoftwareProject(
 projectID INTEGER PRIMARY KEY,
 budget FLOAT,
 dueDate DATE,
 language VARCHAR)

                              ↓

Project::Object.
Project[
 projectID =>> INTEGER,
 budget =>> FLOAT,
 dueDate =>> DATE].
HardwareProject::Project[
 supplier =>> STRING].
SoftwareProject::Project[
 language =>> STRING].
HardwareSoftwareProject::Object.
HardwareSoftwareProject::HardwareProject.
HardwareSoftwareProject::SoftwareProject.
```

Figure 17. Key equality, data overlap and attribute overlap

```
CREATE TABLE Employee(
 employeeID INTEGER,
 departmentID INTEGER,
 CONSTRAINT Employee_PK PRIMARY KEY(employeeID, departmen-
tID))
CREATE TABLE Project(
 projectID INTEGER,
 departmentID INTEGER,
 CONSTRAINT Project_PK PRIMARY KEY(projectID, departmentID))
                              ↓

Department::Object.
Department[
 departmentID =>> INTEGER,
 employeeID =>> Employee,
 projectID =>> Project].
Employee[
 employeeID =>> INTEGER,
 departmentID =>> Department].
Project[
 projectID =>> INTEGER,
 departmentID =>> Department].
```

Figure 18. Key overlap and data equality (or data inclusion)

4.1.5 Mapping Constraints

In SQL, it is possible to specify constraints (like PRIMARY KEY, UNIQUE, NOT NULL, etc.). We map them into Frame Logic's axioms [1], thus preserving all the semantics embedded within a relational database[5].

Figure 19 gives an example of mapping a constraint PRIMARY KEY. An attribute is a *primary key*, if it is unique and total. An attribute is *unique*, when no two tuples in the relation have the same value for that attribute, and no tuple in the relation has two values for that attribute. An attribute is *total* (not null), if all tuples in the relation contain values for that attribute.

```
CREATE TABLE Employee(
 EmployeeID INTEGER PRIMARY KEY)
                              ↓
PrimaryKey(Employee, employeeID).
Forall C, P PrimaryKey(C, P) <-
 Unique(C, P) and Total(C, P).
Forall C, P Unique(C, P) <-
 IdenticalValues(C, P) and SingleValue(C, P).
Forall C, P IdenticalValues(C, P) <-
 Forall I1, I2, IP I1:C and I2:C and
 I1[P->>IP] and IC[P->>IP] and Equal(I1, I2).
Forall C, P SingleValue(C, P) <-
 Forall IC, IP1, IP2 IC:C and
 IC[P->>IP1] and IC[P->>IP2] and Equal(IP1, IP2).
Forall C, P Total(C, P) <-
 Forall IC Exists IP IC:C and IC[P->>IP].
```

Figure 19. Mapping constraints

4.2 Data Migration

The *data migration* process is the migration of data from the relational database into a knowledge base; in particular, tuples in the relational database are mapped into ontological instances. This process is performed in two phases:

- Ontological instances are created. Each instance is assigned with a name that uniquely identifies it, and
- Relationships between ontological instances are created.

In Figure 20, an ontological instance d is instantiated from a concept Department. It has the value 1 for a property departmentID and is referenced by another ontological instance e.

---

[5] Due to the static nature of an ontology, no dynamic aspects of SQL – triggers and referential actions (like ON UPDATE, ON DELETE, etc.) – can be mapped.

```
INSERT INTO Department(
  departmentID)
  VALUES(1)
INSERT INTO Employee(
  employeeID, departmentID)
  VALUES(2, 1)
```

                                          ↓

```
d:Department[
  departmentID ->> 1].
e:Employee[
  employeeID ->> 2,
  departmentD ->> d].
```

Figure 20. Mapping tuples

5 Related Work

While reverse engineering is a widely-studied subject, there are only a few approaches that consider ontologies, as the target for reverse engineering. Among them are:

- *Stojanovic et al.'s approach* [1]: This approach comes most closely to ours. However, it assumes data equality and data inclusion, thus being able to extract only a small subset of semantics embedded within a relational database. Additional ("hidden") semantics can be discovered, by analyzing a set of tuples in the relational database, when their intersection is partial (i.e. data overlap) and when there is no intersection (i.e. data disjointedness)
- *Kashyap's approach* [2]: This approach is similar to Stojanovic et al.'s. However, it requires much user interaction for semantic annotation, thus giving less opportunity for automation. Moreover, the approach does not create axioms. An axiom can be used to further characterize relationships between ontological instances
- *Dogan and Islamaj's approach* [15]: This approach provides simple and automatic schema transformation as well as data mapping: a relation maps to a concept, the tuples belonging to that relation map to ontological instances and attributes of the relation become properties in the concept. However, it ignores inheritance and optimization structures, thus creating an ontology that looks rather "relational".

A majority of the work on reverse engineering has been done on extracting entity-relationship and object models from relational databases. Unfortunately, this work cannot be directly applied to extracting ontologies from relational databases, because of differences between ontologies and database schemata. These differences stem from the fact that:

- An ontology model is richer than a database schema [16]. For example, Frame Logic allows us to organize properties (and not only concepts) into inheritance hierarchies

- An ontology provides more semantics than a database schema does [16]. For example, in a relational database, semantics are not solely contained in the relational database schema, but also in data
- An ontology blurs a distinction between classes and instances [16]. For example, the notion of metaclass – a class whose instances are themselves classes – makes it difficult to distinguish an ontology from ontological instances. It is just a role of concept to be a class or an instance.

6 Conclusion

We have proposed a novel approach to reverse engineering of a relational database to an ontology. Based on an analysis of key, data and attribute correlations, our approach has advantages over the existing approaches in that:

- It allows the user to extract more semantics from the relational database, including inheritance and optimization structures, and
- It reduces user interaction, which is mainly required to confirm the extracted semantics and to give them more appropriate names[6].

Our approach can be applied to migrating data-intensive Web pages, which are usually based on relational databases, into the ontology-based Semantic Web. This migration starts with mapping the schema of a relational database into an ontology ("schema transformation"). The ontology is then used for mapping tuples in the relational database into ontological instances ("data migration"). The ontological instances form a knowledge base [17]. The facts in the knowledge base are then transformed into RDF statements and published on the Web. This publishing makes the Web content machine-understandable.

References

1. L. Stojanovic, N. Stojanovic and R. Volz, Migrating Data-intensive Web Sites into the Semantic Web, In: Proceedings of the 17th ACM Symposium on Applied Computing (SAC) (2002)
2. V. Kashyap, Design and Creation of Ontologies for Environmental Information Retrieval, In: Proceedings of the 12th Workshop on Knowledge Acquisition, Modeling and Management (KAW) (1999)
3. R. Chiang, T. Barron and V. Storey, A Framework for the Design and Evaluation of Reverse Engineering Methods for Relational Databases, In: Data and Knowledge Engineering, Vol. 21, No. 1 (1996), 57–77
4. P. Fraternali, Tools and Approaches for Developing Data-intensive Web Applications: A Survey, In: ACM Computing Surveys, Vol. 31, No. 3 (1999) 227–263

---

[6] Unlike the data migration process, the schema transformation process cannot be completely automated. User interaction is still necessary, when ambiguities occur and semantics cannot be inferred [11].

5. P. Atzeni, G. Mecca and P. Merialdo, Design and Maintenance of Data-Intensive Web Sites, In: Proceedings of the 6th International Conference on Extending Database Technology (1998) 436–450
6. S. Comai and P. Fraternali, A Semantic Model for Specifying Data-Intensive Web Applications using WebML, In: International Semantic Web Working Symposium (SWWS) (2001)
7. S. Lawrence and C. Giles, Accessibility of Information on the Web, In: Nature, No. 400 (1999) 107–109
8. T. Berners-Lee, XML 2000 – Semantic Web Talk, http://www.w3.org/2000/Talks/1206-xml2k-tbl/slide10-0.html (2000)
9. T. Gruber, A Translation Approach to Portable Ontology Specifications, In: Knowledge Acquisition, No. 5 (1993) 199–220
10. M. Erdmann, A. Maedche, H. Schnurr and S. Staab. From Manual to Semi-automatic Semantic Annotation: About Ontology-based Text Annotation Tools, In: Proceedings of the Workshop on Semantic Annotation and Intelligent Content (COLING), P. Buitelaar and K. Hasida (eds.) (2000)
11. A. Behm, A. Geppert and K. Dittrich, On the migration of relational database schemas and data to object-oriented database systems, In: Proceedings of the 5th International Conference on Re-Technologies for Information Systems (1997) 13–33
12. J. Melton and A. Simon, Understanding the New SQL: A Complete Guide, San Mateo, CA: Morgan Kaufmann (1993)
13. M. Kifer, G. Lausen and J. Wu, Logical Foundations of Object-oriented and Frame-Based Languages, In: Journal ACM, No. 42 (1995) 741–843
14. S. Decker, D. Brickley, J. Saarela and J. Angele, A Query and Inference Service for RDF, http://www.w3.org/TandS/QL/QL98 (1998)
15. G. Dogan and R. Islamaj, Importing Relational Databases into the Semantic Web, http://www.mindswap.org/webai/2002/fall/Importing_20Relational_20Databases_20into_20the_20Semantic_20Web.html (2002)
16. N. Noy and M. Klein, Ontology Evolution: Not the Same as Schema Evolution, In: Knowledge and Information Systems, No. 5 (2003)
17. A. Maedche, S. Staab, N. Stojanovic, R. Studer and Y. Sure, Semantic Portal – The Seal Approach, In: Creating the Semantic Web, D. Fensel, J. Hendler, H. Lieberman and W. Wahlster (eds.), MIT Press, MA, Cambridge (2001)

No Registration Needed:
How to Use Declarative Policies and Negotiation
to Access Sensitive Resources on the Semantic Web

Rita Gavriloaie[1], Wolfgang Nejdl[1], Daniel Olmedilla[1], Kent E. Seamons[2], and
Marianne Winslett[3]

[1] L3S and University of Hannover, Germany
{gavriloaie,nejdl,olmedilla}@learninglab.de
[2] Department of Computer Science, Brigham Young University, USA
seamons@cs.byu.edu
[3] Dept. of Computer Science, University of Illinois at Urbana-Champaign, USA
winslett@cs.uiuc.edu

Abstract. Gaining access to sensitive resources on the Web usually involves an explicit registration step, where the client has to provide a predetermined set of information to the server. The registration process yields a login/password combination, a cookie, or something similar that can be used to access the sensitive resources. In this paper we show how an explicit registration step can be avoided on the Semantic Web by using appropriate semantic annotations, rule-oriented access control policies, and automated trust negotiation. After presenting the PeerTrust language for policies and trust negotiation, we describe our implementation of implicit registration and authentication that runs under the Java-based MINERVA Prolog engine. The implementation includes a PeerTrust policy applet and evaluator, facilities to import local metadata, policies and credentials, and secure communication channels between all parties.

1 Introduction

In traditional distributed environments, service providers and requesters are usually known to each other. Often shared information in the environment tells which parties can provide what kind of services and which parties are entitled to make use of those services. Thus, trust between parties is a straightforward matter. Even if on some occasions there is a trust issue, as in traditional client-server systems, the question is whether the server should trust the client, and not vice versa. In this case, trust establishment is often handled by unidirectional access control methods, most typically by having the client log in as a preregistered user. This approach has several disadvantages.

1. Such practices are usually offered in a "take-it-or-leave-it" fashion, i.e., the clients either *unconditionally* disclose their information to the server in the preregistration phase, or cannot access the service at all. The clients cannot apply their own access control policies for their personal information, and decide accordingly whether the server is trustworthy enough so that sensitive information can be disclosed.

J. Davies et al. (Eds.): ESWS 2004, LNCS 3053, pp. 342–356, 2004.
© Springer-Verlag Berlin Heidelberg 2004

2. When the clients fill out the online registration form, it is very hard for the server to verify whether the provided information is valid.
3. Often, much of the information required in online registration forms does not seem directly related to the service that clients want to access. However, since the clients have to unconditionally provide the information, there is no way that they can discuss their misgivings with the server.

A notable example of the latter shortcoming is that traditional access control methods usually require the customer to reveal her exact identity, which, in many cases, is irrelevant to the service the customer requests. For example, suppose that Alice visits the current ACM on-line store. To find out the price of a one-year membership in ACM SIGMOD, Alice must go through a lengthy registration process to obtain an "ACM Web Account" and use that account for all her interactions with the ACM Store. Even if Alice decides to join ACM SIGMOD, she should not have to provide all of the personal information that is requested on the ACM Web Account registration form, such as her fax number. These kinds of registration requests are sufficiently annoying and intrusive that services have sprung up to automatically fill in such forms with false information and keep track of the resulting account names and passwords (see, e.g., http://www.sixcube.com/autofiller or http://www.roboform.com).

Similar access control needs have arisen in the context of the EU/IST ELENA project [13], whose participants include e-learning and e-training companies, learning technology providers, and universities and research institutes (http://www.elena-project.org/). Any potential student or learning provider should be able to connect to the ELENA network and access an appropriate subset of its resources. For example, suppose that E-Learn Associates manages a 1-credit-unit Spanish course in the ELENA network, and Alice wishes to take the course. If the course is accessible free of charge to all police officers who live in and work for the state of California, Alice can show E-Learn her digital police badge to prove that she is a state police officer, as well as her California driver's license, to gain access to the course at no charge.

However, Alice may not feel comfortable showing her police badge to just anyone; she knows that there are Web sites on the west coast that publish the names, home addresses, and home phone numbers of police officers. Because of that, Alice may only be willing to show her badge to companies that belong to the Better Business Bureau OnLine. But with this additional policy, access control is no longer the one-shot, unilateral affair found in traditional distributed systems or recent proposals for access control on the Semantic Web [9, 14]: to see an appropriate subset of Alice's digital credentials, E-Learn will have to show that it satisfies the access control policies for each of them; and in the process of demonstrating that it satisfies those policies, it may have to disclose additional credentials of its own, but only after Alice demonstrates that she satisfies the access control policies for each of them; and so on.

In this paper, we build upon the previous work on policy-based access control for the Semantic Web by showing how to use *automated trust negotiation* in the PeerTrust approach to access control. We start by introducing the concepts behind trust negotiation in section 2. We then introduce guarded distributed logic programs to express and implement trust negotiation in a distributed environment, in section 3. Section 4 describes the PeerTrust execution environment and an application scenario implemented for this paper, and section 5 provides additional information about the PeerTrust implementation. The PeerTrust implementation uses the Java-based MINERVA Prolog engine for reasoning and uses Java applications and applets for everything else, including negotiation capabilities both on the server and the client side, means for secure communication, and facilities to import local RDF metadata, policies, and credentials. The paper concludes with a short discussion of related approaches and further work.

2   Trust Negotiation

Digital credentials (or simply *credentials*) make it feasible to manage trust establishment efficiently and bidirectionally on the Internet. Digital credentials are the on-line counterparts of paper credentials that people use in their daily life, such as a driver's license. By showing appropriate credentials to each other, a service requester and provider can both prove their qualifications. In detail, a credential is a digitally signed assertion by the *credential issuer* about the properties of one or more entities. The credential issuer uses its private key to sign the credential, which describes one or more attributes and/or relationships of the entities. The public key of the issuer can be used to verify that the credential was actually issued by the issuer, making the credential verifiable and unforgeable. The signed credential can also include the public keys of the entities referred to in the credential. This allows an entity to use her private key to prove that she is one of the entities referred to in the credential, by signing a challenge [12]. Digital credentials can be implemented in many ways, including X.509 [7] certificates, anonymous credentials [1, 2], and signed XML statements [3].

When credentials do not contain sensitive information, the trust establishment procedure is very simple. For example, if Alice will show her police badge and driver's license to anyone, then she (more precisely, a software agent acting on her behalf) first checks E-Learn's policy for its Spanish course, which is always available. Then she presents her police badge and license along with the retrieval request. However, in many situations, especially in the context of e-business, credentials themselves contain sensitive information. For example, as discussed earlier, Alice may only be willing to show her police badge to members of the BBB. To deal with such scenarios, a more complex procedure needs to be adopted to establish trust through negotiation.

In the PeerTrust approach to automated trust establishment, trust is established gradually by disclosing credentials and requests for credentials, an iterative process known as *trust negotiation*. This differs from traditional identity-based access control:

1. Trust between two strangers is established based on parties' properties, which are proven through disclosure of digital credentials.
2. Every party can define access control policies to control outsiders' access to their sensitive resources. These resources can include services accessible over the Internet, documents and other data, roles in role-based access control systems, credentials, policies, and capabilities in capability-based systems.
3. In the approaches to trust negotiation developed so far, two parties establish trust directly without involving trusted third parties, other than credential issuers. Since both parties have access control policies, trust negotiation is appropriate for deployment in a peer-to-peer architecture, where a client and server are treated equally.

Instead of a one-shot authorization and authentication, trust is established incrementally through a sequence of bilateral credential disclosures.

A trust negotiation is triggered when one party requests to access a resource owned by another party. The goal of a trust negotiation is to find a sequence of credentials $(C_1, \ldots, C_k, R)$, where R is the resource to which access was originally requested, such that when credential C_i is disclosed, its access control policy has been satisfied by credentials disclosed earlier in the sequence—or to determine that no such credential disclosure sequence exists. For example, when Alice registers for the free Spanish course:

Step 1 Alice requests to access E-Learn's Spanish course at no charge.

Step 2 E-Learn asks Alice to show a police badge issued by the California State Police to prove that she is a police officer, and her driver's license to prove that she is living in the state of California.

Step 3 Alice is willing to disclose her driver's license to anyone, so she sends it to E-Learn. However, she considers her police badge to contain sensitive information. She tells E-Learn that in order to see her police badge, E-Learn must prove that it belongs to the Better Business Bureau.

Step 4 Fortunately, E-Learn does have a Better Business Bureau membership card. The card contains no sensitive information, so E-Learn discloses it to Alice.

Step 5 Alice now believes that she can trust E-Learn and discloses her police badge to E-Learn.

Step 6 After checking the badge and driver's license for validity (i.e., that each credential's contents has not been altered since it was signed, and that it was signed by the right party) and that Alice owns them, E-Learn gives Alice the free registration for this course.

We can view each resource in this example as an item on the Semantic Web, with its salient properties stored as RDF properties. For example, the amount of credit associated with the course can be represented by the RDF property (written as a binary predicate) "creditUnits(spanish101, 1)". Each resource is automatically associated with the appropriate access control policies by means of these properties, as discussed later.

3   PeerTrust Guarded Distributed Logic Programs

In this section, we describe the syntax of the PeerTrust language. The semantics of the language is an extension of that of SD3 [15] to allow the set of all PeerTrust programs to be viewed as a single global logic program. We refer the interested reader to [15, 11] for semantic details.

Definite Horn clauses are the basis for logic programs [10], which have been used as the basis for the rule layer of the Semantic Web and specified in the RuleML effort ([4, 5]). PeerTrust's language for expressing access control policies is also based on definite Horn clauses, i.e., rules of the form

$$lit_0 \leftarrow lit_1, \ldots, lit_n$$

In the remainder of this section, we concentrate on the syntactic features that are unique to the PeerTrust language. We will consider only positive authorizations.

References to Other Peers The ability to reason about statements made by other parties is central to trust negotiation. For example, in section 2, E-Learn wants to see a statement from Alice's employer that says that she is a police officer. One can think of this as a case of E-Learn *delegating evaluation* of the query "Is Alice a police officer?" to the California State Police (CSP). Once CSP receives the query, the manner in which CSP handles it may depend on who asked the query. Thus CSP needs a way to specify which party made each request that it receives. To express delegation of evaluation to another party, we extend each literal lit_i with an additional *Issuer* argument,

$$lit_i \text{ @ Issuer}$$

where *Issuer* specifies the party who is responsible for evaluating lit_i or has the authority to evaluate lit_i. For example, E-Learn's policy for free courses might mention policeOfficer(X) @ csp. If that literal evaluates to true, this means that CSP states that Alice is a California police officer. For example, if all California state police officers can enroll in Spanish 101 at no charge, we have:

eLearn:
freeEnroll(spanish101, X) ← policeOfficer(X) @ csp.

This policy says that the CSP is responsible for certifying the employment status of a given person. For clarity, we prefix each rule by the party in whose knowledge base it is included.

The *Issuer* argument can be a nested term containing a sequence of issuers, which are evaluated starting at the outermost layer. For example, CSP is unlikely to be willing to answer E-Learn's query about whether Alice is a police officer. A more practical approach is to ask Alice to evaluate the query herself, i.e., to disclose her police badge:

eLearn:
policeOfficer(X) @ csp ←
  policeOfficer(X) @ csp @ X.

CSP can refer to the party who asked a particular query by including a *Requester* argument in literals, so that we now have literals of the form

$$lit_i \text{ @ Issuer \$ Requester}$$

The *Requester* argument can be nested, too, in which case it expresses a chain of requesters, with the most recent requester in the outermost layer of the nested term. Using the *Issuer* and *Requester* arguments, we can delegate evaluation of literals to other parties and also express interactions and the corresponding negotiation process between parties. For instance, extending and generalizing the previous example, consider E-Learn Associates' policy for free Spanish courses for California police officers:

eLearn:
freeEnroll(Course, Requester) $ Requester ←
  policeOfficer(Requester) @ csp @ Requester,
  rdfType(Course, "http:.../elena#Course"),
  dcLanguage(Course, "es"),
  creditUnits(Course, X),
  X < = 1.

If Alice provides appropriate identification, then the policy for the free enrollment service is satisfied, and E-Learn will allow her to access the service through a mechanism not shown here. In this example, the mechanism can transfer control directly to the enrollment service. For some services, the mechanism may instead give Alice a nontransferable token that she can use to access the service repeatedly without having to negotiate trust again until the token expires. The mechanism can also implement other security-related measures, such as creating an audit trail for the enrollment. When the policy for a negotiation-related resource such as a credential becomes satisfied, the runtime system may choose to include the resource directly in a message sent during the negotiation, as discussed later.

Local Rules and Signed Rules Each party defines the set of access control policies that apply to its resources, in the form of a set of definite Horn clause rules that may refer to the RDF properties of those resources. These and any other rules that the party defines on its own are its *local* rules. A party may also have copies of rules defined by other parties, and it may use these rules in its proofs in certain situations. For example, Alice can use a rule (with an empty body in this case) that was defined by CSP to prove that she is really a police officer:

alice:
policeOfficer(alice) @ csp
   signedBy [csp].

In this example, the "signedBy" term indicates that the rule has CSP's digital signature on it. This is very important, as E-Learn is not going to take Alice's word that she is a police officer; she must present a statement signed by the police to convince E-Learn. A signed rule has an additional argument that says who issued the rule. The cryptographic signature itself is not included in the logic program, because signatures are very large and are not needed by this part of the negotiation software. The signature is used to verify that the issuer really did issue the rule. We assume that when a party receives a signed rule from another party, the signature is verified before the rule is passed to the GDLP evaluation engine. Similarly, when one party sends a signed rule to another party, the actual signed rule must be sent, and not just the logic programmatic representation of the signed rule.

More complex signed rules often represent delegations of authority. For example, the California Highway Patrol (CHP) can use a signed rule to prove that it is entitled to answer queries about California state police officers, using its database of CHP officers:

chp:
policeOfficer(X) @ csp ←
   signedBy [csp]
   policeOfficer(X) @ chp.

If Alice's police badge is signed by the CHP, then she should cache a copy of the rule given above and submit both the rule and the police badge when E-Learn asks her to prove that she is a California state police officer.

Guards To guarantee that all relevant policies are satisfied before access is given to a resource, we must sometimes specify a partial evaluation order for the literals in the body of a rule. Similar to approaches to parallel logic programming such as Guarded Horn Logic [16], we split the body's literals into a sequence of sets, divided by the symbol "|". All but the last set are *guards*, and all the literals in one set must evaluate to true before any literals in the next set are evaluated. In particular, (a subset of) the guards in a policy rule can be viewed as a query that describes the set of resources for which this policy is applicable. The query is expressed in terms of the RDF characteristics of the resources to which the policy applies. In this paper, access will be granted to a resource if a user can satisfy any one of the policy rules applicable to that resource. (This scheme can be extended to allow negative authorizations and conflict resolution.) For example, if Alice will show her police membership credentials only to members of the Better Business Bureau, she can express that policy as a guard that is inside her police credential but outside the scope of CSP's signature. This is expressed syntactically by adding these additional local guards between ← and "signedBy".

alice:
policeOfficer(alice) @ csp
    ← member(Requester) @ bbb @ Requester
    | signedBy [csp].

Both local and signed rules can include guards. PeerTrust guards express the evaluation precedence of literals within a rule, and any rule whose guard literals evaluate to true can be used for continued evaluation. In contrast, guards in parallel logic programming systems usually introduce a deterministic choice of one single rule to evaluate next.

Public and Private Predicates In trust negotiation, we must be able to distinguish between predicates that can be queried by external parties, and ones that cannot— analogous to the public and private procedures in object-oriented languages. For example, authentication and time-of-day predicates are private. Parties may also have private rules, which are neither shown to nor can directly be called by other parties. Public and private rules and predicates are straightforward to design and implement in definite Horn clauses. The examples in this paper include only public rules.

4   Execution Environment and High-Level Algorithms

PeerTrust's current implementation is targeted at scenarios that arise in the ELENA project, where clients want to access protected Web resources residing in a distributed repository (see Fig. 1). In Fig. 1, Alice and E-Learn obtain trust negotiation software signed by a source that they trust (PeerTrust Inc.) and distributed by PeerTrust Inc. or another site, either as a Java application or an applet. After Alice requests the Spanish course from E-Learn's web front end, she enters into a trust negotiation with E-Learn's negotiation server. The negotiation servers may also act as servers for the major resources they protect (the Learning Management Servers (LMS) in Fig. 1), or may be separate entities, as in our figure. Additional parties can participate in the negotiation,

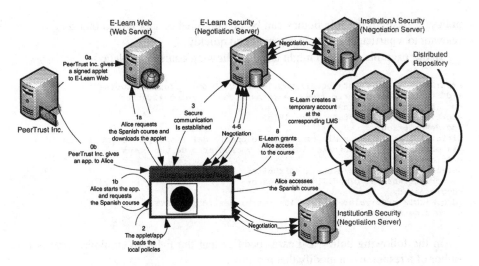

Fig. 1. Resource access control scenario

if necessary, symbolized in our figure by the InstitutionA and InstitutionB servers. If access to the course is granted, E-Learn sets up a temporary account for Alice at the course provider's site, and redirects her original request there. The temporary account is invisible to Alice.

Parties possess credentials that they have either obtained directly from credential issuers or from on-line repositories of issued credentials. We expect that credential issuers will also give parties default, tailorable policies to protect the credentials they have issued. For example, when Alice receives a new credit card, it is to the advantage of the credit card company to help Alice guard against theft or misuse of her card, by giving her a bootstrap policy to protect the card. Issuers can also direct novice users of digital credentials to trustworthy organizations that provide trust negotiation software, so that the users can actually make use of their new credentials. This software should be signed by the organization that produces it, so that users can be sure that the software that they download and run has not been tampered with, and is actually the software produced by the organization. In the PeerTrust 1.0 demo, a trusted party offers trust negotiation software as a signed Java application or applet that any other party can download and use. Other parties offer credentials and policies that can be obtained at run time and (for demo purposes only) assign public and private keys to users new to the demo.

When a client asks to access a resource, the negotiation server must determine what policies are applicable to that resource. As in [9], we do not want to assign policies explicitly to each resource, due to scalability and manageability concerns. Instead, in the context of the Semantic Web, we implicitly assign policies to each resource based on the RDF metadata associated with that resource. These metadata are imported into the negotiation server as facts in the logic program. Such facts are mentioned in the bodies of each policy rule, to define the scope of the policy; rule bodies may include additional limitations such as time-of-day restrictions to further restrict the scope of the policy. If desired, the rule bodies can be precompiled or indexed so that the policies relevant to a particular resource can be found quickly.

In our example, E-Learn might use the following course metadata:

```
<rdf:Description about="http://www.learninglab.de/.../spanishCourse/">
<rdf:type resource="http://www.learninglab.de/.../elena#Course"/>
<dc:language>es</dc:language>
<dc:title>Curso de español</dc:title>
<dc:description>
Dirigido a estudiantes sin conocimiento previo del lenguaje. Se estudiarán
las estructuras gramaticales básicas y vocabulario de uso común.
</dc:description>
<elena:creditUnits>1</elena:creditUnits>
<dc:creator>Daniel Olmedilla</dc:creator>
<dcq:created>
<dcq:W3CDTF><rdf:value>2003-12-15</rdf:value></dcq:W3CDTF>
</dcq:created>
```

In the following policy, E-Learn specifies that the E-Learn employee who is the author of a resource can modify that resource.

eLearn:
modify(Course, Requester) $ Requester ←
 employee(Requester) @ eLearn @ Requester,
 dcCreator(Course, Requester).

The RDF description of the resource may match the bodies of several policy rules, automatically making several policies applicable to the resource. As mentioned earlier, for an access control model based on positive authorizations, the client will be given access if s/he can satisfy any of the relevant policies. If no policies are relevant, then the client does not gain access. If a negotiation succeeds in showing that a client is entitled to access the requested resource, then the negotiation server redirects the client's browser to the correct location for the desired service, as described later.

Because PeerTrust represents policies and credentials as guarded distributed logic programs, the trust negotiation process consists of evaluating an initial logic programming query ("Can this user access this resource?") over a physically distributed logic program (a set of credentials and policies). Because the program is distributed, the help of several parties may be needed to answer a query. From the perspective of a single party, the evaluation process consists of evaluating the query locally to the maximum extent possible, and sending requests to other parties for help in evaluating the aspects of the query that cannot be resolved locally. The "@ issuer" arguments in the logic program tell each party who to ask for help. (When an issuer argument is uninstantiated, one may need to ask a broker for help in finding the relevant parties.)

As with any logic program, a PeerTrust query can be evaluated in many different ways. This flexibility is important, as different parties may prefer different approaches to evaluation. For PeerTrust 1.0, we chose to adopt a *cooperative* model of evaluation. In other words, PeerTrust 1.0 assumes that all parties are using identical trust negotiation software. The constructs used in the first-generation implementation will form the substrate of PeerTrust 2.0, which will adopt an *adversarial* paradigm that gives parties more autonomy in their choice of trust negotiation software and provides additional guarantees of security against attacks. PeerTrust 2.0 will also address the resolution of deadlocks and livelocks, which are not considered in PeerTrust 1.0.

The evaluation algorithm for PeerTrust 1.0 is based on the cooperative distributed computation of a proof tree that, if fully instantiated, will prove that the client is entitled to access the desired resource. Each party uses a queue to keep track of all active proof trees and the expandable subqueries in each of these trees. The proof trees contain all information needed to show that a client is entitled to access a resource, including the policy rules that have been used, the instantiations of variables in those rules, and the credentials themselves. When a party needs help from another party in expanding a proof tree, it sends a traditional logic programming query to the other party. The response to that query includes both the traditional logic programming query answers, as well as proof trees showing that each of the answers to the query really is an answer to the query. (We will refer to this collection of information simply as the "query answer" in this paper.) To provide privacy during negotiation and avoid certain kinds of attacks, queries and query answers must be sent over secure communication channels.

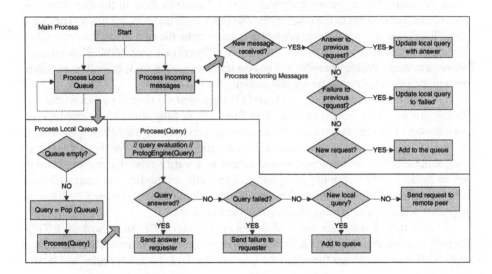

Fig. 2. PeerTrust 1.0 Evaluation Algorithm

The evaluation algorithm used in PeerTrust 1.0 is described in [11]. Briefly, the evaluation algorithm evaluates a logic program using the usual Prolog evaluation strategy, depth-first and left-to-right. PeerTrust 2.0 will include more elaborate evaluation strategies, and, using those, will also allow the different parties to choose from different negotiation strategies as discussed in Yu et al. [18].

Figure 2 shows the high-level modules in the current implementation of PeerTrust, which is identical across all parties. Each party has a queue that contains the queries that it needs to process. Each party has two threads. The first thread reads from the queue and processes one query at a time. Processing involves local query evaluation (using a Prolog inference engine), sending out the answers to newly evaluated queries, and sending new queries to other parties, all depending on whether there are any new subqueries to be processed locally or remotely. Answered queries are deleted from the queue. If we send a query to another party, the query at the requester side is set to status "waiting" (other queries can be processed in the meantime). If the query does not return an answer, this is also forwarded to the requester. The second thread listens for new queries or answers sent by other parties to previously posed queries. It processes these messages and updates the queue accordingly. If a new query is received, we add it to the queue. If an answer is received, the query status (previously "waiting") is updated so the server can continue with its processing (evaluate one of the remaining subgoals).

5   Implementation

PeerTrust Application and Applet The outer layer of PeerTrust's negotiation software is a signed Java application or applet program[4], which implements the queues described in the previous section, parses incoming queries, translates them to the PeerTrust language, and passes them to the inner layer. The inner layer answers queries by reasoning about PeerTrust policy rules and credentials, and returns the answers to the outer layer. The current implementation of the inner layer of PeerTrust uses MINERVA Prolog[5], which provides a Prolog compiler and engine implemented in Java; this offers excellent portability and simplifies software installation.

The first implementation of PeerTrust [11] simulated distributed parties within one Prolog process. The current version, PeerTrust 1.0, is fully distributed, employs secure socket connections between all negotiating parties, and uses Prolog metainterpreters to evaluate queries over sets of policies and credentials. PeerTrust's facilities for communication between parties and access to security related libraries are written in Java. The Prolog meta interpreters, Java code, examples, and traces of their runs on different kinds of examples, as well as a demo application, are available at http://www.learninglab.de/english/projects/peertrust.html.

To import RDF metadata, we modified an open source RDF parser written in SWI-Prolog[6] to work with MINERVA Prolog. The modified parser extracts RDF predicates from XML and transforms them into the internal PeerTrust format for rules and facts.

Public Key Infrastructures and Authentication PeerTrust 1.0 uses Public Key Infrastructure (PKI), specifically X.509 [7], as the framework for how digital credentials are created, distributed, stored and revoked. With an X.509-based approach to trust negotiation, function calls are made at run time to verify the contents of each received credential by determining whether the credential really was signed by its supposed issuer. This may involve looking up the public key of the issuer at a trusted third party. Further, when a policy specifies that the requester must be a specific person mentioned

---

[4] The signature guarantees that the software has not been tampered with.

[5] See http://www.ifcomputer.co.jp/MINERVA/home_en.html.

[6] See http://www.swi.psy.uva.nl/projects/SWI-Prolog/packages/sgml/online.html for the original parser.

in a credential (for example, that Alice must be the police officer whose name appears on the police badge that she has disclosed), then an external function call to an authentication library is needed so that Alice can prove that she is that person, generally by interactively proving that she possesses the private key associated with the public key that in turn is associated with that particular field of the credential.

PeerTrust 1.0 relies on the TLS protocol and its authentication facilities (as implemented in the Java Secure Socket Extension package, JSSE[7]), and uses appropriate signed rules to relate the constants used in the logic programs, e.g., "alice," to Alice's public key. For conciseness, the policies that we present in this paper do not include these details, and are written as though Alice (and every other party) has a single global identity, "alice," and Alice has already convinced E-Learn that she is in fact "alice."

Importing and Using Digitally Signed Rules To guarantee that signed rules are issued by specific parties and that no one tampered with the rule, PeerTrust 1.0 uses digital signatures as defined by the Java Cryptography Architecture and implemented in the java.security.Signature class. Rules are signed with the private key of the issuer, and can be verified with the corresponding public key. PeerTrust 1.0's signature verification is based on MD5 hashes of the policy rules (stored in Prolog plain text format) and RSA signatures.

Authentication When a party submits a credential, in order to verify that it is a party mentioned in the credential, we have to obtain sufficient evidence that the submitter possesses the private key associated with a public key that appears in the credential. Earlier work in trust negotiation proposed an extension to TLS to conduct the negotiation as part of the TLS handshake [6]. The extension leverages the credential ownership mechanisms of TLS to verify credential ownership during trust negotiation.

Another approach to trust negotiation is to establish a standard SSL/TLS session and then conduct the trust negotiation over the secure connection, which is the approach we take in our current prototype. When credential ownership must be verified, there are several possible approaches. If one party disclosed a certificate during the SSL handshake, then any credentials subsequently disclosed during trust negotiation that contain the same public key can rely on the SSL handshake as adequate authentication. Otherwise a proof-of-identity protocol must be introduced over TLS. The protocol must be carefully designed to thwart man-in-the-middle or reflection attacks [12]. PeerTrust 2.0 will support authentication by borrowing from the proof-of-ownership techniques supported in TrustBuilder, the first trust negotiation prototype to support these security features. In TrustBuilder, the negotiation participants push a proof of ownership along with the credentials they disclose.

6 Pulling It All Together: Alice Signs Up to Learn Spanish

The interaction diagram in Figure 3 shows the negotiation details that were sketched in Figure 1, for the case of Alice enrolling in Spanish 101.

---

[7] JSSE can be found at http://java.sun.com/products/jsse/.

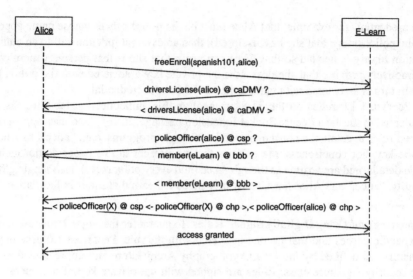

Fig. 3. Negotiation between Alice and E-Learn

After Alice requests free access to the Spanish course offered by E-Learn Associates, E-Learn responds by asking for Alice's driver's license. Alice responds by sending back the appropriate signed proof (shown without its signature in Fig. 3), i.e.,

driversLicense(alice) @ caDMV
signedBy [caDMV].

As the next step, E-Learn asks Alice to prove that she is a California state police officer. Alice can prove this by disclosing her police officer credential signed by CHP plus the rule signed by CSP that says that all CHP officers are CSP officers. The latter rule is freely disclosable, but as shown earlier, Alice's guard on her CHP credential restricts its disclosure to BBB members only. So, rather than disclosing her proof, Alice asks E-Learn about its membership status at the Better Business Bureau. After E-Learn produces a proof of membership signed by the BBB, Alice discloses her CHP credential and CSP's signed rule, and then E-Learn allows Alice to access the Spanish course.

7 Related Work

The Secure Dynamically Distributed Datalog (SD3) trust management system [8] is closely related to PeerTrust. SD3 allows users to specify high level security policies through a policy language. The detailed policy evaluation and certificate verification is handled by SD3. Since the policy language in SD3 is an extension of Datalog, security policies are a set of assumptions and inference rules. SD3 literals include a "site" argument similar to our "Issuer" argument, though this argument cannot be nested, and "Requester" arguments are not possible either, which is appropriate for SD3's target application of domain name service, but restricts SD3's expressiveness too much for our purposes. It also does not have the notion of guards.

The P3P standard [17] focuses on negotiating the disclosure of a user's sensitive private information based on the privacy practices of the server. Trust negotiation generalizes this by basing resource disclosure on any properties of interest that can be represented in credentials. The work on trust negotiation focuses on certified properties of the credential holder, while P3P is based on data submitted by the client that are claims the client makes about itself. Support for both kinds of information is warranted.

Yu et al. [18] have investigated issues relating to autonomy and privacy during trust negotiation. The work on autonomy focuses on allowing each party in a negotiation maximal freedom in choosing what to disclose, from among all possible safe disclosures. Their approach is to predefine a large set of negotiation *strategies*, each of which chooses the set of disclosures in a different way, and prove that each pair of strategies in the set has the property that if Alice and E-Learn independently pick any two strategies from the set, then their negotiation is guaranteed to establish trust if there is any safe sequence of disclosures that leads to the disclosure of the target resource. Yu et al.'s approach to protecting sensitive information in policies is UniPro; PeerTrust supports UniPro's approach to policy protection, through PeerTrust's use of guards in rules.

Recent work in the context of the Semantic Web has focussed on how to describe security requirements in this environment, leading to the KAoS and Rei policy languages [9, 14]. KAoS and Rei investigate the use of ontologies for modeling speech acts, objects, and access types necessary for specifying security policies on the Semantic Web. PeerTrust complements these approaches by targeting trust establishment between strangers and the dynamic exchange of credentials during an iterative trust negotiation process that can be declaratively expressed and implemented based on GDLPs.

Similar to the situated courteous logic programs of [5, 4] that describe agent contracts and business rules, PeerTrust builds upon a logic programming foundation to declaratively represent policy rules and iterative trust establishment. The extensions described in [5, 4] are orthogonal to the ones described in this paper; an interesting addition to PeerTrust's guarded distributed logic programs would be the notion of prioritized rules to explicitly express preferences between different policy rules.

8   Conclusion and Further Work

This paper has tackled the problem of explicit registration needed for accessing protected resources on the Web, where the client has to provide a predetermined set of information to the server. We showed how explicit registration can be avoided on the Semantic Web by placing appropriate semantic annotations on resources that need protection, writing rule-oriented access control policies, and providing facilities for automated trust negotiation. Our PeerTrust language for expressing access control policies is based on guarded distributed logic programs. The Java/Prolog-based PeerTrust 1.0 prototype provides trust negotiation capabilities for servers and clients, with facilities to import and reason about access control policies, digital credentials, and metadata about local resources requiring protection.

PeerTrust 2.0 will include import/export of PeerTrust policies in RuleML format and the use of XML digital signatures (based on the Apache XML Security Suite), as well as interfaces to protect general resources such as Semantic Web services.

References

[1] S. Brands. *Rethinking Public Key Infrastructures and Digital Certificates: Building in Privacy*. The MIT Press, 2000.

[2] J. Camenisch and E. Herreweghen. Design and Implementation of the *Idemix* Anonymous Credential System. In *ACM Conference on Computer and Communication Security*, Washington D.C., Nov. 2002.

[3] D. Eastlake, J. Reagle, and D. Solo. Xml-signature syntax and processing. W3C Recommendation, Feb. 2002.

[4] B. Grosof. Representing e-business rules for the semantic web: Situated courteous logic programs in RuleML. In *Proceedings of the Workshop on Information Technologies and Systems (WITS)*, New Orleans, LA, USA, Dec. 2001.

[5] B. Grosof and T. Poon. SweetDeal: Representing agent contracts with exceptions using XML rules, ontologies, and process descriptions. In *Proceedings of the 12th World Wide Web Conference*, Budapest, Hungary, May 2003.

[6] A. Hess, J. Jacobson, H. Mills, R. Wamsley, K. Seamons, and B. Smith. Advanced Client/Server Authentication in TLS. In *Network and Distributed System Security Symposium*, San Diego, CA, Feb. 2002.

[7] International Telecommunication Union. *Rec. X.509 - Information Technology - Open Systems Interconnection - The Directory: Authentication Framework*, Aug. 1997.

[8] T. Jim. SD3: A Trust Management System With Certified Evaluation. In *IEEE Symposium on Security and Privacy*, Oakland, CA, May 2001.

[9] L. Kagal, T. Finin, and A. Joshi. A policy based approach to security for the semantic web. In *Proceedings of the 2nd International Semantic Web Conference*, Sanibel Island, Florida, USA, Oct. 2003.

[10] J. W. Lloyd. *Foundations of Logic Programming*. Springer, 2nd edition edition, 1987.

[11] W. Nejdl, D. Olmedilla, and M. Winslett. PeerTrust: automated trust negotiation for peers on the semantic web. Technical Report, Oct. 2003.

[12] B. Schneier. *Applied Cryptography, second edition*. John Wiley and Sons. Inc., 1996.

[13] B. Simon, Z. Miklós, W. Nejdl, M. Sintek, and J. Salvachua. Smart space for learning: A mediation infrastructure for learning services. In *Proceedings of the Twelfth International Conference on World Wide Web*, Budapest, Hungary, May 2003.

[14] G. Tonti, J. M. Bradshaw, R. Jeffers, R. Montanari, N. Suri, and A. Uszok. Semantic web languages for policy representation and reasoning: A comparison of KAoS, Rei and Ponder. In *Proceedings of the 2nd International Semantic Web Conference*, Sanibel Island, Florida, USA, Oct. 2003.

[15] J. Trevor and D. Suciu. Dynamically distributed query evaluation. In *Proceedings of the twentieth ACM SIGMOD-SIGACT-SIGART Symposium on Principles of Database Systems*, Santa Barbara, CA, USA, May 2001.

[16] K. Ueda. Guarded horn clauses. In *Logic Programming '85, Proceedings of the 4th Conference*, LNCS 221, pages 168–179, 1986.

[17] W3C, http://www.w3.org/TR/WD-P3P/Overview.html. *Platform for Privacy Preferences (P3P) Specification*.

[18] T. Yu, M. Winslett, and K. Seamons. Supporting Structured Credentials and Sensitive Policies through Interoperable Strategies in Automated Trust Negotiation. *ACM Transactions on Information and System Security*, 6(1), Feb. 2003.

Semantic Annotation Support in the Absence of Consensus

Bertrand Sereno, Victoria Uren, Simon Buckingham Shum, and Enrico Motta

Knowledge Media Institute, The Open University, Milton Keynes MK7 6AA, UK
{b.sereno, v.s.uren, s.buckingham.shum, e.motta}@open.ac.uk

Abstract. We are interested in the annotation of knowledge which does not necessarily require a consensus. Scholarly debate is an example of such a category of knowledge where disagreement and contest are widespread and desirable, and unlike many Semantic Web approaches, we are interested in the capture and the compilation of these conflicting viewpoints and perspectives. The Scholarly Ontologies project provides the underlying formalism to represent this meta-knowledge, and we will look at ways to lighten the burden of its creation. After having described some particularities of this kind of knowledge, we introduce ClaimSpotter, our approach to support its 'capture', based on the elicitation of a number of recommendations which are presented for consideration to our annotators (or analysts), and give some elements of evaluation.

1 Introduction

While the Semantic Web starts to soar, it is nevertheless relying on a precise and exact annotation of the multiple resources it connects. Annotating a document with the actual information it contains is being addressed through a number of projects ([1] for instance), but all of them have in common the desire to translate, in a more formal way, information which is already present in the actual page (*e.g.* the price of an item in an online store or the affiliation of a researcher), and more importantly, which is not going to be contested.

Indeed, such knowledge is to be accepted 'as it is' by the application, the knowledge expert, or the end user. We are on the other hand interested in the annotation of knowledge which does not necessarily fit this description. Consider scholarly discourse: there can be many interpretations about a particular piece of research, and disagreement is an inherent part of it. Unlike many Semantic Web approaches, disagreement and contest are highly desirable here, as we want all the conflicting viewpoints and perspectives to be captured.

Arguments are not necessarily constrained to the field of scholarly debate though, and we can witness their emergence in many domains nowadays, as analysts express their viewpoints about the direction their company should take piece or publish their review of the latest movies, and allow their readers to comment on them, by providing their own arguments for or against.

We are introducing in this article an approach, ClaimSpotter, to assist the formalisation of such knowledge, and we will focus on scholarly debate. We describe

J. Davies et al. (Eds.): ESWS 2004, LNCS 3053, pp. 357–371, 2004.
© Springer-Verlag Berlin Heidelberg 2004

a strategy to provide our annotators (or analysts) with relevant information extracted from the document under consideration. We describe firstly the inherent formalism of this approach and introduce in more detail the characteristics of the knowledge we are interested in, and the difficulties associated with its capture. We will then present the architecture and the components of ClaimSpotter, and report on some preliminary elements of its evaluation. Finally, we will conclude by a discussion and the presentation of some related work.

2   The Scholarly Ontologies Project

The Scholarly Ontologies (or ScholOnto) project [2] aims at implementing a Semantic Web of scholarly documents, enriched with the (possibly contradicting) interpretations made by their readers, who become analysts. These interpretations summarize the core contributions of an article and its connections to related work, which are deemed relevant in the eyes of an analyst. They are formalized as triples (or claims) <node, relation, node>, where the nodes can be chunks of text or (typed) concepts (like a theory, a methodology or an approach), and the relation is an instance of a class defined in a formal ontology of discourse, which organizes the way interpretations can be articulated; figure 1 gives some examples of relations which can be drawn between nodes. Utterances like *In my opinion, the document [3] describes a mechanism to enhance documents with machine understandable information, which supports the notion of Semantic Web, as introduced in [4]*, can be encoded as <enhancing documents with machine understandable information, supports, Semantic Web>, where [enhancing documents with machine understandable information] and [Semantic Web] are two concepts defined by the current analyst and associated to their respective document ([3] and [4]), and connected with an instance of the relation class [example of] (cf. figure 1).

For their annotation, users are encouraged to make links to concepts backed by other documents (*e.g.* [Semantic Web] in the previous example) and to reuse concepts. They may extend the models built by other contributors, adding further claims, or take issue with them if they feel the original interpretation is flawed. Thus, a claim space emerges collaboratively and cumulatively as a complex web of interrelated claims (cf. figure 1), which represents the perspective adopted upon a particular problem by a community of researchers. Representing annotation as claims allows a number of intelligent services, like for instance the tracking of a particular idea and the elicitation of its subsequent reuses [2].

However, we expect that moving from utterances expressed in natural language to a set of ScholOnto claims is not going to be straightforward, as analysts will have to translate their opinions in a claim-compatible form. In the following paragraphs, we will look at the characteristics of this problem.

2.1   Difficulties

We start by emphasising that interpretations are necessarily personal. They contain what has been understood from a document; and they will also be (and

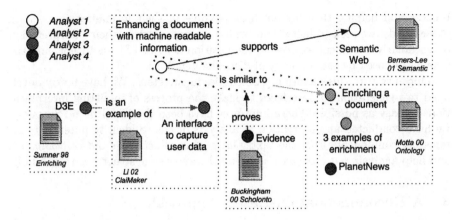

Fig. 1. Multiple interpretations encoded as sets of ScholOnto claims, expressing contributions and connections to and from documents. Analysts 1 and 3 have created two concepts defined in two different documents and linked them with a relation; analyst 2 reuses a concept created by analyst 1 and creates a link to one of his own concept defined in a new document; analyst 4, finally, creates a new concept in his document and connects it to another claim.

should be) influenced by an number of factors upon which we have no control, the most obvious being the analyst's personal research interests. To rephrase it, interpreting a document implies taking a perspective on its contents, and viewing it through a prism which bends it to one's own interests.

Because of the underlying formalisation, yet another difficulty resides in the elicitation of actually *what* to use as nodes and relations, how long (or detailed) they should be and so on, a problem which is likely to be faced by newcomers to any application requiring formalization, as noted by Shipman and McCall [5]:

> "Users are hesitant about formalization because of a fear of prematurely committing to a specific perspective on their tasks; this may be especially true in a collaborative setting, where people must agree on an appropriate formalism."

Formalising means translating, and potentially losing, a part of the original opinion held by an analyst. These opinions will have to fit in the schema of relations, which means leaving aside all the nuances that could not be represented by it. Opinions will appear more clear-cut, and added to their increased visibility, we might witness the rise of a legitimate fear of commitment.

2.2   Our Approach

We are not pretending to solve these problems, but instead seek to provide ways to lighten them, by helping users feeling more confident with the overall process and helping them as much as possible in their formalisation task. In other words, we seek to help them bridge the gap between their interpretation of a scholarly document expressing the position defended by an author, and the schema imposed by the ontology of discourse relations.

Our answer to this daunting problem lies in two steps. We have firstly developed two generations of interfaces to make the process of inputting interpretations as easy as possible. These interfaces have been described in [6]. Secondly, we have conducted an observation of analysts' needs to identify potentially interesting components from the text. Our goal is *to get sense out of documents* and help analysts *put their own sense* on the knowledge structures they build.

3   A Recommendation-Based Approach

To *get sense out of documents*, we are going first of all to look at the task in more detail and get some insight on the underlying formalization process. Although we have to bear in mind that the kind of knowledge we are interested in would be found only implicitly in scholarly documents [7], as it results from a sense-making process, we are investigating the following research question:

> what are the limits of text-based approaches to assist the translation of one's interpretation into a set of formalized knowledge constructs ?

We believe that by combining the Scholarly Ontologies (ScholOnto) repository of claims and some carefully selected components of the document, we can assist the task of claim formulation. We also argue that providing such resources within an interface will substantially improve the overall experience. Our global vision is therefore based on the following aspects: (1) assisting the formulation of claims by proposing an alternative, ScholOnto-aware, view of the document; and (2), wrapping these resources in an environment to actively support the formulation of claims. This enhanced environment would support the first step of a dual-annotation process, composed of:

- an annotation with 'simple' claims, for which machine tools can help by spotting potentially relevant claim elements or valuable areas of the document.
- and in a second step, an annotation with 'complex' claims, which result from a human sense-making process.

3.1   Observation Studies

Our previous use of the expression 'relevant claim elements and areas' was maybe an improper one. We should stress that we are not interested in actually summarising a scholarly document and 'reducing' it to a number of claim-worthy components. Indeed, any particular aspect of it might be of interest to at least one analyst. However, by lifting up some of its components and proposing them to the analyst for further analysis, we hope to reduce the cognitive overload, while still providing her full access to the whole document.

So, how do analysts approach a document, when faced with the task of expressing their interpretation? There has been some literature about how people approach a document (see [8] for instance), and how some components are more likely to be retained for attention than some others. However, we wanted to see if the claim-formulation process had some characteristics of its own. Therefore, we devised an initial experiment. Seven persons (all researchers) were given a short paper (2 pages) and a marker pen. They were asked to answer a number of questions, and to highlight, for each question, the parts (or components) of the document that they were going to use to formulate their answer. The questionnaire was designed to allow an easy mapping into ScholOnto claims, with questions about both the contributions made in the document and its connections to the rest of the literature:

- Q1: what is the problem tackled in this document?
- Q2: how does the work presented try to address this problem?
- Q3: what previous work does it build on?
- Q4: what previous work does it critique?

Our initial hope was to identify a set of components which would be widely used and therefore which could be *recommended* to novice analysts. However, we have witnessed a number of different approaches to answer these questions, as highlighted in the results table (cf. table 1).

Some persons highlighted the keywords and made use of them in their answers. Another person used the title. One person marked an entire section (*Data analysis*) without giving any more detail about which parts of it were going to be used. Some sections were also much more used than some others: most of the participants found their answers to questions Q1 and Q2 in the abstract and the introduction and dismissed nearly completely the remainder of the document. It suggests that the ability to access these components directly would be useful.

A majority of subjects used sentences spread in multiple sections however. Some of these sentences were used consistently to answer the same question: for instance, "*The wealth of digitally stored data available today increases the demand to provide effective tools to retrieve and manage relevant data.*" is used 4 times out of 4 to answer question 1. On the other hand, some sentences, like for instance "*Rather than being a static visualization of data, the interface is self organizing and highly interactive.*" is used three times, and to answer three different questions. It might mean that the questions were not well defined enough, that they were maybe overlapping, resulting in some confusion in our subjects' minds.

In addition to the section they belong to, other aspects or features of a sentence that we could identify include the presence of a citation (especially, of course, to answer questions Q3 and Q4), like "*Latent Semantic Analysis (LSA) [4] has demonstrated improved performance over the traditional vector space techniques.*". Such sentences are considered as describing related work and therefore make valuable elements to consider when interpreting a document's connections to the literature.

	a1	a2	a3	a4	a5	a6	a7
Title							Q1
Abstract							
The paper introduces an approach...	Q2	Q2	Q1	Q2	Q2 Q3	Q1	
Latent Semantic Analysis...	Q2	Q3	Q2		Q2 Q3		Q1
A modified Boltzman...	Q2	Q3	Q3		Q2 Q3		
The approach was implemented...	Q3						
Introduction							
The wealth of digitally stored...	Q1		Q1	Q1	Q1		
Keyword searches over...		Q1		Q1			
...							
Data Analysis						Q3	
Latent Semantic Analysis (LSA) [4]...			Q3	Q3			Q2 Q4
It overcomes...							
We apply LSA to extract...		Q3	Q3	Q2	Q3		
...							
Data Visualisation						Q3	
Rather than being a static...	Q4			Q2			
Data is displayed in an initially...		Q3	Q2 Q3	Q3	Q3	Q2	Q2 Q4
...							
Prototype Systems							
Conclusions							
Initial tests show that the...							
Detailed user studies are in preparation							
First resutls on using an... [3].							
An extended version of this paper...							

Table 1. Partial results of the experimental process, displaying, for each component (section and sentences) of our test document [9] and for each analyst (a1... a7), the question(s) it helped to answer.

Finally, we also noticed that sentences containing an instance of what we assessed to be a highly-subjective verb (like 'to apply', 'to demonstrate', 'to overcome'), which showed a strong level of commitment by the author, were picked. Sentences like *"The paper introduces an approach that organises retrieval results semantically and displays them spatially for browsing."* clearly describe the authors' intention and, therefore, also provide valuable information about the document's contributions and/or the authors' position, which in turn provide valuable material to write a claim.

We understand from this observation that our analysts would have very different needs according to their ways of approaching a document and that no one approach would be suitable for everyone. Among the different elements that we could propose for consideration, the most important to us seems to be the ability to identify areas in the document where an author defends her position and relates it (through praise or criticism) to the literature [10]. What is asked of analysts here is eventually to interpret a document. And interpreting a document also means positioning oneself (by agreeing or disagreeing) with respect to the research carried out and presented in the document, positioning oneself with

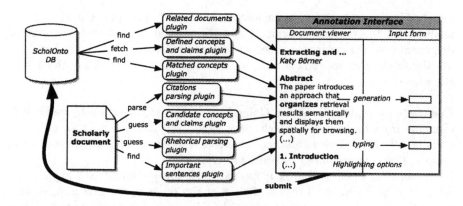

Fig. 2. ClaimSpotter architecture

respect to the arguments being proposed by the authors to defend themselves, and positioning oneself with the citations being made and their underlying motivation [11].

We are proposing a *recommending* approach (similar to the one described in [12]), named ClaimSpotter, based on the recommendation of different components grabbed from the original text and from the ScholOnto repository, leaving it to the analyst to decide whether to use them or not. It is our belief (a belief which has been supported by the observation study) that the ability to identify and recommend such elements from the text would help analysts *get sense out* of the document.

3.2 Recommendors

The first element of the ClaimSpotter architecture is a set of recommendors. We have developed preliminary versions of components to extract the previously mentioned elements from the documents, like references signals or sentences describing the work carried out by the authors. We should stress here that we were not initially interested in the development of up-to-date components; rather, we have developed an architecture for these elements based on a shared XML formalism, which allows them to communicate in a standardized way. More importantly, we should be able to plug into the system more robust and up-to-date components. Figure 2 presents the way these components are organized.

In the following paragraphs, we will describe the initial recommendation components (or plug-ins) we have developed so far.

Defined concepts and claims. Once an annotation is stored in a repository, it becomes an additional source of information for a new analyst. Therefore, we start by extracting as much relevant information as possible from the repository of annotations, including: (i) previously encoded (in any document) concepts matched in the contents of the current document; (ii) concepts defined by fellow analysts for the current document, and (iii) claims defined over the current document (i.e., the claims for which the current document was used as backing). We also fetch concepts and claims made by each of the document's authors, over the whole repository.

Candidate concepts and claims. Going back to the document itself, we identify elements from its contents, which, once again, *might* be used as an object in a claim. We look at elements like acronyms, proper nouns and frequent noun groups. They are presented by order of frequency.

Because our discourse ontology has natural language labels (*uses, applies. . .*), which can be changed to fit the dialect of the domain, we also implement a complementary approach, based on the identifications of areas where these labels appear, augmented with some selected synonyms from the WordNet resource [13]. The ability to recommend a sentence like *"Latent Semantic Analysis as well as (. . .)* **are applied** *for semantic data analysis (. . .)."* (taken from our test document [9]) is potentially very interesting. This should give us a first indication of the particular locations in the document where the author defends her argument. If the analyst shares the point of view of the author, further processing is made on such sentences in order to generate candidate claims like <semantic data analysis, uses/applies, LSA>.

Cited documents. We are also providing a first look at citation contextual parsing, to try to get some insight on the reason motivating each citation. Citation signals (identified manually) are extracted from the text with their context (a couple of sentences before and after the occurrence of the citation). We perform a basic parse of this contextual information (by looking for typical expressions) to guess whether the citation was being supportive or unsupportive. We present these cited documents with their concepts and claims.

Related documents. Additionally, we look at related documents: we extend the notion of relationship between two documents [14], by looking at documents which are related through a claim (in other words, the ones for which at least one analyst has seen a connection). For instance, in figure 1, although documents [4] and [3] are not in a cite/cited relationship, one analyst has related them through a claim. Once such documents are identified, we also fetch their concepts and claims and include them for consideration.

Important areas. We have implemented a simple approach to look at candidate important areas (sentences or sets of sentences) in the document, importance being merely defined here as a combination of the presence of title, abstract and header words in a passage.

Rhetorical parsing The experiment showed the importance of identifying areas containing a description of the author's work. A particularly efficient approach to identify areas where an author defends her position is found in Teufel and

	Category	Confidence
The paper introduces an approach...	OWN	*0.97*
Latent Semantic Analysis...	BACKGROUND	0.67
A modified Boltzman...	BACKGROUND	0.58
The approach was implemented...	OWN	*0.61*

Table 2. Output from the rhetorical parser with the abstract section of our test document [9]. Each sentence is associated with its most likely category. The column on the far right displays the classifier's confidence in the prediction (from 0 (uncertainty) to 1 (certainty)).

Moens' summarizing system [15]. The role played by each sentence (*e.g.* introducing the authors' work, providing background information, or supporting a cited work) is guessed from a number of annotated examples described in terms of an exhaustive range of features including, among many others, the contents of the sentence (presence of meta-discourse constructs [16] or linguistic cues like adverbs and citation signals [10]) and its position in the document.

We experimented with this idea by developing a rhetorical parsing approach, once again to see how it would work. We have focused on a three-category scheme, dealing only with the notion of scientific attribution [17]. We are interested in the sentences describing the research work being carried out by the author (OWN), the work being attributed to external (to the document) authors (OTHER), and the work (or ideas, assumptions, hypotheses, ...) attributed to a research community in general (i.e., where no explicit mention of a person's name is given) (BACKGROUND).

We trained a naïve Bayes classifier with a limited corpus of 230 sentences for the OWN category, 135 sentences for the OTHER category, and 244 sentences for the BACKGROUND category, and a features set composed of the words of each sentence. We nevertheless got some interesting results from the classifier. Table 2 gives an example of rhetorical filtering output. The first sentence, which was heavily used as a basis for annotation in our experiment (cf. table 1) could be lifted up (because of its guessed rhetorical role) and proposed for further consideration.

We also got additional insight in the classifier by looking at its most significant terms (*id est*, the terms which contribute the most to the decision to put a sentence in one category rather than another). We selected the 10 most relevant terms of the classifier, using a χ^2-based filtering computation [18]. Although there was some noise (provided mostly by domain-dependent words, resulting from our annotation corpus), some of the results were rather interesting: the most significant terms for the OWN category included *we, section, paper, our, this* and *describe*; while the terms for the OTHER category were including *[citation]* (a generic expression for each citation in the training documents) and *his*. We can then see that many terms can be used to infer the role played by a sentence, some of them being already captured by the relations labels of the ontology, and some of them having been guessed from our annotated training instances.

3.3   Interface

The second element of our approach is to help analysts put their own sense in documents, which we achieved through the realisation of several input interfaces. We have for instance generated an output filter for the recommendors which allow their integration in ClaiMapper [6], a graphical interface that partially realises the notion of claim space presented earlier (cf. figure 1) and allowing the creation of nodes and their connection into claims.

The ClaimSpotter annotation interface (cf. figure 3) basically acts as a document reader [19] [20], but also allow analysts to access the recommendations *'in situ'*, through different highlighting options in the original text. It is also possible to drag and drop elements from the text into the 'notes panel' on the right side of the interface, allowing one to keep a trace of the elements of interest. Concepts defined by fellow analysts over the current document can also be accessed and reused; claims made by fellow analysts can be duplicated or debated through the creation of additional claims too. Cited and related documents' ScholOnto information (concepts and claims) can be accessed too and imported into the current document.

4   Evaluation

As we have just started our experimental validation, we will simply introduce the course of actions we have taken so far, and present the aspects we want to focus on. To summarise, we are interested in two main aspects: (i) the quality and usefulness of the recommendations, and (ii) their presentation in an interface.

Assessing the recommendations' relevance is going to be a highly subjective matter. Were we interested in capturing a fact in a document, we could check if the correct instance has been recognised, which is impossible here. Because we cannot measure two seminal aspects of annotations, their stability and their reproducibility [21], we have to fall back on some other aspects, like for instance the usefulness of the tool. We could look at the number of claims submitted by the analysts, and try to answer the following questions: *do analysts make more claims when presented with such recommendations?* or *does the presentation of fellows' claims give something for analysts to react against ?* More interestingly, we can also evaluate the intrinsic quality of the claims. If we assume that a claim using a relation 'is evidence for' is stronger than another one using 'is about' (because it bears more commitment for its author), we might want to see how these relations are used over time, and if the presence of the recommended information inspires confidence for the analyst and encourages her to believe that she can make such claims herself. Table 3 lists a number of these aspects that we have started to study.

We started with four analysts, and we should stress immediately that we will not be able to derive any strong conclusions from such a limited sample, but the goal of this section is rather to introduce the experimental process and state a number of observations and comments we have made during the process. These

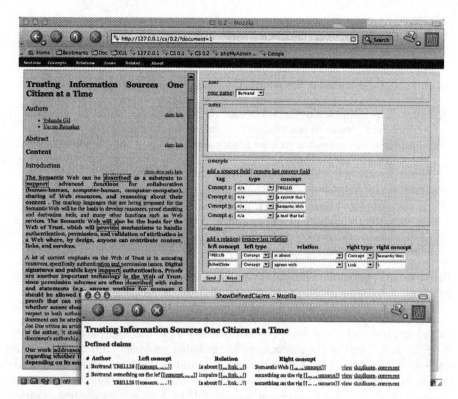

Fig. 3. ClaimSpotter's annotation interface is used to interact with the output of the different recommendors. The main screen separates the workspace into two main areas: a document frame where the view can be customised through highlighting and/or hiding some specific components; and a form frame on the right side where knowledge triples can be created and finally submitted to the ScholOnto database.

four people were given instructions about the task and the Scholarly Ontologies project (two of them were novices, and the remaining two experienced users). They were then asked, for a given paper, to spend a reasonable amount of time annotating it, depending on how much they wanted to say about it. After this time, they were provided with the output from the recommendors and left to decide whether they would like to make changes and add any claims to their interpretation.

To summarise these preliminary results, we could say that there were as many stories as analysts, which is not surprising in itself. For instance, one of our expert users made a lot of use of the recommendations provided, by doubling the number of concepts (from 9 to 16) and claims (from 9 to 18) created. Also of interest was the nature of these newly created claims, 5 out of these 9 being claims about the problem addressed in the document, highlighting maybe the potential usefulness of the tool at spotting OWN statements during the rhetorical parsing step. Our

impact of the recommendors

a)	Do they help her understand what the document is about ?
b)	Do they help her hold an internal model of the document and of its connections to the literature ?
c)	Do they help her break her interpretation into 'acceptable' chunks of text and relations and model it as a structured network of nodes and relations ? [5]
d)	Does the presentation of fellow analysts' claims help her overcome her concerns: commitment, 'what to use as a node ?', 'what did they say ?', ...
e)	Do the recommendations give her additional ideas about the document (which she might not have thought about), additional claims to express, or to counter-argue about a particular point (claim) made by someone else ?

impact of the interface

f)	Is the ability to browse the text, hide some of its components (sections), and to show the recommendations in situation (through highlighting) helping ?
g)	Are the recommendations easily available and accessible ?
h)	Does their presentation make sense ?

Table 3. Evaluation dimensions for our ClaimSpotter interface and the recommendors

second analyst, who was also well acquainted with the approach, also added concepts as a result of the recommendations being provided, and expressed how some of the claims she had made had been found by the tool itself, helping her to (partly) check her results. In that case, the ability to 'understand', as much as possible, the author's argument was useful, by helping the analyst position herself with respect to that argument. Finally, our two novices also had different experiences with the recommendations. One highlighted how it was helping him to go beyond 'simple' claims like <this document, is about, X> and to be able to formulate more in-depth claims. Our last analyst made only limited use of the recommendations, as she was feeling more confident with the document itself, and did not want to be influenced by external factors. Having been able to provide some support (although not easily quantifiable) to three of our four analysts gives us the motivation to perform a more thorough study, including more detailed aspects such as the ones presented in table 3.

5   Related Work

We are expecting these recommendations to support our ontology-supported sense-making annotation process, which is at the boundary of two areas: (1) sense-making approaches typically use free text to capture user stances (*e.g.* [22]); whereas (2) ontology-supported annotation tools aim at capturing knowledge which does not require interpretation and is not likely to be contested.

On the right side of this spectrum, ontology-based annotation tools like CREAM [1] or MnM [23] rely on the presence of the knowledge to capture directly in the document. We have seen that our task, on the contrary, would be more complex, particularly because what we are trying to capture, what we want to "remember, think, clarify and share" [24], will appear only implicitly. For that reason, our approach has tried to build a bridge to assist the formalisation and the population of the ontology as much as possible.

On the left side, the D3E environment, for instance, provides a publishing framework for research papers that allows readers to comment on and to discuss their contents [22]. These comments (and their author) are shown as a threaded discussion, with the ability to initiate several discussions about particular points. An optional categorisation of the nature of the comment can be provided, either 'agreement' or 'disagreement'. Because ScholOnto is based on a formal structure, it is believed that more uses (including intelligent services) could be made of the annotations, admittedly at the cost of formalising this information. TRELLIS is another system which adds formal structure to the semantic annotation by linking statements drawn from web documents using a set of discourse, logical and temporal connectives [25]. TRELLIS is designed to assist analysis of multiple documents in a Web context, implying collaboration between multiple users. However, Tim Chklovski *et alii*. have not reported the use of semantic relations in automatic analysis of data.

We have proposed a bridge between these two worlds by developing and proposing a set of recommendations. They are wrapped up in an approach to assist the formalisation of one's interpretation, which is inspired by the work of Leake *et alii* [12]. This approach proposes methods to assist experts and beginners alike in their task of building and extending a knowledge map by adding concepts and connections (or propositions). Our work shares the same goal, which is to support the construction of a knowledge map (an aspect which is made more obvious when we are using the ClaiMapper interface [6]).

Turning to the recommendors we have implemented, we have already introduced some of the work in rhetorically-directed parsing [10] [26] [15]. Another of our recommendors is based on the parsing of citations. Much work has tried to make use of citation context, for instance, to retrieve documents or to index the contents of the cited document [27] [28]. Additional work has also tried to *understand* the motivation underlying a citation, based on provided set of keywords [26] [29], or on learned lists of contextual words [15]. We expect to bring in some of these works into our architecture and build more and more interesting recommendors.

6   Conclusion

We have presented in this article an approach to support the annotation of a particular class of knowledge which does not necessarily imply a consensus on its interpretation. We have focused on the field of scholarly debate and more precisely on the Scholarly Ontologies project, where multiple and possibly contradicting interpretations can be expressed as a set of knowledge constructs, or claims. Although a claim is, by definition, a statement, and although it does require some elements over which we will not have any control, we have made the hypothesis that the ability to get as much insight as possible into the author's argument would help. Thus we defined an experiment where the subjects were explicitly asked to specify which parts of a document they were more likely to use to answer four questions about the contributions and the connections of a document. Initial conclusions on this experiment have allowed us to characterize the range of elements in the text that these analysts were more likely to consider as a basis to formulate their interpretation as a set of claims. Based on these observations, we hypothesized that a number of components (from claim elements to relevant document areas) would help and we provided mechanisms to extract them from the document, in an attempt to provide support to analysts.

References

[1] Handschuh, S., Staab, S.:   Authoring and Annotation of Web Pages in CREAM. In: Proceedings of the 11th International World Wide Web Conference (WWW2002). (2002)

[2] Buckingham Shum, S., Motta, E., Domingue, J.: ScholOnto : an Ontology-based Digital Library Server for Research Documents and Discourse. International Journal on Digital Libraries **3** (2000) 237–248

[3] Li, G., Uren, V., Motta, E., Buckingham Shum, S., Domingue, J.: ClaiMaker: Weaving a Semantic Web of Research Papers. [30]

[4] Berners-Lee, T., Hendler, J., Lassila, O.: The Semantic Web. The Scientific American (2001) 34–43

[5] Shipman, F.M., McCall, R.: Supporting Knowledge Base Evolution with Incremental Formalization. In: Proceedings of Human Factors in Computing Systems conference. (1994) 285–291

[6] Uren, V., Sereno, B., Buckingham Shum, S., Li, G.: Interfaces for Capturing Interpretations of Research Literature. In: Proceedings of the Distributed and Collective Knowledge Capture Workshop, a part of the Knowledge Capture Conference (KCAP), FL, USA. (2003)

[7] Motta, E., Buckingham Shum, S., Domingue, J.: Ontology-Driven Document Enrichment: Principles, Tools and Applications. International Journal on Human Computer Studies **50** (2000) 1071–1109

[8] Bishop, A.P.: Digital Libraries and Knowledge Disaggregation: the Use of Journal Article Components. In: Proceedings of the 3rd ACM International Conference on Digital Libraries. (1998)

[9] Börner, K.: Extracting and Visualizing Semantic Structures in Retrieval Results for Browsing. In: Proceedings of the 5th ACM International Conference on Digital Libraries. (2000)

[10] Swales, J.M.: Genre Analysis: English in Academic and Research Settings. Cambridge University Press (1990)

[11] Weinstock, M.: Citation Indexes. In: Encyclopedia of Library and Information Science. Volume 5. (1971) 16–40

[12] Leake, D.B., Maguitman, A., Reichherzer, T., Cañas, A., Carvalho, M., Arguedas, M., Brenes, S., Eskridge, T.: Aiding Knowledge Capture by Searching for Extensions of Knowledge Models. In: Proceedings of the International Conference On Knowledge Capture (KCAP), FL, USA. (2003)

[13] Miller, G., Beckwith, R., Fellbaum, C., Gross, D., Miller, K.: Introduction to WordNet : an Online Lexical Database. Technical Report CSL 43, Cognitive Science Laboratory, Princeton University (1993)

[14] Small, H.: Co-citation in the Scientific Literature: a New Measure of the Relationship Between Two Documents. Journal of the American Society for Information Science **24** (1973) 265–269

[15] Teufel, S., Moens, M.: Summarizing Scientific Articles: Experiments with Relevance and Rhetorical Status. Computational Linguistics **28** (2002) 409–445

[16] Hyland, K.: Persuasion and Context: the Pragmatics of Academic Metadiscourse. Journal of Pragmatics **30** (1998) 437–455

[17] Teufel, S., Moens, M.: What's Yours and What's Mine: Determining Intellectual Attribution in Scientific Text. In: Proceedings of the 2000 Joint SIGDAT Conference on Empirical Methods in Natural Language Processing and Very Large Corpora, Hong Kong. (2000)

[18] Yang, Y., Pedersen, J.O.: A Comparative Study of Feature Selection in Text Categorization. In: Proceedings of the 14th International Conference on Machine Learning, Morgan Kaufmann (1997) 412–420

[19] Graham, J.: The Reader's Helper: a Personalized Document Reading Environment. In: Proceedings of the ACM SIGCHI Conference on Human Factors in Computing Systems (CHI '99). (1999)

[20] Boguraev, B., Kennedy, C., Bellamy, R., Brawer, S., Wong, Y.Y., Swartz, J.: Dynamic Presentation of Document Content for Rapid On-line Skimming. In: Proceedings of the AAAI Spring 1998 Symposium on Intelligent Text Summarization. (1998)

[21] Carletta, J.: Assessing Agreement on Classification Tasks: the Kappa Statistic. Computational Linguistics **22** (1996) 249–254

[22] Sumner, T., Buckingham Shum, S.: From Documents to Discourse: Shifting Conceptions of Scholarly Publishing. In: Proceedings of the ACM SIGCHI 1998 Conference on Human Factors in Computing Systems, Association for Computing Machinery (1998)

[23] Vargas-Vera, M., Motta, E., Domingue, J., Lanzoni, M., Stutt, A., Ciravegna, F.: MnM: Ontology Driven Semi-automatic and Automatic Support for Semantic Markup. In: Proceedings of the 13th International Conference on Knowledge Engineering and Management (EKAW 2002). (2002)

[24] Ovsiannikov, I., Arbib, M., McNeill, T.: Annotation Technology. International Journal on Human Computer Studies **50** (1999) 329–362

[25] Gil, Y., Ratnakar, V.: Trusting Information Sources One Citizen at a Time. [30]

[26] Miike, S., Itoh, E., Ono, K., Sumita, K.: A Full-text Retrieval System with a Dynamic Abstract Generation Function. In: Proceedings of the 17th Annual International ACM-SIGIR Conference. (1994) 152–161

[27] Lawrence, S., Bollacker, K., Giles, C.L.: Indexing and Retrieval of Scientific Literature. In: Proceedings of the 8th Conference on Information and Knowledge Management (CIKM'99). (1999) 139–146

[28] Bradshaw, S., Hammond, K.: Automatically Indexing Documents: Content vs. Reference. In: Proceedings of the 6th International Conference on Intelligent User Interfaces, IUI'02, Association for Computing Machinery (2002)

[29] Nanba, H., Okumura, M.: Towards Multi-paper Summarization using Reference Information. In: Proceedings of the IJCAI'99 Conference. (1999) 926–931

[30] Proceedings of the 1st International Semantic Web Conference (ISWC 2002), Sardinia, Italy. (2002)

Uncertainty in Knowledge Provenance

Jingwei Huang and Mark S. Fox

Enterprise Integration Laboratory, University of Toronto
40 St. George Street, Toronto, ON M5S 3G8, Canada
{jingwei,msf}@eil.utoronto.ca

Abstract. Knowledge Provenance is an approach to determining the origin and validity of knowledge/information on the web by means of modeling and maintaining information sources and dependencies, as well as trust structures. This paper constructs an uncertainty-oriented Knowledge Provenance model to address the provenance problem with uncertain truth values and uncertain trust relationships by using information theory and probability theory. This proposed model could be used for both people and web applications to determine the validity of web information in a world where information is uncertain.

1 Introduction

With the widespread use of the World Wide Web and telecommunications making information globally accessible, comes a problem: anyone is able to produce and distribute information on the web; however, the information may be true or false, current or outdated, or even outright lies. The concerns regarding how to determine the validity of web information are receiving more and more attention. Interest in addressing the issue of web information trustworthiness has appeared under the umbrella of the "Web of Trust" which is identified as the top layer of the Semantic Web and is still in its infant stage of development (see [2] slides 26&27).

Knowledge Provenance (hereafter, referred to as **KP**) is proposed in [6] to create an approach to determining the origin and validity of web information by means of modeling and maintaining information sources and dependencies, as well as trust structures. The major questions KP attempts to answer include: Can this information be believed to be true? Who created it? Can its creator be trusted? What does it depend on? Can the information it depends on be believed to be true? This proposed approach could be used to help people and web software agents to determine the validity of web information.

Four levels of KP have been identified, as follows:

- Level 1 (**Static KP**) focuses on provenance of static and certain information;
- Level 2 (**Dynamic KP**) considers how the validity of information may change over time;
- Level 3 (**Uncertainty-oriented KP**) considers information whose validity is inherently uncertain;
- Level 4 (**Judgment-based KP**) focuses on societal processes necessary to support provenance.

J. Davies et al. (Eds.): ESWS 2004, LNCS 3053, pp. 372-387, 2004.

Static KP and Dynamic KP have been studied in [6] and [10] respectively. This paper focuses on uncertainty-oriented KP.

In Levels 1 and 2 of KP, an information creator is either trusted or distrusted, and a proposition is trusted by a provenance requester to have a truth value of "True", "False", or "Unknown". However, it is common to find that a person may trust an information creator to a certain degree rather than completely trust or completely distrust it. Furthermore, a proposition created by the information creator may also be believed to be true to an extent rather than absolutely "True" or "False". The questions here are how to define these types of uncertainty and how to use uncertain values to infer the validity of a proposition.

Level 3, or uncertainty-oriented KP, addresses this type of provenance problem in a world where information is uncertain. This paper focuses on the basic and the most important aspects of uncertainty in provenance, that is, uncertain trust relationships and uncertain truth values. "Degree of trust" (subjective probability) is introduced to represent uncertain trust relationships; "Degree of Certainty", the probability of a proposition to be true, is used to represent uncertain truth values; and an uncertainty-oriented KP model is constructed to infer the degrees of certainty for different types of propositions by applying information theory and probability theory. This uncertainty-oriented KP model can be used to determine the validity of web information with uncertain trust relationships and uncertain truth values.

The content of this paper is organized as follows. Section 2 introduces the related research; section 3 introduces the basic concepts of knowledge provenance; section 4 provides a motivating scenario for developing an uncertainty-oriented KP model; section 5 constructs an uncertainty-oriented KP model by applying probability theory and information theory; section 6 provides an example to use uncertainty-oriented KP for provenance reasoning; and section 7 provides a summary and future research.

2 Related Research

The issue of web information trustworthiness has appeared under the umbrella of the "Web of Trust" that is identified as the top layer of the Semantic Web [2].

No doubt, digital signature and digital certification [18] play important roles in the "Web of Trust". However, they only provide an approach to certifying an individual's identification and information integrity, but they do not determine whether this individual can be trusted. Trustworthiness of the individual is supposed to be evaluated by each web application. For the purpose of secure web access control, Blaze et al [4] first introduced "decentralized trust management" to separate trust management from applications. Since then, trust management has grown from web access control to more general trust concerns in various web applications. PolicyMaker [4] introduced the fundamental concepts of policy, credential, and trust relationship. REFEREE [5] introduced trust protocol; Kinateder and Rothermal [14] developed a distributed reputation system with a trust building model; Herrmann [9] used Jøsang's subjective logic [12] to evaluate the trust values of software components. Twigg [19] applied Jøsang's subjective logic based trust model to support routing decision for P2P and ad hoc networks. Golbeck et al [8] and Richardson et al [16] developed the models of trust propagation in social networks.

Trust management attempts to answer the question of whether an individual is trusted to do a specific action to a specific resource [13]. However, KP needs to answer whether the information created by an individual in a specific field can be believed to be true. Even though KP may be regarded as a specific form of trust management in which the action is understood as telling true information, KP still needs to handle certain problems beyond the current range of trust management. In the context of KP, trust management only considers trust relationships between information users and information creators; however, it does not consider the dependencies among the units of web information. KP needs to consider both of them.

Regarding uncertainty in trust management, uncertainty logics provide various methods for representing and updating uncertainty/belief [3]. Jøsang [12] proposed subjective logic to represent uncertain trust values with an opinion triangle in which an opinion is represented as a triple (b, d, u) where b, d, u denote the degrees of belief, disbelief, and uncertainty respectively, and the sum of them equals to 1. This method can discern the difference between "unknown" and "disbelief", but it requires a degree of uncertainty in addition to degree of belief or disbelief, thus possibly causing some difficulties to users. Gil & Ratnakar [7], as well as Golbeck et al [8] represented uncertain trust relationships by grading with discrete numbers corresponding to a set of linguistic descriptions. The advantages of this method are simple and easy to use. The disadvantages are that users usually have different understandings on the linguistic descriptions, thereby resulting inconsistency in defining and understanding the descriptions of trust relationships. Fuzzy logic has the similar difficulties. Probability is a more direct solution adopted by many researchers to represent uncertain trust relationships, due to its sound theoretical foundation and the common understanding of its meaning. This paper also uses probability to represent both uncertain trust relationships and uncertain truth values, and constructs probability-based provenance reasoning model.

3 What Is Knowledge Provenance?

Knowledge Provenance is an approach to determining the origin and validity of knowledge/information on the web by means of modeling and maintaining information sources and dependencies, as well as trust relationships. This section introduces the basic concepts of KP.

The basic unit of web information to be considered in KP is a "proposition". A proposition, as defined in Proposional Logic, is a declarative sentence that is either true or false. A proposition is the smallest piece of information to which provenance-related attributes may be ascribed. An information creator may define a phrase, a sentence, a paragraph, even a whole document as a proposition. Not only text but also an xml element could be defined as a proposition.

The taxonomy of the propositions in KP is illustrated in figure 1. KP_prop is the most general class of propositions; An Asserted_prop is an assertion that is not dependent on any other propositions; A Dependent_prop is a proposition whose truth is dependent on other propositions; An Equivalent_prop is a copy and its truth value is the same as the proposition it depends on; A Derived_prop is a derived conclusion based on some premises; A Composite_prop could be the "and"/ "or" / "negation" of other proposition(s).

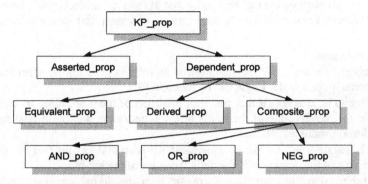

Figure 1. Taxonomy of Propositions in Knowledge Provenance

To use KP, information creators need to annotate web documents with KP metadata to describe the provenance-related attributes, such as who is proposition creator and what is the premise proposition on which this proposition depends. A web browser "plugin" is expected to assist information creators to annotate their web documents; information users (provenance requesters) need to define their personalized trust relationships to tell whom they trust; an online KP software agent (a KP reasoner) will trace KP tags (KP metadata) in web documents across web pages, combining information sources and dependencies, as well as trust relationships, to deduce the origin and validity of tagged information.

3.1 Static Knowledge Provenance

As mentioned earlier, there are 4 levels of KP. Because Level 1, or static KP, is the basis for other levels, this subsection gives a brief introduction to it, before uncertainty-oriented KP is studied. A detailed formal description can be found in [6].

Static KP focuses on static and certain information. Static KP needs to answer the following competency questions that define the requirements for static KP.
- Is this proposition true, false, or unknown?
- Who created this proposition?
- Which knowledge fields does this proposition belong to?
- In these fields, can the information creator be trusted?
- Does the truth of this proposition depend on any other propositions? If so, what?
- What is the digital signature verification status of this proposition?

Terminology
Every Asserted_prop or Derived_prop has an "*assigned truth value*" that is the truth value given by the proposition creator, and every KP_prop has a "*trusted truth value*" that is evaluated and trusted by a specific provenance requester.

In the context of KP, "trust" means that one party believes the information created by another party to be true in a specific field. A trust relationship in KP is defined as a triple (a, c, f) where the provenance requester a "trusts" (directly or indirectly) information creator c in a specific knowledge field f. Here, "trust" means that a believes any proposition created by c to be true in field f; "indirect trust" means that a does not directly know c but trusts c by the media of some references who trust c.

Static KP Axioms

The axioms for static KP are summarized as follows. The formal specification of these axioms in First Order Logic can be found in [6].

- A KP-prop is "trusted", if the creator or publisher of the proposition is "trusted" in a field that covers* one of the fields of the proposition, and the digital signature verification status is "Verified".
- For an asserted, or derived, or equivalent KP-prop that has no creator specified, the creator of the document is the default creator of the KP-prop.
- If a proposition does not have a creator, then the digital signature verification status of the KP-prop is determined by the digital signature verification status of the document.
- The default assigned truth value of a KP-prop is "True". That is, if a proposition creator does not give the truth value of a proposition, the creator implicitly declare the truth value is "True".
- The trusted truth value of an asserted-prop is the same as its assigned truth value, if the asserted-prop is trusted by the provenance requester; otherwise the trusted truth value is "Unknown".
- The trusted truth value of an equivalent-prop is the same as the trusted truth value of the proposition it depends on, if this equivalent-prop is trusted; otherwise the trusted truth value is "Unknown".
- The trusted truth value of a derived-prop is the same as its assigned truth value, if the derived-prop is trusted and the KP-prop it depends on is "True"; otherwise the trusted truth value is "Unknown". Note that it is unnecessary to include everything used to derive the truth value in the dependency.
- The trusted truth value of a negative-prop is the negation of the trusted truth value of the KP-prop it depends on, if the negative-prop is trusted by the provenance requester; otherwise the trusted truth value is "Unknown".
- The trusted truth value of an And-prop is "True" if all the KP-props it depends on are "True"; the trusted truth value of an And-prop is "False" if at least one of the KP-props it depends on is "False"; and the trusted truth value of an And-prop is "Unknown" if at least one of the KP-props it depends on is "Unknown" and none of them is "False".
- The trusted truth value of an Or-prop is "True" if at least one of the KP-props it depends on is "True"; the trusted truth value of an Or-prop is "False" if all of the KP-props it depends on are "False"; and the trusted truth value of an Or-prop is "Unknown" if at least one of the KP-props it depends on is "Unknown" and none of them is "True".

---

* The relations among different knowledge fields could be very complex, which is beyond our topic on KP. We assume that a common recognized taxonomy of knowledge fields is used.

4 Motivating Scenario of Uncertainty-Oriented KP

The following two cases provide a clue for constructing uncertainty-oriented Knowledge Provenance model.

Case 1: Uncertain Truth Values

Consider the proposition found on a web page that "Acupuncture on pain-relief points cuts blood flow to key areas of the brain within seconds" discovered by a scientist in Harvard Medical School. Instead of giving truth value as True (1) or False (0), the proposition creator may assign a numeric truth value between 0 and 1 to the proposition. This numeric truth value represents the degree of confidence (subjective probability) that the creator believes the proposition to be true. When a reader reads this proposition from the web, what numeric truth value does the reader give to this proposition? And how to calculate it? Intuitively, the numeric truth value given by the reader will depend on how much the reader trust the proposition creator and whether this proposition is dependent on other propositions.

Case 2: Uncertain Trust in Information Creators

Further consider the trust relationship between a reader and the proposition creator in the above example. A reader may trust the creator in the field of "Neuroscience" to a certain degree rather than completely "trust" or completely "distrust" it. Here, "trust" means to believe any proposition created by the creator on the topic of "Neuroscience". The degree of trust could be represented with a number in interval [0,1.0] where 1.0 is corresponding to complete trust and 0 is corresponding to complete distrust. For example, the reader trusts the creator to a degree of 0.9, that should be understood as any proposition about "Neuroscience" created by the creator is believed to be true by the reader with a subjective probability of 0.9.

These two cases reveal the following points for building uncertainty-oriented KP:
- The truth value of a proposition may be uncertain. The degree of confidence (subjective probability) for a proposition to be true could be introduced to extend a binary truth value to a numeric truth value.
- A proposition creator may assign a numeric truth value to a proposition, and a numeric trusted truth value of a proposition may be calculated according to how much the provenance requester trusts this proposition and the trusted truth value of the proposition that this proposition depends on.
- Trust relationships may be uncertain. The degree of belief (subjective probability) could be introduced as degree of trust to represent uncertain trust relationships.

5 Uncertainty-Oriented KP Model

This section aims to construct an uncertainty-oriented KP model by applying probability theory and information theory. The following terms defined in static KP need to be used. (Note: in this paper, "KP agent" represents "provenance requester").

assigned_truth_value(x, y): proposition x has truth value of y assigned by its creator.

trusted_truth_value(a,x,y): KP agent *a* trusts that proposition *x* has truth value *y*.
trusted(x,a): proposition *x* is trusted by agent *a*.

Several notations and definitions used in this paper are introduced as follows:
Pr(Y) denotes the probability of event *Y*;
"*TTV$_x$*" denotes *trusted_truth_value(a, x, "True")*, that is, the trusted truth value of proposition *x* (trusted by KP agent *a*) is "True". In our discussion, only one provenance requester (agent *a*) is involved, so, "*a*" does not appear in "*TTV$_x$*". Other notations below are similar.
"*ATV$_x$*" denotes *assigned_truth_value(x, "True")*, i.e., the truth value of proposition *x* assigned by proposition creator is "True";
"*Trusted$_x$*" denotes *trusted(x, a)*, that is, KP agent *a* trusts proposition *x*.
When only one proposition is involved, the footnote representing the proposition can be omitted, e.g., "*TTV$_x$*" is written as "*TTV*".
Consider that a proposition has only two possible determined truth values: "True" or "False", therefore, "$\neg ATV_x$" represents *assigned_truth_value(x, "False")*; and similarly "$\neg Trusted_x$" represents that agent *a* distrust proposition *x*. Note that as a simple method to handle uncertainty, "Unknown" was used to represent a status in which truth value cannot be determined in static KP. In this paper, we will introduce a method to represent uncertain truth value. So, "Unknown" will no longer be used as a truth value.
From the motivating scenario in the last section, we know that proposition creator may assign a numeric truth value to a proposition. This numeric truth value assigned by proposition creator is called **"assigned degree of certainty"** and is used to represent uncertain assigned truth value. It is defined as follows.
Definition 1: the assigned degree of certainty (denoted as *acd*) of a proposition given by the proposition creator is defined as the degree of confidence (subjective probability) of the proposition creator to assign the truth value of "True" to the proposition.

$$acd = Pr(ATV) \qquad (5\text{-}1)$$

Similar to static KP where a proposition has a trusted truth value (trusted by a provenance requester), a proposition may have a numeric trusted truth value. This numeric truth value is called **"degree of certainty"** and is used to represent uncertain trusted truth value. It is defined as follows.
Definition 2: the degree of certainty (denoted as *cd*) of a proposition is defined as the probability in which provenance requester believes the proposition to be "True", that is, the probability of the trusted truth value to be "True".

$$cd = Pr(TTV) \qquad (5\text{-}2)$$

Finally, **"degree of trust"** is defined to represent uncertain trust relationships.
Definition 3: the degree of trust (denoted as *td*) of a proposition is defined as the degree of belief (subjective probability) for the provenance requester to trust this proposition.

$$td = Pr(Trusted) \qquad (5\text{-}3)$$

The degree of trust of a proposition is the maximal degree of trust of the proposition creator in a field that covers (see footnote in section 3.1) one of the fields of the proposition.

In the following, first, the knowledge provenance model for asserted propositions is constructed, and then this same approach is applied to other types of propositions including "Derived", "Equivalent", "AND", "OR", as well as "NEG".

5.1 Uncertain Model of Asserted Propositions

When an asserted proposition has an assigned degree of certainty that represents uncertain assigned truth value given by the proposition creator, what is the degree of certainty (uncertain trusted truth value) of this proposition? According to Axiom 1 of static KP:

$$for\text{-}all\ (a,x,v)$$
$$((type(x,\ "asserted\_prop")\ ^\wedge\ trusted(x,\ a) \qquad\qquad (5\text{-}1\text{-}0)$$
$$^\wedge\ assigned\_truth\_value^{(1)}(x,\ v))$$
$$\text{-}\!>trusted\_truth\_value(a,\ x,\ v))$$

the degree of certainty of an asserted proposition depends on (1) the assigned degree of certainty given by the proposition creator; (2) the degree of trust of the proposition. From the axiom, it is easy to understand, when the degree of trust is 1.0, the degree of certainty is the same as the assigned degree of certainty, as shown in figure 2(a). But when degree of trust is 0 (corresponding to "unknown"), what is the value the degree of certainty? Furthermore, when degree of trust is less than 1.0 and greater than 0, what is the relation among degree of certainty, assigned degree of certainty, and degree of trust?

First, let us consider the case of degree of trust being zero. According to information theory ([17] [15]), "entropy" is used to measure the degree of uncertainty of information, and the entropy of a variable x which has n possible outcomes $v_1, ..., v_n$ is defined as follows.

$$H(x) = -\Sigma_{1,...,n}\ p_i\ log\ p_i \qquad\qquad (5\text{-}1\text{-}1)$$

where, p_i is the probability for the variable to have outcome v_i; for a given n, when all the p_i are equal to $(1/n)$, which is corresponding to the most uncertain situation, entropy $H(x)$ is maximal and equals to $log\ n$; entropy $H(x)$ is minimal and equals to 0 if and only if one p_i is 1.0 and all others are 0, which is corresponding to the most certain situation. In the case of the variable having only two possible outcomes, the entropy becomes:

$$H(x) = -(p\ log\ p + (1-p)\ log\ (1-p)) \qquad\qquad (5\text{-}1\text{-}2)$$

And the entropy has maximal value if and only if $p=0.5$.

In our context of uncertainty-oriented KP, if the degree of trust of an asserted proposition is 0, then no matter what value the assigned degree of certainty is, there is no information for determining the degree of certainty of the proposition, which is corresponding to the most uncertain situation where the entropy should be maximal. As a proposition has only two determined values "True" and "False", in this case, the probability of this proposition to be "True" should be 0.5, that is, the degree of certainty of this proposition should be 0.5. Therefore, based on information theory, we assign 0.5 to the degree of certainty of this asserted proposition when degree of

---

[1] Predicate assigned_truth_value(...) is used to replace the predicate truth_value(...) defined in [fox&huang2003]. They have the same definition.

trust is 0, as shown in figure 2(b). As a matter of fact, this situation of asserted proposition can be extended to other types of propositions. When a proposition is distrusted, no matter what type the proposition is, there is no information available to determine its degree of certainty, so according to information theory the degree of certainty of the proposition should be 0.5. For this reason, we have the following axiom.

Axiom 5-1:

$$for\text{-}all \ (a,x) \ ((type(x, "KP\_prop") \ ^\wedge\neg \ trusted(x, a))$$
$$\text{-}>certainty\_degree(a, x, 0.5)).$$

Now consider the general situation when degree of trust is any real value that ranges from 0 to1.0. Recall axiom 1 of Static KP (formula 5-1-0). We know that the trusted truth value of an asserted-prop is dependent on (1) whether the asserted-prop is trusted by the provenance requester; (2) the assigned truth value given by the proposition creator. By using the sum rule and conditional probability of Probability theory, the probability of the trusted truth value of an asserted proposition to be "True" is calculated with the following formula:

$$Pr(TTV) = Pr(TTV \mid Trusted, ATV) * Pr(Trusted, ATV)$$
$$+ Pr(TTV \mid Trusted, \neg ATV) * Pr(Trusted, \neg ATV) \qquad (5\text{-}1\text{-}3)$$
$$+ Pr(TTV \mid \neg Trusted) * Pr(\neg Trusted)$$

Because whether a proposition is trusted by the provenance requester and what is the assigned truth value of the proposition given by its creator are independent to each other, according to the product rule of probability theory, we have

$$Pr(Trusted, ATV) = Pr(Trusted) * Pr(ATV) \qquad (5\text{-}1\text{-}4)$$
$$Pr(Trusted, \neg ATV) = Pr(Trusted) * Pr(\neg ATV)$$

Apply (5-1-4) and $Pr(\neg Y) = 1 - Pr(Y)$ to (5-1-3),

$$Pr(TTV)$$
$$= Pr(TTV \mid Trusted, ATV) * Pr(ATV) * Pr(Trusted)$$
$$+ Pr(TTV \mid Trusted, \neg ATV) * Pr(Trusted) * (1 - Pr(ATV)) \qquad (5\text{-}1\text{-}5)$$
$$+ Pr(TTV \mid \neg Trusted) * (1 - Pr(Trusted))$$

The conditional probabilities in the above formula can be determined as follows. According to axiom 1 of static KP, when the assigned truth value of a proposition is assigned as "True", and the proposition is trusted, the trusted truth value is "True", that is, the probability in which the trusted truth value is "True" is 1.0, i.e.

$$Pr(TTV \mid Trusted, ATV) = 1.0 \qquad (5\text{-}1\text{-}6)$$

Similarly, when the assigned truth value of a proposition is assigned as "False", and the proposition is trusted, the trusted truth value is "False", that is, the probability in which the trusted truth value is "True" is 0, i.e.

$$Pr(TTV \mid Trusted, \neg ATV) = 0 \qquad (5\text{-}1\text{-}7)$$

According to information theory and our discussion earlier in this section, when a proposition is distrusted, no matter what the assigned degree of certainty given by the proposition creator is, there is no information to determine the degree of certainty, which is corresponding to the most uncertain situation and the "entropy" has maximal value, so the degree of certainty of this proposition should be 0.5, i.e.

$$Pr(TTV| \neg Trusted) = 0.5 \qquad (5\text{-}1\text{-}8)$$

Applying (5-1-6) (5-1-7) (5-1-8) and definitions in (5-1) (5-2) (5-3) to formula (5-1-5), we have

$$cd = td*(acd - 0.5) + 0.5 \qquad (5\text{-}1\text{-}9)$$

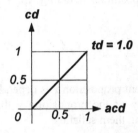

(a) when td=1.0, cd=acd

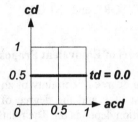

(b) when td=0.0, cd=0.5

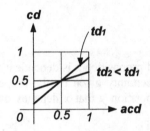

(c) with the decrease of td,
cd close to 0.5

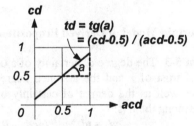

(d) relation among cd,acd,td

$$cd = td*(acd\text{-}0.5) + 0.5$$

cd: degree of certainty (uncertain trusted truth value)
acd: assigned degree of certainty
    (uncertain truth value assigned by proposition creator)
td: degree of trust

Figure 2. Relation among degree of certainty, assigned degree of certainty,
and degree of trust

The relation among the degree of certainty, assigned degree of certainty, and degree of trust of a proposition, revealed by formula (5-1-9), can be illustrated in figure 2. When degree of trust is 1.0 (completely trust), the degree of certainty is the same as the assigned degree of certainty given by the proposition creator (see figure 2 (a)); with the decrease of degree of trust, the degree of certainty is close to 0.5 ("unknown") (see figure 2 (c)); when the degree of trust is 0 (completely distrust), the degree of certainty should be 0.5 ("unknown") (see figure 2 (b)); if assigned degree of certainty $acd = 0.5$, then degree of certainty $cd = 0.5$, no matter what the degree of trust is (see figure 2 (a)(b)(c)).

Theorem 5-1: The degree of certainty of an asserted proposition is dependent on the degree of trust of the proposition and the assigned degree of certainty given by the proposition creator. The relation among them satisfies:

$$cd = td*(acd - 0.5) + 0.5 \qquad (5\text{-}1\text{-}9)$$

The derivation of formula (5-1-9) gives the proof of this theorem.

In the following subsections, the approach used above is applied to set up uncertainty-oriented KP model for other types of propositions including "Equivalent", "Derived", "AND", "OR", and "NEG".

5.2 Uncertain Model of Equivalent Propositions

Theorem 5-2: The degree of certainty of an equivalent proposition x is dependent on the degree of trust of x and the degree of certainty of the proposition y that this equivalent proposition depends on. The relation among them satisfies:

$$cd_x = td_x * (cd_y - 0.5) + 0.5 \qquad (5\text{-}2\text{-}1)$$

The proof of this theorem can be found in [11].

5.3 Uncertain Model of Derived Propositions

Theorem 5-3: The degree of certainty of a derived proposition x is dependent on the degree of trust of x and the assigned degree of certainty given by the proposition creator as well as the degree of certainty of proposition y that x depends on. The relation among them is:

$$cd_x = td_x*cd_y*(acd_x - 0.5) + 0.5 \qquad (5\text{-}3\text{-}1)$$

The proof of this theorem is similar to theorem 5-1 and can be found in [11].

This model has the similar properties of the uncertainty model for asserted propositions (formula (5-1-9). When degree of trust is 1.0 (completely trusted) and the degree of certainty of premise y is 1.0 ("True"), the degree of certainty of derived proposition x is the same as the assigned degree of certainty given by its creator; if degree of trust is 0 (completely distrusted) or the degree of certainty of premise y is 0 ("False") or the assigned degree of certainty of derived proposition x given by its creator is 0.5 ("Unknown"), the degree of certainty of proposition x will be 0.5 ("Unknown"); with the decrease of degree of trust of x and degree of certainty of y, the degree of certainty of derived proposition x is close to 0.5.

5.4 Uncertain Model of Composite Propositions

As the premise of a derived proposition may be a composite ("AND"/ "OR"/ "NEG") proposition, uncertainty-oriented KP needs to answer how to calculate the degree of certainty of a composite proposition.

"AND" Propositions

Consider "AND" proposition $z = (x \wedge y)$. According to product rule of probability theory:

$$Pr(A \cap B) = Pr(A|B)*Pr(B),$$

or

$$Pr(A \cap B) = Pr(B|A)*Pr(A),$$

and if A is conditionally independent to B (i.e., $Pr(B|A) = Pr(B)$), then

$$Pr(A \cap B) = Pr(B)*Pr(A)$$

In order to calculate $Pr(x \wedge y)$, the relation between x and y, either the statement of x and y being conditional independent or the conditional probability $Pr(x|y)$ (or $Pr(y|x)$) needs to be provided by the proposition creator. In the context of KP, this claimed relation between x and y needs to be trusted by provenance requester. So, in KP, that "AND" proposition $z = (x \wedge y)$ is trusted should be understood as the relation between x and y (conditional probability) is trusted. The degree of certainty of z, TTV_z, is calculated as follows.

$$Pr(TTV_z) = Pr(TTV_z|Trusted_z, (x \wedge y))*Pr(Trusted_z, (x \wedge y)) \quad (5\text{-}4\text{-}1)$$
$$+ Pr(TTV_z|Trusted_z, \neg (x \wedge y))*Pr(Trusted_z, \neg (x \wedge y))$$
$$+ Pr(TTV_z| \neg Trusted_z)*Pr(\neg Trusted_z)$$

It is easy to understand that if proposition z is trusted and $x \wedge y$ is true, then z is true; if the proposition z is trusted but $x \wedge y$ is false, then z is false; and if proposition z is distrusted, then there is no information to determine the truth of z, that is, if the conditional probability used to calculate $Pr(x \wedge y)$ is distrusted, then the correctness of the computing result of $Pr(x \wedge y)$ is unknown. So we have:

$$Pr(TTV_z|Trusted_z, (x \wedge y)) = 1.0$$
$$Pr(TTV_z|Trusted_z, \neg (x \wedge y)) = 0 \quad (5\text{-}4\text{-}2)$$
$$Pr(TTV_z| \neg Trusted_z) = 0.5$$

In addition, whether proposition z is trusted is conditionally independent to whether $x \wedge y$ is true. Therefore,

$$Pr(Trusted_z, (x \wedge y)) = Pr(Trusted_z)* Pr(x \wedge y) \quad (5\text{-}4\text{-}3)$$

Furthermore, $cd_y = Pr(y)$, and $cd_x = Pr(x)$, so, we have

$$Pr(x \wedge y) = Pr(x|y)* Pr(y) = Pr(x|y)* cd_y \quad (5\text{-}4\text{-}4)$$

or

$$Pr(x \wedge y) = Pr(y|x)* Pr(x) = Pr(y|x)* cd_x$$

Applying (5-4-2) to (5-4-4) and definition (5-2) (5-3) to (5-4-1), we have the formula to calculate the degree of certainty of "AND" proposition, $z = x \wedge y$, as follows.

Axiom 5-3: if $z = (x \wedge y)$, then

$$cd_z = td_z*(Pr(x|y)* cd_y - 0.5) + 0.5 \quad (5\text{-}4\text{-}5)$$

or

$$cd_z = td_z*(Pr(y|x)*cd_x - 0.5) + 0.5$$

"OR" Propositions

Consider "OR" proposition $z = (x \vee y)$. Because

$$Pr(x \vee y) = Pr(x) + Pr(y) - Pr(x \wedge y) \quad (5\text{-}4\text{-}6)$$

and $Pr(x \wedge y)$ appears in $Pr(x \vee y)$, the relation (conditional probability) between proposition x and y need to be specified and need to be trusted also.

Similar to uncertainty-oriented KP model of "AND" propositions, the degree of certainty of "OR" proposition z is calculated as follows, the proof is omitted.

Axiom 5-4: if $z = (x \vee y)$, then

$$cd_z = td_z*(cd_x + cd_y - Pr(x|y)*cd_y - 0.5) + 0.5 \qquad (5\text{-}4\text{-}10)$$

or

$$cd_z = td_z*(cd_x + cd_y - Pr(y|x)*cd_x - 0.5) + 0.5$$

"NEG" Propositions

Uncertainty-oriented KP model of "NEG" proposition is very simple. Consider "NEG" proposition $x = \neg y$. According to probability theory,

$$Pr(\neg y) = 1 - Pr(y)$$

So, we have

Axiom 5-5: if $x = \neg y$, then

$$cd_x = 1 - cd_y \qquad (5\text{-}4\text{-}11)$$

6 Example

An example to illustrate how to use uncertainty-oriented KP model is given as follows. Some basic concepts of KP involved can be found in section 3.

A reader finds a web page containing the following propositions: (1) asserted proposition (Asserted_prop: "New finding"): "Acupuncture on pain-relief points cuts blood flow to key areas of the brain within seconds"; (2) equivalent proposition (Equivalent_prop: "Brain areas"): "The specific brain areas affected are involved in mood, pain and cravings", which is the copy of another proposition in another web document; (3) derived proposition (Derived_prop: "Implications of finding"): "This finding could help explain why some studies have found acupuncture helpful in treating depression, eating problems, addictions and pain." Assume that this web page is annotated with kp metadata.

The following is an example of annotating one proposition. Other propositions could be annotated in similar way. An example of annotating a whole web document could be found in [6](section 5).

```
<kp:Derived_prop rdf:id="Implications_of_finding"
        is_dependent_on="#Conditions"
        creator ="Bruce Rosen"
        degree_of_certainty = 0.9
        in_field ="Neuroscience"
>
This finding could help explain why some studies have
found acupuncture helpful in treating depression, eating
problems, addictions and pain.
    </kp:Derived_prop>
```

Figure 3 illustrates the major kp metadata associated with each proposition, the dependencies of the propositions, and the provenance reasoning process using uncertainty-oriented KP model. To use KP, the reader needs define his/her trust relationships (shown as "trust_degree" boxes in figure 3). Certainly, a KP agent (KP reasoner) can provide a set of default trust relationships to certain common used information sources. A KP agent will conduct provenance reasoning as requested from the reader. According to theorem 5-3, in order to calculate the degree of certainty of derived proposition "Implications of finding", KP agent needs to obtain the degree of trust of this proposition, the assigned degree of certainty of the proposition, and the degree of certainty of its premise -- the AND_prop "condition1". The latter leads to calculating the degrees of certainty of Equivalent_prop "Brain areas" and Asserted_prop "New finding". And the calculation of the degree of certainty of Equivalent_prop "Brain areas" leads to calculating the degree of certainty of Asserted_prop "Brain_regions". So, the calculation process can be outlined in 5 steps as shown in figure 3 in which each step is represented with a box marked by step number and the formula used. For example, step (1) calculating the degree of certainty of asserted proposition "New finding" by using formula (5-1-9).

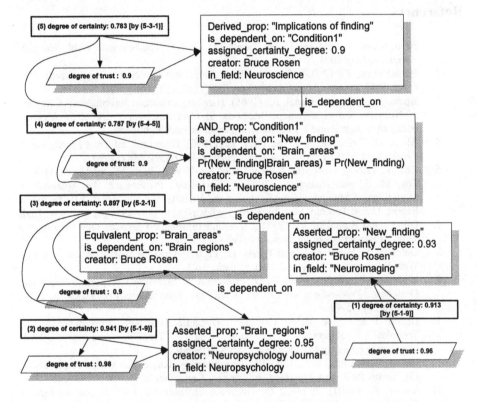

Figure 3. Example of provenance reasoning using Uncertainty-oriented KP

7 Summary

In this paper, we have proposed an uncertainty-oriented KP model addressing the provenance problem with uncertain trust relationships and uncertain truth values.

"Degree of trust" (subjective probability) has been introduced to represent uncertain trust relationships; "degree of certainty", the probability of a proposition to be true, has been used to represent uncertain truth values; and an uncertainty-oriented KP model has been constructed to infer the degree of certainty for different types of propositions by using information theory and probability theory. This uncertainty-oriented KP model could be used to determine the validity of web information in a world where information is uncertain.

As mentioned in introduction section, Knowledge Provenance comprises of four levels: Static, Dynamic, Uncertainty-oriented, and Judgment-based KP. To continue our work, we will develop judgment-based KP that focuses on societal processes necessary to support knowledge provenance.

This research was supported, in part, by Bell University Laboratory.

References

1. Berners-Lee, T., Hendler, J., and Lassila, O., (2001), "The Semantic Web", *Scientific American*, May 2001.
2. Berners-Lee, T., (2003), Semantic Web Status and Direction, *Int. Semantic Web Conf. 2003*, keynote. http://www.w3.org/2003/Talks/1023-iswc-tbl/
3. Bhatnager, R.K., and Kanal, R., (1986), Handling Uncertain Information: A Review of Numeric and Non-numeric Methods, in *Uncertainty in Artificial Intelligence*, edited by L. Kanal and J. F. Lemmer, Elsevier Science Publishers.
4. Blaze, M., Feigenbaum, J. and Lacy, J., (1996), Decentralized Trust Management, *Proceedings of IEEE Conference on Security and Privacy*, May, 1996.
5. Chu, Y., (1997), Trust Management for the World Wide Web, Master Thesis, MIT.
6. Fox, M. S., and Huang, J., (2003), "Knowledge Provenance: An Approach to Modeling and Maintaining the Evolution and Validity of Knowledge", EIL Technical Report, Uni.of Toronto, May 2003, http://www.eil.utoronto.ca/km/papers/fox-kp1.pdf
7. Gil, Y. and Ratnakar, V., (2002), "Trusting Information Sources One Citizen at a Time", *Proceedings of Int. Semantic Web Conf.2002*.
8. Golbeck, J., Hendler, J., and Parsia, B., (2002), Trust Networks on the Semantic Web, University of Maryland, College Park.
9. Herrmann P., (2003), Trust-Based Protection of Software Component Users and Designers, *Proceedings of 1st Int. Conf. On Trust Management, LNCS 2692*, Springer, PP.75-90.
10. Huang, J. and Fox, M. S., (2003), " Dynamic Knowledge Provenance ", EIL Technical Report, University of Toronto, June 2003. http://www.eil.utoronto.ca/km/papers/kp2-TR03.pdf
11. Huang, J., and Fox, M.S., (2003B), "Uncertainty-oriented Knowledge Provenance", EIL Technical Report, University of Toronto, September 2003.
12. Jøsang, A., (2001), A Logic for Uncertain Probabilities, *International Journal of Uncertainty, Fuzziness, and Knowledge-Based Systems*, V.9, N.3, 2001, PP.279-311.
13. Khare, R., and Rifkin, A., (1997), "Weaving and Web of Trust", *World Wide Web Journal*, Vol. 2, No. 3, pp. 77-112.
14. Kinateder, M. and Rothermel K., (2003), Architecture and Algorithms for a Distributed Reputation System, *Proceedings of 1st Int. Conf. On Trust Management, LNCS 2692*, Springer, PP.1-16.
15. MacKay, D.J.C. (2003), *Information Theory, Inference, and Learning Algorithm*, Cambridge University Press, 2003.

16. Richardson, M., Agrawal, R., and Domingos, P., (2003), Trust Management for the Semantic Web, *Proc. of Int. Semantic Web Conf. 2003*, PP.351-368.
17. Shannon, C.E. (1948), A Mathematical Theory of Communication, *The Bell System Technical Journal*, Vol.27, pp379-423, 623-656, October, 1948.
18. Simon, E., Madsen, P., Adams, C., (2001), An Introduction to XML Digital Signatures, http://www.xml.com/pub/a/2001/08/08/xmldsig.html
19. Twigg A., (2003), A Subjective Approach to Routing in P2P and Ad Hoc Networks, *Proc. of 1st Int. Conf. On Trust Management, LNCS 2692*, Springer, PP.225-238.

Collaborative Semantic Web Browsing with Magpie

John Domingue, Martin Dzbor, and Enrico Motta

Knowledge Media Institute, The Open University, Milton Keynes, UK
{J.B.Domingue, M.Dzbor, E.Motta}@open.ac.uk

Abstract. Web browsing is often a collaborative activity. Users involved in a joint information gathering exercise will wish to share knowledge about the web pages visited and the contents found. Magpie is a suite of tools supporting the interpretation of web pages and semantically enriched web browsing. By automatically associating an ontology-based semantic layer to web resources, Magpie allows relevant services to be invoked as well as remotely triggered within a standard web browser. In this paper we describe how Magpie trigger services can provide semantic support to collaborative browsing activities.

1   Introduction

Magpie is a tool supporting the *interpretation of web pages*, acting as a complementary knowledge source, which a user can call upon to gain instantaneous access to the background knowledge relevant to a web resource. Magpie automatically associates a *semantic layer* to a web resource, rather than relying on a manual annotation [8]. Semantic layering relies on the availability of an *ontology* [12] – an explicit, declarative representation of a domain. Ontologies help to assign meaning with the information on a web page, and on the basis of the identified meaning, to offer the user several functionalities based upon semantic services.

The semantic layers produced using the Magpie framework transform an arbitrary web document into a semantically (or contextually) *enriched document*. In previous projects we have developed methodologies for enriching documents with both informal and formal annotations to support organizational learning [19, 21]. Our Enrich methodology was successful applied in domains as diverse domains as aerospace design engineering and widening participation in education. Magpie extends the Enrich framework through the on-the-fly semantic layering of web documents [6].

In earlier papers [6-8] we gave an overview of the Magpie framework and design principles and outlined Magpie's basic functionalities. A key principle underlying the design of Magpie is that the ontology provides an explicit interpretative viewpoint over the web resources. Since different readers of a particular web resource (e.g. a personal home page) will most likely have different degrees of familiarity with the information shown in a web page and with the relevant background domain, they will necessarily require different levels of sense-making support. Hence, the semantic layering and consequently support for semantic browsing using the Magpie framework needs to be sufficiently *flexible* and *extendible* to allow for the different users' needs.

J. Davies et al. (Eds.): ESWS 2004, LNCS 3053, pp. 388-401, 2004.

In this paper we discuss how Magpie can support collaborative semantic web browsing. More specifically, how users can be informed when a colleague finds information in a web page which is relevant to the current user's context. Hence, the framework that has been designed to support an individual user in interpreting web resources can also facilitate community-based knowledge and experience sharing. The economic benefits of 'group-wide interpretation' are gained by providing faster access to the relevant expertise and experience related to the semantically relevant topics or issues *within the group* or community.

The rest of this paper is structured as follows. Section 2 describes a small scenario where Magpie supports collaborative web browsing. We then describe the overall architecture of Magpie in some detail. A review of related work in section 4 is followed by some conclusions.

2   A Scenario of Magpie in Use

Imagine commercial company that specializes in finding interesting technologies and exploiting them for profit. Two members of the company, Gill and Martin, are browsing the web site of the Knowledge Media Institute (KMi) with a goal of finding potentially interesting projects.

Gill brings up her web browser and selects a particular ontology, in this case the AKT Reference Ontology[1], to act as a point of view for browsing. Gill then subscribes to a number of collectors – a specific type of Magpie trigger service. The interface for trigger service subscription is shown in Fig. 1. Using the interface Gill subscribes to the People, Project and People's Projects collectors. Gill also uses the Magpie preferences dialog to indicate that Martin is a co-worker involved in a shared information gathering task.

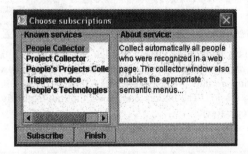

Fig. 1. A screen snapshot of the Magpie interface for subscribing to services

Gill first looks at the home page for the Alice project, shown in Fig. 2, and uses the Magpie toolbar to highlight key ontological concepts on the page; shown in close up in Fig. 3. As can be seen, Magpie preserves the appearance of the page, and offers a toolbar-based user interface to highlight concepts of a particular type. The buttons in the Magpie toolbar are ontology dependent; i.e. they correspond to the selected classes from the specific ontology the user selected. For the AKT reference ontology

---

[1] http://www.aktors.org/publications/ontology/

the key concepts are research area, project, person and organisation. Selecting a button in the toolbar highlights the associated concepts within the page. Thus, the toolbar embodies our rationale to base the interpretation of a web resource on a particular viewpoint. Because the viewpoint to be taken will depend on the specific user's task we leave the choice of ontology up to him or her.

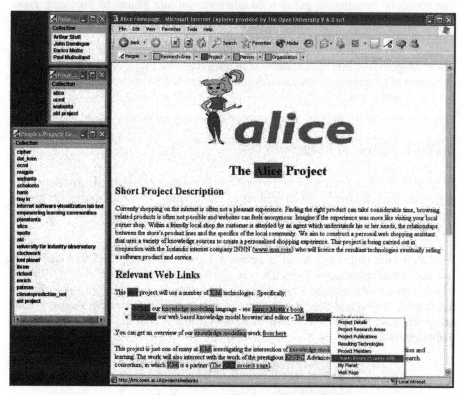

Fig. 2. The Alice project home page viewed through Magpie. Known *people, organizations, projects* and *research areas* are highlighted using the Magpie toolbar (shown in close-up in Fig. 3). On the left-hand side are three Magpie collectors – the top two log the people and projects found in the browsing session. The bottom one shows the (not explicitly mentioned) projects associated with the people found.

Fig. 3. A close-up view of the Magpie toolbar. Each item in the toolbar corresponds to a particular concept in the selected ontology. Selecting a button in the toolbar highlights the associated terms within the current web page.

In Magpie, each annotated and highlighted concept becomes a 'hotspot' that allows the user to request a menu containing relevant functionalities for that item. In Fig. 2, the contextual right-click on the 'WebOnto' concept reveals a menu of semantic services for projects. The choices generally depend on the ontological classification of a particular concept within the selected ontology. Some Magpie functionalities are straightforward (e.g. 'Project Details'). Others are more sophisticated enabling the user to explore the semantic neighbourhood of a particular concept, and to navigate to the web resources that are semantically related but not explicitly linked to. For example, the service 'Shares Research Interests With' responds with a list of projects having common research interests with the WebOnto project. The list as shown in Fig. 4 cannot be found anywhere on the KMi web site. However, the interpretative viewpoint of the selected ontology gives the reader an insider's view. Additionally, the answer to a semantic query, which is a web resource, can be further browsed semantically. Thus, Magpie merges the independent mechanisms for recognizing semantic relevance and browsing web resources.

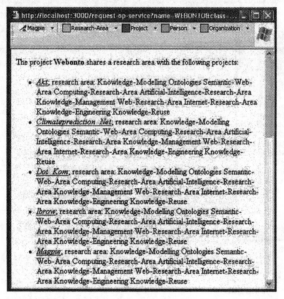

Fig. 4. Results of the semantic query 'Shares Research Areas With' invoked for the 'WebOnto' project by the semantic menu action depicted in Fig. 2. Each bullet shows the name of a project followed by a list of overlapping research areas.

The left-hand side of Fig. 2 shows three Magpie collectors. These are automatically filled by Magpie trigger services, which use a semantic log knowledge base (KB) that keeps a record of a browsing session and the entities found on the web pages. Collectors show a semantically filtered view of the semantic log providing a structured record of user's browsing history. Moreover, all visited pages are semantically annotated with a specific ontology rather than merely indexed by keywords. The top two collectors in Fig. 2 record the people and projects recognized on this and previously visited web pages thus serving as a type of semantic bookmark.

The bottom collector lists those projects that are relevant to the discovered people but were not mentioned explicitly on any visited page. This collector represents what we term a semantic neighbourhood. Items within a Magpie collectors offer the same functionalities as hotspots on a web page; it is possible to right-click them and request appropriate semantic services. Other types of trigger services are discussed in [7].

Now Gill moves to the KMi Stadium project page. As she does a Magpie Contact window pops up. This notifies Gill that her colleague, Martin, was recently, looking at a related technology, Lyceum, which has the same author and owner. The (green) icon to the right of Martin's picture indicates that he is currently online within an Jabber-based instant messaging client, BuddySpace [9], developed in our lab. Selecting the 'Contact' button in the window brings up an instant messaging dialog window.

Note that the above interaction relies on the existence an ontology which specifies the relationships between project, technologies, organisations and people and which has been populated by the appropriate entities.

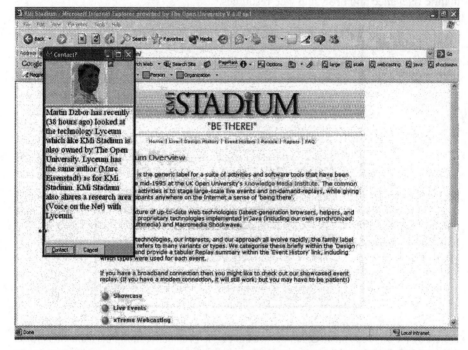

Fig. 5. A screen snapshot showing the collaborative browsing support provided by Magpie. The 'Contact?' window shows that a colleague, Martin, has been browsing a similar page.

3   The Magpie Architecture

In the introduction we stated that a key design principle underlying Magpie was to allow the users who normally have little knowledge of a particular discourse, to browse web resources and take the full advantage of relevant contextual knowledge. This broad aim was elaborated into a set of design requirements we believe are important for designing user-oriented and user-driven applications for browsing and understanding the semantic web. The full list of requirements is given in [8]; here we highlight the key points:

- Magpie should offer semantic web functionality with near-zero additional costs for the users;

- Magpie should provide access to semantic information using a 'one-click' (or less) principle.

We will now describe how the Magpie architecture supports the interactions described in the scenario. The architecture uses an infrastructure that we have developed, called IRS-II [20], which supports the publishing and invocation of semantic services. A key feature of IRS-II is that it is based on the UPML framework [11] and therefore differentiates between tasks, problem solving methods (generic reasoners) and domain models. The split between tasks and problem solving methods enables us to clearly separate the activities of implementing semantic services from making them available in a fashion where they can be easily invoked with little or no overhead to the end-user. We will not say any more about the IRS-II in this paper but will instead focus on the aspects of the architecture related to collaborative web browsing.

3.1   An Overview of the Magpie Architecture

The Magpie architecture (shown in Fig. 6) is essentially that of a mediator. The mediation occurs between the user browsing web pages and the suite of remotely accessible semantic services. Some services are from the 'user-requested' category, while others are 'triggered'. This difference will become obvious in the following sections.

The Magpie architecture consists of a *Service Provider* and a *Service Recipient*. This emphasizes the fact that the document source (i.e. web server) and the source of a semantic service may not be on the same machine. Similarly, a concept of 'client' suggests that an active role is always on the side of a browser with a server passively serving requested data. In the case of our trigger services, it is the server component that drives the conversation to provide information that is semantically relevant but not explicitly requested by the user.

Currently, the Service Provider component of Magpie is built around a suite of tools providing access to a library of domain ontologies, populated KBs, 'handcrafted' semantic services, and a semantic log KB. This library accepts ontologies represented in RDF(S) [1], DAML+OIL [5], and OCML [18] (the latter being the internal representation we use for reasoning). An OWL [23] import/export mechanism is nearing completion. Most of the ontologies relate to a particular domain of discourse (e.g. academic organizations or design).

3.2   Service Recipient Components

The Magpie components on the service recipient ('client') side comprise the Magpie Browser Extension (of Internet Explorer), the Magpie Service Dispatcher, and Trigger Service Interfaces. The Magpie Browser Extension is embedded in the browser as a plug-in and controls the interaction with Magpie facilities. The plug-in preserves as much as possible the appearance of a web page before semantic annotation through the application of semantic layers. Its user interface components visualize entities found in a web page, and enables users to interact with the semantic services through contextual menus.

The Browser Extension also contains a simple parser that annotates the entities from a particular ontology on a web page using an ontology-derived lexicon. Although not as complete as some grammatical named-entity recognition (NER) techniques, the lexicon-based parsing is extremely fast, and thus satisfies our near-zero overhead constraint. While lexicon-based NER is fast, its major drawback is precision and completeness. We are currently working on merging a lexicon-based and a grammar-based NER into the core Magpie plug-in. However, in order to avoid adding ever more complex NER techniques to the browser extension, we also experiment with implementing advanced NER algorithms as (semantic web) services a user would be able to subscribe to.

When evaluated using standard language engineering measures such as precision of recognition and recall, Magpie exhibited a high degree of precision within the domain. When tested outside of the intended domain, the precision fell dramatically, due to the brittleness of the fast lexicon-based NER techniques that the plug-in uses. In our tests, we used Magpie and benchmarked it against GATE [4] and a pattern-based NER tool called eSpotter developed in-house. The NER technique used in Magpie outperformed those in the benchmarked competitors in terms of timing and almost 100% precision of recognition whilst within the tested domain. This satisfies our main criterion to provide NER-based functionality with zero time overhead. The obvious drawback is the quick degradation of recognition performance when leaving the domain for which the lexicon was created.

The *Magpie Service Dispatcher* acts as a dedicated semantic proxy for the user's web browser. It manages the communication between the Browser Extension and the appropriate dispatcher of the service providers. The Magpie Dispatcher delivers user's requests and the provider's responses using customized XML messages. *Collectors* are one form of Magpie Trigger Service Interface that display data pushed by the applicable trigger services.

The Magpie semantic layer comprises customized <SPAN...> tags enclosing named entities linking them with the relevant instances and classes within the chosen ontology. This approach to visualizing semantic layers gives users the control of what types of entities are visible at any time. This improves navigation through the (semantically enriched) content, and avoids overwhelming the users with too much information, which is a problem with some link-recommending systems (see the discussion in [17]). When the entities are recognized, the Dispatcher passes them to a *Central Magpie Service*, which asserts the entities as facts into the *Semantic Log KB*. The purpose of and mechanisms within semantic logging are addressed later.

In addition to highlighting entities and offering semantic service menus, the Magpie infrastructure supports *Trigger Service Interfaces*. These comprise various summarizers, recommenders or collectors. Unlike contextual, menu-based services, the user does not explicitly request a trigger service but subscribes to it (see Fig. 1). When a trigger service is activated information is pushed from the service provider to reflect particular patterns in the log of recognized entities. Nonetheless, a user might not be interested in receiving messages from all trigger service providers.

Collaborative browsing is supported via the trigger service interfaces. The messages are instigated by the browsing activity of registered collaborators.

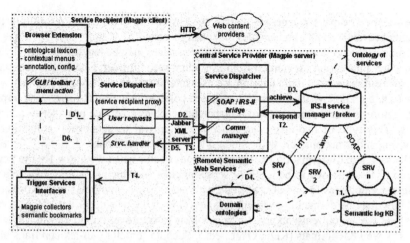

Fig. 6. Schematic architecture of the Magpie framework.

3.3 The Magpie Service Dispatcher

The role of the Service Dispatcher is to handle all interactions between the user, the Magpie-enabled browser and the respective Magpie service providers. In principle, the dispatcher is an alternative to the GET/POST requests available in standard HTTP protocols. Although Magpie supports HTTP requests, a growing number of services are available in formats that do not lend themselves to a seamless integration into a standard web browser. Separating interface and communication gives us several advantages.

The dispatcher abstracts the user's action (e.g. a click selection of a semantic service), and automatically translates this into the appropriate XML-based request to the service provider. Generally, each request may have a specific XML form or template associated with it, and this is automatically 'filled in' by Magpie before being dispatched to the service provider. The dispatcher delivers the XML-coded request on the user's behalf.

This leads to a second benefit. Since the Magpie dispatcher acts on behalf of the user and can be identified as such, it is possible to implement the service request/response communication in an *asynchronous* way. In other words, the communication stream does not have to remain open while the service providers are waiting for the response from the actual service execution. When the response is ready, the service provider can easily send it back to the user who originally requested it (or better to a dispatching agent acting on behalf of the user).

Finally, the asynchronous capability attached to the standard web browser is critical for supporting what we labelled as trigger services. People may be familiar with numerous pop-up windows that are 'pushed' to the user's desktop while browsing. However, the principle of trigger services is totally different. They are not designed for 'blanket coverage' of all users browsing a particular page. They enhance a particular viewpoint facilitated through a particular ontology, and they are only activated, when a specific pattern emerges among the entities on a page. Therefore, the dispatcher prevents 'spam', and enables real push services.

Some of the messages coming from trigger services may be handled directly by the dispatcher thus lifting the burden from the actual web browser. The trigger messages may be re-directed to a more appropriate user interface than a plain web browser window (e.g. a graphic visualization or tree-based collector widget). However, the important feature is that the presence of a dispatcher enables a service provider to address users. This type of *two-way communication* is critical to supporting collaborative browsing and is not possible with standard HTTP based protocols.

Bi-directional information exchange becomes useful when we allow for the negotiation of the ontology to be used for sense-making. In principle, a user may refer to different ontologies to interpret a single web page. Some ontologies may be remote, and they may be defined in different formats. One of the dispatcher based functionalities that we are currently experimenting with is to create an import facility for various key web KR formats (RDF, OWL, etc.). Such an 'ontology-to-lexicon translator' might also allow the user to customize an ontology or select only classes that are needed.

3.4 The Semantic Log and Collaborative Trigger Services

The key to collaborative browsing is the availability of a *shared semantic log*. The URL of each web page browsed is passed, via the service dispatcher, to a web service which downloads the document and extracts the items which match the ontology derived lexicon. The items are then asserted into a semantic log KB as facts. Magpie *watchers* monitor and respond to patterns in the asserted facts. When the relevant assertions have been made for a particular watcher, a semantic service response is *triggered*, and applicable information delivered to the dedicated window in the user's web browser. An example Magpie watcher definition is given below.

```
(def-watcher collect-peoples-projects  peoples-projects
   (found-item ?time ?address ?page-url ?person ?user-id)
   (person ?person)
   (has-project-member ?project ?person)
   (not (found-item ?time2 ?address ?page-url2 ?project))
  :action (collect :peoples-projects ?user-id ?project
                    ?page-url ?address)))
```

Fig. 7. Watcher definition for trigger service "People's Projects" (in OCML). The results of using this method on the semantic log KB are shown in the bottom left-hand collector in Fig. 2.

Collaborative trigger services make use of the fact that users working together will share a semantic log. We can then create watchers which trigger services for collaborators. The definition of the watcher for the alert shown in Fig. 7 is shown in Fig. 8. This definition notifies a user when a collaborator has recently looked at a web page containing a related technology. In this context technologies are related if they cover related research areas, have the same author or are owned by the same organization.

```
(def-watcher alert-collaborator-for-similar-technology  contact
   (found-item ?time1 ?address1 ?page-url1 ?technology1 ?user-id1)
   (found-item ?time2 ?address2 ?page-url2 ?technology2 ?user-id2)
   (within-3-days ?time1 ?time2)
   (are-related-technologies ?technology1 ?technology2)
   (not (= ?user-id1 ?user-id2))
   (not (= ?page-url1 ?page-url2))
  :action
   (alert-collaborator :similar-technology ?user-id1
                       ?user-id12 ?technology1 ?technology2)))
```

Fig. 8. Watcher definition for a collaborative trigger service "People's Projects" written in OCML. The results of using this method with the semantic log KB are displayed in the bottom left-hand collector in Fig. 2.

We know from the studies of Tauscher and Greenberg that on average 58% of visits to web sites are revisits. We do not know if any studies which extend this work for collaborating teams but we presume that colleagues engaged on similar information gathering tasks would come across the same pages. Watchers such as those shown in Fig. 8 prevent the duplication of work and facilitate team knowledge sharing.

4   Related Work

To our knowledge, one technology that strongly resembles Magpie (at least in respect to the appearance) is the KIM plug-in for Internet Explorer. KIM [22] is a Knowledge and Information Management platform for automatic semantic annotation, web page indexing and retrieval. Similarly to Magpie, KIM uses named entities as a foundation of a document's semantics, and assigns ontological descriptions and definitions to the entities in the text. The platform takes advantage of a massive populated ontology containing common 'upper-level' concepts (e.g. locations, dates, organizations or money) and their instances.

Unlike Magpie, the essence of KIM is a NER technique based on the GATE platform [4] but extending the typically flat set of NER rules with ontological hierarchies. The entities are recognized in the text by the KIM server API, and in parallel they are associated with respective instance in the ontology. Here, GATE provides a lot of support in recognizing abbreviations, incomplete names and co-referenced terms. All these functionalities enable KIM to recognize both already-known and new named entities. While the actual annotation is similar to that in Magpie, the generic capabilities of GATE offer one important benefit – KIM is able to extend its knowledge base by inserting newly recognized entities as instances of appropriate ontological classes.

The major difference between Magpie and KIM is the 'aftermath' of recognition. KIM enables the user to explore the semantic definitions/descriptions of the recognized items in a semi-structured format. Rather than showing complex semantic definitions, Magpie allows the user to choose which service s/he is interested in. This enables Magpie to use the reasoning capabilities of ontologies to a much greater extent, and eventually provide a more customized and open-ended user interaction experience. To summarize, we see Magpie and KIM as two complementary tools catering for different user needs.

One of the inspirations for Magpie was the COHSE family of systems [3]. COHSE combines an Open Hypermedia System with an ontology server into a framework for ontological linking. As with Magpie, it uses an ontology-derived lexicon; but instead of annotations it adds links to related web pages. The links are added either by a proxy server or via an augmented Mozilla™ browser. The distinctions between Magpie and COHSE are due to their differing design goals. The goals for COHSE were (i) to separate web links from the web pages and (ii) to make the links conceptual (i.e. potentially generated from an ontology). The goal for Magpie is to support interpretation and information gathering by tapping into relevant conceptual knowledge. Magpie's interface enables ontological differences to be highlighted, and the services provided are dependent on the class of entity found. Magpie also offers trigger services via semantic logs. Neither type of Magpie service is designed to replace traditional links rather they act as an auxiliary knowledge source.

A host of annotating tools and systems have emerged in recent years. For instance, the Amaya editor implementing the Annotea framework [15], the CREAM-based Ont-O-Mat/Annotizer [13], MnM [24], and the SHOE framework [14]. The main difference between these efforts and the approach taken by Magpie and KIM lies in the origin of the annotations. The above tools relied (at least partly) on the manual annotation of a document. Once the annotation was seeded by the user/librarian, the annotation systems typically provide tools to take over from the user and automate the process. For instance, Ont-O-Mat uses the rule learning capability of Amilcare – a tool often used in conjunction with GATE.

Magpie differs from these tools by intertwining entity recognition, annotation, and a formal representation of an ontology. Our approach to entity recognition and annotation results in a near-zero overhead for the users (including document authors) who are not required to annotate their work. Ontologies, on the other hand, provide a shared (and formal) understanding that is more likely to outperform 'free-text' annotations in conveying the same meaning to different users. We admit though that free-hand annotations are superior in terms of personalized and customized interpretation.

Another strand of research that is relevant to the Magpie framework is Letizia [16] and its idea of a reconnaissance agent. This type of agent "looks ahead of the user on the links on the current web page". The authors argue that pre-filtering the web pages may improve the relevance and usefulness of browsing. The functionality similar to that of Letizia ("logged entities reconnaissance") is implemented in Magpie through its semantic logging and ontological reasoning upon the semantic log KB. In [7] we describe a Magpie component which visualizes the semantic neighbourhood of a browsing session through the semantic log.

There are a number of systems which support collaboration though augmented web browsing. The CWB (Collaborative Web Browsing) [10] is one of several systems which allows users to synchronously browse the same web page. One of the novel features of CWB is that it is extremely lightweight and does not rely on a plug-in, binary executable or Java applet. The I2I system [2] allows users to leave calling cards on web pages which state that the user would be happy to talk to other users on a topic related to the web page contents. To our knowledge there are no collaborative web browsing tools which utilize a shared ontology.

5   Discussion and Conclusions

In this paper we described the generic Magpie framework for semantic web browsing focussing on how trigger services can support collaborative sense making on the web. Our infrastructure supports colleagues working together on related information gathering activities. Users are notified about relevant browsing activities of co-users.

Supporting semantic browsing requires a number of key technologies. An ontology which captures a shared viewpoint enables inferences to be made as to when the contents of one web page are related to another. It is vital that the ontology is automatically populated from relevant web resources. Our currently deployed version, which relies on the AKT Reference ontology, uses a mixture of ODBC database interfaces and generic scripts for population – see [6] for more details.

In this paper we also presented a brief summary of our evaluation study, where we benchmarked NER techniques used in Magpie with those used by GATE and another in-house developed NER tool. We concluded that Magpie exhibited superior performance in terms of time needed to process web pages (accelerating NER by as much as factor of 10-15 compared to GATE). Moreover, with such a low time overhead Magpie achieves near-100% precision *within* the domain for which lexicon was intended. The major 'drawback' of the lexicon based technique used in Magpie is a rapid degradation in precision and recall when moving *outside* of the intended domain. However, a complementary tool (eSpotter) which uses patterns and grammars has been tested in conjunction with Magpie, and the envisaged merger of the two technologies promises to overcome the brittleness of ontologically derived lexicons for NER.

A shared (ontology based) semantic log captures knowledge about the interesting entities found by a community of users browsing the web. Pro-active trigger services can be fired whenever interesting patterns of communal behaviour are detected. These patterns can of course indicate overlaps indicating users are looking at related web resources or disjointness indicating that users are looking at complementary web resources. The triggering pattern will naturally depend on users, their task and the type of collaboration. In many settings users will only wish to share a strictly limited portion of their browsing activity.

The final key technology is provided by the Magpie dispatcher which enables a user's browser to be addressed directly. Standard HTTP does not support client addressing, nor the pushing of information to the user in a structured and controlled manner. The Magpie service dispatcher provides this complementary functionality, which in turn is essential for a meaningful distribution of trigger services. Moreover, the messages are passed between the user's dispatcher and the provider's dispatcher before they reach the actual service. The dispatcher also supports the login/password-based authentication of the users, which enables the user to select or subscribe to only to those services s/he is authorized to.

The Semantic Web promises to deliver a system where computational resources can be brought to bear to aid human users in knowledge intensive tasks. Through a combination of the technologies outlined above Magpie is able to link collaborators engaged in shared browsing activities through formally specified relations. Tim Berners-Lee argues that "Semantic Web is about integration of resources rather than browsing the resources"[2]. What is the role of Magpie or Magpie-like technologies that inherently address the issues of *browsing*? While Magpie might not be "*the* semantic browser", it definitely is "a browser for the Semantic Web". In other words, Magpie acts as an *integrator* residing within the user's web browser that facilitates access to the relevant *distributed* knowledge resources.

The Magpie framework is not intended for the purposes of browsing the Semantic Web. Its main contribution to the Semantic Web research community is in allowing users to browse the standard Web whilst utilizing the concepts and relationships captured within a selected ontology. We emphasize that majority of semantic services (whether on-demand or triggered) that are offered through the Magpie framework are published using the standards of semantic web services. Consequently, Magpie behaves more like an end-user interface for accessing and interacting with these distributed services rather than a "browser".

Furthermore, a significant amount of knowledge is available on the standard Web, which is not annotated, and typically coded in a semantically 'flat' format. Another contribution Magpie offers is the utilization of this content and its enrichment using a semantic layering based approach. We believe that this is an important step towards supporting semantically enriched browsing both by individuals and communities.

One of our case studies conducted in the context of an Open University climatology course gives students (beginners!) access to state-of-the-art research findings resulting from the largest climate modelling exercise – climate*prediction*.net. Without Magpie's ability to link these highly complex findings with the course concepts, the students would need to spend considerable effort in terms of study time on consulting their tutors and various traditional sources (e.g. course books). Therefore, we believe that existence of a tool supporting semantically enriched browsing is an important application for early adopters and users of Semantic Web technologies.

Acknowledgements

The Magpie research is supported by the Advanced Knowledge Technologies (AKT) and climate*prediction*.net projects. AKT is an Interdisciplinary Research Collaboration (IRC) sponsored by the UK Engineering and Physical Sciences Research Council by grant no. GR/N15764/01. The AKT IRC comprises the Universities of Aberdeen, Edinburgh, Sheffield, Southampton and The Open University. Climate*prediction*.net is sponsored by the UK Natural Environment Research Council and UK Department of Trade e-Science Initiative, and involves Oxford University, CLRC Rutherford Appleton Labs and The Open University.

References

[1] Brickley, D. and Guha, R., *Resource Description Framework (RDF) Schema Specification*. 2000, World Wide Web Consortium. (URL: http://www.w3.org/TR/2000/CR-rdf-schema-20000327).

---

[2] Quoting Tim Berners-Lee's keynote speech delivered at 2nd International Semantic Web Conference, Sanibel Island, Florida, US, October 2003.

[2] Budzik, J., Bradshaw, S., Fu, X., *et al.*, *Supporting Online Resource Discovery in the Context of Ongoing Tasks with Proactive Software Assistants.* Intl. Journal of Human-Computer Studies, 2002. **56**(1): p.47-74.

[3] Carr, L., Bechhofer, S., Goble, C., *et al. Conceptual Linking: Ontology-based Open Hypermedia.* In *Proc. of the 10th Intl. WWW Conf.* 2001. Hong-Kong.

[4] Cunningham, H., Maynard, D., Bontcheva, K., *et al. GATE: A Framework and Graphical Development Environment for Robust NLP Tools and Applications.* In *40th Anniversary Meeting of the Association for Computational Linguistics (ACL).* 2002. Pennsylvania, US.

[5] DAML-Coalition, *Reference description of the DAML+OIL ontology mark-up language.* 2001, http://www.DAML.org/2001/03/reference.html.

[6] Domingue, J., Dzbor, M., and Motta, E., *Semantic Layering with Magpie,* In *Handbook on Ontologies in Information Systems,* Staab, S. and Studer, R. (Eds.) 2003, Springer Verlag.

[7] Domingue, J., Dzbor, M., and Motta, E. *Magpie: Supporting Browsing and Navigation on the Semantic Web.* In *Proc. of the Intelligent User Interfaces (IUI).* 2004. Portugal.

[8] Dzbor, M., Domingue, J., and Motta, E. *Magpie: Towards a Semantic Web Browser.* In *Proc. of the 2nd Intl. Semantic Web Conf.* 2003. Florida, USA.

[9] Eisenstadt, M. and Dzbor, M. *BuddySpace: Enhanced Presence Management for Collaborative Learning, Working, Gaming and Beyond.* In *JabberConf Europe.* 2002. Germany.

[10] Esenther, A.W. *Instant Co-Browsing: Lightweight Real-time Collaborative Web Browsing.* In *Proc. of the 11th International WWW Conference.* 2002. Hawaii, USA.

[11] Fensel, D. and Motta, E., *Structured Development of Problem Solving Methods.* IEEE Transactions on Knowledge and Data Engineering, 2001. **13**(6): p.913-932.

[12] Gruber, T.R., *A Translation approach to Portable Ontology Specifications.* Knowledge Acquisition, 1993. **5**(2): p.199-221.

[13] Handschuh, S., Staab, S., and Maedche, A. *CREAM - Creating relational metadata with a component-based, ontology driven annotation framework.* In *Proc. of the Intl. Semantic Web Working Symposium (SWWS).* 2001. California, USA.

[14] Heflin, J. and Hendler, J., *A Portrait of the Semantic Web in Action.* IEEE Intelligent Systems, 2001. **16**(2): p.54-59.

[15] Kahan, J., Koivunen, M.-R., Prud'Hommeaux, E., *et al. Annotea: An Open RDF Infrastructure for Shared Web Annotations.* In *10th Intl. WWW Conf.* 2001. Hong-Kong.

[16] Lieberman, H., Fry, C., and Weitzman, L., *Exploring the web with reconnaissance Agents.* Comm. of the ACM, 2001. **44**(8): p.69-75.

[17] Middleton, S., DeRoure, D., and Shadbolt, N. *Capturing knowledge of user preferences: Ontologies in recommender systems.* In *Proc. of the ACM K-CAP.* 2001. Victoria, Canada.

[18] Motta, E., *Reusable Components for Knowledge Modelling.* Frontiers in AI and Applications. 1997, The Netherlands: IOS Press.

[19] Motta, E., Buckingham Shum, S., and Domingue, J., *Ontology-Driven Document Enrichment: Principles, Tools and Applications.* Intl .Journal of Human-Computer Studies, 2000. **52**(5): p.1071-1109.

[20] Motta, E., Domingue, J., Cabral, L., *et al. IRS-II: A Framework and Infrastructure for Semantic Web Services.* In *Proc. of the 2nd Intl. Semantic Web Conf.* 2003. Florida, USA.

[21] Mulholland, P., Zdrahal, Z., Domingue, J., *et al., Integrating working and learning: a document enrichment approach.* Journal of Behaviour and Information Technology, 2000. **19**(3): p.171-180.

[22] Popov, B., Kiryakov, A., Kirilov, A., *et al. KIM - Semantic Annotation Platform.* In *Proc. of the 2nd Intl. Semantic Web Conf.* 2003. Florida, USA.

[23] van Harmelen, F., Hendler, J., Horrocks, I., *et al., OWL web ontology language reference.* 2002, http://www.w3.org/TR/owl-ref/.

[24] Vargas-Vera, M., Motta, E., Domingue, J., *et al. MnM: Ontology Driven Semi-automatic and Automatic Support for Semantic Markup.* In *Proc. of the 13th European Knowledge Acquisition Workshop (EKAW).* 2002. Spain.

Toward a Framework for
Semantic Organizational Information Portal

Emanuele Della Valle and Maurizio Brioschi

CEFRIEL - Politecnico of Milano, Via Fucini 2, 20133 Milano, Italy

Abstract. Information Portals have gathered lot of attention among many organizations interested in a single point of access to their information and services. But developing portals from scratch is sometimes too expensive, so many vendors have proposed frameworks to make it affordable. Notwithstanding the frameworks the market offers seem stuck in a simplicity vs. flexibility trade off imposed by the Web technologies they are built with. Therefore we believe that a technology change is required and that Semantic Web technology can play a key role in developing a new, Semantic, generation of simpler and, at the same time, flexibler frameworks for Organizational Information Portal.

1 Introduction

Any organization[1] daily produces and consumes a great amount of information. The need for managing it goes back to ancient times but since information communication technologies have made it possible to share and store it in an inexpensive way this need seams to have grown stronger year after year. Take the last decade wide deployment of intranet solutions as an example, as they gain in popularity among organizations, they have been populated with services such as: web access to databases, newsletters and forums, and shares full of documents, forms, calendars of events, news and link collections. As a consequence, most organizations have ended up with a huge set of repositories of structured, semi-structured and unstructured information distributed over their intranets. Such amount of information is normally *comprehensible to accustomed users*, but, occasional and novel users would have an hard time in getting to what they are looking for, because they would probably get no automatic answer to such questions as: What information do we have? Where is it? How did it get there? Who put it there? How do I get it? How can I add more? What does it mean? Can you provide context information? Can you provide more specific information?

In the last years portals have gathered lot of attention among enterprises interested in addressing these questions, due to their ability in offering the user a unique and structured access to heterogeneous information and web based services. In particular many vendors[2] have proposed frameworks, for facilitating

---

[1] by "organization" we mean "any large group of people who work together", such as enterprises, public bodies, universities, associations, etc.
[2] BEA, Broad Vision, Hummingbird, IBM, Microsoft, Oracle, Plumtree and Sybase

J. Davies et al. (Eds.): ESWS 2004, LNCS 3053, pp. 402–416, 2004.

the construction of portal solutions specific for enterprises called Enterprise Information Portals (EIPs). However, since we are facing a broader application of EIPs to organizations, rather than only to enterprises, we prefer to refer to such frameworks as Organizational Information Portal Frameworks (OIP-Fs) and we call Organizational Information Portals (OIPs) the Web applications constructed with OIP-Fs.

In a OIP we distinguish several kind of interaction times:

- *browsing time*: when generic members of the organization (we call *users*) either navigate through or search in the OIP in order to find the information or service they need to accomplish their tasks;
- *authoring time*: when authorized members (we call *editors*) publish, update or delete information or services;
- *shaping time*: when an authorized and skilled member (we call *shaper*) forges the interfaces for both users and editors;
- *administering time*: when an authorized and skilled member (we call *administrator*) decides which operations each member can perform on which information source or service.

Moreover the common set of requirements an organization usually ask an OIP-F for are: easiness (velocity and bargain rate) to develop upon; integrability with the broadest set of existing information sources and web-based services; scalability and adaptability in serving users that are accessing the OIP not only within the intranet but more and more from the extranet using portable devices; and, last but not least, long time maintainability. Most of these requirements are partially incompatible: some call for simplicity, others involve flexibility. So a common problem in developing a OIP-F is trading off between simplicity and flexibility.

We believe the market offers OIP-Fs that are stuck in a simplicity vs. flexibility trade off imposed by the Web technologies they are built with. Available OIP-Fs generally suffers from the huge amount of manual work still required for finding, extracting, representing, interpreting, and maintaining organizational information and services. For instance, consider the result set of a web search: how many retrieved pages does a user normally have to read through before getting what he/she is looking for? Right now only a technology change can enable a further step in the direction of developing a new generation of OIP-Fs. This is why we believe the innovative Semantic Web technologies will play a key role: a little semantics, provided by explicitly augmenting resources (both content and services) with metadata, the meaning of which is formally defined using ontologies, can help. It can enable both local constrains and global universality, thus many interoperable structures can be adopted underneath (RDB, XMLDB, etc.). It can endow information management in a distributed and autonomous way, making information reuse possible. Last, but not least, if a little semantics is provided then machines can, in a way, "understand" the content of a resource and its relationships with others resources; thus Semantic Web technologies can help in automatically finding, extracting, representing, interpreting, and maintaining resources. We call this new generation of OIP-Fs based on Semantic

Web technologies, Semantic Organizational Information Portal frameworks, or shortly Semantic OIP-Fs.

In the following we will introduce the four ingredients (section 2) we used in making up our concept of Semantic OIP-F (section 3). Later on, section 4 describes a prototype we have developed as an early proof of our concept. Before concluding, in section 5 we gives a short survey of related works.

2   Ingredients in Our Concept

The innovative idea, first proposed in SEAL [1], is straightforward: can we use metadata defined by ontologies to support the construction of portals? And if so, does it help?

Even if it might appear as a radical new departure actually it is not. On the contrary it is the bringing together of existing and well understood technologies:

- *Web Frameworks*, such as Struts, Jetspeed, Tapestry, WebWork and Cocoon, that, following Model-View-Controller (MVC) design pattern, propose to separate data, business logic, and presentation.
- *Hypertext Architectures* and, in particular, the *WWW conceptual models* such as WebML [2], W2000 [3], HDM [4], OOHDM [5], Araneus [6], and WSDM [7], that are proposals for the conceptual specification and automatic implementation of Web sites.
- *Ontologies*, to model the domain information space, the navigation, the access, the presentation and possibly even the operation offered by a portal.
- *Metadata*, to make resource descriptions available to machine in a processable way.

2.1   Web Frameworks and Model-View-Controller Approach

MVC dates back to the '80s and today it is one of the most recommended architectural design pattern for Web applications. MVC suggests to separate an application in three types of component: a model, some view and a controller. The *model* manages the data of the Web application responding to requests for information about its state (usually from the view), and to instructions to change state (usually from the controller). Each *view* provides data presentation and manages the user input. Finally, the *controller* interprets the user inputs, commanding the model and/or the views to change as appropriate.

The market provide a variety of frameworks based on MVC design patterns for Web application fast development. Just surfing the web looking for such frameworks you might run into Struts ("a flexible control layer based on standard technologies like Java Servlets, JavaBeans, ResourceBundles and XML"), Tapestry ("an alternative to scripting environments such as JavaServer Pages or Velocity) or Jetspeed ("an Open Source implementation of an Enterprise Information Portal, using Java and XML").

2.2 WWW Conceptual Models

We surveyed various model-driven approaches to design Web applications available in WWW conceptual model literature [2, 3, 4, 5, 6, 7]. They show it is possible, and even convenient, to model separately at least the domain information space, the navigation, the access and sometimes also the operations. So, drawing these ideas back to OIP-F development we have formulated the following definitions.

The *domain information model* is a shared understanding of the information the OIP makes available that does not change, or changes slowly, over the time. For instance, in modeling CEFRIEL (our organization) information space we can assert that: CEFRIEL is an **organisation**; organisations are divided into **units**; **people works for** a unit on one or more **projects**; people can be divided into **researchers** and **consultants**; projects can be split in **researches** and **consultancies**; in particular a researcher **investigates** in at least a research project and a consultant **advises** in at least a consultancy; an employee can be both a researcher and a consultant at the same time; and so on. The domain information model once instantiated can capture, at least in part, the organizational memory.

The *navigation models* represent the heterogeneous paths the OIP users can adopt in traversing the organizational memory. They are not necessarily shared among all users, but they are jointly employed by homogeneous categories of users. For instance, taking CEFRIEL organizational memory as an example, researchers usually share a research-project-centric vision, so knowing each other's competency is more important than knowing which unit another researcher belongs to. Thus if the user is a researcher, then navigation paths between researchers and their competency should be stressed, while those between researchers and units should be left in the background. On the contrary, administration staff have a clear vision of the organization chart, but don't care too much about ongoing projects. Thus the navigational model for them should emphasize navigation paths among CEFRIEL, its units and the people who work for them and leave competency in the background instead.

The *access models* represent collections of resources not strictly homogeneous, highly variable and sometimes even related to a specific user, a sort of *views*. For instance, we could offer "recently added" (the collection of all the resources added or updated recently), "most visited" or "last visited" (if we monitored the interaction of the users with the portal), "favorites" and so on.

The *operation models* represent both user operations and system operations. User operations are those directly visible to users. For instance, the operation "include resource in favorites", which allows users to put a reference to the select resource in the collection of their favorites, is a typical user operation. Another common example is a "filter operation", which allows users to specify some selection criteria other a collection in order to select a subset of elements of interest. Contrariwise, system operations are not visible to users, but are triggered by user/editor/administrator/shaper operations. For instance, the function that, triggered by "include resource in favorites", updates the collection of favorites or the operation that "implements" the filtering, are system operations.

In order to design the domain information model WWWCM approaches use existing modeling languages: E-R diagrams in HDM [4], UML class diagrams in W2000 [3] and OOHDM [5], etc. Moreover, they explicitly provide a set of ad-hoc primitives to model navigation (e.g. entity, component, node, slot, structural link, semantic link, etc.), access (e.g. collection, collection center, etc.) and, in case they do, operation (e.g. input, pre-condition, session, etc.). On the contrary we propose to adopt ontologies and metadata.

2.3   Ontology-Oriented Metadata-Based Solutions

Metadata-based solutions have already proved to be able to provide enough *machine-processable* information for automating most information retrieval tasks, but, in a pure metadata based solution, the meaning associated to the metadata is not machine-processable. So a machine can process this metadata but it cannot "reason" upon it. For instance users of a metadata-based search engine might got a smaller result set, containing more relevant resources, but once they have selected one of the retrieved resource, asking the OIP to provide context information or a more specific resource remains impossible.

A good deal of help can come from defining metadata using ontologies. In fact, ontologies, being explicit (hence formal) conceptualisations of a shared understanding of a domain [8] can be used to make metadata machine processable. So, if the meaning of each metadata was defined using an ontology, a machine could, in a way, "understand" it and reason upon it. This way, beside a centralized and controlled approach, a distributed environment, where autonomous entities maintain heterogeneous shared resources describing them with metadata defined by the corporate ontology, becomes feasible.

However, if a single enterprise had chosen some years ago to build up such an ontology-oriented metadata-based solution, from scratch and on its own, it would have ended up in a "disaster" because no standard solution was available. It was the time, instead, for academics to experiment with such ideas. Ontobroker [9] and SHOE [10] are successful examples of such pre-Semantic Web applications.

To the contrary, today metadata-based ontology-oriented solutions are becoming feasible thanks to the ongoing Semantic Web researches that are leading the standardisation process of the related technologies. So far, the W3C has coordinated many activities that have already supplied Resource Description Framework (RDF) [11], a framework for describing web resources with metadata, and Ontology Web Language (OWL) [12], a comprehensive ontology vocabulary that has just become a W3C Proposed Recommendation.

3   Making Up Our Concept

So far we have identified the key ingredients: *Web Frameworks* are the state of the art in developing Web application; *WWW conceptual model* indicates clearly what to model and how to exploit the resulting models; *ontologies* are good formal models; last but not least, *metadata* (especially if defined by ontologies) enable distributed approach to information and service management. But we still have to combine them to make up our concept.

3.1 Our Model

We start considering that even if the global Semantic Web might still be a little bit too ambitious, however, as the standardisation of the Semantic Web technologies proceeds, some pioneering organizations would be able to build "local organizational Semantic Webs" represented by services and documents available over the intranet (or the extranet) annotated with metadata defined by a corporate ontology materialized in a sort of *organizational memory*. So the domain information model, which WWWCM approaches usually explicitly ask the modeler to provide, will be already captured by the organizational memory. But, differently from WWWCM, this organizational memory will be completely decoupled from the Semantic OIP design, because the OIP will be only one, among many other, application to use the information available over the organizational Semantic Web. Therefore a Semantic OIP built using our framework, cannot assume any "a priori" agreement over this domain information model except the use of a common set of primitives provided by the Semantic Web technologies (e.g. XML, RDF, OWL, ect.).

So, we don't require the shaper to model explicitly navigation and access using a specific set of primitives as many WWW conceptual model approaches suggest. We propose, alternatively, to define a navigation and an access terminology modeling respectively navigation and access in a domain independent way, using metadata defined by ontologies and, then, we support the shaper in building navigation and access models mostly using OWL mapping terminology. In fact, we believe navigational models can be build by *mapping* some domain information terms to the navigation terminology, but in building access structure, even if mapping corporate ontology terminology to the access terminology could prove to be useful, the high variability and user specificity of such models might require to explicitly draw new relationships between resources in the corporate memory and also to add ad-hoc resources (e.g. centers of collection). Even so, we expect the latter task to be largely automatized by dynamically querying the organization memory or by profiling the interaction with the users.

Finally if we wanted to model operation using Semantic Web technologies, we could define an operation terminology as in the two previous case; but understanding that we might need to extend such terminology using rules, which are not standardized yet, we prefer to leave this task for future works.

3.2 Our Controller

Decided what to model, we conceive the control operations we want to make available to each user, editor, shaper and administrator at his/her specific interaction time.

At Browsing Time Web users interact with the Web in many ways, but three patterns are commonly recognized: searching, navigation and bookmarking. Users do search when they know exactly what they are looking for, hence they are able to express their requests with sufficient precision. Otherwise users do navigate either when they know how to get to a resource or when they don't know what they are looking for but they understand it as they browse. In both cases users bookmark a resource when they want to store a direct entry point to a particular resource. A semantic OIP should exploit metadata and ontologies in order to improve all interaction patterns. In particular we want to improve searching by resource discovering, navigation by automatic link creation and bookmarking by personal access modeling.

At Authoring Time ontologies, in particular the corporate ontology, can be exploited in supporting the editorial task of adding new resources or describing existing ones. It has already been shown (e.g. in Protégé 2000 [13]) that they can be employed in automating part of process for creating editorial interfaces. But we believe most of the benefits of using Semantic Web technologies should come from reducing the effort required to augment resources with metadata. In the authoring environment we envision, authors are asked only what is strictly necessary, while the rest is inferred.

For instance, the metadata a project team uses for describing project results contains also information regarding the skills of the team members. These skills could be easily used for automatically pre-populating a skill management application, so that the authors were required to confirm what was inferred instead of filling in a tedious job description.

At Shaping Time beside the commonly available controlls that enable visual page composition, we want the shapers to be able to define both navigation and access models. Using OWL mapping terminology via a graphic interface a shaper maps the corporate terminology to the navigation terminology in order to build a navigation model for each category of user. For instance, if we define in the navigation terminology the property `related` and we determinate its presentation functionality, then a CEFRIEL shaper might model a navigation path intended for researchers by mapping the relationship between researchers and their competency to `related`.

Moreover, a shaper can build visually a shared access structure either by mapping the corporate terminology to access terminology or by querying. For instance, a CEFRIEL shaper might build an access structure by defining a query that extract the competency most frequently required in projects of the last two years.

At Administering Time we want to support administrators[3] in authorizing: users to selectively access the resources, editors to describe and publish resources

---

[3] Please note that here we are not interested in fine grain access controll to concepts and instances in the corporate ontology but to the easier problem of managing user access to the portal accessible resources.

available on the organizational Semantic Web and shapers to manage navigation and access models. Administration operation don't probably get too benefit from the introduction of Semantic Web technologies, but defining permission on a concept basis instead of a resource basis might drive some improvement in managing such task, too.

3.3 Our View

We choose not to model presentation explicitly (as some WWWCM have tried), because we recognize that most of the success of a Web application depends on its presentation. In fact, modeling in details such a critical task might prove too complex, in particular because good graphic designer are not supposed to be good modelers and vice versa. However we are not suggesting to code each page from scratch, but to write templates of pages in a MVC approach. This way we aspect the same advantages, in term of visual coherence and accessibility, as modeling but at a more affordable effort.

4 Concept Refinement and an Early Proof of Concept

At the current state of the work we are refining the concept, in particular *we are investigating how to improve navigation by creating links automatically and displaying them in a navigation panel*. The rational behind is strain forward: a Semantic OIP built using our framework can, in a way, understand the meaning of the metadata used to describe a resources; so, when a user asks the Semantic OIP to retrieve a resource at a given URL, it returns the required resource inserted in a navigation panel
that automatically provides the user with links to both context information and more detailed information. In fact, it is possible to provide the user with automatically generated links to context (or more detailed) information as long as the relationship among these resources can be inferred by a *reasoner service*. The challenge is to offer the users clearly understandable metaphors, such as a landmark (the position of a well-known resource that plays the role of reference point), and orientation tools, such as a compass (a navigational instrument for finding directions).

In our vision the semantic EIP can generate, at least, three different kinds of links:

- *access point links* are generated by asking a reasoner service which resources should be reachable according to the current access model. We distinguish between *global* and *contextual access points*. The former type is always visible (such links are sort of landmarks that help users in taking theirs' bearings), while the latter type depends on the retrieved resource (such links are a sort of compass that guides users locally in accessing the information).
- *categorized links* are generated by asking the reasoner service to group together, according to the current navigation model, those resources that are

related via the same property or its subproperties. Links in this category are provided in order to give users an idea of both the context in which the retrieved resource is located and if more detailed information is available.
- *metadata links* should provide the user with both a simple visualization of the metadata describing the retrieved resource and an intuitive navigation of the semantic relationships to other resources.

In order to proof this concept, we have built a first prototype of a semantic OIP-F following the presented approach and we have demonstrated its functionalities by constructing a Semantic OIP to access a "synthetic" organizational memory that describes CEFRIEL (an on-line demo is available at http://seip.cefriel.it). In particular we developed a servlet-based application that uses Velocity for implementing MVC pattern, Jena–2.1[4] to manage RDF triples and RACER 1.7.15 [14] as reasoner service that can "understand" RDF and OWL-DL. An overall architectural vision of our prototype is shown in figure 1.

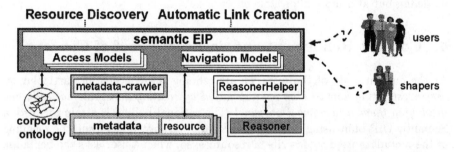

Fig. 1. Logical architecture of the proposed framework for Semantic OIP.

Moreover we have developed a first draft of the navigation and access terminology we have introduced in section 3.1. We got inspired either by common terms used in WWW conceptual modeling and in HTML 4.1 link types[5]. We kept them explicitly as simple as possible, but still rich enough to be useful in proving the concept. On the one hand, our *navigation ontology* defines four properties:

- **contains**: a transitive property to express containment (e.g. a museum contains art)
- **contained**: inverse property of contains
- **seeAlso**: a property to express a relevant connection
- **related**: a symmetric subproperty of **seeAlso**

On the other hand, our *access ontology* defines a class and four properties:

- **Home**: a class whose instances are collection centers or landmarks
- **next**: a transitive property to express precedence in a connected series

---

[4] See http://www.hpl.hp.com/semweb/ for details
[5] See http://www.w3.org/TR/html4/types.html#type-links

- prev: inverse property of next
- down: a transitive property to express dependency in a hierarchy
- up: inverse property of down

Then we define and code a visual behavior for each term in the two terminology in order to automatically generate and present the three different kind of links present in our navigation panel.

The prototype, "understanding" RDF and OWL-DL, can process the metadata that describe the retrieved resource, generating *metadata links* according to the following schema:

```
<resource label>[<list of labels of types>]
<property label>
<resource label>[<list of labels of types>] or literal value
```

All the words between angle brackets are links that retrieve the resource with the corresponding label.

For instance, if a user asks to retrieve CEFRIEL home page, our prototype having "understood" the metadata associated with the page should generate the two following set of links:

```
CEFRIEL[Organisation] has_unit    eTECH[Unit]
Brioschi[HeadOfUnit]  works_for   CEFRIEL[Organisation]
```

The former states that CEFRIEL, which is an organisation, has got eTECH as unit and the later that Brioschi, which is a head of unit, works for CEFRIEL.

The propotype has got 3 boxes containing *categorized links*:

- the *contains* box, that shows links to resources conceptually "contained" in the retrieved one. We chose to use "contained" in a relaxed way; therefore links can appear in this box for different reasons:
  - if the retrieved resource is a rdfs:Class, then the box is populated with links to all its individuals and all its subclasses,
  - if the retrieved resource is related to any other via contains, then the box is populated with links to them
- the *contained* box, that shows links to resources that "contains" the retrieved one. Even in this case, we chose to interpret "contained" in a relaxed way including both rdfs:subclassOf hierarchies and user defined (via contains) hierarchies. So the box is populated with links either to the superclasses or to the resources related to the retrieved one via contained.
- the *related* box, that shows links to resources that are associated to the retrieved resource either via a seeAlso or a related property.

As we explain in 3.1 we don't want to oblige the shaper to use directly the terms defined in the navigation and access ontology, we want instead to play on OWL mapping primitives. Thus, the shaper should not connect resources present in the organizational memory directly with contains, contained, seeAlso and related. They should otherwise map properties, which already exists into the corporate ontology, to those. In particular we choose to map properties using `rdfs:subpropertyOf`. This way the reasoner can easily compute sub-property closure and "understand" that two resources are related (e.g. via `contains`) not only when it is explicitly stated, but also when it is entailed.

For instance, CEFRIEL has got nine Units and in the corporate ontology `has_unit` is the property used to relate CEFRIEL to its Unit, so if a group of users normally interpret the `has_unit` as a containment relationship, a shaper can put in the "navigation model" the triple `has_unit rdfs:subpropertyOf contains`. This way, when CEFRIEL home page is retrieved, links to all the 9 unit of CEFRIEL are placed in the "contains" box.

In the prototype we have provided a special control, visible only at shaping time, to support the mapping task in a WYSIWYG approach. When a user is loged in as a shaper, beside each property in the "metadata links" we show the current mapping for the property. If no mapping is already present a combo box listing the available terminology is shown, otherwise a link labeled "del" give the shaper the possibility to delete the mapping.

Finally the prototype has got as *access point links* a global navigational bar and a contextual navigational bar configurable through the access model. The global navigation bar is populated with links to resources of type `Home`, while for the contextual navigation we use an approach similar to the one illustrated for categorised links. So our prototype populates the boxes labeled "prev", "next", "up" and "contextual navigation" with links to resources, that are associated to the retrieved resource, respectively via a `prev`, `next`, `up` and `down` property.

As we stated before with access models we represents collections of resources not strictly homogeneous, highly variable and sometimes even related to a specific user. In order to build such a model the resources, part of a collection, should be related using the terminology of the access ontology. Thus, the resources that are collection centers should be declared of type `Home`, while the others should be related using `down` and `next` (`up` and `prev` can be inferred).

So, if the corporate ontology already provide relationships that can be exploited for building a collection the mapping approach can be use even here. For instance, if the corporate memory contains a set of courses, whose priority is expressed using the property `dc:requires`[6] and composition using `dc:partOf`, a collection can be created making `dc:requires` a subproperty of `next` and `dc:partOf` a subproperty of `down`.

Otherwise, as we anticipated in 3.1, the high variability and user specificity of such collections might require to draw new relationships, between resources already present in the corporate memory, and sometimes to add ad-hoc resources. For instance, if a shaper wanted to create a "successful story" collection, we should create an ad-hoc HTML document to be used as a collection center and relate resources describing stories of this kind with `next`, starting from the most recent one and going back in time.

In order to show how different views ,of the same corporate memory, can be generated by combining navigation and access models, we develop also a "man-

---

[6] A property of the Dublin Core metadata element set (see http://dublincore.org/).

agement service" (available on-line at http://seip.cefriel.it/seip/manager.html) that can be used to switch between a set of available corporate memories mounting different navigation and access models[7].

Finally, at the time we write this article we are investigating how *improve searching by resource discovering*. In fact if semantic metadata is available, a search engine would not be exclusively based on full text search, but it could make lever on semantics, so it could, in a way, analyse the resources finding those that match the user request. Thus it is no more a matter of searching but it becomes a matter of discovery by matching. Moreover such a semantic search engine wouldnt retrieve only a list of unrelated resources, but it could organize them in a structured collections by exploiting the relationships among the retrieved resources.

5 Related Works

We already discuss the differences between the presented approach and WWW conceptual modeling, we get most inspired from. So in this section we highlight the differences from other works in the Semantic Web community.

An approach that tries, as we do, to combine WWWCM and Semantic Web is *SHDM* [15]. SHDM is a direct extension of OOHDM [5] that use ontologies to define an application conceptual model, extending the expressive power of the original method and use RQL query language to specify flexible navigation model and access structures.

Another similar approach is *OntoWebber* [16]. It proposed to explicit model the Web sites, using ontologies as the foundation for Web portal design and semi-structured data technology for data integration. OntoWebber was the basis for creating the Semantic Web Community Portal.

An approach that presents sameness is *SEAL* [1] and its recent evolution *SEAL-II* [17] that offer a comprehensive set of industrial strength tools for building knowledge portals [18]. With them we share the idea of using semantic annotation and, in particular, ontologies as an affordable way to integrate heterogeneous resources of information. We both use ontologies as a conceptual backbone for building and maintaining portals, but SEAL-II uses pre-semantic web technologies (e.g. F-logic, Ontobroker [9]) while we build our prototype using RDF and OWL-DL.

However SHDM, OntoWebber and SEAL are still oriented to traditional Web Applications. They only take limited advantages from the Semantic Web technologies, considering them a set of richer formal languages to use for accomplishing their goal. Neither of them stress the necessary strong decoupling of the constructed OIP from the organizational Semantic Web. They all propose to design the organizational ontology explicitly for the portal and they assume complete controllability over it. On the contrary, we recognize in a metadata-bases ontology-oriented solution a major progress in interoperability, thus we push for

---

[7] In case you want to try it, please remember to go back to the semantic EIP to see the differences.

a distributed and autonomous approach. In this scenario, the Semantic OIP is only one among many applications that can "understand" the metadata that describes resource contents. Thus we prefer to resign any "a priori" agreement on the organizational memory.

The approach that shows more similarities to our automatic link creation concept is *COHSE* [19]. In fact, its main concern is in linkage and navigation aspects between web pages. It improves the consistency and breadth of linking of web pages by deriving links among them from metadata describing their contents. But it doesn't provide a way to model explicitly different navigation models (for different large group of homogeneous user) and different access models (for specific views tailored to small groups of users) as we do.

KAON [20] is an open-source ontology management infrastructure targeted for business applications. One of its component is KAON Portal that is a simple tool for generating multi-lingual, ontology-based Web portals. With this approach we share the MVC pattern, but while KAON stress more scalability and performance issues, we focus more on giving an homogeneous navigation experience to user despite the heterogeneity that characterise the resources.

Among the other projects we want to highlights *ODESeW* [21], a recently published ontology-based application to automatically generates and manges a knowledge portal for intranets and extranets, *SemIPort*[8], a newly started project we share some objective with, and two really successful examples of pre-Semantic Web application we have already cited: *SHOE* [10] and *Ontobroker* [9].

SHOE provides mechanisms that allows the definition of ontologies and the embedding in HTML pages of metadata referring to those ontologies, then a SHOE enable browser can show these claims to the user and guide him from page to page.

Ontobroker shows many similarity with SHOE. It allows the annotation of HTML pages with metadata, but it provides, with F-logic, a more expressive ontology definition language, that it uses for specification of ontologies, metadata augmentation and queries.

6   Conclusion

We believe that Semantic Web technologies in the next few years will break through as the technology change that developers of OIP frameworks require for moving a step further in the direction of a better trade off between simplicity and flexibility. So we propose a novel approach to a framework for Semantic OIPs that, making lever on Semantic Web technologies, brings many innovation in OIP development:

- it imposes no restriction but the use of RDF and OWL in building the corporate ontology;
- it doesn't require the information carried by the metadata to be coded in any particular way, thus this information is reusable;

---

[8] see http://km.aifb.uni-karlsruhe.de/semiport/partners.html/overview.html

- it enables both resources and metadata management in a distributed and, when necessary, autonomous way as long as resources are network retrievable;
- it offers a homogeneous navigation experience among heterogeneous resources distributed over an Organizational Semantic Web mostly by mapping corporate terminology to the terminology known by our Semantic OIP-F;
- it provides a light weight multi-lingual support.

Furthermore in our prototype we investigate the *visual construction at shaping time of navigation and access models* that we exploit at browsing time via a *resource discovery* feature for retrieving resources (available on the intranet) and *a navigation panel* that contains one of the retrieved resources and a set of automatically generated links. Therefore, a Semantic OIP, built using the proposed approach, will give a unified view of the information present in the organizational Semantic Web, while the organization can keep developing distributed and autonomous information systems on an ad-hoc basis (as required by contingency plans) and singular departments can keep their degree of autonomy in managing such systems.

Acknowledgements

The research has been supported by the MAIS project while the implementation of the prototype reported in this paper has been partially founded by Engineering as part of the activities of the XV Master in Information Technology of CEFRIEL-Politecnico of Milano. We thank our colleagues, in particular Paolo Castagna and Stefano Campanini, for precious contributions, and our student Lara Marinelli.

References

[1] Alexander Maedche, Steffen Staab, Nenad Stojanovic, Rudi Studer, York Sure: SEAL – A framework for developing SEmantic Web PortALs. Lecture Notes in Computer Science **2097** (2001)

[2] Stefano Ceri, Piero Fraternali, Aldo Bongio: Web Modeling Language (WebML): a modeling language for designing Web sites. Computer Networks (Amsterdam, Netherlands: 1999) **33** (2000) 137–157

[3] L. Baresi, F. Garzotto, P. Paolini, S. Valenti: HDM2000: The HDM Hypertext Design Model Revisited. Tech. report, Politecnico di Milano (Jan. 2000)

[4] Franca Garzotto, Paolo Paolini, Daniel Schwabe: HDM — A model based approach to hypertext application design. ACM Transactions on Information Systems **11** (1993) 1–26

[5] D. Schwabe, G. Rossi, S. D. J. Barbosa: Systematic hypermedia application design with OOHDM. In ACM, ed.: Hypertext '96, Washington, DC, March 16–20, 1996: the Seventh ACM Conference on Hypertext: Proceedings, New York, NY, USA, ACM Press (1996) 116–128

[6] Giansalvatore Mecca, Paolo Atzeni, Alessandro Masci, Paolo Merialdo, Giuseppe Sindoni: The ARANEUS web-base management system. In: Proceedings of the ACM SIGMOD International Conference on Management of Data (SIGMOD-98). Volume 27,2 of ACM SIGMOD Record., New York, ACM Press (1998) 544–546

[7] O. M. F. De Troyer, C. J. Leune: WSDM: a user centered design method for Web sites. Computer Networks and ISDN Systems **30** (1998) 85–94

[8] T. Gruber : A translation approach to portable ontology specifications. Knowledge Acquisition **5** (1993) 199–220

[9] Dieter Fensel, Jurgen Angele, Stefan Decker and Michael Erdmann, Hans-Peter Schnurr, Steffen Staab, Rudi Studer, Andreas Witt: On2broker: Semantic-based access to information sources at the WWW. In: WebNet (1). (1999) 366–371

[10] Jeff Heflin, James A. Hendler: Dynamic ontologies on the web. In: AAAI/IAAI. (2000) 443–449

[11] : Resource Description Framework (RDF) Model and Syntax Specification. (2004)

[12] M. Dean, D. Connolly, F. van Harmelen, J. Hendler, I. Horrocks, D. McGuinness, P. Patel-Schneider, L. Stein: Owl web ontology language reference. Recommendation, World Wide Web Consortium (2004)

[13] H. Eriksson, R. Fergerson, Y. Shahar, M. Musen: Automatic generation of ontology editors. In: Proceedings of the 12th Banff Knowledge Acquisition Workshop, Banff, Alberta, Canada (1999)

[14] Volker Haarslev, Ralf Mller: Racer: A core inference engine for the semantic web. In: Proceedings of the 2nd International Workshop on Evaluation of Ontology-based Tools (EON2003), Sanibel Island, Florida, USA (2003) 27–36

[15] Fernanda Lima, Daniel Schwabe: Application modeling for the semantic web. In: LA-WEB 2003 - First Latin American Web Conference, Santiago, Chile, IEEE-CS Press (2003) 802–817

[16] Yuhui Jin, Sichun Xu, Stefan Decker, Gio Wiederhold: Managing Web sites with OntoWebber. Lecture Notes in Computer Science **2287** (2002) 766

[17] Andreas Hotho, Alexander Maedche, Steffen Staab, Rudi Studer: SEAL-II - the soft spot between richly structured unstructured knowledge. Journal of Universal Computer Science **7** (2001) 566–590

[18] Steffen Staab, Alexander Maedche: Knowledge portals: Ontologies at work. The AI Magazine **22** (2000) 63–75

[19] Les Carr, Wendy Hall, Sean Bechhofer, Carole A. Goble: Conceptual linking: ontology-based open hypermedia. In: World Wide Web. (2001) 334–342

[20] E. Bozsak, M. Ehrig, S. Handschub: Kaon – towards a large scale semantic web. In: Proc. of the 3rd Intl. Conf. on E-Commerce and Web Technologies (EC-Web 2002). (2002) 304–313

[21] Oscar Corcho, Asuncin Gmez-Prez, Angel Lpez-Cima, V. Lpez-Garca, Mara del Carmen Surez-Figueroa: Odesew. automatic generation of knowledge portals for intranets and extranets. In D. Fensel, ed.: The Semantic Web, ISWC 2003, LNCS 2870. (2003) 802–817

CS AKTiveSpace:
Building a Semantic Web Application

Hugh Glaser[1], Harith Alani[1], Les Carr[1], Sam Chapman[2], Fabio Ciravegna[2], Alexiei Dingli[2], Nicholas Gibbins[1], Stephen Harris[1], m.c. schraefel[1], and Nigel Shadbolt[1]

[1] School of Electronics and Computer Science, University of Southampton, Southampton, United Kingdom
hg@ecs.soton.ac.uk
[2] Department of Computer Science, University of Sheffield, Sheffield, United Kingdom

Abstract. In this paper we reflect on the lessons learned from deploying the award winning [1] Semantic Web application, CS AKTiveSpace. We look at issues in service orientation and modularisation, harvesting, and interaction design for supporting this 10million-triple-based application. We consider next steps for the application, based on these lessons, and propose a strategy for expanding and improving the services afforded by the application.

1 Introduction

In 2000, the Advanced Knowledge Technologies (AKT) project was launched as a collaborative project between a number of UK universities (Southampton, Aberdeen, Edinburgh, Sheffield and the Open University). The funding was £7.5m and the project was planned to last for six years. The aim was to bring together a range of different disciplines to investigate the issues that were then emerging where large-scale networks and data sources were meeting more intelligent processing than hitherto. Many of these issues have now been captured by the term "Semantic Web" which has gained currency since Tim Berners-Lee's article in Scientific American [2].

As the AKT project progressed, the partners from the different disciplines captured and advanced the state of the art in each area, and a number of Technology Integration Experiments (TIEs) were planned to ensure that the different technologies informed each other. The full range of individual technologies can be found at [3]. One of these TIEs has led to the subject of this paper, the CS AKTiveSpace.

CS AKTiveSpace exploits the wide range of semantically heterogeneous and distributed content that has been collected relating to Computer Science research in the UK. This content is gathered on a continuous basis using a variety of methods including processing SQL using scripts, "screen-scraping" (processing web pages directly from HTML) as well as adopting a range of models for

J. Davies et al. (Eds.): ESWS 2004, LNCS 3053, pp. 417–432, 2004.

content acquisition. The content currently comprises around ten million RDF triples. We made use of the storage, retrieval and maintenance methods we developed in the first two years of the project to support its management. The content is mediated through an ontology constructed for the application domain that was defined in the project, and incorporating components from other published ontologies. CS AKTiveSpace interaction supports the exploration of patterns and implications inherent in the content and exploits a variety of visualisations and multi dimensional representations. Knowledge services supported in the application include investigating communities of practice: who is working, researching or publishing with whom (through ONTOCOPI), and on-demand acquisition: requesting that further knowledge be found from the web about a person. This phase of the project culminated in CS AKTiveSpace winning first place in the Semantic Web Challenge, 2003.

In the following sections, we consider harvesting (knowledge acquisition from structured and unstructured sources), service orientation and modularisation, and user interaction. We look in particular at two of the core services that have been integrated: ONTOCOPI and Armadillo. ONTOCOPI is a community of practice service while Armadillo is a natural language harvesting service used to supplement our triplestore with further information about entities of interest at the user's request. We conclude with a discussion of the lessons learned in these components of the project and look at how these will be focusing our efforts for the next three years.

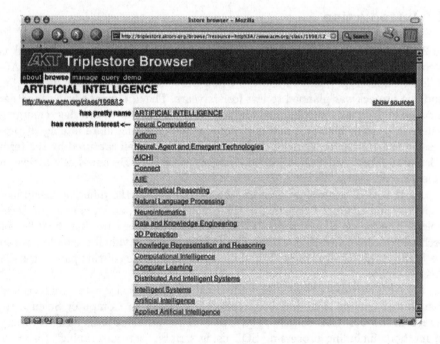

Fig. 1. Browser

2   Ontology Development

The information sources that are aggregated and presented by the CS AKTive-Space are mediated through a common ontology. This ontology, the AKT Reference Ontology, was developed within the AKT project over a six month period, drawing heavily on ontologies written earlier by AKT partners. The reasons for this were twofold: ontology development is a costly exercise, and careful reuse of existing work stands to provide benefits by reducing duplicated effort. Secondly, our choice of a single ontology for the system reduces the amount of translation required. Information from external sources (which may have been expressed in other ontologies) still needs to be translated into the system ontology, creating a 'walled garden' in which it is easier to work.

This closed approach was taken for pragmatic reasons. The alternative being an open approach that might figuratively be described as a meadow in which many ontologies bloom, would have been to use a number of heterogeneous ontologies throughout the system. This approach runs the risk of complicating the design of the system components unnecessarily, because each of the components must either be able to translate between each of the ontologies in use, or be able to invoke a separate translation service that mediates between the ontologies. In addition, these ontologies may have mutual inconsistencies, which raises the cost of deciding upon appropriate mappings between ontology or ontology fragments.

Our closed approach to ontology design has the additional benefit that it is more practical to write tools for information extraction against a single ontology, and much easier to write tutorial materials from which third parties can learn to write their own extraction tools.

Our choice of an ontology for the AKTiveSpace was driven largely by our previous developments, but we hypothesised that we would be able to construct an appropriate interface for an application domain given any suitably expressive ontology for that domain, and that the actual choice of ontology was largely immaterial. This has been borne out in our experiences of building CS AKTive-Space. The selection of elements to be displayed in CS AKTiveSpace brings certain characteristics of the application domain to the foreground (people, publications, institutions, etc) in what is essentially a very abstract ontology for that domain. What is required is that these characteristics can be extracted from our chosen ontology in sufficient detail, regardless of the manner in which they are actually represented in our ontology.

The chief concern with ontology choice is that of the resulting performance of the AKTiveSpace interface. Overly-expressive structures in strangely-structured ontologies may still allow the extraction of the information required by the user interface, but at an exaggerated cost (being the cost of executing queries which have been expressed in that ontology). Our ontology showed itself to be fit for purpose, although some areas were more complex than they needed to be for the specific task performed by the user interface (notable areas were the representations of dates and of publications). However, this was anticipated as a likely consequence of using a largely task-neutral ontology in a more task-specific application.

3   Service Orientation and Modularisation

3.1   Harvesting

To be convincing, the building of a Semantic Web application requires data on a large scale. In the long term, we expect the data on the Web to be marked up, either mechanically or by hand. In the medium to short term, however, suitable heterogeneous sources for our application domain were not available. We therefore devoted effort from the outset to gathering the data we needed, so that when the storage and processing technologies had been built, the data would be there for them to use.

Due to the wide variety of the data sources that we use, we have found it necessary to invest a degree of effort in developing individual services for each of our data sources that mediate and recast these sources in terms of our ontology. These services range from specialised database export scripts to XML transformation tools [4] that have been trained to extract the required content from semi-structured web pages. Although these mediators are based on a common framework of code (which handles the straightforward tasks of database access, HTTP retrieval, RDF construction and the more common patterns in our ontology, such as date and time expression), they each contain specialised capabilities that are tailored to the content and nature of the individual data sources. While the bulk translation of instance data by such a mediator is straightforward, our use of these mediators has shown that the mapping of existing structured and semi-structured data at the schema/ontology level is not a task that can be effectively automated in all cases; the investment of effort in building mediators for our common ontology is reflected in the consequent perceived value of the knowledge base to which they contribute.

The CS AKTiveSpace application requires that a range of content be available for use by the system. As it stands, some of this content already exists in suitable structured forms, while others do not. We adopt a pragmatic attitude that reflects the fact that although the content that we are gathering is the prime mover that drives the interface, we should also be tolerant of inconsistencies in that content. We use a relatively scruffy approach in which we make the immediate best use of the available data sources, perhaps in an imperfect fashion, while anticipating that we will be able to make better use of them in future. Although this comes at a cost (there is an implicit commitment to future knowledge maintenance), such early exploitation of available content is necessary to initiate a community process that should be self-sustaining in the future and so justify the investment of effort.

We employ both push and pull models of knowledge acquisition, where push and pull refer primarily to whether the publisher or consumer are responsible for translating the data into a form which is suitable for the consumer. The push model involves a data source (the publisher) choosing to express its data in terms of the ontology used by the CS AKTiveSpace. The publisher is solely responsible for the translation, so the consumer may simply retrieve the translated knowledge base without any further effort required on its part. In comparison, the pull model requires that the consumer takes a raw data source (which may be published against some other ontology, or which may only exist as a set of unannotated webpages) and construct a knowledge base from that data source.

In some ways, the pull model has advantages over the push model, in that the consumer has a much greater level of control over what information is encoded within the resulting knowledge bases and is better placed to be able to correct inconsistencies or to adapt to changes in the underlying common ontology, However, this comes at the expense of a greater cost to the consumer, both in the acquisition phase of the knowledge lifecycle (when a new data source is acquired), and particularly in the maintenance phase.

We use the pull model predominantly for large, comparatively static data sources (for example, the list of countries and administrative regions given by ISO3166), and as an interim solution for high-value data sources that are of general interest to the community (for example, the Engineering and Physical Sciences Research Council's database of research funding). This gives us a means to 'pump-prime' the system with sufficient data to encourage other members of the community to participate by offering to push their local data sources to us (the viral, rich-get-richer phenomenon that we later describe needs to start somewhere). In the longer term, we aim to encourage the owners of the majority of these pull model sources to move to a push model of delivery.

The hyphen metadata gathered by these mediators consists of 430MB of RDF/XML files containing around 10 million RDF triples describing 800,000 instances of people, places, publications and other items of interest to the academic community.

3.2 Armadillo

Information can be present in different formats on the Web, in documents, in repositories, (e.g. databases or digital libraries). From such resources or their output, it is possible to extract information with different reliability. Systems such as databases generally contain reliable structured data and can be queried using an API or a Wrapper. Wrapper methodologies are Information Extraction methodologies aiming at modelling very regular Web pages such as those produced by databases; wrappers can be induced, i.e. they can be learnt from examples [5], [6]. When the information is contained in textual documents, extracting information requires more sophisticated methodologies. Wrapper induction systems have been extended to cope with less rigidly structured pages [7], free texts and mixtures of them [8]. The degree of complexity increases from rigidly structured to free texts. The more complex the task is then generally the less reliable the extracted information is. Also, as complexity increases more training data is required. Wrappers can be trained with a handful of examples whereas full IE systems may require millions of words [9]. The more the task becomes complex, the more information is needed for training, the more reliable input data becomes difficult to identify.

Armadillo [10] is a service for on-the-fly, user-determined, directed knowledge acquisition, which is used to opportunistically expand a given knowledge base.

Armadillo makes use of a simple methodology, which populates ontologies from distributed information. The system starts from a set of generic strategies, typically wrappers, defining where to search for initial information and what to look for. When data is harvested using these strategies, it is passed to an oracle, such as a reliable database, which is used to verify the results to an initial degree of certainty. Armadillo works because of the inherent redundancy of information on the web. Redundancy is given by the presence of multiple citations of the same information in different contexts and in different superficial formats. This factor is currently used for improving question answering systems [11]. When recognized information is present in different sources, it is possible to use its multiple occurrences to bootstrap recognisers that, when generalized, will retrieve other pieces of information, producing more generic recognisers [12]. The system loops in this manner to discover more and more reliable information.

The Armadillo AKTiveSpace application works in the following way. First a user submits an armadillo request to populate the underlying ontology via the AKTiveSpace site. This request is automatically submitted to a remote Armadillo server, which queues requests until one of many Armadillo clients is available to process it. An Armadillo client uses 3store RDQL queries to determine what knowledge is already asserted regarding the instance to be populated, and to help resolve referential integrity issues [13]. To prevent compounding of any errors this does not collate information that has been previously submitted from Armadillo. With a basic ontology of information, each entity is rated for reliability by utilising the redundancy of its sources. If information has been elicited from numerous sources it is assumed to be more reliable than an entity from only one source. With an aim to locate web pages that contain information suitable for incorporating into the ontology, higher rated entities are used to search for likely pages of interest, using the Google search engine. Armadillo uses Amilcaré for Information Extraction to identify the structure of found pages so that additional entities can be identified. This approach finds additional content for the ontology and each entry is again rated for reliability, this process continuously cycles until a set timeout has occurred. Finally the populated ontology is asserted into the AKT 3store in the form of RDF triples. In this way, future requests for information about the instance in question will potentially return more information.

The Armadillo approach of initially wrapping followed by repeated Information Extraction can be seen to dramatically improve the recall of available data with a minimal loss of precision. This is demonstrated in table 1 showing the performance when eliciting papers for eight individuals; this is detailed further in [10].

	Possible	Actual	Correct	Wrong	Missing	Precision	Recall	F-Measure
Seed	320	152	151	1	168	99.3	47.2	64.0
IE-based	320	217	214	3	103	98.6	66.9	79.7

Table 1. Accuracy of Armadillo in paper discovery

In the table, *Possible* represents the number of pieces of information that the system is expected to extract (i.e. the information as extracted by an oracle, such as a person); *Actual* is the number of pieces of information extracted in total by the system. *Correct* is the number of correct pieces of information extracted by the system, *Wrong* the incorrect extractions and *Missing* the missed pieces of information. *Precision, Recall* and *F-measure* are standard overall measures in the field of information extraction: precision=correct/actual, recall=correct/possible, while F-measure is a weighted mean of the two.

3.3   ONTOCOPI

ONTOCOPI (ONTOlogy-based Community Of Practice Identifier [14]) is a tool that finds sets of similar instances to a selected instance in a knowledge-base. If an ontology (i.e. both the classification structure and the knowledge base of instantiations) represents the objects and relations in a domain, then connections between the objects can be analysed. The aim of ONTOCOPI is to extract patterns of relations that might help define a Community Of Practice (COP). COPs are informal groups of individuals interested in a particular job, procedure or work domain, who exchange insights on tasks connected with work [15]. COPs are very important in organisations, taking on important knowledge management (KM) functions. Increasingly, COPs are being harnessed by organisations to carry out aspects of their KM (for an extended example, see [16]). Community identification is currently very resource-heavy, often based on extensive interviewing. ONTOCOPI supports the task of COP identification by analysing the patterns of connectivity between instances in the ontology. The ONTOCOPI hypothesis is that the informal relations that define a community of practice can be inferred from the presence of more formal relations (such as being the member of a group, the author of a paper, and so on). For instance, if A and B have no formal relation, but they have both authored papers (formal relation) with C, then that indicates that they might share interests (informal relation). It is our working hypothesis that the COPs identified by ONTOCOPI can be reasonable proxies for communities of practice.

Algorithm The ONTOCOPI expansion algorithm generates the COP of the selected instance by identifying the set of close instances and ranking them according to the weights they accumulate from several path traversals. It applies a breadth first, spreading activation search, traversing the semantic relations between instances (ignoring directionality) until a link threshold is reached. The link threshold allows COPs to be of different ranges. A narrow COP of a project may consist of only those entities in direct relation to the project (e.g. project employees, member organisations, themes), while a wider COP may include indirectly related entities, such as the colleagues of the project's members, other projects about the same theme or subject, etc. Consider the example in figure 2. Assume we need to identify the COP of the query instance *A*, using the relationships *has Author*, *memberOf* and *attended*, with the weights 1.0, 0.6, and 0.3

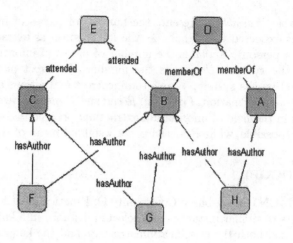

Fig. 2. Example Ontology Network

respectively. All instances will have an initial weight of 1. Activation will spread from the query instance to neighbouring instances in the network, up to a given number of links. In the first expansion, the query instance A will pass on weight to all the instances it is connected to. The amount of weight passed equals the weight of the instance multiplied by the weight of the traversed relationship. In this case, A passes 1×0.6 to D, and 1×1 to H. These will be added to their initial weights of 1. In return, these instances will pass their total weights to all their neighbours, so D for example will pass $(1 + 1 \times 0.6) \times 0.6$ to B and A. Expansion will stop when the link paths are exhausted or the link threshold is reached Instances therefore accumulate weight based on the number of relevant relations they have with the initial instance.

3.4 ONTOCOPI in CS AKTiveSpace

The complete implementation of ONTOCOPI exists as a plugin for Protégé 2000 [17] as presented in Alani et al[14] and O'Hara et al [18]. A less sophisticated version (with less features) has been developed as a web service and linked to 3store. ONTOCOPI can access the ontology and knowledge base stored in 3store via RDQL queries. When a person instance is selected within CS AKTiveSpace, it sends the URI of this instance in a HTTP query to ONTOCOPI, which in turn queries 3store to identify the CoP of the given instance. The result will be a list of person URIs that forms the community of the selected individual. The list is returned back to CS AKTiveSpace as an RDF file.

As explained earlier, community identification in ONTOCOPI is based on analysing knowledge networks of instances and their interconnections. Hence its quality is directly dependent on that of the knowledge source. When integrating ONTOCOPI with CS AKTiveSpace, it was noticed that the quality of the resulting COPs was mostly affected by three main factors in the 3store knowledge base:

1. Richness: This is related to the amount and variety of knowledge in 3store. For example if only a small amount of information is available about a person, and of limited variety (e.g. few authored papers), then the identified COP for this individual will inevitably be shallow and of poor quality. The richness of 3store is always increasing as more knowledge is being harvested from an increased number of sources.
2. Connectivity: Performance of ONTOCOPI will be compromised if the network to be analysed is fragmented and heavily disconnected (i.e. a large number of connections are missing between existing instances). Acquiring more knowledge to establish further connections is therefore important for COP identification.
3. Duplication: One of the persisting problems often encountered when gathering knowledge from multiple sources is that of duplication. Information about the same individuals or objects is often acquired from various sources. It is necessary to have a mechanism for identifying and resolving duplications to maintain the integrity of the knowledge base and the quality if the services it provides. ONTOCOPI's output was greatly improved when *sameAs* attributes were added to 3store. ONTOCOPI's algorithm was modified to take into account these relations when crawling the knowledge network.

4   Server Implementation

4.1   Scale

Due to the volume of data (approximately 15M RDF triples) and degree of interlinking and inference required the RDF data and RDFS schema required storage in a dedicated RDF(S) server application, rather than queries run directly over RDF/XML files. It would have been possible to implement the back-end directly over RDF/XML data with no caching or pre-parsing, but the computational cost would be high enough to prevent interactive use.

The scale of the data combined with the use of RDFS' inferential capabilities required some advances in the area of RDFS storage, these are further described in [19], but mainly involve an efficient RDBMS to RDF mapping and hybrid eager/lazy entailment generation.

The scalability of the system was tested further by asserting an additional 10M triple knowledge base, and the system showed no obvious difference in performance. However the ability to scale to a level of data describing international research is likely to require more work in the area of efficiency and scalability.

4.2   Expressivity

For the most part RDFS was found to be adequately expressive for the description of the resources used in the UK Computer Science data, however there is no way to indicate the equivalence of two RDF resources, so we required the OWL sameAs property for these uses. This property is particularly common where we have multiple documents describing the same individuals, such as a funding body's description of a particular researcher combined with their home institution's description.

The correct handling of this co-reference situation is just one small part of the problem it poses; a larger, and in many ways still unsolved part is the correct automatic identification of co-referent entities.

There is a more subtle issue relating to excessive analysis – and general excessively expressive structures – in ontological structures. For example the Calendar-Date class in the AKT Reference Ontology[20] is structured as shown in figure 3.

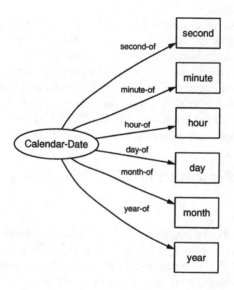

Fig. 3. AKT Reference Ontology date representation

For cases where the interface wishes to display a date in a form understandable by a user this requires a moderately complex query to be executed, whereas a simple string, or XML Datatype date representation can be retrieved and parsed with a single, simple query.

5   User Interface

The CS AKTiveSpace interface (figure 4) lets users explore the domain of Computer Science in the UK. Users can look at particular regions of the country or research areas as defined by the ACM classification system to see who in a given region is working in which areas. Users can also explore a given researcher's community of practice, as well as get a sense of where that person ranks in terms of funding level in an area or other UK rating criteria. The CS AKTiveSpace interaction design emphasises exploration of a domain via a persistent context of the associated attributes in the domain.

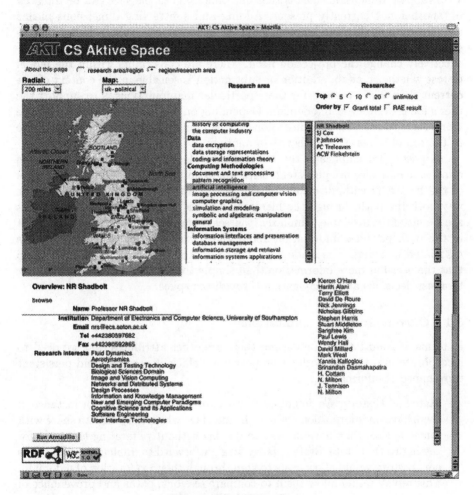

Fig. 4. CS AKTiveSpace

The CS AKTiveSpace interface is informed by the mSpace interaction model for representing high dimensional information domains for access by a range of users [21]. In this model, users are presented with a default projection through the dimensions of the domain space. When the projection is flattened, the result is a hierarchy which can be readily represented in a 2-dimensional view. These projections are referred to as "slices" through the domain space. An mSpace provides several particular manipulations which can be carried out on the slices to better support users' interests in the domains. These affordances are dimensional sorting, swapping and expansion and contraction. In dimensional sorting, users can rearrange the ordering of elements in the slice, changing the dependencies in the hierarchy.

Swapping dimensions means that one dimension in the slice can be replaced by another not currently present. Adding and subtracting dimensions means that the current slice can be contracted or expanded with more or fewer dimensions. With these manipulations, users can either reorganize the current slice or effectively change the projection itself. There are constraints within the model to test whether a swap, addition or subtraction is sensible in the context of the current slice. The rationale for these particular manipulations is to support the user's focus of interest in a domain. Depending on a user's context, it may make more sense to see how the dimensions in the domain all relate to one attribute at the top of a hierarchy rather than another.

mSpaces also emphasise the maintenance of context. Instances in a given dimension of a slice are persistent: selection of an instance reveals the next level of the hierarchy without occluding the previous level of the hierarchy. In this way both the path through the hierarchy and the context of the path elements are persistently available. Similarly, the selection of an instance at any point in the path provides information about that currently selected instance. This associated information is made available to improve the context of selection so that the user has more information than simply the label of an instance in order to assist decisions about navigation through the space.

5.1   Current Interface Limitations

In terms of good interaction design, there are other attributes that we need to incorporate into the UI, both to support more efficient access to and persistent provenance of information.

- State and History: We do not currently capture state, so that, for instance, if users have an information state in the interface which they wish to share with someone else, they have no way to do this without reiterating the steps for getting to that state. State is fairly straightforward to implement. History is not. History would allow users to step through their exploration of a domain. This replay would allow them to compare sessions, paths and provenance of an exploration
- Order: We do not order the attributes in a dimension in any specific way. Adding ordering on each dimension (currently represented by a column) would give the added query on that dimension to see, for instance, either a listing by alphabet or by ranking of the institutions in the list, according to the UK's Research Assessment Exercise ("RAE Result"), or by grant total and so on.
- Number: a simple value to provide per dimension/column is how many elements are in a current dimension/column at any point.

The above list represents refinements to the extant UI. That UI represents an interaction paradigm that is distinct from the Web's primary keyword search/

link click search/browse interaction. We have been focusing on the benefit of this exploration approach, which we view as a complement to search/browse, not as a replacement. As such, an integrated interface would provide both exploration and search/browse. It is not obvious how keyword search would be integrated with the CS AKTiveSpace UI so that users would be able to see the both the context of a given retrieved item as well as the list of possible hits.

The current CS AKTiveSpace has implemented only a subset of the mSpace functions. It presents a default slice, and users can reorganise the dimensions in the slice to support their focus of interest. Users cannot at this time swap, add or subtract dimensions. They do however get detailed information about any instance selected in a given dimension. So, selecting a given researcher, for instance, provides a brief profile of the researcher: contact information, top publications and community of practice information.

One of the reasons why the CS AKTiveSpace interaction is an imperfect mSpace is that, while we knew what the affordances of the model were, we had not yet formalised how best to implement these in a semantic web application. Indeed, we used our efforts to instantiate some of the core mSpace functions as a way to better refine the model and its relation to representing it within OWL. Part of the research now is to fine tune the rules for deploying a complete mSpace over an ontologically defined space, and then testing the deployment against a set of domains. From here, we plan to deploy a framework to make deploying mSpaces in the semantic web as plug and play as possible. Our goal is to make available a set of interface models that semantic web application designers can readily deploy against their domains. Improving and automating interaction deployments for the Semantic Web is also part of the research agenda of the Workshop on Interaction Design and the Semantic Web at WWW2004[3], motivated by our experience with CS AKTiveSpace

The CS AKTiveSpace UI has also shown us that, even with 10 million triples, we do not have sufficient content to provide a truly rich reflection of the domain modelled. The expressive power of these applications, in order to make the kinds of comparisons between X and Y comes with scale. Harvesting data can only take us so far, it seems. So, while we have demonstrated with CS AKTiveSpace a new kind of representation and interaction for Semantic Web applications, we are seeking ways to improve content acquisition so we can better utilise the model's capabilities.

Overall, the interaction design for CS AKTiveSpace has been well received. Demonstrations of CS AKTiveSpace have motivated various industrial, government and funding groups to solicit us on building AKTiveSpaces for aspects of their intranets. That the interaction design is well-formalised we anticipate will help to make this translation process both tractable and effective.

---

[3] http://interaction.ecs.soton.ac.uk/idsw04/

6   Client Implementation

The CS AKTiveSpace client is implemented as an XHTML and ECMA-Script web page, rather than using a piece of external software, such as a Java Applet. We felt that this technique was more in-keeping with the spirit of the semantic web, as it builds on existing web technologies.

6.1   Data Access and Query Execution

Queries are run against the RDF(S) used to inform the client using RDQL [22] queries in HTTP GET requests. The HTTP services queried return XML documents containing the RDQL binding table that satisfies the query.

The scripts running in the web page initialise the display by querying the schema and instances that are required to build the initial state of the interface. For the UK Computer Science data these initial queries can be time consuming over slower Internet links, sometimes taking up to 30 seconds, as they require the transfer of a significant amount of data spread over several hundred requests. If the interface was being rolled out as a production service, with a relatively static schema it would have been advantageous to cache the data required to initialise the client - or pass it in some bulk, compressed, form to reduce the initialisation time.

6.2   mSpace Column Implementation

The design on the column interactions is based upon mSpace [23], but the implementation in RDF required a mapping between the structures present in the RDF schema and the columns.

The mapping chosen for the implementation of this version is the most direct one, mapping directly from column to column in the order they appear on the screen. Although this mapping is quite easy to understand it produces different results for the same query if expressed in a different order – for example. if a research area is chosen before a region, you will not necessarily get the same results as when the region is chosen before the research area.

This implementation has led to a formalisation and more detailed explanation of the column/semantic mapping [21].

7   Concluding Remarks

This paper has discussed the technologies and structure that forms the CS AKTiveSpace. We began by discussing the ontology design choices, and noted that what is required is a sufficiently expressive ontology, and that the structure influences the performance of the application, rather than the capabilities. We then discussed the harvesting of data for the application. For the CS AKTive-Space to be realistic, it was important that a wide range of heterogeneous sources were used; until the semantic web becomes a reality, it will be necessary to build and use targeted tools to acquire data from appropriate sources for particular application areas.

We then discussed one of the services utilised by CS AKTiveSpace - Armadillo. This natural language processor enables the user of the semantic web application to request and initiate further knowledge discovery from the web, as required. Another service was then presented - ONTOCOPI. This service gives the user a sophisticated tool for finding out complex relationships between instances in the space.

The amount of data for an application such as this is high, and we included a section on the server, noting that it can now serve 25M RDF triples in an efficient manner.

In the last section, the most obvious aspect of the application was discussed, the User Interface. This was introduced through the theory behind it, followed by comments on the implementation.

Finally, CS AKTiveSpace shows that a large-scale ontology mediated application can recruit, in a dynamic fashion. heterogeneous information resources and present them in a tractable and efficient manner. The principled composition of these semantic services is the subject of ongoing research within the AKT project.

8   Acknowledgements

This work was supported by the Advanced Knowledge Technologies (AKT) Interdisciplinary Research Collaboration (IRC). The AKT IRC is sponsored by the UK Engineering and Physical Sciences Research Council under grant number GR/N15764/01 and comprises the Universities of Aberdeen, Edinburgh, Sheffield, Southampton and the Open University.

References

[1] Semantic Web Challenge 2003. http://challenge.semanticweb.org/ (2003)
[2] Berners-Lee, T., Hendler, J., Lassila, O.: The semantic web. Scientific American (2001)
[3] The AKT project: The AKT Technologies. http://www.aktors.org/technologies/ (2003)
[4] Leonard, T., Glaser, H.: Large scale acquisition and maintenance from the web without source access. In: Workshop 4, Knowledge Markup and Semantic Annotation, K-CAP 2001. (2001) 97–101
[5] Kushmerick, N., Weld, D.S., Doorenbos, R.B.: Wrapper induction for information extraction. In: Intl. Joint Conference on Artificial Intelligence (IJCAI 1997). (1997)
[6] Muslea, I., Minton, S., Knoblock, C.: Wrapper induction for semistructured web-based information sources. In: Proceedings of the Conference on Automatic Learning and Discovery (CONALD 1998). (1998)
[7] Freitag, D., Kushmerick, N.: Boosted wrapper induction. In: Proceedings of the 17th National Conference on Artificial Intelligence (AAAI 2000). (2000)

[8] Ciravegna, F.: Adaptive information extraction from text by rule induction and generalisation. In: Proceeedings of the 17th International Joint Conference On Artificial Intelligence (IJCAI 2001). (2001)

[9] Yan, T., Garcia-Molina, H.: The sift information dissemination system. In: ACM TODS 2000. (2000)

[10] Dingli, A., Ciravegna, F., Wilks, Y.: Automatic semantic annotation using unsupervised information extraction and integration. In: Proceedings of SemAnnot 2003 Workshop. (2003)

[11] Dumais, S., Banko, M., Brill, E., Lin, J., Ng, A.: Web question answering: Is more always better? In: Proceedings of the 25th Annual International ACM SIGIR Conference on Research and Development in Information Retrieval (SIGIR 2002). (2002)

[12] Brin, S.: Extracting patterns and relations from the world wide web. In: WebDB Workshop at 6th International Conference on Extending Database Technology, (EDBT 1998). (1998)

[13] Alani, H., Dasmahapatra, S., Gibbins, N., Glaser, H., Harris, S., Kalfoglou, Y., O'Hara, K., Shadbolt, N.: Managing reference: Ensuring referential integrity of ontologies for the semantic web. In: Proceedings 13th International Conference on Knowledge Engineering and Knowledge Management (EKAW'02). (2002) 317–334

[14] Alani, H., Dasmahapatra, S., O'Hara, K., Shadbolt, N.: Ontocopi - using ontology-based network analysis to identify communities of practice. IEEE Intelligent Systems 18(2) (2003) 18–25

[15] Wenger, E., McDermott, R., Snyder, W. Harvard Business School Press, Cambridge, Mass (2002)

[16] Smith, R., Farquhar, A.: The road ahead for knowledge management: An ai perspective. American Association for Artificial Intelligence 21(4) (2000) 17–40

[17] Musen, M., Fergerson, R., Grosso, W., Noy, N., Grubezy, M., Gennari, J.: Component-based support for building knowledge-acquisition systems. In: Proceedings of the Intelligent Information Processing (IIP 2000) Conference of the International Federation for Processing (IFIP), World Computer Congress (WCC'2000). (2000) 18–22

[18] O'Hara, K., Alani, H., Shadbolt, N.: Identifying communities of practice: Analysing ontologies as networks to support community recognition. In: Proceedings of the IFIP World Computer Congress (IFIP 02), Montreal, Canada. (2002)

[19] Harris, S., Gibbins, N.: 3store: Efficient bulk RDF storage. In: Proceedings of the 1st International Workshop on Practical and Scalable Semantic Systems (PSSS'03). (2003) 1–20 http://eprints.aktors.org/archive/00000273/.

[20] The AKT project: The AKT Reference Ontology. http://www.aktors.org/publications/ontology/ (2002)

[21] Gibbins, N., Harris, S., schraefel, m.: Applying mspace interfaces to the semantic web. preprint: http://triplestore.aktors.org/tmp/www2004-mspace-model.pdf (2003)

[22] Hewlett-Packard Labs: RDQL - RDF data query language. http://www.hpl.hp.com/semweb/rdql.htm (2003)

[23] schraefel, m., Karam, M., Zhao, S.: mSpace: Interaction design for user-determined, adaptable domain exploration in hypermedia. (2003) 217–235

Cultural Heritage and the Semantic Web

V.R. Benjamins[1], J. Contreras[1], M. Blázquez[1], J.M. Dodero[3], A. Garcia[2], E. Navas[2], F. Hernandez[2*], C. Wert[2+]

[1]Intelligent Software Components, S.A., www.isoco.com
{rbenjamins, jcontreras}@isoco.com

[2]Residenca de Estudiantes, www.residencia.csic.es,
enavas@fundacionginer.org, {cwert, fhc}@residencia.csic.es

[3]Universidad Carlos III de Madrid, www.uc3m.es
dodero@inf.uc3m.es

Abstract. Online cultural archives represent vast amounts of interesting and useful information. During the last decades huge amounts of literature works have been scanned to provide better access to Humanities researchers and teachers. Was the problem 20 years ago one of scarceness of information (precious originals only to consult in major libraries), today's problem is that of information overload: many databases online and many CD collections are available; each with their own search forms and attributes. This makes it cumbersome for users to find relevant information. In this paper, we describe a case study of how Semantic Web Technologies can be used to disclose cultural heritage information in a scalable way. We present an ontology of Humanities, a semi-automatic tool for annotation, and an application to exploit the annotated content. This tool, positioned somewhere in the middle, between a basic editor and a fully automatic wrapper, helps annotators performing heavy knowledge acquisition tasks in a more efficient and secure way.

1. Introduction

Online cultural archives represent vast amounts of interesting and useful information. During the last decades huge amounts of literature works have been scanned to provide better access to Humanities researchers and teachers. Most works are scanned as images, which are available through microfiches, CDs and online databases. More recently, OCR techniques are increasingly applied to provide full text search facilities. Was the problem 20 years ago one of scarceness of information (precious originals only to consult in major libraries), today's problem is that of information overload: many databases online and many CD collections are available, each with their own search forms and attributes. As is the case with general search engines, keyword based search has its limitations. One can only search for specific words and their co-occurrence in documents. This may give acceptable results for 'normal' Web users, in the area of humanities it is not sufficient because one is above all interested in *relations* e.g. between artists, their works, the friends, their studies, who they inspired,

---

* Now at: Digibis: fhc@digibis.com
+ Now at: Patronato General de la Universidad Alcalá www.fgua.es

J. Davies et al. (Eds.): ESWS 2004, LNCS 3053, pp. 433-444, 2004.
© Springer-Verlag Berlin Heidelberg 2004

etc. In this paper, we describe a case study of how Semantic Web Technologies can be used to disclose cultural heritage information in a scalable way. We present an ontology of Humanities, a semi-automatic tool for annotation, and a publication procedure for generating a semantic cultural portal.

The basic idea is the following:

- Build an acceptable ontology of Humanities by involving professionals.
- Use the ontology to semantically annotate existing cultural content.
- Support the annotation process by an "intelligent" editor.
- Publish the results on a website, providing functionalities for semantic navigation, intelligent search and 3D visualization.
- Provide a methodology so that other content providers can publish and exploit their content on the Semantic Web.

1.1 The Humanities Domain

Research in the area of Humanities typically aims at investigating object such as events, persons, and movements, in a historical or cultural context. Applied to art, this includes, for example, paintings (e.g. the Guernika of Picasso), movements (Impressionism or Modernism), painters (Paul Klee) and authors (Cervantes). In this application domain, relations between persons, works, locations, etc. are very important because they constitute large part of the context, which gives meaning to the object of study. Therefore, keyword-based approaches to retrieve information have serious limitations, since those approaches simply ignore the meaning and the interrelations the concepts have. The other approach used in this area relies on RDBMS, which enables a more precise retrieval. However, there are many databases available, each with its own schema. More recently, also thesauri are used to improve retrieval of information by considering synonyms, hyponyms, etc. Ontologies go one step further by allowing the expression of additional relations between domain concepts. In addition, they can play the role of meta models for integration of multiple heterogeneous sources.

1.2 Ontologies

An ontology is a shared and common understanding of some domain that can be communicated across people and computers [15, 16, 3, and 17]. Ontologies can therefore be shared and reused among different applications [12]. An ontology can be defined as a formal, explicit specification of a shared conceptualisation [15, 3]. "Conceptualisation" refers to an abstract model of some phenomenon in the world by having identified the relevant concepts of that phenomenon. "Explicit" means that the type of concepts used, and the constraints on their use are explicitly defined. "Formal" refers to the fact that the ontology should be machine-readable. "Shared" reflects the notion that an ontology captures consensual knowledge, that is, it is not private to some individual, but accepted by a group. An ontology describes the subject matter using the notions of concepts, instances, relations, functions, and axioms. Concepts in the ontology are organized in taxonomies through which inheritance mechanisms can be applied. It is our experience that especially the social part for building a commonly agreed ontology is not easy [2].

In the next section, we outline the ontology of Humanities, along with the methodology followed for its construction. Section 3 presents the semi-automatic annotation tool. In Section 4, we discuss different types of exploitation of the semantic content. Finally, Section 5 presents a discussion of the results and concludes the paper.

2. An Ontology of Humanities

To build the ontology, the Competency Questions Methodology [25] has been used. Competency questions are questions that the experts require the ontology-based application to provide answers for. Answers to the questions provide concrete inputs for the classes, instances and relationships to include in the ontology. In Table 1, we illustrate some of the competency questions used, categorized according to the main concepts they have elicited.

Concept	Competency Question
Person	Who wrote 'Cráter'? Every member of PNV Editors of the Gaceta Literaria journal Painters that participated any exposition in Barcelona in 1923
Works	Which works is about Rafael Laffón? What another name is known for work X? Where did X study? Which publications came out from the congress X?
Places and Dates	Where was X brought up? Where was placed Publisher X? Which authors were born in Madrid? When was group X dissolved?
Activities	Which activities did Ramón Gómez de la Serna play? What did Ramón Basterrá play in the 20's? Who managed publisher X? What post did X occupy?
Organizations	Where did Eusa, Víctor study? Who managed institution X? Who studied in institution X? Who formed group X?
Styles	List of every author qualified as post-modernist Which works are considered as ultraist? Which movements does Picasso belong to? What another name is known for group X?
Events	What events did Antonio Espina participate in Madrid in 1920 and 1921 years? Every congress held in Madrid Who participated in any congress held in Seville in 1920?
Relationships	Which acquaintances did Antonio Espina have with Ramón Gómez? What acquaintance did Antonio Espina have with Mexico? What acquaintance did Antonio Espina have with the group SIC? Enemies of X

Table 1. Competency Questions for the Humanities Ontology

Some of the concepts included in the ontology include: Studies, Profession, Company, Institution, Academic Organization, Person, Work, Expression, Manifestation, Graphic works, Literary work, Musical work, Event, Exposition, Group, Social Group, Movement, Subject. A complete description of the ontology can be obtained from [10]. Each concept of the ontology is described through several attributes.

An important design decision we took was that relationships between concepts are modelled as first class objects. This decisions was taken because often the relationships themselves have attributes that cannot be modelled by its involving concepts. Take for example, the relation "studied_at" between a person and an organization. This relation is qualified by a start and end date, which is not meaningful to person nor location.

The ontology has been constructed with Protégé 2000 [19]. Fig 1 shows a fragment of the ontology in Protégé 2000.

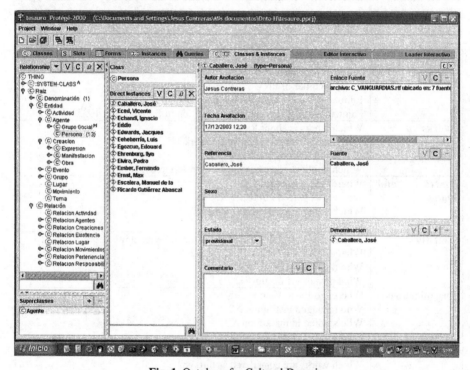

Fig. 1. Ontology for Cultural Domain

As starting point for the ontology, we used two types of existing ontologies:
1. General ontologies to model things like persons, organizations, events, etc. Examples of ontologies considered include: SUO [23], Generalized Upper Model [14], WordNet [27], CyCorp [6]
2. Specific standards for the humanities domain for modelling things like works art, typical relations like 'studied_in', 'inspired_by', etc. We included IFLA [13] a standard of Federation of Library Associations and Institutions, and MARC [18] a XML standard for automatically processable bibliographical information

3. The Semi-automatic Annotation Tool

The annotation task for the Semantic Web takes as input existing content, either structured, semi-structured or unstructured, and provides as output the same content along with a semantic annotation based on ontologies. The semantics as such are defined in ontologies. The annotations provide pointers to these ontologies.

Annotation can be performed in several manners, ranging from completely manual to tool-assisted to fully automatic. As a result of the analysis performed in [5], it turns out that the type of annotation approach to be chosen depends on the rate of structure the content exhibits. More structure allows for more automation, while maintaining the quality of the annotations.

As has been the experience of several researchers and practitioners, the annotation effort is a serious barrier to its widespread use [1, 25 and 26]. Although in the area of humanities manual annotation efforts are considered as necessary and are actually performed, significant improvements are possible ranging from intelligent assistants to (semi)-automatic annotators.

Together with a detailed methodology for ontology management and population we built an intelligent annotation editor. There are considered two kinds of users for the tool:

- **Knowledge engineer** (in charge of ontology schema management): performs major changes on the ontology, especially on the ontology schema, evaluating the final impact on the existing instances.
- **Annotator** (in charge of ontology population): introduces new instances in the ontology and maintain the existing ones.

The annotation tool, a kind of intelligent editor that helps the user to perform annotation tasks for a given source text is developed as a plug-in to the Protégé 2000 tool. As shown in Fig 2, the editor allows loading the source text to be annotated (right hand side). It allows standard editing operations on the ontology and the instances as provided by Protégé 2000 (left hand side). Apart from the standard Protégé functionalities, the user can easily add new instances using a drag-and-drop facility.

For instance, we can say that Picasso is an artist by selecting "Picasso" in the source text and dragging it to the ontology concept "Person" and releasing it. This creates the instance and pops up the Protégé form for creating instances. The annotation process does not change the source text itself (i.e. by putting the ontological tags in the text), rather it creates a link from the instance to the original string in the source text that caused its creation. As such the original string is an occurrence of the instance, and there can be many occurrences of the same instance throughout the text. Thus, if we drag-and-drop the identical string "Picasso" again on "person", then rather than creating a new instance, it creates a new occurrence of the same instance, unless, of course, the user decides otherwise. We can also select a string like "inspired-by" and drag-and-drop it onto the corresponding relation in the ontology (modelled as a class). Now the editor creates in instance of this relationship and pops up the corresponding Protégé 2000 from where the user is prompted among other to complete the domain and range of the relation.

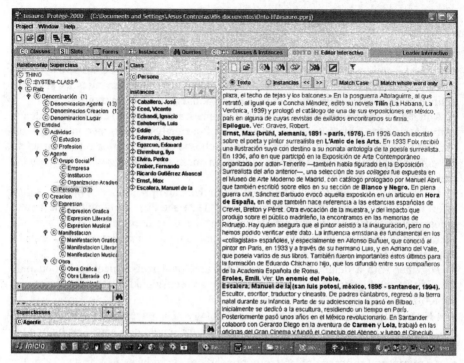

Fig. 2. Assisted Editor for Cultural Text Annotations

Since complete manual annotation is a tedious and error-prone work, we added improvements towards automatic annotation to the editor. Automatic (cascading) creation of instances and a recommendation facility, each of them discussed in more detail below.

3.1 Annotation Rules

In complex domain as described here, when performing massive knowledge acquisition tasks, often exist typical annotation patterns to be performed. For instance, each time a new artistic work is being annotated, it makes sense to also create new instances for its expression and manifestation (as defined in the IFLA standard [13]). In IFLA "work" is defined as the idea of an art work, like that of the Guernika painting of Picasso (Spanish Civil War and the Guernika bombing). The "expression" is a painting (it could as well be expressed in a poem or movie). The "manifestation" is the actual painting that can be enjoyed in the "Reina Sophia" museum in Madrid, Spain. These kind of patterns stem from dependency relations between concepts in the domain ontology.

For these typical annotation sequences we included a rule engine that allows conditional firing of a rule set to add a new instance, check for name conflicts or consult the annotator for ambiguity resolution, among others. The rule engine is based on the open source software [11] and was connected to the cultural domain ontology using an ad-hoc programmed java proxy.

3.2 Recommendations

In order to increase the accuracy and speed of the annotation process the editor includes recommendation functionalities for the annotator. When the users asks for advice for selected words or text parts the systems first checks existing instances in the domain ontology. The check is performed using a Natural Language Processing (NLP) module that decides whether two instances could be the same. This subsystem includes simple lexical and morphological modules possibly augmented with a synonym dictionary. If the selected word or a part of the selected text is identified as a possible new occurrence of an existing instance the system asks the annotator to decide which of the following action should be performed: (i) adding a completely new instance, (ii) modifying on existing instance with a new occurrence (adding new source link) or (iii) discarding any ontology modification. The more instances the ontology contains, the better recommendation the system can offer.

Other way of advising is firing guessing rules. These rules can suggest possible concepts for the selected text. For instance if a selected word starts with capital letter, it is not the first sentence word, and it was not recognized in the morphological module, it will be designated as a proper name and the concepts "NAME" (person's or place's) will be suggested to the annotator.

3.3 Conflict Resolution

One of the most complex concepts in this cultural ontology in the NAME concept. Since almost all things can be named in different ways and the exploitation will stress access to the information using this attribute we took special care modelling it. Each author, place, work, etc. can possess a number of names, variable in the time line or different depending on the relation they participate in. For instance, an author can write a book using one pseudonym, then use his legal name when attending an exposition and use an acronym when writing a new book with two colleges. All these names should point to the same person instance.

That is why the system offers instance duplication detection that warns the annotator of a possible existing instances using the name relations between concepts.

3.4 Search Facilities

We tested our tool by several users. It turned out that search facilities are extremely important in order for the annotator to keep track of what has already been annotated, as well as allowing him to follow different annotation strategies. Two example strategies include: i) following the text from begin to end, and ii) topic (author, work, movement) based. Especially in the latter strategy, search facilities are extremely important. The editor allows the following types of search:

- Marking instance from ontology: Instances already annotated have link to text marking their occurrences. It is very useful for the annotator to check what text was already processed.

- Search instance in ontology: This functionality is often used as part of the recommendations. The user can search for ontology instances that contain part of the text in their source.

All search functionalities take into account that almost all instances are referenced with their 'name' attribute. That is why when searching for occurrences the system identifies instances not only by source but also by their 'name' value related.

3.5 Import Facilities

Since there exists a bibliographic standard for authors and works storage defined upon the XML language called MARC [18], we built an import tool for translating it into the ontology formalism. The tool uses the rule engine and parsers to process XML input file and fill the ontology with acquired instances for persons, and artistic works. As well as the drag and drop functionalities this one also includes conflict detection for avoiding data duplication. Whenever the import tool detects possible data repetition, it postpones the decision to the end of the process and then asks the user to resolve possible actions to be taken: (i) adding new instance, (ii) adding new occurrence of an existing instance or (iii) skipping any action.

4. Exploitation of the Semantic Content

4.1 A Semantic Portal for Cultural Heritage

A small web-based prototype for the cultural ontology built earlier showed us that the knowledge base as modelled by domain experts and knowledge engineers is not always a good candidate to visualize it as is. Since many relations in this domain were modelled as explicit concepts, navigation became tedious and unfriendly.

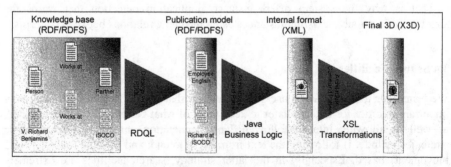

Fig. 3. Explicit visualization ontology for web publication

The main purpose for building ontologies is to provide semantic content for intelligent systems. The knowledge models are designed to offer the appropriate information to be exploited by the software. No visualization criteria are used to build an ontology and often the information is not suitable to be published as it is:

- Concepts may have too many attributes
- When relations are represented as independent concepts (first class objects) the navigation becomes tedious
- Concepts to be shown do not always correspond to modelled ones.

Therefore we felt a need for explicit visualization rules that allow the creation of views on the cultural ontology, in order to visualize only the relevant information in a user friendly way. We introduced the concept of "visualization ontology", which makes explicit all visualization rules and allows an easy interface management. This ontology will contain concepts and instances (publication entities) as seen on the interface by the end user, and it will retrieve the attribute values from the cultural ontology using a query. It does not duplicate the content of the original ontology, but links the content to publication entities using an ontology query language. This way one ontology that represents a particular domain can be visualized through different views.

The visualization ontology has two predefined concepts:

- **Publication entity**: Concept that encapsulates objects as they will be published in the portal. Any concept defined in the visualization ontology will inherit from it and should define these attributes
  - XSL style-sheet associated to the concept that translates its instances to final format (HTML, WAP, VoiceXML, etc.)
  - Query that retrieves all attribute values from the original ontology.
- **Publication Slot**: Each attribute that is going to appear on the web should inherit from this concept. Different facets describe how the attribute will appear on the page.
  - Web label: The label that will appear with the value
  - RDQL: reference to the query used to retrieve the attribute value
  - Link: When the published value should perform some action on mouse click (link, email, button, etc...), the action is described here.

Portal elements are described as children of the Publication Entity and their instances are defined according to the languages the entity will be published in (labels in English, Spanish, etc.), or the channel (whether the transformation style-sheet is going to translate into HTML, WAP, or just XML). In this case, the news library is exported in HTML format.

Back-office management is divided into two tasks:

- Content management on domain ontology: adding new instances or modifying the overall schema.
- Visualization management on publication ontology: modifying how information is shown (look and feel, layout, etc..)

Both tasks are performed using Protégé 2000 editor, since both domain and publication models are defined in RDF language.

4.2 3D Visualization

We have also developed a 3D generation module that allows navigating through the ontology content. For that purposes we have implemented software that translates given domain ontology, applying user defined visualization rules into the X3D [29] standard.

The resulting scene shows instances in a three-dimensional net represented as geometrical bodies with an ad-hoc defined texture. The scene is highly interactive allowing user to move the focus position and interact with the object (clicking on them).

Fig. 4. 3D navigation on domain ontology

5. Discussion and Conclusions

In this paper we presented an approach and tool of for creating a cultural "Semantic Web Island", and we showed examples of how this can be exploited for the benefit of art lovers. One should notice that the mentioned technology is generic and can be applied to any other domain with small modifications, provided there is domain ontology available. An exception to this statement should be considered: cultural domain has some strong requirements on instance names (due to pseudonyms, different typing or languages). Special attention to these particularities has to be paid when modelling humanities or cultural domains.

There are basically two types of tools for annotation (which actually are two extremes of a continuous line):

- Editors to manually annotate content with terms defined in ontologies
- Wrappers to automatically annotate content with ontological terms

When an editor not only allows for mark-up of content, but also provides support (e.g. suggestions of ontology terms for particular content), then it moves up the continuum to the wrapper end. The editor we described in this paper is somewhere in the middle of this continuum.

Our next step is to improve the NLP part of the tool, including shallow parsing, to come closer to automatic ontology population. On the exploitation side, we are working on extending the 3D visualization part to automatically generate thema-oriented online "cultural tours".

6. Acknowledgements

Part of this work has been funded by the European Commission in the context of the project Esperonto Services IST-2001-34373 and SWWS IST-2001-37134 and by the Spanish government in the scope of the project: ONTO-H (PROFIT, TIC): Intelligent access to digital cultural content based on an ontology for Humanities.

7. References

[1] V. R. Benjamins and D. Fensel. Editorial: Problem-solving methods. International Journal of Human-Computer Studies, 49(4):305–313, October 1998. Special issue on Problem-Solving Methods.
[2] V. R. Benjamins, D. Fensel, S. Decker, and A. Gomez-Perez. (KA)2: Building ontologies for the internet: a mid term report. International Journal of Human-Computer Studies, 51(3):687–712, 1999.
[3] W. N. Borst. Construction of Engineering Ontologies. PhD thesis, University of Twente, Enschede, 1997.
[4] CBL. Common business library, 1999.
http://www.commerceone.com/solutions/default.html.
[5] Contreras et al. D31: Annotation Tools and Services, Esperonto Project:
www.esperonto.net
[6] CyCorp: **http://www.cyc.com/**
[7] DAML. http://www.daml.org
[8] S. Decker and F. Maurer. Editorial: organizational memory and knowledge management. International Journal of Human-Computer Studies, 51(3):511–516, 1999. Special Issue on Organizational Memory and Knowledge Management.
[9] Stefan Decker, Michael Erdmann, Dieter Fensel, and Rudi Studer: Ontobroker: Ontology Based Access to Distributed and Semi-Structured Information. In R. Meersman et al. (eds.): Semantic Issues in Multimedia Systems. Proceedings of DS-8. Kluwer Academic Publisher, Boston, 1999, 351-369.
[10] Juan Manuel Dodero, Jesús Contreras, Richard Benjamins, Test Case Ontology Specification Cultural Tour. D9.2, Esperonto Project, www.esperonto.net.
[11] Drools http://drools.org/
[12] A. Farquhar, R. Fikes, and J. Rice. The ontolingua server: a tool for collaborative ontology construction. International Journal of Human-Computer Studies, 46(6):707–728, June 1997.

[13] Federation of Library Associations and Institutions: http://www.ifla.org
[14] Generalized Upper Model:
    http://www.darmstadt.gmd.de/publish/komet/genum/newUM.html
[15] T. R. Gruber. A translation approach to portable ontology specifications. Knowledge Acquisition, 5:199–220, 1993.
[16] N. Guarino. Formal ontology, conceptual analysis and knowledge representation. International Journal of Human-Computer Studies, 43(5/6):625–640, 1995. Special issue on The Role of Formal Ontology in the Information Technology.
[17] G. van Heijst, A. T. Schreiber, and B. J. Wielinga. Using explicit ontologies in KBS development. International Journal of Human-Computer Studies, 46(2/3):183–292, 1997.
[18] MARC http://www.loc.gov/marc/
[19] Protete 2000 tool: http://protege.stanford.edu
[20] RDF. Resource description framework, 1998. http://www.w3.org/TR/WD-rdf-syntax.
[21] RDFS. Resource description framework schema, 1998. http://www.w3.org/TR/1998/WD-rdf-schema-19980814.
[22] A. Th. Schreiber, J. M. Akkermans, A. A. Anjewierden, R. de Hoog, N. R. Shadbolt, W. Van de Velde, and B. J. Wielinga. Knowledge Engineering and Management, The CommonKADS methodology. MIT Press, 2000.
[23] SUO Standard Upper Ontology http://suo.ieee.org/
[24] W. Swartout and A. Tate. Coming to terms with ontologies. IEEE Intelligent Systems and Their Applications, 14(1):19–19, January/February 1999.
[25] M. Uschold and M. Gruninger. Ontologies: principles, methods, and applications. Knowledge Engineering Review, 11(2):93–155, 1996.
[26] D. A. Waterman F. Hayes-Roth, D. B. Lenat. Building Expert Systems. Addison Wesley, 1983.
[27] WordNet: http://www.cogsci.princeton.edu/~wn/
[28] XML. Extensible markup language, 1998. http://www.w3.org/TR/PR-xml-971208.
[29] X3D http://www.web3d.org/x3d.html

Neptuno: Semantic Web Technologies
for a Digital Newspaper Archive

P. Castells[1], F. Perdrix[2], E. Pulido[1], M. Rico[1], R. Benjamins[3], J. Contreras[3], J. Lorés[4]

[1]Universidad Autónoma de Madrid
Ctra. de Colmenar Viejo km. 15, 28049 Madrid
{pablo.castells,estrella.pulido,mariano.rico}@uam.es
[2]Diari Segre S.L.U.
C/ Del Riu nº6, 25007 Lleida
fperdrix@diarisegre.com
[3]iSOCO, S.A.
c/ Fca. Delgado 11 – 2° 28100 Alcobendas – Madrid
{rbenjamins,jcontreras}@isoco.com
[4]Universitat de Lleida
C/ Jaume II nº69, 25001 Lleida
jesus@griho.net

Abstract. Newspaper archives are a fundamental working tool for editorial teams. Their exploitation in digital format through the web, and the provision of technology to make this possible, are also important businesses today. The volume of archive contents, and the complexity of human teams that create and maintain them, give rise to diverse management difficulties. We propose the introduction of the emergent semantic-based technologies to improve the processes of creation, maintenance, and exploitation of the digital archive of a newspaper. We describe a platform based on these technologies, that consists of a) a knowledge base associated to the newspaper archive, based on an ontology for the description of journalistic information, b) a semantic search module, and c) a module for content browsing and visualisation based on ontologies.

1 Introduction

The introduction of information technologies in the news industry has marked a new evolutionary cycle in journalistic activity. Digital media allow an unprecedented dissemination, ease of access, immediacy, economy, virtually unlimited extension, and *à la carte* information delivery, eliminating time and space restrictions, and altering editorial team routines. The creation of new infrastructures, protocols and exchange standards for the automatic (push) or on-demand (pull) distribution and/or sale of information packages through different channels and transmission formats has deeply transformed the way in which the different specialised agents that participate in the news industry (companies, media, groups, agencies, consortiums, professionals, etc.) communicate with each other. Internally, the trend for information producers points to the adoption of integrated platforms that support the whole cycle of contents

J. Davies et al. (Eds.): ESWS 2004, LNCS 3053, pp. 445-458, 2004.
© Springer-Verlag Berlin Heidelberg 2004

elaboration, management, and publication, spanning from the reception of external information (e.g. from news agencies), the elaboration of own contents, layout composition, documentation, archive management, etc.

One interesting consequence of this technological transformation in the media industry has been the emergence, in very few years, of a whole new market of online services for archive news redistribution, syndication, aggregation, and brokering (see for example NewsLibrary [1], the British Library [2], or a list of online U.S. newspaper archives [3]). Newspaper archives are a highly valuable information asset for the widest range of information consumer profiles: students, researchers, historians, business professionals, the general public, and not the least, news writers themselves. Providing technology for news archive construction, management, access, publication, and billing, is an important business nowadays (see for instance NewsViews Solutions [4], ActivePaper Archive [5]).

The information collected from everyday news is huge in volume (e.g. by mid 2003 LexisNexis [6] claimed to handle over 3.3 billion documents), very loosely organised (e.g. compared to a book library), and grows without a global a-priori structure, as news stories add up and evolve unpredictably. This ever-growing corpus of archived news results from the coordinated but to much extent autonomous work of a team of reporters, whose primary goal is not to build an archive, but to serve the best possible information product for immediate consumption. Reporters are often assisted by librarians and archive specialists, who help classify, index, and annotate news as they are sent to the archive, using special-purpose archive management software.

In addition to this, powerful search and navigation mechanisms are needed for information consumers to find their way through. Current technology typically provides keyword-based search (often by fields: body, headline, section, lead, byline), browsing facilities inside newspaper issues, and, in online newspapers, navigation through static hand-made hyperlinks between news materials (e.g. links to earlier background stories).

A wide margin remains yet for taking advantage of the possibilities offered by the digital medium to exploit a newspaper archive. Aspects that can be improved include: a) keyword search falling short in expressive power; b) weak interrelation between archive items: users may need to combine several indirect queries manually before they can get answers to complex queries; c) lack of a commonly adopted standard representation for sharing archive news across newspapers; d) lack of internal consensus for content description terminology between and among reporters and archivists; e) lack of involvement of reporters in the archiving process. We believe the emerging Semantic Web technologies [7] provide a good approach to overcome these limitations.

The Neptuno project[1] has been set up to apply Semantic Web technologies to improve current state of the art in diverse aspects of the production and consumption of digital news. It is being conducted by two universities (Universidad Autónoma de Madrid and Universitat de Lleida), a news media company (Diari SEGRE), and a technology provider (iSOCO, S. A.). This paper presents the results achieved in the

---

[1] http://seweb.ii.uam.es/neptuno/

first phase of the project, which focuses on the construction, management and exploitation of a newspaper archive.

The goal of the work described here is to develop a high-quality semantic archive for the Diari SEGRE newspaper where a) reporters and archivists have more expressive means to describe and annotate news materials, b) reporters and readers are provided with better search and browsing capabilities than those currently available, and c) the archive system is open to integration in potential electronic marketplaces of news products.

According to these goals, a platform has been developed whose main components are:

- An ontology for archive news, based on journalists' and archivists' expertise and practice, and integrating current dominant standards from the IPTC consortium [8].
- A knowledge base where archive materials are described using the ontology. A DB-to-ontology conversion module automatically integrates existing legacy archive materials into the knowledge base.
- A semantic search module, where meaningful information needs can be expressed in terms of the ontology, and more accurate answers are supplied.
- A visualisation and navigation module to display individual archive items, parts or combinations of items, and lists or groups of items.

The Diari SEGRE reporters will be the primary users of the archive exploitation functionalities. A version for the general public is planned as a future extension of the project.

The rest of the paper is organised as follows. The next section describes the creation and management of the newspaper library with the technology previously in use at the Diari SEGRE. After this, an overview of the online newspaper archive industry and current technologies is given. Section 4 describes the definition of an ontology for the Neptuno project, and Section 5 explains the search and visualisation functionalities for the knowledge base. Section 6 describes the platform architecture and the construction of the knowledge base from current archive news databases, providing some implementation details.

2   Document Management at Diari SEGRE

The elaboration of news within a mass media group like Diari SEGRE is fed by diverse information sources, among which in-house newspaper archives are a must. These digital archives are a constant reference for background information search, or browsing related news, in order to complement, clarify, or help place in a certain context the new information a journalist is writing.

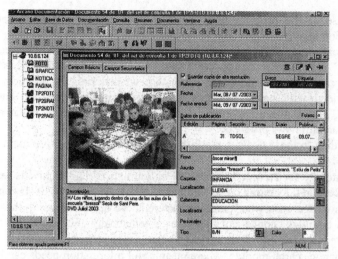

Fig. 1. Current news archive management environment

Most press media nowadays have massive information repositories based on relational database systems, with special-purpose software to manage their contents. The Diari SEGRE newspaper may publish over a hundred news and some fifty photographs everyday, which are automatically uploaded into the digital archive of the newspaper. The archive consists of a database, JPEG image files (published photos), and PDF files (newspaper pages). The archive currently contains all the issues of the newspaper since July 1995 to date. This means nearly 400,000 news and 200,000 photos, which take about 14 Gb total disk space. A software platform named Milenium Arcano [9] (see figure 1), one of the most popular ones in the news sector in Spain and Portugal, is used to manage the archive. Arcano provides functionalities for archive update, manual documentation, and content search.

The news archival process is done by the documentation department, according to the criteria of experts in this department, and the possibilities (and limitations) of the software platform, classifying news using a hierarchical thesaurus, in endless evolution, of available concepts for contents annotation. On the other side, journalists consume this previously stored information when they need to inform themselves on subjects, histories or events, not always with the ideally desirable available time, neither with enough beforehand archive system knowledge to be sure how to formulate their queries and information needs. Because of all this, the differences between archivists' and journalists' mental models (evidenced along this project) call for a more flexible content categorisation and search system, which is the aim of the Neptuno project, by making use of Semantic Web technologies.

3   Online Newspaper Archives on the WWW

Today virtually all press media published on the web have a public access system to their news archive through the web. While a few newspapers keep providing free archive access, in the last few years paid access, by pay-per-view or periodical subscription, is becoming prevalent. Diari SEGRE itself has a service of this kind. The Special Libraries Association News Division (SLAND) maintains a list of online newspaper archives at http://www.ibiblio.org/slanews/internet/archives.html.

Online archives usually provide searching and browsing facilities for archive news. For instance, the search service of the newspaper El País [10] (the one with most readers in Spain), in its most advanced modality, allows queries by section, date, heading, lead, body, author, and type of content (text, photography, graphic, animation, audio, video). This kind of search options, with very slight variations, is representative of thousand other archive services offered on the WWW by media companies from the five continents.

Other more ambitious projects integrate the archives of several newspapers, and even recover the old historic issues conserved in print. NewsLibrary [1], for example, offers online access to more that 200 newspapers and other sources (covering different time spans, the oldest ones starting in 1977), including all first-rank news media. The British Library [2] provides online access to more that half a million articles from five historic newspapers (Daily News, News of the World, Penny Illustrated, The Manchester Guardian, Weekly Dispatch), including conserved issues from as far back as 1851, properly digitized, segmented and graphically treated. ProQuest Historical Newspapers [11] is a similar product that integrates one and a half century of contents (news, advertisements, comic strips, letters to the editor, weather information, and other content genres) of The New York Times (1851-2001), The Wall Street Journal (1889-1987), The Washington Post (1877-1988), The Christian Science Monitor (1908-1991), and Los Angeles Times (1881-1984). These applications allow searching and navigating through old issues, and visualising the pages in HTML or the original format.

With the emergence of this new market, technology and solution providers for the deployment of online archives have proliferated as well, addressing all aspects needed for the development of the application, depending on the starting materials (paper, microfiche, digital), the target environment (web, intranets), and the intended use (internal, public, commercial). This may involve digitation and graphical treatment of materials, archive management and maintenance, integration in the information production chain, publication, access, etc. Many commercial tools exist today to this end, like ActivePaper Archive [5] from OliveSoftware, NewsViews Solutions tools [4], ArchiveIQue [12] from Baseview Products, Canto Cumulus [13], or DC4 [14] from Digital Collections, to name just a few.

These and similar available platforms and applications suffer, at a smaller scale, from the same problems and limitations as the ones highlighted by the Semantic Web perspective: no support for conceptual search; extensive ad-hoc implementation efforts are required for integration with other archives or external information systems; platforms are not open to unforeseen extensions; rigid browsing facilities; no explicit notion of the semantics conveyed by archive documents. The aim of our project is to achieve or enable specific improvements by introducing ontology-based semantics, and exploiting this to provide better and/or novel functionalities in a news archive management system, following and/or improving existing proposals from the Semantic Web field, and contributing our own.

4 An Ontology for a Newspaper Library

The first step in the development of the Neptuno project has been the definition of an ontology to represent and process news information. After evaluating the available languages and standards for ontology definition, we have chosen RDF [15], currently the most mature, stable and widespread standard in the latest projects and developments in the Semantic Web area.

According to the reference methodologies in the Semantic Web, the recommended steps for the construction of an ontology are [16]:

1. Determine the domain and scope of the ontology.
2. Determine the intended use of the ontology.
3. Reuse existing ontologies or controlled vocabularies.
4. Enumerate important terms in the domain.
5. Define the class hierarchy.
6. Create instances.

In the Neptuno project we have taken this recommendation as a general guide, adapting it to our particular case without significant deviations. We describe next the definition process for each of these aspects, and the resulting ontology. The last of the above-mentioned steps, instance creation, which is done automatically in Neptuno, is described later in Section 6 about platform architecture.

4.1 Domain, Scope, and Intended Use

Although, apparently, the selection of the domain should be an obvious question, the journalistic field has the peculiarity of potentially dealing with topics in all fields of human knowledge and current affairs: politics, culture, courts, science, sports, art, economy, etc. It has been necessary to carefully establish a limit in the domains to represent, without which any attempt at approaching completitude would lead to a whole project for each thematic information area.

The conceptual reflection of these thematic areas in our ontology is limited to the definition of generic categories by topics and subtopics, such as "politics", "immigration", "economy", "trade", "stock market", or "sports", as will be described next, but does not include specific classes and entities for these areas, such as "political party", "suffrage", "judge", "lawyer", "sentence", "sportsman", "actress", "theatre play", or "music group", nor the instances of these entity types. The creation of a knowledge base for these entities, that would completely take in the potential informative coverage of a mass media, exceeds the capacity of any single organisation, company or agency that would intend to undertake such an endeavor. On the other hand, the utility of a partial collection, more feasible to construct, is difficult to justify.

As for the intended use, after a thorough analysis, we have come to the conclusion that the management of a newspaper archive is, of all the potentially targetable aspects in the production cycle of a newspaper, possibly the one which offers more and best opportunities for improving processes and products, and best lends itself to the Semantic Web proposals. Among other reasons that sustain this assessment, we can mention a) the quality of the newspaper library contents, which have passed a selection filter (as opposed to the news flow that arrive everyday to the newspaper offices), given that only the news that actually make it to the newspaper pages are stored in the archive; b) the enrichment of contents with metadata, descriptions, and a careful manual categorisation by professional archivists who supervise the transit of news to the archive one by one; and c) the persistence of materials for an indefinite period of time (once again, in contrast to more ephemeral materials from agencies and other sources, that are finally discarded), which allows a continued exploitation of the added value that results from the contributions we propose here.

4.2 Existing Ontologies and Controlled Vocabularies

Our first observation, when considering the reuse of existing ontologies and standards in this field, is that as of now no proper journalistic ontology has been published, as far as we are aware. In this sense our work is a contribution to the growth of the Semantic Web and publicly available ontology collections.

With respect to other kind of controlled vocabularies, different standards have been developed in the area of journalism, such as NewsML [17], NITF [18], XMLNews [19], the IPTC subject reference system [8], and PRISM [20]. NewsML and NITF (News Industry Text Format) are XML-based standards to represent and manage news along their whole lifecycle, including their creation, exchange and consumption. While NewsML is used to represent news as multimedia packages, NITF deals with document structure. XMLNews is a subset of NITF and is based on RDF. It includes a set of tags (such as location, person, or date) that allow annotating news to facilitate information search.

These three standards have been created by the IPTC (International Press Telecommunications Council), an international consortium of news agencies, editors and newspapers distributors. This organism has proposed the Subject Reference System, a subject classification hierarchy with three levels and seventeen categories in its first level.

PRISM (Publishing Requirements for Industry Standard Metadata) was developed by IDEAlliance (International Digital Enterprise Alliance), an industrial board of editorial companies and publishing software manufacturers which includes Adobe, Quark, Condé Nast and Time Inc. It is an XML standard, similar to NewsML, that provides a metadata vocabulary for the editorial industry to facilitate aggregation and syndication of digital contents.

After evaluating all these standards, we have adopted the IPTC Subject Reference System as a thematic classification system for news archive contents. The integration and adaptation of this standard to our ontology has been carried through by a) converting the IPTC topic hierarchy to an RDF class hierarchy, and b) establishing a mapping between the classification system (thesaurus) previously in use at Diari SEGRE, and the IPTC standard. In order to represent the actual archive contents, we have built our own ontology, which is described next.

4.3 Identification of Concepts and Class Hierarchies

Diari SEGRE has a database in which information about news, photographs, graphics and pages is stored. Newspaper contents are classified everyday by archivists using the Milenium Arcano tool. The criteria used for this classification are basically two: the section to which the contents belongs (Sports, Economy, ...) and the topics they deal with. For the latter classification a thesaurus is used that has been elaborated incrementally over time among all archivists, and that is frequently updated as new needs arise.

One of the problems that came up when the daily work of editors and documentalists was analysed is that the way in which editors search information in the database greatly differs from that in which archivists annotate and store this information. For this reason the use of the subject reference system by IPTC was proposed to archivists, who agreed that this could be a solution to the problem.

The ontology to represent the archives of Diari SEGRE has been built by using the Protégé ontology editor [21]. Some of the concepts in this ontology correspond to tables in the existing database, such as News, Photograph, Graphics and Page. All these concepts are subclasses of the Contents concept.

In addition, three ways of classifying contents have been included. In one of them contents are classified by subject following the IPTC subject classification hierarchy. An alternative classification can be made according to contents genre, which has to do with the nature (breaking news, summary, interview, opinion, survey, forecast, etc.) of a news or photograph rather than its specific contents. Finally, a content can be classified according to some keywords that describe it.

These three classifications replace those by section and category in the thesaurus that were used so far by documentalists. A mapping has been established between the old thesaurus categories and those in the IPTC hierarchy. In some cases this correspondence is not one to one so contents are allowed to be classified in more than one category.

Other concepts have been created that do not correspond directly to information stored in the current database, among which it is worth mentioning the NewsRelation concept that allows establishing relationships among news such as "extension", "previous", "comment", etc. The possibility of extending the ontology with other concepts and descriptions remains open. The characteristics of the employed Semantic Web technologies are devised to facilitate this kind of extension.

5 Semantic Search and Navigation

The defined ontology serves to enrich the existing news archive contents with explicit semantic representations, giving rise to a semantic knowledge base. The ontology provides the vocabulary to express descriptions and associate them to the resources stored in the archive. The added value that results from this enrichments pays-off with the possibility to develop advanced exploitation modules like the ones developed in Neptuno, namely, a search module, and a system for ontology visualisation, both integrated in a semantic portal.

5.1 Semantic Search

With respect to search, the availability of semantic information in the knowledge base allows the user to formulate more precise and expressive user queries, and implement a system that is able to use conceptual elements to match information needs against archive contents. Most existing search systems today are keyword/based: the user introduces the relevant words, and the search engine retrieves all the documents that contain them. Occurrences of words are sought in documents, without taking into account:

- The meaning of words (they may have multiple).
- The relation between words in the query.

Which can result in the following problems:

- The system may return many documents with low relevance for the original query.
- It is the user's responsibility to open each document to check its relevance.

This may result in users not finding the sought information, even when it exists or, on the other extreme, cause an information overload due to many documents offered as the response.

A semantic search engine [22, 23] has knowledge of the domain at hand. The availability of a domain ontology that structures and relates the information according to its meaning allows the implementation of a search system where users can specify search criteria in terms of modelled concepts and attributes. The results are presented in a structured form including only the requested information. Contrary to traditional search systems where the answer consists of whole documents, where the user has to find manually the sought information, semantic search systems can return only the requested information (ontology instances).

The search module in Neptuno has been developed following these principles of semantic search. Moreover, the module combines direct search by content classes and class fields, with the possibility to browse the IPTC taxonomy, according to which archive news and documents are classified (see figure 2). The interaction between both aspects of search is twofold. On the one hand, search by fields is restricted to the IPTC categories selected by the user. On the other, Neptuno shows the list of categories to which the results of a search belong. The user can navigate directly to them, or select them to narrow or restrict the search successively.

5.2 Visualisation

Despite the advantages that semantic models provide to retrieve information, one of the problems of these models is supplying a readable and understandable presentation for the end-user. In the model design and construction phase, the expressive value of the model is valued, and no visual or aesthetic aspects are taken into consideration. The main purposes for building ontologies are to provide semantic content for intelligent systems. The knowledge models are designed to offer the appropriate information to be exploited by the software. No visualisation criteria are used to build an ontology and often the information is not suitable to be published as it is:

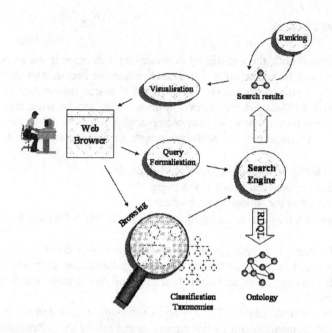

Fig. 2. Navigation and search in the Neptuno platform

- Concepts may have too many attributes.
- When relations are represented as independent concepts (first class objects) the navigation becomes tedious.
- Concepts to be shown do not always correspond to modelled ones.

In our case, in the ontology described in this paper, modelling of concepts and relations in the newspaper archive has not been restricted by publication criteria, as could be the number of attributes of a concept, number of instances, or existence of auxiliary concepts for the representation of relations.

There is a need to differentiate between what is going to be modelled from how it is going to be visualised. That's why we introduce the concept of Visualisation Ontology [24]. This ontology, called publication schema, allows organising the concepts and attributes in order to be published in the portal.

The visualisation ontology represents publication concepts as they should appear in the portal. It does not duplicate the content of the original ontology, but links the content to publication entities using an ontology query language. This way one ontology that represents a particular domain can be visualised through different views.

The visualisation ontology has two predefined concepts:

- Publication entity: Concept that encapsulates objects as they will be published in the portal. Any concept defined in the visualisation ontology will inherit from it and should define these attributes
    o XSL style-sheet associated to the concept that translates its instances to HTML.
    o Query that retrieves all attribute values from the original ontology.

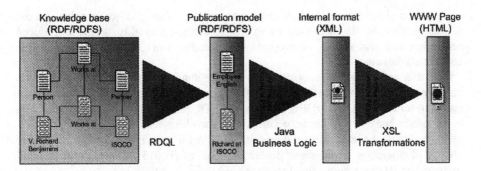

Fig. 3. Publication through visualisation ontology

- Publication Slot: Each attribute that is going to appear on the web should inherit from this concept. Different facets describe how the attribute will appear on the page.
  - o Web label: The label that will appear with the value.
  - o RDQL: reference to the query used to retrieve the attribute value.
  - o Link : When the published value should perform some action on mouse click (link, email, button, etc.), the action is described here.

Portal elements are described as children of the Publication Entity and their instances are defined according to the languages the entity will be published in (labels in English, Spanish, etc.), or the channel (whether the transformation style-sheet is going to translate into HTML, WAP, or just XML). In this case, the news library is exported in HTML format.

Back-office management is naturally divided into two tasks:

- Content management on domain ontology: adding new instances or modifying the overall schema.
- Visualisation management on publication ontology: modifying how information is shown (look and feel, layout, etc.)

Both tasks are performed using Protégé 2000 editor, since both domain and publication model are defined in RDF language.

6 Architecture and Implementation

In Neptuno we have undertaken the introduction of the Semantic Web proposals by following a smooth transition strategy [25], which advises to keep the compatibility (at least initially) with the current technology: browsers, protocols, web and application servers, databases, architectures.

The current version of the Neptuno platform is an extension of previously working systems at Diari SEGRE that does not interfere with technology and procedures previously in use. At the time of this writing we are testing a first prototype. The Neptuno ontology, that is to say the hierarchy of concepts, properties and relationships, has been built manually. It contains 1,330 classes and 44 properties. The manual creation of ontology instances, associated to several hundred thousands news accumulated over the last nine years in the Diari SEGRE archive, would unquestionably be the best way to warrant the highest quality of the introduced semantics, but also an out of proportion, unfeasible work, out of any reasonable cost/benefit balance.

For this reason Neptuno includes a module that populates the ontology with instances that are extracted automatically from the Arcano database, by using a mapping tool from JDBC/ODBC databases to RDF [26]. To limit the volume of data in our preliminary testing phase, we are initially working with a subset of the archive, including only the contents produced in 2003, which comprise 39,084 news and 19,573 photographs. From these contents a total of 95,615 instances and 857,447 sentences in RDF are automatically generated by this module.

The manual creation of instances for new informations and photographs stored in the newspaper archive, at a regular daily pace, from the deployment of Neptuno onwards, is indeed a feasible goal in the future. The introduction of new semantic documentation tools requires, however, a careful work of analysis, design, testing and balancing of the additional burden that such tools may impose on archivists. Meanwhile, we have decided not to interfere with the current environments with which the Diari workers interact, and to generate new instances everyday by the same automatic procedure as used for old materials, without altering the newspaper production pace.

The contents search and visualisation modules operate directly on the knowledge base in RDF. The user poses search requests through a web interface in which (s)he selects the contents class to be searched (News, Photograph, Graphics, or Page), and specifies keywords for the desired fields (heading, author, section, date, subject, etc.) in the selected class. This information is sent to the Neptuno server where the request is formalised as an RDQL query. This query is run on the knowledge base and returns a list of resources (instances) that satisfy the query constraints.

The list of resources is sent to the visualisation module, which generates an HTML page where the list of found instances is displayed in an abbreviated and clickable form. When the user selects an instance, the visualisation module on the server notices the class to which the instance belongs, selects the corresponding publishing entity, and generates a web page where the resource details are shown according to the principles described in the previous section.

Access to the knowledge base from the search and visualisation modules is carried out by means of the Jena library [27] for RDF.

7 Conclusions and Future Work

A newspaper archive is a fundamental working tool for editorial teams, and a potentially marketable product towards different kinds of consumers through diverse distribution channels.

The size and complexity of the stored information, and the time limitations for cataloguing, describing and ordering the incoming information, make newspaper archives a relatively disorganised and difficult to manage corpus. In this sense, they share many of the characteristics and problems of the WWW, and therefore the solutions proposed in the Semantic Web vision are pertinent here.

The work developed so far represents an actual application experience of Semantic Web technologies in a real setting, and makes novel contributions to several of the undertaken aspects: definition of ontologies in a specific domain, semantic search and exploration functionalities, development of a user interface to interact with the knowledge base, transition from a working system with traditional technologies to a semantic-based platform.

Besides these immediate advantages, the work done allows undertaking now higher-level problems from the grounds established so far, which we are starting to undertake at the time of this writing. For example, the expressiveness of the ontology developed in this phase is limited in terms of the semantics that is actually added with respect to the information already present in the current archive databases. As pointed out in Section 6, the manual introduction of this semantics is unfeasible because of its high cost, most of all for old contents. The feasible means to carry out this enrichment are those of semiautomatic kind, by means of metadata extraction modules, based on text analysis and text mining, that generate relationships between news, detect concepts in news bodies, classify contents, etc. This enrichment would enable the development of further capabilities even more sophisticated.

Other goals we are considering from this point are the integration of new sources (external newspaper archives), contents types (text, audio, video) and languages (Spanish and Catalan), the already mentioned enrichment of contents description through automatic methods of text and multimedia analysis, and the automatic adaptation to multiple devices and access channels. We also intend to go further in the improvements achieved so far, increasing for example, the precision of the search system by means of ranking algorithms, increasing its expressiveness with more advanced interfaces, and carrying out a methodological revision of the representation and classification systems (ontology) currently used in the knowledge base.

The ease of this kind of extensions over a platform like the one developed is an important indirect advantage of the work done to this point, and an intentional feature of the used technologies.

8   Acknowledgements

This work is funded by the Spanish Ministry of Science and Technology, grants FIT-150500-2003-511 and TIC2002-1948.

References

1. NewsLibrary, the world's largest news archive, http://www.newslibrary.com
2. The British Library, the world's knowledge, http://www.bl.uk
3. Baumgart, J.: U. S. Newspaper Archives on the Web. Available at http://www.ibiblio.org/slanews/ internet/archives.html
4. NewsViews Solutions, http://www.newsviewsolutions.com

458   P. Castells et al.

5. ActivePaper Archive by Olive Software, http://www.active-paper.com/ap_aparchive.html
6. LexisNexis for law, public records, company data, government, academic and business news sources, http://www.lexisnexis.com
7. Berners-Lee, T., Hendler, J., Lassila, O.: The Semantic Web. Scientific American (2001).
8. IPTC Subject Reference System & NewsML Topicsets, http://www.iptc.org/metadata
9. Milenium Arcano by Protec, http://www.mileniumcrossmedia.com/Arcano/Arcano.htm
10. El País - el archivo - Hemeroteca, http://www.elpais.es/archivo/hemeroteca.html
11. ProQuest Historical Newspapers, http://www.il.proquest.com/products/pt-product-HistNews.shtml
12. ArchiveIQue by Baseview, http://www.baseview.com/products/archiveique.html
13. Canto - Digital Asset Management with Cumuluc, http://www.canto.com
14. DC4, The Digital Collections System, http://www.digitalcollections.biz/dc4.asp
15. Lassila, O., Swick, R.R.: Resource Description Framework (RDF) Model and Syntax Specification. W3C Recommendation 22 February 1999. Available at http://www.w3.org/TR/ REC-rdf-syntax
16. Noy, N.F., McGuinness, D.L.: Ontology Development 101: A Guide to Creating Your First Ontology. Stanford Knowledge Systems Laboratory Technical Report KSL-01-05 and Stanford Medical Informatics Technical Report SMI-2001-0880 (2001)
17. IPTC NewsML, http://www.newsml.org
18. IPTC News Industry Text Format (NITF), A Solution for Sharing News, http://www.nitf.org
19. XMLNews, XML and the News Industry, http://www.xmlnews.org
20. Publishing Requirements for Industry Standard Metadata (PRISM), http://www.prismstandard.org
21. Noy, N.F., Sintek, M., Decker, Crubezy, M., Fergerson, R.W., Musen, M.A.: Creating Semantic Web Contents with Protege-2000. IEEE Intelligent Systems 16(2) (2001) 60-71
22. Guha, R., McCool, R., Miller, E.: Semantic search. 12th International World Wide Web Conference (WWW2003), Budapest, Hungary (2003), 700 – 709
23. Shah, U., Finin, T., Joshi, A., Cost, R.S., Mayfield, J:. Information Retrieval on the Semantic Web. 10th International Conference on Information and Knowledge Management (2002).
24. Contreras, J., Benjamins, V.R., Prieto, J.A., Patón, D., Losada, S., González, D.: Duontology: an Approach to Semantic Portals based on a Domain and Visualisation Ontology. KTWeb, http://www.drecommerce.com/doc/Benjamins-Duontology-a.pdf
25. Haustein, S., Pleumann, J.: Is Participation in the Semantic Web too Difficult? International Semantic Web Conference (ISWC'2002). Sardinia, Italy (2002)
26. Bizer, C.: D2R MAP - A Database to RDF Mapping Language. 12th International World Wide Web Conference (WWW2003). Budapest, Hungary (2003)
27. Jena 2 – A Semantic Web Framework, http://www.hpl.hp.com/semweb/jena2.htm

MIKSI - A Semantic and Service Oriented Integration Platform

Alexander Wahler[1], Bernhard Schreder[1], Aleksandar Balaban[1],
Juan Miguel Gomez[2], Klaus Niederacher[1]

[1] NIWA Web Solutions Vienna, Austria
{wahler, schreder, balaban, niederacher}@niwa.at
[2] Digital Enterprise Research Institute, Innsbruck, Austria
juan.miguel@deri.ie

Abstract. The MIKSI platform provides a novel information and workflow infrastructure for common tasks of marketing and public relations (e.g. producing and sending of press releases). MIKSI is based on a service oriented architecture using web service technology for communication and data exchange. The process flow is implemented in BPEL [1] using RDF [12] for message exchange. The underlying data model consist of RDF(S) repositories, e.g. event and address data as demonstrated in the first prototype. This paper presents the MIKSI platform with emphasize on its architecture, business processes, semantic data model and interfaces, tools, and other technical issues.

1 Introduction

For many, the long-term goal of the Web service effort is seamless interoperation among networked programs and devices. Once achieved, many see Web services as the means of providing the infrastructure for universal plug-and-play and ubiquitous computing. MIKSI commits to this technology and provides an infrastructure for efficient handling of marketing and public relation tasks. The common characteristic of theses tasks, independent from the sector they are applied to, is the integration of different heterogeneous data-sources or services in a line of business processes, which interact with specific target-groups and applications. To integrate complex, stateful interactions among applications, most of the major industry players have proposed some form of business process integration, orchestration, or choreography model. MIKSI is built on the recently released BPEL4WS from IBM, which defines an interoperable integration model that facilitates the expansion of automated process integration.

MIKSI extends current Web Service architectures and takes up the efforts of the Semantic Web Community [9] that has developed languages and computing machinery for making Web content and Web Services explicitly interpretable by computer programs. Efforts include the development of languages like RDF(S), DAML+OIL [15] or OWL [16]. Regarding MIKSI, RDF(S) is the language of our choice and it is primarily used for providing a description of resources and messages via its semantic constructs.

J. Davies et al. (Eds.): ESWS 2004, LNCS 3053, pp. 459-472, 2004.

This paper first describes the MIKSI business processes exemplified through the use case of a Press Release Service. These processes are implemented in the MIKSI platform which is further described with its service oriented architecture in section 3. The fourth part gives an overview of BPEL and analyses the role of BPEL in MIKSI. Section 5 describes the architectural components of MIKSI, section 6 analyses the semantic data model and the role of RDF(S) and ontologies. We conclude with an outlook and related work in section 7.

2 MIKSI - Press Release Services

The development of the MIKSI platform was in close co-operation with case study partners [19], who provided real world examples and data for the first prototype. The integration of an use case from the early beginning provided test beds and steered the development of the MIKSI architecture.

An example of a real world MIKSI module is the "Press Release Service", a common but complex task of many companies and institutions. In our example we describe the press release service of a cultural institution, that daily promotes several events and provides the appropriate information about these events to journalists of daily/weekly and monthly media. In our case study we could identify two main types of public relation activities: periodic mailings and event-driven mailings using respectively different distribution channels (email, snail mail) and different levels of personalisation. While the periodic mailings basically follow a predefined static process with the time period as main attribute, the event-driven mailings are steered by the requirements and interaction of the user (e.g. by a marketing employee). Figure 1 shows an example business process.

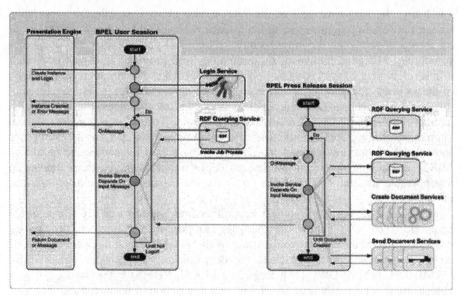

Fig. 1. Part of MIKSI business process architecture with atomic services and BPEL processes.

After the login the user sees all related personal tasks in the "Task Manager". Periodic mailings as described above appear automatically in the task manager – according to specified timing constraints – and can be activated for production, while event-driven mailings have to be created by the user. The creation of a new press release instance is shown in figure 1. The dispatch of "Music Press Release" needs several interactive steps with the user, during which address sources, target groups and events (e.g. concerts) are selected. The press documents are produced automatically by merging the event data with selected templates and preparing the recipient list. Finally the documents are sent. Actually the press release service is implemented as a push service for journalists but in the future MIKSI will be extended with pull services for journalists, which enable a comfortable data exchange and the integration of the MIKSI services in content management systems of press media. All these features are supported by the service oriented architecture of MIKSI.

3 MIKSI - A Service Oriented Platform Using a Semantic Data Model

3.1 MIKSI - Service Oriented Architecture (SOA)

The first approach in the MIKSI development phase was the decision for an appropriate software architecture. The classical 3 tier architecture was evaluated against the approach of a service oriented architecture (SOA), which gained new importance through the upcoming Web Service effort. Service oriented architecture is defined as a specific software platform based on the set of decoupled, well described software components (modules). This modules can be understood as black box components with known, well described interfaces and message exchange protocols. Thus their interfaces and message formats are known und understandable for other modules of the SOA, in order for these components to be used in diverse practical application scenarios. They can be registered, discovered and reused within a SOA framework. A SOA platform can provide its components to other platforms.[21]

SOA components are characterized by the following behaviour:
• Well-defined.
• Self-contained.
• Do not depend on the context or state of other services.

In MIKSI we call these components Atomic Services.

The objectives of SOA are:
• Loosely coupled and interoperable components.
• Component reusability, encapsulation and abstraction of components.
• Flexible creation of complex business processes based on existing components.
In today's SOA approaches each service is exposed via standard web service interfaces, which are described by the Web Services Description Language (WSDL) [7], and accessed through the Simple Object Access Protocol (SOAP) [14]. For the

service requester it is not necessary to have knowledge about the internal business logic of the service, the message exchange protocol and the service description will hide these specific details from the service requester.

The capabilities of MIKSI fulfill the criteria for a service oriented architecture in various ways: First, MIKSI is a scalable platform with reusable components, second, new business processes based on atomic services can be easily added to the MIKSI service repository, and third, MIKSI provides services to other platforms and integrates third party services.

The main components of the MIKSI architecture are atomic services. An example for an atomic service in the MIKSI prototype is the "Send Engine" which sends emails including attachments to a specified list of recipients. This service is a component of the press release process described above; as an atomic service module it is reusable in all implemented business processes and accessible over its WSDL interface for MIKSI or its business partners.

Atomic services within MIKSI are combined into complex business processes and have the following characteristics:

- Centrally managed (deployment, instance creation, destruction).
- Created from existing atomic components (using special visual tools).
- Well described on the architectural level (SOA has knowledge of existing services).
- Stateless or stateful behaviour.
- Support of synchronous and asynchronous operation calls.
- Message exchange based on well known exchange protocols.
- Provision of transaction definitions together with error handling and recovery mechanisms.

3.2 MIKSI SOA Integration Layer

The MIKSI integration layer has been build on the well known SOA architectural standards, SOAP and WSDL. For the creation of composite business processes and their orchestration MIKSI uses the BPEL4WS process flow description language. The flow descriptions are interpreted and executed by our chosen BPEL engine which accesses and invokes MIKSI components independent of their actual technical realization, which means they could be Java classes, EJBs, JMS components or even external components from third party suppliers. An object/component can be used if there is a proper WSDL description of the component access interface. SOAP, WSDL and BPEL4WS as mentioned above build the service integration layer of the MIKSI SOA. This layer acts as an abstraction of the services characteristics by providing a uniform service access interface.

The layered MIKSI SOA bus structure (on the integration layer) is shown in Fig. 2.:

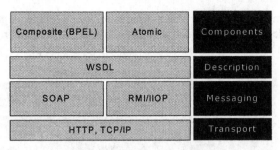

Fig. 2. MIKSI SOA Bus structure

The composition of the business processes is performed by the BPEL4WS service composition framework. In our MIKSI prototype we used IBMs BPWS4J Alphaworks test engine. The role of business processes and BPEL in MIKSI is described in the next chapter.

3.3 MIKSI SOA Application Layer

Components of a SOA are well described, reusable pieces of software with characteristics as mentioned above (well-defined, self-contained, independent). SOAP, WSDL service descriptions and BPEL4WS are elementary parts of the SOA service integration layer. This layer provides the top level abstraction of the SOA Some additional information about the specifics of the MIKSI application layer is following:

- As low level service support we decided to use a persistent data model based on RDFS which is used by J2EE EJB components. These components reside in a JBoss [20] J2EE application server which is responsible for the creation of component instances and the management of the run time system behaviour.
- Transformers, wrappers and send engines are basically J2EE EJB components with extra functionality provided by some java objects libraries.
- Persistent data is stored in a standard relational data base, which is in turn accessed by the Jena RDF framework according to a semantic data model.

The figure below (Fig.2.) shows an application layer based block diagram of the MIKSI SOA. The application server is used to provide a secure, scalable environment for architectural components. All local atomic services and the BPWS4J engine reside inside the application server as EJB components.

3.4 Semantic Data Model

An ontology based data model is used within the MIKSI platform to achieve a high level of flexibility. Several separate ontologies have been created using RDFS, which describe the basic concepts existing within the domain of marketing, including their properties and relationships to other concepts. In the first MIKSI application, three small ontology models – the event model, the task model and the contact model – are used. While RDFS was deemed as the appropriate description language for the semantic data model of the first MIKSI prototype, later versions might introduce more powerful ontology languages such as OWL, in order to benefit from the additional possibilities for describing semantic concepts and relationships.

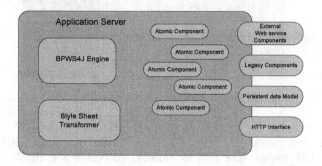

Fig. 3. Block diagram of MIKSI application components

4 Business Processes and the Role of BPEL in MIKSI

4.1 BPEL4WS

BPEL4WS provides a language for formal specification of business processes and business interaction protocols. By doing so, it defines an interoperable integration model that should facilitate the expansion of automated process integration both in public and private environments as stated in [6]. In the environment of the MIKSI platform this concept is used by integrating private services and offering public services.

Business processes can be described in two ways.

- **Executable business processes** model actual behavior of a participant in a business interaction.
- **Business protocols**, in contrast, use process descriptions that specify the mutually visible message exchange behavior of each of the parties involved in the protocol, without revealing their internal behavior. The process descriptions for business protocols are called *abstract processes*.

4.2 Business Processes

In BPEL4WS, a simple business process is, as noted in the introduction, layered on WSDL-defined Web Services. The interaction model of WSDL is essentially a stateless client-server of synchronous or uncorrelated asynchronous interaction. However, BPEL4WS defines business processes consisting of stateful long-running interactions in which each interaction has a beginning, a defined behavior and an end, modeled by a flow. This flow is composed by a sequence of **activities**.   The behavioral context for each activity is provided by a *scope*. A *scope* can provide **fault** handlers, **event** handlers, compensation handlers and a set of data **variables** and **correlation** sets.

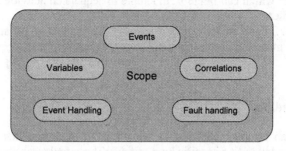

Fig. 4. Functionalities of BPEL4WS

4.3 Activities

Activities are the basic building blocks of the BPEL process. Through the combination of activities we define the flow behavior (sequences, parallel flows, message or event driven activities), points of communications with business partners (receive, invoke), simple initialisation steps or loop and branch activities known from classical programming languages.

4.4 Variables

Variables allow to specify stateful interactions in a business process. Variables provide the means for holding messages that constitute the state of a business process. These messages can be either those that have been received from business partners or those who are to be sent to the business partners. Variables can also hold data which are needed for holding state related to the process and never exchanged with partners. Finally, variables are associated with a *messageType*, which corresponds with a WSDL message type definition.

4.5 Correlation

Correlation deals with conversational and negotiation properties. As previously mentioned, business processes exchange information with messages. These messages have an XML syntax. However this exchange of information can be enhanced by means of correlation. During its lifetime, a business process typically holds one or more conversations with partners involved in its work. Conversations may be based on a sophisticated transport infrastructure which correlates the messages involved in a conversation using some form of conversation identity. For example in MIKSI the correlation mechanism is used to identify one specific user session instance of the BPEL session process (a generated Session ID will be used as the correlation item).

4.6 Event Handling

Each scope can be associated with a set of event handlers when a certain event occurs. Several actions which can range from simple to sequenced activities are taken within the event handler.

In BPEL4WS there are two types of events: Alarms that go off after user-set times or incoming messages corresponding to a request/response or one-way WSDL operation.

4.7 Fault Handling

Each scope can be associated with a set of custom fault-handling activities. Every activity is intended to fit a specific kind of fault. These faults can result from a WSDL operation fault or a programmatic *throw* activity.

4.8 Advantages and Disadvantages of BPEL4WS

In this section we will summarize the disadvantages and advantages BPEL4WS.

Disadvantages:

- *Semantics*: BPEL4WS lacks a complex and enriched syntax for its' data structures. The message and data types are those of the XSD specification in the WSDL model.
- *Mediation*: There are no mediators in BPEL4WS. Business logics and data handling can not be mediated.
- *Process abstraction*: There is no specific link between public and private processes (abstract and executable business processes).

Advantages:

- *Exception and fault handling*: BPEL4WS provides an interesting fault handling and fault tolerance framework based on the notion of scopes. However, it does not allow a real "transactional" mechanism, but the nesting of several actions.
- *Security enabled by WS-Security*: This specification describes a security framework provided by IBM. Because business processes use messages and these messages can be modified or forged, it is recommended to use WS-Security signatures to ensure the integrity of data. Also, messaging protocols can be the target of reply attacks. In addition to the signatures, messages should include a "message timestamp". Recipients can use the timestamp information to detect duplicate transmissions.
- *Compensation*: BPEL4WS deals with compensation handlers, which allow to cope with fault tolerance and exception handling. It is also based in the notion of scopes.
- *Distinction between private / public processes*: The distinction in BPEL4WS between abstract and executable business processes (i.e. public and private

processes) is very suitable for including a B2B protocol engine. In abstract processes, the exchange of messages between the trading partners could be modeled in a B2B syntax. For example, one of the trading partners could define a RosettaNet based syntax for their messages, where the business transactions would be received by the trading partner and interpreted correctly.

- *Industry support*

Comparing these arguments; the deciding points for the usage of BPEL in MIKSI have been the industry support and the distinction between private and public processes. Nevertheless we have been aware of the risk of using a novel business process execution language, which is not standardized yet. This risk is considered in the layered structure of the MIKSI SOA Bus and the design of the architectural components, which are described in the next section.

5 MIKSI Architectural Components

The MIKSI platform uses many well known protocols/standards of a WSDL-SOAP based SOA. But for providing a real service oriented platform with client interaction, dynamic service invocation, access controlling, user authentication and support for system management tasks, we had to add additional components as demonstrated in figure 5:

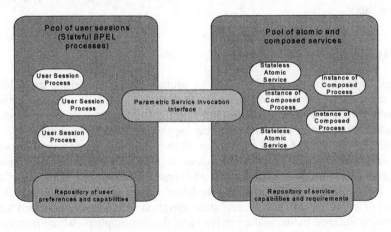

Fig. 5. MIKSI platform component overview.

5.1 MIKSI - Interface for Parametric Service Invocation (Invoker)

The parametric service invocation interface, realized as a stateless EJB, provides better decoupling between business logic, presentation layer and the control mechanisms for the pool of atomic services and processes. MIKSI processes or services are not directly callable by the client, but clients have the possibility to invoke MIKSI components through parametric SOAP calls, which are in turn used by the user session process to determine which one of the underlying business processes should be invoked.

The component for parametric service invocation supports the control of the client's access to the services by checking the capabilities and preferences of clients and services and performs monitoring and reporting functionality. This architectural component can be viewed as an object with embedded knowledge about the state of the system at run time.

5.2 MIKSI Atomic Services

MIKSI Atomic services are typically functional atomic components described by its own WSDL interface description and accessed through the SOAP message exchange protocol. There is a set of initial services such as diverse wrappers (wrappers for accessing persistent data models or legacy applications) and transformers, as well as engines for document creation/transformation. The MIKSI platform can use other SOAP services which could be distributed and belong to other (partner) platforms.

Examples of atomic services include services of fine granularity (e.g. document generation services which implement XSL-FO [22] processing to produce PDF or RTF documents or file manipulation services which enable our business processes to access data from files and store persistent data in files within the BPEL process flow) and more powerful services (such as an atomic mail service, which sends the produced documents to the list of chosen recipients by dynamically generating mailing lists).

5.3 MIKSI User Session Processes

The user session process is a stateful BPEL process used to model the stateful nature of an active user session. It acts as the point of entry for all following user activities. The user session provides mechanisms for user authentication, for the invocation of parameterized operation calls and for safely logging off from the system.

MIKSI uses the BPEL4WS mechanism of correlations to create a new instance of the user session process every time a user logs on. This is done by a one-time invocation of a special operation, which will create an unique user ID as a part of the SOAP input message, instantiating a correlation variable at the same time. After the creation of a specific user session all future operation calls will be performed through this session instance by using the session identification number - which is unique for one pair of user name / user password - for a correlation check.

6 The Role of RDF within MIKSI

6.1 Decision RDF

The first approach during the development of the MIKSI Platform was to convert a legacy rational database to a new data model needed for an improved performance of marketing processes in MIKSI. It quickly became apparent that the usage of RDF [12] would alleviate existing problems and allow continuous extension and enrichment of the semantic core concepts of the chosen domain of cultural marketing.

Generally RDF is all about providing a way of describing resources via metadata. It restricts the description of resources to triplets (subject, predicate, object) and provides interoperability between applications that exchange machine understandable information on the Web. The broad goal of RDF is to define a mechanism for describing resources that makes no assumptions about a particular application domain, nor defines (a priori) the semantics of any application domain. RDF also provides a lightweight ontology system in the form of RDF Schema, which is usually needed to express meaning in a RDF document. It defines the terms that will be used in the RDF statements and gives specific meanings to them.

While considering the benefits of some more powerful ontology languages (such as DAML-S or OWL, [15] [16]), it was found that the requirements of the semantic data model of the MIKSI platform could be fulfilled by the capabilities of an ontology described in RDFS. Three small ontologies have been designed to describe the domains within which the MIKSI platforms first prototype is operating: the domain of events (such as concerts, theatre productions and exhibitions), the domain of contacts (consisting of all sorts of categories of contacts, from the audience to the press) and finally the domain of tasks which describes the common objects of interest one would expect to find in a typical marketing department environment.

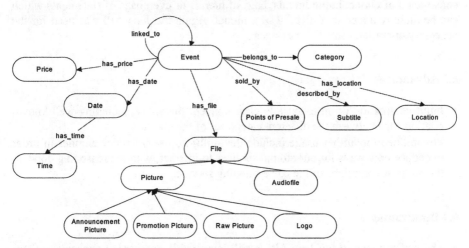

Fig. 6. A sample of the domain of events (showing classes, properties and subclass relationships)

The MIKSI Platform uses Jena [10], a Java API for processing RDF (and its open source implementation of the same name). Jena was developed by Brian McBride of Hewlett-Packard and is derived from earlier work on the SiRPAC API. Jena allows to parse, create, and search RDF models.

Once the decision of building a simple ontology for the domain and using it to build a semantic data model for MIKSI has been made, another way of using RDF in

MIKSI emerged from the need to classify and restrict the possible SOAP messages encountered and produced during the lifetime of a MIKSI task.

6.2 MIKSI Messages

Several problems with SOAP messages prompted the use of a different way to generate and handle messages in MIKSI. Within the context of BPWS4J, standard SOAP messages could not give the amount of flexibility needed: Neither was it possible to use arrays of complex objects, nor SOAP with attachments [23] within the chosen BPWS4J engine, furthermore it was not possible to read, split or initialize these objects within an executing business process and still very complicated to perform dynamic invocation or process composition based on the given messages.

A workaround was to use SOAP as the transport layer for MIKSI RDF messages. According to a lightweight message ontology, a valid instance of a MISKI SOAP Message is generated either by client or server architecture, serialized into plain text and packed into SOAP messages as simple strings and then sent to its corresponding partner. If the client receives a new message, the presentation engine (the prototype uses Cocoon [17]) extracts and parses the string argument, extracting the RDF part to facilitate the generation of a dynamically created HTML page:

The MIKSI messages can have one or more complex sub-messages, which are constructed of either simple literals, bags of literals or even bags of statements which can be directly added to a given RDFS model. Again the Jena API was used for the necessary operations on RDF messages.

6.3 Advantages

- Intuitive creation of an extensible class concept hierarchy, including well known relationships between the different categories of the domain.
- Possibilities for further usage include the ability to use inference engines in order to deduce new ways for our atomic services to interact, with the reasoning done on the pre/post conditions of the corresponding service.

6.4 Disadvantages

- The performance of the Jena API is still improvable and certain concepts are still under development – including a reliable query language (e.g. certain improvements of RDQL are necessary in order to speed up the queries of the persistent ontology model)
- The internal MIKSI XML/RDF messages are mainly used to ease the data exchange between different components of the MIKSI architecture, but of course these messages are not easily understandable by third parties outside of the MIKSI framework. One possible solution would be to continue using XML/RDF messages on the application layer, while returning to the use of standard SOAP messages for the integration layer.

7 Conclusion and Future Work

When the MIKSI project started one year ago, the platform was first designed as a small web services platform for marketing and public relation tasks for cultural institutions. The complex business processes of this domain specific sector required the need for a powerful business execution language for web services, which influenced our decision to use BPEL4WS for the process implementation. During the initial development phase, the bottleneck of the relational data model of addresses and events of our case study partner was recognized, e.g. the categorization "music" of an event is not equivalent to the interest "music" in the address database, which leads to errors and inconsistencies during dispatching of press releases. Instead of implementing simple mediation-systems between these two databases, we decided to integrate a semantic data model based on ontologies.

Both decisions led to MIKSI being a powerful semantic service oriented platform, which goes far beyond an application for cultural institutions. The SOA concept of MIKSI allows the integration with third party services, the fast implementation of new business process and the publication of services. Next development steps will focus on a better dynamic service composition based on a semantic description of the service capabilities and graphical interfaces for the modeling of business processes to open MIKSI for a broader application area in various sectors. Though MIKSI is the first version of a broader vision, there will be a lot of issues in the rapidly emerging field of Semantic Web Services that have to be considered in future releases.

References

1. Curbera, F., Goland, Y., Klein, J., Leymann, F., Roller, D., Thatte, S., and Weerawarana, S.: Business Process Execution Language for Web Services Version 1.1, BEA Systems & IBM Corporation & Microsoft Corporation, 2003, http://www.ibm.com/developerworks/library/ws-bpel/
2. Business Process with BPEL4WS Understanding BPEL4WS, Part 1 – 7, http://www-106.ibm.com/developerworks/webservices/library/ws-bpelcol1/
3. Mcllraith, S.: "Semantic Enabled Web Services", XML-Web Services ONE Conference, June 7, 2002.
4. Fensel, D. and Bussler, C.: The Web Service Modeling Framework, In White paper and Internal Report, Vrije Universiteit, Amsterdam, 2002.
5. The DAML Services Coalition (alphabetically Anupriya Ankolenkar, Mark Burstein, Jerry R. Hobbs, Ora Lassila, David L. Martin, Drew McDermott, Sheila A. Mcllraith, Srini Narayanan, Massimo Paolucci, Terry R. Payne and Katia Sycara), "DAML-S: Web Service Description for the Semantic Web", The First International Semantic Web Conference (ISWC), Sardinia (Italy), June, 2002.
6. Bussler C., Fensel D., Maedche A.: A Conceptual Architecture for Semantic Web Enabled Web Services. SIGMOD Record 31(4): 24-29, 2002 Environments, J. ACM SIGMOD Record, vol. 28, no. 1, Mar. 1999, pp. 47–53.
7. Christensen, E., Curbera, F., Meredith, G., Weerawarana, S.: Web Services Description Languague WSDL 1.1, http://www.w3.org/TR/wsdl
8. The IBM Business Process Execution Language for Web Services JavaTM Run Time. http://www.alphaWorks.ibm.com/tech/bpws4j

9. Berners-Lee, T., Hendler, J., Lassila, O.: The Semantic Web, Scientific American, May, 2001.
10. Jena Semantic WEB Toolkit http://www.hpl.hp.com/semweb/jena.htm
11. Leyman, F. Web Services Flow Languague.
    http://www3.ibm.com/software/solutions/webservices/pdf/WSFL.pdf
12. Lassila, O., Swick, R. Resource Description Framework (RDF) Specification.W3C Recommendation, 22 February, 1999. http://www.w3.org/TR/REC-rdf-syntax.
13. Workflow Management Coalition: The Workflow Reference Model. Document Number TC00-1003, Workflow Management Coalition Office, Avenue Marcel Thirty 204, 1200 Brussels, Belgium, 1994.
14. Box, D., Ehnebuske, D., Kakivaya, G., Layman, A., Mendelsohn, N., Nielsen, H., Thatte, S., Winer, D.: Simple Object Assess Protocol (SOAP) 1.1. W3C Technical report, 2000. http://www.w3.org/TR/SOAP/
15. DAML+OIL Reference description, http://www.w3.org/TR/daml+oil-reference
16. OWL, Web Ontology Language Reference, http://www.w3.org/TR/owl-ref/
17. The Apache Cocoon Project, http://cocoon.apache.org/
18. McGovern, J., Tyagi, S., Stevens, M., and Mathew, S.: Java Web Services Architecture, ISBN: 1-55860-900-8
19. Wiener Werkstätten und Kulturhaus, www.wuk.at
20. JBoss Application Server, http://www.jboss.org/index.html
21. Leymann, F.: Web Services: Distributed Applications without Limits
    http://www.btw2003.de/proceedings/paper/keynote-leymann.pdf
22. Extensible Stylesheet Language (XSL) Version 1.0 W3C Recommendation 15 October 2001, http://www.w3.org/TR/xsl/
23. SOAP Messages with Attachments W3C Note 11 December 2000,
    http://www.w3.org/TR/2000/NOTE-SOAP-attachments-20001211

Semantic Web Technologies for Economic and Financial Information Management

Pablo Castells[1], Borja Foncillas[2], Rubén Lara[3], Mariano Rico[1], Juan Luis Alonso[2]

[1] Universidad Autónoma de Madrid
http://nets.ii.uam.es/
{pablo.castells,mariano.rico}@uam.es
[2] Tecnología, Información y Finanzas
http://www.grupoanalistas.com/
bfoncillas@afi.es
[3] Digital Enterprise Research Institute (DERI) Innsbruck
http://deri.semanticweb.org/
ruben.lara@uibk.ac.at

Abstract. The field of economy and finance is a conceptually rich domain where information is complex, huge in volume and a highly valuable business product by itself. Novel management techniques are required for economic and financial information in order to enable an efficient generation, management and consumption of complex and big information resources. Following this direction, we have developed and ontology-based platform that provides a) the integration of contents and semantics in a knowledge base that provides a conceptual view on low-level contents, b) an adaptive hypermedia-based knowledge visualization and navigation system and c) semantic search facilities. We have developed, as the basis of this platform, an ontology for the domain of economic and financial information.

1 Introduction

The field of economy and finance is a conceptually rich domain where information is complex, huge in volume and a highly valuable business product by itself. A massive amount of valuable information is produced world-wide every day, but its processing is a hard and time-consuming task. Efficient filtering, search, and browsing mechanisms are needed by information consumers to access the contents that are most relevant for their business profile, and run through them in an effective way.

The finance community is a major spender in information technology. The web has created new channels for distributing contents, to which more and more activity and information flow has been shifting for more than a decade. The new web technologies are enabling a trend away from monolithic documents, towards the emergence of new content products that consist of flexible combinations of smaller content pieces, fitting different purposes and consumers, and procuring a more efficient capitalization and reuse of the contents produced.

Along this line, a number of XML standards for financial contents and business have been defined during the last few years, like FpML, XBRL, RIXML, ebXML,

J. Davies et al. (Eds.): ESWS 2004, LNCS 3053, pp. 473-487, 2004.
© Springer-Verlag Berlin Heidelberg 2004

NewsML, IFX, OFX, MarketsML, ISO 15022, swiftML, MDDL, among others [4]. Most of them are concerned with describing business processes and transactions. Some, like XBRL [16], RIXML [15] and NewsML [13], do focus on content structure and provide a rich vocabulary of terms for content classification. Our assessment is that these vocabularies need significant extensions when faced to the actual needs of content managers that deal with advanced financial information. More insightful semantics and a sharper level of representation are required to describe and exploit complex information corpora.

Currently, most of the economic and financial information generated by information providers is mainly textual and, therefore, it cannot be interpreted and processed by computers. This leads to the same problems the management of current Web contents is presenting nowadays. [5] summarizes these problems in the following major points: searches are imprecise, yielding an excessive number of matches; information consumers face the task of going through a big volume of matches in order to get the information required; in addition, the maintenance of the information resources is complex.

The Semantic Web [2] aims at overcoming the problems summarized above by providing an explicit representation of the semantics underlying information sources. Ontologies [8] constitute the backbone technology for the semantic web and, more generally, for the management of formalized knowledge in the context of distributed systems. They provide machine-processable semantics of data and information sources that can be communicated between different agents. Information is made understandable for the computer, thus assisting people to search, extract, interpret and process information.

Semantic Web technologies can naturally be applied to the domain of economic and financial information in order to overcome its current limitations regarding information management. The purpose of our work is to achieve an improvement in current Internet-based economic information management practice by adopting Semantic Web technologies and standards in a real setting. We have undertaken a joint project involving a content provider in this field and two academic institutions, aiming at the development of an ontology-based platform for economic and financial content management, search and delivery [1]. The specific technical objectives of this project are:

- Define an ontology for the economic and financial information domain that must solve the needs of both the content provider and the information consumers.
- Develop ontology-aware tools for content provision and management.
- Develop a hypermedia-based module for content visualization and semantic navigation in web portals.
- Support semantic search in terms of the economic and financial information ontology in order to improve the quality of the results.
- Include a user modeling component to be used in navigation and search.
- Easy to adopt solution for the content provider i.e. improve the steps in the current business process but without major changes in the overall process.

This paper presents a real use case in the field of economic and financial information management, its limitations when dealing with current contents, and the approach we have followed to build an ontology-based tool meeting the domain requirements. The paper is structured as follows: section 2 presents our working domain; section 3 details the approach followed and the tools developed so far; section 4 conducts a discussion about our experiences in the project and the main results achieved; finally, section 5 summarizes the conclusions of our work and points out its limitations and future extensions.

2 Description of the Domain

Tecnología, Información y Finanzas (TIF)[1] is part of a corporation that generates high-quality economic information (equity research notes, newsletters, analysis, sector reports, recommendations), and provides technology solutions for information consumers to access, manage, integrate and publish this information in web portals and company intranets.

The consumer profile of this information is diverse, including financial institutions, banks, SMEs that use the information in decision making and foreign trade activity, and distributors who publish the information in first-rank printed and digital media about Spanish economic activity. Adequating the information and delivery procedures to such heterogeneous customer needs, interests, and output channels, is a big challenge.

A wide group of professionals and domain experts in the company is in charge of daily generating a wide range of valuable economic and financial information, including economic, market, bank, and financial analyses, commercial fair reports, import/export offers and news and manuals, among others.

A number of custom web-based content management systems are used for the different types of information generated in the organization. They support the user in creating, editing and publishing this data. The information generated is introduced in the company database, which feeds the automatic delivery systems and web sites.

The custom content management systems are based on web forms that request the appropriate information for a given content type. These forms are created following an ad-hoc procedure, and they are not related to any explicit conceptual model in the company, only to the correspondent part of the database schema.

Contents are organized and processed on the basis of a (mental) conceptual model, a vocabulary for information structures and classification terms, which is driven by market needs and reflects the view of the company on the information products it provides. This model is present somehow in the current TIF software system for information management, and it is implicit in the design of the database.

Therefore, the semantics of the information stored in the company and its structure is not clearly defined. This makes the generation and maintenance of content managers a time-consuming and error-prone task. Furthermore, the selection of the appropriate information to publish on the web portals and to deliver to the customers is not a trivial task, as the intended meaning of some of the information in the database is not easy to interpret.

---

[1] http://www.grupoanalistas.com/

In this context, our assessment is that the procedures followed in the company can be greatly improved by means of the construction of an explicit and formal definition of the conceptual information model of the organization. Such an unambiguous model would provide a uniform view of the information stored in the company, potentially bringing the following benefits: improvement of the data quality, uniform interpretation of the information by providers and consumers, reduction of the information maintenance effort, and semi-automatic generation of new web portals and delivery systems based on the conceptual model and the user profiles.

3 An Ontology-Based Approach to the Information Management Problem

In order to overcome the current limitations in the management, access and search of the information generated by TIF, we have developed an ontology-based platform that applies semantic web technologies in a real setting and shows the usefulness of such technologies. The main components of the platform architecture (see Fig. 1) are: the economic and financial information ontology, the import (from the TIF database) and export (to different formats) facilities, the content management and provision tools, the visualization interface and the search interface and engine. Each of these components is detailed in the following sections, together with the motivations of the approach followed and the choice of technologies.

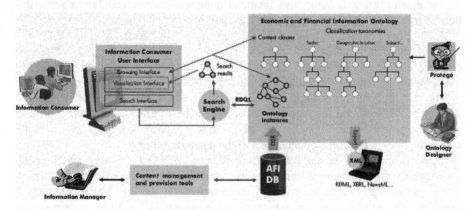

Fig. 1. System architecture

3.1 The Economic and Financial Information Ontology

The role of the economic and financial information ontology is central in our architecture, as it reflects the explicit conceptual model followed in the organization for the generation, management and access of the contents provided. The design of the ontology has been driven by the TIF domain and requirements. The possibility of reusing other ontologies or taxonomies, such as GICS for the classification of sectors, was considered. However, none of them met the TIF requirements, so the reuse of other standards had to be discarded.

The procedure followed to design the domain ontology was incremental, interacting with domain experts in order to produce refined versions of the ontology. Two main steps can be distinguished in the design:

1. First version of the ontology, which was designed based on the existent database schema.
2. Interaction with domain experts from TIF in order to refine the ontology, addition of missing concepts, relations and properties, and assurance of the appropriate coverage of the domain.

The interaction with the domain experts has been the most crucial step for a successful design of the ontology, as they have contributed with numerous and valuable improvements to the first version of the domain ontology. The first step was motivated by the need of making explicit the current structure of the database in order to use it as the starting point for the interaction with the domain experts.

Ontology characteristics

The requirement analysis studies carried out with in-house financial and technical experts have led us to establish four distinct kinds of concepts (classes) in the developed ontology:

1. Content classes. They stand for information products created by financial experts at TIF. Each TIF information product is described by an instance of a content class.
2. Classification categories. No instances are created for these classes. The classes are used directly as values for the *category* property of content instances. The categories form a taxonomy that serves as a classification scheme.
3. Entity classes. They represent all other information items that are not produced by financial experts, but that are used to annotate contents. This includes concepts like companies, banks, organisations, people, information sources, event hosting facilities, etc.
4. Enumerated types for certain property values. They provide sets of values (controlled vocabularies). These classes contain just the *value* and *code* properties, and have a fixed and moderate number of instances.

From our experience in ontology engineering for information systems, the consideration of these four kinds of classes is an interesting and recurrent distinction that arises in many, if not most, information management systems in diverse domains. In fact, although perhaps not explicitly stated, a similar approach can be found in information exchange standards like RIXML [15] and other standards in the controlled vocabulary community [9]. As is usually the case when attempting a subdivision of the knowledge representation primitives, the distinction is not necessarily always a sharp line. Our proposed scheme responds to a careful study of experts' and users' needs and domain understanding, information system development know-how, and the capabilities of the underlying technological support (e.g. web-based navigation, internal information organisation and storage).

The developed ontology provides explicit connections between contents, categories, and other entities, that were only implicit in the current implementation. These relations are now well characterized, and can be further described in as much detail as needed, as the employed semantic web technology allows. As will be described later, this is exploited in our platform to support more expressive and precise search capabilities, and for the semi-automation of the generation of user interfaces and forms for search, information visualisation, and content provision.

Ontology language

Regarding the choice of the ontology language used to define the ontology, the following criteria were followed:

- Maturity of the language, including its degree of standardization.
- Sufficient tool support for the design and maintenance of the ontology.
- Appropriate expressiveness for modelling of the domain.

Following these criteria, RDF(S) was chosen. The rationale behind this choice is:

- RDF(S) is a W3C recommendation, which provides a guarantee of its maturity and stability. OWL was also considered, but as it is still in the process of becoming a W3C recommendation, its stability was not clear enough.
- RDF(S) is the most widely supported language by the available tools. That fact reduces the risks in the development and the time necessary to implement our architecture.
- After numerous meetings with domain experts from TIF, it was shown that the expressivity of RDF/RDFS was enough for the TIF business activity. The transitive closure of subPropertyOf and subClassOf relations, the domain and range entailments, and the implications of subPropertyOf and subClassOf, were the only inference mechanisms used. These are supported by the "simple" RDFS inference level of Jena. No further expressivity or inference mechanisms were required to meet the provider requirements for the generation of the information and the requester requirements for its consumption.

Tool support

Among the ontology development tools available with support for RDF, Protégé-2000[2] was selected because of its maturity, ease-of-use and, what is more important, its scalability and extensibility.

Protégé-2000 has thousands of users all over the world who use the system for projects ranging from modelling cancer-protocol guidelines to modelling nuclear-power stations [6]. It provides a graphical and interactive ontology-design and knowledge-base development environment. It helps knowledge engineers and domain experts to perform knowledge-management tasks. Ontology developers can access relevant information quickly whenever they need it, and can use direct manipulation to navigate and manage an ontology.

In addition to highly usable interface, two other important features distinguish Protégé-2000 from most ontology-editing environments: its scalability and extensibility. Developers have successfully employed Protégé-2000 to build and use ontologies consisting of 150,000 frames. Supporting knowledge bases with hundreds of thousands of frames involves two components: (1) a database backend to store and query the data and (2) a caching mechanism to enable loading of new frames once the number of frames in memory has exceeded the memory limit.

---

[2] http://protege.stanford.edu

One of the major advantages of the Protégé-2000 architecture is that the system is constructed in an open, modular fashion. Its component-based architecture enables system builders to add new functionality by creating appropriate plugins. The Protégé Plugin Library[3] contains contributions from developers all over the world. Plugins for other ontology languages such as DAML+OIL and OWL assures an easy evolution of our ontology if a higher expressiveness is required in the future.

The result of our conceptual work in cooperation with the domain experts, using RDF(S) as ontology languages and Protégé-2000 as the ontology development tool, is an ontology that has been approved by the company as appropriately reflecting its business domain and that fits to the huge volume of information already present in the organization i.e. the current information can be easily expressed in terms of the ontology. Fig. 2 partially shows the resulting ontology. All the elements of the ontology are described in Spanish. No multilingualism support has been considered, as the business activities of TIF are mainly focused on the Spanish market.

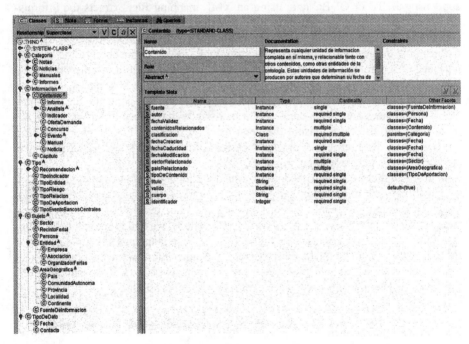

Fig. 2. Ontology in Protégé-2000

3.2 Linking to Existing Data

As exposed in the previous sections, TIF has a number of experts in economy and finances that daily generate economic and financial information that is stored in the TIF information systems. Several applications make this information arrive to the

---

[3] http://protege.stanford.edu/plugins.html

customers for its consumption, either via the information delivery systems (XML delivery) or via the various web portals TIF feeds with this information. Our project has been conceived as an extension and improvement of the current exploitation system. Therefore, all the information already available in the organization had to be annotated using the ontology described in section 3.1, while keeping some other applications in the company (assessment systems, knowledge management system, etc.) working properly. For this reason, in addition to the annotation of the information for the delivery systems and web portals, the information has to be also stored in the company databases to keep these other systems running.

Our solution was designed to achieve the improvement of our target applications (delivery systems and web portals) with the restriction of not having any impact in other company applications.

The first step was to annotate the contents already available using our domain ontology. For this task, we used the open source tool D2R. D2R connects to RDBMSs supporting JDBC or ODBC and, using an XML mapping file, extracts the information from the RDBMS and generates RDF instances.

An XML mapping file has to be created for each concept in the ontology. The file defines how the results of an SQL query on the RDBMS are mapped to the concept attributes. An ontology concept requires in some cases information from several database entities. How this information is gathered is defined in the SQL query.

We have generated such mappings and, from the available contents, the appropriate RDF instances have been created. These instances have been in turn stored in the organization RDBMSs to ensure the persistency of the data. For this purpose, Jena has been used. Jena retrieves the RDF instances of the ontology from the files generated using D2R and stores them in the RDBMSs.

A problem that we faced was how to, after the annotation of available information, deal with the new information daily generated in the company. As we had the constraint of keeping all the information (existing and to be generated) stored in the existing database schema for its use by other applications, we had to maintain two copies of the organization information. In order to reuse the mappings already defined for the information annotation of existing data, the new information generated is first stored in the RDBMSs and then such mappings are used by D2R to annotate this information. The ontology instances are then stored in the RDBMSs.

3.3 Information Search

Our platform provides a search module where customers, content providers, content managers and administrators can query the knowledge base. Our search module improves the facilities provided by the information management system version running at TIF before our project was started in several ways. Whereas the former system only provided keyword-based, full-text search, and a simplified, ad-hoc, partial form of structured search, our module supports full structured search in terms of any dimension of the ontology, and allows setting different levels of detail and difficulty of use, depending of the intended user profiles.

In our system the user interacts with an HTML search form interface where s/he can select concept types in the ontology (content classes), and provide search keywords for properties of the class. Thus the user can formulate expressive information needs in terms of classes, properties, and relations among contents and concepts. The search forms are automatically generated by a generic mechanism from ontology class descriptions. The search form generation mechanism shares much functionality with (actually it can be viewed as a particular case of) the visualization module, described in the next section. Here we describe the features that are specific to the search forms generation.

The search form generation mechanism provides a default procedure to generate forms adapted to the structure and field types of classes, and the possibility to define custom form design by means of search form templates for classes. For the default procedure, the properties of content classes have a boolean "searchable" metaproperty, with which ontology designers can control whether or not the generated search forms should include an input control where search values for the property can be supplied. The generation procedure selects different HTML/JavaScript controls depending on the type of the searchable property.

The default mechanism provides an instant search facility as a by-product of the ontology and knowledge base construction. However, it is usually necessary to create a custom form design in accordance with the global application look and feel and brand image considerations. This is achieved in our system by creating form templates for each content class, where all aspects of the design can be defined in as much detail as desired. Our template definition language is based on JSP, where custom tags have been defined to provide a simple vocabulary for expressing property references and other ontology graph traversal expressions. The language also includes primitives to easily specify HTML or JavaScript input components, and facilities to define global layout constructs. Wherever details are not explicitly indicated in the template, the system tries to provide appropriate default solutions. An example of the semantic search form for a given class of the ontology is given in Fig. 3.

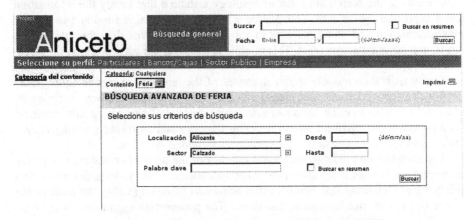

Fig. 3. Semantic search form for a "Feria" concept

It has been studied that it is generally more adequate to provide customers with fairly simple and easy to use search interfaces [7], whereas experts and content managers, who are aware of many internal information details, can benefit from more complex and powerful search facilities. This is supported in our platform by creating different templates for different user profiles and usage modes, thus enabling the creation of as large and varied an array of power levels and modalities as needed (see [12] for an overview of user interface approaches for searching), in a highly modular way, very easy to extend. In our current implementation, the set of searchable properties and the search form design for each class have been provided by information management experts and graphic designers from TIF.

The possibilities to use the ontology vocabulary to formulate information needs in our system go beyond specifying property values for content classes. The search module allows the user to combine direct search, using content classes and fields, with navigation through the classification taxonomies included in the ontology. This approach follows the classic combination of searching and browsing in systems like Yahoo! and others [11]. The user can restrict the direct search to selected taxonomy categories. With the search results, the system returns the list of categories to which the results belong, using which the user can narrow or widen his/her search, or go back to browsing.

The search module converts the information need conveyed by the user into an RDQL query, which is executed against the ontology, yielding a set of RDF instances that match the query. The list of instances is presented to the user in an understandable way in a web page. The user can click on instances, which are then displayed in detail in a full page (or a large page area). The way individual instances and lists of search results are presented to the user is controlled by a visualization module that is described next.

3.4 Information Visualization

The results of the search are a list of ontology instances that satisfy the information need expressed by the user. Our platform includes a specialized module to present this information and allow the user to run through them, visualize the information units, and navigate across units. This module is based on our early work on the Pegasus tool [3].

The visualization module shows instances of the ontology in dynamically generated web pages. Each class of instance is presented in a different way, showing its data and relations to other instances selectively. Instead of hardwiring this treatment in a program, our platform allows defining the presentation of each ontology class independently, using one or several visualization models per class.

The presentation model of each class establishes the parts of an instance that have to be shown, in what order and under what appearance. This model is defined with a fairly simple language that permits referencing and traversing easily the parts of the semantic network that have to be visualized. The presentation engine selects dynamically the appropriate view for an instance at the time it has to be presented, according to the instance class, and other conditions, if any. The visualization module takes also care of presenting in the same page other instances related with the one being visualized, or of generating hyperlinks to them instead, in order to navigate across ontology relations.

The presentation language is based on JSP, with a library of custom tags which allow creating, besides free HTML and JavaScript code, a) ontology access expressions, b) HTML / JavaScript primitives that display ontology constructs, and c) layout constructs. The presentation models currently defined for the ontology classes have been constructed by inserting the appropriate ontology references and presentation constructs, into the HTML / JavaScript code provided by professional page designers at TIF.

The presentation language also includes the possibility to express conditions on user profiles, the access device, the state of the application, or the characteristics of the information itself to be presented. This way, any aspect of presentation can dynamically adapt itself to the execution context. These conditions can determine the choice of one or other presentation model for an instance, or at a more detailed level, establish the aspect of small parts of the presentation, the inclusion or not of certain information fragments, the generation of hyperlinks, or the selection of one or other page component (lists, tables, trees, etc.).

Currently three presentation models have been defined for the implemented application: extended view, to show instances with maximum detail in a page; summary view, to show lists of instances, for example the ones that result from a search; and minimum view, to be used for example as the text of the link to an instance. Fig. 4. shows an example of an extended view for an instance of the Fundamental Analysis concept.

Fig. 4. Extended view of a Fundamental Analysis instance

The explicit ontology allows describing more meaningful and precise user profiles, which can express preferences on specific topics, content classes, or even abstract content characterizations. The user models defined to this date include a) professional profiles, and b) subscription profiles of content consumers. The subscription profile carries access permissions to different parts of the ontology, as a consequence of which the user will have hidden access to different information areas. The professional profile defines a scale of interests for different subjects and types of materials, which determines the order (priority) and amount of information that is shown to the user, depending on the typology and relevant subject areas for his/her profile

3.5 Content Management and Provision Tools

Content managers themselves are actually users of a highly expressive version of the search and browsing facilities. Efficiency and precision in locating the right contents, and ease of navigation through them, are essential for authors who classify and link pieces together to define global information structures. These search facilities are provided as a complement of the content provision tools for content managers.

The tools for inputting contents, currently in use at TIF, have been adapted to allow defining richer semantics in terms of the ontology. In addition to filling forms with fields for instance properties, managers can create rich interrelations among contents or to external entities. The user interface for content managers is based on web forms that are generated automatically according to the content class. These data input forms are created by the system exactly the same way as search forms (see section 3.3): a) there is a default mechanism that takes into account property types to generate appropriate input controls, and b) one can instead define an input form template for each class.

The main difference is that content input and content search requirements usually need differently designed forms, therefore designers should create two different templates for each class accordingly. For example, not all class attributes need to be used for search, but it is likely that they all need to be provided values when a new instance is created by a content manager. Likewise, the set of fields that should be exposed when instances are shown to the end information consumer need not be the same as (typically they are a superset of) the ones that appear in a search form, and may be a subset of all fields required by an instance creation form.

4 Experiences and Results

Our first observation is that at the time of this writing no proper ontology was available for the description of economic and financial information. Most standards for information exchange (most based in XML) in the field are specifically oriented to business processes and transactions, and only have small descriptions for economic data, rigid forms, or content packaging information (title, author, source, time stamps, etc.). Only a few provide extensive enough vocabularies for dealing with semi-structured, semantically rich information contained in documents like the ones TIF produces. NewsML [14] provides the IPTC Subject Reference System, a thematic taxonomy that includes a section for economy, but with much too broad terms for highly specialized financial analysts like TIF professionals. RIXML [15] provides or adopts several controlled vocabularies for aspects like subject, industrial sector, intended audience, and geographic location.

These standards are difficult to adopt from the beginning because of the particularities and specialization of the provider's business, and the inevitable regional bias. For instance, the GICS industrial sector subdivision standard adopted by RIXML considers the shoe industry as a single sector, while in Spain, the shoe sector being a highly developed industry, a finer subcategorization is desirable, e.g. distinguishing sports shoes, sandals, boots, men / women shoes, etc. Rather than integrating the standards, we have developed or own taxonomies, and we are currently defining export/import mappings to standards.

Besides contributing an ontology for a domain where no proper ontology had been defined before, our work has motivated a major revision and improvement of the existing categorization taxonomy used at TIF, which had been incrementally built on-demand over the years, without a clear a-priori evolution plan. A cleaner, more consistent and better organized classification scheme, and a better and clearer understanding by the industrial partner of its own domain, has resulted from this project.

A second observation is that whereas Semantic Web technologies have reached a significant maturity level, we still miss certain tools or features that we felt should be basic. For instance, we are not aware of any freely available tool to dynamically link ontology instance properties to database records so that data are retrieved at runtime, or even instances are created from data on demand. Instead, we are using a mechanism to statically dump the whole database to create a huge RDF graph with all possible instances, which is not optimal, and launch this mechanism every day to update the graph with new data. We have found other minor, though no less important, limitations in commonly used Semantic Web tools as well, like the lack of an operator for string comparison in RDQL/Jena.

Another small detail that required more attention and effort than expected is that of text normalization for search purposes, which requires conversion of texts to upper-case form, removal of accents, maintaining a record of lexical variants for nouns (e.g. "John Doe", "Doe, John", "J. Doe", "Doe, J.", "Doe", "J.D."), etc. We have not included support for spelling errors and typos.

A public demo of our system and further information about the project is currently available at http://nets.ii.uam.es/aniceto/. The total set of data and documents produced and stored by TIF since the old system was put to work in 1998 amounts to 159,429 records stored in different DB tables, taking 5.1 Gb disk space (including a number of documents in PDF format). This volume of information has given rise to 180,831 instances and 2,705,827 statements in the RDF knowledge base, taking 1.3 Gb in the MySQL Jena format. The current version of the ontology includes 196 classes and 99 properties.

5 Conclusions

The development of a significant corpus of actual Semantic Web applications has been acknowledged as a necessary achievement for the Semantic Web to reach critical mass [10]. The work presented here is a contribution in this direction, and provides a testing ground for our research.

We have developed a platform for economic and financial information management using state-of the art Semantic Web technologies and standards. The platform includes an ontology-driven knowledge base, where information products are enriched with semantic descriptions. The platform provides means for content provision, access, and administration of this knowledge repository. The information access facilities include semantic-based search, exploration and visualization facilities. The advantages of the search, visualization, and management modules do not lie only in their application to the particular case at hand. Besides improving the end-user experience, they provide important advantages for developers, as flexible, general-purpose modules, portable to other ontologies, easy to configure, supporting a variety of options and power vs. simplicity levels. We actually intend to prepare these modules to make them publicly available.

Many aspects of our work so far can be improved. For instance, while our ontology defines various relations between content classes, such relations are poorly described by current data at TIF. The new ontology-based content management tools allow and encourage interrelating contents, once our platform is deployed, but the information will still be missing in previously existing contents. Due to the size of the legacy materials (over 5 Gb), the most feasible way to enrich old contents would be through (supervised) text analysis and (semi)automatic metadata extraction. Contents managers would also benefit from such a service, which can be used to assist manual annotation, relieving managers from part of this effort.

Another major direction for our future work is to extend the adoption of Semantic Web technologies to package, integrate and commercialize financial services currently offered by TIF. We are starting an extensive analysis of current financial services in the company in order to identify basic (atomic) services, implement them as web services, and study potential compositions into more complex and added-valued web services by using ongoing business process definition languages. This work intends to include semantic description of the service functionalities in order to enable dynamic discovery of services and contingency plans in case of error. The semantic descriptions of the services will make use of the TIF economic and financial ontology defined in the work presented in this paper.

Acknowledgements

This work is funded by the Spanish Ministry of Science and Technology, grants FIT-150500-2003-309, TIC2002-1948.

References

1. J. L. Alonso, C. Carranza, P. Castells, B. Foncillas, R. Lara, M. Rico. Semantic Web Technologies for Economic and Financial Information Management. 2nd International Semantic Web Conference (ISWC'03), Poster Session. Sanibel Island (Florida), 2003.

2. Berners-Lee, T., Handler, J., Lassila, O.: The Semantic Web, Scientific American, May 2001.
3. P. Castells and J. A. Macías. An Adaptive Hypermedia Presentation Modeling System for Custom Knowledge Representations. *World Conference* on the WWW and Internet (Web-Net'2001). Orlando, 2001.
4. Coates, A. B.: The Role of XML in Finance. XML Conference & Exposition 2001. Orlando, Florida, December 2001.
5. Ding, Y., Fensel, D.: Ontology Library Systems. The key to successful Ontology Re-Use. In: Proceedings of the First Semantic Web Working Symposium. California, USA: Stanford University 2001; S. 93-112.
6. Gómez-Pérez, A., Angele, J., Bechhofer, S., Corcho, O., Domingue, J., Légér, A., Missikoff, M., Motta, E., Musen, M., Noy, N. F., Sure, Y., Taglino, F., McGuiness, D., Ramos, J. A., Stumme, G., Bouillon, Y., Fernández-López, M., Stutt, A., Handschuh, S., López, A., Maier-Collin, M., Christophides, V., Plexousakis, D., Magkanaraki, A., Ahn, T. T., Karvounarakis, G.: OntoWeb deliverable 1.3: A survey on ontology tools, available at http://www.ontoweb.org, 2002.
7. S. L. Green, S. J. Delvin, P. E. Cannata and L. M. Gómez. No Ifs, ANDs or Ors: A study of database querying. International Journal of Man-Machine Studies, 32 (3), pp. 303-326, 1990.
8. Gruber, T. R.: A translation approach to portable ontology specifications, Knowledge acquisition, 5(2), 1993.
9. K. Fast, F. Leise and M. Steckel. What Is A Controlled Vocabulary? Boxes and Arrows, December 2002. Available at http://www.boxesandarrows.com/archives/what_is_a_controlled_vocabulary.php.
10. S. Haustein and J. Pleumann. Is Participation in the Semantic Web too Difficult? International Semantic Web Conference (ISWC'2002). Sardinia, Italy, 2002.
11. M. Hearst, A. Elliott, J. English, R. Sinha, K. Swearingen, K-P. Yee, Finding the Flow in Web Site Search, Communications of the ACM, 45 (9), September 2002.
12. M. A. Hearst. User Interfaces and Visualization. In R. Baeza-Yates and B. Ribeiro-Neto, Modern Information Retrieval. Addison-Wesley, 1999, pp.257-323.
13. International Press Telecommunications Council (IPTC). Subject Reference System & NewsML Topicsets, http://www.iptc.org/metadata, 1999.
14. International Press Telecommunications Council (IPTC). NewsML, http://www.newsml.org, 2000.
15. Research Information Exchange Language, RIXML, http://www.rixml.org, 2001.
16. eXtensible Business Reporting Language, RBXL, http://www.xbrl.org, 1998.

Author Index

Lecture Notes in Computer Science

For information about Vols. 1–2913

please contact your bookseller or Springer-Verlag

Vol. 2981: C. Müller-Schloer, T. Ungerer, B. Bauer (Eds.), Organic and Pervasive Computing – ARCS 2004. XI, 339 pages. 2004.

Vol. 2980: A. Blackwell, K. Marriott, A. Shimojima (Eds.), Diagrammatic Representation and Inference. XV, 448 pages. 2004. (Subseries LNAI).

Vol. 2979: I. Stoica, Stateless Core: A Scalable Approach for Quality of Service in the Internet. XVI, 219 pages. 2004.

Vol. 2978: R. Groz, R.M. Hierons (Eds.), Testing of Communicating Systems. XII, 225 pages. 2004.

Vol. 2977: G. Di Marzo Serugendo, A. Karageorgos, O.F. Rana, F. Zambonelli (Eds.), Engineering Self-Organising Systems. X, 299 pages. 2004. (Subseries LNAI).

Vol. 2976: M. Farach-Colton (Ed.), LATIN 2004: Theoretical Informatics. XV, 626 pages. 2004.

Vol. 2973: Y. Lee, J. Li, K.-Y. Whang, D. Lee (Eds.), Database Systems for Advanced Applications. XXIV, 925 pages. 2004.

Vol. 2972: R. Monroy, G. Arroyo-Figueroa, L.E. Sucar, H. Sossa (Eds.), MICAI 2004: Advances in Artificial Intelligence. XVII, 923 pages. 2004. (Subseries LNAI).

Vol. 2971: J.I. Lim, D.H. Lee (Eds.), Information Security and Cryptology -ICISC 2003. XI, 458 pages. 2004.

Vol. 2970: F. Fernández Rivera, M. Bubak, A. Gómez Tato, R. Doallo (Eds.), Grid Computing. XI, 328 pages. 2004.

Vol. 2968: J. Chen, S. Hong (Eds.), Real-Time and Embedded Computing Systems and Applications. XIV, 620 pages. 2004.

Vol. 2967: S. Melnik, Generic Model Management. XX, 238 pages. 2004.

Vol. 2966: F.B. Sachse, Computational Cardiology. XVIII, 322 pages. 2004.

Vol. 2965: M.C. Calzarossa, E. Gelenbe, Performance Tools and Applications to Networked Systems. VIII, 385 pages. 2004.

Vol. 2964: T. Okamoto (Ed.), Topics in Cryptology – CT-RSA 2004. XI, 387 pages. 2004.

Vol. 2963: R. Sharp, Higher Level Hardware Synthesis. XVI, 195 pages. 2004.

Vol. 2962: S. Bistarelli, Semirings for Soft Constraint Solving and Programming. XII, 279 pages. 2004.

Vol. 2961: P. Eklund (Ed.), Concept Lattices. IX, 411 pages. 2004. (Subseries LNAI).

Vol. 2960: P.D. Mosses (Ed.), CASL Reference Manual. XVII, 528 pages. 2004.

Vol. 2958: L. Rauchwerger (Ed.), Languages and Compilers for Parallel Computing. XI, 556 pages. 2004.

Vol. 2957: P. Langendoerfer, M. Liu, I. Matta, V. Tsaoussidis (Eds.), Wired/Wireless Internet Communications. XI, 307 pages. 2004.

Vol. 2956: A. Dengel, M. Junker, A. Weisbecker (Eds.), Reading and Learning. XII, 355 pages. 2004.

Vol. 2954: F. Crestani, M. Dunlop, S. Mizzaro (Eds.), Mobile and Ubiquitous Information Access. X, 299 pages. 2004.

Vol. 2953: K. Konrad, Model Generation for Natural Language Interpretation and Analysis. XIII, 166 pages. 2004. (Subseries LNAI).

Vol. 2952: N. Guelfi, E. Astesiano, G. Reggio (Eds.), Scientific Engineering of Distributed Java Applications. X, 157 pages. 2004.

Vol. 2951: M. Naor (Ed.), Theory of Cryptography. XI, 523 pages. 2004.

Vol. 2949: R. De Nicola, G. Ferrari, G. Meredith (Eds.), Coordination Models and Languages. X, 323 pages. 2004.

Vol. 2948: G.L. Mullen, A. Poli, H. Stichtenoth (Eds.), Finite Fields and Applications. VIII, 263 pages. 2004.

Vol. 2947: F. Bao, R. Deng, J. Zhou (Eds.), Public Key Cryptography – PKC 2004. XI, 455 pages. 2004.

Vol. 2946: R. Focardi, R. Gorrieri (Eds.), Foundations of Security Analysis and Design II. VII, 267 pages. 2004.

Vol. 2943: J. Chen, J. Reif (Eds.), DNA Computing. X, 225 pages. 2004.

Vol. 2941: M. Wirsing, A. Knapp, S. Balsamo (Eds.), Radical Innovations of Software and Systems Engineering in the Future. X, 359 pages. 2004.

Vol. 2940: C. Lucena, A. Garcia, A. Romanovsky, J. Castro, P.S. Alencar (Eds.), Software Engineering for Multi-Agent Systems II. XII, 279 pages. 2004.

Vol. 2939: T. Kalker, I.J. Cox, Y.M. Ro (Eds.), Digital Watermarking. XII, 602 pages. 2004.

Vol. 2937: B. Steffen, G. Levi (Eds.), Verification, Model Checking, and Abstract Interpretation. XI, 325 pages. 2004.

Vol. 2936: P. Liardet, P. Collet, C. Fonlupt, E. Lutton, M. Schoenauer (Eds.), Artificial Evolution. XIV, 410 pages. 2004.

Vol. 2934: G. Lindemann, D. Moldt, M. Paolucci (Eds.), Regulated Agent-Based Social Systems. X, 301 pages. 2004. (Subseries LNAI).

Vol. 2930: F. Winkler (Ed.), Automated Deduction in Geometry. VII, 231 pages. 2004. (Subseries LNAI).

Vol. 2929: H. de Swart, E. Orlowska, G. Schmidt, M. Roubens (Eds.), Theory and Applications of Relational Structures as Knowledge Instruments. VII, 273 pages. 2003.

Vol. 2926: L. van Elst, V. Dignum, A. Abecker (Eds.), Agent-Mediated Knowledge Management. XI, 428 pages. 2004. (Subseries LNAI).

Vol. 2923: V. Lifschitz, I. Niemelä (Eds.), Logic Programming and Nonmonotonic Reasoning. IX, 365 pages. 2004. (Subseries LNAI).

Vol. 2919: E. Giunchiglia, A. Tacchella (Eds.), Theory and Applications of Satisfiability Testing. XI, 530 pages. 2004.

Vol. 2917: E. Quintarelli, Model-Checking Based Data Retrieval. XVI, 134 pages. 2004.

Vol. 2916: C. Palamidessi (Ed.), Logic Programming. XII, 520 pages. 2003.

Vol. 2915: A. Camurri, G. Volpe (Eds.), Gesture-Based Communication in Human-Computer Interaction. XIII, 558 pages. 2004. (Subseries LNAI).

Vol. 2914: P.K. Pandya, J. Radhakrishnan (Eds.), FST TCS 2003: Foundations of Software Technology and Theoretical Computer Science. XIII, 446 pages. 2003.